Netscape DevEdge® Web Developer's Library

Netscape DevEdge® Web Developer's Library

edited by
Paul Dreyfus

Netscape Communications Corporation

Netscape® Press

Mountain View, California

Netscape DevEdge® Web Developer's Library
Published by
Netscape Press
501 East Middlefield Road
Mountain View, CA 94043

Library of Congress Card Number: 99-066778

ISBN: 0-7645-4585-X

Printed in the United States of America

10 9 8 7 6 5 4 3 2 1

1B/QY/RQ/ZZ/FC

Distributed in the United States by IDG Books Worldwide, Inc.

Distributed by CDG Books Canada Inc. for Canada; by Transworld Publishers Limited in the United Kingdom; by IDG Norge Books for Norway; by IDG Sweden Books for Sweden; by IDG Books Australia Publishing Corporation Pty. Ltd. for Australia and New Zealand; by TransQuest Publishers Pte Ltd. for Singapore, Malaysia, Thailand, Indonesia, and Hong Kong; by Gotop Information Inc. for Taiwan; by ICG Muse, Inc. for Japan; by Intersoft for South Africa; by Eyrolles for France; by International Thomson Publishing for Germany, Austria and Switzerland; by Distribuidora Cuspide for Argentina; by LR International for Brazil; by Galileo Libros for Chile; by Ediciones ZETA S.C.R. Ltda. for Peru; by WS Computer Publishing Corporation, Inc., for the Philippines; by Contemporanea de Ediciones for Venezuela; by Express Computer Distributors for the Caribbean and West Indies; by Micronesia Media Distributor, Inc. for Micronesia; by Chips Computadoras S.A. de C.V. for Mexico; by Editorial Norma de Panama S.A. for Panama; by American Bookshops for Finland.

For general information on IDG Books Worldwide's books in the U.S., please call our Consumer Customer Service department at 800-762-2974. For reseller information, including discounts and premium sales, please call our Reseller Customer Service department at 800-434-3422.

For information on where to purchase IDG Books Worldwide's books outside the U.S., please contact our International Sales department at 317-596-5530 or fax 317-596-5692.

For consumer information on foreign language translations, please contact our Customer Service department at 800-434-3422, fax 317-596-5692, or e-mail rights@idgbooks.com.

For information on licensing foreign or domestic rights, please phone +1-650-655-3109.

For sales inquiries and special prices for bulk quantities, please contact our Sales department at 650-655-3200 or write to IDG Books Worldwide, 919 E. Hillsdale Blvd., Suite 400, Foster City, CA 94404.

For information on using IDG Books Worldwide's books in the classroom or for ordering examination copies, please contact our Educational Sales department at 800-434-2086 or fax 317-596-5499.

For press review copies, author interviews, or other publicity information, please contact our Public Relations department at 650-655-3000 or fax 650-655-3299.

For authorization to photocopy items for corporate, personal, or educational use, please contact Netscape Communications Corporation, Copyright Permission, 501 East Middlefield Road, Mountain View, CA 94043 or fax 650-528-4124.

For general information on Netscape Press books in the U.S., including information on discounts and premiums, contact IDG Books Worldwide at 800-434-3422 or 650-655-3200. For information on where to purchase Netscape Press books outside the U.S., contact IDG Books International at 650-655-3021 or fax 650-655-3295.

is a registered trademark under exclusive license to IDG Books Worldwide, Inc., from International Data Group, Inc.

John Kilcullen, *CEO, IDG Books Worldwide, Inc.*

Steven Berkowitz, *President, IDG Books Worldwide, Inc.*

Richard Swadley, *Senior Vice President & Group Publisher,IDG Books Worldwide, Inc.*

Netscape Press and the Netscape Press logo are trademarks of Netscape Communications Corporation.

Credits

IDG Books Worldwide

Acquisitions Editor
Jim Sumser

Development Editor
Eric Newman

Copy Editors
Lauren Kennedy
Brian MacDonald
Julie M. Smith
Chandani Thapa

Project Coordinators
Linda Marousek
Tom Debolski

Book Designer
Daniel Ziegler Design

Graphics and Production Specialists
Mario Amador
Stephanie Hollier
Jim Kussow
Jude Levinson
Ramses Ramirez

Quality Control Specialist
Chris Weisbart

Proofreading and Indexing
York Production Services

About the Editor

Paul Dreyfus was the editor of *View Source*, Netscape's online technical magazine for developers at `http://developer.netscape.com/viewsource` from 1996 to 1999. He built the publication from a handful of articles on client-side Web development to a virtual online library with more than 250 tutorials on all aspects of Web application scripting and programming. During his tenure as *View Source* editor, Mr. Dreyfus also managed Netscape's Technology Evangelism team.

Previously, Mr. Dreyfus was editor-in-chief of *Apple Directions*, the Apple Computer, Inc., monthly developer business newsletter. He came to the high-tech industry from the book publishing world, where he was managing editor of Boston Publishing Company, which produced the critically acclaimed 27-volume illustrated history of the Vietnam war, *The Vietnam Experience*, published by Time-Life Books. He has an M.A. in rhetoric from the University of California.

Currently, he's a director in America Online's Netscape Business Solutions business unit. He lives in San Jose, California, with his wife and two children.

This book is dedicated to my parents, Pierre and Dorothy Dreyfus. They tried to teach me that with a little patience and hard work you can accomplish almost anything. This book and View Source *magazine are proof that their lesson finally penetrated my thick skull. Thanks to both of them for their patience and hard work with me.*

Foreword

Marc Andreessen — Netscape Communications cofounder, America Online chief technical officer

When I wrote the code that eventually became Netscape Navigator (and after that, Communicator), I'm not sure what I would have believed less likely: that the code would help launch a business worth hundreds of millions of dollars, or that we'd end up giving its source away for free over the Internet. What ended up happening with this code is testament to the flat-out unpredictability of software development. Even if you try to picture your own success, you can never imagine the shape it will take. As they say, life sometimes gets in the way of your plans.

But from the beginning, we knew that our success would depend on developers like you. If anything, we may have underestimated the critical role folks such as you would play in the overall success of Netscape and the Internet. You've clearly taken the industry and the medium far beyond where even the brightest Netscape visionaries imagined we'd be by now. A few short years ago, *e-commerce* was a typographical error; today, it is creating unprecedented technical and business innovation, opportunity, and wealth.

We've accomplished this together. Netscape provided the tools and suggested a path for you to follow; you grabbed the tools, changed them to suit your needs, and expanded that path into a superhighway.

Right from the start, one of the significant tools we gave developers was open access to Internet application source code. The Internet was built on open standards, and we wanted to keep it as free of proprietary approaches as possible. So, in the very first release of Navigator, we built in the View Source command so everyone could see how everyone else developed his or her Web pages. Hence, all you had to do was select View Source, and up popped a window with the complete source code for any page you were viewing, letting you use the code (and try to better it) in your own application. (Now you use the Page Source command in the View menu.)

That concept eventually led to our releasing the source code for Communicator itself — and that of other Netscape products, such as our Directory Server Software Development Kits — through the mozilla.org Web site (`http://www.mozilla.org`). There you can download the entire source for Communicator and change or modify it in any way you want to better suit your needs. If you'd like (and we encourage you to do this), you can contribute your ideas back by sending in your code.

View Source magazine was built with a similar vision. When Paul Dreyfus came on board to launch our fledgling developer online technical journal in 1996, he believed that if he could convince a few creative people to write up their Web development techniques (really opening their source!), others would follow suit. After all, where else on the Web could you show off your programming expertise, attach your name to it, and be certain that it would be read by people who could appreciate what you'd done?

That concept bore fruit in a major way. Starting with a couple of articles a month, *View Source* was soon attracting so much content that, at one point, Paul and his team of "*View Sourcerers*" were updating the *View Source* Web site every third week with four or five new articles. Readership began in the low hundreds; by 1998, an average of 50,000 people per week looked at the front page. The *View Source* archive, containing well over 200 articles as of this writing, has grown to become a comprehensive online reference library for Internet technical tutorials. And it's still expanding; see for yourself at `http://developer.netscape.com/viewsource`.

This book is our way of thanking the visionaries who originally contributed to *View Source*, and the readers who benefited from their work and then turned around and contributed new ideas. You can think of *View Source* as a smaller version of mozilla.org; without your creativity and hard work, neither would have been successful.

We also hope that efforts such as these continue to inform, educate, and inspire your development efforts. Keep viewing and sharing the source, and you never know: that little Web project you're working on today could be tomorrow's multi-million-dollar business.

Preface

This book contains the collective principles and techniques that constitute the Netscape Communications–approved way of building Web-based applications for small workgroups. All the techniques and code described here will help you develop applications that are stored and/or run on Netscape's Web server, Netscape Enterprise Server (or, in a very few cases, Netscape Application Server), and can be accessed using Netscape Communicator and other standard browsers, including Microsoft Internet Explorer.

No book on this subject can be comprehensive: To fully understand the Netscape technologies you can use to build Web applications, you need to read the thousands of pages of documentation Netscape publishes on its developer Web site, DevEdge Online, at `http://developer.netscape.com`. Instead, the book provides chapters — selected from the DevEdge *View Source* technical journal for developers — on the subjects and issues of most general interest and applicability. Techniques described here can be used to help solve problems that are not addressed in the official documentation and can also help you create your own specific development solutions.

The material provided in this book and on the accompanying CD-ROM is authoritative; Netscape and the authors of each chapter have endeavored to provide tutorial information and code examples that work, as is, provided you use the designated versions of Netscape's software products. For more specifics on the Netscape products and technologies you need to use, see the book's general introduction, "Developing Web Applications That Can Grow," and information in the specific chapters.

Each chapter has been written by experts and thoroughly reviewed by Netscape technical staff for accuracy and usability. (See the Netscape License Agreement on the CD-ROM that accompanies this book to understand the limitations to warranties about the information in this book and on the CD-ROM.)

Who Should Read This Book

Netscape DevEdge Web Developer's Library will benefit anyone developing an application that users access over the Web. It's intended particularly for those of you writing applications that serve a user base in the low hundreds. This book will help you if you have any of the following jobs:

- Technical staff within a corporate information systems department

- Information systems consultants, resellers, or integrators (including regional and global systems integrators)

- Networking deployment staff in small, medium, or large corporations

- Do-it-yourself programmers working on Web-based projects

- Students developing Web applications for class projects

- Technical business/management decision makers trying to gain an understanding of Web application business requirements

It will help you understand and write every part of your application, from its user interface to the code that provides access to relational databases and other back-end systems. It will also help you develop strategies to help you expand your current small workgroup-sized application to serve a larger user base.

What You Should Know Before You Read This Book

Most of the techniques described here are based on applications of the Netscape JavaScript language, which is embedded in HTML pages stored on an HTTP server. JavaScript is a scripting language that is interpreted by Web browsers and, when applicable, compiled to run on the Netscape Enterprise (Web) Server. Its syntax is more intuitive than those of lower-level, compiled languages, and it's comparatively easy to get JavaScript applications up and running. You don't need to be a sophisticated programmer to understand much of this book's content.

This said, you should have basic familiarity with programming principles and techniques if you're going to gain maximum benefit from this book. The editor and authors assume that readers have the following:

- A basic understanding of the terminology associated with programming

- A thorough understanding of the HTML language

- At least introductory knowledge of and experience with JavaScript

- General familiarity with the World Wide Web and Internet architectures and technologies

- Experience writing Common Gateway Interface (CGI) scripts

- Familiarity with relational database management systems (RDBMS) and the Open Database Connectivity (ODBC) standard

How This Book Is Organized

Netscape DevEdge Web Developer's Library has 45 chapters contained in four parts. Supporting material for many of the chapters — including code examples, working applications, and graphics — can be found on the CD-ROM that accompanies this book. The following sections describe what you find in each part of the book. More complete descriptions of each section can be found in the general introduction to the book as well as in the introductions to each section.

Part I: Web Application Concepts

Part I provides general descriptions of key technologies that are either developed or strongly supported by Netscape. You'll need to understand the concepts introduced in these chapters to benefit fully from the tutorials and code in later chapters and on the CD-ROM. Note that some of the material in this section introduces important technologies that are not explained in the book but that you're encouraged to explore further on your own.

Part II: Innovative Client-Side JavaScript Techniques

The second part of the book shows you how to write JavaScript scripts that run on Netscape Communicator and other standard browsers, including Microsoft Internet Explorer. These scripts provide the features of your application that a user sees and interacts with — the so-called user interface. Most of the chapters in this section are written by Danny Goodman, a longtime author, teacher, and consultant on scripting technologies. The chapters and accompanying files on the CD-ROM contain working code that's been tested by the authors and Netscape technical staff.

Part III: Server Development, I: Scripting for Workgroups

The chapters in Part III show you how to write lightweight programs for Netscape Enterprise Server that provide database connectivity and other standard features of modern Web-based workgroup applications. You'll learn how to write JavaScript that's compiled and run on the server to provide robust functionality to small workgroups (that is, those consisting of fewer than approximately 200 users). All the features described in this section can be accessed with Netscape Communicator and other standard Web browsers. The chapters and files on the CD-ROM contain a great deal of working, tested code that you can copy and paste into your application.

Part IV: Server Development, II: Building Applications for Scalability

The last part helps you grow your applications to meet the needs of larger workgroups, up to the thousands (and, theoretically, millions). You'll learn how to design JavaScript applications for future scalability — that is, so that they can grow to serve ever-increasing user bases. You'll also learn about how to use advanced technologies/products, including the Lightweight Directory Access Protocol (LDAP), Java servlets, and Netscape Application Server, to build larger-scale applications. This section by nature is the least comprehensive of the four because this topic is so vast and, currently, relatively unexplored.

The CD-ROM

Many chapters contain references to code examples, applications, graphics, and supporting documentation that we've included on the CD-ROM that comes with the book. An important part of the CD-ROM is the "Welcome and Software Download" file (actually an HTML page). The file contains links you can follow to download the Netscape Communications software products needed to run the examples, if you don't have those products already. We urge you to load the CD-ROM and familiarize yourself with its organization before reading the book. This will make it easier for you to find what you're looking for as you read each chapter. We've included separate folders for each chapter that refers to supporting materials, including the chapter number in the folder name to make it easier to find material on the CD-ROM.

Contributors

The following list provides background information on the book's contributors:

■ **Mike Abney** (Chapter 43) is one of the original developers at Net Explorer, Inc., a leading provider of online technology solutions that specializes in custom application development, systems integration, technology consulting, and new media production. Mike spent two years building object-oriented applications in Java. He attended Texas A&M University, where he received a B.S. in Computer Science from the College of Engineering with a minor in Environmental Design from the College of Architecture. This background gives Mike a unique perspective on the design of object-oriented systems, particularly in the area of human interaction.

■ **Paul Colton** (Chapter 37) is president and CEO of Live Software Inc. (Santa Clara, California) Paul has more than ten years' experience as a software engineer and technical director and has been developing applications in Java since its inception. Paul is the lead developer of the JRun Servlet Engine product line as well as of the JRun Scripting Toolkit product, an advanced Java-based HTML scripting system. He has written several articles in computer science-related trade journals and was a contributing author of the first edition of the book *Java Unleashed*.

- **Tony Dahbura** (Chapter 45), a lead systems engineer at Netscape, has been developing applications in various programming languages for 20 years. He has written for various technical magazines, dating all the way back to the Apple II days. Tony has developed code for many government and private agencies. Of all the languages he has programmed, the Java language interests him the most, from its syntactic perspective to its machine independence, so Java development is where he's spending most of his development efforts these days. When not writing software and speaking to folks about development, Tony enjoys sailing and scuba diving.

- **Duane K. Fields** (Chapters 19, 30, and 36) is a Web applications engineer with IBM's Tivoli Systems, designing interactive tools for internal and external customers. Duane is an active writer and a frequent speaker on the technical and aesthetic aspects of developing and running commercial Web sites.

- **Danny Goodman** (Chapters 2 and 10–18) writes the "JavaScript Apostle" column for *View Source*, and is a JavaScript/DHTML consultant and the author of two hot-selling books in the Web authoring world: *Dynamic HTML: The Definitive Reference* and the *JavaScript Bible, 3d edition*.

- **Robert Husted** (Chapters 1, 6, 20, 25, 32, and 33), formerly a Netscape Technology Evangelist for Web and application server technologies, is coauthor (with JJ Kuslich) of *Server-Side JavaScript: Developing Integrated Web Applications*. Currently the intranet technical lead for Qwest Communications, Robert develops server-side JavaScript and Java servlet-based applications. Robert is a frequent contributor to *View Source* magazine.

- **JJ Kuslich** (Chapters 22, 23, 29, 34, and 35) is an Internet applications designer and developer at Application Methods, the e-commerce services subsidiary of RMI.NET. He's worked extensively on the design and development of several server-side JavaScript applications, ranging from database-oriented sample applications to real-world e-commerce sites. He's also worked on the requirements and design of multitiered e-commerce applications. With Robert Husted, he is the coauthor of *Server-Side JavaScript: Developing Integrated Web Applications*. He's also a regular *View Source* contributor.

- **Roni Korenshtein** (Chapter 44) is a consultant specializing in object-oriented design and development. He has been designing and developing object-oriented tools, technologies, and applications for the past ten years in Smalltalk, C++, and Java for companies such as IBM, Nortel, E*Trade, Certicom, and e*solutions. Roni holds 11 patents in computer security, user interface, storage and retrieval, compilers, and object-oriented frameworks.

- **Eric Krock** (Chapter 8) is a product manager for Netscape's Communicator browser product. One of the founding members of technology evangelism at Netscape, Eric has worked on JavaScript, DHTML, and Netscape's commerce applications. In that capacity, Eric contributed much of the original sample code, applications, TechNotes, and articles to the DevEdge Online Web site in its early days.

- **Victoria Gilbert** (Chapter 21) was a technical writer in Netscape Communication's documentation group. She has worked in a variety of positions, including handling expert systems development, engineering management, marketing coordination and training, quality assurance, and publications management. Finally, she decided that what she likes most is explaining things to programmers. Since then, Victoria has concentrated on designing and writing developer documentation.

- **Glen Long** (Chapter 24) is a consultant with the London practice of the Thomson Technology Consulting Group (TTCG), which specializes in providing technology consulting to the publishing industry. He is experienced in designing and developing architectures and applications for the Web and spent much of 1999 working with Netscape Enterprise Server. In his spare time, Glen likes to eat and sleep.

- **Benoît Marchal** (Chapter 28) runs his own consulting company, Pineapplesoft sprl. His interests include distributed applications, object-oriented programming and design, system programming, handhelds, and computer languages (notably Java). He also enjoys teaching and writing.

- **Damian Mehers** (Chapter 27) is a consultant who has worked for Digital Equipment Corporation's European Systems Integration group, based in Geneva, Switzerland. He delivers Advanced World Wide Web Application Development and Integration courses, workshops, and consults customers throughout Europe and beyond. Damian has more than ten years' experience in application development and integration, largely focused on the middleware arena. For the past three years, he has concentrated on the integration of the World Wide Web with new and existing applications. The views he expresses here are his own and do not represent Digital Equipment Corporation

- **Vishi Natarajan** (Chapter 44) is the principal designer and architect at e*solutions, Inc., a leading provider of consulting services using Netscape Application Server technology. Vishi has designed and developed many enterprise Web solutions using NAS and has a lot of experience in design, development, and deployment of e-commerce Web sites using NAS.

- **Mike Polikoff** (Chapter 26) is a native of Deerfield, Illinois, and a graduate of Emerson College in Boston. He currently works as a Web developer for Bank of America in Chicago. He enjoys playing cards, playing on his computer, and playing cards on his computer.

- **Caroline Rose** (Chapter 4), a lead editor and occasional writer for *View Source*, has her own editing/writing business in Palo Alto, California. The original writer for the Inside Macintosh series of technical books from Apple Computer, Inc., Caroline was also the editor of *develop*, Apple's technical journal for developers.

- **Bob Schlicher** (Chapters 41 and 42) is a principal software architect with AlterNet Communications, a consulting firm that specializes in design, development, and integration of distributed business applications using middleware solutions. He's presently consulting and developing distributed enterprise solutions for Unisys on the Genesis Project at Norwest Financial Services and for Lockheed Martin/Oak Ridge National Laboratory on advanced distributed computing designs.

- **Mark Wilcox** (Chapters 31, 38, and 39) is the Web administrator for the University of North Texas. Regular readers of *View Source* know him as the "LDAP Heavyweight" columnist. His book *Professional LDAP Programming* was published in May 1999. He's been working with the Lightweight Directory Access Protocol and the Web long before it was fashionable to do so. When not working with Web technologies, he likes to spend time with his wife.

- **Gregg Williams** (Chapter 9) is a technical writer, editor, and journalist with 20 years of experience explaining complex technologies to various audiences. He was the first senior editor at *BYTE* magazine, and he evangelized cutting-edge technologies at Apple Computer; he is currently a senior technical writer at Vitria Technology. In his copious free time, he covers the emerging field of Internet-based publishing (IBP) at Pubspace: `http://www.pubspace.com`.

- **Michelle Wyner** (Chapter 40) was the Netscape Technology Evangelist for all things LDAP, JavaScript, and DHTML. She currently is the LDAP Enforcer (aka Technology Evangelist) for the Netscape-Sun Alliance. When not swearing at Windows and loving Linux, she can be found playing roller hockey on any of three teams, or pickup outside at the Netscape rink.

Conventions

This book uses some special conventions that make the material easier to follow and understand:

- Menu choices use a notation like File ⇨ Edit, which means choose File from the menu bar, and then choose Edit.

- *Italic text* indicates new terms or placeholders, and is sometimes used for emphasis.

- `Monotype text` indicates code, onscreen text, or Internet addresses.

Acknowledgments

I don't see how any book can be created by a single person. It's just too much work. That goes double for this book, which was truly a collaborative effort. I'm just the point person in front of a small army of exceptionally bright, talented, and passionate people.

First, I have to offer my warmest thanks to the true authors of this book, the men and women who wrote the *View Source* articles that became that chapters you are about to read. As you'll see, I owe a huge debt of gratitude to Danny Goodman and Robert Husted, who wrote more chapters than anybody. Let me say that it's rare to find people with their combination of skills: really great programming and really great writing. In my experience, you rarely even get one of those skills, but Danny, Robert, and the rest of the authors are (unfairly) blessed with both. (I'm jealous.) Please see the author biographies for more on all the writers.

The long list of people who made this book possible should really begin with Elliot. Elliot Bergson was the first editor of the Netscape Home Page way back in 1995 and 1996 when the Netscape Home Page was the true center of the Web universe. Not to overstate his contribution, but his genius led the way to today's Netcenter and other portal Web sites. Along the way, he proposed *View Source* magazine in 1995; he also named it after the View Source command that was replaced by the Page Source item in Navigator 4's View menu.

The concept for *View Source* was then carried forward by its original editor, Jennifer Mulcaster, who developed the first articles (with Danny Goodman) along with the other five jobs she was doing. Early *View Source* patron saints also included Lynn Carpenter, who hired me as the magazine's full-time editor, and Donna Simonides, the first Vice President of Netscape Developer Relations. (Thanks especially to Donna's bosses at the time, who kept her so busy that she probably didn't even know she was letting me spend $12,000 a month to get the magazine's editorial content off the ground.) Then came Mark Coggins, both a snappy dresser and one of the best managers I've ever worked for. Marty Cagan and Danny Shader were also early "true believers" who helped launch Netscape Developer Relations and *View Source* into orbit. Atri Chatterjee, Todd Lowdon, and Debra Kuhns picked up where they left off. Thanks to them as well.

The DevEdge Online Web site team at the time, led by another Netscape original, Fay Mark, made *View Source* happen, first every month, then every other week. Thanks, Fay, for getting it in a big way and giving *View Source* prominence and attention. Thanks also to her team for all the great support right from the start and up to this day — especially to the steadfast Lee Ming Yeh, but also to Rebecca Grant, Richard Hall, Lori Landesman, Christen Lee, Paul Macadam, and Sarah Oh.

Next, of course, are the "*View Sourcerers*" — the authors and editors who did the real work. You are too numerous to mention here (although some of your work appears in this book), but let me say this about all of you collectively: You are unbelievable. The "if you build it, they will come" concept introduced in the book *Field of Dreams* is supposed to be a fantasy, but in the case of *View Source*, it's absolutely true. I had this wild idea that if we published a few articles, developers from the community at large would follow suit and contribute their ideas. Believe it or not, that actually happened. Thanks especially to Angus Davis, the first developer who offered up his own idea — and the author of the first article I published at *View Source*. For those of you paying close attention, you'll probably be as surprised as I was to learn that Angus was all of 19 years old when he wrote for *View Source* the first time. (From the mouths of babes . . . .)

I'd also like to single out Caroline Rose and Lorraine Anderson, the two editors extraordinaire who make the authors and Netscape — and me — look better with each successive issue of *View Source*. Without their editing skills, and their patience with my so-called publication process, *View Source* and this book would not exist. And without the occasional Scrabble game, Caroline, it's possible that I wouldn't exist. Thanks to both of you. Thanks also to Anne Szabla, another terrific editor who worked during *View Source*'s early days, and to Gregg Hurwitz for his brief but influential stint as assistant managing editor.

Constant sources of inspiration for the ideas that became *View Source* articles (and chapters in this book) were the members of the Netscape Technology Evangelism team, some of whom I was lucky to manage. Heartfelt thanks to all who ever held that title, for your ideas and for your passion in building Netscape, especially in the early years. I'll try to remember all of you: Steve Abell, Christie Badeaux, Christian Ey, Benjamin Feinman, Tim Hickman, David Huntley, Robert Husted, Eric Krock, Mark Lavi, Mike Lee, Lea Lucente, Jim Pelke, Alec Plumb, Bill "Garlic" Rouady, and Michelle Wyner.

I can't offer a complete list of contributors without acknowledging the DevBabes — more formally, the great folks who staffed the Netscape Developer

Response Center. Eva, Ali, Tabitha, Shannon, Jane, and especially my buddy Pat — you guys make it fun, interesting, and worthwhile.

I must also thank Gregg Williams, perhaps the most talented technical writer I've worked with, and Greg "Joz" Joswiak, another great manager I've worked for. They taught me what I needed to know about developers when I worked with them in the Apple Developer Group. Further, my mentor from years ago, Bob Manning, gave me the experience and confidence (and occasional shot of whiskey) I needed to undertake this. Without them, I never would have had the tools to build *View Source*.

Now, to the "bookmakers": Suzanne Anthony and, especially, Susan Walton of Netscape Publisher Relations put the idea for this book in front of the right publishers and finally sold IDG Books on the idea. Lysa Lewallen helped me with the proposal (as did Caroline Rose). Jim Sumser believed enough in the idea to want to publish it, and Eric Newman developed a trying manuscript. (Usually editors have to work on the prose of only one writer; Eric had to edit more than a dozen at once.)

The authors also asked me to thank the following people for their help in preparing the individual articles that became the chapters in this book: Ian Bond, Brian Byun, Frank Chen, Pat Flanders, Rick Fleischman, Karl Florida, Ken Graham, Basil Hashem, Leif Hedstrom, Karen Horwitz, Tim Howes, Scott Johnston, Scott Jolly, Rich Kadel, Thomas Lee, Clayton Lewis, James Mace, Rajesh Mahajan, Eric Mann, Roseanna Marchetti, Steven Martin, Rand McKinney, Willy Mena, Prasad Mokkapati, Jill Nicola, Kim Padgett, Junaid Razzak, Steve Sarette, Chander Sarna, Marcellino Tanumihardja, Jim Wagner, Eckart Walther, Jonathan K. Weedon, David Weiden, Rob Weltman, Rich Yaker, Stephen Yen, and Doug Yoshinaga.

All the people I've just mentioned, as well as the authors whose work you are about to read, went far out of their way to help assure that this book's content is accurate. Any mistakes you find are mine, and mine alone.

Finally, I need to thank my family: my daughter, Samantha, whose energy and creativity always challenges me to use mine; my son, Henry, whose hard work and discipline inspire me to rise above my difficulties; and my wife, Robin, whose love and belief in me give me the confidence to succeed.

Contents at a Glance

Part I

Part II

Part III

Part IV

Server Development, II: Building Applications for Scalability 455

Contents

Part I

Part II

Using JavaScript for Innovative Client-Side and Interface Development

Part III

Part IV

Introduction: Developing Web Applications That Can Grow

The purpose of this book is to get you home at a reasonable hour. A lot of the books sitting right next to this one are probably trying to interest you in some cutting-edge technology, inviting you to try something new and different with the vague promise that it will make you a really "cool" developer.

Interesting, that word *cool*. When it comes to software development, I guess it conjures up an image of someone who lives in New York or San Francisco, travels to a minimal loft-space full of computer hardware (if he or she doesn't live there) sometime around 11 in the morning, takes off his teenie-weenie sunglasses (or doesn't, if he's *really* cool), and programs all night in a language you and I have barely heard of. When he's done, he'll have an elegantly coded widget that may or may not do something that someone wants to do. Even if it does, it will take hours, even days, of integration, porting, and testing to work with any other piece of working software. Cool? Indubitably. Practical? Not.

To me, cool is all about doing something that's really useful, doing it well, and doing it quickly. It's about taking well-wrought tools and making something that people use to make their lives better or easier. It's about doing it so that what you've done can be reused by others. And, most of all, cool is about getting away from the keyboard and getting to the other parts of life, whatever they are for you.

If you prefer my approach to cool, this book is for you. Using this book doesn't mean you can't wear teenie-weenie sunglasses or stay up compiling code all night, if that's what you want to do. (Just don't page me after 10 p.m., please.) It does mean that your efforts will result in a chunk of code that, more than likely, will be instantly usable.

This book is designed to help you develop scalable Web-based applications for workgroups, using well-established Netscape-endorsed technologies. There are a couple of keywords here. First, there's *Web based*. By that, we mean applications that are contained within, or accessed through, HTML pages housed on an HTTP server, such as Netscape Enterprise Server. Users find and use these applications' features over the Web using a standard Internet browser — that is, Netscape Navigator and Netscape Communicator, as well as Internet Explorer.

Next, there's *scalable:* If you're familiar with the latest market-speak, you'll know that the term refers to applications that can grow to meet the needs of ever-increasing numbers of users. You'll also know that it's one of the bugaboos of Web development.

Using Netscape Enterprise Server (and other HTTP servers), it's relatively simple to develop applications that meet the needs of smallish groups of people — say, up to 100 or 200 users. Lightweight scripting languages, such as JavaScript and CGI, let you write many of the features that will make a Web application look, feel, and even behave like a desktop application. You can code fairly complex features, such as relational database integration and all kinds of user interactivity. But what do you do when you want that application to meet the needs of many hundreds, thousands, and even millions of users?

This book will help you write the simple applications for smallish groups of people. From our experience with Netscape developers, we figure that's what most Web developers need. We also know that there's a small but increasing number of developers whose applications will have to grow beyond the needs of that workgroup. Many of you have to think about thousands of users in an enterprise intranet for a multinational corporation with users who span the globe. Some are opening a part of your corporate intranet to your partners and customers to do business with them in an extranet. A few of you are even launching a full-blown business over the next big public Internet site. And all of you probably need to know that, just in case, your application can grow to serve more simultaneous users. For all of you, we offer practical ideas for enabling your application to grow — to "scale" and meet the needs of a larger user base.

Finally, there's the term *Netscape-endorsed technologies*. Here, we mean technologies and products built by Netscape. You'll see that much of the book's focus is on writing JavaScript applications, those that process on either the client or the server.

The code in this book is written to run on Netscape products, especially Netscape Navigator/Communicator and Netscape Enterprise Server. You'll also see material about the Lightweight Directory Access Protocol (LDAP), of which

Netscape was among the first adopters and evangelists. (For example, Netscape was the first company to release a directory server product based on LDAP.) Further, you'll learn about Netscape's pioneering product in the application server space, Netscape Application Server. Along the way, you'll read about parts of one of the *de facto* languages of Internet development, Java.

All the Netscape products you'll need to run the software examples in this book can be downloaded at no charge from Netscape's Web site. To help you find Netscape software products and download them, the CD-ROM that comes with the book includes a file called "*Welcome and Software Download*," actually an HTML page. It includes an introduction to the CD and its contents, as well as links to the locations on the Netscape Web site where you can download the following software:

- Netscape Communicator, including the Netscape Navigator browser

- Netscape Enterprise Server, Netscape's HTTP/Web server product (you can download a development and test version of this product)

- Netscape Directory Server and Netscape Directory Server SDKs (C++, Java, and PerLDAP versions)

All the tutorials and examples in this book and on the CD have been written by Netscape-affiliated experts and reviewed by Netscape technical staffers. They represent our best effort to provide Netscape-endorsed techniques and concepts for Web development. When you've completed reading this book, we hope you'll have a better understanding of what it means to conceive of and develop an application the Netscape way.

The Best from DevEdge Online and *View Source*

No one person can write authoritatively about this wide variety of technologies, products, and programming issues. For this book, we've assembled a group of more than a dozen technical experts, most of them with hands-on experience in developing Web applications. The one thing they have in common is that they've all contributed to *View Source* magazine, Netscape's online technical journal for developers, which is on the Web at `http://developer.netscape.com/ viewsource`. *View Source* is part of Netscape Communications' award-winning developer Web site, DevEdge Online, which you can find at `http://developer.netscape.com`. We selected the chapters you'll read here from its 200 or so technical articles, combing through them to find the very best, most reliable, Netscape-endorsed development information.

Among the writers, you'll find the *View Source* JavaScript Apostle columnist, Danny Goodman, scripter extraordinaire and author of the *JavaScript Bible* (IDG Books Worldwide). You'll also see work from another regular columnist, "LDAP Heavyweight" Mark Wilcox, the author of *Implementing LDAP*, as well as from two top server-side JavaScript programmers, Robert Husted and JJ Kuslich, who recently published the definitive book in their field, *Server-Side JavaScript*.

Similarly, it's unlikely that we can provide a single volume — even a large one, like this — that treats all these topics in a complete fashion. Rather than even try to do what it would take many books to accomplish, we've chosen chapters of particular creativity and usefulness. The chapters describe general principles/ideas/programming techniques that you'll be able to use, as is. You should also be able to expand on them to meet your particular needs. Look at this book as a tasty appetizer to a full-course meal, but one that can help you cook the meal yourself.

Using the CD-ROM

This book simply would not be complete — or even usable — without the CD-ROM. Most of the files on it contain one of the following elements:

- Working code examples referred to in the chapters. You should be able to copy and paste this code into your own application and/or, following the instructions in the chapters, get the code up and running quickly and easily.

- Netscape documentation that either explains the basics of (or elaborates upon) concepts and techniques written about in the chapters. As you'll see, some of the tutorials are, literally, guides to Netscape documentation, to help you accomplish something and learn your way around a document at the same time (for future reference).

- Illustrations that were either too large or too complex to include in the book.

You'll need the following Netscape software products to run the sample applications from the CD-ROM. Note that not all this software is required to run each of the examples:

- Netscape Communicator; we recommend Version 4.5 or later

- Netscape Enterprise Server; we recommend Version 3.1 or later

- Netscape Directory Server; we recommend Version 3 or later

- Netscape Directory Server SDKs, Java, C++, and PerLDAP versions

NOTE

Some of the chapters in Part IV refer to Netscape Application Server, which is not available for free download as this book went to press.

We selected files and software from DevEdge Online that we felt were vital to your attaining an understanding of the material and to work with the examples we've provided. We couldn't fit everything we wanted to on the CD-ROM, so in some cases we refer you to locations on DevEdge and other Web sites for additional information, documentation, and software. We invite you to type the URLs into your browser and follow every cross-reference for an even deeper understanding of the concepts and tutorials presented here.

ON THE CD-ROM

We recommend that you start with the file on the CD-ROM called *"Welcome and Software Download"*; it provides a brief guide to the CD-ROM as well as URLs and links to the software products you'll need to run the examples. You can view the file (it's written in HTML) in any browser.

A Word on Compatibility and Reliability

As we've said already, this book can't hope to be a complete guide to all the subjects above. Instead, we've chosen the best information we can find that, we hope, will spur you on to tackle a great many problems not specifically discussed here. And, if we can't be comprehensive, we can at least strive to be authoritative. That's why we've assembled this group of experts to write this book.

We can also strive to be reliable and give you code examples that actually run the first time you try them. We assure you to the lengths of our ability (and to the lengths our lawyers will let us) that the techniques and code in this book work, as does the code on the CD-ROM. Our expert authors wrote most of these examples to solve problems they encountered doing real-live web development projects. (Please, however, see the standard Netscape Software License statement on the CD-ROM that accompanies this book; it applies to both the sample code on the CD as well as the code in the book. The important information to take away from the Netscape Software License agreement is that we provide the code in the book and on the CD-ROM on an "as-is" basis with no representations or warranties about its accuracy, quality, or completeness.)

We know that the applications work today with Netscape Communicator 4.*x*, and that most of it will also run with Microsoft Internet Explorer 4.*x*, as well. (We have not tested the applications with Internet Explorer 5, as that product was released as this book went to press.) All the Web server code in the book was written to run with and has been tested on Netscape Enterprise Server 3.*x*. LDAP code has been tested against Netscape Directory Server 4.*x*. And AppLogics and other application server code have been tested with Netscape Application Server 2.*x*.

Will all the code run tomorrow, with newer versions of Netscape software? It's the goal of the Netscape-Sun Alliance that will develop and release future versions of Netscape products that code that runs on today's software will also work with future versions, with minimal or no code rewriting. But, clearly, we can't guarantee that the code in this book will work with all future versions of Netscape software products.

To be sure you have the latest information about developing applications that work with Netscape products, please be sure to read DevEdge Online at `http://developer.netscape.com`. There, Netscape will post any updates you'll need to get your code to work with new products. Also, should any of the chapters and examples in this book require rewriting to work with new products, the editors of *View Source* will do their best to provide new versions. So, if these examples don't work, the best thing to do is to visit *View Source* at `http://developer.netscape.com/viewsource` and look for the updates. (Again, no promises here, but we'll do the best we can.)

Keeping up to Date

This book is not intended to provide you a look at cool, cutting-edge technology, as we've stated throughout this introduction. Instead, it's about tried-and-true development techniques you can use to get your job done faster, cheaper, and — we hope — better.

Needless to say, those techniques will change as technology moves ahead. Today's reliable techniques will go the way of all other outmoded ideas and be replaced by new methods of doing the same things — we hope in better ways.

A book like this can't change with the times and update itself. A Web publication can, however, and that's one of the beauties of the Web. We urge you to look at future articles in *View Source* magazine (again, that's at `http://developer.netscape.com/viewsource`) as an extension of this book in online form, just as this book is really an extension of the online magazine in book form. *View Source* was founded on the principle of providing reliable, creative solutions to common Web development problems. If you keep reading *View Source*, you'll not only have this book's 45 chapters at your disposal, you'll have hundreds of how-to articles — a virtual library — to speed your development efforts, with today's and tomorrow's technologies.

You'll not only be really cool. You'll also be able to go home earlier.

PART

I

Web
Application
Concepts

Web Application Concepts

This section of *Netscape DevEdge Web Developer's Library* is intended for those of you new to Web application development, or new to Netscape's technologies. The chapters here introduce you to concepts you'll need to understand in order to use the "how-to" chapters that appear later in the book. The material is presented approximately in order of complexity, starting with simpler, basic information and moving to more complex concepts.

The content is broken down into three main areas: The first subject is JavaScript, Netscape's lightweight, easy-to-use scripting language for Internet application development. Second, you'll find information on LDAP, the Lightweight Directory Access Protocol, which can make your applications easier to develop and more useful. Third, the authors describe advanced technologies and products you use to add complex features to an application and to make it useful for larger numbers of users, including CORBA, Netscape Application Server, Electronic Data Interchange (EDI), and Enterprise Java Beans (EJB).

1

All About JavaScript

Robert Husted — *intranet technical lead, Qwest Communications*

I f you've ever built Web pages, you've probably used JavaScript, Netscape's light-weight scripting language for building Web applications. And if you've ever built applications for Netscape's Web server, Netscape Enterprise Server, you've, at the very least, encountered server-side JavaScript and the Netscape programming tool/environment, LiveWire. Even a brief or limited encounter with these technologies may have peaked your curiosity, and the following questions may have come to mind:

■ What is the difference between client-side JavaScript (CSJS) and server-side JavaScript (SSJS)?

■ What is the relationship between SSJS and LiveWire?

■ How does SSJS compare with CGI?

■ How do SSJS and the Netscape Application Server (NAS), Netscape's industrial- strength Web application server, relate to each other?

This chapter addresses these questions to help you better understand the growing world of JavaScript.

A Holistic Look at JavaScript

What is the difference between client-side JavaScript and server-side JavaScript? To answer this question, it's best to look at JavaScript holistically and discuss all parts of the technology. JavaScript is composed of the following:

■ **Core JavaScript:** the base JavaScript language

■ **Client-side JavaScript (CSJS):** an extended version of JavaScript that enables the enhancement and manipulation of Web pages and client browsers

■ **Server-side JavaScript (SSJS):** an extended version of JavaScript that enables back-end access to databases, file systems, and servers

Figure 1-1 shows JavaScript technology graphically. Core JavaScript is the foundation upon which CSJS and SSJS are built.

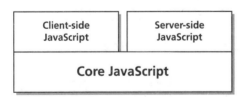

Figure 1-1: How core JavaScript, client-side JavaScript, and server-side JavaScript relate

Core JavaScript Defined

Core JavaScript encompasses all the statements, operators, objects, and functions that make up the basic JavaScript language. Originally called LiveScript, JavaScript is a cross-platform, object-oriented scripting language created by Brendan Eich of

Netscape. JavaScript is the world's most popular programming language; it is used on more platforms and in more languages than any other programming language in history, and it has been licensed by more than 175 companies for inclusion in their Web tools. JavaScript is even available as a standalone scripting language. You can thus take advantage of the booming popularity of JavaScript by integrating it into your own products.

You may have heard of ECMA Script — this is the version of JavaScript that has been standardized by ECMA (a European association for standardizing information and communications systems). The ECMA specification is based on JavaScript 1.1 and includes only the core JavaScript language. No client-specific or server-specific objects or functions were included in the ECMA standard.

The following objects are part of core JavaScript:

- array

- date

- math

- number

- string

As you can see, core JavaScript contains objects that are applicable to both client and server. If you know core JavaScript, you can easily write client-side and server-side JavaScript. Again, the only distinction is that client-side and server-side JavaScript have additional objects and functions that you can use that are specific to client-side or server-side functionality. Any JavaScript libraries (.js files) you create in core JavaScript can be used on both the client and the server without any changes whatsoever.

Client-Side JavaScript

You probably already know client-side JavaScript (CSJS), which means you also know core JavaScript. CSJS, the single most popular language on the Internet, is used in more than 3.5 million Web pages. It composed of core JavaScript along with additional objects, such as the following:

- document

- form

- frame

- window

The objects in CSJS enable you to both manipulate HTML documents (check form fields, submit forms, create dynamic pages, and such) and the browser itself (direct the browser to load other HTML pages, display messages, and so on).

ON THE CD-ROM

You'll find a wealth of official Netscape JavaScript documentation on the CD-ROM that accompanies this book, including the core and server-side guides and reference manuals. In addition, the entire CSJS object model is detailed in "Danny Goodman's JavaScript Object Roadmap and Compatibility Guide," which can be found on the CD-ROM that accompanies this book. Follow this path to find the materials that support Chapter 1: Sample Code and Supporting Documentation ⇨ Part I ⇨ Chapter 1. For a guide to the contents of the contents of the CD, see the CD file called *Welcome and Software Download*.

Server-Side JavaScript

Server-side JavaScript (SSJS) is composed of core JavaScript and additional objects and functions for accessing databases and file systems, sending e-mail, and so on. SSJS enables developers to create database-driven Web applications quickly and easily by leveraging their existing knowledge of JavaScript. It's used to create and/or customize server-based applications by scripting the interaction between objects.

ON THE CD-ROM

The entire SSJS object model for the Netscape Enterprise Server is detailed in "Server-Side JavaScript Object Roadmap and Compatibility Guide," on the CD-ROM that comes with this book; follow this path to find it: Sample Code and Supporting Documentation ⇨ Part I ⇨ Chapter 1.

SSJS is included with the Netscape Enterprise Server and is ideal for creating Web applications that can be run on any platform, on any browser, and in any language. Does it make sense to create something in Visual Basic or PowerBuilder that can be run on only one platform, when you can create a Web application with SSJS that can be run on any existing platform (such as UNIX, Macintosh, and Windows)?

SSJS is also available in the E-Commerce applications — BuyerXpert, SellerXpert, CommerceXpert, and so on — from Netscape, so that customers can customize their applications. The objects employed in the commerce products' implementation of SSJS are different from those used on the Enterprise Server because the data access engines are different. However, the core language is the same.

CSJS versus SSJS

Table 1-1 is a comparison between CSJS and SSJS. Note that the only syntactical difference between CSJS code and SSJS code is that for CSJS you use a <SCRIPT> tag rather than a <SERVER> tag in your HTML document. Remember, however, that SSJS provides a different set of objects than CSJS does. If you try to use CSJS objects in your server application, errors result. Note that CSJS can be served by any server, but it can be displayed only by JavaScript-enabled browsers. SSJS must be served by a JavaScript-enabled server, but it can be displayed by any browser.

TABLE 1-1: CLIENT-SIDE JAVASCRIPT AND SERVER-SIDE JAVASCRIPT

	CLIENT-SIDE JAVASCRIPT	SERVER-SIDE JAVASCRIPT
Tags	<SCRIPT>	<SERVER>
Execution	Client browser (interpreted)	Server (compiled into SSJS byte code)
Compilation	Not compiled	Application file (.web)
Client	JavaScript-enabled	Any browser
Server	Any server	JavaScript-enabled

LiveWire and SSJS

If you're at all familiar with Netscape Enterprise Server, you've probably heard the terms LiveWire and server-side JavaScript used interchangeably although they're two distinctly different technologies. When Netscape released the LiveWire product in 1996, it contained site management utilities and provided database connectivity via SSJS on Netscape Enterprise Server 2.0. In 1997, Enterprise Server 3.0

included LiveWire, and it was no longer a separate product. Netscape began to refer to the database access engine itself as LiveWire to distinguish it from the language that the database applications are written in, SSJS.

Figure 1-2 shows how SSJS interacts with LiveWire to connect with a variety of databases (DB2, Informix, Oracle, Sybase, and ODBC-compliant databases). SSJS provides developers with a collection of objects (such as the database, DbPool, and cursor objects) that interact with the LiveWire database access engine to communicate with a database. At the same time, some of the objects that are part of SSJS (the file, SendMail, and state management objects) do not interact with LiveWire. Remember that LiveWire involves database access only, whereas SSJS encompasses database access and additional server-side functionality.

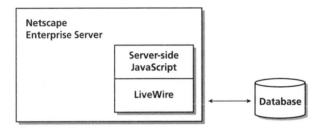

Figure 1-2: How SSJS and LiveWire interact

SSJS versus CGI

So how do SSJS and the LiveWire database access engine stack up against CGI? SSJS is faster and more efficient for Web applications, particularly those that access a database. In internal Netscape tests, SSJS was three times faster than Perl CGIs for database access. There are distinct advantages and disadvantages to each approach, as detailed in Table 1-2.

TABLE 1-2: SERVER-SIDE JAVASCRIPT AND CGI COMPARED

SSJS	CGI
ADVANTAGES	ADVANTAGES
Provides state management capabilities.	Is very portable—can be run on any CGI-enabled Web server.

SSJS	CGI
ADVANTAGES	**ADVANTAGES**
Is based on a standardized language (ECMA Script/JavaScript).	Can be programmed in a variety of languages (C, Java, Perl, and so on).
Provides built-in database access via the LiveWire Database Service.	Means that client and server programs can be written in JavaScript.
Allows code reuse between client and server applications.	Extends functionality using Java (via LiveConnect).
Caches database connections for faster performance.	Runs three times faster than CGI. Scales better than CGI.
DISADVANTAGES	**DISADVANTAGES**
Requires a JavaScript-enabled Web server.	Is slow; a separate process is spawned every time the CGI is executed (which is taxing on the server).
Requires that the application run in-process with the Web server.	Makes state management difficult to implement.
	Makes database access available only via separate libraries.

Don't overlook the important advantage to using a common development language. If you use SSJS to create your Web applications, you use JavaScript on both the client and the server. You can concentrate on a single language syntax when you create both the client and the server parts of your application. The syntax is also similar to Java syntax, providing more synergy and code reuse in your development efforts.

SSJS and Netscape Application Server

In 1998, Netscape introduced the Netscape Application Server (NAS) for use in enterprise-scale, mission-critical applications that support hundreds and thousands of concurrent users. In contrast, SSJS on the Netscape Enterprise Server is intended for use in workgroup applications that support fewer than a hundred concurrent users.

The TechNote "Communicating with NAS AppLogics from SSJS," which can be found on this book's CD-ROM, details the process for communicating between SSJS and NAS, a process facilitated by Netscape's LiveConnect technology. Using LiveConnect, you can communicate with any Java application running on your server, including a NAS AppLogic. You can create critical portions of your application in NAS and then communicate with them via SSJS. This way you can later migrate your entire application to NAS or reference a given service from another application without having to modify the AppLogic.

The Future of JavaScript

CSJS is supported in the Netscape Navigator Web browser and has been distributed with the free source available at the mozilla.org Web site, `http://www.mozilla.org`. SSJS is available in the Netscape Enterprise Server and the Netscape E-Commerce series of products (CommerceXpert, BuyerXpert, SellerXpert, and so forth). Netscape's support of SSJS has continued to increase, and SSJS will be supported in future Netscape products.

The JavaScript engine is now available for licensing by third parties for inclusion in their client and server products and various tools. The engine is available in either C/C++ or Java. (This is how the client browser exposes objects such as window, document, and form, and how the Netscape Enterprise Server exposes the database, DbPool, and other such objects that interact with the LiveWire database service.) If your client or server application needs a scripting language, you might consider licensing JavaScript, the most popular programming language in history.

2

Java versus JavaScript: The Impact of Dynamic HTML

Danny Goodman — *consultant and writer*

An e-mail message from a reader in response to my *JavaScript Bible* raised a provocative question that I hear all the time: "What advantages does JavaScript have over Java?" On the surface, this question is hardly new. Ever since Netscape put the "Java" in JavaScript (JavaScript began life at Netscape under the name LiveScript), plenty of folks have rightfully asked this question. By now, a healthy majority of the Web-authoring world knows the basic differences between the two languages and development environments. What makes this question new to me now, however, is the context in which it was asked.

The correspondent had just finished designing a user interface that required dynamically changing segments of body content on a page without reloading the entire page. Although I don't know the deployment considerations that the correspondent faced, such as cross-browser compatibility, backward compatibility with older browser versions, and so on, I do know that in the end, he wrote a Java applet to perform a development task he had hoped would be accomplished more quickly in JavaScript and Dynamic HTML (DHTML). This event prompted him to ask me the question he did.

As the interest in DHTML increases, it is an excellent time to reassess the roles of Java applets and JavaScript in client-side interactivity.

Why Use Java Applets?

The Java programming language was originally designed for the burgeoning world of network programming. Concepts such as data streams, sockets, and URLs were part of the native class libraries from the very start. The language was targeted at building network-centric applications. The subsequent notion of running a Java program inside a browser window as an applet certainly attracted a lot of Web developers to Java: Here was a chance to get one version of executable code onto a client machine of almost any operating system. At the same time, a Java applet could add some zing to the otherwise flat and fairly crude HTML publishing medium. This was the dream.

In reality, however, a lot of applets that grace public Web pages these days don't have much to do with networking. They scroll banners, wave flags, and present prettily formatted text content in ways that HTML 3.2 wasn't equipped to handle. I do wonder, though, about the heavy reliance on Java applets for so much animation on a Web page. If Java had been intended to be such an animation-friendly universe, wouldn't double-buffered graphics for smooth paint–clear paint sequences be automatic, rather than require extra code?

Although I have reservations about many of the ways developers use Java applets, they do have a place today in Web application development, especially when they play to Java's strength as a network-oriented programming language. I'll pick up on this thread later in the chapter.

JavaScript: What Is It Good For?

Client-side JavaScript has opened a path to programming for many authors who knew little more than HTML. The accessibility of JavaScript — you don't have to learn a language and an Integrated Development Environment (IDE) to get results — enables authors to develop and modify pages quickly. Scripts embedded in the document also begin running right away, and often do their job faster than a Java applet equivalent. Of course, security and privacy concerns prevent JavaScript from being a true network-oriented language on its own (without the help of a security layer such as signed scripts), so there are plenty of tasks authors would like JavaScript to do on the network for which the language is not suited.

Netscape Navigator 3 gave us the chance to blend JavaScript and Java together when LiveConnect made its appearance. From the client side, LiveConnect enables scripts to communicate with Java applets and access native Java classes (without any applets) with the same ad hoc ease as scripting. The security bugaboo still gets in the way, however, preventing unsigned JavaScript and LiveConnect from taking full advantage of Java (that is, JavaScript cannot use the Java classes to read a server data file).

More facilities in JavaScript 1.2, the version found in Communicator, make JavaScript even more powerful as both a general-purpose and a Web-oriented scripting language. The long-awaited switch control structure and the outstanding implementation of regular expressions make the language more than ready for prime time. (Adobe Systems, for example, has adopted the core JavaScript 1.2 language for scripting the Acrobat Forms object model.)

The DHTML Factor

Now comes Dynamic HTML with its promise to provide positioning of content (which can be adapted to path animation), much-improved content formatting with style sheets, and even hiding, showing, loading, and unloading segments of content on a page without reloading a fully reconstituted page. Font sizes need no longer be measured on a cross-your-fingers relative 1-to-7 scale; they can be specified with real point sizes. If you want the left and right margins of a paragraph to be 1.25 inches wide, you can set them this way rather than twiddle with hidden-border tables and transparent GIFs. You can even specify a custom downloadable font to achieve your look, just as the desktop publishing Big Kids do.

A significant benefit to doing all this in DHTML, opposed to using a Java applet that formats interactive content, is that downloading HTML source code is generally faster than waiting for an applet and its data to download. You clearly get a more immediate bang for the byte with DHTML.

But if you've been following my *View Source* articles on DHTML, you're aware that creating cross-browser content that looks and acts the same everywhere is no Sunday picnic. The timing of browser releases and W3C final recommendations for related standards has yielded uneven implementations at the moment, even though both Netscape and Microsoft pledge to uphold the recommendations going forward.

I suspect it is this uneven-implementation problem that led my e-mail correspondent ultimately to choose a Java applet as his deployment medium.

Hammer and Nails

An old proverb reads:

> When all you have is a hammer, everything looks like a nail.

Allow me to port the proverb to the computing world:

> When all you know is one programming environment, everything looks like a problem to solve with it.

Authors of several Web sites I've visited in the past month appear to be quite proud of their accomplishments with Java and creating applets. One site's home page displays a streaming text banner that scrolls five different headlines in a continuous loop. Each headline is actually a link to a different product line area on the Web site. I was not aware of this the first time I visited the site because the banner text didn't appear to be an HTML link in any way; the black text has no underline or other indication to draw me to click on the text. And now that I know the banner phrases are hot links, it's even more irritating when I return to the site to catch up on the latest offerings. You see, the links are not rendered on the page in any other way than as Java applets. So I have to wait for the applet to load and start, and then wait for the desired headline to appear before I can click on it.

Another site I periodically visit demonstrates yet another problem with the applet-only approach. Its home page also includes applet-generated hot spots (animated images this time) that are portals into the rest of the site. But for a while the applet wouldn't download into my browser properly, and as a result, I was locked out of the rest of the site. There was not an HTML link to be found, and I wasn't about to load up on a half-dozen bookmarks for one site. Even with the main-page applet fixed, the nested pages include a series of applets that act as cross-page navigation buttons. Because the site contains material I want to reference often, I tried to save the site for later viewing in an offline reader. But each time a page loads in the reader, it yearns for the applet class files on the host server. At no time do the applets contribute to the content of the page, but they certainly do get in my way. I now must view the page only while online, even though I would benefit from having the information available on a laptop far from a network connection.

Applets aren't the only culprits in the school of design that insist on making life difficult for visitors. Another Web site provides a hot spot on an image as the portal to the content portion of the site — except that the hot spot is at the bottom of a 110KB image. Oh, how clever. You force me to see your fancy, ego-pumping Web site image before going any further. As they say in Brooklyn, fuhgeddaboudit.

JavaScript Hammers

Before you think I'm jumping only on the backs of Java applet programmers and image freaks, let me also say that plenty of JavaScript is thrown at wasteful and disruptive nonsense on more Web pages than I care to count. Once you have a working knowledge of client-side JavaScript, it's easy to let that knowledge get the better of you and your Web page. Some scripters may not believe that my own home page doesn't have one line of JavaScript code in it. Imagine, ScriptBoy has no scripts on his home page!

It's not so much that I worry about backward compatibility with older browsers — the vast majority of my Web site visitors use modern browsers. It's just that I don't find an appropriate application of JavaScript on that page; it wouldn't add to the content or the experience of visitors to the page. This is certainly not the case in other parts of my site where there is often a lot of script action going on behind the scenes (for example, script action flagging users to view what's new in a section since their last visit to the pages).

And, as if to break my own rules, I found myself involved with a project that had brought out the client-side JavaScript hammer when a server-based solution (complete with read-only database access) would normally have been the appropriate tool. In the end, client-side JavaScript saved the entire project because the application had to be deployable as a self-contained solution on CD-ROM. It's an odd feeling to at one moment wince at the thought of forcing client-side JavaScript to do a server's job, but at the next moment smile proudly after replicating sophisticated server functionality entirely with JavaScript code that lives in HTML files.

At the Brink of DHTML

Deciding which technology offers the best solution for a design problem becomes harder all the time. In particular, this a very difficult time for creative Web authors who might like to embrace Dynamic HTML. You may be wondering if you should use style sheets for formatting or let some established Java-based content creation tools make pretty pages out of your text content. Should you introduce some click-and-drag interactivity or path animation with element positioning, or should you design an applet to do the job?

It's a period of painful transition as we wait for evidence of critical mass of DHTML-equipped browsers visiting our sites — unless you're in the enviable position of designing pages for a single DHTML-capable browser, such as Communicator. Everyone wants their pages to look sexy and wants to remain competitive, using whatever means. Or, for example, you may have a corporate style sheet for print that you want to adapt for the Web site, but HTML 3.2 simply can't do it. What's a Web author to do?

New Question, Age-Old Answer

My sense is that, despite all the hammers in which we invest our time, money, and energy, we must put the visitor first. The more I surf the Web, both to explore new sites and to revisit familiar territory, the more impatient I become. It is frustrating to see that page loading is fast (the server and network are doing their jobs), but there is so much stuff loading into the home page — tons of images, applets, and sounds — that it is impossible to get inside the site quickly. And I'm an old guy who wasn't brainwashed with years of "Sesame Street" segment pacing, much less MTV jump cuts. I can't imagine what it's like for the younger surfers who were born with TV remotes and game controllers already in hand.

The need for speed generally works against Java applets that do not contribute significantly to content when client-side JavaScript or Dynamic HTML can do the job. Still, there are times when only an applet will do, and, therefore, I write more *faceless* applets. A faceless applet does its network-related work as quickly and unobtrusively as possible, while content rendering and user interfaces are done in HTML. LiveConnect enables my JavaScript code to communicate with the faceless applet.

As for DHTML, at the time of this writing, the browser base to support it is admittedly limited, but it will only grow over time. Maintaining two sets of pages, one for the latest browser technology and one for all the rest, is a great strategy if you can afford the time and money and it does not bog down your ability to keep the site content fresh. You can, of course, embed style sheets in pages that provide nicely formatted content for new browsers and plain content for older ones. This is not a bad strategy at all. And it may be worth the effort to start now: There is a lot to learn about DHTML, so the sooner you start to get some code under your fingernails, the better equipped you'll be when you eventually make the switchover.

So what about my e-mail correspondent? Did he make the right choice in doing his dynamic content application as an applet instead of in DHTML? Knowing how difficult it is to create a cross-browser page that does the type of swappable text content he needed (and the fact that he mentioned Version 3 browsers in his comments), I believe he did the right thing. When his browser base graduates to the next round of browsers, however, it will be time to revisit the applet and maybe redo it as DHTML to add some speed to getting that page going. And if he were designing the page for a single DHTML-equipped browser today, I'd strongly recommend avoiding the applet altogether and heading straight for the zippy DHTML solution.

3

JavaScript on the Server: Internet Application Development without Native Code

Paul Dreyfus — *senior manager, Technology Evangelism, Netscape Communications*

Maybe you've seen this *Dilbert* comic strip: It shows one of the regular characters saying to a guy who looks like Santa Claus, "I know who you are. That scruffy beard, the red suspenders, smug expression. You're a UNIX programmer." The Santa lookalike replies, "Here's a nickel; go out and get yourself a real computer."

The demand for UNIX programming and programmers has grown astronomically along with the growth of the Internet. A couple of years ago, no one (except perhaps UNIX programmers) would have believed that UNIX could become so hot. But there's no question that with the spread of the Internet, UNIX programming, especially when used to add functionality to and to create applications for Internet/intranet servers (most of which sit on hardware running UNIX), is in demand like never before. The same goes for professional C/C++ programmers for CGI and other types of server development on a variety of platforms.

This is great if you're a UNIX or C/C++ programmer, but not so great if you seek the services of one. There are only so many professional "native language" programmers, and if you're lucky enough to find a good one, he or she may be expensive.

The good news is that you don't have to know UNIX, C/C++, Pascal, and other languages designed for writing native code to accomplish a great many server-programming tasks today. I'm not talking about Java, either. Java is less complex than many native programming languages because of its object-oriented nature and because the code you create using Java runs "as is" — that is, without alterations for specific platforms (or so they say), and on all platforms with a Java virtual machine. However, it is still generally best to have professional programmers who are comfortable writing native code do Java programming. I'm talking about the server-side JavaScript solution provided by Netscape's LiveWire development tool. JavaScript enables you to add features to Netscape Enterprise Server using an easy-to-understand scripting language instead of having to write low-level, native code. It lets you produce cross-platform code that runs in the same way on both UNIX and Windows NT/2000 versions of the servers — an improvement on native languages, which generally don't produce cross-platform code. JavaScript can be used to write both small and large Web-based applications that run more efficiently than their CGI counterparts. And, in doing all the above, it enables a whole new class of previously nonexpert programmers to create sophisticated Internet applications that can access and modify corporate databases and build dynamic Web pages.

Is this bad news if you're a UNIX, C, or Pascal programmer who's been making a living writing CGIs and other server software? No. There's tremendous demand for what you do, and this demand swill likely increase as more and more businesses set up intranets. However, LiveWire and server-side JavaScript are great news if you're trying to set up an intranet — or develop an application for a public Web site — and you don't really think of yourself as a programmer.

JJ Kuslich, a consultant with Application Methods, Inc., and the developer of a great many Web applications based on a variety of languages and environments, says this about server-side JavaScript:

JavaScript is a simple language with a short learning curve. Yet, given the database connectivity extension that LiveWire provides, it's possible to create a Web site that allows dynamically created pages filled with data from corporate databases. JavaScript and LiveWire make this orders of magnitude simpler than was previously possible with C/C++ code and CGI scripts. Plus the execution is generally faster than CGIs. Essentially, JavaScript and LiveWire are excellent replacements for CGI technology — faster, simpler, more powerful. Using LiveWire will give you an advantage because you won't need expensive specialists to maintain the code (in most cases), yet, at the same time, it gives you a nice breadth of capabilities.

The rest of this chapter describes server-side JavaScript and what you can do with it. If you're developing Web-based applications — especially for viewing, entering, and/or modifying information in databases — you'll learn why you want to take a close look at JavaScript (if you haven't already). If you're inexperienced at programming, JavaScript will enable you to do things that you probably didn't know you could do. Even if you're an old hand with UNIX or C/C++, you'll be able to save time and accomplish some of the same things — and maybe more — that you've been doing with the CGI approach to server programming.

Using JavaScript to Develop Web-Based Applications

Code created with JavaScript runs on Enterprise and FastTrack servers using the JavaScript runtime, part of the LiveWire development environment that ships with Netscape Enterprise Server. LiveWire also includes the JavaScript server-side compiler and the database connectivity library, a set of JavaScript objects; these last components are what I focus on in the rest of this chapter.

LiveWire's server-side JavaScript solution, in its broadest description, can be used to develop Web-based applications, or, to be a bit more precise, used to make Web servers carry out the tasks you and your users want them to do. Web-based application can be generally defined as the code that sits on a Web server and performs specific tasks — either on the client or on the server, depending on how the code is written. The code is accessed by the end-user through a Web page.

Server-side JavaScript doesn't enable you to program a server to do anything, but it does let you program the features that are among the most in demand today: database connectivity and what's known as *state maintenance*. Actually, though database connectivity is what many LiveWire developers think of first, Netscape engineers originally designed server-side JavaScript to provide both the database object and a set of state maintenance objects — that is, the code that enables servers to keep track of clients and what the clients are doing when they're connected to the server. Additionally, if there's a feature you can't add to your application with JavaScript, you can do it using C; the resulting code can be tied into your application using the C-call application programming interface that's part of the Netscape Enterprise Server.

The chapters in Part III of this book, "Server Development, I: Scripting for Workgroups," provide more detailed descriptions of how you can use server-side JavaScript, including code examples. For now, though, I take a quick look under the hood of this part of LiveWire to give you an idea of its features and what you can do with it, starting with its state maintenance objects. For a lot more detail about each of the following subjects, you'll want to reference the *Netscape LiveWire Developer's Guide* (for Netscape Enterprise Server Version 2.*x* and earlier) and *Writing Server-Side JavaScript Applications* (for Netscape Enterprise Server 3.*x* and later); the following sections include pointers to specific parts of the *Netscape LiveWire Developer's Guide* document.

ON THE CD-ROM

Netscape LiveWire Developer's Guide and *Writing Server-Side JavaScript Applications* are on the CD-ROM that comes with this book. To find these documents, follow the path, Sample Code and Supporting Documentation ⇨ Part I ⇨ Chapter 3.

What Is Server-Side JavaScript?

Starting with the basics, let's first define server-side JavaScript. All JavaScript code resides within an application, actually an HTML page, sitting on a Web server. Depending on how it's tagged, the code executes either on the server or on the client that's connecting to the application or the HTML page. To create client-side JavaScript code — code that executes on the client computer — you use the `<script>` tag; for server-side JavaScript, which executes on the server, you use the `<server>` tag.

How do you determine whether to have your JavaScript code run on the client or the server? This is a complicated question is a good subject for a separate book. To give you a quick answer though, here's what the *LiveWire Developer's Guide* says on the subject:

As a rule of thumb, use client scripts for the following:

■ Validating user input; that is, checking that values entered in forms are valid

■ Prompting a user for confirmation, and displaying error or informational popups

■ Performing aggregate calculations (such as sums or averages) or other processing on data retrieved from the server

■ Conditionalizing HTML, performing other functions that do not require information from the server

Use server scripts for:

■ Maintaining information through a series of client access

■ Maintaining data shared among several clients or applications

■ Accessing a database or files on the server

■ Calling external libraries on the server

■ Dynamically customizing Java applets, for example, visualizing data using a Java applet

To sum up, you generally use server-side JavaScript for state maintenance, to provide a connection between a Web application and a database, or to access functionality from code written in other languages. Also, to make Web application development easier, LiveWire provides a variety of JavaScript functions that are designed to run only on servers. These functions can generate dynamic HTML, redirect a client to another URL, flush the server's output buffer, and encode special characters so they can be used in a URL, among other tasks. For more detail on this subject, see Chapter 5 of the *LiveWire Developer's Guide*.

State Maintenance Objects

You may have heard that HTTP is a stateless protocol. This means that nothing inherent to the protocol helps a server know whether a client has visited the server before, what processes the server has run on the client's behalf, what data the server has previously served to a particular client, and even how many times the server has been accessed. These are all tasks that have to be written in to the server, and JavaScript provides an easy way to do this.

You can use the following four predefined state objects — objects that let a server maintain persistent data about how it's being used — that you build into your application and control using JavaScript:

- *The server object,* which contains global data for the entire server, keeps track of all requests served by the server and lets the server share data among different applications and clients. You may use the server object to keep track of the number of times an application has been called.

- *The application* or *project object* contains data that enables the application to share data with multiple clients. For example, you can keep track of the number of times clients connected to the server have requested an application to complete a specific task.

- *The client object* contains data specific to an individual client. For example, you can keep track of a client's actions using the same application multiple times.

- *The request object* contains data about the latest request made by a client.

More information on how you use these objects and the LiveWire object framework is in Chapter 4 of the *LiveWire Developer's Guide*.

Database Access with JavaScript

Perhaps the most commonly sought Web-based applications are those that provide database access. There's a virtual tidal wave of organizations that want to have their cake and eat it too, by both updating their networks with Internet technologies and by still letting those new networks use the information they've stored in relational, and other, databases.

Traditional programming methods for accessing databases from Web servers — specifically, writing CGIs — can be quite difficult, requiring you to write complex low-level code. Server-side JavaScript lets you accomplish this far more simply, using the JavaScript database connectivity library provided with LiveWire. In brief, JavaScript code in your application can be written to obtain information from the database and display it in a standard HTML page. It also enables users to enter data into the database as well as modify existing data.

JavaScript lets your Web application access information stored on Informix, Oracle, Sybase, and any other relational databases that accord with the Open Database Connectivity (ODBC) standard for Windows NT-based systems. These applications are said to be *three-tier*, or *client-server-server applications*, because they connect a client (tier one) sitting on a user's system with a Web server (tier two) that in turn connects to a server containing database information (tier three). These applications can be used either over the public Internet or in private intranets and extranets.

When your application uses JavaScript database access methods, LiveWire opens a connection with the database, which is then reused for multiple requests. What happens then depends on the JavaScript you've written in to your application to control the object. You can use JavaScript to have the object accomplish many of the tasks usually associated with retrieving and working with information from a database, including the following:

- Connecting to and disconnecting from the database

- Beginning, committing, and rolling back a structured query language (SQL) transaction

- Displaying results of an SQL query creating updateable cursors for viewing, inserting, deleting, and modifying data

- Accessing binary large objects (blobs) for multimedia content such as images and sounds

Additionally, Netscape Enterprise Server contains a multithreaded JavaScript virtual machine to enable multiple processes to execute simultaneously. It also enables a pool of database connections that can be shared by multiple concurrent requests as well as multithreaded client libraries for Oracle, Sybase, and Informix database systems. These features are designed to make your job as a developer that much easier.

You can find specific information on how you can use the database object in the *LiveWire Developer's Guide* and *Writing Server-Side JavaScript Applications*. Many of the chapters in Part III of this book also describe how to use server-side JavaScript for database connectivity.

A Word on Scalability and Performance

Scalability and performance are important issues for most developers. You want to be sure that you're investing in code that's scalable and can grow to meet increasing demands. You also want your software to run well on your hardware platform so that it makes your users productive and doesn't overtax the server's processing overhead.

With both these issues, it's hard to make a definitive statement regarding the direction to take. Current evidence strongly suggests that JavaScript code is scalable to a point and can meet many of the needs of large enterprise — even mission critical — development jobs, and that it performs in a manner that's at least as good as, if not better than, CGIs and other server enhancements.

Again, to quote JJ Kuslich, this time on the subject of scalability:

> Sample applications that we've written are quite large. In one, we have around 97 custom server-side functions written in JavaScript, contained in 15 server-side JavaScript libraries and about 40 HTML pages, many of which also contain [other] server-side code. The application includes a total of about 8000 lines of JavaScript and HTML code. To tell you the truth, I've been pleasantly surprised at the scalability of JavaScript. It's a simple language, and requires some clever coding at times, but the fact that we're able to do all that we've done is impressive. There are certainly improvements to be made, but I would say even in its current state it is capable of both small-scale and large-scale applications.

It would be a mistake, however, to blow the capabilities of server-side JavaScript applications out of proportion. Though they can accomplish a lot, there have some known limitations. For example, there are some limits to the amount of information the state objects can capture. And the model for database access is page- or form-based, meaning that the client communicates with the server by submitting entire HTML pages instead of being able to submit individual functions containing discrete bits of data. Finally, you can't currently use the database object and JavaScript to access data from legacy systems, such as older IBM mainframes.

With regard to performance, by their very design, Web applications created with JavaScript run more efficiently than CGIs. With CGI solutions, the server has to both spawn an incidence of the CGI and create a connection with the database, undertaking a two-step process. With JavaScript solutions, the server has already established the connection and is reusing it — a more economical solution. Also, with a CGI, the program running on the server and the CGI are separate, and the server has to work with two files. With JavaScript, all the code is contained in one file, which means the server doesn't use as much processing overhead to run the program.

How do JavaScript-based server applications perform in high-traffic situations? Netscape engineers and technical support people answer the question this way: JavaScript is currently being used predominantly for intranet sites, which don't usually experience high volume. However, Netscape tech support engineers have worked on sites employing server-side JavaScript-based solutions that are hit at least 100,000 times a day without performance difficulties, at least from the JavaScript code.

A good rule of thumb when it comes to writing Web applications with server-side JavaScript is that such applications will grow to meet the needs of (or, as they say in the industry, *scale*) up to about 100 simultaneous users. A greater number of users might tax the server to the point that it becomes less reliable, although some creative application designers have figured out how to make their applications scale higher. However, for 100-plus user applications, developers are turning increasingly to Java servlets, described in Part IV of this book in the chapter " Server Development, II: Building Applications for Scalability."

Conclusion: JavaScript in Your Future

As the title of this chapter suggests, JavaScript's great promise is that it enables you to program servers without writing complex, native code. In many ways, we're well down the road to this promise: JavaScript provides a simple-to-use but powerful way to build state maintenance and database access into Web applications, a method that helps you expand your applications to meet the demands of future users. This chapter, however, is just an introduction, an invitation to learn more. Part III of this book has a lot of specific ideas, along with code, to show how you can use JavaScript for server-side programming — without having to program in native languages.

4

Directories and LDAP: Universal Access to Directory Information

Caroline Rose — *editor and writer*

W hen you think of an information directory, you most likely envision a centralized database containing names, phone numbers, e-mail addresses, and other information about people in an organization. And no doubt you can easily imagine the advantages centralized directories offer the people who use and maintain them. But do you know that directories are much more than just "white pages" or a method for finding e-mail addresses; have you thought about what directories mean to you as a developer? If not, I give you some food for thought in this chapter, and if you already appreciate directory services but not the solutions that have existed to date, I've got some good news for you. Lightweight Directory Access Protocol (LDAP), the Netscape Directory Server, and Netscape's variety of client-side directory tools have a great deal to offer Internet developers.

Who Cares?

If directories make you think, "What city, please?" think again. They're not just for keeping track of people's phone numbers, e-mail addresses, and physical addresses. Directories do more than merely store information about people; they can also contain information to be shared or centralized, such as software configuration preferences, access privileges, group memberships, and calendar information. They can also be used to keep track of things such as conference rooms or network resources (such as printers or fax machines).

To name only a few useful directory applications:

- Tracking users' software configuration preferences in a directory can give them the mobility they need to work from any location. Rather than being stored in a local registry or preferences file, accessible only from a single computer, this information can essentially travel around the network with the user.

- Tracking access privileges in a directory enables network administrators to keep users out of parts of the network that are off limits to them. Storing access control rights in the directory enables multiple applications to have easy access to the same security settings.

- Centralizing user account and password information can minimize password management and disparate sign-ons across applications.

- Managing Web site configuration information in a centralized directory makes site administration simpler. One configuration change in the directory can easily be applied to all the servers at the site.

Directories that follow a standard, open protocol move applications and software vendors from a desktop-oriented focus to a network-centered one. Instead of being limited to looking up addresses in a local address book, users can search external directories that follow the standard protocol. Frequently changing customer mailing lists can be accessed just as easily by a desktop sales management application as by a mail server that does the company's automated mailings; it can also be accessed by an external Web server application from an organization that's purchased the right to use the list. The barriers around global access are removed as the adoption of the protocol becomes widespread — which is certainly the case with LDAP.

LDAP has the potential to do for directories what HTTP and HTML did for documents — and Netscape provides the tools that let you unlock that potential.

The Evolution of LDAP

Historically, directory-type information was often stored in an application-specific private database, possibly shared across small workgroups through LAN file sharing using some kind of proprietary protocol. Or an application-specific networked directory would use a protocol that was proprietary to the application (for example, Lotus Notes or Microsoft Exchange) or to the operating system (as in the case of the Novell NDS Directory), restricting use of the directory to people using that application or operating system. The need for a standard, open protocol became evident, but the eventual ISO standard, X.500, was complex and cumbersome to implement, and it was not acceptable as an Internet solution.

Along came LDAP, the Internet directory protocol (based on a client-server model) that was defined by the Internet Engineering Task Force (IETF) and initially developed at the University of Michigan at Ann Arbor. At first LDAP was just a simplified ("lightweight") front end to X.500, but even then it spurred a lot of development. It soon evolved into a standalone protocol and sparked even more interest. LDAP is not only a simpler protocol to implement than X.500 (especially in clients), but because it's under IETF change control, it will naturally evolve to meet Internet requirements.

LDAP is one of the very few Internet protocols that have become associated with a well-documented, well-known, and easy-to-use API. The LDAP API has been widely adopted; LDAP products and services are currently offered by more than 40 vendors, including Netscape, Novell, Oracle, Microsoft, and IBM.

What's What: The Basics

Before going any further, let's take a closer look at some of the basic terms and tools associated with directories and LDAP.

An LDAP directory client (or *LDAP client* for short) accesses a directory by interacting with an LDAP server through the LDAP API, a set of functions (or classes) that request the server to perform operations defined by the LDAP protocol. For example, the server responds to a search request by searching the directory and returning a list of the matching entries. Netscape Communicator is an example of an LDAP client; Communicator's address book feature enables a user to look up a person's e-mail address in various directories located on LDAP servers — not only the user's personal address book but also a corporatewide directory or an Internet-wide directory such as Four11 (`www.four11.com`).

The Netscape Directory Server software package contains all the components necessary for building an LDAP directory service, including the LDAP server, an HTML-based client interface, and the Netscape Directory Client Software Developer's Kit (SDK) for creating custom LDAP clients. The Netscape Directory Server also is capable of replicating directory data, controlling access to the directory, and managing the types of information stored in the directory (more on these features later).

The Netscape Directory Client SDK consists of client-side software for accessing LDAP directory servers through the LDAP API. You can use this SDK to build an LDAP client or to make your existing application *directory-enabled* (sometimes called *LDAP-enabled*). Figure 4-1 illustrates the client-server relationship between a directory-enabled application and an LDAP server.

NOTE

The latest version of the Netscape Directory Client SDK can be downloaded at no charge from the Netscape Web site. See the CD file called *"Welcome and Software Download"* for instructions and links to the Web site.

The Netscape Directory Client SDK provides three different kits; which kit you use depends on whether you program in C, Java, or Perl.

The LDAP C SDK is a set of C-based LDAP API libraries as well as command-line utilities for some directory operations. The command-line utilities are convenient for testing and for use with scripting languages such as Perl. The LDAP Java SDK consists of the LDAP Java Classes, a library implemented entirely in Java that supports the functionality of the LDAP API through an object-oriented interface. This interface is consistent with data access objects in JavaSoft's Java Development Kit (JDK). You can also use a PerLDAP version of the SDK to create LDAP clients, although you'll also need the C version of the SDK if you're going to use Perl. (PerLDAP provides hooks into the C SDK APIs.) The chapters in Part IV of this book show you how to create clients using all three methods.

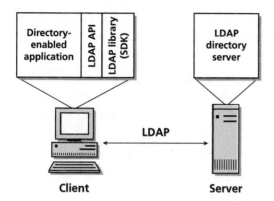

Figure 4-1: The LDAP client-server relationship

The LDAP Java Classes are included as part of Netscape Communicator 4.0 and can be used to incorporate LDAP access into an applet in a Web page. Furthermore, LiveConnect makes the LDAP Java Classes available to JavaScript. The LDAP Java SDK also supports using JavaBeans components to provide LDAP access.

About LDAP Directories

Entries in an LDAP directory contain information about an object, such as a person. The entries are usually organized into a hierarchical tree. Each entry in the hierarchy is a collection of attributes, and which attributes are used depends on the type of entry. Each attribute has a type plus one or more values. For example, an entry for a person can have attributes for the person's name, phone number, e-mail address, and so on.

The types of information that can be stored in a directory are defined by a schema in the directory server. The default schema describes people and groups in an organization. You can extend the schema by adding your own attributes or even your own entry types. You can, for instance, expand the standard entry for a user to include a driver's license number just as you can create a new entry type that describes printers on a network.

The Client-Server Interaction

Here I look at the client-server interaction between a directory-enabled application and an LDAP server. I assume an application written in C, although of course both the LDAP C and the LDAP Java SDKs, and PerLDAP provide similar functionality.

The client connects to the server using a function in the LDAP C SDK. Simultaneously, or as a second step, the client can authenticate itself to the server. It does this by passing the server the user's name and password or other credentials — for example, an X.509 certificate — depending on the authentication mechanism chosen. An authenticated client may be able to access more information than one that isn't authenticated. A secure connection with encrypted data transmission is also available through the Secure Sockets Layer (SSL).

Once connected and authenticated, the client can access the directory through functions in the LDAP API that perform the following operations, among others:

- Find directory entries based not only on a search filter but also on the starting point and scope of the search, the specific attributes to return, and size and time limits

- Add and delete entries

- Modify and rename entries

These operations can be performed synchronously or asynchronously. When finished, the client calls a function to close its connection to the server.

It's as simple as this. But perhaps as you consider whether to directory-enable your application, you're concerned about the lack of control inherent in relying on a centrally located directory rather than on a local file. If so, note that LDAP servers offer a replication feature, which essentially keeps multiple copies of a directory around. Replication serves as a failsafe mechanism as well as a means to place copies local to the user community, thereby reducing wide-area network bandwidth requirements. In addition, your application can cache information read from a directory; this way, if the directory server is ever down or if your application is disconnected from the network, the application can still run (although perhaps with out-of-date directory information).

An Example of Directory Enabling

As a simple example, suppose a Web-based purchase request application presents a form for the user to fill out. The user is prompted to enter an employee number, a department, and a phone number, as well as a manager's e-mail address for approval. Directory-enabling the application makes it possible for the form to be automatically filled out with the data and transmitted to the user's manager. This saves time and money and avoids typing errors that might cause the request to be misrouted or rejected.

Directory-enabling is as simple as embedding a little bit of JavaScript in a Web page that gets executed when the form is posted. A connection is made with the directory server, and the directory is searched to find the user's manager. The user's employee number, department, and phone number are extracted from the user's directory entry, the manager's e-mail address is extracted from the manager's entry, and an e-mail message containing the request is sent to the manager.

Once the manager approves the request, another bit of JavaScript can be executed to search the directory for the request's proper next destination, perhaps the purchase agent responsible for dealing with the vendor in question. Again, this can be accomplished via a simple directory search operation.

So you can see that without much work, an application can gain quite a lot of power when it becomes directory enabled. Chapters in Part IV of this book take a closer look at this process, complete with code.

Going Forward

I hope this brief introduction has inspired you to look further into taking advantage of directories and LDAP in your development efforts. Keep in mind these benefits:

- **Universal access.** LDAP is the Internet directory standard and is widely adopted and implemented by vendors everywhere.

- **Simplicity.** Although it provides a wealth of features, LDAP is a relatively simple protocol with a straightforward API.

- **Extensibility.** You can easily, dynamically extend beyond the standard schema, tailoring the LDAP directory to suit the needs of your application.

- **Access control and security.** LDAP connections can be authenticated (requiring a password or other credentials) and secured through SSL.

- **Multiplatform development.** C, Java, PerLDAP, and JavaScript APIs are available, making LDAP directory services accessible from virtually any language, platform, or development environment you choose.

To get started, you'll want to look at the Directory SDKs on the CD-ROM included with this book.

LDAP is becoming as standard for directory information just as HTTP is for document transport over the Web. No doubt you'll want to join the growing world of developers and users who have discovered the power that directories and LDAP can provide.

5

CORBA: Theory and Practice

Paul Dreyfus — *senior manager, Technology Evangelism, Netscape Communications*

CORBA — the Common Object Relation Broker Architecture defined by the influential Object Management Group (OMG) — defines how software objects distributed over a network can work together independent of client and server operating systems. There's much more to CORBA than this. I'll provide a more complete introduction to the subject in a moment, but for those who'd like to know what to do before hearing all the whys and wherefores, I start with the three main CORBA "developer action items," organized roughly by developer types:

■ **Web application and component developers:** Develop small software objects, each object providing a discreet service instead of writing large, general-purpose applications. Write these objects using Java, especially JavaBeans (although you can also use C and C++), and make them CORBA compliant by giving them an *Interface Definition Language* (IDL) specification. You can use other languages, as well, but they require that you do more work to make the resulting objects CORBA compliant.

■ **Enterprise developers:** Divide your "legacy" code and other older code into smaller objects and write an IDL specification for them. This "exposes" the object's services to other CORBA objects across the Internet, making it possible for other CORBA objects to see and communicate with your objects. One of the great advantages to CORBA's is that it offers you a way to preserve your current code base and give it an interface (through IDL) that makes it accessible using Internet technology.

■ **Tool developers:** Add support for CORBA to your Internet development environments. In order for IDL-defined objects (or services) to be accessible to the vast array of client and server systems on the Internet, an object's IDL specification has to be compiled into language-specific code. If you're a tool developer, the Internet development community depends on you to make that process easy by adding language-specific IDL compilers to your product. Additionally, developers will look to you to provide facilities with your tool to let them integrate CORBA objects into their applications.

I'll come back to each of these items later, so don't worry if you aren't entirely satisfied by the above descriptions. For now, let's talk about the CORBA vision and its underpinnings.

CORBA Theory from Marc Andreessen

Marc Andreessen, one of the co-founders of Netscape, played a large role in popularizing the CORBA standard, making the decision in 1996 to build CORBA compliance into every Netscape browser and server. At the time, the vast majority of Web sites — even those called *applications* — served up static, HTML-based content. Some sites connected to relational databases, but very few enabled Web users to gain access to applicationlike services and perform the tasks typically associated with standalone computer applications.

Marc, among other visionaries, knew that CORBA could change all this. Using CORBA, developers would be able to provide users access — over the Web — to a vast range of *services*, such as using information from old and new databases, tracking inventory, keeping medical records, controlling corporate finances, searching for information, purchasing, banking — you name it. These services could be implemented as small software objects stored on servers of all types; CORBA would enable objects written in virtually any language to interact over the Internet. The objects themselves could provide access to previously written applications sitting on mainframes and other systems, or they could provide access to newer application software designed specifically for Internet use. Additionally, each of these objects would be small software components rather than large applications; they could be updated and distributed far more quickly and easily than older, traditional software.

At the time, the 700-plus members of the OMG — including IBM, Apple Computer, Oracle, Hewlett-Packard, Digital Equipment Corporation, and Microsoft — had endorsed CORBA, and many companies had implemented CORBA-based information technology solutions. CORBA-based solutions remained unavailable to most Web users, however, because the majority of browsers and servers didn't yet support the standard. To make the CORBA vision real, support for it would have to become a standard commodity item, available to every Internet user, via every Internet server.

Responding to its leader's vision, Netscape took a huge step toward "commodifying" CORBA. The first step in Netscape's CORBA strategy was to integrate CORBA software, called an *ORB* or object request broker, into all its products. The ORB would give all Netscape Communicator users access to any existing and all future CORBA-compliant software objects.

The next steps were up to the developer community — that is, *you*. Marc Andreessen called on developers to give Web users access to CORBA's benefits by following the action items outlined just above. But before getting to CORBA practice, and what you can do, let's talk more about CORBA theory so you can understand those benefits.

A Short History

Long ago, before the popularity of the Internet and the Web — that is, way back in 1989 — the OMG formed to define an open software architecture that would let different vendors' software objects work together over a network. The OMG founders saw that the proliferation of different proprietary network and operating systems often demanded that good folks like you develop entirely different versions of the same network-based, client-server applications. They wanted to define an open way to write these applications such that the same code could be used regardless of the operating system and network connection. Since then, the OMG has grown to become the world's largest software consortium. Its members' collective work resulted in the CORBA 2.0 specification, adopted in 1994, which achieved the goals of defining an open architecture for platform- and network-independent object computing.

CORBA grew at the same time as three influential trends, which lent credence to the CORBA vision. First, the software development community realized the importance of object-oriented programming techniques, even though they'd been around for the better part of two decades. Second, industry leaders, including IBM, Microsoft, and Apple, were advocating new application models based on small, task-specific components instead of large, general-purpose monoliths. These components would be easy to write and update because they were small. Developers could more conveniently, and more cheaply, upgrade only those parts of their software that were out of date, and users wouldn't have to purchase entirely new versions of the entire package. And the small components could be distributed over a network more easily than their gargantuan ancestors could. The more enlightened of these component architectures promised a cross-platform future where all components could work together entirely independent of the underlying operating system.

Third, just after the release of CORBA 2.0, in early 1995, the Java programming language burst forth, almost as a proof of the concepts behind the object-oriented, component software architecture visions. Java provided an object-oriented development environment for producing small software components that could run on any operating system with a Java virtual machine. And Java added a new wrinkle to the vision: The components could be used over the Internet, which by then was well into its popularity surge.

CORBA easily fit the new component- and Internet-based approach to building and using software. It defined a way to divide application logic into objects that would be distributed over a network, some sitting on clients, others on a variety of servers. It also defined a way for those objects to communicate and use each other's services.

CORBA also ingeniously specified a way for older software to be reused in the new environment. In this way, unlike many competing schemes, CORBA formed a two-way "bridge" for software developers and users. The CORBA specification bridges the proprietary code of the past with the open, Internet-based applications of present. It also bridges the present with the distributed Internet-based object computing future where users will not only be able to search for subjects within simple HTML pages but also for objects that can perform services.

The Netscape Vision and CORBA

Given CORBA's openness, and its bridge to the past and future of computing, it's no wonder that hundreds of companies and institutions have adopted CORBA already and that Netscape has made CORBA one of its cornerstone technologies. CORBA defines an architecture for the communication of software services, in the form of objects, to communicate with one another over the network. Client objects, using the Internet Inter-Orb protocol (IIOP), communicate with other objects sitting on servers, or even on older host systems connected to the network. Working together, these objects are said to be a *distributed application* — an application with parts distributed across the network.

The CORBA specification gives you a way to write software objects that can communicate with other CORBA objects across the network, regardless of the language used to create them or the server's operating system. With CORBA, you can write an object that sits on a client system within one corporation, and that object can then reach out across the Internet and use the services — or view the information — contained in another object, or set of objects, sitting on a server in another corporation.

That's the CORBA theory. The rest of this chapter describes some of CORBA's more practical aspects.

CORBA Practice

CORBA can be described in terms of its *component* parts:

- The architecture itself, which defines services and protocols that dictate how objects communicate with one another.

- The software modules that manage the communication between objects; these modules are called *object request brokers*, or ORBs.

■ A language, called *Interface Definition Language* (IDL), that you use to provide a specification for a CORBA object, making the object—and the service(s) it provides—visible to other CORBA objects.

■ The objects themselves, which actually provide services.

Architecture and ORBs

CORBA defines a protocol—IIOP, the Internet Inter-ORB Protocol—governing how objects communicate over the network. For those of you familiar with the Open Systems Interconnect (OSI) model of network protocols, IIOP runs atop TCP/IP on the Application Layer. Unlike HTTP, which is a stateless protocol, IIOP allows state data to be preserved across multiple invocations of objects and across multiple connections.

The CORBA architecture also provides a set of services that help objects interact with one another. (The term *services* here might be confusing. In the CORBA world, *services* means both the services provided by the CORBA architecture to help objects communicate and the services provided by the objects themselves.) The services are among the efficiencies provided by CORBA: You write your objects' code—the code that provides the object's services—and IDL specification; CORBA takes care of how your object identifies itself, finds other objects, learns of network events, handles object-to-object transactions, and maintains security. The services include the following:

■ A naming service, which enables a CORBA client to locate a named CORBA object. Every CORBA object has its own unique name.

■ An event service, which provides an asynchronous messaging layer to complement the synchronous nature of standard CORBA communications. Publishers and subscribers each connect to an event channel; publishers send messages (events) to the event channel, and subscribers receive these messages (events) asynchronously.

■ A transaction service, which defines transactions between objects.

■ A security service, which provides security functions, such as encryption, authentication, and authorization, to protect data and to control user access to objects and their services.

ORBs are fundamental to the architecture. For any client or server to be a part of the CORBA scheme, it must include an ORB to help it find and communicate with CORBA objects. Once outfitted with an ORB, a client or server can use the services of any CORBA object on any server or host on the network, communicating using the IIOP protocol.

Interface Definition Language

CORBA also defines a special language, IDL, that provides a language-neutral way of describing a specification for a CORBA object and the service(s) it provides. IDL enables components written in different languages to communicate with one another using IIOP and the rest of the CORBA architecture. (Objects with IDL-defined interfaces are said to be CORBA compliant.)

Currently, it's easiest to provide an IDL specification for objects written in C, C++, and Java because the OMG has completed mapping schemes (or translation guides) from IDL to these languages. Also, there are already compilers that employ these mapping schemes to translate IDL to C, C++, and Java. (OMG is constantly working on IDL mappings for other languages.)

CORBA objects may sit on different types of systems — Windows or UNIX servers, IBM 3090 or DEC VAX mainframes. They may even be written in different languages. In fact, the objects don't need any inherent knowledge of one another's existence. As long as the interface to the service provided by the object is written in IDL, all the objects can communicate and use one another's' services through ORBs sitting on clients, servers, database systems, mainframes, and other systems on the network.

Multitiered Applications: How CORBA Works

Because CORBA objects can reside on such a variety of systems, CORBA is said to enable "multitiered" applications. In fact, the concept of "n-tiered" applications (that is, with a client communicating with any number of servers and data sources) that is so prevalent in "marketectural" literature today originated in the CORBA world. Through the ORB sitting on the user's browser, that user can have access to the services of objects sitting on a multitude of servers and hosts. A CORBA object, using IIOP and the client ORB, can use the services of an object on a Web server (through the server ORB), which in turn can use one or more objects on relational databases or legacy systems (as long as each system includes an ORB). In this way, an object can be both a client and a server object: An object that resides on a server or host — acting as a server — can provide services to a client object. The same object — acting as a client — can request the services of another server object.

A client object requests the services of other objects through an ORB that resides on the client system. (It's not called a request broker for nothing.) Using IIOP, the client ORB then reaches across the network, looking for ORBs on other systems and the server objects that can provide the requested services. Each object has a unique name, which has been provided according to the CORBA naming service, that identifies it and its services to other objects. Once the ORB has found the requested service/object, the client object communicates with the server object, still using IIOP. Each object's IDL interface tells the other object how to use its services and how to construct the results generated by these services.

An example will make this more compelling; let's look at a parcel-tracking application. Let's say that, using the Internet, a user wants to track delivery of a package. The user enters a URL into a Web browser (the client, or tier 1) that points to the delivery company's Web server. The server (tier 2) uses HTTP to send a Web page to the user; this page contains an embedded Java applet, which is the client component of the parcel-tracking system. Note that so far nothing described up to this point is different from a traditional HTTP Web transaction.

Next, the user enters a parcel-tracking number into the appropriate field in the Java applet. Using the client-side ORB, the applet then generates and sends an IIOP message across the network, looking for a specifically named server object that can obtain the status of the parcel. The ORB on the server (tier 3) with the appropriate parcel-tracking object picks up the message and invokes the object's status-finding method. Through the server ORB, the object then generates another IIOP message looking for an object on a legacy system — let's say, an IBM mainframe — (tier 4) that contains all the parcel company's data.

Upon obtaining the last request through its ORB, the mainframe containing the data-tracking object determines the status of that parcel from its database and returns an IIOP message with the information to the server object. The server then routes the information — again with IIOP and the ORBs — to the Java applet running on the client, which displays the results to the user. All this happens at the blink of an eye, as it would with a standard desktop application.

Creating CORBA Objects

The architecture and ORBs provide the mechanism for CORBA communications — that is, the rules that objects have to pay attention to if they're to work together. The objects themselves are small software modules that provide some kind of a service, such as access to a database, account management, or inventory tracking. There are two general ways to create CORBA objects, depending on whether you're creating new objects or trying to turn existing code into an object.

Creating New Objects

If you're starting from scratch, you can develop CORBA-compliant objects most easily using Java or C++. This is because IDL-to-Java and IDL-to-C++ compilers are readily available to you as integral parts of Netscape Enterprise Server 3.x. You can also find IDL-to-C compilers — as well as other compilers for use with other languages — from other vendors.

Whether you use Java or C++ depends on your preferences and the solution you're trying to develop. Java is probably more flexible, although C++ may offer better performance, depending on your server environment. If everything else is equal, Netscape suggests using Java because of its cross-platform nature. Your Java object will work on any operating system with a Java virtual machine.

To give you a feel for what's at stake in the creation of a Java or C++ CORBA object, here are the basic steps you'd follow:

1. Using IDL, write a specification for the objects.

2. Using the appropriate compiler, compile the IDL code into Java or C++ code "stubs" and "skeletons." The client uses the stubs, while the server skeletons provide the framework that you fill in with the code for the service your object is to provide.

3. Write the Java or C++ code to implement the service.

4. Compile the code created in the previous step.

The specific techniques you'd use to create new Java and C++ CORBA objects are described in the Netscape Internet Service Broker documentation that's on the CD-ROM. You'll want to start with the *Netscape Internet Service Broker for C++ Programmer's Guide* and the *Netscape Internet Service Broker for Java Programmer's*

Guide. They can be found by following the path, Sample Code and Supporting Documentation ⇨ Part I ⇨ Chapter 5.

ON THE CD-ROM

Netscape Internet Service Broker for C++ Programmer's Guide, Netscape Internet Service Broker for Java Programmer's Guide, and other Netscape CORBA documentation can be found on the CD-ROM that accompanies this book. Find it by following the path, Sample Code and Supporting Documentation ⇨ Part I ⇨ Chapter 5.

Reusing Existing Code

One of the advantages to CORBA is that it provides a path for advancing legacy systems and other existing code bases, into the cross-platform, Internet-based present and future. If you're involved in this kind of project, you have some tough decisions to make. Should you throw out what exists and start from scratch, say, with Java? Should you try to reuse your entire system? Or should you proceed on the middle path and rewrite some services while retaining the existing code for others?

Helping you make this decision is far beyond the ken of this chapter. If you've decided, however, to reuse your code, your course is often similar to the one you'd take if you were creating new CORBA objects. You first need to decide which parts of your code you'd like to reuse, and then define a specification for them using IDL.

What you do with the IDL specification for the code, and the code itself, will differ widely depending on your specific situation; and creating stubs and skeletons for existing code, and then connecting them to the code itself, can be quite complex. For advice on how to proceed, it is helpful to look at the OMG web site at http://www.omg.org.

CORBA Limitations and Opportunities

Although CORBA is a mature, time-tested technology, it's not without limitations; for example, network security is still an issue because you can't communicate across a firewall directly with IIOP. To overcome this and enable IIOP transactions across a firewall, CORBA currently uses HTTP tunneling, converting IIOP packets into HTTP packets so the firewall can recognize and direct them. Netscape, OMG, IONA, and others are working to enable transparent IIOP communications across firewalls; one potential fix to the security issue is an object proxy that will work with firewalls so that proxy servers could understand IIOP. Also, OMG has developed a guide to using Secure Socket Layer (SSL) for sending IIOP packets, which is part of the current CORBA specification.

Another limitation happens to be a great opportunity for those of you building tools for Internet application development. As noted earlier, language-specific IDL compilers constitute a crucial part of the CORBA object development process, taking IDL specification code and turning it into native language stubs (for client objects) and skeletons (for server-based objects). However, CORBA currently supports only a handful of languages, and there are now very few IDL compilers, even for the supported languages.

If you develop Internet application tools, you can both differentiate your product and move the CORBA vision a little closer to reality by including IDL compilers — at least for C, C++, and Java — with your tool. If you're the kind of developer who wants to boldly go where others haven't, you can also determine mappings from IDL to the unsupported languages of your choice. Additionally, you can provide tools to create IDL specifications from object interfaces written in other languages — for example, a Java-to-IDL or C++-to-IDL processor. This would enable developers to define objects in their favorite language without having to learn IDL. In any case, there's a huge opportunity — and a great need — for tools that support CORBA object development and CORBA component developers. Wouldn't you rather offer CORBA support with your tools than have your competitor do it first?

Additionally, there's a need for tool vendors to provide support for integrating CORBA objects with Web-based applications. Many Web application development tools support a variety of standards and languages, letting developers build applications using Java, JavaScript, C, C++, UNIX, and other components.

Despite these limitations, Netscape and others have bet heavily on CORBA. True, adoption of CORBA is not as widespread as its backers might like it to be, and even though most CORBA-compliant objects currently sit behind firewalls, CORBA solutions currently number in the thousands. Companies numbering in the thousands support CORBA through membership in the OMG. Additionally, a variety of companies have very publicly lined up behind and/or adopted CORBA. These companies include IONA, which has produced its own ORB products; Oracle; McDonnell Douglas Aerospace; Digital Equipment Corporation; MITRE Corporation; Andersen Consulting; and, of course, Netscape. (You can read the stories of these and other successful CORBA adopters on the OMG Web site.)

Netscape: Enabling CORBA for Internet and Intranet Users

Netscape's goals have been to turn CORBA into a commodity, enabling it for use across intranets, extranets, and the Internet, by integrating it into its product line and working with others to extend IIOP and other CORBA technologies. Toward this end, Netscape originally licensed technology from Visigenic Software and formed partnerships with Sun, IBM, and Oracle to develop CORBA-based technologies.

In line with its vision of the networked enterprise, the first step of Netscape's CORBA strategy is to make CORBA an integral part of every client and server across its installed base. Netscape includes the following with its new Communicator and SuiteSpot product lines:

- Netscape Communicator ships with the Netscape Internet Service Broker for Java — a Java ORB — making it possible for clients to use the services of CORBA-compliant objects.

- Netscape Enterprise Server (NES), Netscape's standard Web server, includes both Java and C++ ORBS, called the *Netscape Internet Server Brokers* for Java and C++. Included with the server is a single-user developer license and all the tools that come with it, including IDL compilers, network agents, and miscellaneous utilities.

- NES also includes the Web Application Interface (WAI), which augments the Netscape server application programming interface (NSAPI). WAI has an IDL specification and lets your server "plug-in" and other server-side software objects communicate with CORBA objects on the network. For an interesting approach to integrating CORBA with NES, see Chapter 27, "Integrating LiveWire and CORBA" in Part III of this book.

- The Netscape Application Server (introduced in the next chapter) includes CORBA support. For information on how to integrate NAS with CORBA, see the TechNote "Integrating NAS, Netscape Extensions, and CORBA," on the CD-ROM that comes with this book. To find it follow the path, Sample Code and Supporting Documentation ➪ Part I ➪ Chapter 5.

Unlike other CORBA solutions that are based on proprietary protocols, Netscape's implementation makes strict use of IIOP, the open protocol that runs on top of TCP/IP.

The CORBA Promise and You

As I hope you've seen from this chapter, contributing to the progress of the CORBA vision holds great promise for you and for your users. You can develop software objects that are reusable or turn your existing code base into reusable objects. Or, if you develop Web application-building tools, you can incorporate CORBA support into your products.

The Internet world is moving rapidly toward CORBA for three main reasons:

- CORBA is a time-tested technology that's already used in many large corporate applications.

- CORBA embraces virtually every computing operating system and language.

- CORBA provides a standard, open means of interoperability between software objects distributed across the Internet.

As I look at it, it's fairly simple: If you don't support CORBA, you risk having to redo your software yet again for future, not-yet-conceived solutions. If you adopt CORBA, you join a great many others in giving your software an immediate place in today's and tomorrow's networked enterprise.

6

Netscape Enterprise Server and Netscape Application Server: What's the Difference?

Paul Dreyfus — *senior manager, Technology Evangelism, Netscape Communications*
Robert Husted — *intranet technical lead, Qwest Communications*

All Web sites serving up basic HTML-based content depend on standard Web servers. Such Web servers "speak" the HTTP protocol as they handle basic HTTP requests from browsers and serve up HTML pages.

Most Web servers, including Netscape's Enterprise Server (NES), also enable you to offer a fair amount of applicationlike services to users over the Web, primarily access to information stored in relational databases. The initial chapters in this book introduce some of the Web server programming concepts you need to understand before you develop such basic Web-based applications.

Increasingly, developers and e-commerce vendors want to provide "real" desktoplike applications over the Web. Such applications might access data and application services from legacy systems (in addition to relational databases), conduct high-volume transactions, or serve hundreds of thousands, or even millions, of simultaneous users.

Standard Web servers, including NES, can be pushed beyond their programming and performance limits by such Web applications. Using CORBA, which is described in the previous chapter, is one way around the limitations of a Web server. CORBA, though, can be a difficult programming solution for all but the most expert programmers. Further, Web servers often choke on high loads and sophisticated applications, even those written according to the CORBA specification or those using other higher-capacity APIs. (See the book's general introduction for a brief discussion of other APIs available on the Netscape Enterprise Server.)

Increasingly, Web developers are turning to application servers for high-availability applications that employ a variety of services from multiple databases and other back-end systems and offer them to a great many users. Netscape has been a pioneer in this field with the Netscape Application Server (NAS); it hails as a best-of-class programming and runtime environment for advanced Web applications.

In this chapter, we're going to introduce you to application servers in general, NAS in particular, and explain what's really behind the performance, scalability, and reliability claims Netscape makes about NAS. Along the way, we'll also introduce you to Netscape Enterprise Server (NES) and how it works, comparing its application environment with that of CGI. The purpose of this chapter is to help you understand when you can rely on NES, and when you need to make the expensive jump to NAS. We'll show you why NAS provides a faster, highly reliable runtime environment than NES for complex Web-based applications (that is, applications that provide a dynamic user interface, access multiple databases, interact with legacy systems, provide users read and write access to files, and so on).

Different Architectures, Different Purposes

We should start by pointing out that we're not saying that NAS is better than Netscape Enterprise Server, Netscape's Web server, is. Each was designed to accomplish a specific purpose. In the early days of the Web, when people primarily used it to publish information, developers were simply interested in serving up HTML documents using the HTTP protocol. Netscape Enterprise Server was designed to do just that, and to be a general-purpose runtime environment for relatively light-weight application code. It does both these jobs very well. Now, people use the Web to serve highly complex applications — not unlike the ones we run natively on our desktop computers. Application servers have been introduced for the special purpose of working in tandem with Web servers to process complex application code — something Netscape Application Server is extremely good at doing.

Web servers are designed primarily to respond to HTTP requests by returning HTML pages to users. The various ways to do database access and application development on Web servers are add-ons to the basic functionality rather than well-designed and optimized solutions for Web applications. The add-ons achieve their work through server plug-ins, language interpreters (such as Perl), and so forth. So the processing that takes care of them can't really be considered "native" to the Web server environment. This poses several problems, as you shall see.

Unlike any Web server — and, perhaps, any other application server — NAS was designed from the ground up to perform high-end processing (including dynamic user interface generation, database access, legacy access, and commerce transactions) for Web-based applications. In 1995, Keng Lim founded Kiva Communications to develop a concept that, at this time, was entirely new: One day, Web applications would require a runtime environment that provided 'round-the-clock reliability, robust application logic processing, and the capability to serve many thousands, even millions, of users without a hitch. His concept became the Kiva Enterprise Server. Netscape Communications purchased Kiva in late 1997 and built Kiva Enterprise Server into the Netscape Application Server. As a result, the architecture of NAS is primarily focused on providing heavy-duty, reliable processing capabilities that can grow to meet the needs of a virtually unlimited user base.

This is a high-level "marketectural" comparison of a Web server and NAS. Now let's look at the issue a little more closely and a little more technically.

Web Servers and CGI:
A Way into Databases

Web server engineers recognized fairly early in the game that exposing corporate data via the Web would be very useful. The earliest way of doing this was via the

Common Gateway Interface (CGI), which could be programmed in a variety of languages, including C/C++ and the UNIX scripting languages (such as Perl and tcl).

Figure 6-1 shows how a CGI script works. The Web browser makes a request (such as `http://server.domain.com/cgi-bin/myCGI.pl`) that references a program on the server rather than a standard Web page. The Web server runs the requested program (myCGI.pl) and passes the output back to the Web browser. Thus, when you make a CGI request you're not asking for an HTML document; you're actually requesting the output from the specified program on the server.

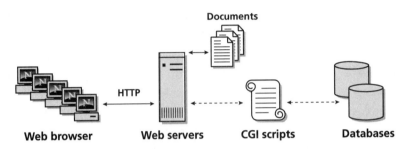

Documents

HTTP

Web browser   **Web servers**   **CGI scripts**   **Databases**

Figure 6-1: Obtaining data via a CGI Script

The biggest limitation to this scheme is that the Web server has to start up a new process every time a CGI script is invoked. Once that process is finished, it goes away. In other words, CGI processes don't persist from one invocation to the next. This results in high processing overhead, which limits the number of CGI scripts that can run at a given time and slows down the Web server when they do run. (There's a commercial solution to this called *Fast CGI* that keeps CGI scripts running in memory, and thus speeds up the performance of CGI-based applications.)

There are other limitations that lead to increased overhead and slow performance, such as the fact that the server must ensure that the Perl interpreter is running for all Perl CGI scripts. C/C++ CGI scripts run faster but are more complex so that C/C++ CGI development requires more sophisticated programming skills than Perl CGI development does. For instance, if you want to enable database access using C/C++, you must use some form of database-dependent embedded SQL. In Perl, you must use a database-dependent library to facilitate connections. In both cases, if you ever switch databases, you have to rewrite a lot of your code. Also, every time a CGI script obtains information from the database, it has to open a connection to the database and then close it once it's done. Opening and closing connections are two of the most processing-intensive requests you can make to a relational database management system (RDBMS), and a CGI script must do this every time it's executed.

Another drawback to CGI development is that because the HTML code that makes up a Web page is tightly integrated with the actual program code (in C/C++, Perl, and so forth), changing the appearance of a Web page that's created via CGI requires modifying the actual CGI program. The skills required for CGI coding far exceed those required for basic HTML coding. Changing even one word on the HTML page requires the skills of a more expensive Web developer rather than a less expensive HTML coder. In addition, the fact that CGI scripts can be coded in a variety of languages — your Web site might have C/C++ CGI scripts, Perl CGI scripts, and UNIX shell CGI scripts — means that if your CGI programmer leaves, you'll have to find a replacement who knows all these languages in order to maintain your CGI-based applications.

In summary, then, CGI scripts can give system administrators big headaches because they slow down the server machine and heavily tax databases due to the processing overhead they incur. Also, if you don't settle on a single language and a set of coding standards for your CGI scripts, you'll end up with a maintenance nightmare that leads to developer dissatisfaction, high maintenance costs, and more bugs. Last, if you use a CGI solution, you may end up paying far too much money for hardware to support its inherent inefficiencies.

Despite all these drawbacks, CGI scripts were (and still are) quite popular at the workgroup level (small number of users) because they're relatively easy to develop, they work, they can easily be moved between Web servers (for those rare occasions when you change Web server vendors), and they've been around for a while. They're an ideal solution, for example, for one-off system tasks such as parsing log files. They're a good general-purpose solution for shops that aren't overly concerned with Web site performance or maintenance.

But CGI scripts are a poor solution for database-driven Web applications and sites that must be maintained over time, despite the fact that a number of famous Web site applications — in fact, some of the pioneers of the concept of Web-based commerce — run on CGI.

Web Servers and Server-Side JavaScript: Improved Applications

There are other options for building and processing Web server applications with measurable advantages over CGI. For example, server-side JavaScript (SSJS) is a technology for building Web server applications that was introduced by Netscape in 1996 and was duplicated shortly thereafter by Microsoft (thus, demonstrating that it's a good workgroup-size or department-size solution). The SSJS runtime engine (which is an NSAPI plug-in) runs in-process with the Web server (see Figure 6-2), so it's available all the time. Because the Web server doesn't have to instantiate a new process every time SSJS is needed (as it does with CGI), it can handle requests faster and more efficiently.

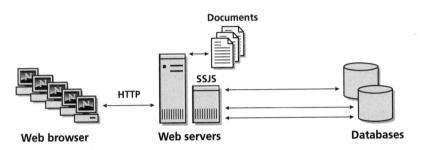

Figure 6-2: Obtaining data via server-side JavaScript

Unlike a CGI script, where the HTML code is inline with the program logic, an SSJS program is written in JavaScript and stored in an HTML page (similar to the way client-side JavaScript is implemented), so the Web pages that make up your application can be modified by an HTML coder rather than by a programmer. Unlike CGI-based applications, which generally comprise two languages (client-side JavaScript on the front end, and Perl or C/C++ on the back end), SSJS applications are coded only in JavaScript, so there's more consistency in the way your applications are written. In addition, because SSJS is a superset of the same core JavaScript language that's used on the client, you can share code between your client-side programs and your server-side programs. And because JavaScript is an extremely popular programming language, it's easier to find programmers who know JavaScript than those who know Perl or C/C++.

SSJS applications are more database-friendly and can execute faster than CGI scripts because database connections are always available; SSJS applications don't have to connect to a database and disconnect from it for each request as CGI scripts do. This is because SSJS objects persist as long as the Web server is running. The DbPool object can remain permanently connected to a database and can also create multiple connections simultaneously to several different databases (SSJS supports access to Oracle, Informix, Sybase, DB2, and all ODBC databases), making SSJS quite efficient at providing instantaneous access.

With SSJS, you can take full advantage of the so-called three-tier architecture. With a two-tier client-server architecture, the client connects directly to a database without first going through a Web (or any other) server. This is expensive for both database processing and licensing; each client has to have a separate license to access the database. With a three-tier architecture, multiple clients access a Web server, which maintains shared connections to the database. Less processing overhead occurs on the database, and you can more efficiently use a smaller number of database licenses than you can with traditional two-tier client-server architectures.

Figure 6-3 contrasts two-tier and three-tier systems. You can see that in a two-tier system every client must have a dedicated connection to the database. This means that during periods when the user is reading or entering data, the database connection sits idle. Users must also connect to the database and disconnect from it at least once a day. (For security reasons, a client is not connected to the database all the time.) By comparison, three-tier systems use database connections more efficiently. Fewer database connections are required because they're shared among all users, and you can support more users with fewer connections. The connections are used more efficiently because there's a relatively continuous flow of traffic across the shared connections. Last, the connections can be maintained for the life of the application (because users log in to the application on the server and not to the database).

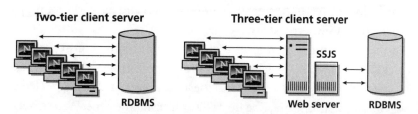

Figure 6-3: Comparing two-tier and three-tier systems

SSJS also provides state and session management capabilities as part of the SSJS runtime environment. Session management is a way of determining whether a user is logged in, monitoring user activity, providing a record of user actions, storing user information that must be available to different pages of the same application, and keeping track of information that must persist across multiple HTTP requests. State management monitors application usage, detecting such things as what an application is doing and how many users are using it so that information and resources can be shared between users. SSJS has four objects available for state and session management:

- **The `server` object:** used for sharing information between applications (seldom used)
- **The `project` object:** mostly used for state management
- **The `client` object:** used for session management
- **The `request` object:** used for providing page-based information and easy access to values that are passed to a page.

These objects are always running and are always available to the application. The developer has to decide, though, whether session information is stored with the client (so if the server goes down and is restarted the user doesn't lose any session information) or on the server (so that you can support browsers that don't enable client cookies).

SSJS is an improvement over CGI (which is stateless), but it's not ideal because state and session information can't be shared between servers. This is the biggest reason why it's difficult to scale SSJS beyond the workgroup or departmental level. If you didn't use state/session information in your SSJS application, it could scale well beyond the workgroup level. As it is, if you have a multiple-server environment, users can be in trouble if one server goes down in the middle of a process. Users might lose order and/or database information and have to submit it all over again to get back to where they were, even if they're redirected automatically to another server. Users might even have to go through the entire log-in process again.

As you can see, SSJS isn't really ideal for mission-critical, enterprise-scale applications where there are many users and the application (including related state and session information) must be up and running all the time. Web servers simply weren't designed for processing application logic for database access, distributed state and session management, mission-critical processing, and so forth; they're mostly for Web page (HTML) access with add-ons to provide minimal application-type functionality.

Scalable Application Services

Scalable Application Services (NAS) improves on this scheme greatly by sharing state and session management across servers in the same cluster. A cluster is composed of two or more server machines that are grouped together so that if one server goes down, the remaining servers take up the slack. Since state and session information is shared in the cluster, no transactions are lost.

NAS was designed from the ground up to provide application services in such a way that the number of users and the number of simultaneous requests sent to a given application aren't an issue. If your user base grows, you just plug in another application server to handle the load and you don't have to make any changes to your application. You can add any number of server machines to a cluster to support a given application. For example, Hong Kong Telecom's customer care and billing application supports more than 200,000 users; E*Trade's Mutual Fund application was developed in two months and supports 275,000 subscribers; ISN's First Auction site was developed in four months and its "flash" auctions support 8,000-plus concurrent users.

NAS applications are composed of HTML pages and application logic (AppLogic) modules. As shown in Figure 6-4, a Web server handles requests, and if they reference an application, they're forwarded to the application server for processing. The requests are received by the KXS (Kiva executive) process and forwarded to either a KCS process (which runs C/C++ AppLogic modules) or a KJS process (which runs Java AppLogic modules). Each KCS and KJS process maintains a specified number of threads (completely configurable by the system administrator) and executes AppLogic modules to completion on those threads. This provides a faster response than a CGI script or an SSJS program and doesn't slow down your Web server. When an AppLogic module has finished running, the results are sent back to the Web server and returned to the client browser.

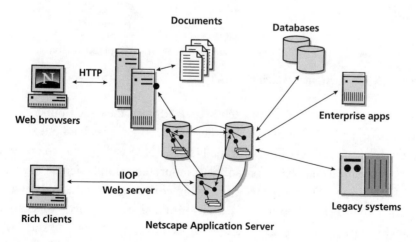

Figure 6-4: How NAS fits in

Because you can add any number of servers, specify any number of KCS and KJS processes, and maintain any number of threads on each process, you can fine-tune your NAS environment to whatever configuration gives your application the best performance. This type of detailed application performance tuning generally results in the need for less hardware requirements and a more efficient use of the existing servers. You can't do this with CGI, SSJS, or any other existing Web solution.

So how does NAS guarantee 24 × 7 (24-hour-a-day, 7-day-a-week) availability? Figure 6-5 shows how NAS works internally. If a KCS or KJS process goes down, the KXS process restarts it. But what happens if the KXS goes down? Well, there's an additional administrative process (KAS) that monitors KXS and restarts it if it fails. There's even some checking by NAS to ensure that KAS is always running. Even if all the processes go down and the other NAS servers in the cluster have to take over, NAS sends out e-mail and fax-mail alerts immediately to notify the system administrator. Contrast this with CGI or SSJS on a Web server: If the server goes down, there's almost no way of knowing it until a customer or employee calls in to complain. With NAS you'll know there's a problem long before the customer finds out; you'll probably even be able to fix it before your application slows down.

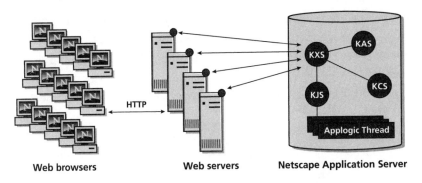

Figure 6-5: The internal workings of NAS

With NAS, the HTML is completely separated from the code (unlike a CGI script, where the HTML is inline with the code, or the somewhat better SSJS model, where the code is inline with the HTML). NAS enables you to create applications as a team. Your designers can focus on presentation logic (HTML pages, Java GUIs, and so on), your programmers can concentrate on business logic (AppLogic modules and extensions), and your database administrators can focus on data logic (SQL queries, views, stored procedures, functions, and such, which are stored in query files and are separate from the AppLogic code). Every member of your Web team can be busily engaged in writing robust applications without getting in one another's way.

Parting Advice

Is NAS for everyone? In a word: no. Some sites are small and don't need a lot of application-support muscle. Some companies can afford only one computer and a robust Web server like Netscape Enterprise Server. However, it's nice to know that NAS is an option when you need it.

You may be wondering what you can do right now if you suspect you'll need NAS in the future as your Web site traffic grows and your Web applications mature. Here are some suggestions:

- If you create CGI scripts, consider using C/C++. This way you won't have to rewrite everything when you move to NAS.

- If your Web developers aren't comfortable with C/C++, Perl is a good alternative. However, use Perl CGI scripts only for one-off tasks that will always support a relatively small number of users and only if you have a team of efficient Perl scripters. Remember, if you want to move a Perl application to NAS, you'll have to rewrite it in C/C++ or Java.

- Create small database applications in SSJS. It's an easy solution for quickly creating workgroup-size database-driven applications and is strongly supported by Netscape (both now and in the future). There are even efforts afoot to support SSJS on other Web servers.

- Create your larger, mission-critical applications in Java. (Java servlets function as CGI scripts do except that Java servlets continue to run between requests and can support some state and session management.) This way, you can reuse your code when you move to NAS.

Remember that when creating Web applications, one size does not fit all. Every site has different requirements, focus, and audience. CGI scripts are great if you plan to change Web servers frequently, have a lot of Perl or C/C++ expertise in your shop, aren't overly concerned about maintenance, and are willing to settle for a dated, general-purpose solution. SSJS is ideally suited to workgroup-size database-driven applications. Java servlets are great for larger-scale Web applications (including database applications) if your developers are already comfortable with

Java. NAS is the perfect solution for high-traffic sites or for applications that must scale into the hundreds, thousands, and even millions of users.

Every solution has its tradeoffs. Some solutions are easy to code and fast and cheap to implement, but lack scalability; others are robust, scalable, and reliable, but require more coding discipline. However, the end goal is always the same — creating a solution that will best serve your customers at the lowest total cost to your company (including initial costs, development costs, and long-term maintenance costs). Web server solutions are great while your site traffic is still growing, provided you always keep an eye on where you need to go in the future. As your customer base grows, you'll find that application servers like NAS will best help you meet your customers' needs.

7

Looking into Enterprise JavaBeans

Duane K. Fields — *internet systems engineer, Tivoli Systems*

The introduction of the Enterprise JavaBeans (EJB) specification by Sun Microsystems and its adoption by major application server companies like Netscape promise to ease and speed the development of mission-critical applications. With the 4.0 release, Netscape Application Server provides support for EJB (as well as for Java servlets and Java server pages); and this will make your job of coding complex Web applications easier than ever.

EJBs are reusable business logic components for use in distributed, multitier application architectures. You can get up and running quickly by building applications around the growing number of EJB components, which provide functionality that traditionally has represented the biggest challenge to creating Web-based applications.

For example, if you were developing a high-end e-commerce application, you might purchase one EJB that performs real-time credit card approval, another that manages a customer database, and another that calculates shipping costs. You would then tie these together within your application server by customizing the runtime properties of the beans, and there you would have it — an order processing system. The application server would automatically handle sticky issues such as balancing loads, maintaining security, monitoring transaction processes, sharing resources, ensuring data integrity, and so on.

This chapter introduces you to Enterprise JavaBeans, gives you an overview of how applications are designed around EJBs, and shows you how to create and access a simple EJB. I can't offer a lot of detail here; if you'd like to get the complete story on EJB, visit the Sun Microsystems EJB Web site, `http://java.sun.com/products/ejb/docs.html`. EJBs are different from the plain JavaBeans that you may be familiar with, so let's start by looking at those differences.

Enterprise JavaBeans Versus Ordinary Beans

You may be wondering how Enterprise JavaBeans relate to the JavaBeans you've been hearing about for the past couple of years that work with application builders. The two types of beans actually don't have much in common from a technical perspective, even if the philosophy behind them — to enable developers to drop reusable components into their applications — is similar.

"Ordinary" beans are Java classes, typically graphical user interface (GUI) components, designed to conform to a series of programming conventions so that integrated development environments like Symantec Visual Cafe or IBM's VisualAge for Java can inspect the beans and enable you to hook them together into applications. Your development environment can then generate appropriate Java code to work with the beans. For example, a bean might represent a special kind of text field or list box, and the development environment could then ease the code development process by graphically enabling you to configure this bean and call the right methods for the desired functionality.

EJBs are similar components, but EJBs follow a completely different set of conventions and interfaces and aren't for use inside development environments. The purpose of EJBs is to encapsulate business logic (for example, the steps involved in depositing money into an account, calculating income tax, or selecting which warehouse to ship an order from) into server-side components. In the EJB paradigm, an application is implemented as a set of business-logic-controlling EJBs that have been configured in application-specific ways inside an "EJB container" such as an application server. Clients are then written to communicate with the EJBs and handle the results. The standardized interfaces exist to enable the EJB container to manage security and transactional aspects of the bean.

Fitting Application Servers into EJB Containers

EJBs work in concert with an EJB container, typically integrated into an application server such as Netscape Application Server (NAS). EJB containers must support Sun's Enterprise JavaBean specification, which details the interface between beans and other application server elements. EJBs can be used with any application server or other system providing an EJB container that implements these interfaces. EJB containers can also exist in other systems such as transaction monitors or database systems.

Application servers in particular are excellent environments to host EJB containers because they automate the more complex features of multitier computing. Application servers manage scarce resources on behalf of the components involved in the design. They also provide infrastructure services such as naming, directory services, and security. And they provide bean-based applications with the benefit of scalability — most application server environments will let you scale your application through the addition of new clusters of machines.

EJB containers offer their beans a number of important services. Although you may not deal with these services directly because they're generally kept under the covers, EJBs couldn't function without them. These services include the following:

- **Life cycle management services:** Enable initialization and shutdown of beans.

- **Security services:** Enable beans to work with a wide variety of authentication schemes and approval processes.

- **Transaction services:** Manage such things as rolling back transactions that didn't fully complete and handling final commitment of transactions, plus transactions across multiple databases.

- **Persistence and state management services:** Enable beans to keep information between sessions and individual requests, even if the container's server must be rebooted.

The EJB container also provides a communications channel to and from its beans, and it will handle all its beans' multithreading issues. In fact, the EJB specification explicitly forbids a bean from creating its own threads. This ensures thread-safe operation and frees the developer from often complicated thread management concerns.

Building Applications Around EJBs

Now let's examine how to build an application around some EJBs. Because the role of EJBs is to define the core business logic of your application, you need some way other than EJBs to deal with presentation issues like generating Web pages to communicate results. If you're building a Web-based application around EJBs, you can break up your architecture into three main areas:

- The business logic (the core business transactions and processing), provided by EJBs

- The presentation logic (the logical connection between the user and EJB services), provided by Java servlets

- The presentation layout (the actual HTML output), provided by Java Server Pages (JSPs)

For example, in a banking application, a servlet might use the services of an EJB to determine whether users are business or consumer customers and direct them to an appropriate JSP-controlled Web page to show them their account balance.

 CROSS-REFERENCE
You can learn a lot more about Java servlets from Chapters 36 and 37 of this book.

In this model, Java servlets control the logic and flow throughout the application. The presentation layout (the HTML) is isolated from the program logic through JSPs. This means your HTML designers can work independently on the look and feel of your pages while your engineers focus on code development. And by sticking to standards-based technologies such as JSPs and servlets, you can ensure portability and scalability of all the aspects of your distributed, multitier application.

Comparing Types of EJBs

There are two primary types of EJBs: session and entity beans.

Session beans provide a service, usually work with objects passed in as parameters, and generally disappear between transactions. Session beans take their name from the fact that they're usually instantiated by the client and exist only for the duration of a single client-server session, where the session bean performs operations on behalf of the client. In the e-commerce example, there might be a session bean that calculates shipping charges based on input parameters such as the shipping address and the weight of the order.

There are two types of session beans: *stateless* (the most common type) and *stateful.* Stateless beans simply perform a service and don't have any persistent data, whereas stateful beans maintain some data between requests but are generally short lived. Stateful beans are responsible for handling their own data persistence issues.

Entity beans represent persistent objects, which are maintained across requests. An entity bean, for example, might represent a particular inventory item or a purchase order. Each entity bean is uniquely identified. One of the key features of entity beans is that they employ container-managed persistence — that is, it's the job of the EJB container (for example, the application server) to maintain the entity. This frees the developer from the often-complex job of maintaining persistence across requests and reboots.

Generally, for designs requiring persistence in beans, entity beans are used because the container will provide for persistence of data. However, the EJB specification doesn't require that application servers support entity beans and container-managed persistence of data. Because they're essentially an optional feature, you'll achieve maximum portability and flexibility of deployment by designing applications primarily around session beans, and stateless session beans at that. Until server-managed persistence of entity beans becomes commonplace, you're stuck implementing persistent objects yourself.

You'll also make your application easier to scale if you avoid using persistent objects like stateful session beans and entity beans. If you deploy stateful session beans in a clustered environment, for example, you have to worry about the fact that you must maintain access to beans between requests even if subsequent requests are being handled by different servers from the cluster. Say you have an entity bean representing an invoice that stays around throughout requests and you deploy that bean as part of an application built on a clustered environment. You will be forced either to make sure that all subsequent user requests are confined to the original server (thus reducing the benefits of a clustered environment) or to manually hand off the information between servers during each request.

Creating a Simple EJB

Now let's look at the procedure for creating a simple EJB. In this example, we'll develop a shipping bean that could be used in any application needing to ship packages. Such a bean might be part of an e-commerce package or provided by a shipping agent as a convenience to its customers. This shipping bean will perform services such as shipping the package, calculating charges, and tracking the package. Though we won't actually code the entire bean in this example, we'll do enough to give you a feel for what beans look like, how you might interface with them, and how they interact with application servers and client applications.

Because stateless session beans offer the most flexibility and portability, we'll implement our shipping bean as this type.

Creating the Bean Interfaces

When you create a bean, you must first create the home and remote interface classes. These form the contract that client applications will use to access the services of the bean. The interface classes only specify the available services and methods; they don't implement them. Both classes are expressed in RMI syntax, Sun's scheme for remote method invocation. RMI programmers, noting that EJB calling conventions look very similar to their RMI equivalents, may wonder how EJBs differ from solutions based on RMI. The major difference is that with RMI, the programmer is responsible for handling transaction and security issues, while these issues are handled for EJBs by their container.

The remote interface is how the bean is exposed to clients that want to interact with it. It provides for a set of services that will ultimately be implemented by the container the bean is deployed into and involves very little coding, as shown in the code snippet below. You will, however, need to create equivalent methods inside the main JavaBean class, which we'll see later. The remote interface extends `javax.ejb.EJBObject` and `javax.ejb.Remote`.

```
package commerce.shipping;

import javax.ejb.*;
import java.rmi.RemoteException;

public interface Shipper extends EJBObject, java.rmi.Remote
{
    public String genTrackingNum() throws RemoteException;
    public dollarAmount calcCharge(ZipCode origZip, ZipCode
destZip)
        throws Remote Exception;
}
```

The *home interface* (also known as the *local interface*), as shown in the next example, provides a set of methods that enable clients to control the life cycle of beans — in other words, the creation and destruction of beans by the container. It extends the `EJBHome` interface and must implement at least one `create()` method, which will be called by the container to invoke the bean into existence. We can overload the `create()` method to allow several different possible initializations. In this case, we'll include an alternative `create()` method that lets us create a shipper bean with a "priority level" (next day, rush, and so on). If we create an entity bean, we have to define a `finder()` method as well, which will be used by the container to locate specific instances of the entity bean.

```
package commerce.shipping;

import javax.ejb.*;
import java.rmi.RemoteException;
import java.rmi.Remote;

public interface ShipperHome extends EJBHome {
```

```
    public Shipper create() throws CreateException,
RemoteException;
    public Shipper create(int priority) throws
CreateException, RemoteException;
}
```

Writing the Enterprise JavaBean Class

The home and remote interfaces that we just created have very little code and even less functionality. The actual bean class is where the business logic resides. We implement the interface of the type of bean we create — for example, a session bean. We then implement the methods defined in our remote interface and any methods specified by the bean type we're implementing, as this example shows:

```
package commerce.shipping;

import javax.ejb.*;
import java.rmi.*;

public interface ShipperBean implements SessionBean {
    private transient SessionContext context;
    private transient Properties props;
    private int priority;

    // These methods are required by the SessionBean
interface and
    // allow the bean to react to life-cycle events such as
activation
    // or removal. If you had an advanced bean that needed to
manage
    // database connections or other resources, you would
open and close
    // them here. Most SessionBeans will use empty
implementations.
    public void ejbActivate() {
System.err.println("Actived..."); }
    public void ejbRemove() {
System.err.println("Removed..."); }
```

```java
    public void ejbPassivate() {
System.err.println("Passivated..."); }

    // These methods are called by the container to associate
the
    // bean with its context within the container. Typically,
a bean
    // keeps a reference to its context.
    public void setSessionContext(SessionContext context) {
        this.context = context;
        properties = context.getEnvironment();
    }

    // These methods are analogous to the create() methods we
created in our
    // home interface and will be called by the container. We
therefore need
    // to implement the same method signatures as before.
Note, however, that
    // we don't return an object, as that's handled by the
container's
    // implementation of the home interface.
    public void ejbCreate() {
        System.err.println("New Shipper Bean created");
    }

    public void ejbCreate(int priority) {
        this.priority = priority;
    }

    // Now for the "business logic" methods defined in our
remote interface.
    public String genTrackingNum() throws RemoteException {
        // Insert code to generate the next tracking number.
        return trackingNumber;
    }
```

```
    public dollarAmount calcCharge(ZipCode origZip, ZipCode
destZip)
        throws RemoteException {
        // Calculate shipping charges.
        return totalCharges;
    }
}
```

Packaging and Deploying the Bean

To deploy an EJB means to load it into our application server's container. Beans are packaged into Java archive (JAR) files along with a special version of the JAR's manifest file (essentially its table of contents) and a serialized instance of a `DeploymentDescriptor` object, which tells the container how to interact with the bean. The deployment descriptor specifies how the bean is supposed to be used in this particular application. For example, it might dictate who has access to the bean, the specifics of starting and concluding transactions, and such.

Although the contents of a bean package are prescribed in the EJB specification, the actual tools that package and build deployable beans are left to the design of the application server developers. Most application server developers provide tools you can use to build your deployment descriptors.

Accessing the Bean

Clients don't interact directly with beans. Instead, all requests for interaction are handled by wrapper interfaces generated by the container the beans have been deployed into. This shields the client from management services that may be implemented differently from container to container. Access is through the home interface we defined earlier.

Before we can use the home interface to ask the container to create an instance of the bean, we have to acquire a reference to it. This is accomplished using JNDI — the Java Naming and Directory Interface. We access the home interface by placing a lookup call to the server and requesting the class name of the bean. The class name we're looking for was defined in the `DeploymentDescriptor` object we created at deployment time. Once we've acquired this reference, we can ask the server to invoke any of the defined service methods.

I should mention that EJBs are accessible from CORBA clients as well. The EJB specification will enable CORBA clients to interact with EJBs by presenting them through a CORBA-accessible interface. This provides seamless access between CORBA and Java.

Tying Java Technologies Together

Enterprise JavaBeans are making it possible to build distributed applications with pluggable components from a variety of vendors. They enable developers to implement solutions that take advantage of previously difficult-to-implement features such as distributed transaction management and multithreading, now provided by the EJB container. And the introduction of EJBs means that the whole family of Java technologies — RMI, JDBC, JNDI — is tied together into an enterprise computing platform well equipped to handle the serious demands of mission-critical computing.

8

Electronic Data Interchange (EDI) on the Internet

Eric Krock — *product manager, Netscape Communications*

E lectronic data interchange (EDI) is a technology poised for explosive growth as the Internet provides an affordable way for businesses to connect and exchange documents with customers and suppliers of any size. EDI is the electronic exchange of business documents, data, and other information in a public-standard format. It cuts the cost of managing business-to-business transactions by eliminating the need for labor-intensive manual generation and processing of documents. Even if you and your company don't use EDI internally or EDI over the Internet today, you will in the future, so it's worth learning about it now.

Some of America's largest companies, such as Boeing and its suppliers, have been using EDI for many years now to exchange business documents. EDI requires a network connection between the two companies exchanging documents, and a guarantee that that network connection is secure. Until the advent of the Internet and encryption software, such a guarantee required either a dedicated line running between the two companies or a connection on both sides to what's called a *value-added network* (VAN). A VAN is a proprietary messaging system that works something like sending attached files by e-mail. Because VANs have both high start-up and annual costs as well as per-message transmission fees, EDI has traditionally been too expensive to deploy except between the largest companies that have thousands and thousands of transactions with each other per year.

The Internet has now given us a network to which everyone is connected, and the development of encryption technology means that business documents can be securely exchanged over this public network. Consequently, EDI can be rolled out from a large company to all its suppliers, no matter how small they are, because to hook up, all they need is a PC and an Internet connection. Electronic commerce software enables the companies to send, receive, encrypt, and track business documents as they flow back and forth.

This chapter will familiarize you with EDI technology — the need it fills, who's using it, how it works, how it can be applied, what's involved in adopting it, and the software products that Netscape offers to get you up and running before your competition is.

The Need for EDI

One top manager at J.C. Penney says that if you're not doing EDI, there's a question as to whether you will be doing business at all. In today's competitive environment, where the Internet is eliminating all geographic and cultural barriers to the competition, if you don't squeeze all the unnecessary costs out of your system, you'll be replaced by somebody else who does. EDI enables businesses to squeeze the costs of faxing, phoning, manual document handling, and dedicated proprietary network connections out of their systems.

Although the initial public offerings of business-to-consumer Internet commerce companies like Amazon.com have received a lot of public attention, the real profits will be made in business-to-business e-commerce. This is because the number of transactions here is so great, and the cost of managing those transactions is so high. By doing these transactions electronically over the Internet, and enormous amount of money can be saved. For example, one food-processing company cut the cost of administering a purchase order from 70 dollars to 93 cents when it began transmitting purchase orders via EDI.

The business costs that EDI reduces so drastically are the settlement costs. Once two companies have agreed to make a transaction, they have to settle that transaction by shipping the goods, recording that the goods have been received, sending the payment, and recording that payment has been received. A transaction that is settled manually usually involves slow and labor-intensive methods of communication and introduces the possibility of errors.

Let's look at all the communication that might take place in the course of a single transaction. A person first looks through a paper or CD-ROM product catalog, and then he or she faxes a purchase order to the supplier company. The purchaser receives acknowledgment of the order back via fax. Some time later, however, the purchase might need to phone or fax the supplier to make a change to the purchase order or to check on its status. And then, when the goods are shipped, the purchaser receives some kind of shipping notice by fax. An invoice is sent in the mail, and then the purchaser must generate a check and mail it off to the supplier. So, as you see, in the course of a single transaction, many pieces of paper are handled and several calls are made, all of which cost time and money. Even when computers are used to generate and record information, that information generally is printed out, faxed, and then entered again at the other side.

EDI makes all these transactions happen electronically. It replaces human-to-human communication with application-to-application communication. For instance, a purchase order is sent electronically from one company's internal accounting system to another's. Business documents of other kinds are exchanged in a similar manner. There's no need for phone calls, faxes, or generating and sending paper through the mail.

You can see that the potential for cost savings is huge. And as I mentioned earlier, in the past, these cost savings used to be available only to the large companies that could afford to hook up to a VAN; now, thanks to the Internet, the savings are available to virtually every and any company.

In addition to reducing corporate buying and selling costs, EDI can also speed up the exchange of business information; this enables a company's entire chain of suppliers to respond more quickly to changes in demand, and makes just-in-time production really possible. With EDI, the Internet can tie a company's entire chain of suppliers together in one seamless electronic network. Imagine, for example, that when Boeing decides it wants to create a new plane, it sends out a request for the seats to a supplier. The supplier sends out subrequests for the support struts that are needed, and whoever makes the support struts sends out subrequests for the metal that's needed. All this can take place electronically and instantaneously from end to end, instead of having to be done one step at a time manually.

How EDI Works

What makes EDI possible today is a set of standards developed by large businesses in the 1970s. The ANSI (American National Standards Institute) X12 subcommittee sets EDI standards in North America. A related organization, the Data Interchange Standards Association, supports the X12 standards development process, maintains and publishes the standards, and provides educational seminars, conferences, and other information services. These standards define how to format and exchange business documents electronically. They define a language for representing purchase orders, invoices, mortgage applications, health insurance reimbursement forms, shipping forms, and other documents that companies commonly exchange. In all, more than 180 standard document types have been defined.

In ANSI X12 nomenclature, each standard type of EDI document (such as purchase order, purchase-order acknowledgment, invoice, and so on) is assigned its own three-digit identifying number. Purchase orders are document type 850, so EDI professionals often use the terms *purchase order* and *850* interchangeably. But keep in mind that *850* refers to a purchase order that has been formatted for exchange according to the ANSI X12 standard, whereas *purchase order* could refer to a purchase order in any format.

The ANSI X12 standards are in use today at many large companies, including Ford, other automakers, aerospace companies, and insurance companies. A similar global standard called EDIFACT, developed under the auspices of the United Nations, is more widely used outside North America.

The way EDI works is illustrated in Figure 8-1. Company A sets up a purchase order using its internal business software. Next, EDI software, such as Netscape's ECXpert with its built-in mapping software, maps (or translates) the purchase order from the internal format to the standard ANSI X12 850 document format. Then Company A sends that ANSI 850 document to Company B, either over a VAN or encrypted in EDIINT format over the Internet. Company B receives that 850, and its mapping software then imports the purchase order into its own internal business applications.

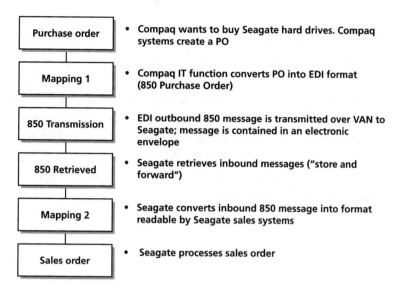

Figure 8-1: A systems view of an EDI transaction

It's also possible to use EDI when only one of the trading partners (EDIspeak for "companies that buy from and sell to one another") has EDI software. There are several ways to use EDI with partners that lack their own EDI-compliant systems.

In one approach, a large company with EDI software accepts documents from its smaller suppliers in some agreed-upon format, and then maps those documents first into ANSI X12 documents and finally into its internal systems. For example, a company might allow its trading partners to submit purchase orders as Excel documents attached to e-mail messages. The Excel documents can then be first mapped into ANSI X12 850 purchase orders by mapping software and then imported into an internal accounting system by ECXpert through its built-in support for legacy integration.

In another approach, a large company with EDI software sets up a Web site to host a trading community for its trading partners. Trading partners can log in to the Web site and then send EDI documents to and receive EDI documents from any of the other trading partners by using a simple HTML forms interface. Small trading partners need not even understand EDI syntax; they just fill out HTML forms, and new EDI documents are automatically created behind the scenes as necessary. Netscape TradingXpert makes it easy to build such trading communities and comes with built-in support and sample HTML user interfaces for the most common EDI document types.

In reality, a single EDI transmission may include a large number of documents, as shown in Figure 8-2. Each document is called a *transaction*. All the transactions that are destined for the same department at the partner company are bundled together into what's called a *functional group*. For instance, one functional group might go to the order-processing department, while another functional group might go to the finance department. One EDI transmission can include two or more functional groups and is called an *interchange*. It is like taking multiple purchase orders and putting them all into an envelope addressed to Order Processing, taking another bunch of documents and putting them into an envelope addressed to Finance, and then putting those envelopes into a big manila folder addressed to, say, Boeing, and mailing it.

- **Big envelope**
- **Little Envelope**
- **Document**

- **Interchange**
- **Functional group**
- **Transaction**

 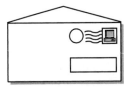

Figure 8-2: The anatomy of an EDI transmission

Within a transaction, each line is called a *segment,* and each piece of information on that line is called an *element.* The ANSI X12 standards define for each kind of document the data elements that can be used, the kinds of segments those data elements are combined into, and the order of the elements and segments.

Of course, the software on the other side, receiving the data, needs some way to tell where each transaction, functional group, and interchange starts and ends. As shown in Figure 8-3, standard, easily recognizable headers and trailers define the beginning and end of the interchange, each functional group, and each transaction.

Each document's definition consists of a name, a three-digit code, a description of what the document is used for, the header information, the body or line-item information, and the trailer-summary information. Figure 8-4 shows a partial definition of an ANSI 850 document, or purchase order.

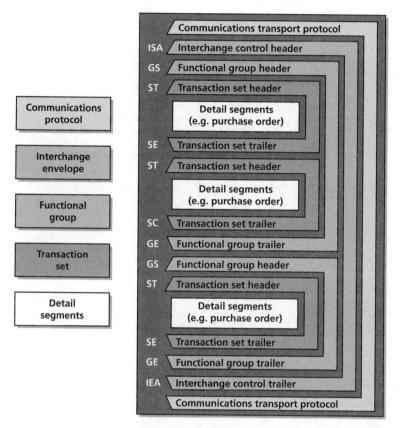

Figure 8-3: How the different parts of an EDI transmission are delimited

Mapping software takes a standard business document such as an invoice and transforms it into an ASCII text file in the ANSI X12 format for that document. Each line of information in a printed invoice, for example, is mapped to a segment, and each piece of information is mapped to an element, as shown in Figures 8-5 and 8-6. The segments are then combined to create the finished ANSI X12 invoice, as shown in Figure 8-7. Note that EDI documents use asterisks as delimiters to show where data elements begin and end, just as HTML documents use angle brackets to show where HTML tags begin and end.

850 Purchase Order
Functional Group • PO

This Draft Standard for Trial Use contains the format and establishes the data contents of the Purchase Order Transaction Set (850) for use within the context of an Electronic Data Interchange (EDI) environment. The transaction set can be used to provide for customary and established business and industry practice relative to the placement of purchase orders for goods and services. This transaction set should not be used to convey purchase order changes or purchase order acknowledgment information.

Table 1

NOTE	POS. NO.	SEG. ID	NAME	REQ. DES.	MAX USE	LOOP REPEAT
	010	ST	Transaction set header	M	1	
	020	BEG	Beginning segment for purchase order	M	1	
	030	NTE	Note/special instruction	F	100	
	040	CUR	Currency	O	1	
	050	REF	Reference numbers	O	>1	

Figure 8-4: Partial definition of an ANSI 850 (purchase order)

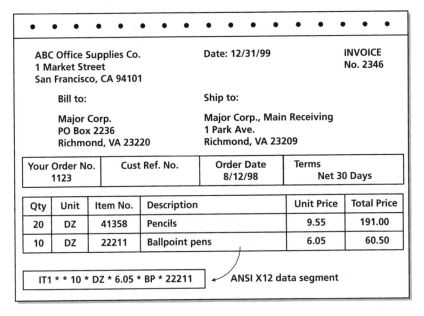

Figure 8-5: A typical invoice, with a line of information mapped to a segment

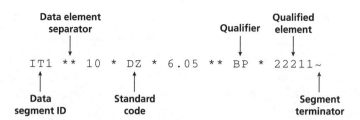

Figure 8-6: An ANSI X12 data segment, up close and personal

```
BIG*970817*2346*970812*1123
PER*AP*FRED JONES*TE*8042506789
N1*BT*MAJOR CORP.*92*012345678
N3*PO BOX 2236
N4*RICHMOND*VA*23220
N1*ST*MAJOR CORP.*92*0123457801
N2*MAIN RECEIVING
N3*1 PARK AVE
N4*RICHMOND*VA*23209
ITD*08*3*****30
IT1**20*DZ*9.55**BP*41358
PID*F****PENCILS
IT1**10*DZ*6.05**BP*22211
PID*F****BALL POINT PENS
TDS*25150
CAD*M****UPS
CTT*2
```

Figure 8-7: The invoice in ANSI X12 format

Of course, regardless of whether you send an EDI document over a VAN or the Internet, it's important to know that your trading partner received it. When Company A sends Company B a business document, Company B sends back a functional acknowledgment. A functional acknowledgment just means, "We got your document"; it doesn't have any legal authority.

When you receive a document from a trading partner, it's also important to be certain that the document was in fact sent by the company that claims to have sent it (rather than forged by someone else), and to be certain that it wasn't modified or corrupted during transmission. Proprietary VANs generally provide a guarantee that data will be transmitted unharmed from one side to the other and that messages come from the company they claim to be from. In the Internet world, documents are signed with digital certificates to accomplish the same thing. EDIINT, the standard for exchanging EDI documents over the Internet, defines how documents can be signed by the sender. The receiving software verifies the digital signature. Any EDI software that's compliant with the EDIINT standard (including Netscape's ECXpert) understands how to sign a business transaction, encrypt it, and then decrypt it on the other side.

Applications of EDI

EDI can be applied in the realms of both corporate selling and corporate purchasing. On the selling side, a supplier company can create a Web site where corporate customers can browse its catalog electronically and make purchases online. EDI software such as Netscape's SellerXpert makes this easy by providing the capability to load data into a catalog and begin selling online right out of the box. Conversely, a large company such as GM or Boeing can ask its trading partners to supply their catalog information electronically, and it can then set up a site where its purchasing staff, or even employees throughout the enterprise, can browse supplier catalogs. Software like Netscape's BuyerXpert can be used to import supplier data and set up one consolidated catalog internally.

In order for EDI to be used in these ways, there needs to be a common understanding of how the buying and selling companies are going to interact. Which side is going to transmit the purchase order? What's going to be received in return? How will the workflow for approvals be handled? These kinds of questions are answered by the Open Buying on the Internet (OBI) standard.

The workflow between buyer and seller typically goes as follows: The buyer browses a catalog on the seller's site, finds the product he or she is looking for, and indicates that he or she wishes to purchase the product. The seller's site then creates a purchase-order request and sends it to the buyer company for approval by management. The buyer company's software receives the purchase-order request and checks the business rules that have been defined internally to decide where that purchase-order request should be sent for approval. It might go to the buyer's manager if the amount is less than $1,000 or to the company's vice-president if it's more than this amount. The appropriate authority in the buyer's company receives the purchase-order request and approves it; thus, it becomes an approved purchase order, which is then routed back to the selling company and processed. OBI defines the handshake for passing off these documents and handling the workflow for approval.

Netscape is one of the first companies to ship OBI-compliant software. Netscape ECXpert, SellerXpert, and BuyerXpert are all fully OBI compliant. At a conference on EDI held in early 1999, CommerceNet sponsored an interoperability test in which Netscape and other companies with OBI-compliant software demonstrated that they could indeed exchange business documents over the Internet using this technology.

Adoption of EDI

EDI is already firmly established in very large companies in a number of industries: transportation, manufacturing, insurance-claims processing, and so on. These companies have enjoyed significant cost savings as well as other advantages for years. But smaller companies have been left out because they haven't been able to afford the large fixed investment in hardware, software, and expensive VAN connections that EDI requires. As discussed earlier, the Internet has changed all that. The obvious move, then, at this point is to migrate over time from VANs to the Internet, and to roll out the proven EDI technology over the Internet to everyone in the supply chain who until now couldn't participate. In fact, smaller suppliers will find their large customers mandating the small suppliers participate if they want to continue to sell parts.

The EDIINT standard, now in draft form, defines how to do EDI transactions over the Internet. It explains what kinds of certificates are used, which kinds of encryption are supported, which algorithms you can choose from, and so on.

Although EDI technology is complex, it's even more challenging to form business relationships that will allow the potential cost savings of EDI to be realized. In order to achieve these cost savings, a company has to coordinate carefully with its trading partners. As with many standards, the ANSI X12 specification has a great deal of flexibility built into it, and different companies will use a standard document type in different ways. For example, two companies might both use ANSI 850s, but they need to agree on which company's part numbers will be used as the contents of data elements. Companies need to coordinate to make certain that they assign the same interpretation to each field in the standard form and agree on the kind of data that will appear. They also need to agree if data will be transmitted as S/MIME e-mail attachments, HTTP submissions, or FTP batch transfers.

It is hopelessly expensive and time consuming to negotiate such agreements separately with every single company in your industry. To avoid this problem and speed adoption, many industries now have their own additional, industry-specific protocols for using EDI over the Internet. For example, the Gas Industry Standards Board and the Automotive Industry Action Group have each formulated protocols for EDI over the Internet in their respective industries.

Requirements for an E-Commerce Solution

What should a company look for when it selects the EDI software to implement an e-commerce solution? There are many different factors to take into consideration. Following are the most important EDI software factors:

- It must be easy to use so that it can be rolled out to all the employees in the enterprise.

- It should conform to the EDIINT standard and the OBI standard for maximum interoperability.

- It must be adaptable to business logic—in other words, it's got to be able to internalize rules such as all purchase orders over $1,000 need a vice-president's signature.

- It must complement and integrate with existing EDI systems; no company can throw out its existing EDI hardware and software or its VAN connections until the very last supplier has moved to EDI over the Internet, which may take a very long time.

- It must integrate on the back end with internal legacy applications; companies can't afford to throw out or rewrite their legacy applications running on mainframes for purposes such as accounting, reporting, and order processing.

- It needs to support a database of all the partners from whom it will accept EDI documents and the agreements it's reached with each partner on how these documents will be handled.

- It should be able to process a high volume of data per day, with close to 24x7 availability.

- It must be able to handle input from all over the world in a variety of formats. An international company, for example, may receive business documents from the United States in ANSI X12 format, as well as business documents from overseas in EDIFACT format.

■ It must support the submission of documents by a variety of means, including VANs, encrypted e-mail, HTTP submissions, and FTP transmissions.

■ It must be year-2000 compliant, which means that it must support the 4010 revision level of the ANSI X12 standard. (Obviously, this will cease to be an issue in the year 2000.)

■ It must have mapping support built in, both to transform incoming ANSI X12 or EDIFACT documents into legacy-application formats and to transform documents arriving in other formats to EDI format.

Netscape's CommerceXpert Product Family

Netscape's CommerceXpert line of products meets all the requirements listed above and offers companies a complete, integrated suite of EDI software. This means that when a company adopts some or all of the products in this line, it doesn't have to invest further in consulting and software development to integrate solutions purchased from separate suppliers. This is one of the factors that made CommerceXpert attractive to Citigroup (formerly Citicorp), which has acquired lifetime rights to the CommerceXpert product family.

Following is a brief description of each of the CommerceXpert products:

■ **ECXpert** fits at the center of a company's trading network. It enables the sending, receiving, encrypting, managing, and tracking of business documents as they flow back and forth. ECXpert includes mapping software that's capable of mapping from any file format into any other file format. It has built-in support for the protocols agreed upon by the Gas Industry Standards Board and the Automotive Industry Action Group.

■ **BuyerXpert** enables a company to import electronically the catalog data from all its suppliers and create one consolidated catalog that its purchasing staff can use. Because BuyerXpert is OBI compliant, it can handle the routing of purchase-order requests for approval according to an individual company's business rules.

■ **SellerXpert** enables a company to set up a catalog that's accessible over the Internet so that corporate customers can visit the Internet site to make buying decisions. Like BuyerXpert, SellerXpert is OBI compliant to support cross-company workflow and routing of purchase-order requests for approval.

- **TradingXpert** enables a company to set up a trading community Web site for the convenience of all its trading partners. Trading partners can log in and use a simple HTML forms interface to send and receive EDI documents. This way, any trading partner with a browser and Internet access can participate in the trading community.

- **MerchantXpert** is Netscape's business-to-consumer e-commerce solution. It enables a company to set up a Web site that sells directly to the public. It includes features specifically for enabling business-to-consumer e-commerce such as transaction settlement using credit cards.

- **PublishingXpert** enables a company to publish content for profit by selling access to that content over the Internet. The content can be anything from streaming video to HTML pages, and PublishingXpert offers flexible pricing, billing, and subscription schemes.

- **BillerXpert** enables companies to do electronic bill presentation by e-mail and offers statement review, approval, and settlement services on their Web site.

Shifting EDI from VANs to the Internet

Companies can now augment their existing EDI infrastructure using the Internet to roll out this cost-saving technology to those suppliers that could never participate before. They can also cut costs further over time by eventually shifting all of their business-document transactions from expensive, proprietary VANs to communication over the Internet. And they can make this changeover at a pace that they and their trading partners are comfortable with.

A key factor in successfully making this changeover is selecting the right enabling software. Netscape CommerceXpert is a complete family of e-commerce solutions that's robust, secure, scaleable, standards compliant, and easy to use. Offering the broadest and deepest out-of-the-box functionality of any e-commerce products on the market today, CommerceXpert gives companies a competitive edge by enabling them to get their e-commerce solution up and running sooner. In a world where customers can be gained or lost worldwide at the speed of light, the companies that offer the best service on the Internet the soonest will dominate their industries by cutting costs, increasing customer loyalty, and winning new customers.

9

Directory and Security Services: Netscape's Ready-Built Application Infrastructure

Gregg Williams — *technical writer and editor*
Paul Dreyfus — *senior manager, Technology Evangelism, Netscape Communications*

When you design a new network application or update an older system to make it accessible over a network (whether it is an intranet, an extranet, or the Internet), you face the task of building a user information infrastructure. This infrastructure determines who has access to the system, it guarantees that unauthorized users can't access the system, and it enables you to manage such administration details quickly and easily throughout the life of the system. Wouldn't it be nice to be able to add this infrastructure without having to program it yourself?

As many developers have already discovered, Netscape technologies can make this dream a reality. Netscape offers a platform-independent, standards-based, scalable, extensible set of products that provide directory, security, and remote administration features for your network applications. You get immediate access to these complex technologies without having to design, implement, debug, or maintain them. You can create a higher-quality, more powerful product in less time and at a much lower cost. And you can create a wider variety of network-based solutions than you would otherwise be able to do — which can translate into new business opportunities for your company.

This set of Netscape products offers three groups of technologies:

- **Directory technologies** to centrally store user and application information; currently implemented by Netscape Directory Server and the associated Netscape Directory Software Development Kit (SDK)

- **Security technologies** to authenticate and secure interactions from client to server and server to server; implemented by Netscape Security Services and Netscape Certificate Server

- **Remote administration technologies** to centrally monitor and administer distributed applications and users within a common framework; implemented by Netscape Console

These products (see Figure 9-1) are based on open-standard technologies, primarily the Lightweight Directory Access Protocol (LDAP) that's rapidly becoming the de facto industry standard for directory development.

After giving an overview of the benefits of using these Netscape technologies, this chapter describes the directory, security, and administration products, and how you can start using them.

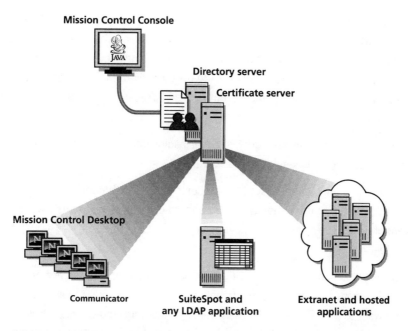

Figure 9-1: Netscape Security, Directory, and Administration Products

Benefits of Using the Netscape Technologies

Whether you're creating a new network application or network-enabling an existing system, here are the chief benefits you can derive from a flexible, powerful, scalable, and easy-to-administer central store of user data:

■ **Faster and less expensive development.** When you use the Netscape technologies, you don't need to spend time developing and maintaining an administration framework or a central store of user information. With such an infrastructure in place, you can spend your time and valuable programming resources on the features of your system that benefit your users—the features they actually see.

- **More efficient, extensible use of user data.** Your system can look up data about users more quickly and more easily if it's all stored in a central location, meaning your users gain quicker access to information and services. Additionally, every application that's part of your, or your customers', systems can use the same central store of data and the same security and administration; you don't have to add a separate user store for each new application.

- **Lower management costs.** Because you're managing only one repository of user information, the cost of management goes down.

- **Lower cost of upgrading the system.** You don't have to go through major upgrades of your store of user information when you want to upgrade your system's features. Your central store of user data will work with the new features the same way as with the existing features.

- **Capability to open your system to a greater number of users.** Say you first design an application that's accessible only to intranet users behind a corporate firewall and that you later want to open it to extranet users from outside your corporation. With Netscape's directory technologies, you can simply add the names of new users to the central storehouse without having to go through a major upgrade of your application's user information storehouse. Netscape's technologies can scale upward to meet the needs of hundreds of thousands of users. Small systems currently use these technologies for simple authentication of dozens of users; Netscape's Netcenter uses them to handle millions of users. If your user base grows, you can simply add more servers to handle the load and let the Netscape technologies handle replication and other synchronization issues.

- **Simpler access for users.** You can provide users with a single ID to log on to multiple applications. Instead of having to remember multiple passwords and user names, users can use this single ID for all applications that access the LDAP-based directory from any location. When users leave the company, you then need only to remove their user information from that central directory to end their access to all the applications in your system.

These are all benefits that current Netscape developers are bringing to their corporations and users. For example, Security Dynamics' SecurSight family of products uses an embedded Netscape Directory Server to help customers maintain tight network security regardless of the number of users. Perhaps most important, embedding the Netscape Directory Server has saved Security Dynamics a year of development time and subsequent resources.

"Through SecurSight, Security Dynamics will help enterprises deliver to their end-users and business partners information anytime, anywhere, securely," said

Scott Schnell, senior vice president of marketing and corporate development. "Critical to this vision is giving our SecurSight customers the choice of where to store user security information. By partnering with Netscape, we will be offering our customers the leading implementation of LDAP available today."

Applying the Directory Technologies

Netscape Directory Server is a sophisticated storehouse of application and user information that can be accessed from anywhere on your intranet or extranet — or, in the case of the Internet, from anywhere in the world. A key distinguishing feature of directory servers is that the database is optimized for fast reads and is hierarchical rather than relational. Directory servers aren't limited to storing user information (such as employee name, phone number, and e-mail address). Rather, they're useful for storing any kind of structured information that needs to be shared or centralized.

A directory server can store all user information in one place, where any networked application can access it. This means you don't have to implement separate directories for each of your applications. And system administrators like applications that use a directory server because it means less work for them when they have to maintain user information or install a new application (that is, if the new application uses an existing directory server).

A directory server can be called on by an application to authenticate users (that is, to verify their identities and confirm the networked services they're authorized to use). This improves the user experience by enabling users to access multiple applications and databases after a single sign-on process. It also means the application can enable users to access only data to which their status entitles them. For example, a company can allow employees to access all the data in the company's product database, while customers see only certain products and the correct pricing information for their customer type.

And a directory server can store application configuration data, enabling you to create applications that are *location independent*. Users can sit at any computer connected to the network, identify themselves to your application, and receive the same computing experience, customized the way they've set it up and with access to the same data, regardless of their physical location.

Netscape Directory Server Advantages

Netscape Directory Server is based on the LDAP architecture, as mentioned earlier. Directory servers that support LDAP — including Netscape Directory Server — offer several advantages:

- They can be customized on the fly; that is, new data fields can be added at any time.

- Data can be duplicated across multiple servers for greater data integrity or split across multiple servers to improve access speed.

- They enable you to update your application without having to build a new user information database for it. When you want to open up an intranet application to partners over an extranet or over the Internet, you can use the same storehouse for new user data, or a new application can access the same user information database.

CROSS-REFERENCE

Chapter 4, "Directories and LDAP: Universal Access to Directory Information," provides more details about the benefits of LDAP.

Netscape Directory Server provides these additional advantages over other LDAP-based directory servers:

- Netscape Directory Server runs on every major platform, including LINUX.

- Netscape Directory Server is easy to embed in your application using C or Java with the free Netscape Directory Software Development Kit (SDK). You need to add only a few lines of C or Java code to enable your application to access Netscape Directory Server's user authentication, security, and other features. To see just how easy it is, read the chapters on LDAP in Part IV of this book.

- Netscape Directory Server is a top-performing, most scalable LDAP directory server currently available, by a large margin. It can handle well over 3,000 search operations per second and more than 20 million entries on a single server; recent benchmarks showed it to be 230 times (that's 23,000 percent) faster than Novell Directory Services (NDS). Among the factors that contribute to its performance: it ships with a database that's optimized for LDAP clients performing typical directory queries in which read operations greatly outnumber write operations; the server has been optimized to work with today's multiprocessor server hardware; and, administrators can tune Directory Server to maximize its performance depending on the circumstances in which it's being used.

■ Netscape Directory Server includes NT Sync, a program that enables bidirectional synchronization between the server and the Windows NT 4.*x* user-account database. Also, third-party and custom solutions enable Netscape Directory Server to synchronize with NDS and other directory servers. What this means is that you don't have to write your own synchronization code to have Directory Server work with other directories.

■ Any LDAP-compatible application you create using the Netscape Directory SDK will work with Windows NT/2000 and its LDAP-compatible Active Directory servers. By using the Netscape Directory SDK to directory-enable your application, you save time in building directory functionality, while providing the capability to synchronize with other major directories, data validation and normalization, and other features too. The time you save— and the flexibility you add to your applications—helps both you and your customer. Further, the costs of development and owning the application become lower over time because Netscape Directory SDK is easier to maintain and upgrade.

■ Because the source code to the Netscape Directory SDK is freely available through mozilla.org (`www.mozilla.org`), you can completely customize the Directory Server to work with any application. For more information on the Netscape Directory SDK free source and its opportunities, see "Embedding Netscape Directory Server in Your Application Using the C and Java Directory SDKs" in Part IV of this book.

■ Netscape Directory Server is optimized to work with Internet applications—not network operating systems. This means it doesn't have the limitations of other LDAP-based directory servers that are designed to work with one or another network operating system (NOS). These limitations include potentially creating security holes when used over the Internet, making it harder to replicate directory data between multiple directory servers over the network, and limiting the way information can be stored in the directory.

NOTE
Netscape Directory Server and the Netscape Directory SDK can be downloaded for free from the Netscape Web site. See the file on the CD-ROM called *Welcome and Software Download* for instructions and links to the site.

Let's take a closer look at the last advantage because it's an important factor differentiating Netscape Directory Server from other LDAP-based directory servers.

Netscape Directory Server defines a security model that's independent of the underlying network operating system. Users and groups in the Netscape directory aren't operating system principals. In other words, they can't be given NOS privileges — such as read or write access to file servers, access privileges to network printers, backup operator rights, and access to trusted domains — unless the application is specifically designed this way. This is especially important in extranet and Internet applications where users come from outside an organization's firewall: Administrators don't want to use a directory server that accidentally grants external users access to internal resources. With Netscape Directory Server, you can't mistakenly grant users access to any NOS resources.

Further, Netscape Directory Server uses LDAP itself to send replication adds to, changes to, and deletions from the central directory to other directories across the network. Because most firewalls can be configured to enable LDAP traffic, this means that Directory Server updates can work across firewalls. Other LDAP-based directory servers, which are designed to work with specific operating systems, carry replication requests with remote procedure calls (RPCs), which can't cross most firewalls.

Also, directory servers that are built to work with specific network operating systems tend to use restrictive naming models that can limit the way the directory is used for specific applications. Netscape Directory Server supports the standard LDAP naming model, which provides complete flexibility in how you store user information in the server's database.

How Corporations Are Using Netscape Directory Server

BC Telecom, Inc., Canada's second largest telecommunications company, recently took advantage of Netscape Directory Server to revamp approximately 250 applications, including its customer service, human resources, communications, and forms-routing systems. The existing systems, based on proprietary mainframe technologies (specifically MVS and VM), were expensive and didn't allow for the type of flexibility and growth BC Telecom required for the future. The company wanted to migrate to easier-to-use, more flexible, scalable, open-standards-based Internet technologies. It also needed to update other MVS-based applications for year-2000 compliance.

Their first step was to centralize all user data with Netscape Directory Server. Each of the previous systems relied on its own directory. By combining all the directories, BC Telecom made the job of its development team faster, cheaper, and easier. Instead of having to rebuild the directory for each system one by one, they built with Directory Server a single repository of user information that each new application could use. Directory Server supplied the infrastructure that BC Telecom used to rapidly build and deploy its new systems and applications.

Rick Waugh, senior systems analyst at BC Telecom, says, "The fact that Netscape Directory Server supports LDAP makes it much faster and easier to manage user accounts across a wide range of applications and services. It's saving us a lot of time, and we can now make the repository available for people to write [new] applications to."

Another company that's made widespread use of Netscape Directory Server is Ford Motor. Ford is using Netscape Directory Server as the foundation for the Ford Supplier Network, an extranet that lets Ford deliver information and applications to its suppliers around the world. By providing a service-ready infrastructure, Netscape Directory Server enables Ford to simplify administration and reduce the cost of ownership for its sophisticated extranet. With more than 200,000 directory entries for people and other resources stored in a central directory, Ford's extranet system is one of the largest directory deployments to date.

Ford has found that directory performance is crucial to the successful deployment of its extranet applications; its developers have found that even small degradations in directory performance result in unusable applications. Netscape Directory Server provides the high levels of performance and reliability that Ford requires. Additionally, Netscape Directory Server meets Ford's requirements for rapid development and deployability; its engineers wrote more than 100 directory-enabled applications with Directory Server in 6 months.

Netscape Directory Server: Developer Use and Availability

You can use Netscape Directory Server, available for free for development purposes, to provide the directory services your application needs. Incorporating Netscape Directory Server gives you—and your customers—all the advantages that come from using a high-performance, secure, and scalable LDAP-based directory server. And it saves you development costs and helps you bring your product to market more quickly.

Continued

Netscape Directory Server: Developer Use and Availability *(continued)*

By bundling Netscape Directory Server with your application, you can provide your customers with a complete solution. A number of software vendors—including Bay Networks, Fabrik Communications, Hewlett-Packard, Netegrity, and VASCO Data Security—have already embedded Netscape Directory Server in their products. To read more about one developer's experience, see the View Source article, "SiteMinder 3.0: Directory-Enabled Access Control with Netscape's Directory Server," included on the CD-ROM that's part of this book.

Your application can access Netscape Directory Server (or any other LDAP-based directory server) from C or Java using the free Netscape Directory SDKs. To learn how to embed Directory Server in your application, see "Embedding Netscape Directory Server in Your Application Using the C and Java Directory SDKs" in Part IV.

The usefulness of the SDKs is enhanced by the fact that Netscape has made the source code available (also for free). The source code enables you to better understand how the SDK works and enables you to customize the SDK to meet specialized needs. For more about the advantages of the source code release, see the just-mentioned *View Source* article.

ON THE CD-ROM

The *View Source* article "SiteMinder 3.0: Directory-Enabled Access Control with Netscape's Directory Server," can be found on the CD-ROM that accompanies this book. Follow this path to find it: Sample Code and Supporting Documentation ⇨ Part I ⇨ Chapter 9.

Security Technologies

Internet-based applications center on data transactions of various sorts engaged in by a variety of people, such as employees, customers, and business partners. These applications must address various security issues in order to protect the company's network and the data on it. Safeguards must be in place to ensure that people can get to the information if they're entitled to it and cannot gain access to the information if they are not entitled to it.

Netscape has done the hard work of implementing two important security functions: point-to-point security and authentication. Now this expertise is available to you through Netscape Security Services (NSS), a software development package that lets you integrate Secure Sockets Layer (SSL) and public-key security capabilities with your application. NSS provides you with access to the same security technologies that millions of Netscape users have depended on for years. Even better, its powerful API gives you quick access to these technologies without requiring you learn the complicated low-level details. NSS provides a range of security solutions and multiple levels of control over what data can be accessed so that you can choose the appropriate level of security for your application.

Point-to-Point Security

Point-to-point security helps ensure that anyone who intercepts information being transmitted across a network is unable to put the information to use. This is accomplished by encoding the information before sending it and decoding it upon receipt.

NSS implements several leading cryptographic standards — including Secure Sockets Layer (SSL) 2.0 and 3.0, several key-encrypted algorithms from RSA (DES, Triple-DES, RC2, and RC4), and FORTEZZA — in a modular way. You can choose from among the supplied cryptography modules or add your own, choosing the *strength* of encryption to match the value of the information being protected.

NSS also offers cryptographic token support through the RSA-endorsed PKCS #11 standard (also known as Cryptoki). This enables your application to use industry-standard hardware acceleration to provide faster and more secure access to data. PKCS #11 is also compatible with other hardware security devices such as smart cards and Java rings.

In addition, many customers (especially those in government and financial institutions) require software that's certified to meet existing security standards. The software underlying NSS is validated to the Federal Information Processing Standard (FIPS) 140-1 Level 2 standard. This validation greatly reduces the time needed for your application to obtain certification from the National Institute of Standards and Technology.

Authentication

It's important not only to keep information secret, but also to ensure that the people who send or receive a message are who they say they are. For this, you need authentication, which is usually accomplished through the mechanism of certificates.

A certificate is an electronic document that's extremely difficult to forge, issued by a source and trusted by both the sending and receiving parties. Various companies are in the business of issuing certificates, and some also sell software that enables you to issue your own certificates. Issuing your own certificates can be more cost-effective than purchasing certificates from an outside vendor and is appropriate for some situations.

NSS provides industry-leading support for authentication through its SSL support for X.509 v3 certificates. NSS also provides a utility for directory-based management of certificates. And Netscape sells Netscape Certificate Server to enable you to issue your own certificates.

Netscape Certificate Server and NSS: Developer Use and Availability

You can use Netscape Certificate Server as part of any application that uses certificates to authenticate users.

You can use NSS to add security to any application or any server—and compatible security services are already built into the millions of Netscape servers and clients in use today.

You can use NSS in many contexts to create new business solutions that wouldn't otherwise be practical—and do it quickly and economically. For example, you could use it to create banking servers that enable banks to transmit sensitive customer information securely between offices. Or, by placing an NSS-enabled server on the Internet and having customer employees access it using Netscape Communicator, you could deliver a Virtual Private Network (VPN) solution. Select Netscape partners, including CheckPoint Software Technologies, RedCreek, and Litronic, are already using the first version of Netscape Security Services.

To get further information about NSS, Netscape Certificate Server, and other security products from Netscape, visit the Security Developer Central Web page within DevEdge Online at www.developer.netscape.com/tech/security.

Remote Administration Technologies

Most Internet-based applications manipulate data that needs to be administered, and yours is probably no exception. A custom scheme for doing this administration means more work for you. Worse yet, it makes more work for your customer-administrators, who have to learn yet another user interface.

Netscape has designed Netscape Console to provide a single, consistent user interface and architecture for administering Internet-based applications. Netscape will be using it to provide consistent administration for its future products (beginning with Netscape Communicator 5.0). Version 1.0 of Netscape Console will provide a framework for administering user and group data, with more features to come in later versions.

Netscape Console, which requires Netscape Directory Server, offers the following advantages:

- The console provides a consistent user interface for administering client and server software and for maintaining directory-based user information.

- It's written in Java so customers can do their administration from any Java-enabled computer platform.

- The Nescape Console introduces the concept of *delegated administration.* This feature enables an administrator to give selected users access to parts of the directory database. Through delegated administration, customers using your Console-enabled application can improve quality and decrease costs by enabling their users (and their outside customers) to maintain their own records.

Netscape has integrated Netscape Console into its latest line of servers, with the version 4.*x* numbering scheme, and into Netscape Communicator 5. Netscape is using Console to enable remote administration of Apollo servers. It's also using Mission Control Desktop, an application created using Netscape Console, to enable administrators to configure and update Communicator 5.0 across a network.

In addition, a variety of companies have committed to using Netscape Console in their products. The list includes American Internet Corp., AXENT Technologies, BMC Software, Business Objects, Check Point Software Technologies, Legato Systems, Marimba, Novera Software, Resolute Software, SR Gen, Trusted Information Systems, and Ukiah Software.

Netscape Console: Developer Use and Availability

You can use Netscape Console to add remote administration services to your application quickly and inexpensively. Your customers will benefit from interacting with a common, consistent administration user interface.

As of this writing, release of the Netscape Console SDK and freely available source code through the Netscape Web site are imminent. This SDK will enable you to design your administration functions to work within the Netscape Console framework. In addition, you'll be able to extend Netscape Console to call non-Java administration software, thus enabling you to leverage work you've already done. To check on the SDK's availability, see Netscape DevEdge Online at `www.developer.netscape.com`.

Advanced Tools for Network "Plumbing"

Network applications generally require a sophisticated infrastructure. But trying to program this by yourself can be expensive and eat up huge amounts of time and engineering resources. By using the Netscape technologies described in this chapter, you can greatly reduce the cost of implementing the directory, security, and remote administration services your network applications need. By providing advanced tools for addressing the "plumbing" details, these Netscape technologies can give you new business opportunities and enable you to deliver better systems and products faster.

PART

II

Using JavaScript for Innovative Client-Side and Interface Development

Using JavaScript for Innovative Client-Side and Interface Development

This section tells you how to build user interfaces — the part of your Web application that the user sees — using client-side JavaScript. It provides a lot of how-to information about the "Netscape-preferred" way of building your user interface: client-side JavaScript.

The chapter titles should be self-explanatory. Each chapter is intended as a self-contained unit — you can read them in whatever sequence you'd like. They're ordered according to degree of difficulty, so you'll probably get the most out of this section if you read the chapters in the order in which they're presented.

Each chapter shows you how to do something that's not explained in the Netscape JavaScript documentation. But just in case, official Netscape documentation is included on the CD-ROM that comes with the book. It's all in the materials that support Chapter 1. If you come across any objects or concepts that you don't understand, refer to the documentation for a complete explanation.

## 10

CSS-Positioning: The Dynamic HTML Neutral Zone

Danny Goodman — *consultant and writer*

Those who write leading-edge Web applications that must work on a broad spectrum of browser platforms can expect to develop different versions of their code for some time to come — if not indefinitely. Standards efforts are always welcome in this area, but as happens so often, the browser makers can and do develop new features and technologies much faster than standards bodies can study and adopt them.

It's happening again in the realm of Dynamic HTML (DHTML), a broad area that includes the ability to change more HTML page content and appearances on the fly than ever before. In this chapter, I focus on one fun aspect of DHTML:

scripting the precise positioning and visibility of elements on a page. More specifically, I demonstrate techniques you can use to create a single DHTML page and scripts that accommodate the different object models in Netscape Communicator 4 (which includes Navigator 4) and Microsoft Internet Explorer 4.

Finding Common Ground

Precise positioning of elements on a page is covered by a W3C recommendation commonly called CSS-Positioning (CSS-P), which you can find on the Web at http://www.w3.org/TR/REC-CSS1. This is an extension of the same body's valiant work in establishing a CSS standard (Cascading Style Sheets, Level 1; or CSS1), a standard supported by Navigator 4 and Internet Explorer 4 — and to some extent by Internet Explorer 3. The CSS-P recommendation (which has now been folded into the CSS Level 2 recommendation) specifies a vocabulary for setting numerous attributes of distinct entities that can be positioned, layered, hidden, and shown on the page.

Over and above this common standard, Netscape and Microsoft have applied these concepts to their own document object models and have developed different ways of conceptualizing these positionable entities. Netscape calls these items *layers* and has even created a <LAYER> tag to facilitate adding such items into a document. Microsoft, on the other hand, refers to such items as *styles*. The challenge we scripters face is controlling Netscape's layers and Microsoft's styles to accomplish the same job.

Explaining the details of each of these objects extends way beyond the scope of this chapter, but I'll simply say that the vocabulary for scripted properties and methods of Netscape layers has little in common with that of Microsoft styles. These problems can be conquered with a bit of version checking in scripts or custom API creation, shown later. In the meantime, here's how to create these objects so that both Navigator and Internet Explorer can use them.

In an effort to be respectful and diplomatic at the same time (if not downright weasely), I will hereafter refer to generic instances of these objects as *positionable thingies*.

Creating Positionable Thingies

Once you've determined the kinds of elements you want to have on your page, the next HTML task is to create those elements as positionable thingies that both browsers will treat as first-class objects. You have several syntactical ways of embedding the HTML that defines properties of positionable thingies in your documents, but the one I currently favor is defining the properties within a <STYLE> tag set inside the <HEAD> tag, as follows:

```
<HTML>
<HEAD>
<STYLE TYPE="text/css">
   <!--
   #thingy1Name {attributes}
   #thingy2Name {attributes}


   ...


   -->
</STYLE>
</HEAD>
```

The attributes for each item must include the position attribute. Table 10-1 shows the most common attributes you would set for a positionable thingy.

TABLE 10-1: COMMON POSITIONAL THINGY ATTRIBUTES

ATTRIBUTE NAME	VALUES
Position	Absolute|relative
Left	Pixel position relative to outer element
Top	Pixel position relative to outer element
Visibility	Visible|hidden|inherit
z-index	Integer layer position in stack

The syntax for these attributes is different from those of the normal HTML attribute settings you may be used to. All attributes for a given object are grouped together inside one set of curly braces, attribute names are separated from their values by colons, and multiple attributes are delimited by semicolons. Therefore, to set an absolute-positioned item named `myImage` to a top-left position of 200, 250, and initially hide it, you would use the following syntax:

```
#myImage {position:absolute; top:200; left:250;
visibility:hidden}
```

It may take you a while to cease using the equals sign between attribute name and value, as you're accustomed to doing in HTML tags.

The other half of the formula is an HTML tag in the document that associates content with the positioning attributes named and defined in the `<STYLE>` tag. A convenient tag to use for this is the `<SPAN>...</SPAN>` tag set (the `<DIV>...</DIV>` tag set is also a good choice when using absolute positioning for the item). In that tag, you add an ID attribute that points to the name of the item properties defined earlier, like this:

```
<SPAN ID=myImage>
    [HTML content of any kind here]
</SPAN>
```

No matter where in the `<BODY>` section this `<SPAN>` tag occurs, it obeys the positioning attributes of the like-named definition in the `<STYLE>` tag. I must also emphasize that in Navigator 4, a `SPAN` or `DIV` element is not treated as a layer (for hiding and showing, for example) unless the element has a position style attribute assigned to it.

Referencing Positionable Thingies

For JavaScript to access a positionable thingy, your script must be able to reference the object. This is one area in which the different object models force scripters to deal with incompatibility head-on. A Navigator layer is contained by its document. Moreover, a layer itself contains a document that holds all the content for that layer. Therefore, a reference to a layer created in the main document looks like this:

```
document.layerObjectName
```

In this syntax, `layerObjectName` is the name you've assigned to the layer. If you need to adjust the content of that layer, the reference must go one level deeper. For example, to access an image object that lives in a layer, the reference would be as follows:

```
document.layerObjectName.document.images["imageName"]
```

In other words, you use the same approach for building references between nested layers and their documents as you do when building references between nested frames.

The Internet Explorer syntax, on the other hand, includes a way to globally reference all styled objects inside the main document. A reference to the `all` property of the document can reach a uniquely named styled object in the following manner:

```
document.all.styledObjectName.style
```

To reach an image object that lives in one of these style objects, the reference doesn't have to specify the object's style property, but must point directly at the uniquely named image object:

```
document.all.imageName
```

Getting back to positionable thingies: To make a property accessible by both browsers, you need to construct your references either along separate paths (based on the browser version) or by creating what I call *platform equivalencies*.

The "separate paths" methodology entails setting global variables as flags for each platform. For example, you would open your page's scripts with the following segment:

```
var isNav4, isIE4
if (parseInt(navigator.appVersion) >= 4) {
    if (navigator.appName == "Netscape") {
        isNav4 = true
    } else if (navigator.appVersion.indexOf("MSIE") != -1) {
        isIE4 = true
    }
}
```

With these variables in place, you can use them elsewhere to branch to the platform-specific references:

```
if (isNav4) {
    document.layer1.visibility = "hidden"
    document.layer2.visibility = "visible"
}
if (isIE4) {
    document.all.layer1.style.visibility = "hidden"
    document.all.layer2.style.visibility = "visible"
}
```

Or by doing a little more work up front, you can set some global variables to comparable portions of both platform references, and assemble one reference that works for both platforms:

```
var range = ""       // empty for Navigator 4
var styleObj = ""    // ditto
if (parseInt(navigator.appVersion) >= 4) {
    if (navigator.appVersion.indexOf("MSIE") != -1) {
        range = ".all"
        styleObj = ".style"
    }
}
...
eval("document" + range + ".layer1" + styleObj +
".visibility = 'hidden'")
eval("document" + range + ".layer2" + styleObj +
".visibility = 'visible'")
```

What you gain in fewer statements per property change, you lose in increased complexity of syntax — you must make sure your eval() statement has all the dots in the right places. This "platform equivalency" methodology works best when your scripts make many changes to only a few objects, and those changes are to the properties that Navigator and Internet Explorer have in common. There's an example later in this chapter where the two-path approach to property access works better.

Property Match-Ups

One added complexity to scripting both platforms for CSS-Positioning is that the two object models don't always see eye-to-eye on the names of key properties. Each object model features many properties that supplement the standard in the model's own unique way. Our job is to script for the common denominator.

That denominator encompasses three basic modifiable properties of positionable thingies:

- Location

- Visibility

- Stacking order (z-index)

Additional properties let you set background image and color and the item's clipping region. When the property names and value types for both platforms are the same, it makes for an easy time; when they're not, it's time to do some platform branching.

Table 10.2 shows a selection of properties for the Navigator layer and Internet Explorer style. Items that are the same for both appear in bold.

TABLE 10-2: LAYER VERSUS STYLE CSS-P PROPERTIES

NAVIGATOR LAYER PROPERTY	COMMENTS	IE STYLE PROPERTY
Left	The Microsoft style object has a left property, but the value is a string including the unit of measure (for example, "20px"). To perform math on the left property of the style object, use the pixelLeft property.	PixelLeft
Top	The same situation as with left and pixelLeft	PixelTop

Continued

TABLE 10-2: *(continued)*

NAVIGATOR LAYER PROPERTY	COMMENTS	IE STYLE PROPERTY
`Visibility`	The Netscape layer object returns possible values of `show`, `hide`, and `inherit`; the Microsoft style object returns `visible`, `hidden`, and `inherit`. But the layer object can be set to the style object property value names without complaint.	`Visibility`
`Zindex`	100 percent agreement on the integer values of this stacking order property.	`ZIndex`
`Background`	Value is a URL of a background image.	`background`
`BgColor`	Different property names, but the same color values, including Netscape plain-language names.	`backgroundColor`

Unlike the Navigator layer object, the Internet Explorer style object does not have methods for moving the object. But both objects change their locations if you modify their respective positioning properties. One other important difference is that if a style object doesn't have one of its properties explicitly assigned in the <STYLE> tag, the property value is an empty string; the layer object assigns default values to virtually all properties, whether they appear in the <STYLE> tag or not.

Dealing with these inconsistencies in a complex document can become tedious. Fortunately, you have one additional alternative for distancing yourself further from day-to-day concerns about platform inconsistencies: Generate your own set of APIs in JavaScript to take care of both platforms. Such an API consists of a function that stands in for each of the positioning tasks that your positionable thingies need on the page. You essentially create your own metalanguage for CSS-P for moving, hiding, showing, and restacking objects in your application. If you build a library of these functions, you can link it into any CSS-P page as an external .js file.

A Not So Fishy Story

To see how well one can meld the Navigator layer and Internet Explorer style objects together in one application, I converted one of Netscape's "swimming fish" layer demonstrations to CSS-Positioning format with animation scripts that — to the user — work identically on both platforms (see Figure 10-1). The application is the more complex of the two demonstrations: It's the one that changes the z-order of layers so that the fish swims in a different pattern between three colored columns depending on the swimming direction.

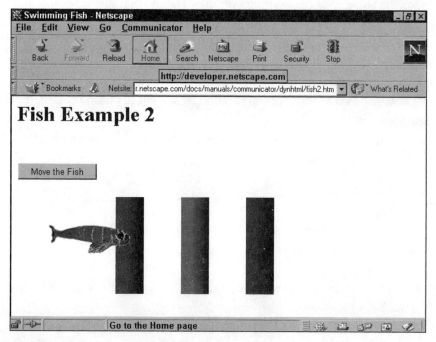

Figure 10-1: The Fish Example

If you're using Netscape Navigator 4 or later, you can view Fish Example 2 to see how the original version works. The Fish example can be found on the CD-ROM that comes with this book, and it uses the <LAYER> tag and the layer object properties and methods.

ON THE CD-ROM

The examples referred to in this chapter, and the source code for them can be found on the CD-ROM that accompanies this book. We urge you to look at the examples as you read this text. Follow the path, Sample Code and Supporting Documentation ⇨ Part II ⇨ Chapter 10. If you're not running Netscape Communicator, Version 4.0 or higher, you'll need to download it from the Netscape Web site, where it's available for free. To learn how, see the file on this CD named *Welcome and Software Download.*

Now look at the CSS-P version, Fish Example 3, also on the CD. If you're not following along with the examples on the CD, note that this version of the example looks just like the version in Figure 9-1, only it's written in CSS-P. The full source code is also available on the CD-ROM. I've added a couple of extra touches, such as a Stop button and status bar messages that reveal a little more about what's going on as the fish swims.

Let me go over the source code section by section to reveal my design decisions along the way.

The first order of business is to create the positionable thingies by using standard CSS-style syntax:

```
<HTML>
<HEAD>
<TITLE>Swimming Fish</TITLE>
<STYLE TYPE="text/css">
   <!--
   #bluepole {position:absolute; top:150; left:160; z-
index:1;}
   #redpole {position:absolute; top:150; left:260; z-
index:4;}
   #greenpole {position:absolute; top:150; left:360; z-
index:2;}
   #fish {position:absolute; top:170; left:40; z-index:3;}
   #waiting {position:absolute; top:100; left:50;}
   #fishlink {position:absolute; top:100; left:10;
visibility:hidden;}
   -->
</STYLE>
</HEAD>
```

The objects include three colored poles, a fish object that displays different images depending on the swimming direction, a "Please wait" message that shows as images load, and an object containing the control buttons (initially hidden from view). Only the pole and fish objects need to have their z-index attributes set because the other objects don't get involved with the stacking order part of this example.

In the next section, some script statements establish key global values for the entire page:

```
<SCRIPT LANGUAGE="JavaScript">
// set browser platform global vars
var isNav4, isIE4
var range = ""        // empty for Navigator 4
var styleObj = ""
if (parseInt(navigator.appVersion) >= 4) {
   if (navigator.appName == "Netscape") {
      isNav4 = true
   } else {
      isIE4 = true
      range = ".all"
      styleObj = ".style"
   }
}
```

As you'll soon see, I need both the two-path and platform equivalency methods of handling the different platform syntax. The statements above cover me both ways, setting variables for platform flags (isNav4 and isIE4) and for the joint reference components (range and styleObj.

Some additional preloading of image objects and global variables follows:

```
// pre-cache both fish images and assign to objects
// for easy image swapping later
var fishForward = new Image()
fishForward.src = "images/fish1.gif"
var fishBackward = new Image()
fishBackward.src = "images/fish2.gif"
// global switch for fish direction
var direction = "forward"
```

```
// global ID for fish motion timeout
var timeoutID
```

There are only two fish images, each one an animated GIF. One faces to the right ("forward" in this application); the other faces left. A global value stores the direction in which the fish is currently swimming. Another holds the timeout ID for the repetitious calls to the function that inches the fish along its path.

The first function — showForm() — is called by the window's onLoad event handler:

```
// show 'waiting' message while images load
// then hide it and show the animation buttons' layer/style
function showForm() {
    // both browsers covered in each statement
    eval("document" + range + ".waiting" + styleObj +
".visibility = 'hidden'")
    eval("document" + range + ".fishlink" + styleObj +
".visibility = 'visible'")

    // commented out is the two-path method for comparison

//   if (isNav4) {
//       document.waiting.visibility = "hidden"
//       document.fishlink.visibility = "visible"
//   }
//   if(isIE4) {
//       document.all.waiting.style.visibility = "hidden"
//       document.all.fishlink.style.visibility = "visible"
//   }
    return false
}
```

The sole job of this function is to swap the visibility of the waiting and fishlink (button) objects after all the images load. I demonstrate the platform equivalency method of addressing the objects in both platforms. Because the visibility property is the same on both platforms, this approach works well here. So that you can better understand what's going on, the code also includes (commented out) the two-path method of doing the same action. This method may use many more lines of code, but to me it is much more readable and maintainable.

Next comes the master function that moves the fish when the user clicks the "Move the Fish" button:

```
// start that fish swimmin'
function moveFish3() {
    // cancel current ID so repeated invocations
    // don't trigger multiple timeouts
    clearTimeout(timeoutID)
    // set status bar message
    showFishLayer()
    // Nav4 returns integers for left;
    // IE4 returns "nnpx". Must use pixelLeft in IE4
    if (isNav4) {
        var position = document.fish.left
    }
    if (isIE4) {
        var position = document.all.fish.style.pixelLeft
    }
    if (direction == "forward") {
        moveForward(position)
    } else {
        moveBackward(position)
    }
    // call this function again after 10 ms to nudge fish
    timeoutID = setTimeout("moveFish3()", 10)
    return
}
```

The moveFish3() function's first task is to clear any existing timeoutID value. Failure to do so will cause additional clicks of the button to start what look like separate timeout threads, causing the fish to swim faster and faster as more in-stances of the setTimeout() statement per second invoke this function.

Next I call the showFishLayer() function that displays information about the current path in the status bar. (I'll discuss status bar messages in more detail later.)

Moving the fish requires setting its horizontal location to the right or left by 5 pixels, depending on the direction. To start the process, I must get the current position (since I won't be using the Netscape `layer.moveBy()` method here). As described earlier, the two platforms have different property names for the location values: `left` and `pixelLeft`. The platform equivalency method fails here because one statement cannot conveniently be used for both platforms. Thus, I call upon the global platform flags set earlier to create two paths to set the position variable to the current setting.

Depending on the current direction (global variable), I then hand off processing to `moveForward()` or `moveBackward()`, passing the current position as a parameter. Once the desired routine has finished, the `setTimeout()` method sets a wake-up call to invoke this same `moveFish3()` function in 10 milliseconds.

The first function that actually moves the fish object shifts it to the right by 5 pixels:

```
// nudge fish to the right 5 pixels until
// it reaches right edge; then turn him around
function moveForward(position) {
    if (position < 450) {
        if (isNav4) {
            document.fish.left += 5
        }
        if (isIE4) {
            document.all.fish.style.pixelLeft += 5
        }
    } else {
        setPoles("new")
        changeDirection()
    }
}
```

I chose to change the Navigator layer's left property, but I could have also used the `moveBy()` method. For Internet Explorer 4, setting the `pixelLeft` property is the way to move a style horizontally. Regardless of platform, this motion works only while the position of the fish object is less than 450 pixels. If the position reaches that level, two functions change the z-order of the poles and direction of the fish.

Moving the fish in the opposite direction is very similar:

```
// nudge fish to the left 5 pixels until
```

```
// it reaches left edge; then turn him around
function moveBackward(position) {
   if (position > 10) {
      if (isNav4) {
         document.fish.left -= 5
      }
      if (isIE4) {
         document.all.fish.style.pixelLeft -= 5
      }
   } else {
        setPoles("reset")
        changeDirection()
   }
}
```

Adjustments to the position are negative values because the object needs to move to the left (a decreasing left position) — until, that is, the position reaches 10, at which time the pole z-order is changed once again and fish direction is again swapped.

Changing direction requires changing a couple of settings:

```
// swap image in the mainFish layer/object and
// change global direction value
function changeDirection() {
   // different references for image in layer/style
   if (isNav4) {
      var fishImg =
document.fish.document.images["mainFish"]
   }
   if (isIE4) {
      var fishImg = document.all.mainFish
   }
   if (direction == "forward") {
      direction = "backward"
      fishImg.src = fishBackward.src
   } else {
      direction = "forward"
      fishImg.src = fishForward.src
```

```
        }
        return;
    }
```

I first get a reference to the image contained in the fish object. Notice that the Navigator reference follows the hierarchy through the layer to the document on the layer. Then, depending on the current setting of the direction global variable, the image is swapped in the image object, and the global value is changed.

Changing the pole order requires changing the zIndex property values for four objects. This is a good place to demonstrate the power of creating your own API for a particular positioning task. I define one function, setZIndex(), which takes care of all the platform dealings for the zIndex property in one place.

```
// cross-platform API for setting zIndex property
function setZIndex(objectName, zOrder) {
    var theObj
    if (isNav4) {
        theObj = eval("document." + objectName)
    }
    if (isIE4) {
        theObj = eval("document.all." + objectName + ".style")
    }
    if (theObj) {
        theObj.zIndex = zOrder
    }
}
```

To change the order of each object, I invoke my API, passing the object name and the desired zIndex property value, like this:

```
// change the stacking order of the poles and the fish
function setPoles(type) {
    // call my cross-platform API for zIndex
    setZIndex("bluepole", ((type == "reset" ) ? 1 : 3))
    setZIndex("redpole", ((type == "reset" ) ? 4 : 1))
    setZIndex("greenpole", ((type == "reset" ) ? 2 : 4))
    setZIndex("fish", ((type == "reset" ) ? 3 : 2))
    return
}
```

I had arbitrarily assigned a type to the two orders: reset (the original) and new (the order for backward swimming). I use that type (passed as a parameter to the `setPoles()` method) to help shrink the tests of all four objects' `zIndex` settings to simple conditional expressions. The last two functions stop the fish and set the status bar, respectively:

```
// give him a rest
function stopFish3() {
   clearTimeout(timeoutID)
   window.status = ""
}
// fish in front or behind red pole?
function showFishLayer() {
   window.status = (direction == "forward") ? "Fish BEHIND
red pole and IN FRONT OF others." : "Fish IN FRONT OF red
pole and BEHIND others."
}
</SCRIPT>
```

The message in the status bar shows the user what to look for in the ordering of pole and fish objects.

Now we come to the HTML that generates the elements on the page:

```
<BODY BGCOLOR="#ffffff" onload="showForm();">
<H1>Fish Example 3</H1>
(For cross-platform CSS-P deployment)
<SPAN ID=waiting>
   <H2>Please wait while the fish loads...</H2>
</SPAN>
<SPAN ID=fishlink>
   <FORM>
   <INPUT type=button value="Move the Fish"
onClick="moveFish3(); return false">
   <INPUT type=button value="Stop the Fish"
onClick="stopFish3(); return false">
   </FORM>
</SPAN>
```

The first two objects are contained by <SPAN> tags, with their ID attributes pointing to the corresponding positioning style attributes defined at the head of the document. One object contains nothing more than an <H2>-level block of text. When the page finishes loading the images, that object is hidden, and the second object, containing a form with two buttons, is shown.

The balance of the HTML creates the objects for the poles and fish:

```
<SPAN ID=bluepole>
    <IMG SRC=images/bluepole.gif>
</SPAN>
<SPAN ID=redpole>
    <IMG SRC=images/redpole.gif>
</SPAN>

<SPAN ID=greenpole>
    <IMG SRC=images/greenpol.gif>
</SPAN>

<SPAN ID=fish>
    <IMG NAME="mainFish" SRC=images/fish1.gif>
</SPAN>

</BODY>
</HTML>
```

The fish object displays the forward-facing image at the outset. The pole images could be listed in the HTML in any order because their z-order is hard-coded by their position attributes in the head.

It is important to note that I changed the sequence of the HTML tags from what was in the original layer version of this example. One concern I had was how the appearance would degrade in non-DHTML browsers. The layout in the document looks much better in older browsers, although it's not nearly as intelligent as the positioned version (and the button scripts should be blocked for non-DHTML browsers, too).

Wrapping up the Fish

I hope this discussion and demonstration show that where there are mutually agreed-upon standards, we can, in those immortal words, "all get along" when our audience demands it. Dynamic HTML has millions of cool applications waiting to be written, and the great thing is that every modern browser can run them.

11

JavaScript and User Interface Design

Danny Goodman — *consultant and writer*

I believe a common misconception among Web application developers is that user interface design belongs solely to the operating system gods, who determine the look and feel of computer screen elements: windows, menu bars, icons, and so on. It is to such developers that I gleefully offer the following pop quiz:

Q. User interface guidelines for HTML documents are based on which graphical user interface (GUI) standard?

   a. Macintosh

   b. Windows 3.1

c. Windows 95/NT 4.0

d. X-Windows

Of course, this is a trick question. The correct answer is:

e. None of the above

To the keepers of the *graphical user interface* (GUI) crown jewels, this might sound like blasphemy. After all, each GUI environment has been fine-tuned over time by engineers and designers who have extensive experience in human-to-computer communication. Developers even have formal guidelines to follow to make sure their applications uphold the teachings of the Church of the Holy Interface.

Web sites, however, seem to be a whole other animal. Their heritage is not tied to one existing interface design. In fact, I see a strong design parallel between many Web sites and the content of thousands of multimedia CD-ROM products. Once the designer gets inside the operating system's window, all design guidelines go out the window. Elaborate graphics, unique navigation schemes, and custom interface elements occupy the content space.

Surprisingly, I have yet to hear of any visitor backlash regarding the lack of consistency from site to site. The variety may even be alluring to Web surfers who regard each port of call as an adventure.

Despite the wide latitude afforded by the Web, I believe that there are a number of user interface issues that we need to consider when attempting to enliven our sites with JavaScript, LiveConnect, JavaScript Style Sheets, and other cool tools that Netscape gives us for free. Each generation of Navigator offers us a number of opportunities to advance the state of the Web site art, provided we take intelligent advantage of them.

To get the ball rolling, I'd like to share my thoughts and experiences about several common issues that bring together JavaScript and user interface design. In particular, we'll be looking at the following:

- Applying scripting to match your audience

- Handling loading delays

- Validating client-side forms

- Assisting with new plug-in installation

- Deploying sound and other rich media

- Enabling advanced mouse rollover behavior

This certainly is not an exhaustive list, but it covers interface problems that many of us face on a daily basis as we develop Web applications.

Designing for Granny

Whether you consider your site to be analogous to a published work or a living program (or any combination thereof), the old rule for authors and programmers still applies: know your audience. For instance, if your site appeals to a broad consumer audience, you may well help visitors feel more comfortable by adding `onMouseOver` event handlers to links to set the status bar (at the bottom of the browser window, as shown in Figure 11-1) to a plain-language description of what the visitor will see when he or she clicks on that link.

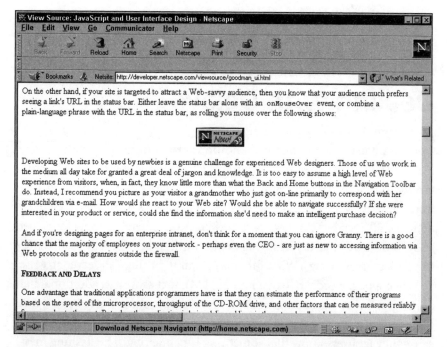

Figure 11-1: Rolling the mouse over the "Netscape Now" image causes a plain language description to appear in the status bar. If the user clicks on the image, the browser will go the Web site described in the status bar.

On the other hand, if your site is targeted to attract a Web-savvy audience, then you know that your audience much prefers seeing a link's URL in the status bar.

Either leave the status bar alone with an `onMouseOver` event, or combine a plain-language phrase with the URL in the status bar.

Developing Web sites to be used by newbies is a genuine challenge for experienced Web designers. Those of us who work in the medium all day take for granted a great deal of jargon and knowledge, and it's too easy to assume a high level of Web experience from visitors. Actually, they know little more than what the Back and Home buttons in the Navigation Toolbar do. Instead, I recommend you picture as your visitor a grandmother who is on-line primarily to correspond with her grandchildren via e-mail. How would she react to your Web site? Would she be able to navigate successfully? If she were interested in your product or service, could she find the information she'd need to make an intelligent purchase decision?

And if you're designing pages for an enterprise intranet, don't think for a moment that you can ignore Granny. There is a good chance that the majority of employees on your network — perhaps even the CEO — are just as new to accessing information via Web protocols as the grannies outside the firewall.

Providing Feedback, Dealing with Delays

One advantage that traditional applications programmers have is that they can estimate the performance of their programs based on the speed of the microprocessor, throughput of the CD-ROM drive, and other factors that can be measured reliably from one day to the next. But when the application is being delivered live via the network, all such benchmarks become irrelevant. There's no way for a client to know how much traffic is clogging the network or how heavily loaded the server is (or if it's even running). What fun it is to wait for a sluggish server at T1 speed!

When a page needs to load a lot of HTML text as well as additional items such as images, Java applets, plug-ins, and plug-in data, the progress messages and indicator in the Navigator status bar are the Web designer's best friends. This is because they let users know that something is happening. The flashing messages and moving progress indicator are subtle forms of entertainment, and at least through Navigator 4, JavaScript doesn't offer scripters any additional interface aids for notifying visitors of loading in progress. That's why I'm often dismayed when designers use JavaScript to open new windows with the status bar turned off. Although I don't disagree that the progress messages in the status bar may be intimidating to newbies, I find it even more unsettling when there is absolutely no feedback indicating that something is happening. Remember, not everyone can see his or her modem lights.

In these days of 400-plus MHz processors and 24X CD-ROM drives, computer users are accustomed to very fast responses to any action. Network or server delays — also called *latency* — are the bane of the consumer Internet. Unless you're on an intranet blessed with a lightning-fast network and processing power, you need to approach page design with this latency in mind. Designing fancy pages on your local hard disk (with images already cached from earlier viewings of the pages while under construction) gives you a very false sense of performance. Clear your caches and access the site from a typical network connection to get a taste of your own design medicine.

Forms Validation

Before client-side scripting was available, all validation of form fields and elements was performed by a server-side *Common Gateway Interface* (CGI) program when the complete form was submitted. Such a CGI works with all forms-enabled browsers, including those that aren't scripting enabled.

When a form has many elements in it, however, CGI-based validation is not particularly user-friendly. Most typically, the CGI reports an error about one of the fields and redisplays the entire form (scrolled to the top), and it's up to the user to locate the errant field and make the correction. By the time the form redisplays, the user has lost mental focus of the content needed for that field, and the text cursor may be many fields away from the one needing attention.

As a user, I prefer to be signaled as soon as possible after I make a mistake in a form. This is where client-side form validation can help. Even on the client side, there are two approaches to form validation.

Scripting Batch Validation

One approach mimics CGI-based batch validation. An `onSubmit` event handler in the `<form>` tag invokes a custom function that checks the validity of all the form elements. If there is a problem, the submission can be halted by letting the last statement of the event handler evaluate to return false. The following code shows a skeletal listing of such a validation routine, including a shortcut to handle the return true or return false statements of the event handler.

```
<HTML>
<HEAD>
<SCRIPT LANGUAGE="JavaScript">
function validate(form) {
    // an example with the First Name field
    if (form.firstName.value == "") {
        alert("The First Name field is required.")
        form.firstName.focus()
        form.firstName.select()
        return false
    }
    // other tests would go here, returning false in an
error condition

    // if processing reaches here, then everything is OK to
be submitted
    return true
}
</SCRIPT>
</HEAD>
<BODY>
...
<FORM NAME="orderform" ... onSubmit="return validate(this)">
  First Name:<INPUT TYPE="text" NAME="firstName" SIZE=35>
...
</HTML>
```

Real-Time Validation

The second approach verifies each entry in real time as the user clicks or tabs out of the field. Each field has an onChange event handler that triggers a function for the required kind of validation. Typical validation tasks include checking whether the field contains any characters at all, whether the entry is a number, and the number of characters of the entry.

I suggest creating individual functions for each basic validation task, and letting each field's onChange event handler summon the function appropriate for the kind of data in the field. Each error function should include an alert() method to describe the nature of the problem and should then select the text in the affected field. The selection performs these two user-friendly tasks:

- It highlights the field in question

- It prepares the current content for retyping of correct information

Unfortunately, it's fairly easy to fool the onChange event handler. If a real-time validation function detects an error and highlights the field, the user can tab or click out of the selected field without making a change to the erroneous entry and without further validation. To counteract this problem, you can perform validation both in real time and at submit time.

In the dummy form (shown in Figure 11-2), the Description field may have an entry of any kind, whereas the Quantity field requires an integer.

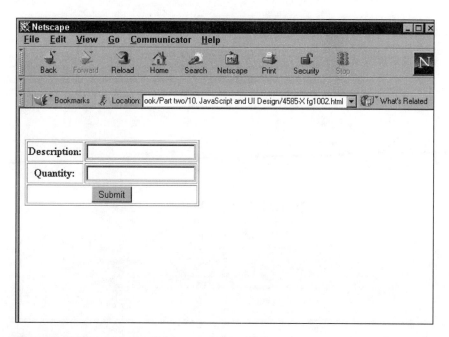

Figure 11-2: A "dummy" form created in HTML

ON THE CD-ROM

The form that appears in Figure 11-2 can also be found on the CD-ROM that accompanies this book, in the file "Chapter 11 Dummy Form." Find it by following the path, Sample Code and Supporting Documentation ⇨ Part II ⇨ Chapter 11. Open the form using Netscape Navigator, and it will help you understand the material that follows.

If you're using the version of the form that's on the accompanying CD-ROM, try entering various kinds of information into the fields, and tab to the next field to validate the entry. Next, try to fool the real-time validation:

1. Enter **Widgets** in the Description field.

2. Enter **33e** in the Quantity field.

3. Press the Tab key. An alert reveals the error in the Quantity field (shown in Figure 11-3).

4. After closing the alert, press the Tab key again.

You have just let an erroneous entry get through the real-time validation checks. But now click the Submit button to catch any last minute errors, and you'll again see the alert shown in Figure 11-3.

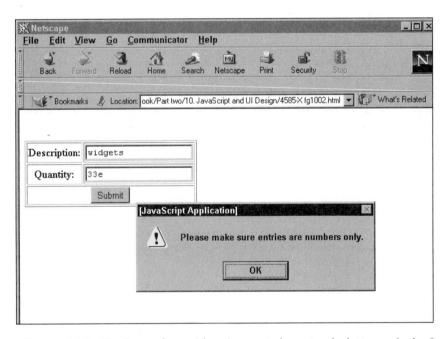

Figure 11-3: The dummy form with an incorrect element—the letter e—in the Quantity field. Our validation routines catch the error and alert the user.

The code below shows the HTML and script for the combined validation routines used in the above form. (To simplify the code below, the form's table tags have been removed.)

```
<SCRIPT LANGUAGE="JavaScript">
// general purpose function to see if an input value has
been entered at all
function isNotEmpty(field) {
    var inputStr = field.value
    if (inputStr == "" || inputStr == null) {
        alert("This field requires an entry.")
        field.focus()
        field.select()
        return false
    }
    return true
}

// general purpose function to see if a suspected numeric
input
// is not empty and is a positive integer
function isNumber(field) {
    if (isNotEmpty(field)) {
        var inputStr = field.value
        for (var i = 0; i < inputStr.length; i++) {
            var oneChar = inputStr.substring(i, i + 1)
            if (oneChar < "0" || oneChar > "9") {
                alert("Please make sure entries are numbers
only.")
                field.focus()
                field.select()
                return false
            }
        }
        return true
    }
    return false
}

// One last check before submission
function finalCheck(form) {
```

```
            var proceed = true
            proceed = isNotEmpty(form.description)
            if (!proceed) return false
            proceed = isNumber(form.quantity)
            if (!proceed) return false
            return proceed
      }
      </SCRIPT>
      </HEAD>
      <BODY>
      <FORM onSubmit="return finalCheck(this)">
      Description:<INPUT TYPE="text" NAME="description"
      onChange="isNotEmpty(this)"><BR>
      Quantity:<INPUT TYPE="text" NAME="quantity"
      onChange="isNumber(this)"><P>
      <INPUT TYPE="submit" VALUE="Submit">
      </FORM>
```

I'm a big fan of client-side forms validation. Even though you still need to use a validation CGI that runs on the server to accommodate nonscripted clients, I'd much rather have all the validation conversations between the user and form handled without taxing the server or the user's patience.

To Plug-In or Not to Plug-In

Even though plug-ins have been around for only a short time, they've certainly livened up many Web sites with a huge variety of rich media. But I've also seen many sites that have abused the privilege at the expense of visitors.

Two user interface issues accompany the use of plug-in media in your Web site:

■ Whether the plug-in is installed in a user's system

■ Delays caused by loading the plug-in and associated data

JavaScript can help you with the former, but some good judgment is needed to address the latter.

Navigator 3 and later come with objects (`plugin` and `mimeType`) that let JavaScript query the browser about which plug-ins are currently installed and the MIME types supported by those plug-ins. On its own, Navigator intercepts HTML instructions (in `<EMBED>` tags) that call upon the client to load a plug-in that's not already installed in the Plug-ins directory. Navigator directs users to a Web page within the Netscape site where they can read generic information about plug-ins. But you can be more helpful in your page by directing plug-in–less visitors directly to the vendor whose plug-in your data requires.

The next code example shows two functions—`mimeIsReady()` and `pluginIsReady()`—that you can use to check to see if a visitor's browser is already installed with a particular plug-in or if it supports a specific MIME type.

```
// Pass "<type>/<subtype>" string to this function to find
// out if the MIME type is registered with this browser
// and that at least some plug-in is enabled for that type.
function mimeIsReady(mime_type) {
    for (var i = 0; i < navigator.mimeTypes.length; i++) {
        if (navigator.mimeTypes[i].type == mime_type) {
            if (navigator.mimeTypes[i].enabledPlugin !=
null) {

                return true

            }

        }

    }
    return false

}


// Pass the name of a plug-in for this function to see
// if the plug-in is registered with this browser and
// that it is enabled for at least one MIME type of any
kind.
function pluginIsReady(plug_in) {
    for (var i = 0; i < navigator.plugins.length; i++) {
        if (navigator.plugins[i].name.toLowerCase() ==
plug_in.toLowerCase()) {
            for (var j = 0; j < navigator.plugins[i].length;
j++)
```

```
{
            if (navigator.plugins[i][j].enabledPlugin) {
                return true
            }
        }
        return false
    }
}
return false
}
```

Of the two functions shown in the above example, `mimeIsReady()` is perhaps the more reliable: It checks whether any installed plug-in is enabled for a specific MIME type (represented as a `<type>/<subtype>` string pair). A problem experienced with the `pluginIsReady()` function among early plug-in generations is that many popular plug-ins have a different name for each platform version.

By running the appropriate test on a visitor's browser before reaching the plug-in-enabled page, you can short-circuit Netscape's built-in plug-in instructions and present more complete and direct instructions about how to download and install the plug-in required for your site. Most plug-in vendor installation instructions advise the user to quit and relaunch Netscape Navigator so that Navigator will recognize the newly installed plug-in. This is unnecessary because you can instruct Navigator to refresh its internal list of available plug-ins (from the Plugins directory) without relaunching. Simply add the script line

```
navigator.plugins.refresh()
```

before the statement that calls either of the plug-in checking functions in the previous example.

Exercising Good Judgment

New plug-in installation is not a smooth operation for a casual visitor to your site. Will a visitor become even more confused if your page offers up friendly advice about installation that contradicts the vendor's instructions to quit and relaunch Navigator? And even after the plug-in is installed, will the user want to wait for the plug-in to load and the content to transfer?

Because of these delays, I recommend that you use plug-ins and Java applets only when they will be delivering mission-critical content or functionality. For example, if the page is from a product catalog that provides QuickTime movie clips of product demonstrations, then the delay in loading the QuickTime plug-in and the movie file may be worthwhile for visitors who are genuinely interested in your product. The same goes for content such as RealAudio, where the rich media is the content.

In contrast, I dislike sites that waste my time loading all this stuff when its contribution to the site is mere fluff. Gratuitous animations and sounds more often than not distract the visitor from the true content of the page. My attitude may make me sound like an old curmudgeon. In truth, I enjoy clever use of multimedia, but my reference point is the typical response time of a multimedia CD-ROM. When a 150K Shockwave file of unknown content starts trickling across the net at a blazing 1.2K per second, I'm outta there before I ever see what you've spent days creating. Unless the promised content of the site is something of extreme interest to me, I'm also not likely to put it in my list of URLs to visit during my next free sunny afternoon while sipping Swiss Mocha in the garden.

Along the same lines, I have visited many sites that try to use sound as either background music or as sound effects synchronized with user actions — especially with the JavaScript-aided mouse rollover changes gaining popularity. (See the next section, "Rollover Behavior," for more about this subject.) When a home page begins loading a plug-in (such as LiveAudio) and a background music soundtrack, the delay before the music starts across a dial-up connection can be so long that the sound doesn't play before I've read the page and found a link to click on. Or the sound will start so late that it startles me as if it's coming out of nowhere.

Synchronizing sounds with user actions is difficult, at best. Your site's first impression has to be its best, so if there are any initial delays in synchronization, the effect is lost. If you can load the plug-in and sound silently and invisibly on an index page (with the appropriate <embed> tag attributes), you may have luck with synchronization in more deeply nested pages of your site. But always check the effectiveness by clearing the caches and opening the URL from the server.

One last point about sound: Not every visitor will like your taste in background music or sound effects; not every visitor will want the neighbor in the next cubicle to hear Web surfing sounds wafting from the speaker. If your pages play sounds by default, always provide a button or other setting to turn the sound off.

Rollover Behavior

Image-swapping mouse rollovers are becoming increasingly popular thanks to the `Image` object introduced in Navigator 3.0. But the most common way to script mouse rollovers produces what I regard as an unwanted user interface effect. While the image changes when the mouse pointer rolls atop the image, the user can roll the pointer away from the image immediately after a mouse click on the image, at which time the image changes back to its original state. If that image (acting as a button or link) is performing some task, it should stay highlighted at least for a moment while the click does its work.

For one site, I created a rollover script that not only keeps the clicked image highlighted for two seconds but also prevents any other image from being clicked while the first image completes its task. The technique involves setting a global Boolean variable to track whether the mouse button is locked out of action. The next example shows some of the key functions that make this happen (omitting the code for precaching images).

```
<HTML>
<HEAD>

<TITLE>Locking Rollovers</TITLE>
<SCRIPT LANGUAGE="JavaScript1.1">

// global variable for 'locked' status
var locked = false

// pre-cache all 'off' button images
var offImgArray = new Array()
// pre-cache all 'on' button images
var onImgArray = new Array()

if (document.images) {
    // statements to load (pre-cache) image arrays and .src
properties (snipped)
    ...
}
```

```
// functions that swap images & status bar
function imageOn(i) {
    if (!locked && document.images) {
        document.images[i].src = onImgArray[i].src
    }
}
function imageOff(i) {
    if (!locked && document.images) {
        document.images[i].src = offImgArray[i].src
    }
}
function setMsg(msg) {
    window.status = msg
    return true
}

// lock 'on' image for 2 seconds, then navigate to button's
URL
function visit(URL,i) {
    if (!locked) {
        locked = true
        var id = setTimeout("finish(\'" + URL + "\'," + i +
")",2000)
    }
}
// to be run after 2 second delay from click on an image
function finish(URL,i) {
    locked = false
    imageOff(i)
    window.status = ""
    location = URL
}
</SCRIPT>

</HEAD>
<BODY>
<CENTER>
```

```
<A HREF="javascript:visit('catalog.html',0)"
onMouseOver="imageOn(0); return setMsg('Catalog')"
onMouseOut="imageOff(0); return setMsg('')"><IMG
SRC="images/catalogoff.gif" WIDTH="120" HEIGHT="45"
BORDER="0" ALT="catalog"></A>
<A HREF="javascript:visit('specials.html',1)"
onMouseOver="imageOn(1); return setMsg('Specials')"
onMouseOut="imageOff(1); return setMsg('')"><IMG
SRC="images/specialsoff.gif" WIDTH="120" HEIGHT="45"
BORDER="0" ALT="specials"></A>
<A HREF="javascript:visit('contacts.html',2)"
onMouseOver="imageOn(2); return setMsg('How to Contact Us')"
onMouseOut="imageOff(2); return setMsg('')"><IMG
SRC="images/contactsoff.gif" WIDTH="120" HEIGHT="45"
BORDER="0" ALT="contact us"></A>
</CENTER>
</BODY>
</HTML>
```

The key to this example is the `visit()` function that is called from the links as-sociated with each image. The parameters include the URL of the destination and an index integer of the image within the precached image arrays, as shown in the following:

```
HREF="javascript:visit('catalog.html',0)"
```

When a user clicks on the image/link, the function acts only if the locked global variable is false; otherwise, the page ignores the click. When the click is accepted, that action sets the locked variable to true and creates a `setTimeout` to invoke the `finish()` function, passing the same URL and index value that `visit()` received.

Although the locked variable is true, the `imageOn()`, `imageOff()`, and `visit()` functions may still be invoked by user actions — rolling over or clicking on images. But the logic of all three functions bypasses the core routines whenever the locked variable is true or if the browser does not support the `Image` object.

Two seconds later, the `finish()` function unlocks the locked global variable, turns off the rollover image, empties the status bar, and, finally, navigates to the chosen URL. During that two-second delay, the highlighted image has remained intact (regardless of the mouse pointer location), and no other image link can be clicked to intercept the previous navigation. The overall feel of this technique is much more like what you'd experience in a multimedia CD-ROM design. Visual feedback more closely resembles what users are accustomed to throughout their navigation around their GUI desktops and documents.

Netscape Communicator also includes more granular mouse event handlers. These let us control the interface in response to a press or a release of the mouse button atop an object and allows our scripted pages to even more closely resemble our favorite desktop GUIs. Many of the chapters in the rest of this section of the book give you ideas about how to do that.

The Price of Freedom

The issues and examples I've shown here are only a few examples of the lively debate about scripting's impact on Web page design for users of all experience levels. The fact that page designers have neither guidelines nor commandments to follow for user interface elements gives them — and you — immense freedom to experiment and improve over the "best of the Web." But with this same freedom comes the great responsibility to do the right thing by your visitors. It may be difficult for a graphically creative genius to view a new creation through the eyes of Granny with the 28.8Kbps modem. But if you fail to do that, then you'll simply impress your savvy friends while alienating the rest of the Web universe.

12

Dueling Event Models: A Cross-Platform Look

Danny Goodman — *consultant and writer*

The upgraded event model introduced to Netscape developers in Netscape Communicator 4.0 made some dramatic improvements to the way the browser handles events. Scripts written in JavaScript 1.2 or later now do a very credible job with events — when the page is intended for a Communicator-only audience. But if visitors to your site include Internet Explorer 4 (IE4) users, you might not know that some of the advanced features of Communicator's event model don't work the same way in IE4. As I'll show in this chapter, it is possible to take advantage of both browsers' event models in the same document. This will become more important to you over time as you add scripted *Dynamic HTML* (DHTML) designs to your pages.

Understanding Basic Events

Events are the lifeblood of scripting and interactivity in a document. They're the initiators, the links between the user and the document. The number and granularity of events available to JavaScript increased substantially with the advent of Communicator and with one exception (the DragDrop event, whose utility in Communicator requires signed scripts), all the events in Communicator are supported in IE4. Table 11-1 shows the events supported in both browsers and the objects from both browsers that support them. Each browser has additional event or object support that is not cross-platform, but as the table proves, the basics are well covered where the two browsers meet.

TABLE 12-1: EVENTS SUPPORTED IN COMMUNICATOR AND IE4

EVENT	OBJECT(S)
Abort	Image
Blur	window, text, textarea, password, select
Change	text, textarea, select
Click	link, area, button, radio, checkbox, reset, submit
Dblclick	Link
Error	window, image
Focus	window, text, textarea, password, select
Keydown	text, textarea, password
Keypress	text, textarea, password
Keyup	text, textarea, password
Load	window, image
Mousedown	link, button, radio, checkbox, reset, submit
Mouseout	link, area
Mouseover	link, area
Mouseup	link, button, radio, checkbox, reset, submit
Move	Window
Eset	Form

EVENT	OBJECT(S)
Resize	Window
Select	text, textarea, password
Submit	Form
Unload	Window

One event not listed in Table 11-1 is the Mousemove event. This important DHTML event is supported in both browsers but in different ways, as I discuss later in this chapter.

Assigning Event Handlers to Objects

Probably the most common way of assigning a script action to an event is via the HTML attribute associated with that event. Event attributes combine the word "on" with the event name (for example, onClick). You can assign an in-line script inside the tag, as in

```
<INPUT TYPE="button" NAME="myButton" VALUE="Click Here"
onClick="alert('Howdy')">
```

or invoke a separate script function defined elsewhere in the document:

```
<INPUT TYPE="button" NAME="myButton" VALUE="Click Here"
onClick="handleClick()">
```

For all the events and objects listed in Table 11-1, you can add the associated event attribute to the object's tags and expect identical behavior in both browsers.

A second way of assigning event handler functions to objects first became available in Navigator 3, and is available in both Communicator and IE4. The same event handlers you know from HTML tag assignment can also be set as properties of the object. To ensure compatibility with both browsers, make sure the name of the event handler in these assignment statements is the all-lowercase version of the HTML attribute, as in

```
document.forms[0].myButton.onclick = handleClick
```

The right side of this kind of assignment statement contains a reference to the function to be invoked when the event fires. Such references omit the parentheses normally associated with functions. One other caveat regarding this type of event handler assignment: the assignment statement must appear in the document after the function and the object have been defined; otherwise, a script error pops up as the document loads.

If you've looked at DHTML code written exclusively for IE4, you may have seen one additional way that this browser links a script to an object and event. In IE4, a <SCRIPT> tag can be earmarked for a specific event of a specific object by way of extra tag attributes that Communicator ignores. The tag set contains only statements that are to run when the IE4 object's event fires (that is, there is no function definition inside that tag set). You cannot use this assignment technique in a cross-platform page, however, because Communicator treats the tag like any other <SCRIPT> tag and runs the statements as the document loads. Destination: Script Error City.

Event Propagation

If you've been comforted so far by how much the two browsers have in common, please take a seat and fasten your seatbelt. The ride gets a little bumpy from here on.

Not every page must concern itself with event propagation, but for interactive content that features a large number of objects sharing scripted behaviors, it can be convenient to dissect and operate on all related events at an object higher up the document object model hierarchy. Instead of assigning similar or identical event handlers to a dozen objects, one event handler in, say, the document object takes care of the whole thing.

For efficient handoff of an event to another object, the browser must have a mechanism that allows an event to traverse the hierarchy. Both Communicator and IE4 have such mechanisms. Unfortunately for cross-platform development, each mechanism is the antithesis of the other: Communicator events trickle down the hierarchy; IE4 events bubble up the hierarchy.

Trickle-Down Events

Communicator's event-trickling mechanism is described more fully in my *View Source* article "Getting Ready for JavaScript 1.2 Events," which you can find on the

CD-ROM. I'll hit the highlights here to help you understand the differences between Communicator and IE4 event propagation.

ON THE CD-ROM

The *View Source* article "Getting Ready for JavaScript 1.2 Events," which more fully describes Communicator's event mechanism, can be found on the CD-ROM that accompanies this book. Follow the path Sample Code and Supporting Documentation ⇨ Part II ⇨ Chapter 12.

When a user clicks a button viewed in Communicator, the browser initially sends that event to the window object. From there it goes to the document object. Lastly, it reaches the target of the click, where an `onClick` event handler can process the event. But if you want the event to be processed or preprocessed in the window or document level, you must turn on event capture for either object (or both). Window and document objects in Communicator have a `captureEvents()` method that lets you specify precisely which event types the objects should grab as they pass through. Event types are properties of the Event (capital "E") object. Therefore, for the document object to capture the click event intended for a document's button, you tell the document to capture all click events:

```
document.captureEvents(Event.CLICK)
```

You must also assign an onClick event handler to the document object:

```
document.onclick = handleClick
```

With these statements in place in the loaded document, when a user clicks on any object that is capable of reacting to a click event, the `handleClick()` function is invoked. It is up to the statements inside the handleClick() function to examine more details about the event (as described later in the section "Event Objects"). This function can do its work and simply gobble up the event, or it can route the event to its intended target (or another target, for that matter).

CROSS-REFERENCE

See the section "Event Objects" later in this chapter for more details.

To summarize Communicator's propagation mechanism:

- Events start at the window level and automatically go to the intended target object unless the document object is explicitly instructed to capture that event type.

- A capturing window or document level must have an event handler assigned to that object for that object type.

- Whether or not the event ultimately reaches its intended target is up to the event handler assigned to the window or document object that captures that event.

Bubble-Up Events

Internet Explorer 4's propagation mechanism initially directs an object's event to the intended target. The event invokes an event handler if one is defined for that object. Under normal conditions, after that event handler function does its thing, the event then continues up the containment hierarchy.

I must point out that there is a distinction between the document object hierarchy you're accustomed to in Communicator and IE4's containment hierarchy. The latter is based on HTML elements that are containers (that is, that have start and end tags). For example, consider the following skeletal document:

```
<HTML>
 <BODY>
  <FORM>
   <DIV>
    <INPUT TYPE="button">
   </DIV>
  </FORM>
 </BODY>
</HTML>
```

In IE4, virtually every container element can have an onClick event handler assigned to it. Therefore, if a user clicks the button, the click event traverses the container hierarchy, passing through <DIV>, <FORM>, and <BODY> in that order. If you want the document-level object to handle all click events from several related buttons, you can place a single onClick event handler in the <BODY> tag and omit onClick event handlers for the buttons and all intervening objects.

To prevent an event from bubbling up, you must cancel event bubbling for the current event. This gets into the event (lowercase "e") object discussion coming up, but here is one way you can keep a click event held within a button object:

```
<INPUT TYPE="button" ... onClick="handleClick();
window.event.cancelBubble=true">
```

You can also include the cancelBubble statement inside the function invoked by the event handler. It affects only the current event being handled.

To summarize IE4's propagation mechanism:

- An event starts at its intended target and invokes an event handler if one is defined.

- Unless explicitly instructed to cancel, the event bubbles up the containment hierarchy after the event handler of the target (if an event handler is defined) executes its last statement.

- Events bubble all the way to the top of the containment hierarchy, unless canceled along the way.

Working Together

As opposite as these two systems appear, they can work quite well together if your intention is to write event handlers high up the object hierarchy that are to be shared among several related objects. Only a tiny bit of platform-specific branching is needed because both browsers share a lot of the right syntax.

The example following this paragraph shows a very simple document that handles all click events at the document level. Thus, all clicks on either the document or the button ultimately invoke the sayHey() function. The code at the beginning of the script is a generic routine that sets platform-flag global variables for use throughout the document. The sayHey() function is the function that is to be invoked by a click of the mouse button. Called by the onLoad event handler, the init() function turns on event capture for Communicator users, causing all click events to be directed to whatever function is referenced by the document object's onClick event handler, defined in the subsequent statement. Both browsers have the document object's onclick event handler set to call the sayHey() function. When this is run in IE4, the click event from the button bubbles up to the document object, where the event is handled.

Here's the full example:

```
<HTML>
<HEAD>
<TITLE>New Window</TITLE>
<SCRIPT LANGUAGE="JavaScript">
var isNav4, isIE4
if (parseInt(navigator.appVersion) >= 4) {
    isNav4 = (navigator.appName == "Netscape") ? true : false
    isIE4 = (navigator.appName.indexOf("Microsoft" != -1)) ?
true : false
}
function sayHey() {
    alert("Hey!")
}
function init() {
    if (isNav4) {
        document.captureEvents(Event.CLICK)
    }
    document.onclick = sayHey
}
</SCRIPT>
</HEAD>
<BODY onLoad="init()">
<FORM>
<INPUT TYPE="button" NAME="myButton" VALUE="Click Here">
</FORM>
</BODY>
</HTML>
```

Mousemove events in Communicator are not affiliated with any object. You're expected to capture this event at the window or document level, and assign a function to the object's onmousemove property. Just as in the event handler assignment in the init() function of the previous code example, setting the onmousemove property of a document object will be recognized by both browsers.

The above example obviously lacks an important feature: the ability to distinguish between a click on a button and a click on the document background. That's where event objects — and their entirely different treatments in the two browsers — come into play.

Event Objects

When an event occurs in either Communicator or Internet Explorer 4 — whether the event is the result of a user action or a system action — the browser generates an event (lowercase "e") object that contains myriad details about the event. For mouse events, for example, this object knows where on the page the event occurred, the object under the cursor at that instant, and which modifier keys, if any, were held down at that moment. It is not only a shared script that may need to know this information about an event. For example, if you want to guard against the entry of numbers into a text field as the user types, the script must be able to inspect each typed character and determine whether the typed character is an allowable one. This is precisely the kind of information that the event object carries with it.

Communicator's event object is automatically passed to functions invoked by event handlers that had been assigned as event properties. Therefore, with the following kind of event handler definition

```
document.onclick = handleClick
```

the function in Communicator can catch the event object as a parameter variable:

```
function handleClick(evt) {
    // statements
}
```

For event handlers defined as tag attributes, the event keyword can be passed in much the same way as you pass this keyword:

```
<INPUT TYPE="button" ... onClick="handleClick(event)">
```

Inside the function, the properties of the event object can be examined to help the function decide how to react to the event.

IE4's event object is a different animal. It is treated as a property of the window object. In other words, there is always an event object hanging around in the window. When a user or system action fires an actual event, the event object picks up the properties of that event and holds onto them until the event handler processing that event finishes its job. At idle time, the event object intentionally loses everything it knew about the most recent event. During processing, scripts can examine the properties of this window.event object for the kind of event-specific details described earlier.

Event Object Properties

Confounding cross-platform development a bit more is that the browsers share precious few event object property names. This means that unless you devise your own set of APIs to bridge the gap (as shown for CSS-Positioning tasks in Chapter 9, "CSS-Positioning: The Dynamic HTML Neutral Zone"), you'll have some additional platform-specific branching in your main document scripts to handle the different property names and reference syntax.

Table 12-2 shows the primary event object properties for each browser — at least the ones whose functionality is identical in both browsers. Each browser has additional, platform-specific properties. Items in common are shown in boldface.

The coordinate properties are pretty straightforward, so I'll devote two examples to presenting little laboratories you can use to experiment with the event object under different browser circumstances. Although both examples use the common tag-based event handler declarations, there is no reason you cannot apply what you'll see in the examples into pages that use the cross-platform event propagation described earlier. The exact implementation depends heavily on the structure of your documents and the events you design into them.

TABLE 12-2: COMMUNICATOR AND IE EVENT OBJECT PROPERTIES

| COMMUNICATOR | | | INTERNET EXPLORER 4 | |
PROPERTY	VALUES	PROPERTY DESCRIPTION	VALUES	PROPERTY
modifiers	Event object properties	Modifier keys pressed when the event occurred	Boolean	altKey ctrlKey shiftKey
pageX	pixel count	Horizontal coordinate of event in content region of browser window	pixel count	clientX
pageY	pixel count	Vertical coordinate of event in content region of browser window	pixel count	clientY
screenX	pixel count	Horizontal coordinate of event relative to entire screen	pixel count	screenX
screenY	pixel count	Vertical coordinate of event relative to entire screen	pixel count	screenY
target	Object	Object that is to receive, or that fired, the event	object	srcElement
type	event name	String value of event name (e.g., "click", "mousedown", "keypress")	event name	type
which	Integer	Mouse button or keyboard key code (but some code values differ with browser)	integer	button keyCode

Detecting Modifier Keys

The first event object laboratory, shown in the next code example (just below), presents a standard link and text input field. Both the onMouseDown event handler of the link and the onKeyPress event handler of the text field invoke the same function — a poor man's cross-platform event propagation scheme if I ever saw one. The function branches to look at the platform-specific event object and determine which of the four possible modifier keys are pressed when the event occurs. There is an extra lesson in this example, as you'll soon see. If you're using a level 4 browser, you can view this example, which can be found on the CD-ROM.

ON THE CD-ROM

The code below is also included in an HTML file on the CD-ROM that accompanies this book; the file is labeled, Chapter 12 Example 1. You can open it and play with it using Netscape Navigator or IE, Version 4 or later. Find the HTML file by following the path: Sample Code and Supporting Documentation ⇨ Part II ⇨ Chapter 12.

```
<HTML>
<HEAD>
<TITLE>Modifiers Keys Properties</TITLE>
<SCRIPT LANGUAGE="JavaScript">
var isNav4, isIE4
if (parseInt(navigator.appVersion) >= 4) {
    isNav4 = (navigator.appName == "Netscape") ? true : false
    isIE4 = (navigator.appName.indexOf("Microsoft" != -1)) ?
true : false
}

function checkMods(evt) {

    var form = document.forms[0]
    if (isNav4) {
        form.modifier[0].checked = evt.modifiers &
Event.ALT_MASK
```

```
        form.modifier[1].checked = evt.modifiers &
Event.CONTROL_MASK
        form.modifier[2].checked = evt.modifiers &
Event.SHIFT_MASK
        form.modifier[3].checked = evt.modifiers &
Event.META_MASK
    } else if (isIE4) {
        form.modifier[0].checked = window.event.altKey
        form.modifier[1].checked = window.event.ctrlKey
        form.modifier[2].checked = window.event.shiftKey
        form.modifier[3].checked = false
    }
    return false
}
</SCRIPT>
</HEAD>
<BODY>
<B>Event Modifier Keys</B>
<HR>
<P>Hold one or more modifier keys and click on
<A HREF="javascript:void(0)" onMouseDown="return
checkMods(event)">
this link</A> to see which keys you are holding.</P>
<FORM NAME="output">
<P>Enter some text with uppercase and lowercase letters:
<INPUT TYPE="text" SIZE=40
onKeyPress="checkMods(event)"></P>
<P>
<INPUT TYPE="checkbox" NAME="modifier">Alt
<INPUT TYPE="checkbox" NAME="modifier">Control
<INPUT TYPE="checkbox" NAME="modifier">Shift
<INPUT TYPE="checkbox" NAME="modifier">Meta
</P>
</FORM>
</BODY>
</HTML>
```

Both calls to the checkMods( ) function pass the Communicator event object. The function defines a parameter variable for the incoming object, and that variable is used in the branch for Communicator processing; it is ignored for IE4 processing. That's because IE4 references to the event object look to the window object for its event property.

Each browser also has a very different way of determining when a modifier key has been pressed in concert with an event.

- In Communicator, the event object's modifiers property is compared (with a bitwise AND operator) against the constants held by the Event (capital "E") object (an object that works here a lot like the Math object). The Event object has a separate constant value for each of the four modifier keys. If you AND the constant against the modifiers property, you get true if the constant value is a component of the modifiers value.

- For IE4, the event object has separate properties for each of three modifier keys (there is no property for the meta key). Each of these properties is a simple Boolean value, which allows the lab to set the checked property of the checkbox objects based on which modifier key or keys were held down during the event.

When you use this example on either browser, you'll experience some unexpected behavior in the text field. The browser does not yield its sovereignty over numerous Ctrl+key combinations or any Alt+key combinations. This may cause you to narrow your sights for defining accelerator key combinations for your pages.

Using Button and Key Codes

The final example of this survey shows you how to extract information about which mouse button or which keyboard key is involved in an event. The next example lists another laboratory page for experimenting with these features. Results of the event object properties for this information are shown in the status bar as you click a button or type into a textarea. Like the lesson about modifier keys and text fields in the previous, this lab holds an extra lesson. But first, let's look at the code.

ON THE CD-ROM

The code below is also included as an HTML file on the CD-ROM that accompanies this book; the file is labeled, Chapter 12 Example 2. You can open it and play with it using Netscape Navigator or IE, Version 4 or later. You can find it by following the path: Sample Code and Supporting Documentation ⇨ Part II ⇨ Chapter 12.

```html
<HTML>
<HEAD>
<TITLE>Button and Key Codes</TITLE>
<SCRIPT LANGUAGE="JavaScript">
var isNav4, isIE4
if (parseInt(navigator.appVersion) >= 4) {
   isNav4 = (navigator.appName == "Netscape") ? true : false
   isIE4 = (navigator.appName.indexOf("Microsoft" != -1)) ?
true : false
}
function checkWhich(evt) {
   var theKey
   if (isNav4) {
      theKey = evt.which
   } else if (isIE4) {
      if (window.event.srcElement.type == "textarea") {
         theKey = window.event.keyCode
      } else if (window.event.srcElement.type == "button") {
         theKey = window.event.button
      }
   }
   status = theKey
   return false
}
</SCRIPT>
</HEAD>
<BODY>
<B>Button and Key Codes From Event Objects</B> (results in
the status bar)
<HR>
```

```
<FORM NAME="output">
<P>Click on this
<INPUT TYPE="button" VALUE="Button"
onClick="checkWhich(event)">
with either mouse button (if you have more than one).</P>
<P>Enter some text with uppercase and lowercase letters:<BR>
<TEXTAREA COLS=40 ROWS=4 onKeyPress="checkWhich(event)"
WRAP="virtual"></TEXTAREA></P>
</FORM>
</BODY>
</HTML>
```

I cheat a bit again for the purposes of the demonstration by calling one function from both the onClick event handler of the button and the onKeyPress event handler of the textarea. The function that handles the event must branch to accommodate the different ways each browser extracts button and key information.

- For Communicator, the which property of the event object is an integer whose range of values depends on the event type. For a button, the which value is 1 for the primary button; for a keyboard key, the which value is the ASCII value of the character associated with the key. Therefore, the script extracts one value regardless of the event or object type.

- For IE4 processing, the script examines the kind of object that originally received the event (window.event.srcElement). The type property of relevant objects reveals the kind of object receiving the user action. For a textarea, the script needs to read the keyCode property of the event object. For standard English characters, the values are the same as Communicator's which property. To get the mouse button used to click the screen button, the script reads the window.event.button property. While this value is an integer as it is in Communicator, the values are different: A click of the primary mouse button is a value of 0.

The bonus lesson in this example is that even though the event objects are supposed to report different values for the right mouse button (if you have a multiple-button mouse), in practice the browsers don't let you trap for this user event. Right-clicks in Windows, for example, display a context-sensitive pop-up menu, without passing the event to the page.

Momentous Events

When I first learned of the different event models in the two browsers, I wondered how they could possibly be reconciled for cross-platform development. To my delight, I discovered that there was significant overlap in the implementations. And even where the approaches are opposite of each other, it isn't too difficult to devise scripts that accommodate many features of both models in one document since the respective syntaxes scarcely step on each other.

13

Browser-Friendly Dragging in Dynamic HTML

Danny Goodman — *consultant and writer*

I f you cut your teeth on command-line interfaces and dot-command formatting in word processors, the notion of using a mouse to manipulate items on the screen may have been a shocker the first time you saw it. If the year was 1984, and you thought this was cool, or the "right way" to compute, you probably bought a Macintosh. Since that time, graphical user interface (GUI) choices have increased to the point where only real geeks use command-line interfaces (and still manage to get a lot of work done in the process).

For the mass audience, the GUI has been the portal to accessible computing. The idea of pointing to a picture of something that represents a real-life object attracts a class of user who may be keyboard-phobic or simply doesn't want to memorize a vocabulary of crazy commands. A new user generation is accustomed to click-on-it interactivity wherever there is a computer screen and, soon, a TV screen.

Interactivity is more than just clicking on stuff; it's also dragging stuff around. "Direct manipulation," some UI pros call it. Accomplishing this on a Web page prior to version 4 browsers required help from the outside, in the form of Java applets and other types of media played through plug-ins. But the positioning powers of Dynamic HTML (DHTML) bring direct manipulation straight into low-bandwidth HTML documents. In this chapter, I give you the basic tools to start putting draggable elements into your DHTML documents — and have the pages run equally well in both Communicator and Internet Explorer, versions 4 and later.

Meeting the Cross-Browser Challenge

Dragging objects around on the page summons several Dynamic HTML powers that are not always implemented the same way in both browsers. Fortunately, there is enough similarity in how the browsers work that you can script draggable objects without too much conditional branching.

DHTML facilities required for dragging objects are:

- Absolute positioning of elements
- Stacking of elements
- Event manipulation

The example application in this chapter includes two draggable images. For the sake of simplicity, the HTML that generates these positionable elements is the same for both browsers: each IMG element is wrapped inside a DIV element. It wasn't necessary for this application to use the Navigator LAYER element. As noted in Chapter 10, "CSS-Positioning: The Dynamic HTML Neutral Zone," Navigator treats a LAYER element and an absolute-positioned DIV element the same for the purposes of scripting an element's position and stacking order (z-order). Establishing proper references to the object being dragged is where the most intensive script branching occurs because the browsers use different object models for controlling position and z-order.

Speaking of differences, the event models at first glance seem anything but compatible. Chapter 12, "Dueling Event Models: A Cross Platform Look," shows how Navigator's trickle-down model and Internet Explorer's bubble-up event model seem to collide with each other. Despite the nearly opposite ways that Navigator and Internet Explorer have of handling events, the amount of browser-specific event code for the example application is very small. As you'll see in this application, the two models can easily meet in the middle, sharing most of the event-handling code.

The Cross-Platform Challenge

If you work exclusively in Windows with code that lets users hold the mouse button down on an element to drag it, you'll likely miss a potential problem for Macintosh users of your page. Unbeknown to most Windows-only Web authors, browsers in the one-button-mouse Macintosh world display the contextual pop-up menu when the user holds down the mouse button and doesn't move the mouse for more than about one second. As soon as that contextual menu appears, no more events are passed through to the page. Since dragging requires constant access to the mouseMove event, this situation is a showstopper. If the user knows to begin dragging immediately, the contextual menu doesn't appear, but you cannot rely on the user to know that or to have the precise coordination to carry it out.

At first this was enough of a problem for my dragging programs that I altered the user interface entirely: all users had to click on an element to "pick it up"; then, with the mouse button released, the user could drag the element around on the screen. Another click "dropped" the item into position. Ugh! Fortunately, there is a way to prevent the contextual pop-up menu from appearing on the Mac without interfering with normal operation in Windows. I'll point out the fix when I get to that point in the code.

An Overview of the Process

The basic structure of the script for dragging is relatively simple. Only three event types are in play: mouseDown, mouseMove, and mouseUp. Each event performs a specific task.

The mouseDown event must determine which element the user has selected for dragging. This allows the script to assemble a global variable reference to the object, which subsequent processing will use over and over during dragging. Whenever that global variable has a reference in it, the script knows that the user has pressed the mouse button down on an element. At the same time, the element is brought to the top of the stacking order so that it floats atop all other draggable elements and doesn't ever "submarine" under another object (except for form controls in Navigator, which are always in front of any draggable element).

Actual dragging occurs in response to the mouseMove event. This event fires each time the mouse pointer moves, whether the mouse button is held down or not. The scripts must be constructed in such a way that they ignore mouseMove events when no element is being dragged. Here is where the reference in the global variable comes in handy again. If there is a reference stored there, it means that the user is pressing down on the element, in which case each moveMove event adjusts the position of the element on the screen; otherwise, the moveMove event is ignored.

The final stage is when the user releases the mouse button. When the mouseUp event fires, the element's stacking order is reset and the global variable is set to null (to keep the mouseMove event from doing anything when no element is selected).

Inside the Code

Before we look at the code, it will be helpful to see how the application works. You can see a static version in Figure 13-1. If you'd like to see the way it really works, you'll have to view it in your browser; the application can be found on the CD-ROM that comes with this book. (Look for Chapter 13, "Browser-Friendly Dragging in Dynamic HTML.")

ON THE CD-ROM
The application that's illustrated in Figure 13-1 can be found on the CD-ROM that accompanies this book. To find it, follow the path, Sample Code and Supporting Documentation ⇨ Part II ⇨ Chapter 13. It can be viewed in either Netscape Navigator or Internet Explorer, versions 4 and later.

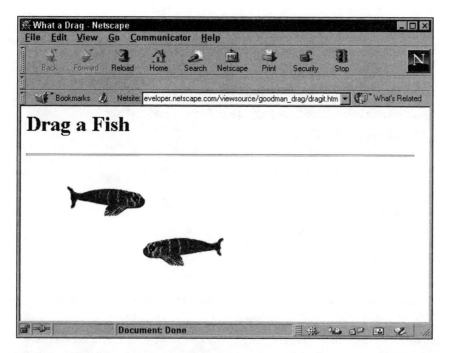

Figure 13-1: The dragging application uses two animated GIF images (fish) as the drag-gable objects, but any HTML-generated content can be used in place of the images.

The HTML document begins by setting the positioning style attributes using Cascading Style Sheet-Positioning (CSS-P) syntax. The z-index attribute for both items is set to 0, which means that they initially appear stacked according to source code order.

```
<HTML>
<HEAD>
<TITLE>What a Drag</TITLE>
<STYLE TYPE="text/css">
   #fish1 {position:absolute; left:50; top:100; width:144;
z-index:0}
   #fish2 {position:absolute; left:110; top:145; width:144;
z-index:0}
</STYLE>
```

Scripting begins with some utilities used by other functions later on. The first order of business is to set a pair of global variables (isNav and isIE) that are used for browser-specific branching.

```
<SCRIPT LANGUAGE="JavaScript">
// Global variables for platform branching
var isNav, isIE
if (parseInt(navigator.appVersion) >= 4) {
    if (navigator.appName == "Netscape") {
        isNav = true
    } else {
        isIE = true
    }
}
```

Next come two functions that I borrowed from a set of cross-browser Dynamic HTML APIs I use. If this application were more DHTML-intensive, I would probably link in the entire API. But since only two functions are needed here — for setting the z-order and moving an element — the in-document download is more economical.

```
// ***Begin CSS custom API Functions***
// Set zIndex property
function setZIndex(obj, zOrder) {
    obj.zIndex = zOrder
}
// Position an object at a specific pixel coordinate
function shiftTo(obj, x, y) {
    if (isNav) {
        obj.moveTo(x,y)
    } else {
        obj.pixelLeft = x
        obj.pixelTop = y
    }
}
// ***End API Functions***
```

More global variables are declared next. The one named `selectedObj` will hold a reference to the selected element while the user has the mouse button held down. Its value is set when the user first presses down on the mouse button (later in the code; see the code sample that begins `// Find out which element has been "pressed" into service`). An equally important pair of global variables (`offsetX` and `offsetY`) will hold integers representing the offset from the top and left edges of the element to the coordinate of the actual mouse position. As you'll see, these values are used so that the dragged object tracks with the cursor in the same place where the user first pressed the mouse button.

```
// Global holds reference to selected element
var selectedObj
// Globals hold location of click relative to element
var offsetX, offsetY
```

The function that sets the `selectedObj` global variable is the most involved of the entire application. The big deal about this is that each browser's document object model treats its positionable elements and properties differently. Moreover, the differences in event models play a role here as well.

For Navigator, the script copies the event coordinates relative to the page to a pair of variables (`clickX` and `clickY`). This is done for a bit of performance help because these values are used repeatedly inside a `for` loop. Saving a copy of these Navigator event object properties to `clickX` and `clickY` means that the property expressions don't have to be evaluated each time through the loop.

Heavy-duty action occurs inside the `for` loop. The purpose of the loop is to see whether, based on the coordinates of the mouseDown position, the mouse button was pressed inside the rectangle of a draggable element. Therefore, the loop will cycle through all Navigator layer objects (each "positionable thingy" is a layer object in Navigator). But because layers might overlap each other, the script must check the layers from the frontmost layer backward — the assumption is that the user expects to activate the actual object directly underneath the mouse pointer, and not an unseen element buried further back. Therefore, the `for` loop starts with the highest-indexed layer and works its way backward.

Since there is no quick method that lets a script find out whether an x,y position falls within a rectangle, the script does the job the long way. Using a copy of each layer in turn, the script compares the event coordinates against the coordinate space occupied by the element. This gets a bit tricky because the height and width of the positioned element are most accurately depicted by its clipping rectangle's height and width, not the element's height and width. The right edge coordinate, for example, is determined by adding the clipping width to the left edge coordinate.

If the mouseDown event is inside one of the layers, the `selectedObj` global variable is set to the reference of that layer object. That object is also brought to the front by setting its `zIndex` value to an arbitrarily high value (100). The process of selecting the element for Navigator is complete, so the return statement bails out of the function at this point.

```
// Find out which element has been "pressed" into service
   function setSelectedElem(evt) {
   if (isNav) {
       // Declare local var for use in upcoming loop
       var testObj
       // Make copies of event coords for use in upcoming
loop
       var clickX = evt.pageX
       var clickY = evt.pageY
       // Loop through all layers (starting with frontmost
layer)
       // to find if the event coordinates are in the layer
       for (var i = document.layers.length - 1; i >= 0; i--)
{
           testObj = document.layers[i]
           if ((clickX > testObj.left) &&
             (clickX < testObj.left + testObj.clip.width) &&
             (clickY > testObj.top) &&
             (clickY < testObj.top + testObj.clip.height)) {
               // If so, then set the global to the layer,
bring it
               // forward, and get outa here
               selectedObj = testObj
               setZIndex(selectedObj, 100)
               return
           }
       }
```

For Internet Explorer, the bubble-up event model means that the mouseDown event already knows which element was selected. This element is actually the IMG element that is wrapped inside the DIV element. Therefore, the script uses the IE object model property to fetch a reference to the image's parent element. As long as the parent is one of the fish DIV elements, that DIV element's style property is assigned to the selectedObj global variable. As mentioned in Chapter 10, adjustments to position properties in IE4 require adjustments to an element's style property.

```
    } else {
        // Use IE event model to get the targeted element
        var imgObj = window.event.srcElement
        // Make sure it's one of our fish
        if (imgObj.parentElement.id.indexOf("fish") != -1) {
            // Set the global to the style property of the
element,
            // bring it forward, and say adios
            selectedObj = imgObj.parentElement.style
            setZIndex(selectedObj,100)
            return
        }
    }
```

If the user pressed the mouse button down on something other than one of the "positionable thingies," the script reconfirms that no element is active for dragging by setting the global value to null.

```
    // The user probably clicked on the background
    selectedObj = null
    return
}
```

The function that does the real work of moving the element to track the mouse is rather compact. Because this function is called with every mouseDown event (shown later, in the last bit of code, just before the section "Where to Go from Here"), the first task is to filter out events that occur when no element is selected. But if one of the fish is selected, the function branches to handle the different ways each browser treats coordinate measures and the corresponding event object properties. Regardless of the browser, the call to move the element ultimately goes to the shiftTo() function from the API group above (see the code sample above that begins // ***Begin CSS custom API Functions***).

For Navigator, the event object is passed as a parameter to the dragIt() function. To get the coordinate point for the element, subtract the horizontal and vertical offsets (stored as global variables at mouseDown time) from the event's mouse position (the element movement is done to the element's top left corner). For IE4, subtract the same offset values from that browser's way of fetching the event coordinates. IE4 for Win32 normally responds to the user's moving the mouse with the mouse button down by displaying the "not allowed" icon in the pointer, halting further event propagation. But as a result of returning false in a function invoked by an event handler, the mouseMove event does not continue on to the system: The script maintains control over the event, allowing the user to drag without any hassle. This return false trick saves the day for the Macintosh in a moment.

```
// Drag an element
function dragIt(evt) {
   // Operate only if a fish is selected
   if (selectedObj) {
      if (isNav) {
         shiftTo(selectedObj, (evt.pageX - offsetX),
(evt.pageY - offsetY))
      } else {
         shiftTo(selectedObj, (window.event.clientX -
offsetX),
            (window.event.clientY - offsetY))
         // Prevent further system response to dragging in
   IE
         return false
      }
   }
}
```

The engage() function is invoked in response to the mouseDown event. This pivotal function first invokes the setSelectedElem() function (above, in the code sample that begins // Find out which element has been "pressed" into service) to find the selected object and assign that object's reference to the selectedObj global variable. When such a selection is made, the offset measures of the mouseDown event location relative to the selected element are saved to the `offsetX` and `offsetY` global variables. Each browser has its own way of determining this offset. For Navigator, the page coordinates of the selected object are subtracted from the event's page coordinates; for IE4, the event object precalculates these offset values and has properties that return those values.

At the end of the `engage()` function is the key to letting Macintosh users hold the mouse button without having the contextual menu pop up. Using the return false technique inside this event handler function prevents the event from reaching the element and system. The system never knows it's supposed to display that pop-up menu.

```
// Set globals to connect with selected element
function engage(evt) {
   setSelectedElem(evt)
   if (selectedObj) {
      // Set globals that remember where the mouseDown is in
relation to the
      // top left corner of the element so we can keep the
element-to-cursor
      // relationship constant throughout the drag
      if (isNav) {
         offsetX = evt.pageX - selectedObj.left
         offsetY = evt.pageY - selectedObj.top
      } else {
         offsetX = window.event.offsetX
         offsetY = window.event.offsetY
      }
   }
   // Block mouseDown event from forcing Mac to display
   // contextual menu
   return false
}
```

When the user releases the mouse button (the mouseUp event), the dragged object is returned to the low z-order soup. The ever-important `selectedObj` global is also set to `null` so that mouseMove events across the page are ignored by the `dragIt()` function (above, in the code sample that begins `// Drag an element`) until the user next presses the mouse button down on a fish.

```
// Restore elements and globals to initial values
function release(evt) {
   if (selectedObj) {
      setZIndex(selectedObj, 0)
      selectedObj = null
   }
}
```

When the page loads, it must set the scene for handling the events. It's easiest on many levels to assign event handlers as object properties rather than as handlers inside the element tags. For Navigator, especially, it means that the page can use the DIV element, which does not have event handlers associated with it.

The BODY element's onLoad event handler invokes the init() function. For Navigator, a quick branch to the setNavEventCapture() function turns on event capture at the document level. Only the three events involved with dragging are set to be captured. Back in the init() function, the onmousedown, onmousemove, and onmouseup event properties are set to the references of the functions that do the work for each event. Despite the differences in event models, these event property assignments are identical for both browsers.

```
// Turn on event capture for Navigator
function setNavEventCapture() {
   if (isNav) {
      document.captureEvents(Event.MOUSEDOWN |
Event.MOUSEMOVE | Event.MOUSEUP)
   }
}
// Assign event handlers used by both Navigator and IE
(called by onLoad)
function init() {
   if (isNav) {
      setNavEventCapture()
   }
   // assign functions to each of the events (works for both
Navigator and IE)
   document.onmousedown = engage
   document.onmousemove = dragIt
   document.onmouseup = release
```

```
        }
    </SCRIPT>
    </HEAD>
    <BODY onLoad="init()">
    <H1>Drag a Fish</H1>
    <HR>
    <DIV ID=fish1><IMG NAME="fishPic1" SRC="fish1.gif" WIDTH=144
    HEIGHT=73 BORDER=0></DIV>
    <DIV ID=fish2><IMG NAME="fishPic1" SRC="fish2.gif" WIDTH=144
    HEIGHT=73 BORDER=0></DIV>
    </BODY>
    </HTML>
```

Where to Go from Here

With the basic dragging functionality at your fingertips, I can think of several ways to extend dragging in applications. In examples at my Web site at http://www.dannyg.com, I compare the position of a released item against a fixed target position to see if the user has positioned the element correctly. If the release position is within a few pixels of the target, the script finishes the job by snapping the element into the exact target position and marks the item as correct. Other experiments you can try include changing the image so that the image object's src property loads a different image based on the direction in which the user drags the element from moveMove to mouseMove. You should also be able to constrain movement by checking whether the Shift key is being held down as the user drags an element, and then allow the element to be dragged only horizontally or vertically.

14

JavaScript Date Object Techniques

Danny Goodman — *consultant and writer*

R eaders who belonged to the Macintosh community in the late 1980s may remember my personal information management (PIM) commercial product, called Focal Point. One of the modules of this PIM was the ever-popular appointment calendar. Perhaps the most valuable lessons I learned from creating and upgrading that application were the intricacies of programming dates and time, both the internal algorithms and user interfaces designed for a worldwide audience.

This experience makes me, I suppose, hypersensitive to the implementation of date and time in a programming environment, such as JavaScript, not that I have any intention of implementing an appointment calendar in JavaScript. (Except as a client-side assistant to a substantial server-based program, the language is not suited to this kind of application.) But given the powers of the Date object in JavaScript in Navigator, I'm surprised by the lack of date- and time-oriented scripting in Web pages.

The purpose of this chapter is to explain the concepts behind JavaScript's Date object and describe a few practical implications of this object in both plain and forms-based HTML pages. Along the way, I also point out some of the pitfalls and bugs you'll need to work around, including a few discoveries made in the interim.

CAUTION

This chapter discusses the Date object only as implemented in Navigator 3. Later versions of Navigator/Communicator have followed the Navigator 3 model and have dealt with some of the gremlins described later in this chapter.

Where the Date Object Comes From

Many scripters have seen the JavaScript object roadmap I devised, which you can find on the CD-ROM that comes with the book. On this roadmap, the Date object stands apart from the window-document object hierarchy because a date is a computational object, rather than one that reflects "physical" elements in an HTML page. The object has no fewer than 22 methods (even more in Navigator 4) that give the scripter access to every time and date component of the object.

ON THE CD-ROM
Look for "Danny Goodman's JavaScript Object Roadmap and Compatibility Guide" on the CD-ROM that accompanies this book. You'll find it in the folder with the materials that support Chapter 1. (Path: Sample Code and Supporting Documentation ⇨ Part I ⇨ Chapter 1.)

The idea for the Date object and its methods didn't fall out of the sky as a feature unique to JavaScript; the syntax is borrowed directly from Java 1.0. In fact, once you master the JavaScript Date object, you will have also mastered 95 percent of Java's original Date object. (However, Java 1.1 added enhanced date-handling powers with a new object called Calendar.)

Creating a Basic Date Object

Because of its Java heritage, using the Date object requires what in Java is a very common occurrence: creating an instance of — *instantiating* — the object before any statement can examine, change, or perform operations on a date. For example, to create a default Date object (whose date is today's date as indicated by the client system's internal clock), the syntax is the following:

```
var today = new Date()
```

When no parameters accompany the Date() object constructor, JavaScript automatically reads the client's internal clock setting and creates the object with the date and time at the instant at which the object is created. Therefore, after executing the above statement, the arbitrarily named variable today is a reference to a Date object in memory that holds the current date and time. In other words, the object takes a snapshot of the client's system clock; the content of this date/time "photo" doesn't change unless a script statement invokes one of the Date object's methods that modify the object.

NOTE
To view the examples referenced in this chapter, open the HTML version of the chapter (which can be found on the CD-ROM that accompanies this book) using Netscape Communicator, which you can download from the Netscape Web site for free. (See the file on the CD called Welcome and Software Download for instructions.) To get the most out of the information in this chapter, you should follow along using your computer and the HTML version, which will allow you to play with the live examples as you read about them here. To find the HTML version, follow the path, Sample Code and Supporting Documentation ⇨ Part II ⇨ Chapter 14.

There are several more interesting ways to create a Date object — all of which entail assigning a specific date and time to the object other than the current moment. For the sake of completeness, Table 14-1 shows all Date object constructor formats for assigning specific dates.

TABLE 14-1: DATE OBJECT CONSTRUCTORS

SYNTAX	EXAMPLE
new Date("Month dd, yyyy hh:mm:ss")	new Date("September 11, 1997 08:30:00")
new Date("Month dd, yyyy")	new Date("September 11, 1997")
new Date(yy,mm,dd,hh,mm,ss)	new Date (97,8,11,8,30,00)
new Date(yy,mm,dd)	new Date(97,8,11)
new Date(GMTmilliseconds)	new Date(873991800000)

To fully appreciate how these Date object constructors work, let's put the Date object under a microscope to see what it's doing internally.

Inside the Date Object

When you create a Date object with the current time and date, there is a lot more going on inside JavaScript than you may be aware of. If you have trouble figuring out what time it is in a neighboring time zone, then the Date object's innards are going to make your head hurt.

To truly understand all this, you need a working knowledge of the recognized world time reference point, which runs through Greenwich, England. Two common names for this time zone are Greenwich Mean Time (GMT) and Coordinated Universal Time (UTC). Although there are tiny differences between the two (the difference between atomic clocks and astronomical observations), for most purposes, you can regard them as equal. If you are interested in how these terms came about, you might want to refer to the excellent online sources The Time Service Department of the U.S. Naval Observatory, at `http://tycho.usno.navy.mil/`, and Greenwich 2000, at `http://time.greenwich2000.com/index.htm`.

The basic point to understand about GMT and time zones around the world is that if you know the time at GMT, you can determine the local time anywhere on the planet because each time zone is measured relative to GMT, by international convention. When the sun is directly overhead the GMT zone, for example, all time zones to the east (through Russia, Asia, Australia, and part way across the Pacific Ocean until you reach the International Date Line) are later in the day than noon; the noonday sun has already been there, done that. Conversely, all time zones to the west (across the Atlantic, through North and South America, and onward across the Pacific up to the International Date Line) are earlier in the day and have lunchtime to look forward to. Figure 14-1 represents a snapshot of the world's time at exactly noon GMT.

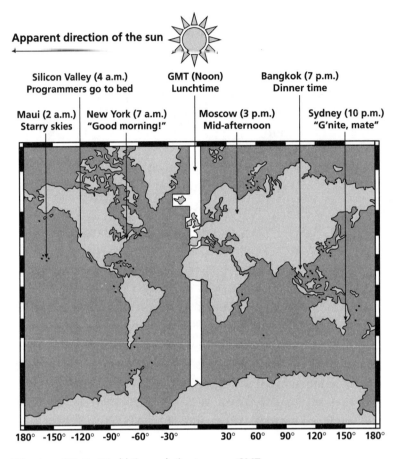

Figure 14-1: World time relative to noon GMT

To eliminate the vagaries of the world's time zones (some of which shift during part of the year for the equivalent of America's Daylight Saving Time), the JavaScript (and Java) Date object stores its information as GMT time. More precisely, the date value is stored as the number of milliseconds before (positive) or after (negative) zero hours GMT on January 1, 1970.

Entering Date Object Values

If you have played at all with the Date object, you may be quite confused about why GMT has to come into the picture at all. After all, if you sit in front of a Windows-based PC at Netscape's world headquarters in Mountain View,

California, and get the value of the current date and time, you see a value that looks like this:

```
Thu Mar 20 23:09:48 Pacific Standard Time 1999
```

On a Mac OS computer in the same location, the value looks like this:

```
Thu Mar 20 23:09:48 1999
```

If you're following along on your computer with the HTML version of this chapter, take a look at the HTML-file example in "Try It on Your Client" to see how it looks in your system. What you see there, however, is the Date object display being automatically converted to your client's time zone — even though it's the GMT date and time that's stored in the Date object. Also, when you use the Date object methods that get and set components of a Date object (year, month, date, day of the week, hour, minute, and second), those values are reflected in your client's local time, not GMT. In fact, the only values that reveal the Date object's GMT date are the millisecond measurement (accessible via the `getTime()` method) and the GMT string conversion (via the `toGMTString()` method).

If you're not following along on your computer, Figure 14-2 shows you what the current date and time look like on a Windows 95 system running Communicator 4.5.

All these conversions to local time, of course, rely on the proper setting of the client computer's clock and relevant Control Panel settings about the time zone of the computer's physical location. In a sense, this is a wild-card issue — as a scripter, you can never be sure that the client's clock and time zone are set correctly.

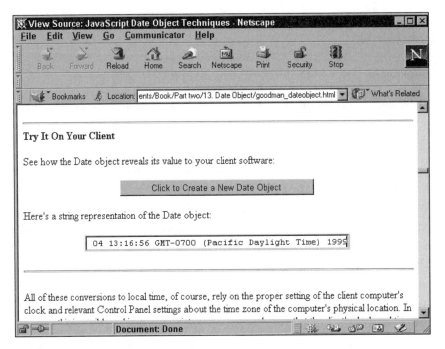

Figure 14-2: Creating a Date object on a Windows 95 system, in Communicator 4.5

Date Object Methods and Values

Given the potential confusion between GMT and local date and time values, I think it's a good idea to look at some specific values of a Date object's components and see precisely which values are GMT-based and which are local. To help you do that, I put together the table "Date Object Methods," which you'll have to look at in the HTML version of this chapter on the CD-ROM because it's actually constructed using JavaScript and employs drop-down lists to make it easier for you. (Figure 14-3 shows a part of this large table, including one of the drop-down lists.) It shows all Date object methods and examples of their values. In the Method column of the table, `dateObj` is a placeholder for any variable that references a previously created Date object. You can experiment with a number of dates and time selections and view the results in the table.

ON THE CD-ROM

To get the most out of the discussion that follows, you should go to the CD-ROM that accompanies this book, open the HTML version of this chapter in your browser, and look at the table "Date Object Methods." (Path: Sample Code and Supporting Documentation ⇨ Part II ⇨ Chapter 14.)

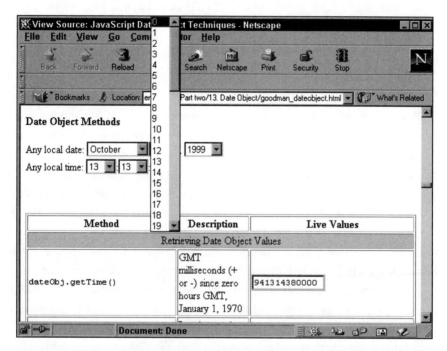

Figure 14-3: A small portion of the Date Object Methods table. The full version is in the HTML version of this chapter on the CD-ROM accompanying this book.

Obtaining an Accurate Date

Because your scripts are at the mercy of an accurate client clock setting, I don't advise relying exclusively on the client to supply the precise GMT time value if your application needs that data for a form's date or time field. For example, if it requires the exact time of a form submission, you might want to use a form submission CGI do the timestamping with the server's clock (assuming you have control over that machine's clock settings).

If your scripts use dates for calculations or comparisons, consider carefully how you generate Date objects. Bear in mind that visitors are most likely to be located in time zones other than yours. Therefore, if you attempt to create a Date object for a specific date and time, the GMT Date object value for visitors from other time zones will be different from the value you use to test out your page. Consider the following Date object constructor statement:

```
var myDate = new Date(1999,11,24,18,0,0)
```

Those constructor values represent 6:00 P.M. on December 24, 1999. For some-one in the Eastern Standard Time zone, the object's GMT value of `myDate` is 1:00 P.M. on December 24; for someone in the Pacific Standard Time zone, the object's GMT value is 10.00 A.M. on December 24.

To establish a firm GMT date and time in an object, you need to use one of the last two methods shown in the chart in the HTML version of the chapter on the CD-ROM, "Date Object Methods" (`Date.parse()` and `Date.UTC()`) to first ob-tain the GMT millisecond value. (Part of the chart appears in Figure 14-3.) You can then use that millisecond value as a parameter to the `Date()` constructor.

Each of these methods requires a specific parameter to do its job. `Date.UTC()` may be the simpler of the two to use, provided you know the GMT time you wish to create. The parameters consist of a comma-delimited list of integer values cor-responding to the year, month, date, hour, minute, and second, in that order.

If you aren't comfortable with converting your local time to GMT just yet, you can use the `Date.parse()` method instead. Its parameter is a string patterned af-ter a date format established by the Internet Engineering Task Force. What I like about this format is that you can specify either the GMT time or the local time along with an offset from GMT. For example, let's say you are in New York (Eastern Standard Time) and want to create a Date object that corresponds to 6:00 P.M. EST on Christmas Eve. Any of the following statements will do the trick:

```
var myDate = new Date("24 Dec 1999 23:00:00 GMT")
var myDate = new Date("24 Dec 1999 18:00:00 GMT-0500")
var myDate = new Date("24 Dec 1999 18:00:00 EST")
```

In the second version, the GMT × 0500 indicates that the time zone is five hours west of GMT. JavaScript (as influenced by Java) also knows the most common time zone abbreviations used in the western hemisphere (EST, EDT, CST, CDT, MST, MDT, PST, and PDT). That no other time zones are allowed is a sign that the early Java model suffered from an American myopia when it comes to global dates and times. Even so, the application of the GMT format, plus or minus an amount of time represented by the hhmm value after GMT, means that this system can be used around the globe.

Doing the Math

When it comes to scripting date calculations, such as the number of days between dates or the date six weeks from today, you can use the milliseconds value of Date objects. I also find it convenient to define some global variables in documents that perform date arithmetic, as shown in the following:

```
var MINUTE = 60 * 1000
var HOUR = MINUTE * 60
var DAY = HOUR * 24
var WEEK = DAY * 7
```

I use all-uppercase names because I treat these values like constants — a common stylistic convention. With these variables predefined, I can use them as shortcuts in calculations. For example, to calculate the number of days between dates, take the difference between two Date object values and then divide that by the DAY variable, as shown here:

```
var today = new Date()
var xmas = new Date(1999,11,25)
var shoppingDays = (xmas - today) / DAY
```

Notice that you can subtract two Date objects directly to determine their difference in milliseconds. But for other calculations involving Date objects and other value types, you must first convert the objects to milliseconds via the getTime() method. For example, say you want to create a new object, futureDate, with the date and time for precisely six weeks from now.

First, you'd capture the current date as (GMT) milliseconds; next, you'd add that value to six times the product of the WEEK global variable, as shown in the following code:

```
var today = (new Date()).getTime()
var futureDate = new Date(today + (WEEK * 6))
```

Some Bugs and Gremlins

The most difficult part of working with the Date object is dealing with some platform-specific bugs (primarily on the Mac OS platform) and one annoying inconsistency.

The Mac OS version of Navigator exhibits a couple of problems you should be aware of. One occurs only when the Date & Time control panel has Daylight Saving time turned on. When Daylight Saving is engaged, JavaScript miscalculates the conversion between local and GMT date values by one hour (in Navigator 2, this discrepancy was an entire day). For example, consider the following Date object constructor and the result:

```
new Date("July 4, 1999 12:00:00")

        // result on Daylight Saving Mac --> Fri Jul 4 13:00:00
1997
```

To handle this problem, I define one more global variable in any page that includes date calculations. This variable, DATEADJUSTMENT, is calculated for every platform, just in case there's an unknown bug lurking on a platform I can't test. Here are the statements that set the variable:

```
function adjustDate() {
    var base = new Date()
    var testDate = base
    testDate = testDate.toLocaleString()
    testDate = new Date(testDate)
    DATEADJUSTMENT = testDate.getTime() - base.getTime()
}
```

Each time a new date is created, the DATEADJUSTMENT value must be subtracted from it. The process of creating an accurate Date object this way requires that you create two Date objects; the adjustment must be factored for both constructors, as shown in the following:

```
var nowInMS = (new Date().getTime() - (2 * DATEADJUSTMENT)
var nowDateObject = new Date(nowInMS)
```

When this date adjustment bug doesn't afflict the client, the variable does contain a small number of milliseconds (the time it takes to execute the `adjustDate()` function). But unless you're calculating times at that granularity, the tiny adjustment won't affect normal date and time calculations.

Mac OS Time Zones

Another, more serious bug affects Mac OS users whose time zone settings place them at GMT or eastward to the International Date Line. The problem is that JavaScript miscalculates the time zone offset entirely, causing Date objects created from the internal clock or via constructors that use local values (that is, all but the constructor for GMT milliseconds) to be one full day later than the intended date.

At the heart of the matter is that, on the Mac OS, JavaScript counts the time zone offset westward from GMT all the way around the Globe instead of using negative numbers east from the GMT to the International Date Line. The time zone offset for Sydney, Australia, should be -600; on Mac OS computers, however, JavaScript renders it as a positive 840. The erroneous counting continues all the way to GMT, whose offset value is rendered as 1440 (60 minutes times 24 zones) instead of zero.

The strange behavior here is that the Mac OS reflects the proper local time and date components but gets the Date object GMT value wrong by one full day. Therefore, if your script requires an accurate GMT version of the local date, the script needs to factor this zone error whenever the GMT value is involved.

To adjust for this potential error, I add one more global variable definition to the `adjustDate()` function, as follows:

```
function adjustDate() {
    var base = new Date()
    var testDate = base
    testDate = testDate.toLocaleString()
    testDate = new Date(testDate)
    DATEADJUSTMENT = testDate.getTime() - base.getTime() -
zoneError
    ZONEERROR = (base.getTimezoneOffset() >= 720) ? DAY : 0
}
```

To create a Date object with the corrected GMT value, here is how to use both date adjustment global variables:

```
var nowInMS = (new Date().getTime() - (2 * DATEADJUSTMENT) -
ZONEERROR)
var nowDateObject = new Date(nowInMS)
```

This last code sample works accurately on all Navigator 3.0 platforms that I've been able to test by setting them to a variety of time zones around the world.

One Inconsistency

JavaScript makes one departure from the Java Date object that could have a negative impact on scripts using dates that reach to the year 2000 and beyond. If your date treatments must be Y2K compliant, you need to script around the problem or use techniques available in more modern versions of the browsers (see Chapter 15, "JavaScript and the Year 2000 (Y2K) Problem").

At issue is the way JavaScript treats the year component of a Date object. According to the Java specification, years are integers after the year 1900. In other words, if you use the getYear() method for a Date object that holds a 1999 date, the returned value should be 99. This is how both Java and JavaScript work for dates prior to 2000.

Java, however, remains true to the algorithm into the future, where the year 2001 is represented by 101. JavaScript, however, treats all years beginning with 2000 as the actual year value: 2001 is 2001. This jump in values could trip up a script that relies on a returned year value in sequence with years prior to 2000.

I prefer to do away with ambiguities such as starting the year counts with 1900. Therefore, if you must be compatible with browsers prior to Version 4, I recommend processing all values that come from the getYear() method through a filter function that adds 1900 to any returned value that is less than 100. The good news is that the setYear() method and all Date object constructors that take an integer value for the year accurately handle four-digit numbers. Use 'em.

One Last Compatibility Tidbit

Although I have not performed exhaustive tests on all Navigator platforms, the most intelligent implementation I've seen is on the Windows 95 platform. At least for North America, if you specify in the Date/Time control panel that you want Windows 95 to automatically adjust your clock for Daylight Saving, your Date object handling gets an added bonus: The correct offset to GMT is calculated for you for any date throughout the year.

For example, Pacific Standard Time is eight hours earlier than GMT, while Pacific Daylight Time is seven hours earlier. If you live in the Pacific time zone and create a Date object for local noon in December (when standard time is in effect), the GMT equivalent is set to 8:00 P.M. If you create a Date object for noon on some day in August, though, the GMT equivalent is properly set to 7:00 P.M. no matter what time of year the script runs to create that object. This is very smart.

In contrast, the GMT offset for Daylight Saving time on the Mac OS is governed by the current state of the system clock — whether or not Daylight Saving time is turned on. Therefore, if you are in the winter months in North America and create a Date object for a July 4 fireworks event at 9:00 P.M., the GMT time will be calculated on the winter months' standard time offset. When July comes around, the Daylight Saving conversion will display the event as starting at 10:00 P.M. — too bad you missed the show.

It can be fun to experiment with changes to the control panels and their effects on the Date object. Be aware, however, that Navigator picks up information about the client's clock setting (and time zone offset) when it launches. If you make a change to the control panel, you must quit and relaunch Navigator for the changes to affect your script experiments.

Date Object Validation

It may be tempting to use the Date object as a way to help validate date and time entries in forms whose fields get submitted to CGI programs for further processing. What's easy to forget, however, is that there are numerous accepted date and time formats in use around the world. Unless you've used software that's been localized for other countries, you probably haven't seen the large variety of formats currently in use. In the United States, for example, the short date format is mm/dd/yyyy. In many other parts of the world, the month and date positions are switched. In still other parts of the world, there might be different delimiter characters between the components, such as a dash (-) or a period (.) instead of a slash (/). The same is true for time formats.

The JavaScript Date object is not smart enough to know whether 3/4/1999 is March 4, 1999, or April 3, 1999. Nor can any script that you write parse such a text field entry. And just because you supply a sample entry in your form or label doesn't mean that the visitor will follow it.

All this leads me to suggest that you divide date and time entry fields into multiple components, each of which can be easily validated with JavaScript. For example, the form illustrated in Figure 14-4 provides three fields for date entry, each of which is backed up by a healthy validation script to check for range and integers. It validates your entry as you complete each field — one item at a time. You can play with this form in the HTML version of this chapter that's on the CD-ROM.

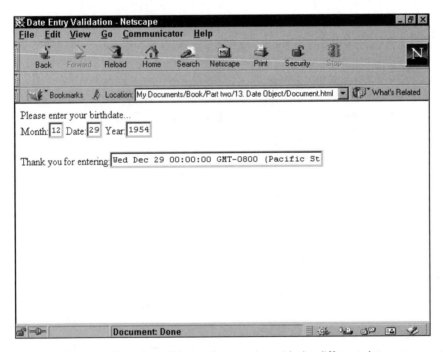

Figure 14-4: A form for validating date entries, with the different date components broken into different fields

ON THE CD-ROM

A working version of this form can be found in the HTML version of this chapter on the CD-ROM that accompanies this book.

Here's the source code for this form and validation functions.

```
<HTML>
<HEAD>
<TITLE>Date Entry Validation</TITLE>
<SCRIPT LANGUAGE="JavaScript">
<!--
// Date Entry Validation Example by Danny Goodman
(http://www.dannyg.com)
// **BEGIN GENERIC VALIDATION FUNCTIONS**
// JavaScript sees numbers with leading zeros as octal
values, so strip zeros
function stripZeros(inputStr) {
var result = inputStr
while (result.substring(0,1) == "0") {
result = result.substring(1,result.length)
}
return result
}

// general purpose function to see if an input value has
been entered at all
function isEmpty(inputStr) {
if (inputStr == "" || inputStr == null) {
return true
}
return false
}

// general purpose function to see if a suspected numeric
input
// is a positive integer
function isNumber(inputStr) {
```

```javascript
for (var i = 0; i < inputStr.length; i++) {
var oneChar = inputStr.substring(i, i + 1)
if (oneChar < "0" || oneChar > "9") {
return false
}
}
return true
}

// function to determine if value is in acceptable range for
this application
function inRange(inputStr, lo, hi) {
var num = parseInt(inputStr)
if (num < lo || num > hi) {
return false
}
return true
}
// **END GENERIC VALIDATION FUNCTIONS**

function validateMonth(field) {
var input = stripZeros(field.value)
if (isEmpty(input)) {
alert("Be sure to enter a month value.")
select(field)
return false
} else {
if (!isNumber(input)) {
alert("Entries must be numbers only.")
select(field)
return false
} else {
if (!inRange(input,1,12)) {
alert("Enter a number between 1 (January) and 12
(December).")
select(field)
return false
}
```

```
        }
        }
        calcDate()
        return true
        }

        function validateDate(field) {
        var input = stripZeros(field.value)
        if (isEmpty(input)) {
        alert("Be sure to enter a date value.")
        select(field)
        return false
        } else {
        if (!isNumber(input)) {
        alert("Entries must be numbers only.")
        select(field)
        return false
        } else {
        var monthField = document.birthdate.month
        if (!validateMonth(monthField)) return false
        var monthVal = parseInt(monthField.value)
        var monthMax = new
        Array(31,31,29,31,30,31,30,31,31,30,31,30,31)
        var top = monthMax[monthVal]
        if (!inRange(input,1,top)) {
        alert("Enter a number between 1 and " + top + ".")
        select(field)
        return false
        }
        }
        }
        alert("Falling through???")
        calcDate()
        return true
        }

        function validateYear(field) {
        var input = stripZeros(field.value)
```

```
if (isEmpty(input)) {
alert("Be sure to enter a month value.")
select(field)
return false
} else {
if (!isNumber(input)) {
alert("Entries must be numbers only.")
select(field)
return false
} else {
if (!inRange(input,1900,2005)) {
alert("Enter a number between 1900 and 2005.")
select(field)
return false
}
}
}
calcDate()
return true
}

function select(field) {
field.focus()
field.select()
}

function calcDate() {
var mm = parseInt(document.birthdate.month.value) - 1
var dd = parseInt(document.birthdate.date.value)
var yy = parseInt(document.birthdate.year.value)
document.birthdate.result.value = (new
Date(yy,mm,dd)).toString()
}
//-->
</SCRIPT>
</HEAD>
<BODY>
<FORM NAME="birthdate">
```

JavaScript and the Year 2000 (Y2K) Problem

Danny Goodman — *consultant and writer*

Imagine a scene from "The Y-Files":

On this overcast afternoon, Skelly and Moldau drive a nondescript sedan to the front of a small, 1940s-vintage house on tree-lined Maple Street in a Philadelphia suburb. As they walk toward the covered front porch, the house appears a bit unkempt but not shabby, with very little sign of activity. They reach the front door and push the button that sounds a faint buzzer from inside. A long moment later, the door opens slowly, squeakily. An old man, perhaps in his early seventies, squints through the screen door to identify his callers.

"Who are you?" his strong but weathered voice says.

"Are you John Thorpe?" Moldau asks.

"Who wants to know?" the aged man barks back.

"Are you John Thorpe, who worked for Giantco from 1965 to 1976?" Moldau inquires again.

"I'm an old man. I can't be the one you're looking for. Go away! Get off my property!"

With that, the old man starts closing the door. But Skelly is quick to fling open the screen door and block the front door with her foot. In the scuffle, she comes within inches, face to face, of the angry, wrinkled man. "Mr. Thorpe," she begins with a sense of urgency, "you worked on the programs for many of Giantco's computer systems. Those programs are still being used today for inventory control, customer billing, and payroll. Your experience with the code will help us prepare the programs for the year 2000. Tens of thousands of jobs depend on your COBOL and FORTRAN skills. You've got to help us, and we're prepared to reward you handsomely." Moldau pulls out a consulting contract from his jacket pocket and quickly unfolds it to show the man.

A few seconds later, Skelly senses less pressure on the door opposing her force. With a sigh of resignation, the man says softly, "Yes, I'm John Thorpe. Come in."

Perhaps without so much drama, but with no less urgency, organizations that employ large-scale computer systems are frantically looking for help in avoiding potential snafus when programs deal with dates after the good ol' 1900s. The situation is called the Year 2000 Problem, commonly called the Y2K Problem because (a) it fits better into trade journal headlines; and (b) why use plain language when an insider abbreviation sounds cooler?

But it's not just the big programs that can get tripped up by the year 2000 and beyond. Even small-scale programs for personal computers and JavaScript date calculations can fall on their faces if the programmer doesn't foresee the problem. In this chapter, I describe the situation for JavaScript authors and show you how to build prevention into your scripts today. I also discuss the user convenience issue of allowing two-digit year entries in dates and how it can work until the end of the year 9999.

The Nature of the Problem

The brunt of the Y2K problem is that for years programmers assumed that a two-digit year entry implied the twentieth century's "19" prefix (yes, I know the year 2000 is part of the twentieth century; please do not e-mail me). Plenty of paper forms we've filled out over the years preprinted the "19" part of the year and left a blank for us to fill in just the last two digits. In other cases, we've been encouraged to use the mm/dd/yy format (or dd/mm/yy for some parts of the world) for quick date entry on a paper or computer-screen form.

All that comes crashing down for these programs when the year being entered is 2000 or later. Entries of "00" and "01" are interpreted by these programs as being 1900 and 1901 instead of 2000 and 2001. If that date is an expiration date, for example, your credit card may have expired seventy years before you were born. Oops.

JavaScript: getYear() and setYear()

Chapter 14 covers the Date object, so here I'll focus primarily on methods that govern retrieving and setting the year value of an instance of the Date object. If you're not vigilant, this is precisely where the Y2K problem will bite you.

The getYear() and setYear() methods have been associated with the Date object since the first release of JavaScript. You can easily dispense with the Y2K problem as it relates to the setYear() method by simply passing a four-digit year as the parameter to the method in all cases. Yes, there are some ranges in which you can pass a two-digit year as a parameter and have it interpreted properly, but using these magic ranges will only get you into trouble. Follow the simple rule of always using four-digit values as the setYear() parameter, and you'll be in good shape on that end.

The getYear() method, however, is a can of worms, especially if you're insisting on compatibility back to Netscape Navigator 2; getYear() changed its behavior between Navigator 2 and 3.

In Navigator 2, getYear() returns an integer value of a date object's year minus 1900. Therefore, for a date object from 1995, getYear() returns 95; for a date object from 2003, getYear() returns 103. Moreover, the Date object in Navigator 2 is limited in its range. It can handle no date before January 1, 1970 (Greenwich Mean Time), and not too far into the 21st century either.

Starting with Navigator 3, however, the value returned by `getYear()` changes for dates other than those in the 1900s. For example, for a date object from 1995, `getYear()` still returns 95, as it does in Navigator 2; for a date object from 2003, however, `getYear()` returns the four-digit version, 2003. For dates prior to 1900, `getYear()` returns the four-digit version. Therefore, only the 1900s have two-digit values returned (and the Date object bottoms out at the year 100).

Handling getYear() Anomalies

How you decide to handle the `getYear()` behavior depends on the range of dates your scripts work with. Ideally, you'd like one solution to work with all browser versions, with little or no version branching. Because in the worst case (Navigator 2) the `getYear()` method returns the year value minus 1900, you can examine the returned value and add 1900 to it if the value is less than 1900:

```
var dateObj = however you reach a date
var theYear = dateObj.getYear()
theYear += (theYear < 1900) ? 1900 : 0
alert("Four-digit year is:" + theYear)
```

If you need to work with date objects whose values are before 1970, the `Date` object in Navigator 2 won't be of any use. This means that you'll be restricted to Navigator 3 or later. Since the `Date` object from this version onward knows dates down to 100, you need to perform the special case only for values less than 100:

```
var dateObj = however you reach a date
var theYear = dateObj.getYear()
theYear += (theYear < 100) ? 1900 : 0
alert("Four-digit year is:" + theYear)
```

Values starting with 2000 will be returned as four-digit values automatically, so the calculation will be performed only for year values in the 1900s.

As for cross-browser concerns, you can treat Internet Explorer 3 as if it were Navigator 2, with the same bottom-year restriction of 1970 and with `getYear()` for 2003 returning 103. Internet Explorer 4's `Date` object behaves like Navigator 4's `Date` object.

Help in Navigator 4

One of the by-products of the ECMAScript effort (as written in the ECMA-262 standard) is a more Y2K-friendly `Date` object. Because the `getYear()` and `setYear()` methods had been long deployed in browsers up through Navigator 3 by the time ECMAScript stabilized, the standard had to be compatible with existing scripts. It did so by defining `getYear()` and `setYear()` as they existed in Navigator 2. But ECMAScript also made provisions for more consistent year handling in the future.

To provide for easier handling of four-digit years, the ECMA-262 standard added a pair of methods, `setFullYear()` and `getFullYear()`, which represent the data entirely in four-digit years. As stated previously, the old `setYear()` method as implemented in browsers accepts full year values; the `setFullYear()` method was added for the sake of having parallel get and set methods in the ECMAScript `Date` object.

Both of these new methods are implemented in JavaScript 1.2, as deployed in Navigator 4, Enterprise Server 3, and Internet Explorer 4. If you're using date calculations only in server-side JavaScript, you can use the new methods on the server without worrying about compatibility with older client versions.

You should be aware of one extra caution flag. In the Windows versions of Navigator, the `document.lastModified` property returns a date value displaying a two-digit year. If your script design relies on the returned value to generate a Date object, you will have to use some of the other techniques described in this chapter to massage the value only in the Windows version of the browser (using browser detection techniques).

Continuing to Use Two-Digit Year Entry

With all this concern about four-digit years, there are still many instances in which two-digit year entries are not only preferred, but economically desirable. For example, one organization I've worked with has an elaborate Enterprise Server application that requires a large amount of data entry on more than a dozen separate forms. Many of the forms have date entry fields, most of which are so critical to the application that a date value must be entered twice (in two adjacent fields) to ensure that the user has not made an entry error (the two date values must match exactly before the data can be submitted). In this situation, requiring operators to type two extra characters for each date field will have a noticeable impact on productivity in the long run.

In implementing the client-side date field validations for this application, I broke my usual rule of forcing date entry by way of three select lists (see Chapter 14). This was not the sin that it might appear to be because the application is used on an intranet by well-trained users who all adhere to one known date format (mm/dd/yy). Cultural differences in date entry styles were not an issue.

But productivity was a vital issue, so I created a validation routine that not only validates the mm/dd/yy entry but also automatically feeds a four-digit-year date back to the field if the validation is successful. This four-digit-year date is not merely for entertainment; rather, the back-end database requires four-digit years in its date field. Therefore, it is incumbent on the validation routine to turn a two-digit year entry into a four-digit year: If a user enters 1/1/99, the validation routine replaces the entry with 01/01/1999, which is suitable for inserting into the database.

The charter from the client was to set the epoch for two-digit year entry to start in 1930 and end in 2029. Therefore, any two-digit year entry will be converted to the four-digit year in that range. The relevant portion of the date validation routine that handles the date entry is as follows (expanded a bit for learning clarity):

```
if (yyyy < 100) {
    // Entered value is two digits, which we allow for
1930-2029.
    if (yyyy >= 30) {
        yyyy += 1900
    } else {
        yyyy += 2000
    }
}
```

This range suits the typical dates entered into this application. Of course, if someone enters a four-digit year outside this range, the year is accepted as is.

The unfortunate side effect of the above technique (sometimes called "windowing") is that it creates a Year 2030 Problem for the application. As users approach that year, there will be less opportunity to use two-digit year entries because they won't apply to years past 2029 unless the program is modified. Some programmers might chuckle at the thought of worrying about something 30 years in the future;

so did the FAA computer programmers who are now making sure that air traffic control computers don't start losing track of planes before Dick Clark finishes rockin' in the New Year for 2000. We should all be learning from the manifestations of the Y2K problem that we can't assume an application will be obsolete before these kinds of issues crop up.

A Permanent Fix

The solution to the Year 2030 Problem in the previous example is to generate a routine that allows two-digit year entries within a 99-year window that automatically moves forward with each passing year. The example code below shows a JavaScript 1.2-level function that accepts a two- or four-digit integer value as a parameter. For two-digit entries, the function figures out where the year fits within the span programmed into the function, and then turns the entry into the appropriate four-digit year.

Most of the code in the example calculates the century values that need to be added to the two-digit entry. Some of the statements can be combined for compactness, but I left them in their expanded form to allow comments for each step along the way. One variable, loCutOffset, determines how many years prior to the current year the window begins. In the example, this value is set to 70. Therefore, in 1998, the entry 28 is converted to 1928; when that value is entered in 1999, the entry is converted to 2028 because the bottom edge of the conversion window will have shifted upward by 1 to 1929. This makes sense for applications in which the dates being entered also tend to slide along with time — membership start dates, license expiration dates, and the like.

```
// Converts two-digit year to four-digit year within a
sliding
// "conversion window." Parameter yyyy is an integer.
function makeFullYear(yyyy) {
    if (yyyy < 100) {
        // Minimum range begins this number of years before
the current year.
        var loCutOffset = 70

        // Today's full year -- requires JavaScript 1.2
```

```
        var curFullYear = (new Date()).getFullYear()
        // Today's century (first two digits of the year)
        var curCent = Math.floor(curFullYear/100)

        // Actual full year of allowable range minimum
        var loFullYear = curFullYear - loCutOffset
        // Actual full year of allowable range maximum
        var topFullYear = curFullYear + (100 - loCutOffset)

        // Century (first two digits) of minimum
        var loCent = (Math.floor(loFullYear/100) < curCent) ?
Math.floor(loFullYear/100)
                        : curCent
        // Two-digit year of minimum
        var loYear = loFullYear - (loCent * 100)

        // Century (first two digits) of maximum
        var topCent = (loCent == curCent) ? curCent + 1 :
curCent

        // Compare two-digit user entry to two-digit range
minimum.
        if (yyyy >= loYear) {
            // If entry is equal or above minimum, add the
entry to the minimum century.
            yyyy = (loCent*100) + parseInt(yyyy, 10)
        } else {
            // If entry is below minimum, add the entry to the
maximum century.
            yyyy = (topCent*100) + parseInt(yyyy,10)
        }
    }
    return yyyy
}
```

I've set up the function in the example within a sample application that lets you experiment with how it works if you were to go forward or back in time. In the example, you can choose one of four years that the function believes it's living in. You can enter a two-digit year and see how well it's converted within the sliding "window of time" established by the function. The example is shown in Figure 15-1. You can also find the example on the CD-ROM that accompanies this book in the file Chapter 15 Example Application; it's viewable in your browser.

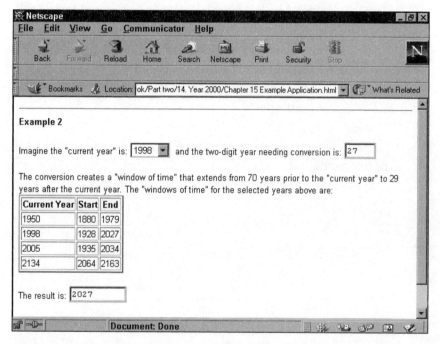

Figure 15-1: A sample date application that lets you experiment with the previous code example

ON THE CD-ROM

The sample application shown in Figure 15-1 can be found on the CD-ROM that accompanies this book. Look for the file Chapter 15, Example Application, which can be viewed in your Web browser. To find it, follow the path, Sample Code and Supporting Documentation ⇨ Part II ⇨ Chapter 15.

With this kind of open-ended treatment of date entry, I can rest assured that even in my retirement years, users will have the convenience of two-digit year entry without anyone's having to muck with the code — or send out agents to track me down.

Which brings us back to Maple Street outside Philadelphia, as Skelly and Moldau walk back to the car with a signed contract tucked away in a pocket...

"How did you know that the man was Thorpe?" Moldau asks Skelly.

"Did you see the shirt he was wearing?" Skelly says to Moldau with an air of self-confidence. "It was an old white dress shirt."

Moldau is still in the dark. "I'm sure a lot of retired guys wear their old shirts," he says, exasperated.

"Yes," Skelly adds, "but every cuff, collar, and edge of his shirt was frayed — except for the pocket."

"You mean. . . ."

"Yes, he wore a pocket protector most of the time he owned that shirt. He fit the profile."

[Cue weird "Y-Files" music theme.]

16

Detecting a JavaScript Client

Danny Goodman — *consultant and writer*

U nless you're developing HTML pages for an intranet environment —
where you know the browser version on virtually every client machine —
you're perhaps painfully aware that not everyone accessing your pages can
benefit from your scripting efforts. At one extreme is the client running the latest
release version of a browser capable of interpreting the most modern version of

JavaScript and a sophisticated document object model. At the other extreme are those visitors who use text-only browsers, such as Lynx. In between are dozens of browser brands and versions. Some can interpret earlier versions of JavaScript; others understand only Internet Explorer's document object model; and still others haven't a clue about the HTML scripting embedded in your documents.

Managing browser-specific features has been a problem for Web authors and Web masters ever since the first HTML extension found its way into early browsers. With each new generation of modern browsers, the universe of visitors to our pages fragments ever more, forcing us to make difficult decisions about how to treat a variety of browsers. If you're a scripter, it's only natural to think about using JavaScript as an aid to sorting out browser versions.

Whoops! No JavaScript

Sometimes I think we scripters get too entwined in our JavaScript-enhanced worlds to distinguish between the forest and its trees. I've lost count of the number of newsgroup requests for a script to help a page detect whether or not the browser is JavaScript enabled. Perhaps the existence of the `javaEnabled()` method of the Navigator object leads some scripters to expect a corresponding `javaScriptEnabled()` method.

What these folks fail to realize is that a non-JavaScript browser cannot run such a script ... or any script. Therefore, you cannot script an `if...else` control structure to `document.write()` one batch of stuff to a page if JavaScript is enabled and a different batch of stuff if JavaScript isn't there (or if it's turned off).

Another dream tactic is to employ a script to overwrite HTML that would be displayed in non-JavaScript browsers. This, too, isn't possible: Any standard HTML in a document will appear in all browsers from Lynx to Communicator. JavaScript cannot inhibit HTML content display.

Determining the Real Need

Although I can't cover every possible scenario in which you might like to distinguish between JavaScript- and non-JavaScript-aware browsers, I see three basic strategies you could use to accommodate browsers with different levels of JavaScript awareness. They are the following:

- Automatic branching from the `index.html` page to a home page optimized for the scripting capability of the browser

- Using a single link to navigate to a JavaScript or non-JavaScript page based on the browser capability

- Executing scripts only in JavaScript-enabled browsers

I believe you can adapt one of these methods to fit most script versus nonscript situations — including those that might otherwise seem hopeless. Solutions range from the very simple to ones that take a fair amount of forethought and careful execution. In all cases, think of JavaScript as a page enhancement tool: When the browser is JavaScript enabled, the page does something more than when the page is viewed in a non-JavaScript browser.

A Branching Index Page

In keeping with my belief that scripting should work silently in the background, without great fanfare, I avoid deploying `index.html` pages that rely on the site visitor's knowing about his or her browser. Though Web page authors are extremely sensitive to browser brands and levels, the increasingly large audience of non-nerds surfing the World Wide Web has little, if any, emotional attachment to the browser being used at any moment. To provide an `index.html` page with two or more links labeled for specific browsers won't help someone who doesn't know exactly what's inside his or her WebTV box.

NOTE

The height of geek bravado must be a site I visited recently (URL withheld so as not to embarrass the page's author) that provided a link labeled for users who had browsers that were HTML 3.2-compatible and a link for those whose browsers weren't up to that level.

But you can craft the `index.html` page to branch to many different tracks through your site. The tactic is based on your first displaying a nearly contentless `index.html` page that isn't the true home or welcoming page to your site. Instead, it displays a lone image of any size (perhaps a logo) in the same page location as that image appears in the true home page for each of your browser-dependent tracks.

Here's a typical `index.html` page that provides branches to two tracks in a site: a scripted track that starts at `home1.html` and an unscripted track that starts at `home2.html`. Here's what it looks like:

```
<HTML>
<HEAD>
  <TITLE>GiantCo OnLine</TITLE>
  <SCRIPT LANGUAGE="JavaScript">
  <!--
      window.location = "home1.html"
  //-->
  </SCRIPT>
  <META HTTP-EQUIV="REFRESH" CONTENT="0;
URL=http://www.giantco.com/home2.html">
</HEAD>

<BODY>
<CENTER>
   <A HREF=home2.html><IMG SRC=images/giantcoLogo.gif
HEIGHT=60 WIDTH=120 BORDER=0 ALT="GiantCo Home Page"></A>
</CENTER>
</BODY>
</HTML>
```

Here is how three different levels of browsers react to this `index.html` page:

■ A JavaScript-enabled browser executes the script in the <HEAD> section and automatically navigates to home1.html, the JavaScript-enabled home page. If the image loads into index.html (via a fast network connection), then the image becomes precached for use in home1.html. If the image doesn't load, then the window stays blank for a fraction of a second, and the browser passes by the index page without the site visitor noticing it.

■ A modern but non-JavaScript browser follows the <META> tag, whose attributes instruct the browser to navigate to (REFRESH) the unscripted home page (home2.html) after no delay. Again, if the image loads, it's precached for use in home2.html. (Note: If you haven't used the <META> tag for refreshing before, closely follow the sample code for attribute and quote placement.)

■ A text-only or old graphical browser remains at this index.html page. In a text-only browser, the ALT description of the image appears as a link to be "clicked," leading one to the unscripted home2.html page. A graphical browser shows the image alone. Although there is no link border around the graphic, I believe a user will try to click on the image to see if anything happens, especially when the link appears in that browser's equivalent of Navigator's status bar during a mouse roll-over.

Let me add the following four points about the example:

■ Notice that the tag contains no color attributes. Even if the home pages have background colors or patterns set, it is best to leave the index.html page plain. Otherwise, the screen will flash from color to plain to color in the switch from index.html to the home page.

■ I chose not to display a link border around the image so that the border doesn't appear and then disappear for those with JavaScript-enabled or modern browsers.

■ If you want to make sure that the JavaScript-enabled browser is compliant with, say, JavaScript 1.2 only, then change the <SCRIPT> tag's LANGUAGE attribute to "JavaScript 1.2". In that case, all browsers running earlier versions of JavaScript will respond to the <META> tag instead.

■ You can use the script in the <HEAD> portion to perform any kind of browser validation checks you like before setting the location object. For example, if your super-duper scripted home page requires a plug-in, you can check for it there. Or if you have further subdivisions of your home page tracks based on browser operating system platform, you can check the value of appVersion for that information.

Taking Advantage of Multifunction Links

You can always interlace a script within a page's HTML to `document.write()` a link (or any other feature for that matter) that you want only JavaScript-enabled browsers to see. But if you want a single link to be able to branch to one of two possible destinations based on the scripting ability of the browser, you can use JavaScript to help out.

For this technique, create the link to the non-JavaScript destination as follows (as you normally would):

```
<A HREF="nonJSCatalog.html">Product Catalog</A>
```

To force this link to navigate to a JavaScript-enabled page, you need to add a special enhancement to the `onClick` event handler for this link: `return false`. Just as a form's `onSubmit` event handler cancels the submission of the form if its final statement evaluates to return false, so, too, does a link ignore the `HREF` attribute if the `onClick` event handler ends that way. Therefore, to add the JavaScript destination to the link, use the following code:

```
<A HREF="nonJSCatalog.html"
onClick="location.href='JSCatalog.html';return
false">Product Catalog</A>
```

Without the `return false` statement, the visitor will end up at the `HREF` attribute's location. You can still add `onMouseOver` and `onMouseOut` event handlers to the link to show friendly status-bar descriptions of the link for JavaScript-enabled browsers.

Script Execution

Because only a JavaScript-enabled browser can respond to object event handlers, you can be sure that plain button clicking, select object choosing, and any other user action will be ignored by a non-JavaScript browser. But what about the cases in which you have, say, JavaScript 1.1 features that will cause script errors in

JavaScript 1.0-only browsers, such as Navigator 2.0x and Microsoft Internet Explorer 3.0?

If you want an event handler to operate differently for JavaScript 1.0 and 1.1, you can create two separate <SCRIPT> segments in your document with identically named functions that are called by the event handler. One <SCRIPT> tag specifies LANGUAGE="JavaScript", whereas the other specifies LANGUAGE="JavaScript1.1". The key here, however, is to make sure that the JavaScript 1.1 tag set is lower in the document than its corresponding JavaScript 1.0 version, as shown in the following example:

```
<HTML>
<HEAD>
   <SCRIPT LANGUAGE="JavaScript">
   <!--
      function doIt() {
        // statements for JavaScript 1.0 browsers
      }
   //-->
   </SCRIPT>
   <SCRIPT LANGUAGE="JavaScript1.1">
   <!--
      function doIt() {
        // statements for JavaScript 1.1 browsers
      }
   //-->
   </SCRIPT>
</HEAD>
<BODY>
<FORM>
   <INPUT TYPE=button VALUE="Click Me" onClick="doIt()">
</FORM>
</BODY>
</HTML>
```

Similarly, you can mask JavaScript 1.0–level browsers in the LANGUAGE="JavaScript" segment by leaving the statements in the function blank or by displaying an alert for the user about what extra functionality a JavaScript 1.1–level browser brings to the user experience.

Another possibility is to use the JavaScript 1.1 feature that lets you set the event handler property of an object from a script. If you restrict the action of setting the event handler to a JavaScript 1.1 script, then only JavaScript 1.1 browsers will respond to user action, as shown in this example:

```
<HTML>
<HEAD>
    <SCRIPT LANGUAGE="JavaScript1.1">
    <!--
        function doIt() {
            // statements for JavaScript 1.1 browsers


        }
    //-->
    </SCRIPT>
</HEAD>
<BODY>
<FORM>
    <INPUT TYPE=button NAME=joeButton VALUE="Click Me">
    <SCRIPT LANGUAGE="JavaScript1.1">
    <!--
        document.forms[0].joeButton.onclick=doIt
    //-->
    </SCRIPT>
</FORM>
</BODY>
</HTML>
```

In this example, the button object does not have an explicit event handler in its tag. Instead, the reference to the doIt() function defined earlier in the document is assigned to the onclick property of the button. (The property name for an event handler is always in lowercase.) The <SCRIPT> tag for this assignment must come after the <INPUT> tag that creates the button to make sure the button object exists before its event handler property can be set. In the document defined in this example, only JavaScript 1.1–level browsers respond to user action in any way.

Object Checking

One final way to ensure that a particular operation will succeed only in browsers capable of that operation is to use object detection. The best example of this is the well-known Dynamic HTML rollover technique called a *rollover*. Many designers and scripters employ an onMouseOver and onMouseOut event handler for an image link to swap the art file associated with the Image object during a mouse rollover. But the Image object is found only in browsers that treat an image as an object in its document object model (Navigator 3 or later; Internet Explorer 3.01 for Macintosh; Internet Explorer 4 or later for Windows). Any attempt at setting the src property of an Image object in older browsers yields an unfriendly script error.

To head off this problem without having to write a complex browser version detection script, you can instead wrap the image swapping code inside an if construction that checks for the presence of the Image object in the browser's object model:

```
function swapImag() {
    if (document.images) {
        // image swapping statements here
    }
}
```

If a browser can work with image objects, the expression document.images returns a value (an array of images in the page, even if it is an empty array because there are no images); otherwise, the expression evaluates to a value that the if condition regards as being false. Use this technique also to surround any image pre-caching script statements you include in your page.

Additive JavaScript

If you examine the implementations suggested throughout this chapter, you might see that I tend to treat JavaScript as an additive feature of a page wherever possible rather than rushing ahead to make two completely separate tracks through a site.

Creating multiple tracks within a Web site makes the maintenance chore all the more difficult.

Perhaps the ideal situation is a page that functions well on its own without JavaScript. By interlacing some <SCRIPT> tags within the basic HTML of the page and some of the event handler techniques described here, you can script added functionality into the page rather than having to generate an entirely separate track. Visitors who have the latest browsers have a more interactive and enjoyable experience at your site, and people with older browsers will be none the wiser.

This technique won't work all the time, of course. Some of the areas of my Web site, for example, simply require JavaScript or the user will see next to nothing on the page. (You can find it at http://www.dannyg.com.) But it means that I can keep the need for parallel pages at a minimum, simplifying the maintenance task.

That Elusive Script

Although there is no magic property, method, or script that detects JavaScript in a browser, you can indeed use JavaScript to enhance the plain HTML page or navigate to fully scripted pages — and still accommodate nonscriptable browsers. It may take a little extra thought and planning, but the results will invite a wide audience to your site without your having to dumb down your pages to the lowest common denominator.

17

Advanced JavaScript Debugging Techniques

Danny Goodman — *consultant and writer*

N etscape's JavaScript Debugger component for Netscape Communicator has been one of the most welcome hunks o' code to reach my desktop in a long while. In his *View Source* article on the JavaScript Debugger, Angus Davis presents a good overview of how to use the debugger in your client-side development. (The article can be found on the CD-ROM that accompanies this book.) Still, there are many occasions when I fall back on some of my older debugging techniques to give me a different perspective on what's happening inside my code.

ON THE CD-ROM

You can find Angus Davis's *View Source* article about how to use it on the CD-ROM that accompanies this book. Follow the path, Sample Code and Supporting Documentation ⇨ Part II ⇨ Chapter 17.

In this chapter, I provide you with a simple but powerful external `.js` library file that preserves a trace of designated values while a script runs. You specify which values are to be monitored and where in the code this happens. As an added bonus, this library file also measures time intervals between tracking statements — all the better to help you identify where performance bottlenecks are slowing down your program. If you're trying to debug code while running in Navigator 3, you can use this debugging method in lieu of the Communicator-level debugger. Some of the techniques here can also apply to server-side JavaScript.

Patrolling for Bugs

I've long held that 90 percent of the bugs in JavaScript code are related to unexpected expression evaluation and faulty object references. At times you think that an expression has one type of data in it, when, in truth, something entirely different is there (a benefit and penalty of using a loosely typed language); object references can also go awry if you accidentally duplicate object names or overlook the nesting of objects in their containers (for example, a text box inside a form inside a document).

Single-stepping through running code is an extremely valuable debugging aid when you know where the problem is. But often your application has grown so large that you may be able to debug it more efficiently by seeing a trace of execution with intermediate values along the way. For example, you'd like answers to these kinds of questions:

- How many times is that loop executing?

- What are the values being retrieved each time through the loop?

- Why won't the `while` loop exit?

- Are comparison operators behaving as I'd planned in `if-else` constructions?

- What kind of value is a function returning?

With thoughtfully placed calls to my external library's debug() method (see the code listing that follows), the report you get after running your script can answer questions like these and many more.

The debug.js Library File

The following example is the listing for the debug.js library file. It consists of one global variable and one function.

```
var timestamp = 0
function debug(flag, label, value) {
    if (flag) {
        var funcName = debug.caller.toString()
        funcName = funcName.substring(10,
funcName.indexOf(")") + 1)
        var msg = "In " + funcName + ": " + label + "=" +
value
        var now = new Date()
        var elapsed = now - timestamp
        if (elapsed < 10000) {
            msg += " (" + elapsed + " msec)"
        }
        timestamp = now
        java.lang.System.out.println(msg)
    }
}
```

When this file loads into a document, the timestamp variable becomes a global variable in the document. This variable is used to store the last time the debug() function is called. The value must persist so that subsequent calls to debug() permit calculations of the time differences between the previous and current invocations.

The debug() function takes three parameters. The first, flag, is a Boolean value. Later in this chapter, I discuss how flag comes into play with the calls to this function. The second parameter is a string that identifies, in plain language, the value being traced. And the value itself is passed as the third parameter.

Virtually any type of value or expression can be passed as the third parameter — which is precisely what you want in a debugging aid.

The bulk of the debug() function executes only if the flag parameter is true. The first task is to extract the name of the function from which debug() was called. By retrieving the rarely used-caller property, debug() grabs a string copy of the entire calling function. A quick extraction of a substring from the first line yields the name of the function. The second task is to start building the message text that records this particular trace. The message identifies the calling function followed by a colon; after that comes the label text passed as the second parameter, plus an equals sign and the value parameter. Here is the format of the output message:

```
In funcName: label=value
```

By itself, the message contains a fair amount of information. But I take it one step further by calculating the current time from the system clock. By subtracting the value of the timestamp variable from the current time, I get an elapsed time. If that elapsed time is less than ten seconds, I append the elapsed time (in milliseconds) in parentheses to the message. Then I update the timestamp global variable.

The final statement is a LiveConnect call to a native Java class method. Experienced Java programmers will recognize the System.out.println() method as the one that writes a value to the Java Console window. If you haven't done any Java programming, you may not even know that Navigator 3.x has a Java Console window available in the Options menu. (In Communicator 4 and later, you can find it in the Communicator menu under Tools.) Java applet errors are automatically written to this window, even if the window is hidden. Similarly, you can use the LiveConnect direct call to a built-in Java method, java.lang.System.out.println(), to write anything you like to the window. Anything written to that window is appended to the end of whatever text is already inside. Therefore, you can write as many debug messages as you like to that window, and they'll all be there for you to see after the script runs.

Loading Debug()

To include this debugging library in your document, add the following <SCRIPT> tag set at the beginning of the document's head section:

```
<SCRIPT LANGUAGE="JavaScript" SRC="debug.js"></SCRIPT>
```

The syntax assumes that you have saved `debug.js` in the same directory as your HTML document. Also, if you're running the page from a server (instead of a local hard disk), the server must be configured to transmit files with the `.js` extension as the MIME type "application/x-javascript". Netscape servers are set up to do this by default. If you run the page from a local hard disk, no other preparation or configuration is needed.

Setting up Your Document for Debug()

As you build your document and its scripts, you need to decide how granular you'd like debugging to be: global or function by function. This decision affects the level at which you place the Boolean "switch" that turns debugging on and off.

You can place one such switch as the first statement in the first script of the page. For example, specify a clearly named variable and assign either `false` or `0` to it so that its initial setting is "off":

```
var DEBUG = 0
```

To turn debugging on at a later time, simply change the value assigned to `DEBUG` from 0 to 1:

```
var DEBUG = 1
```

Be sure to reload the page each time you edit this global value. Also, though you can use any variable name you like, avoid the reserved keyword `debugger` (all lowercase). I chose all-uppercase `DEBUG` to help me locate and delete relevant statements once the page is ready to deploy.

Alternatively, you can define a local `DEBUG` variable in each function for which you intend to employ debugging. One advantage of using function-specific debugging is that the list of items to appear in the Java Console window will be limited to those of immediate interest to you rather than all debugging calls throughout the document. You can turn each function's debugging facility on and off by editing the values assigned to the local `DEBUG` variables.

Calling Debug()

All that's left now is to insert the one-line calls to debug() according to the following syntax:

```
debug(DEBUG,"label",value)
```

By passing the current value of DEBUG as a parameter, you let the library function handle the decision to accumulate and print the trace. The impact on your running code is kept to a one-line statement that is easy to remember. To demonstrate, the next example consists of a pair of related functions that convert a time in milliseconds to the string format "hh:mm". To help me verify that values are being massaged correctly, I insert a few calls to debug().

```
function timeToString(input) {
    var DEBUG = 1
    debug(DEBUG,"input",input)
    var rawTime = new Date(eval(input))
    debug(DEBUG,"rawTime",rawTime)
    var hrs = twoDigitString(rawTime.getHours())
    var mins = twoDigitString(rawTime.getMinutes())
    debug(DEBUG,"result", hrs + ":" + mins)
    return hrs + ":" + mins
}

function twoDigitString(val) {
    var DEBUG = 1
    debug(DEBUG,"val",val)
    return (val < 10) ? "0" + val : "" + val
}
```

After running the script, I display the Java Console window in Navigator to see the following trace:

```
In timeToString(input): input=869854500000
In timeToString(input): rawTime=Fri Jul 25 11:15:00 Pacific
Daylight Time 1997 (60 msec)
In twoDigitString(val): val=11 (0 msec)
```

```
In twoDigitString(val): val=15 (0 msec)
In timeToString(input): result=11:15 (220 msec)
```

NOTE

To find the Java Console, look under the Options menu in Navigator 3.x and earlier; in Communicator 4 and later, you can find it in Communicator menu. Later versions of Communicator 4.x include the Java Console in the Tools item in the Communicator menu.

Having the name of the function in the trace is helpful in cases in which you might justifiably reuse variable names (for example, i loop counters). The function names also help you see more clearly when one function in your script calls another.

About the Timer

In the trace results of this example, you might wonder how some statements appear to execute literally "in no time." You have to take the timing values of this debug scheme with a grain of salt. For one thing, these are not intended to be critical benchmarks. Some of the processing in the debug() function itself occupies CPU cycles. And with rapid-fire execution in the small scripts of the example, the timings are not very meaningful. But in a more complex script — especially one involving numerous calls to subroutines and nested loops — you can place the debug() function calls in statements that aren't deeply nested so that the intervals won't be too small to be of value. In any case, regard the values as relative, rather than absolute, values. And always run the script several times to help you see a pattern of performance.

Viewing in Real Time

I faced another debugging challenge recently while using a computer with a small monitor that prevented me from viewing both the Java Console and browser window at the same time. I wasn't convinced that a nested for loop construction

was iterating enough times through a pair of related lengthy arrays. To help me vi-
sualize how the loops were working as they ran, I modified the debug() function
to write the results not to the Java Console, but to the status bar at the bottom of
the browser window.

To do this, I replaced the line in debug() that calls the
System.out.println() function with a statement that sets the window.sta-
tus property:

```
window.status = msg
```

For this monitoring, the timing wasn't crucial, so I commented out the lines in
debug() that added the elapsed time to the message. I placed the call to debug()
in the innermost loop, showing both of the loop-counting variables:

```
debug(DEBUG,"i,j", i + "," + j)
```

When I ran the script, the status bar whizzed through the values of the for loop
counters i and j:

```
i,j=0,0
i,j=0,1
i,j=0,2
...
i,j=1,0
i,j=1,1
(etc.)
```

In the status bar, I could examine the rhythm of updating the values to see
where some parts of the loop were slower than others based on the array data being manipulated. (Notice, incidentally, how the debug() function evaluated the
third parameter to let me join multiple values in a single debugging message.) And
when the script stopped, the status bar showed the final values, so I could see how
far the loops got.

Server-Side Application

After seeing how helpful this debugging system was on the client side, I looked to see if it could be useful on the server side. Although the Netscape Enterprise Server application manager provides a convenient trace function that's very good at detecting and revealing syntax errors, it does not provide a way to view intermediate values of expressions in your scripts. But you can modify the debug.js file to operate as a server-side library file (compiled into the application).

CROSS-REFERENCE

Please see Part III of this book, "Server Development, 1: Scripting for Workgroups," for detailed information about using server-side JavaScript for application development.

Instead of writing trace results to the Java Console, use the server-side write() method to output the accumulated trace message to the current document. You can use the same DEBUG flags either globally or within each function (I recommend the latter in a complex server application). Of course, the finely crafted display of the HTML output for the screen will be littered with your debug messages whenever you have the DEBUG switches turned on. But that's OK because you should clear up all bugs and turn off (or remove) the DEBUG flags before deploying the application.

Stomp 'em Your Way

By standardizing a way of generating debugging reports, you can greatly simplify the task of debugging your code. For every HTML document you have under construction, include debug.js as a library file. As you write each new function definition, automatically include a debugging switch (var DEBUG = 0) as the first statement. Then, when you're ready to capture values in trial runs of your script, insert the three-parameter calls to debug() wherever they'll reveal intermediate and resulting values to show you what's going on inside your script while you blink. Over time, you may also wish to modify the way the output is formatted or the kinds of parameters you send to the debug() function. Be aggressive, and don't let creepy crawly critters get in your way.

18

Client Side Persistence without Cookies

Danny Goodman — *consultant and writer*

I don't know if this happens to you, but my blood pressure jumps a few points every time I read an article in the mainstream press about browser cookies being used for all kinds of dastardly tracking of web surfer habits (the same kind of tracking that server logs have been doing forever). Although I'm not aware of existing sites that hack their way into cookie data they shouldn't be seeing, the tone of all those news reports makes it seem as though you'd better turn off the cookie feature in your browser before some nerdy stalker finds out you have holes in your underwear as you sit in front of your computer.

This all-too-common user disconnection of cookies makes life more difficult for those of us who employ cookies as a kind of super-global variable that persists across all navigation around our sites. Pages can come and go, browser windows can be resized, and the user can click the Reload button all he or she wants without destroying a valuable variable needed by a script somewhere. What you need, then, is a way to maintain some data during a surfing session without resorting to cookies.

There are two techniques in common use today. One is to encode the global data as the search segment (following a ? symbol) in the current URL of the document. I've experienced inconsistent behavior with this approach in some non-Netscape browsers. The appended values also appear in the Location bar of the browser window, exposing them to user manipulation — intentional or accidental. The other technique, detailed in this chapter, uses what amounts to one or more text input elements positioned out of sight. By way of example, I'll provide a first pass at a simple shopping cart that works on a wide range of scriptable browsers.

Why You Need Persistence

If you've done much application building with client-side JavaScript, you know that the most global scope of a variable is the document in which it is defined. A global variable disappears from a window or frame when the document unloads. Therefore, if your goal is to pass a value from the script of one document to a script in the next document that loads into the same window or frame, you need some other place to store that value temporarily. A cookie is certainly convenient. Even though a cookie is accessed as a property of a document object, all cookie values generated by documents from the same domain and server are available to all documents served from that same server. Turn off cookies, however, and that route is no longer available.

Appending persistent data to the URL of the next document (assuming the next document is accessed from a link within your own document collection) can work. Some scripters assign the value as a search suffix (with the ? symbol divider) or a hash suffix (with the # symbol divider). At the destination, a script can extract the `location.search` or `location.hash` property to grab the data. But I've seen applications of this scheme that get confused when the user is left to his or her own devices for navigating around the site. Sometimes even an inopportune click of the Back button can cause the appended data to be garbled or lost. And, because I'm a geek, if I see such extra data in the Location bar, I get distracted as I try to figure out what the appended data is doing or what information is being carried around.

I'd rather hide that extra data from the user, and let it work like magic. Unfortunately, some convenient ways of hiding data, such as the hidden input element or global variables stored in other frames, are not persistent enough. Resizing the window, clicking the Reload button, or clicking the Reset form button can destroy data that's plugged into a hidden element after it loads. And global variable values can also disappear upon reload and (in some browser versions) upon resize. But the next best and most persistent HTML element available is the text input element or its compatriot, the textarea element. Except in Internet Explorer 3, a document reload does not alter the contents of a text input element. And if you can place that element in a form by itself, there will be no Reset form element to wipe out its content.

The trick with the text-input element is hiding it from the user without resorting to version 4-specific Dynamic HTML element positioning. More to the point, you want the document holding the field to remain in the browser window during the user's visit. The way I go about this is to create a (nearly) hidden frame for the persistent document as part of a frameset. I'll come back to the frameset issue later.

Establishing a Data Structure

Perhaps the most challenging part of implementing persistent data for a text field is designing a data structure for your data. If the data is a single value, it really isn't a problem: Simply plant the data into the text field and retrieve or modify it as needed during site navigation. But for a more complex application, such as a shopping cart, you have the responsibility of determining how the data must be formatted. For example, if the data you want to preserve is from a form, you must generate a string version of what might otherwise be considered a database record. It's up to you to establish a delimiter structure. If your data may include a variable number of such records, you must write even more elaborate scripts to replicate the management of this "database" data.

One tactic is to mimic the way JavaScript exposes cookie data. Each cookie consists of a string of name/value pairs. All scriptable Navigator versions can store up to 20 name/value pairs in a cookie associated with a server. The name and value portions of the script representation of a cookie are separated by an equals sign (=); multiple name/value pairs are delimited by semicolons:

```
name1=value1;name2=value2;name3=value3
```

Unfortunately, since you aren't truly using the `document.cookie` object for text field data, you don't have the benefit of the browser's cookie management facilities for updating the value of a particular name/value pair. It will be up to your scripts to manage the name/value pairs.

Despite the convenience of JavaScript arrays for storing the equivalent of fields and records, they don't help you with the persistence issue. Whether you intend to use cookies or the text input element tactic, all persistent data must be in string form. You cannot store JavaScript arrays in cookies or text fields without first converting them to strings. Though newer versions of JavaScript simplify these conversions (with the `stringObj.split()` and `arrayObj.join()` methods), if you want your persistent data structures to work with older scriptable browser versions, you'll have to roll your own conversion routines.

As demonstrated in the shopping cart example later, I chose to build a variable-length string that acts as a database file. Each record has four fields: product name, stock number, price, and quantity. Fields are colon-delimited; records are semi-colon-delimited. As a user shops through the catalog, new entries are appended to the "database." When it's time to review the shopping cart contents, scripts extract the records and fields. The pieces are distributed into elements of a dynamically generated form. With the form in view, users can make changes to the quantity of an item. For each change to the form, a script reconstructs the database data from the visible and hidden form element values. If the user sets the quantity of an item to 0, the item is not rebuilt into the "database."

A variant of this scenario is to use many text fields rather than just one. In other words, the hidden frame document essentially contains an array of text input elements that mimics the item entries of the shopping cart or order form. You can get away with this provided you create enough of these fields to accommodate the most ambitious customer of your site. Or if you have a limited selection of products, you can maintain the array of fields such that there is one row of fields for each of the products in your online catalog. There is no one best way to structure your data for persistence; the type and amount of data drive the design decisions.

Designing the Frameset

You can create a hidden frame within a frameset if you put the hidden frame at the end of a frameset row or column, provided you use percentage measures for the ROWS or COLS attributes, and define the hidden frame size with an asterisk

(<FRAMESET ROWS="100%,*">). For the example in this chapter, however, I specify the "hidden" frame to be at the top and slightly visible so that you can expand the view during construction and watch the values in the text fields within that hidden frame. Here's the frameset definition for the sample online catalog:

```
<HTML>
<HEAD>
<TITLE>Welcome to Widget World</TITLE>
</HEAD>
<FRAMESET ROWS="0,100%" BORDER=0 FRAMEBORDER="no">
  <FRAME NAME="cartFrame" SRC="cart.html" NORESIZE
SCROLLING="no">
  <FRAMESET COLS="20%,80%">
    <FRAME NAME="toc" SRC="toc.html">
    <FRAME NAME="display" SRC="widget1.html">
  </FRAMESET>
</FRAMESET>
</HTML>
```

For the demonstration, I've chosen a fairly traditional navigation frameset. A left-hand column that acts as a table of contents occupies 20 percent of the window width, whereas the content display area occupies the other 80 percent. I've placed the "hidden" frame in its own row above the frames that users will be working with.

If you don't want to use multiple frames for the visible portion of the page, you can simply create a two-row frameset. Even a frame-averse visitor won't be the wiser.

Inside the Shopping Cart

Rather than go through a tedious line-by-line explication of the code involved in the sample shopping cart, I'll provide an overview of the architecture and basic operation. You can find a complete set of files on this book's accompanying CD-ROM; feel free to explore the well-commented code at your leisure. (To do so, use the Page Source item in the Communicator View menu bar.) It will be helpful to open the catalog and navigate through it while reading about its structure. For a glimpse of what it looks like, see Figure 18-1.

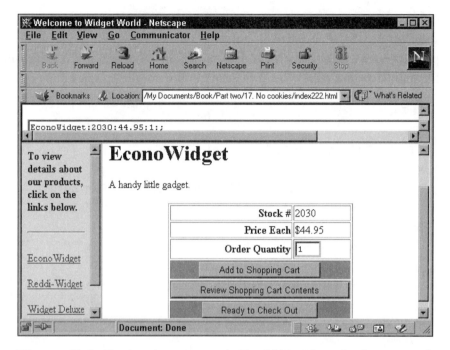

Figure 18-1: The shopping cart example. The "hidden" frame has been exposed slightly to show the text field containing data generated by using the shopping cart.

ON THE CD-ROM

A working version of the shopping cart example can be found on the CD-ROM that accompanies this book. You're encouraged to open the shopping cart example (called Chapter 18 Shopping Cart Example) in your browser and follow along with the text in this chapter. We've included a version of the shopping cart with the "hidden" frame slightly exposed to make it easier for you to play with it. Also, be sure to view the well-commented source code for the example, especially the code for the file `cart.html`. To find the files, follow the path: Sample Code and Supporting Documentation ⇨ Part II ⇨ Chapter 18.

The frameset shown in the previous code listing is contained by the `index.html` page. This is where users start to view the catalog. In a real environment, there would probably be a more "warm and fuzzy" opening page welcoming the visitor to the site and explaining the online shopping that's available.

Almost all the scripting is contained by the cart.html file, which loads into the "hidden" frame. Buttons that appear in the other frames frequently reference functions in this top row frame. Again, this frame also contains the text input field that stores the data while the user navigates freely through the catalog.

The left visible frame holds a document named `toc.html`. For the demonstration, it's nothing more than a simple navigation aid to reach any of the three products featured in this abbreviated catalog of widgets.

Each of the three widget models in the demo product catalog has its own HTML page. You also get a demonstration of a technique that works for small online catalogs whose audience is likely to be using more modern browsers. Information about the products is stored as objects in the `products.js` file that's linked into each of the product pages. Bill Dortch of hIdaho Design (`http://www.hidaho.com`) is a pro at this kind of catalog and has implemented very sophisticated online catalogs that are easy to maintain. Of course, the browser must be modern enough to be able to link in external JavaScript (`.js`) files. On the other hand, if you're trying to appeal to the widest audience, your product pages will either be dedicated HTML pages or be served up from a database on the server via a CGI program.

Controlling the Shopping Cart

On each product page there is not only information about the widget model, but also three buttons. One button adds the item to the shopping cart. The user can enter the quantity on the product page and adjust it later. A second button takes the user to a page that displays the contents of the shopping cart. And the third button goes to the checkout page, which shows the cart contents and provides fields for entry of name, address, and other order information.

Adding an entry to the shopping cart simply appends a formatted record to the hidden text field. In other words, the button's event handler passes product information to a function in `cart.html` that adds the record to the "database" text field:

```
function addToCart(title, stock, price, qty) {
  var output = title + ":" + stock + ":" + price + ":" + qty
+ ":;"
  document.cart.cartData.value += output
}
```

I've chosen to create a data structure that uses colons to delimit fields within the semicolon-delimited record. This demonstration (along with most client-side shopping carts I've seen) does no validation with regard to existing entries of the same item. It wouldn't be all that difficult to add that level of validation, and in a production environment I would do so.

When the user asks to review the shopping cart contents, a script in the hidden frame document converts the string in the text field to an array for scripting convenience. The array is passed to the function that assembles the table (makeTable()). This function breaks up each "database record" into another array of database fields (via the itemSplit() function). The script uses the data from the database field array to assemble the table. Here's the main function that creates the table:

```
function makeTable(cartArray) {
    var item, extension
    var runningTotal = 0
    var table = "<TABLE BORDER=1>\n"

    table += "<TR><TH>Quantity<TH>Stock No.<TH>Item
Name<TH>Price<TH>Total</TR>\n"

    // Loop through array to generate one table row per
array entry.
    for (var i = 0; i < cartArray.length; i++) {
        // Extract one record at a time and convert it to an
array.
        item = itemSplit(cartArray[i])

        // The quantity field, including an event handler to
recalculate the table
        table += "<TR><TD><INPUT TYPE='text' NAME='qty" + i +
"' SIZE=4 VALUE='"
            + item[3] + "'"
        table +=
"onChange='parent.cartFrame.recalc(this.value," + item[2] +
","
            + i + ")'>"
```

```
        // Copy three parts of the record to hidden fields
for data integrity.
        table += "<INPUT TYPE='hidden' NAME='stock" + i + "'
VALUE='" + item[1]
            + "'></TD>"
        table += "<INPUT TYPE='hidden' NAME='title" + i + "'
VALUE='" + item[0]
            + "'></TD>"
        table += "<INPUT TYPE='hidden' NAME='price" + i + "'
VALUE='" + item[2]
            + "'></TD>"

        // Hard-wire the product stock num, title, and price.
        table += "<TD>" + item[1] + "<TD>" + item[0] +
"<TD>$" + item[2]

        // Calculate the extension for the item and format it
for dollars and cents.
        extension = format((item[3] * item[2]),2)

        // Accumulate running total.
        runningTotal += parseFloat(extension)

        // Put extension into a field; the onFocus event
handler inhibits user
        // modification.
        table += "<TD>$<INPUT TYPE='text' NAME='extend" + i +
"' SIZE=8 VALUE='"
            + extension + "'"
        table += "onFocus='this.blur()'></TR>\n"
    }
    // Keep a hidden number of rows.
    table += "<TR><TD COLSPAN=3> <INPUT TYPE='hidden'
NAME='itemCount'
        VALUE='" + i + "'><TD>Order Total:<TD>$"
```

```
          // Display grand total in a text field.
          table += "<INPUT TYPE='text' NAME='grandTotal' SIZE=10
             VALUE='" + format(runningTotal, 2) + "'
      onFocus='this.blur()'></TR>"
          table += "</TABLE>"
          return table
      }
```

All product information is displayed in a table, with interactive text fields for the item quantities, price extensions, and grand total. The table is "live" in that any change to a quantity automatically recalculates the extension and grand total. It also reconstitutes the entire database by recombining all the data components previously written to hidden input elements in the table. This assures that the persistent data is always up to date and always reflects what the user sees in the table. If the user clicks in the navigation frame or on the Back button to get to a product page, the shopping cart data is intact.

NOTE

As you'll you'll surely notice in the code, the table consists of form elements whose names contain index values to indicate which row the element is in (for example, `quantity0`, `quantity1`, and so on). In the `for` loop that iterates through the rows of elements, the code uses the `eval()` function to create object references from string equivalents. If it weren't for an oversight in Internet Explorer 3, it would be more convenient to simply treat multiple instances of the like-named group of elements as an array (for example, `quantity[0]`, `quantity[1]`, and so on). All scriptable versions of Navigator and IE 4 turn like-named elements into an array of that name; IE 3 does not. To accommodate that browser, I use the longer way around. In practice, the explicit naming might also help the server deal with incoming data when the order form is submitted.

Included on the shopping cart review page is a button labeled Refresh. This button simply reruns the routines that assemble the review page, deriving data from the shopping cart text field again. If the user entered 0 for the quantity of an item earlier, that item is no longer in the cart and does not appear in the refreshed cart review table.

At checkout time, the same string-parsing routine builds the table to display the contents. In the demonstration, another table of fields provides entry space for name and address info. In a real order form, other controls would provide places to indicate payment method, shipping costs, sales tax, and the like. For the convenience of a CGI program processing the order, the table includes all product info, most of which is in hidden input elements. So that you can see how the form elements are organized and the type of data stored in each element, I've created a special demo version that lets you e-mail the form's contents to yourself. If you're using Navigator, the form data (as name/value pairs) is embedded in an e-mail message body.

As long as the page remains in the browser cache during the current browser session, Navigator will restore the shopping cart data even if the user navigates to other Web sites and unloads the online catalog frameset. Thus, just as with a cookie, the user can go elsewhere and then return to the site and continue shopping.

Other Applications

I used a shopping cart example in this chapter because e-commerce is all the rage. But the same techniques can be used in other applications that require persistent data across pages within a Web site. At my site (`http://www.dannyg.com`), you can look at an extensive client-side application, called Decision Helper, which is implemented in two ways: with and without cookies. The user can scarcely tell the difference, if at all.

Without the cookie feature turned on in the visitor's browser, there is no way to silently (without signed script permission dialogs, for example) save information between browser sessions. A cookie bearing an expiration date in the future will stick around on the user's hard disk until the next session following that date. Users who have irrational fears of cookie crimes may be missing convenience features at their favorite sites (such as flags that indicate what's new since their last visit). It's their loss. At least your Web site can pass variables between pages even if visitors have cookies turned off.

19

Form-Data Handling in Client-Side JavaScript

Duane K. Fields — *internet systems engineer, Tivoli Systems*

It's typical for Web developers to use server-side applications to handle form data; server-side JavaScript provides a more convenient, cross-platform alternative to traditional CGI applications. For more about that, be sure to see Chapter 25, "Form-Data Handling in Server-Side JavaScript" in Part III of this book. In this chapter, I explore a new technique for working with form data through JavaScript that operates entirely on the client.

The HTML form provides one of the most critical features of Web-based applications, enabling the user to input information into the application. Traditionally, forms have been handled on the server, first by CGI applications in Perl or C, and increasingly through more efficient technologies such as server-side JavaScript (SSJS). In some cases, however, it's possible to avoid the server altogether by processing the form data entirely on the client. Doing so dramatically reduces the complexity of deployment and configuration issues surrounding your application and enables you to implement interactive applications in environments that were previously inaccessible, such as when hosting through an ISP that doesn't provide sufficient access to develop server-side solutions.

I'll begin by discussing how handling form data on the client works, and why you might want to do this. I introduce a client-side JavaScript (CSJS) routine that you can use to emulate SSJS's request object, enabling you to handle form data on the client as easily as you could on the server or through a Perl CGI. To show the benefit of this technique, I present a fairly complex sample application at the end of the chapter.

Taking the Client-Side Approach

In the client-side approach, you specify your form's action handler to be another HTML document instead of passing the data to a server-side script or application. As long as the HTML that contains the form definition is using the GET method, it doesn't require any changes or differences in design in order to work properly in a client-side implementation. Because of this, existing forms can easily be retrofitted to a client-side architecture, or you can use identical forms (with different actions) to perform the same duties in both server-side and client-side situations.

For example, you might see a form definition like this for a CGI:

```
<FORM ACTION="formhandler.cgi" METHOD=GET>
```

And like this for a CSJS handler:

```
<FORM ACTION="formhandler.html" METHOD=GET>
```

Since you're using the GET method of delivering data, the values from the form are then encoded as a string of value pairs appended to the action handler URL. The real work in implementing the client-side approach is in the HTML document that's the receiver of the form's action. You must extract the form data from the end of the URL and then perform whatever actions are needed on the data. Later, I'll show you a reusable JavaScript routine that makes accessing URL data a breeze.

Why Stay on the Client?

Why would you want to use the client-side approach to handling form data? In some situations, you may have no choice. For many users, ISP access restriction may prohibit development of server-side applications. In addition, a client-side approach has a number of unique benefits. Although SSJS, Perl, and CGI will always put some additional load on the server, a purely client-side application has no impact on the server beyond serving the HTML documents. A client-side approach can even be used to create an "offline" application that doesn't require a server at all, allowing a more flexible approach for users who are on the go.

The client-side approach does have some limitations; it's not applicable in all cases. The client-side approach can't record data to a file or a database, for example. And since it uses the GET method of delivering form data, it's limited to transferring 4K of information.

In summary, the client-side approach has these advantages:

- Can be used online or offline

- Has the lightest possible impact on the server load

- Doesn't require privileged access to the server

- Reduces server configuration requirements

On the other hand, it has these disadvantages:

- Doesn't enable persistent data

- Can't handle large (greater than 4K) data transfers

- Requires client to have JavaScript support

- Makes program logic visible to end user

Creating the Client-Side Request Object

A CSJS routine can be used to emulate a powerful feature of SSJS — the request object. If you're already familiar with programming in SSJS, you're halfway there. If not, let me explain. The request object is used to provide your application with information about the current transaction. The request object is initialized with a property for each named input element in an HTML form.

For example, consider the following fragment from an HTML form:

```
<FORM ACTION="handler.html" METHOD="GET">
Client Name:    <INPUT TYPE=TEXT NAME="name">
Company Name:   <INPUT TYPE=TEXT NAME="company">
Delivery Zone: <INPUT TYPE=TEXT NAME="zone">
</FORM>
```

Once delivered to "handler.html," the request object will have three properties (name, company, and zone), which correspond to the values the user entered into the form elements of the same name. You could then use those values directly in "handler.html," as shown in this example:

```
document.write("Dear " + request.name);
document.write("Thanks for ordering...");
```

Or you could use the values for decision making:

```
document.write("Delivery to " + request.company + " will
cost ");
if (request.zone == "A")
    document.write("$500");
if (request.zone == "B")
    document.write("$200");
```

The request object is automatically created by SSJS each time a new page is loaded. The request object doesn't exist in CSJS, so you must create it yourself each time. The following routine decodes the form data stored in the URL and assigns it to corresponding properties of the request object, just like SSJS. This routine must be called before you can access the form data directly. A handy way to do this is through the document body's onLoad handler.

```
// This routine returns an object similar to SSJS's
// request object. Used to process forms on the client, in a method
// similar to SSJS.
//
// Usage: request=createRequestObject();
//        document.writeln("The Name was " + request.name);
//
function createRequestObject()
{
    var request   = new Object();          // Creates a new request object.
    var nameVal   = "";                    // Holds array for a single name-value pair.
    var inString = location.search;        // Strips query string from URL.
    var separator = ",";                   // Character used to separate multiple values.

    // If URL contains a query string, grabs it.
    if (inString.charAt(0) == "?")
    {
        // Removes "?" character from query string.
        inString = inString.substring(1, inString.length);
        // Separates query string into name-value pairs.
        keypairs = inString.split("&");
        // Loops through name-value pairs.
        for (var i=0; i < keypairs.length; i++)
        {
            // Splits name-value into array
(nameVal[0]=name, nameVal[1]=value).
            nameVal = keypairs[i].split("=");
            // Replaces "+" characters with spaces and then
unescapes name-value pair.
```

```
          for (a in nameVal)
          {
     &n bsp;    nameVal[a] = nameVal[a].replace(/+/g, "
")
     &n bsp;    nameVal[a] = unescape(nameVal[a]);
          }
          // Checks to see if name already exists in
request object
          // (since select lists may contain multiple
values).
          if (request[nameVal[0]])
          {
     &n bsp;    request[nameVal[0]] += separator +
nameVal[1];
          }
          else
          {
     &n bsp;    request[nameVal[0]] = nameVal[1];
          }
        }
      }
      return request;
}
```

Example: A Sales Quote Generator

A common application for salespeople is to generate personalized sales quotes
based on customer information provided via an HTML form such as the one
shown in Figure 19-1. The information is used to trigger inclusion of customized
chunks of text such as discount schedules or recommendations for companion
products. For example, given the customer's name and order information, such an
application might generate a letter like the one shown in Figure 19-2.

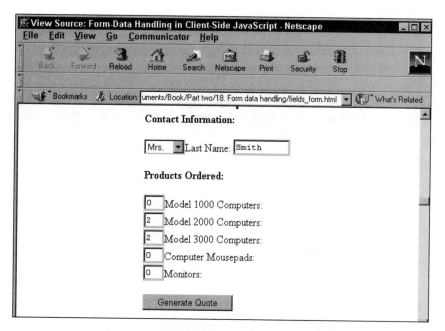

Figure 19-1: A sample HTML form for customer information

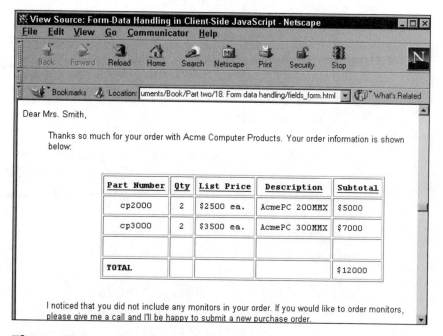

Figure 19-2: A sample sales quote letter

Automating this type of process is a boon to salespeople because it gives them an easy way to generate a professional-looking response to the customer that also includes additional sales or other information keyed off the customer's order. Although this application could be generated on the server, it would be more useful if it could be run offline from a notebook computer, enabling salespeople to create quotations quickly and easily, wherever they are. Here is the code for such an application:

```html
<HTML>
<HEAD>
<SCRIPT LANGUAGE="JavaScript">

function createRequestObject()
{
    var request    = new Object();      // Creates a new
request object.
    var nameVal    = "";                // Holds array for
a single name-value pair.
    var inString   = location.search;   // Strips query
string from URL.
    var separator = ",";                // Character used
to separate multiple values.

    // If URL contains a query string, grabs it.
    if (inString.charAt(0) == "?")
    {
        // Removes "?" character from query string.
        inString = inString.substring(1, inString.length);
        // Separates query string into name-value pairs.
        keypairs = inString.split("&");
        // Loops through name-value pairs.
        for (var i=0; i < keypairs.length; i++)
        {
            // Splits name-value into array
(nameVal[0]=name, nameVal[1]=value).
            nameVal = keypairs[i].split("=");
```

```
            // Replaces "+" characters with spaces and then
unescapes name-value pair.
            for (a in nameVal)
            {
                nameVal[a] = nameVal[a].replace(/+/g, " ")
                nameVal[a] = unescape(nameVal[a]);
            }
            // Checks to see if name already exists in
request object
            // (since select lists may contain multiple
values).
            if (request[nameVal[0]])
            {
                request[nameVal[0]] += separator +
nameVal[1];
            }
            else
            {
                request[nameVal[0]] = nameVal[1];
            }
        }
    }
    return request;
}


// Creates a client-side table describing our inventory. The
beauty of
// this routine is that it could easily be populated
(through SSJS, for example)
// from a living database to keep the client-side version up
to date. This
// function could be kept separate from the main program and
imported by
// using something like <SCRIPT SRC="inventory.js">.
function createClientDB()
{
    // Part number, description, price.
```

```
        addInventoryItem("cp1000", "AcmePC 166MHZ", 1500);
        addInventoryItem("cp2000", "AcmePC 200MHZ", 2500);
        addInventoryItem("cp3000", "AcmePC 300MHZ", 3500);
        addInventoryItem("m755", "Mouse Pad", 3500);
        addInventoryItem("crt9332", "Monitor", 3500);
    }


    // Adds a row to our offline database table.
    function addInventoryItem(partNum, description, price)
    {
        // Creates the new inventory array that will serve as our
    offline
        // version of a database table if it doesn't yet exist.
        if (typeof products == "undefined")
            products = new Array();
        // Creates a new inventory object.
        var o=new Object();
        o.partNum=partNum;
        o.description=description;
        o.price=price;
        // Adds the new object to the products table.
        products[products.length]=o;
    }


    // Creates a table displaying the customer's order
    information.
    function printOrder()
    {
        var grandTotal=0; // The total value of the order.
        var subTotal=0;    // The price x quantity for an item.
        var d=document;    // Shortcut to save some typing.
        // Prints our column headings.
        d.writeln("<CENTER><TABLE BORDER CELLPADDING=5>");
        d.writeln("<TR ALIGN=CENTER VALIGN=CENTER>");
        d.writeln("<TD><B><TT><U>Part Number</U></TT></B></TD>");
        d.writeln("<TD><B><TT><U>Qty</U></TT></B></TD>");
        d.writeln("<TD><B><TT><U>List Price</U></TT></B></TD>");
```

```
   d.writeln("<TD><B><TT><U>Description</U></TT></B></T
D>");
   d.writeln("<TD><B><TT><U>Subtotal</U></TT></B></TD>" );
   d.writeln("</TR>");


   // For each item in the inventory "database," checks for
a nonzero order amount.
   for (i=0; i < products.length; i++)
   {
      // Steps through the database item by item.
      item=products[i];
      // Makes sure that the request property exists to
avoid a JS error
      // caused by referring to nonexistent object
properties.
      if (eval("typeof request."+item.partNum) !=
"undefined")
        {
         // Sets the quantity property of our item to the
value passed
         // in from the form data. We protect ourselves from
problems
         // by running everything through parseInt.

item.quantity=eval("parseInt(request."+item.partNum+")");
         if (item.quantity > 0)
          {
            // Displays a line item for this row.
            subtotal=(item.price*item.quantity);
            d.writeln("<TR
ALIGN=CENTER><TD><TT>"+item.partNum+"</TT></TD>");

d.writeln("<TD><TT>"+item.quantity+"</TT></TD>");
            d.writeln("<TD><TT>$"+item.price+"
ea.</TT></TD>");

d.writeln("<TD><TT>"+item.description+"</TT></TD>");
```

```
            d.writeln("<TD
ALIGN=LEFT><TT>$"+subtotal+"</TT></TD></TR>");
            // Tracks the total for later.
            grandTotal += subtotal;
        }
      }
    }
    // Closes up the table and prints the grand total of all
line items.
    d.writeln("<TR
ALIGN=LEFT><TD><B><TT>TOTAL</TT></B></TD><TD>  </TD>");
    d.writeln("<TD> </TD><TD> </TD><TD><TT>" );

d.writeln("$"+grandTotal+"</TT></TD></TR></TABLE></CENTER>")
;
}


// Builds our request object.
request=createRequestObject();
</SCRIPT>
</HEAD>

<BODY BGCOLOR="#FFFFFF">
<FONT FACE="Arial,Helvetica">
<SCRIPT LANGUAGE="JavaScript">
// Prints the greeting -- for example, "Dear Mr. Green
Jeans."
document.writeln("Dear "+request.salutation+"
"+request.lname+",")
</SCRIPT>
<P>
Thanks so much for your order with Acme Computer Products.
Your order information is shown below:<P>

<SCRIPT LANGUAGE="JavaScript">
// Builds an easy-to-access table of inventory information.
createClientDB();
```

```
// Displays a line-item detail of the customer's order.
printOrder();
</SCRIPT>

<P>

<SCRIPT LANGUAGE="JavaScript">
// Checks for special situations. In this case, we want to
try to sell the
// customer monitors if none were ordered.
if (parseInt(request.crt9332) == 0)
{
    document.writeln("I noticed that you did not include any
monitors in your order. ");
    document.writeln("If you would like to order monitors
please give me a call ");
    document.writeln("and I'll be happy to submit a new
purchase order.<P>");
}
</SCRIPT>

Your order should arrive in a few weeks. Thanks again for
your business.
</FONT>
</BODY>
</HTML>
```

Going Further

We could expand this application by integrating it with a production database. An SSJS application could be used to generate new client-side data nightly, keeping the application up to date. It could even be coupled with a server-side version that speaks directly with the live database — giving you online and offline versions of your tool.

Another application that works well with the client-side technique is an expert system. For example, you ask the user a series of multiple-choice questions, and based on the input, return suggestions appropriate for the situation. To do this, your form would send the answers to the action-receiving page, where they would be compared to an array of answers matched to solutions.

20

Unleashing the Power of mailto URLs

Robert Husted — *intranet technical lead, Qwest Communications*

The `mailto` URL HTML function is extremely useful but sadly underutilized. What's particularly useful is that you can preformat a message by supplying things like the subject line of the message in the URL. You can specify who should be copied (cc) or blind-copied (bcc), and even fill out the body of a message! In this chapter, I look at how to take advantage of these powerful features of `mailto` URLs. There are some things to watch for; for instance, if you don't know about hex encoding, all the blank lines will be missing from your message body. The chapter also gives some JavaScript tips that will help you preformat your programmatic email messages.

The Basics of mailto URLs

In its simplest form, the `mailto` URL looks like this:

```
mailto:name@company.com
```

The corresponding HTML anchor tag, which you place inside your document, is as shown in this example:

```
<A HREF="mailto:name@company.com">send email</A>
```

This tag would be attached to text in your document that, when viewed in a browser, would provide a link. When readers click on the link, the browser causes a mail window to appear with `name@company.com` already filled in on the To: line of the message.

NOTE

This works in every browser I tested it in, but be forewarned that not all browsers recognize `mailto` URLs.

If you want to specify values for additional properties, such as cc, bcc, and subject, you can add them to the URL as name/value pairs (`name=value`). Each property name is followed by an equals sign (=) and then the value to appear for that property. The first name/value pair starts with a question mark (?) to separate it from the e-mail address, and subsequent name/value pairs are separated by an ampersand (&). For example, here's a `mailto` URL with cc and subject values specified (with the separator characters highlighted for readability):

```
mailto:erickrock@netscape.com?cc=bob@acme.com&subject=The
Readme File
```

The HTML anchor tag looks like this (with hex-encoded text for the value of the subject property, as explained in the next section):

```
<A
HREF="mailto:erickrock@netscape.com?cc=bob@acme.com&subject=
The%20Readme%20File">send email to Eric</A>
```

Clicking the corresponding link in the HTML (again, when the file is viewed in a browser) causes a mail window to appear with the To, Cc, and Subject lines already filled in, as shown in Figure 20-1.

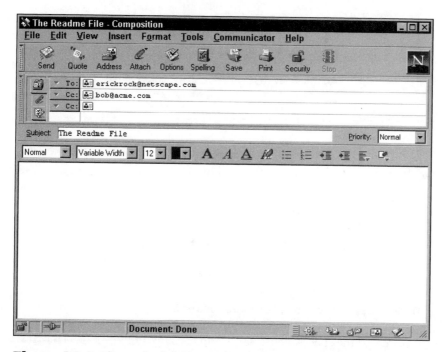

Figure 20-1: The result of clicking on a link containing a ~~mailto~~ URL with cc and subject values specified

What URL Notation Looks Like

Table 20-1 summarizes the separator characters and other special notation that can appear in a URL.

TABLE 20-1: SPECIAL NOTATION IN A URL

NOTATION	MEANING
?	Appears just after the e-mail address, separating it from the first name/value pair.
=	Separates each name and value, in the form `name=value`.

Continued

TABLE 20-1: *(continued)*

Notation	Meaning&
&	Separates name/value pairs, as in `name1=value1&name2=value2`.
%	Precedes an ASCII character code in hexadecimal, in the form `%xx`, as a way of representing that character. For example, `%0A` represents a newline (line feed) character. See more on hex encoding below.
+	Another way to represent a space. For example, the value `Bjorn Free` could appear in the URL as `Bjorn+Free`.

In JavaScript, you can hex-encode a string — that is, substitute the `%xx` notation for all characters other than letters and numbers (and a few special characters) — by using the `escape()` function, as follows:

```
var myString = "Odds & ends for tonight!"
var myEncodedText = escape(myString);
```

This code puts the following value in the variable myEncodedText:

```
Odds%20%26%20ends%20for%20tonight%21
```

Notice that the spaces, ampersand, and exclamation point have been converted to their ASCII character code equivalents: `%20`, `%26`, and `%21`, respectively. Without hex encoding, this string could not be used as a subject value in a URL because the ampersand would be interpreted as a separator between name/value pairs.

Be sure to hex-encode only the subject and message body values in a `mailto` URL. Although the `escape()` function will not encode letters or numbers (or the characters `* @ - _ + . /`), it will encode the `?` and `&` separator characters, which would mess up your URL.

Forms That Can Help

The form shown in Figure 20-2, and available in HTML on the CD-ROM that accompanies this book, will help you create a `mailto` URL that includes cc, bcc, and subject values and a formatted message body (one that can contain newline characters, tabs, and so on). Simply enter the values for the various properties and then click the Create URL button to generate a `mailto` URL.

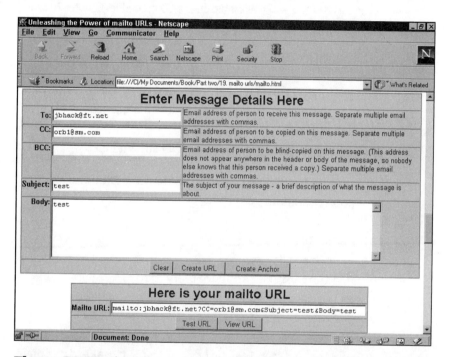

Figure 20-2: A form that can help you generate your own ~~mailto~~ URL

The `mailto` URL generated by the form as filled out in the Figure 20-2 is `mailto:johndox@netscape.com?CC=elainewang@netscape.com&BCC=bbiloxi@iiop.net&Subject=CORBA%20Connectivity`. The HTML form itself is available on the CD-ROM that comes with this book.

ON THE CD-ROM

The CD-ROM that accompanies this book includes the HTML form illustrated in Figure 20-2; it's in the file, Chapter 20 mailto URL Example. Open it in your browser. After you've filled out the form, the `mailto` URL you generate will appear in the box below the form. You can copy and paste the URL into any HTML document to create a link that causes a preformatted mail message to appear when a reader clicks the link. You can also use the buttons in the form to generate the mail message for you, and to test the URL you just created. Source code for the form is also available on the CD in the file, Chapter 20 Example Source Code. To find it, follow the path: Sample Code and Supporting Documentation ⇨ Part II ⇨ Chapter 20.

What if you want to do this directly from JavaScript? You may not want a URL, but instead you may want to create a mail window if a user clicks a button (like the test URL shown in Figure 20-2).

In that case, you could use code similar to that shown here:

```
// POP UP A PREFORMATTED EMAIL MESSAGE WINDOW
function popupMessage() {

  // SET MESSAGE VALUES
  var to = "person@company.com";
  var cc = "another_person@company.com";
  var bcc = "yet_another_person@company.com";
  var subject = "A Preformatted Email Message";
  var body =
      "Chandler,\n\n\tI'm sorry, I can't make it tonight. " +

      "I have to rearrange my sock drawer. " +
      "\n\nSincerely,\n\nMonica"

  // BUILD MAIL MESSAGE COMPONENTS
  var doc = "mailto:" + to +
      "?cc=" + cc +
      "&bcc=" + bcc +
      "&subject=" + escape(subject) +
      "&body=" + escape(body);
```

```
    // POP UP EMAIL MESSAGE WINDOW
    window.location = doc;
}
```

You can test the JavaScript code with a simple form like this one:

```
<FORM>
<INPUT TYPE=BUTTON NAME=Test Value="Mail Window Test"
onClick="popupMessage()">
</FORM>
```

That's all there is to it. Now you know how to create robust `mailto` URLs in your HTML documents and how to pop up windows containing preformatted e-mail messages using JavaScript.

Server Development, I: Scripting for Workgroups

Server Development, I: Scripting for Workgroups

This section shows you how to write server-side JavaScript applications that can serve the needs of workgroups numbering in the low hundreds. The JavaScript shown in this part is surrounded by `<server>` tags, which means it runs on the server — Netscape Enterprise Server to be precise. Another difference is that, by and large, the scripting shown here is more complex. It does things that are a little more arcane to the average person, as well, such as maintaining the state of an application. Also, much of what follows pertains to accessing databases; you'll be a lot more comfortable with it if you understand relational database programming, especially with the Open Database Connectivity (ODBC) standard.

The chapters in this section refer to server-side JavaScript documentation from Netscape. The *Server-Side JavaScript Guide* and the *Server-Side JavaScript Reference*, as well as several other server-side JavaScript goodies, are included on the CD-ROM. We recommend that you follow all the references from the chapters; they will greatly increase your ability to use server-side JavaScript.

21

Setting Up and Managing Database Connections Using Server-Side JavaScript

Victoria Gilbert — *former technical writer, Netscape Communications*

This chapter introduces you to the process of using the LiveWire Database Service and *server-side JavaScript* (SSJS) to connect your application to DB2, Informix, ODBC, Oracle, or Sybase relational databases. I'll show you how to choose the best connection methodology for your application and how to manage connection pools. We're starting with this part of server-side JavaScript's functionality because it's probably the most basic part of any web application, beyond the simple HTML pages themselves. This chapter also serves as an introduction to a lot of the material in Netscape's document *Writing Server-Side JavaScript*

Applications, which you should familiarize yourself with before you attempt writing any in-depth applications using server-side JavaScript and Netscape Enterprise Server (NES) 3.0. The document is on the CD-ROM that comes with this book.

NOTE

This chapter is based on Chapter 8 of the Netscape document *Writing Server-Side JavaScript Applications*. This chapter makes numerous references to *Writing Server-Side JavaScript Applications*, and we urge you to follow them as a way of getting to know that document. Note that the techniques described here, and in that document, pertain to Netscape Enterprise Server Version 3 and higher. For older versions of Netscape Enterprise Server, please see the Netscape *Live Wire Developers Guide* document. Both documents can be found on the CD-ROM that accompanies this book (in the folder with material for Chapter 3, follow the path: Sample Code and Supporting Documentation ➪ Part I ➪ Chapter 3).

Connecting to a Database: Different Approaches

There are two basic ways to connect to a database with the LiveWire Database Service — part of Netscape Enterprise Server (NES) Version 3 and later. You can use DbPool and Connection objects, which were introduced with NES 3.0, or you can use the older database object.

Connecting with DbPool and Connection objects

If you connect with DbPool and Connection objects, you create a pool of database connections for working with a relational database. First, you create an instance of the DbPool class and then access Connection objects through that DbPool object. DbPool and Connection objects separate the activities of connecting to a database and managing a set of connections from the activities of accessing the database through a connection.

This approach offers a lot of flexibility. Your application can have several database pools, each with its own configuration of database and user, and each pool can have multiple connections for that configuration. This allows simultaneous access to multiple databases or to the same database from multiple accounts. You can also associate the connection pool with the application itself instead of with a single client request and thus have transactions that span multiple client requests. You make this association by assigning the pool to a property of the `project` object and then removing the assignment when you're finished with the pool.

Connecting with the Database Object

If you connect with the database object, you use the predefined `database` object for connecting to a database with a single connection configuration of database and user. The `database` object performs all activities related to working with a database. You can think of the `database` object as a single pool of database connections.

This approach is somewhat simpler, as it involves using only the single database object and not multiple `DbPool` and `Connection` objects. However, it lacks the flexibility of the first approach. If you use only the `database` object and want to connect to different databases or to different accounts, you must disconnect from one configuration before connecting to another. Also, when you use the `database` object, a single transaction cannot span multiple client requests, and connections to multiple database sources cannot simultaneously be open.

As described in the following sections, you need to consider two main questions when deciding how to set up your database connections:

- How many configurations of database and user do you need?
- Does a single database connection need to span multiple client requests?

Table 21-1 summarizes how the answers to these questions affect how you set up and manage your pool of database connections and the individual connections. The following sections discuss the details of these possibilities.

Managing Connections Pools

At any given time, a connected `DbPool` or `database` object and all the connections in the pool are associated with a particular database configuration. That is, everything in a pool is connected to a particular database server, as a particular user, with a particular password, and to a particular database.

TABLE 21-1: CONSIDERATIONS FOR CREATING THE DATABASE POOLS

NUMBER OF DATABASE CONFIGURATIONS?	WHERE IS THE POOL CONNECTED?	WHERE IS THE POOL DISCONNECTED?	WHAT OBJECT(S) HOLD THE POOL?	DOES YOUR CODE NEED TO STORE THE POOL AND CONNECTION?	HOW DOES YOUR CODE STORE THE POOL AND CONNECTIONS IN THE PROJECT OBJECT?
1, shared by all clients	Application's initial page	Nowhere	database	No	—
1, shared by all clients	Application's initial page	Nowhere	1 DbPool object	Yes	DbPool: Named property; Connection: 1 array
Fixed set, shared by all clients	Application's initial page	Nowhere	N DbPool objects	Yes	DbPool: Named property; Connection: N arrays
Separate pool for each client	Client request page	Depends[a]	Many DbPool objects	Only if a connection spans client requests	DbPool: 1 array; Connection: 1 array

[a] If an individual connection does not span client requests, you can connect and disconnect the pool on each page that needs a connection. In this case, the pool is not stored between requests. If individual connections do span requests, connect on the first client page that needs the connection and disconnect on the last such page. This can result in idle connections, so your application will need to handle that possibility.

If your application always uses the same configuration, then you can easily use a single `DbPool` object or use the database object and connect exactly once. In this case, you should make the connection on your application's initial page.

If your application requires multiple configurations, either because it must connect to different databases, or to the same database as different users, or both, you need to decide how to manage those configurations.

If you use the `database` object and have multiple configurations, you have no choice. You must connect, disconnect, and reconnect the `database` object each time you need to change something about the configuration. You do so under the control of the client requests. In this situation, be sure you use locks to gain exclusive access to the database object. (Locks are fully discussed in "Sharing Objects Safely with Locking" from *Writing Server-Side JavaScript Applications*.) Otherwise, another client request can disconnect the object before this client request is finished with it. Although you can use the database object this way, you're probably better off using `DbPool` objects.

If you use `DbPool` objects and have multiple configurations, you could still connect, disconnect, and reconnect the same `DbPool` object. However, with `DbPool` objects you have more flexibility. You can create as many pools as you need and place them under the control of the `project` object. (See "Session Management Service" in *Writing Server-Side JavaScript Applications* for information on the `project` object.) Using multiple database pools is more efficient and is generally safer than reusing a single pool (either with the database object or with a single `DbPool` object).

In deciding how to manage your pools, you must consider two factors: how many different configurations you want your pools to be able to access, and whether a single connection needs to span multiple client requests. If you have a small number of possible configurations, you can create a separate pool for each configuration. "Sharing a Fixed Set of Connection Pools" in *Writing Server-Side JavaScript Applications* discusses this approach.

If you have a very large or unknown number of configurations (for example, if all users get their own database user ID), there are two situations to consider. If each connection needs to last for only one client request, then you can create individual database pools on a client page.

However, sometimes a connection must span multiple client requests (for example, if a single database transaction spans multiple client requests). Also, you may just not want to reconnect to the database on each page of the application. If so, you can create an array of pools that is shared. "Sharing an Array of Connection Pools" in *Writing Server-Side JavaScript Applications* discusses this approach.

Whichever approach you use, when you no longer need an individual connection in a pool, clean up the resources used by the connection so that it is available for another user. To do so, close all open cursors, stored procedures, and result sets. Release the connection back to the pool. (You don't have to release the connection if you're using the database object.)

If you do not release the connection, when you try to disconnect the pool, the system waits before actually disconnecting for one of two conditions to occur:

■ You do release all connections

■ The connections go out of scope and get collected by the garbage collector

If you create individual database pools for each user, be sure to disconnect the pool when you're finished with it. For information on cursors, see "Manipulating Query Results with Cursors" in *Writing Server-Side JavaScript Applications*. For information on stored procedures and result sets, see "Calling Stored Procedures" in *Writing Server-Side JavaScript Applications*.

CROSS-REFERENCE
You can also read about stored procedures in Chapter 23 of this book. Additionally, for more information on building cursors with server-side JavaScript, see the *View Source* article "Input and Output with HTML Forms" on the CD-ROM that accompanies this book, in the file Chapter 23 Input and Output with HTML Forms. You can find it by following the path: Sample Code and Supporting Documentation ➪ Part III ➪ Chapter 23.

Sharing a Fixed Set of Connection Pools

Frequently, an application shares a small set of connection pools among all users of the application. For example, your application might need to connect to three different databases, or it might need to connect to a single database using four different user IDs corresponding to four different departments. If you have a small set of possible connection configurations, you can create separate pools for each configuration. You use DbPool objects for this purpose.

In this case, you want the pool of connections to exist for the entire life of the application, not just the life of a client or an individual client request. You can accomplish this by creating each database pool as a property of the project object. For example, the application's initial page could contain these statements:

```
project.engpool = new DbPool ("ORACLE", "myserver1", "ENG",
    "pwd1", "", 5, true);
project.salespool = new DbPool ("INFORMIX", "myserver2",
"SALES",
    "pwd2", "salsmktg", 2);
project.supppool = new DbPool
("SYBASE","myserver3","SUPPORT",
    "pwd3", "suppdb", 3, false);
```

These statements create three pools for different groups who use the application. The `project.eng` pool has five Oracle connections and commits any uncommitted transactions when a connection is released back to the pool. The `project.sales` pool has two Informix connections and rolls back any uncommitted transactions at the end of a connection. The `project.supp` pool has three Sybase connections and rolls back any uncommitted transactions at the end of a connection.

You should create this pool as part of the application's initial page. That page is run only when the application starts. On user-accessible pages, you don't create a pool, and you don't change the connection. Instead, these pages determine which group the current user belongs to and uses an already established connection from the appropriate pool. For example, the following code determines which database to use (based on the value of the `userGroup` property of the `request` object), looks up some information in the database and displays it to the user, and then releases the connection:

```
if (request.userGroup == "SALES") {
    salesconn = project.salespool.connection("A sales
connection");
    salesconn.SQLTable ("select * from dept");
    salesconn.release();
}
```

Alternatively, you can choose to create the pool and change the connection on a user-accessible page. If you do so, you'll have to be careful that multiple users accessing that page at the same time do not interfere with each other. For example, only one user should be able to create the pool that will be shared by all users. For information on safe sharing of information, see "Sharing Objects Safely with Locking" in *Writing Server-Side JavaScript Applications*.

Sharing an Array of Connection Pools

I just described how you can use properties of the project object to share a fixed set of connection pools. This approach is useful if you know how many connection pools you need at the time you develop the application and furthermore if you need only a small number of connections.

For some applications, you cannot predict how many connection pools you will need. For others, you can predict, but the number is prohibitively large. For example, assume that, for each customer who accesses your application, the application consults a user profile to determine what information to display from the database. You might give each customer a unique user ID for the database. Such an application requires each user to have a different set of connection parameters (corresponding to the different database user IDs) and hence a different connection pool.

You could create the DbPool object and connect and disconnect it on every page of the application. This works only if a single connection does not need to span multiple client requests. Otherwise, you can handle this situation differently.

For this application, instead of creating a fixed set of connection pools during the application's initial page or a pool on each client page, you create a single property of the project object that will contain an array of connection pools. The elements of that array are accessed by a key, based on the particular user. At initialization time, you create the array but do not put any elements in the array (since nobody has yet tried to use the application), as shown here:

```
project.sharedPools = new Object();
```

The first time a customer starts the application, the application obtains a key identifying that customer. Based on the key, the application creates a DbPool pool object and stores it in the array of pools. With this connection pool, it can either reconnect on each page or set up the connection as described in "Maintaining a Connection Across Requests" from *Writing Server-Side JavaScript Applications*. The following code either creates the pool and or obtains the already created pool, makes sure it is connected, and then works with the database:

```
// Generate a unique index to refer to this client, if that
// hasn't already been done on another page. For information
// on the ssjs_generateClientID function, see
// "Uniquely Referring to the client Object"
if client.id == null {
   client.id = ssjs_generateClientID();
```

```
}
// If there isn't already a pool for this client, create one
and
// connect it to the database.
project.lock();
if (project.sharedPools[client.id] == null) {
   project.sharedPools[client.id] = new DbPool ("ORACLE",
      "myserver", user, password, "", 5, false);
}
project.unlock();

// Set a variable to this pool, for convenience.
var clientPool = project.sharedPools[client.id];

// You've got a pool: see if it's connected. If not, try to
// connect it. If that fails, redirect to a special page to
// inform the user.
project.lock();
if (!clientPool.connected()) {
   clientPool.connect("ORACLE", "myserver", user, password,
      "", 5, false);
   if (!clientPool.connected()) {
      delete project.sharedPools[client.id];
      project.unlock();
      redirect("noconnection.htm");
   }
}
project.unlock();

// If you've got this far, you're successfully connected and
// can work with the database.
clientConn = clientPool.connection();
clientConn.SQLTable("select * from customers");
// ... more database operations ...

// Always release a connection when you no longer need it.
clientConn.release();
}
```

The next time the customer accesses the application (for example, from another page in the application), it uses the same code and obtains the stored connection pool and (possibly a stored `Connection` object) from the `project` object.

If you use `ssjs_generateClientID` and store the ID on the client object, you may need to protect against an intruder obtaining access to that ID, and hence to sensitive information.

NOTE

The `sharedConns` object used in this sample code is not a predefined JavaScript object. It is simply created by this sample and could be called anything you choose.

Just a Beginning

This is just a start to learning about server-side JavaScript and using it to set up and manage database connections. If you want to become an accomplished server-side JavaScripters, follow the cross-references in this chapter, read more of Writing Server-Side JavaScript Applications on the CD-ROM, and read the other chapters in this section of the book. Server-side JavaScript is a relatively new phenomenon, and I expect that, armed with the basics discussed here, your imagination can develop truly innovative applications of this technology.

22

Creating Flexible Data Views Using Server-Side JavaScript

JJ Kuslich — *application developer, Application Methods, Inc.*

In Chapter 3 of this book, "JavaScript on the Server: Internet Application Development without Native Code," we introduced you to the concept of using server-side JavaScript — part of the Netscape LiveWire development tool — to develop Internet and intranet applications, particularly for connectivity with relational databases. As a software consultant, I've used LiveWire and server-side JavaScript to develop a variety of specific Web-based database access solutions. Since there's so much demand for knowledge about developing database-enabled Web sites, I thought I'd share some of my experiences using and building upon the simple database constructs from server-side JavaScript. I think you'll find that these constructs open a wide world of possibilities for Web-based applications.

In this chapter, I'll demonstrate a few fundamental techniques you can use to create interactive database-access applications using server-side JavaScript, and show you how to create flexible "views" on databases. For you die-hard SQL experts, I'm not speaking of strict SQL views, but rather simply creating result sets and displaying them to the user in a useful format. I'll demonstrate some useful ways to display and organize data from databases on HTML pages. I'll also present techniques that go beyond the simple examples presented in *Writing Server-Side JavaScript Applications*, which describes developing applications for Netscape Enterprise Server 3.*x*, and the examples presented in *LiveWire Developer's Guide*, for use with older versions of Netscape Enterprise Server. Both documents can be found on the CD-ROM that comes with this book

ON THE CD-ROM

The *Netscape LiveWire Developer's Guide* and *Writing Server-Side JavaScript Applications* documents can be found on the CD-ROM that comes with this book. They are in the folder containing supporting materials for Chapter 3, under Sample Code and Supporting Documentation ⇨ Part I ⇨ Chapter 3.

A basic understanding of HTML, SQL, and JavaScript and its database access objects will help you understand the techniques I describe. However, if you're not very familiar with these topics, don't worry. Some of the code samples presented here may pass you by, but the underlying concepts will still help you on your way to designing database applications. For those readers who aren't familiar with the JavaScript objects that provide database access, I'll start by giving a brief overview of them. For a complete description of all of their capabilities, I encourage you to refer to the *LiveWire Developer's Guide*.

Accessing a Database with JavaScript

LiveWire supports connectivity to Informix, Oracle, Sybase, and any other relational databases that use the ODBC standard for Windows NT/2000-based systems. Developers access databases with the Netscape Enterprise Server through the server-side JavaScript database object, which has several methods for performing operations on a database. Among the more commonly used methods of the database object are the following:

- `connect` for establishing a connection to the database with a specific set of user privileges

- `execute` for executing pass-through SQL statements

- `cursor` for establishing a cursor object on a database

- `SQLTable` for printing a simple HTML table based upon a SQL query

- transaction control and error reporting methods

In LiveWire, cursors are primarily used for conducting queries and performing operations on the returned data; you should familiarize yourself with how they work (if you haven't already). Essentially, a cursor is a pointer to a set of record — a result set — that results from an SQL query. Calling the `database.cursor()` method returns a cursor object that points to the result set from an SQL query. Cursors provide a uniform interface to database operations such as inserting, updating, and deleting rows from a table, as well as navigating a result set. They do all this without having to know the specifics of the database management system (DBMS) they're connected to. In a corporate environment where several types of databases — such as Oracle, SQL Server, and so on — may exist, JavaScript cursor objects give developers a tremendous advantage.

As I just mentioned, calling the `database.cursor()` method will establish a cursor containing a result set from an SQL query. The cursor method actually creates a cursor object in JavaScript that represents the cursor, and as such the cursor object has its own set of methods. Performing operations on a cursor is as simple as calling methods and referring to properties, just as with other JavaScript objects.

Some of the most widely used properties and methods of the cursor object are the following:

- The `cursorColumn` property is an array that represents a particular column in the result set. Columns may be as elements of an array or by column name.

- The `insertRow`, `updateRow`, and `deleteRow` methods are used for inserting, updating, and deleting rows in the result set.

- The `next` method allows navigation through the result set.

The following code is an introductory example that demonstrates how to use the objects and methods I just mentioned. The code sample illustrates connecting to a database, writing some values from a table called *Customers* to the screen in HTML, then updating two other fields and writing them back to the Customers table. Just about any database application in JavaScript will contain some or all of the fundamental methods and properties referenced in this example.

```
// Connect the database MYDATABASE on server MYSERVER
database.connect("INFORMIX", "myServer", "informix",
"informix", "MyDatabase");

// Establish an updatable cursor on a sub-set of the
CUSTOMERS table

custCursor = database.cursor("select * from CUSTOMERS where
LASTNAME='Andreessen'", true);

// One next() must be called initially whenever a cursor is
established
custCursor.next();

// Write some data values, firstName and address, to the
screen
write("Name: " + custCursor.firstName + "<BR>");
write("Address: " + custCursor.address + "<BR>");

// Set some data values and update the row in the CUSTOMERS
table
custCursor.income = custCursor.income * 10;
custCursor.description = "CTO of Netscape";
custCursor.updateRow("CUSTOMERS");

// Close the cursor and disconnect from the database
custCursor.close();
database.disconnect();
```

Please refer to Chapter 6 of the *LiveWire Developer's Guide* for specific information on each of the objects, methods, and properties mentioned in this example.

The Fine Line Between Input and Output

HTML tables are commonly used to organize output from database tables or queries because they're a natural construct for visually organizing and displaying data from relational database tables. Yet there are times when there is either too much data to display cleanly on a single screen, or you aren't quite sure what data the user wants to see. Fortunately, HTML was designed for just such situations. You can take advantage of HTML hyperlinks to give users different views of a data set depending on the data they're already viewing. In other words, part of one query's output can become input to a new query that will display a more specific view of the data set chosen.

For example, let's say we're working with a database that stores information about a company's employees and departments in two tables, Employee and Department. The Department table contains a department number (the primary key), manager, location, and budget information. The Employee table contains each employee's Social Security number, name, address, number of dependents, salary, and department number. The table has a composite key consisting of the Social Security number (SSN) and the department number — deptNumber. The table is linked to the Department table through the deptNumber field, as shown in Figure 22-1.

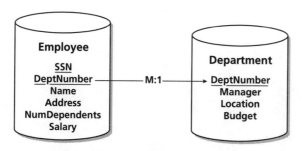

Figure 22-1: The Department and Employee database tables, linked through the deptNumber field

We've designed some simple HTML reports that output the contents of each table upon request. However, suppose a user would like to see the list of all employees in a particular department. What's the best way to create this association and allow users to perform such a look-up operation? One option would be to make an HTML form that allows ad hoc queries on each table, construct a query engine, perform error checks on all of the form input, format the output, and so on. Although such a utility may be useful, it would take hours to design, build, and test. Instead, we can take advantage of the reports we already have to let our users obtain the information they want. Surely the solution that leaves us time enough for a few games of air hockey is the right one, so let's delve into modifying those HTML reports.

First, let's take a look at how one of the standard reports might be constructed from data in the Department table. The HTML code shown in the next example will display information on any given department. No employee or other information has been related to department information at this point.

```
<HTML>
<HEAD>
<TITLE>Department Data</TITLE>

<SERVER>
       // Connect the database COMPANYDATABASE on server
MYSERVER
       database.connect("INFORMIX", "myServer", "informix",
"informix", "CompanyDatabase");
</SERVER>

</HEAD>
<BODY>

<TABLE BORDER=2>
<TR>
   <TH>Department No.</TH>
   <TH>Manager</TH>
   <TH>Location</TH>
   <TH>Annual Budget</TH>
</TR>

<SERVER>
       // Establish a cursor on the Department table
```

```
    deptCursor = database.cursor("select * from
DEPARTMENT");

    // Iterate across every record in the result set
    // and write out selected fields in a table row.
    // Note that next() returns true as long as there are
more rows
    while ( deptCursor.next() )
    {
        write("<TR>");
        write("<TD>" + deptCursor.deptNumber + "</TD>");
        write("<TD>" + deptCursor.manager + "</TD>");
        write("<TD>" + deptCursor.location + "</TD>");
        write("<TD>" + deptCursor.budget + "</TD>");
        write("</TR>");
    } deptCursor.close();
</SERVER>

</TABLE>

</BODY>
</HTML>
```

You'll notice I didn't use the `database.SQLTable` method to simply print out all the fields in the table at once. The `SQLTable` method has its uses in certain situations, but it's very limited and inflexible for formatting and manipulating the output. I'll want to reformat the data displayed in this report, so I've chosen to use a more "manual" method for constructing the HTML table.

To accomplish my goal of performing a lookup, I need to find a way to allow users to use the information presented on the Departments report to find more detailed information about that department, namely, its employees. Yet, all that's on my report is some HTML text that just sits there staring at the users, allowing them no interactivity. Fortunately, HTML has an excellent way to add interaction to a Web page — hyperlinks! We can use them here to take users to a report displaying the employees who work in a selected department. Figure 22-2 illustrates the desired interaction.

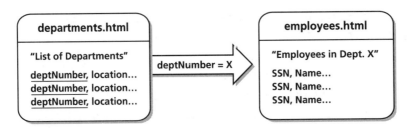

Figure 22-2: The Departments and Employees reports employ an HTML link to take users from one report to the other.

To add this interactivity to the Departments report, I'll add a hyperlink to the deptNumber field that will jump to the report for employees. By itself, such a link will simply jump to the Employees report, showing all employees regardless of their department. I need to add code that passes some information to that report when the user clicks the link, narrowing the query to only employees in a particular department. To do so, I'll use URL encoding to pass along the department name so the results will be limited to only those in the selected department.

URL encoding is a way of adding variable names and associated values, referred to as "name-value pairs," to the URL for the link. In general, such links look like the following:

```
<A HREF="myUrl.html?var1=value1&var2=value2&...">my link</A>
```

In the line just shown, var1=value1 is an example of a name-value pair; each name-value pair is separated by an ampersand (&) character. On the server, this name-value data is available as properties of the request object in the destination page, in this case myUrl.html. For more detailed information on URL encoding and the request object, see Chapter 8 of the *LiveWire Developer's Guide*.

To add the data to the URL for the Department report, I'll have to modify the first line of HTML column output that above was merely printing out the department number, as shown in the next example.

```
write("<TD> <A HREF='employees.html?dept=" +
        escape(deptCursor.deptNumber) +
        "'>" + deptCursor.deptNumber + "</A> </TD>");
```

For instance, for a department number of '37', the code in the previous example will generate the following HTML output:

```
<TD> <A HREF='employees.html?dept=37'>37</A> </TD>
```

If the user clicks the link, the department number will be available to `employ-ees.html` as the property `request.dept` with a value of "37". The code for this operation may appear a bit intimidating at first, so let's examine it line by line.

The first line of code in the example just above writes out the HTML column tag `<TD>` and the first part of the URL in the anchor tag. The second line URL-encodes, or "escapes," the value to be placed in the URL as the value for `dept`. Encoding the value is necessary when the value passed contains spaces, punctuation, or other non-alphanumeric values. Finally, the third line of the example just above writes the department number that will appear to users as the link they can click; it then closes the anchor and column tags, completing that column of the HTML table.

We need to make one final modification, this time to the Employees report, and make use of the data passed via URL encoding to narrow the report to only employees indicated by the `deptNumber` parameter. Imagine that `employ-ees.html` originally used a simple `database.SQLTable` method to display employee data, which would look like the code shown in the next example.

```
<HTML>
<HEAD><TITLE>Employee Data</TITLE>
</HEAD>
<BODY>

<SERVER>
      database.SQLTable("select * from EMPLOYEE");
</SERVER>

</BODY>
</HTML>
```

Altering this statement to account for the data we will be passing to it is a simple matter. With server-side JavaScript, data passed via URL-encoded parameters are available to the application in the request object. When a user clicks on a link from the department's page, `employees.html` will have the department number available as `request.dept`. We can now modify the above query with the code shown in the next example.

```
<SERVER>

var selectionString = "";

// If the value is not null, select employees from a
particular
// department
if (request.dept != null)
     selectionString = " where department=" + request.dept;

database.SQLTable("select * from EMPLOYEE" +
selectionString);

</SERVER>
```

The code in this example will display a list of employees from a particular department if the department number is provided in the URL. Otherwise, it will display all employees as it did before the changes were made.

The ultimate result of the code changes we've made to the departments and employees pages will be an application that displays data on departments where every department number will be a link to a list of employees in that department. When the user clicks a department number, the application presents a list of employees for that department and only that department. If no department number is specified in the URL, all employees will be listed. With little more than a half dozen new lines of code, we've transformed simple HTML reports into dynamic, hyperlinked documents that perform database queries and display the results on the fly.

The Sorted Details

The foregoing example shows a useful way of connecting data and HTML links for the purposes of displaying data so that users can control how they view data. The example can be taken a bit further to let users sort the result sets by any column simply by clicking on the column name at the top of the HTML table. The code in the next example shows how you'd begin to modify the code from the second example (above, starting with the comment 'Connect the database COMPANYDATABASE on server MYSERVER') to implement this "sort by column name" feature.

```
<TABLE BORDER=2>
    <TR>
        <TH>
<AHREF="department.html?orderby=DEPTNUMBER">Department
No.</A></TH>
        <TH><A
HREF="department.html?orderby=MANAGER">Manager</A></TH>
        <TH><A
HREF="department.html?orderby=LOCATION">Location</A></TH>
        <TH><A HREF="department.html?orderby=BUDGET">Annual
Budget</A></TH>
    </TR>

    <SERVER>
            var orderString = "";

            // If the parameter passed in via URL encoding is
not null
            // add an "order by" clause for the field
indicated
            //
            if (request.orderby != null)
                orderString = "order by " +
request.orderby;

            // Establish a cursor on the Department table
with an ordered result set
            deptCursor = database.cursor("select * from
DEPARTMENT " + orderString);
```

Now, with the additional code displayed in this example, whenever a user clicks on a column name, the same page (`department.html`) will be requested again. This time, it will include a parameter included in the URL that tells the server to construct the cursor and order the result set by the column selected. It's important to note that the value of the `orderby` parameter in this example contains a string that exactly matches the column name as it's defined in the Department database. For the case presented, the URL parameter and corresponding column name must match exactly, since it is used directly in the SQL "order by" statement, or the query will not work properly.

"Drilling Down" for Useful Views of Data Sets

In addition to the modifications illustrated here, we could add even more useful features to our application. We could limit the number of fields displayed from the Employee table so that the user doesn't have to scroll to see every data field for a particular employee's data. We could make the application show only three or four columns of information on the initial page, such as Social Security number, name, and supervisor. We could then create a dynamic link on each employee's name that, when it's clicked, would take the user to a detailed report containing data from all the fields for a single employee. This "drill-down" technique is very useful for large data sets and data sets with large numbers of fields.

As I've shown, there are many ways in which URL-encoding and hyperlinks can help turn an application that had little or no interactivity into one that gives users a great deal of control over what data they'll see and how it will be presented to them. Using hyperlinks to turn output into input also reduces development time, and therefore reduces project costs. These techniques show ways to create interesting and interactive presentations of database information.

23

Database Pools and Stored Procedures in Server-Side JavaScript

JJ Kuslich — *application developer, Application Methods, Inc.*

This chapter focuses on database pools and stored procedure access, two important features added to server-side JavaScript with the introduction of Netscape Enterprise Server 3.0. First, I'll describe in detail common design strategies using the `DbPool` object, showing which strategies are appropriate for given development scenarios. I'll also demonstrate some implementation techniques for applying those design strategies to some of the particular design problems. Finally, in the second part of the chapter, I'll discuss some techniques for using stored procedures effectively in your server-side JavaScript applications. It's also important to know how to create cursors with server-side JavaScript; for that I refer you to my *View Source* article "Server-Side JavaScript: Input and Output with HTML Forms," which can be found on the CD-ROM that accompanies this book.

ON THE CD-ROM

Please refer to the *View Source* article "Server-Side JavaScript: Input and Output with HTML Forms," which can be found on the CD-ROM that accompanies this book. It provides a good overview of creating database cursors with server-side JavaScript. It's in the file called "Chapter 23 Input and Output with HTML Forms." Find it by following this path: Sample Code and Supporting Documentation ➪ Part III ➪ Chapter 23.

Wherever appropriate, I'll also point out some tips, tricks, and "gotchas" I've discovered while using server-side JavaScript and Netscape Enterprise Server on projects for some of my commercial clients. You can find the official list of known problems and gotchas on the Netscape Web site at `http://home.netscape.com/eng/server/webserver/3.0/`.

NOTE

The scripting techniques described in this chapter apply only to server-side JavaScript running on Netscape Enterprise Server, version 3 and later. For earlier versions of Netscape Enterprise Server, please refer to the *LiveWire Developer's Guide*, which you can find on the CD-ROM that accompanies this book in the folder with material supporting Chapter 3. You can find it by following this path: Sample Code and Supporting Documentation ➪ Part I ➪ Chapter 3.

Design Strategies for Using Database Pools

The LiveWire Database Service for Netscape Enterprise Server 3.*x* includes a powerful object, DbPool, for creating and maintaining pools of database connections that can coexist. Older versions of the server provided the `database` object for performing similar tasks. There are a number of advantages to using the `DbPool` object over earlier versions of LiveWire, including increased performance. However, the real power of database pools comes from the additional design problems, or scenarios, that you can now address in your applications.

There are a few common strategies for connecting to databases using `DbPool` objects. Table 8.1 from Chapter 8 of *Writing Server-Side JavaScript Applications*, which can be found on the CD-ROM that comes with this book, outlines some of the details of employing the strategies with LiveWire. Before you start to write a LiveWire application, you should take some time to think about how your users will access the application, what level of access they'll require, and other general security and data access issues. Once you've outlined these scenarios, you can apply one or any combination of the strategies mentioned below. Each strategy was derived from real-world approaches to design scenarios similar to ones you're likely to face with your clients. These strategies should give you a good basis for creating good connection and database access designs for your applications.

ON THE CD-ROM

The Netscape document *Writing Server-Side JavaScript Applications* can be found on the CD-ROM that accompanies this book in the folder with materials that support Chapter 3. You can also find the Netscape *LiveWire Developers Guide* in the same place. Follow the path: Sample Code and Supporting Documentation ⇨ Part I ⇨ Chapter 3.

The first strategy listed in the first row of the table deals with the old LiveWire 1.0 strategy for connecting to databases by using the database object. Although it's still valid for the new version of LiveWire, I'm going to discuss only the three new strategies presented in the table and give some more specific information about how to best implement them in your own applications. Table 23-1 shows a mapping of design problems, or scenarios, to recommended connection strategies. Don't forget that the real world often throws more than just one scenario at you, so it's perfectly valid to use a combination of strategies to solve the problem at hand.

TABLE 23-1: DESIGN PROBLEMS AND STRATEGIES

SCENARIO	STRATEGY
Need a connection to a single data source and all application users have same level of access	One global pool per application
Need to connect to more than one data source in the application	Fixed set of global pools per application
Well-defined groups of users (for example, Marketing, Engineering) require different levels of access to the data	
Only a handful of users need connections	
Database access is rare and occurs only on a few pages in the application	One local pool per page

Using a Single Global Pool

This "one connection fits all" strategy uses a single DbPool object, usually created on the application's initial page, to service all database requests. Once you create it, you make the DbPool object persistent by storing it in the project or server object. Unlike earlier versions of server-side JavaScript, Enterprise Server 3.0 allows you to store objects in the project and server objects.

Use this strategy if your application connects only to a single data source and does not require different levels of user permissions. This strategy requires only one user account and set of permissions on the database server. Many Web applications do not use database server security for authenticating individual users of the application; instead, they use a custom solution for user authentication or a Lightweight Directory Access (LDAP) server, like Netscape Directory Server. (See Chapters 4 and 9 of this book for high-level descriptions of LDAP and Netscape Directory Server.) Then, once authenticated, all valid users have the same level of access to the data. Still other applications do not care who the users might be at all and don't have any user authentication process; the users are anonymous. In this case, you would create one generic account on the database server and use that account when creating the pool of connections.

Application Security

Those of you who are security conscious might have already noticed that the connection scheme described in the discussion on creating a fixed set of database pools uses weak security. A sophisticated user or system attacker could bypass the system and gain access to any of the user groups by manipulating and sending back rigged cookie values as if they had already logged on successfully. There are a number of clever ways to improve the security of this scheme if that's necessary. The simplest, brute-force way to ensure security with such a connection strategy is to store only the username and password as client properties and go through the authentication process on every page in the application. The user wouldn't have to physically log in on each page; rather, the application would use the stored username and password to try to log the user on to each page. This way, even if attackers were to fake a cookie value and send an altered username and password, they'd still need to pick a valid username and password. Thus they'd be no better off than trying to hack in through the login screen. Of course, storing passwords in the client variable is not perfectly secure either, depending on the method of client object maintenance you choose. There are other, more efficient ways to enhance the security of the system. However, though security is an important issue, it's not directly relevant to the concepts I'm discussing in this chapter, so I'll set this issue aside for now. The connection strategy being described is perfectly valid without any additional security for many different internal applications where the intent of the login scheme is not to keep intruders out but simply to keep users from accidentally or carelessly altering or viewing sensitive data.

Using a Fixed Set of Global Pools

Some applications require more control over database access than a "one connection fits all" scheme allows. Consider the common scenario of an application that has a few groups of users defined. For example, all Marketing users have the same set of rights over the data, but as a group, Marketing has different permissions from Engineering's. Engineering may have only read-only access to customer data, whereas Marketing has read and write access to the same data. Although you could use server-side JavaScript to design a custom access-control scheme that implements the data access rights, it's more common for such rules to be set at the database server level. Setting them at the database server protects the data from any application that might try to access the data, not just a single application that has implemented the rules. It also eliminates the need to reimplement the rules in every application, or to upgrade every application as the rules change.

There are two common ways to employ user groups for database access. The simplest way is to give all the users in a particular group, such as Human Resources, the username and password for their group account on the database server and use that account to validate users. Another way is to set up a separate list of usernames and passwords for every individual user of the system and associate each individual user account in the application with a group account on the database server. An individual user would log in with his own username and password, the application would validate his user account, and, if successful, it would then secretly log him on to the database server using the database server's group username and password. This second strategy is certainly more secure, since average system users would never know the real username and password that access the database server. However, such security may not always be necessary—in which case simply giving the group username and password to each user in a group may be sufficient.

I'll illustrate how to implement the second strategy. In this scenario, I've created four database pools on the initial page of the application. Three pools are related to each account on the database server that represents the user groups: Marketing, Engineering, and Shipping. A fourth account has special privileges related to user validation, which will be described below.

Table 23-2 shows what the database accounts might look like and what groups they're associated with.

TABLE 23-2: DATABASE SERVER ACCOUNTS

USERNAME	PASSWORD	GROUP
LoginOnly	Pass000	Login
Mktg	Pass123	Marketing
Engr	Pass456	Engineering
Ship	Pass789	Shipping

The connection pools will be stored in an array in the project object and referenced throughout the application to access data. The code in the following example is used on the initial page to create the pools and store them in the project object, indexed in an array simply by their group name.

```
// Create an array of DbPool objects for use throughout the
application.
project.poolArray = new Array();
project.poolArray["Marketing"] = new DbPool("INFORMIX",
"ol_informix", "mktg", "pass123", "applicationDB", 10);
project.poolArray["Engineering"] = new DbPool("INFORMIX",
"ol_informix", "engr", "pass456", "applicationDB", 20);
project.poolArray["Shipping"] = new DbPool("INFORMIX",
"ol_informix", "ship", "pass789", "applicationDB", 3);

// Create one pool for conducting user logins.
// This user account only has SELECT rights on tblUser.
project.poolArray["Login"] = new DbPool("INFORMIX",
"ol_informix", "loginOnly", "pass000", "applicationDB", 1);
```

The fourth pool belongs to a special user account on the database server that will be used *only* for logging individual users in to the system. The account used with this pool has very specific user rights on the database server, which allow it to execute only SQL SELECT statements (read-only) on a single table, tblUser. To be even more security conscious, you could put the SQL query that will look up usernames and passwords into a stored procedure, and give the rights to execute that one stored procedure only to the special login account. This way, the LiveWire application calls the stored procedure and has no direct access to the tables until a user is validated. Table 23-3 contains a list of usernames and passwords for each of the individual users of the system, and also contains the name of the group (for example, Marketing) to which the user belongs.

TABLE 23-3: DATA IN TBLUSER

USERNAME	PASSWORD	GROUP
SallyR	Sal1	Marketing
JoeB	Joe2	Engineering
DaleS	Dale1	Shipping

When individual users log in, the application looks in tblUser to find a matching username and password. If one is found, the application uses the associated group name to find the pool in the array of DbPool objects that has the matching connection and privileges for that user.

The next example shows how the login process works. This process takes place using two pages: loginform.html and loginhandler.html. The page loginform.html contains an HTML form that lets a user log in to the system. When the user clicks the Submit button, the username and password are passed to loginhandler.html, which actually conducts the login process. Using the configuration described, the loginhandler.html page will use the code in the example to perform user validation.

```
// Validate users using the "secret" account on the database
server.

// Get a connection from that pool.
loginConn = project.poolArray["Login"].connection();

// Create a cursor on tblUser using the username and
// password entered by the user from loginform.html.
// If the username and password are valid, the cursor
// should contain one row. If either one is invalid,
// the cursor will contain no rows, indicating a failed
// login attempt.
var sql = "SELECT group FROM tblUser WHERE username='" +
          request.username +
          "' AND password='" +
          request.password + "'";
loginCursor = loginConn.cursor(sql);

// If no record was found, the login was invalid so redirect
to an error page.
// Otherwise, redirect to the application's main menu page.
if (!loginCursor.next())
    redirectPage = "Error.html";
else {
```

```
    // Assign group name to client property
    client.group = loginCursor.group;
    redirectPage = "MainAppForm.html";
}


// Clean up database connections
loginCursor.close();
loginConn.release();
loginPool.disconnect();

// Redirect based upon login attempt.
redirect(redirectPage);
```

The application then stores the group name retrieved from the secret login process in a property of the client object and uses it on any subsequent pages in the application as an index to find the appropriate connection pool in the project object. For example, for any given page in the application, grabbing a connection for previously validated Marketing user SallyR would set client.group = "Marketing". The code would grab a connection from the database, as shown in the next example.

```
// Grab a connection to the database
pageConn = project.poolArray[client.group].connection();
custCursor = pageConn.cursor("select * from tblCustomers");

// ... do things with the cursor
custCursor.close();
pageConn.release();
```

Another valid development scenario for which you could employ the connection grouping strategy would be applications that talk to multiple database servers, possibly even servers of different types (for example, Informix, Oracle, and so on). In such a scenario, you could establish one pool of connections for each database server, or you could choose to have groups of connections for each different database server. Whichever the case, some variation of the connection grouping strategy can also be employed to support the multiple database server scenario.

Using One Local Connection per Page

Some of your applications might call for using a separate connection pool either for every user or for every page of the application. Perhaps each user of your system requires slightly different access rights on the database server, so you need to make sure that each page of the application uses the account associated with the current user. Perhaps the application rarely accesses the database — and even then, only on a few pages. Rather than opening a pool on the initial page and keeping it open for the entire application, you can create a pool only on the pages that require a database connection.

For these scenarios, you'll want to create and disconnect the connection pool on every page that requires database access. The manual *Writing Server-Side JavaScript Applications* describes how to implement this scenario, so I won't rehash that material here. The second example above (beginning with the comment 'Validate users using the "secret" account on the database server') also uses this strategy in part to perform the secret login. Suffice it to say that this strategy is fairly simple to implement, though it's also the least efficient strategy in terms of performance. Repeating the creation of a connection pool every time a user hits a page requiring database access can be expensive. For this reason, you should avoid this strategy for heavily accessed pages when possible.

Connection Strategies Summarized

Three connection strategies really do cover a number of different scenarios you may come across when you design Web database applications. Don't forget that the strategies can be applied in combination, and even with slight modifications, to cover even more scenarios. For instance, for the single global connection scenario, you don't have to create the pool on the initial page; you could create it on some other page in the application. Just be careful in such a case that you apply locking properly to avoid deadlock situations when multiple users hit the same page simultaneously. When connecting on the initial page, you don't have to worry about locking because the initial page is fired only upon application or Web server initialization.

Calling Stored Procedures

Along with database pools, the ability to call stored procedures using server-side JavaScript on Netscape Enterprise Server 3.0 and later warrants a more in-depth discussion. Any client-server developer will tell you that stored procedures are necessary parts of most client-server applications. They are reusable, they run on the database server (freeing up resources on your Web server), and they offer good performance. Because stored procedures are compiled inside the database server, they'll execute faster than an SQL query, which the database server will have to interpret before it can execute it. They're also a great tool for automatically implementing integrity rules on the server. Many of you will write LiveWire applications to access legacy databases, and you might run into databases that already have oodles of stored procedures implemented. With Enterprise Server 3.0, you can take advantage of those stored procedures and do true client-server development for the Internet or intranets.

The hardest part about using stored procedures with LiveWire will probably be writing the stored procedures themselves. Once you have the stored procedures, using them in server-side JavaScript applications is straightforward, provided you follow the rules outlined in Chapter 9 of *Writing Server-Side JavaScript Applications*. Some of the rules for setting up the stored procedures and retrieving data from them change depending on what database server you're using, so make sure you understand the requirements of your particular database server(s) before writing your code.

Note that all the examples on stored procedures assume Informix as the database server. Refer to Chapter 9 of *Writing Server-Side JavaScript Applications* for specific rules that apply to stored procedures for other database servers.

Calling a Stored Procedure

To use any results from a stored procedure, you must first execute it. For stored procedures that return no data, this is generally the only step required. Executing a stored procedure through LiveWire is a very simple process: All you need to know are the name of the stored procedure and the input parameters, and you have enough knowledge to run the stored procedure successfully. The code below is all that is necessary to call the stored procedure `spGetEmployees()` with parameters `departmentID` and `managerName`.

```
// assume dbconn is a valid connection object connected
to an Informix database
departmentID = 7;
managerName = "JJ Kuslich";
spEmps = dbconn.storedProc("spGetEmployees", departmentID,
managerName);
```

Take note that data types matter when you pass in parameters to the stored procedure. If you pass in the string ' 7 ' instead of the number 7 for the `empID` value, and `empID` has an Integer data type in the stored procedure definition, you could receive an error from your database server reporting the data type mismatch.

Note also that some database servers forgive data type mismatches more than others do. Informix gives an error message for mismatched data types; other servers might not care. In general, it's better to follow good programming practice and use the right data types. You should also pay attention to data types if there's a chance your application might need to switch database servers at some point in the future, or if you're accessing multiple database types in the same application.

Retrieving Data from a Stored Procedure

For stored procedures that return values during their execution, one or two more steps are necessary after you create the `storedProc` object to squeeze out all the information returned. There are three places you can look for returned values: return values, output parameters, and result sets. Because return values and output parameters aren't used by all databases (and, frankly, because using them isn't as interesting as using result sets), I'm going to discuss only what you can do with result sets. You can find detailed information about return values and output parameters in *Writing Server-Side JavaScript Applications.*

Result sets are extremely similar to LiveWire cursors. Aside from the fact that result sets are read-only (that is, they aren't updateable), they behave exactly like cursors. You may think that the similarity makes them unusually boring because you already know everything about cursors; however, I think you'll find them very interesting if you consider the possibilities for writing routines that work for both cursors and result sets. Everyone knows that code reuse leads to shorter development cycles, lower costs, and happier programmers. Let me describe exactly how result sets work, and you'll see just how similar they are to cursors.

You create `resultSet` objects very simply by calling the `resultSet()` method of the `storedProc` object. For instance, continuing with the code snippet above, suppose that the `spGetEmployees()` stored procedure returns the names of every employee in the given department who works for a given manager. After creating the `storedProc` object, you could retrieve the results in a `resultSet` object with the following line of code:

```
rsEmployees = spGetEmps.resultSet();
```

After this statement is executed, any rows returned by the stored procedure will be stored in the `resultSet` object, `rsEmployees`. From this point on, you use the `resultSet` object in exactly the same way you would use a cursor.

- You use the `next()` method to advance the `resultSet` object through the records.

- You must advance the `resultSet` object once to initialize it, because just after creation, the `resultSet` object points to the position just before the first record in the set.

- When you reach the end of the set, `next()` returns false.

- When you're done with the `resultSet` object, call its `close()` method and reclaim the resources it was using.

The `resultSet` object behaves exactly like a `cursor` object. The only real differences between the two are that they are created in different ways, and the resultSet object is read-only. You cannot assign values to any `resultSet` values. For instance, the assignment statement `rsEmployees.empID = 7` would not assign the value 7 to the property `resultSet.empID`; it would simply have no effect.

Depending on what database server you're using, you might find one more odd difference between `resultSet` objects and cursors. With Informix and DB2, you cannot refer to properties of the `resultSet` object by column name but instead must refer to them by their index. For these databases, the order of the returned columns matters, and adds another potential source of bugs in your code that you have to watch out for. The next two code examples illustrate the effects of this restriction. (With all other supported databases, you can use column names and ignore their order in the result set.)

Suppose that the stored procedure spGetEmployees() returns a result set containing the employee ID (empID), employee name (empName), and employee phone number (empPhone), in that order, for every employee in the given department who works for a given manager. If the procedure were written in Oracle, Microsoft SQL Server, or Sybase, you would use the code in the following example to display the results.

```
// Assume dbconn is a valid connection object created at
some earlier stage
// Get all employees in department 7 who work for manager
Joe Jackson

spGetEmp = dbconn.storedProc("spGetEmployees", 7, "Joe
Jackson");
rsEmps = spGetEmp.resultSet();
while(rsEmps.next()) {
    write("ID: " + rsEmps.empID + "<BR>");
    write("Name: " + rsEmps.empName + "<BR>");
    write("Phone: " + rsEmps.empPhone + "<BR>");
}

rsEmps.close();
```

Suppose you want to perform exactly the same operation as in this example, but for a stored procedure written for Informix. You would have to change the three bold lines above to the following:

```
write("ID: " + rsEmps[0] + "<BR>");
write("Name: " + rsEmps[1] + "<BR>");
write("Phone: " + rsEmps[2] + "<BR>");
```

I highly recommend creating constants at the beginning of your code to represent the index values of the returned columns. Using constants will make your code more readable by associating meaningful identifier names with meaningless column index numbers. Also, if a column ever changed positions because of a change in the stored procedure, you would have to change every reference to that column if you refer to it directly. If you use constants instead, you need to change the index value only once for the assignment of the index to the constant. The next example shows how you could use constants to improve the code from the snippet just above:

```
// Create "constants" to represent column index values
var EMPID = 0;
var EMPNAME = 1;
var EMPPHONE = 2;


// dbconn is a valid connection object created at some
earlier stage
// Get all employees in department 7 who work for manager
Joe Jackson
spGetEmp = dbconn.storedProc("spGetEmployees", 7, "Joe
Jackson");
rsEmps = spGetEmp.resultSet();


while(rsEmps.next()) {
   write("ID: " + rsEmps[EMPID] + "<BR>");
   write("Name: " + rsEmps[EMPNAME] + "<BR>");
   write("Phone: " + rsEmps[EMPPHONE] + "<BR>");
}


rsEmps.close();
```

I think you'll agree that the code in this example is much more readable than the code that used numbers to reference the columns. Were this a larger piece of code, where the return values were referred to several times, I think you would also agree that if the positions of the columns were ever to change, it would be much more convenient and much less error-prone to simply replace the index values in the constants than to change the values at every reference point.

Of course, JavaScript doesn't really have constants. I'm just using normal JavaScript identifiers and the concept of constants. Using all capital letters visually differentiates my pseudo-constants from normal identifiers and lets me know that I should never be changing the value of those particular identifiers anywhere in my code other than where they are defined. It's not foolproof, but I've found that it works well as a way to introduce pseudo-constants into JavaScript.

Another limitation of LiveWire to be aware of is that resultSet objects cannot be nested with all database servers; in other words, you cannot have more than

one open at a time. So, for example, the code in the next example, which uses a
nested while loop structure, would not work in LiveWire with Informix.

```
// THIS CODE WILL NOT WORK IN LIVEWIRE RUNNING AGAINST
INFORMIX BECAUSE IT NESTS RESULTSET OBJECTS.
// Assume dbconn is a valid connection object created at
some earlier stage
// Get all departments for the company Application Methods
spGetDept = dbconn.storedProc("spGetDepartments",
"Application Methods Inc.");
rsDept = spGetDept.resultSet();

// Loop through all departments and display employee
information for each
while(rsDept.next()) {

    // Get all employees in the particular department
    spGetEmp = dbconn.storedProc("spGetEmployees",
rsDept.deptID);
    rsEmps = spGetEmp.resultSet();

    // Loop through and write out employee information
    while(rsEmps.next()) {
        write("ID: " + rsEmps.empID + "<BR>");
        write("Name: " + rsEmps.empName + "<BR>");
        write("Phone: " + rsEmps.empPhone + "<BR>");
    } // end inner while loop
    rsEmps.close();

} // end outer while loop

rsDept.close();
```

To work around this limitation, you could preload the data from the inner loop into an array structure and then loop through the array in the inner loop instead of the `resultSet` object. To be more efficient about it, you could better handle the case above by simply using a different stored procedure that performs a join on the Employee and Department tables and returns a single result set that contains all the employees for a given department. In general, you'll want to look for this type of workaround rather than trying to implement a potentially inefficient kludge in server-side JavaScript.

A Launching Pad for Solving Real-World Problems

When you put your knowledge of cursors together with what you've learned about `DbPool` and stored procedure access, you'll have the knowledge you need to create powerful, scalable solutions using Netscape Enterprise Server 3.0 and LiveWire. As I've shown, you can have an expanded world of choices for connecting to a database from LiveWire with the new `DbPool` object. Cursors give you control over output from SQL queries and give you a convenient way to update data. Accessing stored procedures gives your application scalability, performance, and code reuse across applications for building industrial-strength client-server applications for the Internet or intranets. The techniques described here — like those shown throughout this book — give you a launching pad for solving your real-world business problems through the effective use of Netscape tools and appropriate design strategies.

24

Changing a Web Application's Look and Feel without Touching the Source Code

Glen Long — *consultant, The Thomson Technology Consulting Group*

W eb publishing has come a long way since the days of static HTML. Technologies such as Netscape's *server-side JavaScript* (SSJS) make it possible to develop highly dynamic sites that not only pull the very latest information directly from a database, but also tailor the presentation of that information to the needs of the individual user. New services can be prototyped, developed, and deployed quickly in a highly scalable environment. As developers for the Web, we've never had it so good.

But if there's one thing I miss about static HTML, it's the immediacy of it. I could simply edit a file, press "Reload" on the browser, and see the changes. No recompile, no restart; just a reload. With SSJS, there's a price to pay for dynamic content: a simple change to the presentation requires a change to the application source and a recompile. This can be a real bottleneck if the person writing the code isn't the person designing the presentation. Certainly the two skills are different enough that it doesn't make sense to have one highly dependent on the other. If nothing else, it's not very conducive to teamwork to require an application rebuild every time someone wants to test a change to the HTML!

I believe there's an elegant solution to this situation — and that solution is presentation templates. With presentation templates, developers can have the best of both worlds, by separating the look and feel of an application from the programming logic that generates the content. Then changes to the presentation can be made by design experts, without requiring any time from the programmer. This chapter will show you how to do this.

Application Logic Versus Presentation Logic

At design time, it's usually fairly simple to separate the concepts of *application logic* and *presentation logic*. Application logic is all about interacting with databases, performing calculations, iterating over data sets, and so on. Presentation logic deals with things like menus, list boxes, buttons, and wizards. In other words, application logic determines what the application does, and presentation logic determines what it looks like.

Unfortunately, clear though this separation may appear during design, it's often surprisingly tricky to preserve through the development phase. The code for the application logic becomes entwined with the code for the presentation, and the two become dependent in a way that feels unnecessary and yet somehow unavoidable.

Heavily object-oriented systems can alleviate this problem by making use of the model / view / controller (MVC) design pattern, which originated with Smalltalk-80. This divides the presentation aspect further into view (the basic on-screen appearance) and controller (how the interface reacts to user input). The view tries to ensure that the appearance reflects the current state of the model, while the controller allows the model to be manipulated via the interface. Many user interface gurus advocate the MVC approach to GUI design, which encapsulates the presentation in the view object to increase flexibility and reuse; in fact, the JDK 1.2 offers a pluggable look and feel.

This said, a full MVC approach isn't really appropriate for form-based Internet applications. The Web is inherently less interactive than a traditional desktop application, and this tends to diminish the role of the controller. And since Web applications are essentially client-pull, the client view can't easily be notified of changes to the server model (as is the case with MVC) — the client can simply request the current state of the model. Still, a pragmatic approach that borrows some of the simpler concepts of the MVC pattern (such as separating the logic from the presentation) and translates them to the development environment of choice can yield some genuine benefits without the overhead of a more complete strategy.

Separating the look and feel of an application from the programming logic makes a lot of sense for all but the most basic of applications — and it makes for a cleaner design, promotes a more parallel style of development, and means that a change to one component is less likely to require a change to the other. Server-side JavaScript provides a framework in which it's simple to implement such a mechanism and apply it either selectively or across all applications.

The Anatomy of an SSJS Application

Let's start with a quick refresher on the anatomy of an SSJS application.

The source for an application can comprise both HTML (.html) files and JavaScript (.js) files, and these are compiled into a single object (.web) file. The HTML files generally correspond to the actual pages of the application (the presentation logic), and the JavaScript files contain standalone functions that can be called from any page (the application logic).

Embedding JavaScript code and function calls into HTML pages is easy — you just use the <SERVER> tag. Code is executed by the server, and the client sees only the results.

Here's a simple example that calls a JavaScript function to obtain a message for the day:

```
<H2>Message of the Day</H2>
<SERVER>
    var today = new Date();
    write(getMessageOfTheDay(today));
</SERVER>
```

This results in the following HTML being sent to the client:

```
<H2>Message of the Day</H2>
Only 127 shoppings days left until Christmas!
```

This is all well and good for relatively simple applications, but for really dynamic pages we often need to do the reverse — that is, embed HTML code inside the JavaScript. And the most obvious way to do this — using the `write()` function to explicitly print the required HTML — is rather less elegant.

Consider the example shown in Figure 24-1, a simple list of "to do" items generated from a database. The code used to generate this example follows the figure.

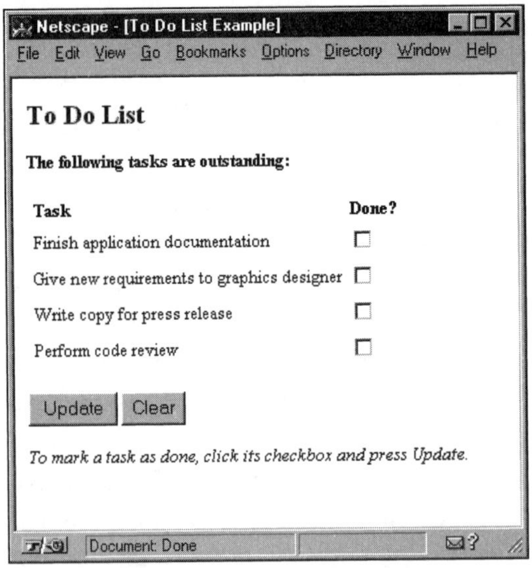

Figure 24-1: A simple To Do List application

```
<HTML>
<HEAD>
<TITLE>To Do List Example</TITLE>
</HEAD>
<BODY BGCOLOR="#FFFFFF">
<H2>To Do List</H2>
<TABLE>
<TR>
<TD><B>Task</B></TD><TD><B>Done?</B&g
t;</TD>
</TR>
<FORM>
<SERVER>
    cursor = database.cursor("SELECT id, task FROM ToDo");
    while (cursor.next()) {
        write("<TR>");
        write("<TD>" + cursor.task + "</TD>");
        write("<TD>");
        write("<INPUT TYPE=\"checkbox\" NAME=\"done\"");
        write(" VALUE=\"" + cursor.id + "\">");
        write("</TD>");
        write("</TR>\n");
    }
    cursor.close();
</SERVER>

</TABLE>
<BR>
<INPUT TYPE="submit" VALUE="Update">
<INPUT TYPE="submit" VALUE="Clear">
</FORM>
</BODY>
</HTML>
```

See how quickly things start to get messy? The HTML is a pain to type (I hate escaping all those quotes!) and a real struggle to read and maintain. The look and feel is so tightly woven into the application logic that each is obscured by the other.

It's not easy to work out what the JavaScript or the HTML is trying to achieve. And, as mentioned earlier, a simple change to the presentation — such as underlining the items in the list, say — requires a change to the application source and a recompile.

So why not separate the look and feel from the application logic? Server-side JavaScript makes some provision for this by allowing functions (the application logic) to be broken out into JavaScript source (.js) files, leaving mainly HTML (the presentation logic) in .html files. Unfortunately, it's inevitable that some application logic will have to remain in the .html files. (One obvious example is the while() loop required to bring multiple rows back from a database cursor.)

The solution is to pull as much HTML as possible out of the application source and put it into presentation templates instead.

Introducing Presentation Templates

Presentation templates are essentially logical chunks of HTML that live in their own directory, completely outside of the compiled application. The application refers to them by name, and then a simple mechanism (an object called a template engine, which I'll explain in a minute) ensures that the required template is loaded into memory and populated with the required data. This is achieved by allowing templates to contain not only the standard HTML tags but also special placeholder tags to indicate where the dynamic information should be inserted.

Here's an example of what a very simple template might look like. (Remember our message of the day earlier on?) This template has a single placeholder for the message text.

```
<H2>Message of the Day</H2>
<%message_of_the_day%>
```

To display the message differently, we would just change the template:

```
<TABLE>
<TR>
<TD><IMG SRC="motdlogo.gif"></TD>
<TD><%message_of_the_day%></TD>
</TR>
</TABLE>
```

Note that in these example templates, the placeholder tags have the form `<%property_name%>`. There's nothing special about the use of `<%` and `%>` to delimit the tags — it's just the syntax that I've chosen.

But where do the values that replace the placeholders come from? They're explicitly passed into the function that expands the template. SSJS provides a very convenient mechanism for passing around key-value pairs: they can be stored as properties on an object.

What, you ask, is the function for expanding templates? It's actually a method belonging to a custom JavaScript object, which I'll now describe.

The TemplateEngine Object

The functionality that supports presentation templates is provided by an object that I've called `TemplateEngine`. `TemplateEngine` is a lightweight (that is, fairly simple) JavaScript object that "knows" the following things:

- Where to look for templates
- How to populate a specific template, given a set of properties

I'll describe how to create and use the object, and then I'll show you the source code so that you can use it in your own applications.

Creating a Template Engine

A template engine is created as follows:

```
engine = new TemplateEngine("\data\templates");
```

This particular engine will expect to find its templates in the directory /data/templates. (The examples in this chapter assume a UNIX platform and file paths, but all code will convert trivially to NT.)

Populating a Template

An individual template is expanded using the expand method of the new object:

```
expanded_html = engine.expand("MyTemplate", props);
```

`MyTemplate.html` is a file in /data/templates and props is a JavaScript object that holds the properties required to populate the template.

Using the Properties Object

The use of an object to store properties is a fairly succinct way of passing a set of keys and associated values to a method. Sometimes it's necessary to create a transient object specifically for the purpose of passing template properties, as in the following example:

```
for (x=1; x < 10; x++) {
    var obj = new Object();
    obj.x = x;
    obj.x_squared = x * x;
    obj.x_cubed = x * x * x;
    write(engine.expand("SquaredAndCubed", obj));
}
```

This short code fragment generates the squares and cubes of the integers from 1 to 10. The template `SquaredAndCubed.html` might contain the following:

```
When x is <%x%>, x squared is <%x_squared%> and x cubed is
<%x_cubed%>. <BR>
```

On other occasions, the properties object comes for free in the form of an object that already exists — a JavaScript cursor, for example:

```
var cursor = database.cursor("SELECT * FROM MyTable");
while (cursor.next()) {
    write(engine.expand("MyTemplate", cursor));
}
cursor.close();
```

Other possible "freebie" objects are the request, project, and server objects.

Creating Template Directory Paths

When you create a template engine, you don't have to pass just one template directory; you can pass an entire directory path (separated by colons, UNIX-style):

```
engine = new TemplateEngine("/dir1:/dir2:/dir3");
```

When you call expand( ), the engine will look first in dir1, then dir2, and so on until it finds the template you requested. This capability enables a useful strategy for getting a consistent look and feel across applications while preserving customized aspects of individual applications, which I'll discuss a little later.

Template Caching and Verbose Mode

Template caching and verbose mode are useful features of the TemplateEngine object.

By default, templates are cached in memory the first time they're requested. This is obviously more efficient than loading them from disk each time (okay — so they probably get cached by the OS anyway, but bear with me). However, it does mean that any changes to templates are reflected only after an application restart.

During the development phase, you can force templates to be loaded on each request:

```
engine.setCaching(false);
```

In verbose mode, headers and footers that give the template name as an HTML comment are added to each expanded template:

```
<!-- Start of template: SquaredAndCubed.html -->
When x is 3, x squared is 9 and x cubed is 27. <BR>
<!-- End of template: SquaredAndCubed.html -->
```

This can be useful for debugging purposes and is enabled with

```
engine.setVerbose(true);
```

And Now, the Source Code

Here's the code for the TemplateEngine object:

```
// Constructs a new TemplateEngine object that
looks for templates
// in the given path.
// Example: engine = new TemplateEngine("/dir1:/dir2");
```

```
function TemplateEngine (path) {
    this.path = path.split(":");
    this.cache = new Object();
    this.caching = true;
    this.verbose = true;

    this.expand = TemplateEngine_expand;
    this.load = TemplateEngine_load;
    this.setCaching = TemplateEngine_setCaching;
    this.setVerbose = TemplateEngine_setVerbose;
}


// Method on the TemplateEngine object that returns
the result of
// expanding the specified template using the specified
properties.
// Example: expanded = engine.expand("MyTemplate", myprops);

function TemplateEngine_expand (template, props) {
    // If we're not caching, just try to load the template.
    if (!this.caching) {
        html = this.load(template);
    }
    else {
        // Try to fetch the template from the cache.
        html = this.cache[template];

        // Perhaps this is the first time it has been
requested.
        if (html == null) {
            // Try to load the template and cache it.
            html = this.load(template);
            if (html != null) {
                this.cache[template] = html;
            }
        }
    }
}
```

```
    // If the template could not be found, just return null.
    if (html == null) {
        return null;
    }

    // If no properties have been supplied, create an empty
object.
    if (props == null) {
        props = new Object();
    }

    // Define the regular expression for the placeholder
tags.
    re = /<%\s*(\w+)\s*%>/;

    // Defensive programming - keep a counter to avoid
infinite loops.
    counter = 0;

    // Expand the template...
    while(re.test(html)) {
        if (counter++ > 1000) { return html; }

        // Get an array of matches
        matches = re.exec(html);
        // Extract the matched text and the property name.
        match = matches[0];
        property = matches[1];

        // Fetch the property value from the properties
object.
        value = props[property];

        // If the property wasn't found, use an empty
string.
        if (value == null) {
```

```
            value = "";
        }

        // Finally, replace the placeholder tag with the
value.
        html = html.replace(match, value);
    }


    // If we're in verbose mode, display some comments.
        if (this.verbose) {
            header = "<!-- Start of template: " + template +
" -->\n";

            footer = "<!-- End of template: " + template + "
-->\n";

            return header + html + footer;
        }
        else {
        return html;
    }
}


// "Private" method on the TemplateEngine object that
searches the
// template path for the given template and returns the
contents of
// the first match. This method need not be called
explicitly, but it
// will need to be changed if running under NT.

function TemplateEngine_load (template) {
    // Try to load the template from directories in the
path.
    for (i = 0; i < this.path.length; i++) {
        dir = this.path[i];
```

```
            // Note Unix-style path...
            filename = dir + "/" + template + ".html";
            contents = getFileContents(filename);

            if (contents != null) {
                return contents;
            }
        }

    return null;
}

// Method on the TemplateEngine object that sets the caching
policy.
// Example: engine.setCaching(true);

function TemplateEngine_setCaching (bool) {
    this.caching = bool;
}

// Method on the TemplateEngine object that sets
verbose mode.
// Example: engine.setVerbose(false);

function TemplateEngine_setVerbose (bool) {
    this.verbose = bool;
}

// Utility function that returns the contents of the
given file
// as a string.
// Example: contents = getFileContents("myfile.txt");

function getFileContents (filename) {
        // Open the file for reading.
        var file = new File(filename);
        var success = file.open("r");
```

```
        // If the file open succeeded, read the contents
line by line
        if (success) {
                contents = "";

                while (!file.eof()) {
                        contents += file.readln() + "\n";
                }
                file.close();
                return contents;
        }
        else {
                return null;
        }
}
```

A Design Strategy for Templates

I've been using templates in my applications for a while, and it seems to work well to have a single template engine for each application that's reused across the pages. This can be neatly achieved by creating a `TemplateEngine` object in the application's initial file and storing it on the project object, thus:

```
project.TEMPLATE_ENGINE = new
TemplateEngine("/appdir:/globaldir");
```

The engine is then created once, when the application is started, and is available for use by all pages in the application. Building on this idea, I've created a helper function called EXPAND (shown in the next long code example) that implicitly uses this stored object and helps make the syntax for expanding templates a bit cleaner. So instead of

```
write(project.TEMPLATE_ENGINE.expand("MyTemplate", props));
```

you can simply use

```
write(EXPAND("MyTemplate", props));
```

The EXPAND() function also generates helpful warnings if the project template engine hasn't been created or if a requested template can't be found. Here's the function itself:

```
// Helper function that returns the result of
expanding the given
// template using the given properties. Assumes that a
TemplateEngine
// object has already been created and stored on the project
object.
// Example: expanded = EXPAND("MyTemplate", myprops);

function EXPAND (template, props) {
    // Check that the project template engine has been
created.
    if (project.TEMPLATE_ENGINE == null) {
        write("Warning: project.TEMPLATE_ENGINE has not been
set");
    }

    // Try to expand the template.
    expanded = project.TEMPLATE_ENGINE.expand(template,
props);

    // Check that the template was found.
    if (expanded == null) {
        write("Warning: template " + template + " could not
be found");
    }
    return expanded;
}
```

Getting a Consistent Look and Feel Across Applications

I said earlier that the ability to pass a directory path when creating a template engine can enable a strategy to get a consistent look and feel across applications while preserving customized aspects of individual applications.

Consider a dynamic site consisting of a number of separate applications. Some elements of the presentation that could all live quite happily in template files will be common to all of the applications — headers and footers, copyright messages, graphical banners, and so on. But there will also be some templates that will be specific to the individual applications.

Here's the clever bit. We can store the sitewide templates in one directory, say /data/templates/global, and the application-specific templates in a separate directory, one for each application, say /data/templates/myapp. When we create the template engine for an application, we'll tell it to look in the application-specific directory first and then the global one:

```
engine = new

TemplateEngine("/data/templates/myapp:/data/templates/global
");
```

So the application-specific templates will be used in preference to the global ones where the names are the same. To put it another way, you now have a templating mechanism that exhibits object-oriented behavior, where specific templates can be used to override more general ones where necessary.

A Simple Example

In this last section, I'll add templating to the To Do List example shown in Figure 24-1 to show what a simple templated application might look like. We'll see how easy it is to create a very different look for the application with a few changes to the templates. The application code isn't complete enough to compile (you'd need the right tables in your database anyway) but should help to demonstrate the key concepts in practice.

The application source, shown in the next example, consists of `initial.html` (the initial file) and `todo.html`. Other files are implicit: a file that contains the code for `TemplateEngine` and the `EXPAND` function, and the file update.html, which is the target for the `POST`ed form.

`initial.html`

```
<SERVER>
    path = "/templates/todo:/templates/global";
    project.TEMPLATE_ENGINE = new TemplateEngine(path);
</SERVER>
```

`todo.html`

```
<SERVER>
    write(EXPAND("HTMLHeader"));
    write(EXPAND("PageHeader"));
    write(EXPAND("ToDoListStart"));
    cursor = database.cursor("SELECT task, id FROM ToDo");
    while (cursor.next()) {
        write(EXPAND("ToDoListItem", cursor));
    }
    cursor.close();
    write(EXPAND("ToDoListEnd"));
    write(EXPAND("PageFooter"));
    write(EXPAND("HTMLFooter"));
</SERVER>
```

The templates, shown in following code example, are `HTMLHeader`, `PageHeader`, `ToDoListStart`, `ToDoListItem`, `ToDoListEnd`, `PageFooter`, and `HTMLFooter`. `HTMLHeader` and `HTMLFooter` will probably be stored in the global template directory, whereas the rest are application specific.

Notice that all the HTML sits outside the application and can be modified without affecting the compiled application. Any or all of the templates can be modified to change the look and feel of the application. For example, to change how the application's footer looks, you would simply change the `HTMLFooter` template. I'll demonstrate how to modify a few of the templates to completely change the way our To Do List looks.

HTMLHeader.html

```
<HTML>
<HEAD>
<TITLE>To Do List Example</TITLE>
</HEAD>
<BODY BGCOLOR="#FFFFFF">
```

PageHeader.html

```
<H2>Task Manager</H2>
<B>The following tasks are outstanding:</B>
<P>
<FORM ACTION="update.html" METHOD="POST">
```

ToDoListStart.html

```
<TABLE>
<TR>
<TD><B>Task</B></TD>
<TD><B>Done?</B></TD>
</TR>
```

ToDoListItem.html

```
<TR>
<TD><U><%task%></U></TD>
<TD><INPUT TYPE="checkbox" NAME="done"
VALUE="<%id%>"></TD>
</TR>
```

ToDoListEnd.html

```
</TABLE>
```

PageFooter.html

```
<BR>
<INPUT TYPE="submit" VALUE="Update">
<INPUT TYPE="reset" VALUE="Clear">
</FORM>
<I>To mark a task as done, click its checkbox and press
Update.</I>
```

```
HTMLFooter.html
```

```
</BODY>
</HTML>
```

The whole page will look just like the one you've already seen in Figure 24-1.

So let's say we fancy giving the application a bit of a facelift. Instead of a table, we'd like to present the tasks as an ordered list. We'd also like to show the priority for each task (which we know to be one of the available fields in the ToDo database table). It would also be nice to make the whole thing look a little less conservative. We need make only a few template changes, as shown in this example:

```
HTMLHeader.html
```

```
<HTML>
<HEAD>
<TITLE>To Do List Example</TITLE>
</HEAD>
<BODY BGCOLOR="#80FFFF">
```

```
PageHeader.html
```

```
<FONT FACE="Arial" SIZE="+2"><U>To Do
List</U></FONT><P>
<B>The following tasks are outstanding:</B>
<P>
<FORM ACTION="update.html" METHOD="POST">
```

```
ToDoListStart.html
```

```
<OL>
```

```
ToDoListItem.html

<LI> <FONT FACE="Arial" SIZE="-1"><%task%>
[<%priority%>] </FONT>
<INPUT TYPE="checkbox" NAME="done" VALUE="<%id%>">

ToDoListEnd.html
</OL>
HTMLFooter.html

<P>
<CENTER>
Copyright &copy; 1998 Template Enabled Design Ltd.
</CENTER>
</BODY>
</HTML>
```

After these changes, the same page would look more like Figure 24-2.

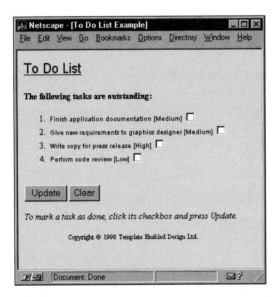

Figure 24-2: A new look for our To Do List application

Thus, we've given the page a whole new look without having to change a single line of application code. We just edit the templates, restart the application, and reload the page.

Simplifying User Interface Design

Separating an application's presentation logic from its application logic by using templates means that maintaining the look and feel of a dynamic application becomes a much more lightweight process. The application developer needs to be involved only when a functional change is required (which is as it should be). And the user interface designer can make changes to the presentation and see the results almost immediately. Life is suddenly much simpler.

In fact, almost as simple as it was in the days when static HTML ruled the Web.

## 25

Form Data Handling in Server-Side JavaScript

Robert Husted — *intranet technical lead, Qwest Communications*

I n Chapter 19, Duane Fields explored the subject of using client-side JavaScript to handle data from HTML-based forms. In this chapter, I'll explore using server-side JavaScript for tasks related to handling form data.

One application that seems to appear on every Web site is the form-data handler Common Gateway Interface (CGI). This CGI collects data from a form submission, packs it into an e-mail message, and ships it to someone in the company or organization. CGIs are used instead of simple `mailto` commands to ensure that required fields have been entered and to provide some sort of feedback to the user, indicating that the submitted data has been received. The example SSJS application discussed in this chapter can replace a large number of these existing CGIs on your Web site, giving you the following benefits:

- Central control of data submitted via forms on your Web site. You need to change the code in only one place to make a change to the way all forms are handled on your site.

- Easy creation of additional e-mail-enabled forms. Since the functionality of the application is controlled by the calling form, no additional programming is required. Anyone on the site can create an e-mail-enabled form that instantly conforms to company standards. This gives the IS department greater control over the way form data is collected, routed, and stored on the site.

- An ability to send HTML-formatted e-mail. The server-side JavaScript SendMail object, which we'll use in this chapter's sample application, makes it easy to send HTML-formatted e-mail, so you can mail the form data in a rich text format.

- Fewer CGIs on your site. Nobody likes an unruly Web site; you can eliminate up to 80 percent of the CGIs on your site by using this one application.

- Easy-to-maintain code. Perl, because of its extreme flexibility in syntax, is generally difficult to read and maintain, while JavaScript's syntax is similar to those of the popular C/C++ and Java languages, all of which are easily maintained.

NOTE
The SendMail object works with Netscape Enterprise Server, version 3.x and later.

Introducing the SendMail Object

I used the server-side JavaScript SendMail object to create the example application described in this chapter. For those of you interested in getting started immediately with this new object, here is the syntax for sending a basic e-mail message:

```
var msg     = new SendMail();           // CREATE SENDMAIL
OBJECT
```

```
msg.To       = "john@doughboy.com";    // RECIPIENT OF
MESSAGE
msg.From     = "bill@company.com";     // SENDER OF MESSAGE
msg.Subject = "Hawaii Sweepstakes";    // SUBJECT OF MESSAGE
msg.Body     = "Hey John, you WON!";   // BODY OF MESSAGE
msg.send;                              // SEND THE E-MAIL
MESSAGE
```

The `SendMail` object will be explained in more detail below. For now we'll focus on what you can do with this new object. You can use it to easily send e-mail directly from your SSJS application. For example, you could do any of the following with the `SendMail` object:

- Send form data via e-mail (the example application accomplishes this task).

- Send notifications to managers about all open Purchase Orders in a database.

- Send out a weekly departmental newsletter in HTML format.

- Send a quarterly feedback form to all company employees—and a daily "tickler" to all employees who have not yet filled out the form.

- Automatically send an e-mail message on Friday morning to everyone in your group reminding them to update their weekly status reports.

- Send an e-mail message to the department manager every morning with a list of open vacation requests.

The possibilities are virtually endless. Read on to learn how to use the `SendMail` object to solve form-data collection issues and to send HTML-formatted e-mail.

Controlling Form Data Through Hidden Fields

You've probably created at least one CGI that handles data submitted via HTML forms. However, since most of these CGIs tend to be very similar in functionality, it makes sense to create a single application that handles form data. The application should be coded in such a way that the form creator can control the CGI's functionality by using hidden fields in the form.

Let's say you want to control whom the e-mail is sent to and what the subject is from your calling form but don't want your users to see that information. By using hidden fields in your HTML form, you can secretly send the data you need without confusing the user with additional entry fields. In the form, you would have the following code:

```
<FORM ACTION="http://machine.domain.com/forms"...>
...
<INPUT TYPE=HIDDEN NAME=TO VALUE="bob">
<INPUT TYPE=HIDDEN NAME=SUBJECT VALUE="Hawaii Sweepstakes
Offer">
...
</FORM>
```

Fields of type HIDDEN are not displayed when the HTML page is rendered in the browser window. Users will never see these fields, yet they will be submitted with the rest of the fields. In our server-side application we would have the following code to get the two HIDDEN values shown above:

```
var sendTo  = request.TO;
var subject = request.SUBJECT;
```

NOTE
Field names are case-sensitive.

Now that we have the values, we can send the form data to the specified person (bob) with the subject Hawaii Sweepstakes Offer. If we produce another promotion, say, for a new Porsche, and we want the e-mail to go to Susan, we don't need to create a new JavaScript application; we just have to create a new form with the following fields in it:

```
<INPUT TYPE=HIDDEN NAME=TO VALUE="susan">
<INPUT TYPE=HIDDEN NAME=SUBJECT VALUE="Porsche Promotional
Offer">
```

Once we've created the SSJS application, we can easily e-mail-enable any form on our Web site and control where the data is sent and what the subject is, without having to alter our JavaScript program. Extending this idea, we can create a full-featured application that will handle nearly any form on our Web site. That's the purpose of the example application.

The Example Application

The example application, originally a Perl CGI that took over a week to code and refine, was coded in SSJS in less than a day. One advantage that I noted immediately was my ability to reuse the skills I'd learned from using client-side JavaScript (CSJS) to code the server-side application, since the language is the same (JavaScript). Traditionally, developers have written their client-side functions in JavaScript and their server-side programs in Perl, C/C++, and so on. Switching back and forth between two different language syntaxes can get confusing and just commenting the code can get you into trouble (comments in JavaScript start with "//" whereas comments in Perl start with "#" — you cannot mix the two without introducing serious errors into your code). Using one syntax greatly improves your programming efficiency, reduces the likelihood of errors, and allows for greater code reuse.

ON THE CD-ROM

Two versions of the sample application for this chapter can be found on the CD-ROM that accompanies this book, one that works on the UNIX version of Netscape Enterprise Server 3.x, the other that works on the server's Windows NT version. Look for the files named Chapter 25 Forms ApplicationNT and Chapter 25 Forms ApplicationUNIX. Find them by following the path Sample Code and Supporting Documentation ⇨ Part III ⇨ Chapter 25.

The example application lets you do the following:

■ Send formatted e-mail messages containing form data to a recipient (or mail alias) at a given company. For example, let's say Bob has a Hawaii Sweepstakes Promotion with a form on the Web site. The example application will enable you to send Bob the data from the form so that he can randomly select a winner. All you have to do is add some hidden fields to Bob's form; you don't have to program a new CGI to handle Bob's form data.

- Check to ensure that required fields have been filled out. Certainly you would not want a form to be submitted if the name, phone number, and reply e-mail address fields were blank or if all fields were blank.

- Display a short HTML-formatted response to the user. After submitting a form, users like to see a confirmation that their data has been received—something like "Thank you for your interest in our Hawaii Sweepstakes; your data has been forwarded and you will be hearing back from us soon."

- Send an automated e-mail confirmation message to the user. Sometimes it's nice to send an e-mail confirmation that the form data has been received. This confirmation can be used either in addition to or instead of the HTML-formatted response just mentioned.

- Write pipe-delimited data to a specified log file (provided the subdirectory already exists). Pipe-delimited data looks like `|John|Doe|415.555.1212|john@doughboy.com|` and it's very easy to import such delimited data directly into a database.

- Redirect the user to another page (rather than returning a short HTML-formatted response). This makes it possible for you to display a customized HTML-formatted response to the user.

NOTE
If you plan to use the example application on your Internet site, please disable portions of the automated e-mail confirmation message and HTML-formatted response functionality as directed by comments in the code.

Now we'll look more closely at what the example application does. (An explanation of how to implement and use the application is included in the application's help document, so I won't discuss that here.)

Checking for Required Fields

The first step in handling the form data is to check for required fields. To do this, simply parse the comma-delimited list of required field names specified in the calling form. (This is somewhat lengthy and therefore won't be shown here; you can find it in the application source code on the CD-ROM.) If no required fields are missing, loop through all the fields, adding the name/value pairs to the outgoing e-mail message or log file entry.

The following code allows you to loop through all form values that were submitted with the POST method (the preferred method for submitting form data):

```
for (var propName in request) {
    // EXCLUDE DEFAULT REQUEST OBJECT PROPERTIES FROM MESSAGE
    if (propName == 'ip' ||
        propName == 'protocol' ||
        propName == 'method' ||
        propName == 'agent' ||
        propName == 'auth_user' ||
        propName == 'auth_type' ||
        propName == 'uri') {
    }
    // EXCLUDE FORM-HANDLING NAME/VALUE PAIRS (HIDDEN FIELDS)
FROM MESSAGE
    else if (propName == 'TO' ||
            propName == 'SUBJECT' ||
            propName == 'TITLE' ||
            propName == 'REQUIRED' ||
            propName == 'LOG_DIR' ||
            propName == 'LOG_FILE' ||
            propName == 'REDIRECT' ||
            propName == 'HTML_FORMAT' ||
            propName.indexOf('e-mail_REPLY') != -1 ||
            propName.indexOf('e-mail_REPLIER') != -1 ||
            propName.indexOf('HTML_RESPONSE') != -1) {
    }
    else {
        ...
        // ADD THE NAME (propName) AND VALUE
(request[propName]) TO THE MESSAGE
        message += "\n" + unescape(propName) + " = " +
unescape(request[propName]);
        ...
    }
}
```

Sending HTML E-Mail Using the SendMail Object

You can send plain text or rich text e-mail directly from your JavaScript application using the new SendMail object. Once all the name/value pairs from the form have been packed into a variable, you're ready to send an e-mail message containing the form data to the user specified in the calling form. (Only the username is specified; the domain name is hard-coded in the application to prevent other companies from using your scripts to process their form submissions.) The message variable can contain HTML tags if you're sending HTML e-mail, so you can either read the contents of an HTML file into the variable or construct your HTML-formatted message on the fly.

Here's how the code would look for a plain text message:

```
var message = "Congratulations Bob, you've won a trip to
Hawaii!";
```

And here's how it would look for a rich text message, with font sizing and other niceties:

```
    var message = "<P><FONT SIZE=+3>Congratulations
Bob!</FONT>\n" +
                "<P>You've won a trip to Hawaii!";
```

```
var to      = "bob@company.com";
var from    = "hawaii@company.com";
var subject = "Hawaii Promotion";
```

To send plain text or rich text e-mail directly from your JavaScript application, first create a SendMail object, as shown here:

```
var msg     = new SendMail();  // CREATE SENDMAIL OBJECT
```

Next specify the e-mail address to which the e-mail will be sent (To), the reply address (From), the subject of your message (Subject), and the content or body of the message (Body), as follows:

```
msg.To      = to;       // RECIPIENT OF MESSAGE
msg.From    = from;     // SENDER OF MESSAGE
msg.Subject = subject;  // SUBJECT OF MESSAGE
msg.Body    = message;  // BODY OF MESSAGE
```

If you want to send rich text e-mail, use the following code to tell the `SendMail` object to send an HTML-formatted e-mail message:

```
// USE THE VALUES BELOW FOR SENDING HTML E-MAIL (PLAIN TEXT
IS THE DEFAULT)
if (request.HTML_FORMAT) {
    msg["Content-Type"] = "text/html;";
}
```

By specifying that the `Content-Type` is "`text/html;`", you instruct the `SendMail` object to send an HTML-formatted message rather than a plain text message. If your HTML document has relative links (`/announcements/an-nounce_24Jan97.html`) for graphics and URLs instead of fully qualified links (`http://machine.domain.com/announcements/announce_24Jan97.html`), you can use the following code to tell the mail client where the relative links begin:

```
// TELLS CLIENT WHERE RELATIVE LINKS BEGIN.
// (BASETAG EQUIVALENT -- USED IF LINKS IN THE HTML DOCUMENT
ARE NOT ABSOLUTE)
msg["Content-Base"] = "http://machine.domain.com/";
```

Now you can send the e-mail message, using the following code:

```
// SEND MESSAGE
if (!msg.send()) {
    // MESSAGE NOT SENT, DISPLAY ERROR MESSAGE
    write("SendMail Error: <b>" + msg.errorCode() + "</b> " +
msg.errorMessage() + "\n");
}
```

Installing the Application on Your Server

If you want to install and test the example application, you need to do the following:

1. Enable server-side JavaScript using Netscape Enterprise Server Administration (select `Server/Programs/Server Side JavaScript`).

2. Specify your mail server using Netscape Enterprise Server Administration (select `Server/Server Preferences/Network Settings/MTA Host:`).

3. Build the SSJS application (run the `build` file).

4. Add the application in Netscape Application Manager (`http://host/appmgr`).

When you test the application (`http://host/forms`), the help file will be displayed by default to tell you more about the application, including how to control it from the calling form. The help file includes a sample form to help you test the application. Please refer to this sample any time you have questions about setting up your own forms.

Taking Advantage of Server-Side JavaScript

You'll find that server-side JavaScript is easier and faster for development of Web applications than traditional CGI approaches. You'll also realize benefits as you use a common language syntax (Java/JavaScript) in all of your development efforts. This chapter is designed to provide you just one way of putting server-side JavaScript to work in your web applications. I hope this and the other chapters in this section of the book will fuel your imagination for other ways of taking advantage of this easy way of developing applications.

26

Managing SSJS Client Sessions with SessionManager

Mike Polikoff — *Web developer, Bank of America*

Server-side JavaScript (SSJS) offers a default Session Management Service that enables the storage of persistent data (on four predefined objects: request, client, project, and server) and the sharing of this data for clients across requests, projects across clients, and the server across projects, clients, and requests. In turn, the JavaScript Application Manager offers several client object maintenance techniques so that a client can be uniquely identified and referred to within the context of a single SSJS application. What the current implementation of SSJS doesn't offer, however, is a simple tool and API for managing session expirations, viewing reports detailing the number of open sessions in progress, and storing client-specific session content.

CROSS-REFERENCE

For a high-level introduction to server-side JavaScript state and session management, see Chapter 3 of this book.

This is where the SessionManager application comes into play. SessionManager, an SSJS application, was developed using Java, JavaScript, and HTML. Its intent is to provide a simple tool and API for managing client sessions for a group of SSJS applications. Rather than replacing the existing methodology, it's layered on top of the Session Management Service, providing a high-level abstraction and API for managing sessions either from the SessionManager interfaces or programmatically from within the target application itself.

This chapter serves as an overview of the SessionManager application and the benefits of separating session logic from the business and presentation layers in an SSJS application. As such, it assumes a basic understanding of SSJS programming and, though the SessionManager application is designed to be technique independent, a familiarity with the `client` object session maintenance techniques. For more information on writing SSJS applications, be sure to see *Writing Server-Side JavaScript Applications* on the CD-ROM that accompanies this book; for information specific to `client` object maintenance, see "Techniques for Maintaining the Client Object" in this document. The document can be found by following the path, Sample Code and Supporting Documentation ⇨ Part I ⇨ Chapter 3.

Before you read this chapter further, be sure to take a look at the source code for the SessionManager application so that you can follow along with it as you read. You can find it on the CD.

ON THE CD-ROM

Source code for the SessionManager application described in this chapter can be found on the CD-ROM that accompanies this book. Look for the file, Chapter 26 SessionManager; follow the path, Sample Code and Supporting Documentation ⇨ Part III ⇨ Chapter 26.

About Client Sessions in SSJS

Before I look at the SessionManager application, let's examine how client sessions work in SSJS. Experienced SSJS programmers are familiar with the client object; it is essentially an empty object to which properties can be assigned and values can be stored between client requests. A unique `client` object is constructed for each client to access an SSJS application and, after a default or programmatically determined period, destroyed, its object space collected by the SSJS garbage collector. Though SSJS documentation might refer to sessions in terms of the `request`, `project`, and `server` objects, both this chapter and the SessionManager application refer to a session only in terms of the `client` object. A session is defined as starting when a client accesses an SSJS application and ending when the client leaves or the session times out.

The client expiration mechanism for SSJS applications is built in. By default, client sessions managed using a server-side maintenance technique expire after ten minutes, while sessions managed on the client expire either upon one's leaving the application (client URL encoding) or when the browser is exited (client cookie). In either case, the expiration period can be modified by calling the `client.expiration()` method and passing in the number of seconds the client session should live before expiring. Each time the server receives a request from a valid client session, the expiration value is reset. When the session expiration period ends or when the application explicitly calls the `client.destroy()` or `client.expiration(0)` methods, the session expires and the runtime engine cleans up the old `client` object.

Though simple to implement, this client expiration mechanism can be problematic on at least three counts. First, to control client expiration behavior, it's necessary to call the `client.expiration()` method not only on every application page but also *after* the client object has been modified and before any call to the global `redirect()` method. This requirement can easily be overlooked, and such an oversight can be troublesome to detect during debugging. Any application page that doesn't explicitly call the `client.expiration()` method inherits the default expiration duration.

Second, there's no built-in mechanism for alerting a client about an expired session. A client who steps away from an application for any length of time beyond the expiration period and then attempts to pick up where he or she left off can suddenly discover something amiss. Because the original session has expired, on the next client request, the SSJS runtime engine creates a *new* session for the client, devoid of any of the properties or values that may have been stored prior to the last request. This can lead to any number of application malfunctions; code dependent upon values stored on the client may pass undefined, or functions expecting strings may receive null values. In a worst-case scenario, the undefined value could be passed to a Java method using server-side LiveConnect, resulting in the throwing of a `java.lang.NullPointerException` and the application screen's going white. Unfortunately, compensating for the possibility of such an occurrence involves repeated value checking and tedious coding on every application page that can be affected.

Third and finally, although the SSJS runtime engine automatically handles garbage collection when a client object expires and is destroyed, it doesn't necessarily clean up all the session data associated with that session. For instance, suppose you wish to store a customized object to represent each client accessing your application. It can be as simple as a constructor with several predefined properties and accessor methods to get and set the values of these properties. Because object references can't be stored on the `client` object, they must be stored either on the `project` object or on the `server` object. The upshot is that you have your custom object stored in a global memory space and a unique identifier to reference this object stored on the client. Although this allows for a clean object-oriented application design, it also opens the possibility that the custom object could outlive the client's expiration. For when the `client` object expires, only the unique identifier is destroyed, not the custom object itself, and unless explicitly removed or overwritten, the custom object will live until either the application or the server instance is restarted.

Overview of SessionManager

We designed the SessionManager application not only to minimize the shortcomings of the existing client expiration mechanism but also to provide a GUI tool for remote session monitoring as well as an abstracted API for managing application session logic. By session logic, I mean any code that exists for the sole purpose of session maintenance, such as expiration calls, conditional variable checking, data assignments, and URL redirection. Ideally, the functionality to accomplish this purpose should be accessible with a minimal number of method calls. The SessionManager API provides exactly this.

SessionManager was also designed with the underlying goal that no code specific to the SessionManager application should have to be compiled as part of an application interested in registering for the SessionManager service. Only the SessionManager methods, which are initialized on the server object and are thus available to all SSJS applications running on the same server instance, need to be used, and these are embedded in your application pages like any other JavaScript code. For the most part, this code should not exceed more than one or two lines on any given page.

For the sake of brevity and because only a handful of methods will ever be used in applications whose sessions are managed by SessionManager, I'll dispense with further details of the application's architecture and concentrate instead on more in-depth descriptions and examples of the core methods. I trust that the source code for the application, which is on the CD-ROM, will suffice to answer more design-oriented questions.

Using SessionManager Methods

SessionManager is nothing more than an SSJS application that makes its services available to other SSJS applications via the `server` object. When initialized, the application stores an instance of the SessionManager object on the `server` object, as the value of the property `server.session.Manager`. This being the case, all SessionManager method calls are made through this object reference.

At its simplest, SessionManager needs to use only two methods to track and manage client sessions for any given application: `registerProject()` and `trackSession()`. I'll discuss these methods first, and then describe methods for customizing session configuration options, storing session content, and handling session expiration and cleanup.

Registering the Application

SessionManager is built on the concept of registered applications, meaning that any SSJS application that intends to use the services of SessionManager must first register with it. This should be handled on the registering application's initial page, which is run only once when the application is first initialized.

The `registerProject()` method takes two mandatory arguments: a reference to the application's project object and the name of the application exactly as it's registered with the JavaScript Application Manager. The following typical call would register an application called "my_project":

```
server.session.Manager.registerProject(project,
"my_project");
```

Passing in the exact application name serves two purposes:

- It ensures uniqueness across applications registered with SessionManager. (The JavaScript Application Manager can't configure multiple applications with the same name.)

- It provides the SessionManager instance with a mechanism for obtaining the application name without explicitly passing it in subsequent method invocations. (It does so by parsing the URI property of the current `request` object.)

The `registerProject()` method stores a reference to the `project` object in a Hashtable, keyed by the application name. In fact, all the storage facilities used by SessionManager, both for registered applications and their client sessions, are instances of `java.util.Hashtable`. This provides the added benefit of implicit locking—all accessor methods of Hashtable are synchronized—and ensures data integrity without explicitly calling `project.lock()`, as you would when storing custom objects using the technique mentioned above.

Tracking the Session

Now that your application is registered with SessionManager, the client sessions it creates are eligible to be tracked, which occurs when you invoke the `trackSession()` method. This method is the heart and soul of the SessionManager API. It's responsible for creating and expiring sessions, setting and updating expiration times, and handling invalid sessions. As such, its implementation is the most complex of all SessionManager method implementations, but its invocation signatures remain simple.

The `trackSession()` method requires as its first argument a reference to the `client` object for the client session to be tracked. This is known as the *target session*, and the client requesting a target session is known as the *target client*. Optionally, `trackSession()` also takes a unique string key and a Boolean redirect command. Thus, it's designed to handle four different argument combinations, as shown in the following calls:

```
server.session.Manager.trackSession(client);
server.session.Manager.trackSession(client, key);
server.session.Manager.trackSession(client, boolean);
server.session.Manager.trackSession(client, key, boolean);
```

The optional string key serves as the session key for the target session. If, for a new session, the key is unspecified, a random key is generated using the global server-side function ssjs_generateClientID( ). For those applications that require usernames and passwords, supplying a username as the session key makes it easier to track sessions using the SessionManager GUI tool; otherwise, it offers no benefit over randomly generated session keys. If you do choose to specify a session key, it must be unique within the scope of the registered application, though not across all applications registered with SessionManager. The drawback to this is the fact that as in the Session Management Service currently in place, a single client session can't be tracked across multiple applications.

The optional Boolean argument, on the other hand, tells the trackSession( ) method what to do if it should encounter an invalid session — that is, a session that either doesn't exist or has expired. It has two options: It can (1) create a new session for the target client, or (2) redirect the target client to a predetermined HTML page, specified by the timeout URL. This could be an application log-in screen, the default home page for the application, or a page simply notifying the client that his or her session is invalid. SessionManager provides methods to specify the timeout URL in addition to other session configuration options, and these will be discussed later. If not specified, the Boolean redirect command defaults to false, and the SessionManager creates a new session for the target client.

Now that you have a clearer idea of the parameters expected by the trackSession( ) method, I will examine in detail the logic followed by the method.

The method is invoked with a reference to the target client and, optionally, a string session key and/or a Boolean redirect command. If a session key is specified, trackSession( ) checks the session pool for a session indexed by that session key. Note that every registered application maintains its own session pool, and the only session pool checked is the one from which the client is calling, known as *the target application*. This is why a session key need be unique only within the scope of an application.

On the other hand, if a session key isn't specified, the method checks the target client for an existing session key and, if one is found, checks the target application's session pool for a session indexed by the session key stored on the client. Note here that in the event that a session key is specified as one of the parameters to trackSession() and a different session key is also stored on the client, the specified session key takes precedence and only that key will be checked. This means that if you're not careful, it's possible to create duplicate sessions for a single client using different session keys. The session key that was specified as a parameter will overwrite the session key stored on the client, and the session indexed by the latter session key will eventually expire.

In either case, whether the session key was specified explicitly or stored on the client, trackSession() has now searched the session pool of the target application and has either found a matching session or has not. If not, this indicates that the target client had at one point begun a session that expired and has been garbage collected. If so, there's the possibility that the session might have already expired but hasn't yet been garbage collected. Details of session expiration and garbage collection will be discussed later.

If the session exists and hasn't yet expired, trackSession() simply resets the expiration and returns — simple enough. If no session exists or a session exists but has expired, the session is considered invalid, and the Boolean redirect command determines the fate of the client. If true, the client is redirected to the timeout URL for the target application. If false or not specified (remember, the Boolean argument defaults to false), either a new session is created (if none was found in the session pool) or the session's expiration is reset (if a session was found in the session pool).

But what happens if a session key is neither specified nor stored on the client? This will be the case, for instance, if a client has never before begun a session with the application. Essentially, trackSession() treats this case the same as it would an invalid session: if it's told to redirect the client to the timeout URL, it does so; otherwise, it creates a new session and adds it to the target application's session pool.

So the flow of control for trackSession() can be summed up with the following instruction set:

1. The trackSession() method is invoked.

2. If a session key is specified, go to Step 4; otherwise, continue.

3. The target client is checked for an existing session key. If one is found, continue; otherwise, go to Step 7.

4. The registered application's pool of sessions is checked for a matching session key. If one is found, continue; otherwise, go to Step 7.

5. The target session's expiration time is checked. If the session is valid, continue; otherwise, go to Step 7.

6. The session's expiration is reset. Go to Step 10.

7. The Boolean redirect command is checked. If true, go to Step 9. If false and coming from Step 5, go to Step 6; otherwise, continue.

8. A new target session is created. Go to Step 10.

9. The client is redirected to the timeout URL.

10. The `trackSession()` method returns.

I warned you that the implementation is complex! Fortunately, you should never have to worry about it. On each application page, all you need is a single call to `trackSession()`, and the SessionManager will take care of all the gory details. Typically, you'll find that the standard use of the `trackSession()` method follows this pattern:

1. A client logs in to or visits a registered application.

2. A call is made to `server.session.Manager.trackSession(client)` or `server.session.Manager.trackSession(client, "unique_id")`.

3. On subsequent pages of the application, a single call to `server.session.Manager.trackSession(client,true)` will either extend the life of a valid session or redirect the client to the timeout URL.

Customizing Session Configuration Options

With all the references to session expirations and timeout URLs, you're probably wondering just how SessionManager determines when a session has expired and where to redirect the client when it has. SessionManager thinks in terms of *session groups* — that is, collections of sessions that share configuration options. Configuration options include properties for setting the session timeout and the timeout URL. In the case of SSJS applications, each registered application defines its own session group, which is the same as the session pool described above.

When an application registers with SessionManager, it's assigned default values for both the session timeout and the timeout URL as well as an error URL, which is simply a redirection page that's used in the event an exception is thrown by SessionManager. The default session timeout is the same as the default expiration of the `client` object (ten minutes), and SessionManager includes two simple HTML pages to serve as the default values for the timeout URL and the error URL, respectively.

All configuration options are customizable, both the SessionManager default options and the options for each registered application. To accomplish this, SessionManager defines two methods, `setDefaultSessionConfigOption()` and `setSessionGroupConfigOption()`. As with the `registerProject()` method, these methods should be called only on the initial page of the target application, after the call to `registerProject()`.

The configuration methods take two standard arguments: the property name of the option you wish to modify and the value you want it set to. In addition, the `setSessionGroupConfigOption()` method, because it's specific to one application, requires the name of the application as it was registered. For a list of the currently available configuration options, you can use the SessionManager GUI tool, under the Configuration menu, or call its `getSessionConfigOptions()` method, which returns an array of all configuration option names.

The following lines of code customize the configuration options for the application "`my_project`" registered earlier in this chapter:

```
server.session.Manager.setSessionGroupConfigOption("my_proje
ct","session_timeout", 3600);
server.session.Manager.setSessionGroupConfigOption("my_proje
ct","timeout_url", "expire.html");
server.session.Manager.setSessionGroupConfigOption("my_proje
ct","error_url","error.html");
```

Note a couple of things about configuring session options: First of all, the `session_timeout` value must be a JavaScript number, indicating the session life in terms of seconds. In the case above, sessions for the application "`my_project`" will live for one hour. Second, the `timeout_url` and `error_url` values should be the addresses of HTML documents. You can use relative addresses (addresses without the protocol, port, and host specified) as long as the page is part of the registered application; otherwise, if the URL is external to the application (as the default SessionManager URLs are), you should use absolute addresses.

Using the setSessionGroupConfigOption() method to configure your registered application session-management schema affects that application and that application only. It's entirely possible to register ten applications with SessionManager and configure all ten with different session timeouts. However, if you have five applications that use the same timeout and error URLs and the same session expiration period, SessionManager also gives you the ability to customize the default session configurations and simply permit the five applications to inherit these options. To do so, use the setDefaultSessionConfigOption() method. Note that this method is applicable only to the SessionManager application; using the method in the context of any registered application will generate an error.

For example, open the initial page of the SessionManager application (init.html) in your text editor of choice. You'll find the following code near the bottom of the page:

```
var session_timeout = null;
var timeout_url = null;
var error_url = null;
//server.session.Manager.setDefaultSessionConfigOption("sess
ion_timeout",session_timeout);
//server.session.Manager.setDefaultSessionConfigOption("time
out_url",timeout_url);
//server.session.Manager.setDefaultSessionConfigOption("erro
r_url",error_url);
```

Simply set one of the variables to the new default value (the same restrictions described previously apply here) and uncomment the method call for that configuration option. When you recompile SessionManager and restart it from the JavaScript Application Manager, any registered application that doesn't override the default configuration options in its initial page will pick up the new default values. An important note here: Restarting the SessionManager application has no effect on existing sessions. This means both that existing sessions aren't destroyed (though you might encounter a problem if a registered application makes a call to SessionManager at the same time as the SessionManager application is restarting) and that existing sessions won't pick up the new configuration options until the first time they call the `trackSession()` method after the new configurations take effect.

Storing Session Content

Using just the four SessionManager methods I've described provides a registered application with a customizable, easily managed session-tracking device. But it's also lacking. After all, a session in and of itself is no more than a reporting and timing device: It enables you to find out how many unique client sessions are open in your application at any given time, when those sessions began, and when they're due to expire. Although this is valuable information, what the `client`, `project`, and `server` objects offer in the existing SSJS Session Management Service is more valuable still: a storage facility for housing persistent client-, project-, or server-specific data. In the SessionManager application, this is known as the *session content*.

Every session opened with SessionManager is represented by a `Session` object. A reference to this object is returned with every call to `trackSession()`. So a call such as the following on a typical application page

```
var mySession = server.session.Manager.trackSession(client,
true);
```

performs all the necessary session management functions, and then stores a reference to the Session object for the target client in the variable `mySession`. Note that the reference to this session is guaranteed to be valid; if the target session were found to be invalid, SessionManager would have redirected the client to the timeout URL before the method could return, and the code on the target page beyond that point wouldn't be executed. Likewise, if the call to `trackSession()` didn't include the Boolean redirect argument, SessionManager would simply have created a new session or extended the life of the existing invalid session and then returned a reference to the newly validated Session object.

This `Session` object contains all information specific to the client session it represents. The information is available through several accessor methods, most of which are needed only by SessionManager. Two of them, however, you'll find useful for storing persistent session content specific to that client session: setContent() and getContent().

All session content stored by SessionManager is contained in a single JavaScript object, much as the session content is stored on the client object in the existing Session Management Service. This is the object you pass to setContent() and that's returned when calling getContent(). In fact, if you simply create an instance of the root JavaScript Object object and store it as the session content for the mySession object above

```
mySession.setContent(new Object());
```

you have, in essence, duplicated the functionality provided by the client object. You can then assign properties to this session content object much as you would to the standard client object. The following code returns the content object and stores it in the variable myContent:

```
var myContent = mySession.getContent();
myContent.foo = "bar";
```

Be aware, though, that if you haven't set the session content for mySession, getContent() will return null, and the above property assignment will result in an error.

To return for a moment to the idea of a custom client object constructor mentioned in "About Client Sessions in SSJS," you might instead create a custom object with any number of predefined properties and methods and set this object as the session content. Using this technique, you have the capability to store object references on the client object, or at least the illusion of it.

No matter which approach you take to storing session content, it should be emphasized that the SessionManager API doesn't replace the content strategy implemented by the current Session Management Service. Using the SessionManager API, you can still assign any number of properties (dependent, of course, on your client object maintenance technique) to the client object. These properties will expire at the same time the session expires, or they can be caused to expire manually using the methods described in the next section.

Handling Session Expiration and Garbage Collection

Ideally, session expiration and garbage collection in SessionManager would function as they do in any other SSJS application — that is, transparently. The built-in expiration mechanism runs as a series of background threads in the SSJS runtime engine and handles client expiration and cleanup automatically. This is the cleanest (no pun intended) model for garbage collection. Unfortunately, SessionManager is an SSJS application itself, and as such, it has no more access to the native client data structures and is no more capable of starting its own daemon threads than any other SSJS application.

This being the case, SessionManager takes a middle-of-the-road approach to session expiration and memory management. On the one hand, as noted above, the `trackSession()` method automatically handles an expired session based on the value of the Boolean redirect argument. If `true`, the method cleans up all session content, removes the `Session` object for the target client from the session pool, and deletes the session key from the `client` object, then redirects the client to the timeout URL. If `false`, the session life is extended (or created anew), and no cleanup is necessary. On the other hand, this approach takes into account only the client who returns to the target application. It's just as likely, perhaps more so, that the client won't return, thereby abandoning a session that will quietly expire and continue to live in the session pool. Outside the remote possibility that a different session will later be created using the same session key, the expired session will live until the application or the server instance is restarted.

To avoid this possibility, SessionManager provides two explicit methods for handling session expiration: `expireSession()` and `expire()`. As the naming convention indicates, the former expires a single session, dictated by the `client` object passed to it, whereas the latter handles the cleanup for any expired sessions within the same session pool.

For example, some applications, such as registration or online commerce services, have defined beginnings and endings to them. These can be considered transaction applications: a client begins a session, completes the transaction, and ends the session. In this case, the application can safely terminate the session upon the completion of the transaction. With SessionManager, you can do so by calling `expireSession()`:

```
server.session.Manager.expireSession(client);
```

This removes the session from its session pool and marks it for garbage collection by the SSJS runtime engine.

However, as mentioned earlier, the possibility always exists that a client in the middle of such a transaction won't complete it. In this case, the call to `expireSession()` will never be executed on the target session, and the session will live in memory until the application is restarted.

SessionManager compensates for this by implementing the `expire()` method, which searches the session pool for the target application, checks the expiration times of each open session, and cleans up any that have expired. An application page, then, might consist of the following session-management code:

```
server.session.Manager.expire();
server.session.Manager.trackSession(client);
```

Essentially, this directs SessionManager to first clean up any expired sessions in the session pool for that application, and then open a new session for the target client.

You probably recognize the drawbacks inherent in such a system. Moving session expiration from a background thread to an explicit method call effectively moves the onus for session management from the runtime engine to the client. This has two less-than-desirable side effects: (1) session management runs on the client's processing time, and (2) session management is dependent on client requests. In other words, expired sessions always remain in memory until the next client request, and it's the next client that is burdened with the extra processing needed for cleaning up after them.

SessionManager, for its part, attempts to minimize excess overhead by restricting session management to the target application. If ten applications are registered with SessionManager, each is responsible for terminating its own sessions. The call in the example above, for instance, checks only the sessions open in the session pool for that application, not the nine other registered applications. This saves processing time by limiting the number of sessions the `expire()` method must check before returning.

To further optimize session management, your application can benefit by following these simple suggestions:

- Don't call `expire()` on application pages already overloaded with heavy processing loads, such as multiple or complex database connections, LDAP queries, and file system access.

- Don't restrict calls to `expire()` only to pages that are accessed so infrequently as to cause session buildup.

Generally, a good place for expiration calls is on the home page of your application, a page that's frequently accessed, thereby keeping expired sessions to a minimum, and that might otherwise be static.

Don't let the drawbacks I've just described deter you. All things considered, session expiration and cleanup as implemented in SessionManager is an efficient process. This doesn't mean that it can't still benefit from good design practices.

The SessionManager GUI Tool

The SessionManager application itself is built using the SessionManager API methods described above. Accordingly, it offers interfaces for monitoring sessions, configuring session options, and managing session expirations remotely.

The interfaces provide two session views: one global, of all applications registered with SessionManager, and the other specific to a single application. The global view summarizes the activity for all registered applications, including application names, the number of sessions open in each application, and the times when the applications registered with SessionManager. The more detailed application view provides a listing of all sessions open with the specified application. This includes the session key, the time when the session was initially opened, and the time when the session is due to expire.

These views generate the type of data useful for reporting purposes. But the application view also provides a mechanism for manually terminating any given session, in the form of a button next to the expiration time for each session. The expiration is accomplished when a call is executed to `expireSession()`. Care should be taken before using this to terminate a session, and because this functionality is available, care should also be taken to restrict access to the SessionManager application in a production environment.

Finally, all session configuration options covered in "Customizing Session Configuration Options," above, can be viewed and modified through the

Configuration interface of SessionManager. Note, however, that changes to the configuration options of an application via this method are good only until the target application or the server instance is restarted. For this reason, it's recommended that configuration options be set using the `setDefaultSessionConfigOption()` and `setSessionGroupConfigOption()` methods on the target application's initial page unless the need arises to modify a configuration option without also restarting the application.

Advancing the SessionManager Application

More advanced session management applications than SessionManager can be imagined. In the perfect world, much of the SessionManager API would be integrated with the SSJS runtime engine, thereby enabling the API to access the native client data structures and overcome some of the shortcomings described in this chapter.

But even without this type of integration, there's plenty of room for more diverse functionality within SessionManager. For instance, the application could provide a resource management API for permitting the application to monitor the system resources associated with open sessions. This is another area of the SSJS programming environment much in need of improvement since there are no methods for handling things such as database connections opened across client requests. Also, it could incorporate a remote connection API for better management of persistent connections to databases and LDAP-enabled directories opened by individual SSJS applications. In fact, the resource management that these two APIs collectively represent has already been built into some of the interfaces in the SessionManager GUI.

In the end, the SessionManager application has two primary goals: (1) to enhance built-in session-management functionality without requiring that each registered application compile source code specific to SessionManager as part of its Web file, and (2) to provide a simple API that isn't intrusive and requires no more than a few lines of code per application page. You'll likely find that the SessionManager accomplishes these goals and then some.

## 27

Integrating Server-Side JavaScript and CORBA

Damian Mahers — *consultant, Digital Equipment Corporation*

Beginning with Netscape Enterprise Server 3.0, Netscape introduced tight integration between the server-side JavaScript database access libraries called *LiveWire* and the *Common Object Request Broker Architecture* (CORBA). CORBA integration is provided through the Netscape Internet Service Broker, Netscape's object request broker (ORB). ORBs pave the way for the deployment of Web-enabled applications as part of an organization's overall distributed object strategy.

In this chapter you'll see, step by step, how to create a CORBA client and server (written in Java), how to access Java objects from LiveWire, and finally how to access a CORBA-based server from LiveWire. I'll begin, however, with an overview of the various approaches to Web-enabling applications, including a reminder of the very real business benefits.

Approaches to Web-Enabling Applications

Rendering an application accessible from a Web browser has many benefits. There is no client software to deploy because the Web browser becomes the client. End users are familiar with using a Web browser to access information. They expect to be able to access information sources from their browser, even if, for example, the information is sitting inside a "legacy" application running on a mainframe.

Setting this up is easier than you might think, especially if the legacy application has already been rendered remotely accessible through an API (typically through a distributed object middleware layer such as CORBA).

The mechanisms used to Web-enable applications have evolved rapidly. Let's take a look at the main ways that new and existing applications can be Web-enabled.

The Common Gateway Interface

The original mechanism for accessing external software from a Web server was the Common Gateway Interface (CGI). CGI programs generally work as shown in Figure 27-1.

Although it is both easy to use and widely supported, CGI does have drawbacks, not the least of which is that it involves the creation of a new process with every single request from a Web browser. Not only does this imply a performance penalty, but it's also somewhat inelegant.

Server-Side APIs

Several alternatives to CGI have evolved. Web server APIs, such as Netscape's Netscape Server API (NSAPI), do address the performance issue, but they can be rather complicated to use. (The NES 3.0 CORBA-based Web Application Interface [WAI] goes a long way toward simplifying matters.) Such server-side APIs work as shown in Figure 27-2.

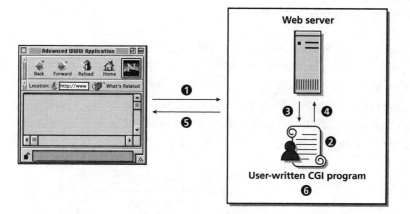

Figure 27-1: How a CGI works: (1) The Web browser accesses a resource on the Web server. (2) The Web server sees that the user is trying to access a CGI program, so it runs the program. (3) The Web server passes information to the user-written CGI program. (4) The CGI program accesses an application (for example) and dynamically generates HTML. (5) The Web server passes the HTML back down to the browser. (6) The CGI program terminates.

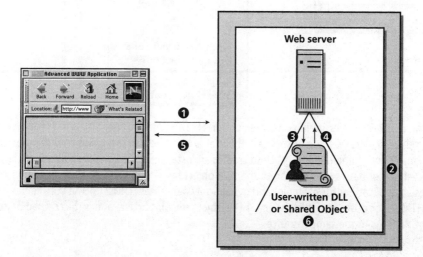

Figure 27-2: How server-side APIs work on Netscape Enterprise Server: (1) The Web browser accesses a resource on the Web server. (2) The Web server sees that the user is trying to access a resource that maps to a DLL or a shared object, so it uses the DLL/shared object. (3) The Web server passes information to the DLL/shared object by calling functions in it. (4) The DLL/shared object accesses an application (for example) and dynamically generates HTML. (5) The Web server passes the HTML back down to the browser. (6) The DLL/shared object remains loaded, and is thus reused on subsequent requests to the same resource.

Server-Side Java

Java programs run inside a piece of software called the *Java Virtual Machine* (JVM). The JVM can be embedded inside other programs, such as Web browsers. It's also possible to run the JVM inside a Web server so that software that you write in Java can handle requests from Web browsers and generates a response. Netscape Communicator and Netscape Enterprise Server both include JVMs. Figure 27-3 shows how Java runs on a Web server such as NES.

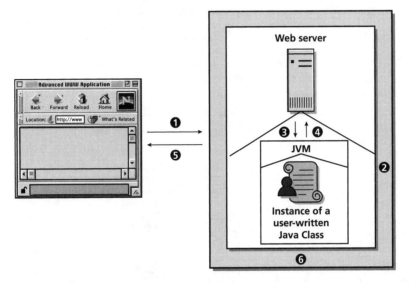

Figure 27-3: Java running on a Web server: (1) The Web browser accesses a resource on the Web server. (2) The Web server sees that the user is trying to access a resource that maps to a Java object, so it initializes the JVM and creates an instance of the corresponding Java class. (3) The Web server passes information to the Java object by calling methods in it. (4) The object accesses an application (for example) and dynamically generates HTML. (5) The Web server passes the HTML back down to the browser. (6) The object remains active, and is thus reused on subsequent requests to the same resource.

Server-Side JavaScript

This chapter focuses on a fourth alternative — server-side JavaScript, combined with distributed component technology in the form of CORBA. In a typical Web page, a user accesses simple HTML files on a Web server, and the Web server sends HTML pages back down to the browser. Server-side scripting with JavaScript involves embedding scripting commands inside the HTML file. These scripting commands are interpreted and executed by a scripting engine built into the Web server. What gets sent back down to the Web browser is the HTML originally in the file, plus any HTML dynamically generated by the embedded scripting commands. This process is shown in Figure 27-4.

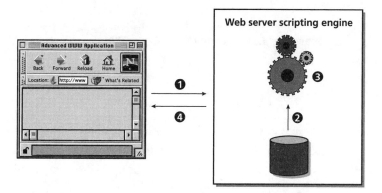

Figure 27-4: How a server-side script works: (1) The Web browser accesses a resource on the Web server. (2) The Web server fetches the HTML file. (3) The scripting engine that runs inside the Web server executes scripting commands embedded in the HTML file. (4) The Web server passes the original HTML back down to the browser, combined with HTML generated by the scripting commands.

CROSS-REFERENCE

In case you haven't read this book in the order in which the chapters appear, please refer to Chapter 3, "JavaScript on the Server," and Chapter 6, "Introduction to Netscape Application Server," for more details about how server-side JavaScript and other server-side applications work.

Here's an example of what server-side JavaScript commands look like:

```
<HTML>
<HEAD><TITLE>Example LiveWire</TITLE></HEAD>
<BODY>
<SERVER>
write("<H1>Hello World</H1>");
</SERVER>
</BODY>
```

```
</HTML>
```

The scripting commands are JavaScript, but note that this JavaScript (delimited by the <SERVER> tag) is executed on the Web server. If you were to view the page source in the Web browser, you would see the following HTML:

```
<HTML>
<HEAD><TITLE>Example LiveWire</TITLE></HEAD>
<H1>Hello World</H1>
</BODY>
</HTML>
```

You can use server-side JavaScript to access files and databases, invoke functions in DLLs or shared objects, and access Java objects. It's through the latter that the whole world of CORBA can be accessed — and I'm about to show you how.

Gearing Up

First, let me emphasize that this isn't rocket science! Try it out yourself.

Typically when getting started on a project, I take a simple working example that can be copied, changed, and improved. I strongly recommend that you spend the two hours or so that it will take to try the simple exercises in this chapter.

If you have no previous experience with Netscape's Web servers, LiveWire, CORBA, or Java, then so much the better — a sound first step is to try things out, hands-on. The point of this chapter is to take you step by step through the whole process. First, though, you'll need to install some software.

Installing the Software

In this chapter, I assume that you're using Windows NT. If you're using a UNIX variant, you should have no problems working out the UNIX equivalents to the commands and directories in this example. Here's what you have to do:

1. Install the current version of the Java Development Kit (JDK), which you can download from the JavaSoft Web site at
   http://www.javasoft.com/products/index.html. I'll assume that you've in-

stalled the kit in the default directory (`c:\jdk1.1.5`). Update your `PATH` environment variable to include `c:\jdk1.1.5\bin`, as described when you install the kit.

2. Set the `CLASSPATH` environment variable to include `c:\netscape\suitespot\wai\java\nisb.zip` and `c:\netscape\suitespot\wai\java\WAI.zip`.

3. If you haven't already, install Netscape Enterprise Server, which you can download for free from the Netscape web site. For information on how to do so, see the file named *Welcome and Software Download*.

4. The default installation directory for Enterprise Server is `c:\netscape\suitespot`. Update your `PATH` environment variable to include `c:\netscape\suitespot\wai\bin` and `c:\netscape\suitespot\bin\https`.

5. Complete the installation by enabling WAI Management and Web Publishing, as described in the Netscape TechNote, "Enabling CORBA on Enterprise Server." For test purposes, I generally set access privileges to "allow anyone anyplace all".

ON THE CD-ROM

The CD-ROM that accompanies this book includes the TechNote "Enabling CORBA on Enterprise Server." The TechNote is in the file called "webnaming"; to find it, follow the path Sample Code and Supporting Documentation ⇨ Part III ⇨ Chapter 27.

If you're unsure how to set the `CLASSPATH` and `PATH` environment variables, execute the commands listed below before doing anything else:

```
set PATH=%PATH%;c:\jdk1.1.5\bin
set
PATH=%PATH%;c:\netscape\suitespot\wai\bin;c:\netscape\suites
pot\bin\https
set
CLASSPATH=c:\jdk1.1.5\lib\classes.zip;c:\netscape\suitespot\
wai\java\nisb.zip
set
CLASSPATH=%CLASSPATH%;c:\netscape\suitespot\wai\java\WAI.zip
;.
```

Some Background on CORBA and Java

When you install Netscape's Enterprise Server 3.*x*, you get a complete CORBA implementation, including development tools. There's far more to CORBA than I can explain in this chapter. If you're not at all familiar with CORBA, you might want to start with a look at Chapter 5, "CORBA: Theory and Practice."

For now, bear in mind that CORBA enables you to split up software so that different chunks can run in different places and talk to each other — a form of object-oriented client-server software. CORBA does the magic of letting a chunk of software invoke methods in remote objects. (See Figure 27-5.)

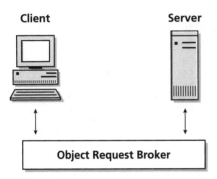

Figure 27-5: Client and server accessing remote objects through CORBA

One of the nice things about CORBA is that the different chunks of software can be written in different languages. The CORBA specification defines language bindings for various languages. CORBA will do the magic of converting the parameters and return values from one language to another if, for example, the client chunk is in Java and the server chunk is in C++ or COBOL, as shown in Figure 27-6.

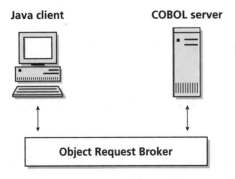

Figure 27-6: Java client and COBOL server accessing remote objects through CORBA

The CORBA implementation that comes with Netscape Enterprise Server supports both Java and C++ language bindings.

Creating and Building a CORBA Client and Server

In this first step, you'll build a very simple CORBA client and server in Java. CORBA clients invoke methods in CORBA object implementations (servers).

Creating the Aardvark Interface File

The methods that can be invoked on an object implementation are defined in a CORBA Interface Definition Language (IDL) file. IDL files define interfaces in a language-independent manner. An interface definition describes all the methods that can be invoked remotely, as well as the method parameters, whether the parameters are to be passed into the method call, out of the method call, or both. But there's obviously a lot more to it than this.

The IDL file that you'll be using models the dietary habits of the aardvark. The Aardvark interface (shown just below) contains one method, called feed(), used to feed an aardvark. The sole parameter, food, indicates the kind of food being fed. The aardvark can return a string from the method, indicating what it thought of the food it was fed.

```
interface Aardvark {
  string feed(in string food);
};
```

Now, do the following:

1. Create the interface shown above in a file named Aardvark.idl. You'll be running this file through an IDL compiler, which spits out source code files that can be used by both the client and the object implementation (the server).

2. Run the IDL compiler that generates Java files, called idl2java: using the command

   ```
   idl2java Aardvark.idl
   ```

The compiler will generate the glue that lets your CORBA client invoke methods in a remote CORBA object that you create. The client side of the glue is known as a *stub*, and the server side is known as a *skeleton*.

Updating the Aardvark Implementation File

In addition to generating the stubs and skeletons, the `idl2java` command generates an example object implementation file — in this case, an example Aardvark implementation. The file `_example_Aardvark.java` contains the example implementation. Follow these steps:

1. Rename _example_Aardvark.java to AardvarkImpl.java. Use this command:

    ```
    rename _example_Aardvark.java AardvarkImpl.java
    ```

2. Open `AardvarkImpl.java` in your favorite editor, and do a global replace of "_example_Aardvark" with "AardvarkImpl" (excluding quotation marks). You probably noticed some HTML comments in the file; these were automatically generated for you. Check out the Javadoc home page at `http://www.javasoft.com/docs/index.html` for more information about those comments.

3. Move down to the default implementation of the `feed()` method, which will look something like the code shown here.

    ```
    public java.lang.String feed (
        java.lang.String food
    ) {
        // implement operation...
        return null;
    }
    ```

4. Enter a more sensible implementation of the `feed()` method, as shown just below. (We all know that aardvarks eat ants, but not many people know that aardvarks also enjoy good sushi.)

    ```
    public java.lang.String feed (
        java.lang.String food
    ) {
        System.out.println("Someone is trying to feed me " +
    food);
    ```

```
    if (food.equals("ants") || food.equals("sushi"))
        return "Yumm!";
    else
        return "Blaach";
}
```

Creating the Server and Client Programs

You'll need a server to create an aardvark and make it available so that it can be fed from clients, and of course, a client program to feed the aardvark. Follow these steps:

1. Create the server file shown here:

```
****added netscape.WAI.naming(...);***
public class Server {
  public static void main(String[] args) {
    try {
    org.omg.CORBA.ORB orb =
        org.omg.CORBA.ORB.init();//Initialize the ORB.
    org.omg.CORBA.BOA boa = orb.BOA_init(); // Initialize
the BOA.
    AardvarkImpl joe = new AardvarkImpl("Joe"); // Create
"Joe" the Aardvark.
    boa.obj_is_ready(joe);      // Tell the ORB that "Joe"
is ready to be fed.
    netscape.WAI.Naming.register("http://localhost/joe",
joe);
boa.impl_is_ready(); // Wait for incoming requests.
  }

  catch(org.omg.CORBA.SystemException e) {
System.err.println(e); }
  }
}
```

2. Create a client program as shown in the next code sample. The client takes as a parameter the kind of food to be fed to the aardvark.

```
public class Client {
  public static void main(String args[]) {
    try {
      org.omg.CORBA.ORB orb = org.omg.CORBA.ORB.init();
// Initialize the ORB.
      org.omg.CORBA.Object obj =
netscape.WAI.NameUtil.resolveURI("http", "localhost", 80,
"/NameService/joe");
      Aardvark joe = AardvarkHelper.narrow(obj);
      System.out.println("Joe says: " +      // Invoke the
remote feed() method.
                            joe.feed(args.length > 0 ?
args[0] : "mozzarella"));
    } catch(org.omg.CORBA.SystemException e) {
System.err.println(e); }
  }
}
```

3. Build the client and the server. The other files, such as the Aardvark implementation, will automatically be rebuilt. Use these commands:

```
javac Client.java
javac Server.java
```

Running the Aardvark Client and Server

Now, we want to run our new client and server. Follow these steps.

1. Run the server in the background, using this command:

```
start java Server
```

2. If you get the following error message just after starting the Web server, wait ten seconds, and try again. The naming service seems to take some time to "warm up":

```
java.net.ConnectException: Connection refused
```

```
org.omg.CORBA.COMM_FAILURE[completed=MAYBE, reason=Http-
server communication problem]
```

3. Finally, feed Joe by running the client. Don't forget to pass in the extra parameter, telling Joe what you're feeding him. Use this command:

```
java Client jelly
```

Building a Server-Side JavaScript Application

Now we'll build the trivial server-side JavaScript application we looked at earlier.

Creating the HTML Source File

Create the source file, hello.html, as shown in the next code example. Because LiveWire can be funny about case sensitivity and spaces in filenames, I suggest you keep things simple and create the source file in a directory such as c:\labs\livewire.

```
<HTML>
<HEAD><TITLE>Example LiveWire</TITLE></HEAD>
<BODY>
<SERVER>
write("<H1>Hello World</H1>");
</SERVER>
</BODY>
</HTML>
```

Compiling the HTML Source File

Having created the source file, you now need to "compile" it into an intermediate format, using the jsac command. Compile the hello.html file with this command:

```
jsac -o hello.web hello.html
```

This creates the "compiled" version of the source file in `hello.web`.

Activating Server-Side JavaScript

After compiling the source file, you need to install it in the Web server. Before you can do that, you must enable server-side scripting in Netscape's Web server, using the Netscape Server administration interface as shown in Figure 27-7.

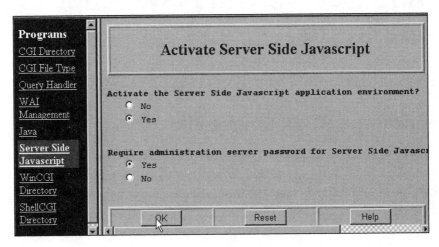

Figure 27-7: Activating server-side JavaScript through the Netscape Server administration interface

Installing the JavaScript Application

Once you've enabled server-side JavaScript, you'll be presented with a link to the JavaScript Application Manager, which can be used to install and maintain JavaScript applications so that they can be accessed from Web browsers.

Install your new hello application by clicking the Add Application button and filling in the resulting form, as shown in Figure 27-8.

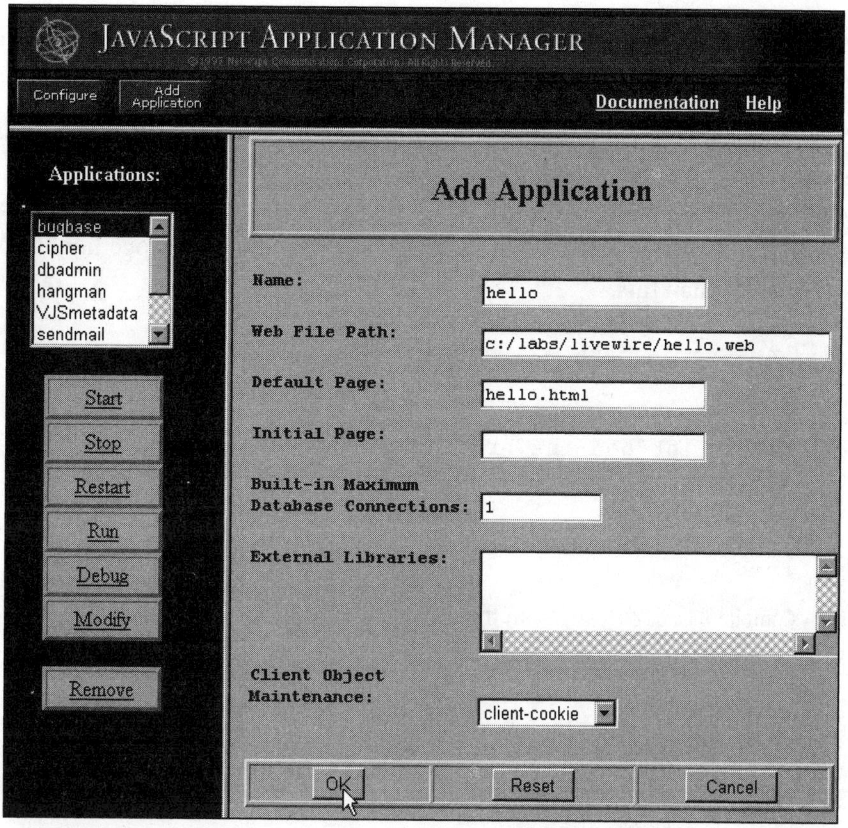

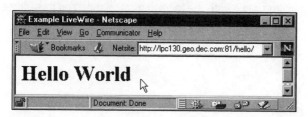

Figure 27-8: Installing the JavaScript application with the JavaScript Application Manager

Once your application is installed, try accessing it by clicking the Run button. This starts up a separate browser window. You should see something like what is shown in Figure 27-9.

Figure 27-9: A browser window running your application

Accessing Java Classes from LiveWire

Now that you've successfully installed your JavaScript application, we're going to move to the next step, which is accessing Java objects from LiveWire. To do that, you'll need a Java object. Here's a very simple one to try it out: a class that exposes one method, named add(), which simply adds two numbers together. It can't get any simpler than this.

1. Create Simple.java, as shown here:

```
public class Simple {
public int add(int nr1, int nr2) {
return nr1 + nr2;
}
}
```

2. Compile Simple.java with this command:

```
javac Simple.java
```

3. Before trying to access the Java class from LiveWire, create the following small Java program to try it out:

```
public class Test {
public static void main(String[] args) {
Simple s = new Simple();
System.out.println("14343 + 3232=" + s.add(14343, 3232));
}
}
```

4. Compile the test program and run it with the following commands. You'll see something like Figure 27-10.

```
javac Test.java
java Test
```

5. Compiling Simple.java produced a file named Simple.class. To make the Simple class available from LiveWire, copy Simple.class to the directory c:\netscape\suitespot\js\samples using this command:

```
copy Simple.class c:\netscape\suitespot\js\samples
```

Figure 27-10: Running the test program

6. Modify your JavaScript application to access the new `Simple` class, as shown with this example:

```
<HTML>
<HEAD><TITLE>Example LiveWire</TITLE></HEAD>
<BODY>
<SERVER>
write("<H1>Hello World</H1>");
var s = new Packages.Simple();
write("Simple says that 346 + 321 = " + s.add(345, 321));
</SERVER>
</BODY>
</HTML>
```

7. Rebuild your JavaScript application using the `jsac` command that you used previously.

8. Go to the JavaScript Application Manager and click the Restart button, so that your modified JavaScript application is reloaded.

9. Access the `hello JavaScript` application from your Web browser; it will look just like what you see in Figure 27-9.

Accessing the CORBA Server from LiveWire

So far you've done the following:

- Built a CORBA client and server, written in Java

- Created a JavaScript application

- Built a small Java class and accessed an instance of that class from your JavaScript application

Now we'll bring all these together.

As a consequence of building your CORBA client and server, you also built the Java CORBA stubs that enable a Java client to talk to a remote Aardvark CORBA object implementation. You can use those very same stubs to access an Aardvark from server-side JavaScript. Follow these steps:

1. Copy the client stubs that were generated as part of the creation of the CORBA client to the `c:\netscape\suitespot\js\samples` directory, so that they can be used to access your Aardvark CORBA object implementation from LiveWire. Use these commands:

   ```
   copy Aardvark.class c:\netscape\suitespot\js\samples
   copy AardvarkHelper.class c:\netscape\suitespot\js\samples
   copy _st_Aardvark.class c:\netscape\suitespot\js\samples
   ```

2. As shown in the next bit of code, update the JavaScript application so that rather than accessing an instance of the `Simple` class, you access an `Aardvark` object implementation via the CORBA Java stubs you just copied.

   ```
   <HTML>
   <HEAD><TITLE>Example LiveWire</TITLE></HEAD>
   <BODY>
   <SERVER>
   var obj = netscape.WAI.NameUtil.resolveURI("http",
   "localhost", 80, "/NameService/joe");
   var joe = Packages.AardvarkHelper.narrow(obj);
   write("Joe says " + joe.feed("mozzarella"));
   </SERVER>
   </BODY>
   </HTML>
   ```

3. Recompile `hello.html` using the `jsac` command.

4. Restart the hello application using the JavaScript Application Manager.

5. Make sure that you still have your CORBA server running. If not, start it with the command you used when creating the CORBA client and server.

6. Edit your Web Server's `obj.conf` file, which you will find under `C:\Netscape\Suitespot\https-hostname\config\obj.conf` and modify the line that starts with `Init classpath=` so that it includes `WAI.zip`: `Init classpath="C:/Netscape/SuiteSpot\\wai\\java\\WAI.zip;C:/Net.` Having saved the new version of `obj.conf`, go to the Web Server Adminstration

interfaces, and click on the "Apply" button, which you will find at the top and to the right of the page.

7. Finally, try accessing your JavaScript application.

Getting Input from the User

A final embellishment would be to allow the person using the browser to specify the name of the aardvark and the food it should be fed. To do this, follow these steps:

1. Update `hello.html` as shown here:

```
<HTML>
HEAD><TITLE>Example LiveWire</TITLE></HEAD>
<BODY>
<SERVER>
if (request.aardvarkName != null && request.aardvarkFood
!= null)
{
var obj = netscape.WAI.NameUtil.resolveURI("http",
"localhost", 80, "/NameService/joe");
var joe = Packages.AardvarkHelper.narrow(obj);
write("Joe says " + joe.feed(request.aardvarkFood));
}
</SERVER>
<H1>Please feed the Aardvarks</H1>
<FORM>
Aardvark name? <INPUT TYPE="TEXT" NAME="aardvarkName"
VALUE="Joe">
<P>

The food? <INPUT TYPE="TEXT" NAME="aardvarkFood"
VALUE="mozzarella">
<INPUT TYPE="SUBMIT">
</FORM>
</BODY>
</HTML>
```

2. Recompile `hello.html` using the `jsac` command.

3. Restart the application using the JavaScript Application Manager.

4. Now try feeding Joe as shown in Figure 27-11.

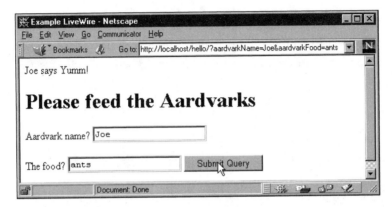

Figure 27-11: Feeding Joe the Aardvark

Tying It All Up

Figure 27-12 shows the "big picture" of what's happening in the last section above.

The CORBA objects being accessed from LiveWire typically represent one tier of a multitiered architecture, perhaps encapsulating some business logic, fetching information from several applications, and integrating it together to offer a higher-level interface.

One of the benefits of using server-side scripting coupled with distributed object technology is that the objects can be reused. Not only can you feed the aardvark via a Web browser, you can also create a C++ GUI client that talked CORBA to the aardvark.

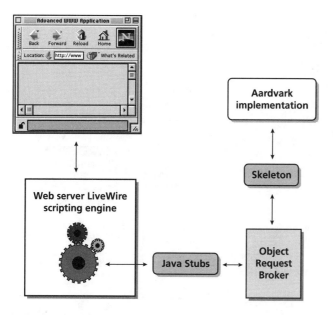

Figure 27-12: The big picture

When consulting on Web-enabling applications, I often see that applications have two kinds of users. The first kind wants easy access to application information, generally operating in a simple, "read-only" mode; this kind of application usage is a perfect candidate for being Web-enabled. The other kind of user demands a high degree of application interactivity, perhaps more than can be offered from a Web application interface.

Rather than maintain two separate code bases, it often makes sense to factor out the common application code into a set of objects that can be used not only from the Web interface, via server-side JavaScript, but also from other clients, such as Visual Basic. (See Figure 27-13.)

If you're not already using CORBA as a way of providing distributed access to your business objects, take a good look. The tight integration between LiveWire and CORBA is a perfect example of the way you can reuse a deployed object infrastructure to provide a Web interface to new and existing applications.

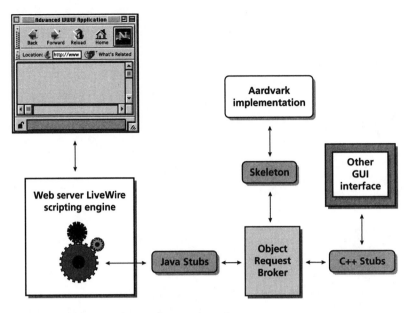

Figure 27-13: Adding a GUI interface client

28

E-Shop in JavaScript: Using Server-Side JavaScript for E-Commerce

Benoît Marchal — *principal, PineappleSoft sprl*

Mary clicks the title of the latest book from her favorite author, enters her credit card information, and relaxes. The book will be in her hands to-morrow morning, and it took her only a few minutes to order. That's electronic shopping at its best!

If you dream of running an electronic shop, or e-shop, this chapter will help you. I'll show you how to build an e-shop with server-side JavaScript (SSJS). My description of this JavaScript shop, JSShop, will give you a look under the hood, whether you finally use JSShop as a template, write your own code, or buy a commercial product. Furthermore, JSShop is a complete SSJS application and can serve as an example of how to write one even if you're not interested in e-shops. Complete source code is available on the CD-ROM that comes with this book.

ON THE CD-ROM

Look for complete source code for JavaScript electronic shop in the file, Chapter 28 JavaScript Eshop. You can find it by following the path Sample Code and Supporting Documentation ⇨ Part III ⇨ Chapter 28.

This chapter assumes you are familiar with HTML, SSJS, and SQL. Additionally, if you haven't already, be sure to read Chapter 3, "JavaScript on the Server."

Developing an Effective E-Commerce Solution

I strongly believe there's no one way to develop e-commerce solutions. Successful e-shops have to differentiate themselves from the many other e-commerce offerings available to Web purchasers. Therefore, it's important to define the audience before building an e-commerce application.

JSShop is a simple yet effective e-shop application that can serve as a model for small businesses with a limited range of products, or be used for experimentation. In terms of functionality, it doesn't compete with commercial solutions such as Netscape's CommerceXpert sophisticated e-commerce products. JSShop supports flexible navigation, searches, and a shopping basket. It doesn't manage sales, banners, or customer profiles; nor does it validate credit cards online, although these features can be added if needed.

Finally, so that the code remains readable, JSShop doesn't contain fancy HTML. It's easy to improve the way JSShop looks, but don't overdo it: an e-shop doesn't need the sleekest design to be effective.

NOTE

JSShop was tested on Netscape FastTrack Server 3.01 with an InterBase 5.0 database; it will also run on Netscape Enterprise Server.

How JSShop Is Organized

JSShop is organized around three basic activities:

- **Browsing:** Enables shoppers to browse through the product range. Products are organized in categories for easy navigation. Each product has a page associated with it.

- **Searching:** Offers a faster track to a particular product for those shoppers who don't need or want to browse.

- **Filling the shopping basket and checking out:** Enables shoppers to register and order the goods they desire.

JSShop is implemented in nine HTML pages with embedded JavaScript statements and four JavaScript (`.js`) files with top-level functions. The HTML pages, which I'll describe in subsequent sections, are as follows:

1. Index page

2. Category page

3. Product page

4. Shopping cart

5. Checkout page

6. Confirmation page

7. Search page

8. Error page

9. Delete page

SSJS works in a transactional mode: pages are called to serve requests and die after processing. In JSShop, information is stored in a database and pages are generated on the fly instead of persisting. This means that JSShop is a database-driven site, which is easier to maintain than static HTML pages — especially if there are many products.

JSShop is driven by five database tables, shown with their fields and links in Figure 28-1.

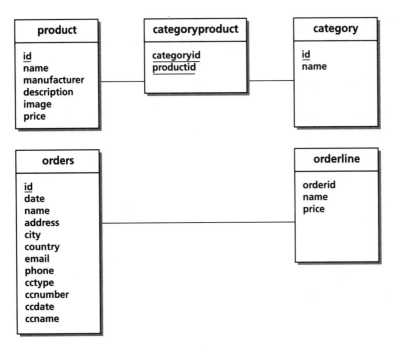

Figure 28-1: JSShop's database schema

- The *product* table stores the price and other product information.

- *Orders* stores information about the shopper, such as name and address, as well as credit card information.

- The *category* table supports browsing. Products can be grouped in categories with like items (for example, a shop may have a Books category that contains two books on JavaScript and one on Web writing). They can be attached to more than one category (for example, the JavaScript books can also be referenced from another category on JavaScript). It's important to support flexible categorization and offer many options since shoppers have different sensibilities and are more likely to click on terms with which they're familiar. Note that in larger shops, it makes sense to offer subcategories or even subsubcategories. However, you must also keep in mind that levels translate into more clicks for shoppers, and most people want to reach the product of interest with as few clicks as possible (something known as instant gratification). For very small shops, it makes sense to list all the products on the home page and forgo categories.

- The *categoryproduct* table models the relationship between products and categories.

■ *Orderline* stores product information attached to an order. Note that the information in the orderline table is with some of the information in the product table to help minimize errors. An alternative design would have linked from orderline to product; however, the product table changes often as products are added, removed, and priced differently, and a link is sensitive to these changes, whereas a copy always reflects what the shopper saw.

Now I'll describe each of the HTML pages in JSShop.

The Index Page

Index, the code for which follows, is the home page. It links to the various categories and features a search form.

```
<HTML>
<HEAD><TITLE>JSShop</TITLE></HEAD>
<BODY>
<H1>JSShop</H1>
<SERVER>
var conn = dbconnect();
var categories = conn.cursor("select * from category order
by name");
if(!(categories && (conn.majorErrorCode() == 0)))
   reportdberror(conn,categories);
while(categories.next())
   write(addClient("<P><A HREF=\"category.html?categoryid="
+
escape(categories.id)) + "\">" + categories.name + "</A>");
dbdisconnect(conn,categories);

</SERVER>
<FORM ACTION="search.html">
<INPUT NAME="search">
<INPUT TYPE="SUBMIT" VALUE="Search">
<INPUT TYPE="HIDDEN" VALUE='`ssjs_getClientID()`'
NAME="NETSCAPE_LIVEWIRE_ID">
</FORM>
<P><A HREF="shoppingcart.html">See shopping cart</A>
</BODY>
</HTML>
```

Index reads the categories from the database and turns them into a list of hyperlinks. The code also takes care to pass the category identifier as a reference in the hyperlink. We'll see in the next section how the category page uses this information.

Index, like every other page in JSShop, includes a link to the shopping cart. In a supermarket, shoppers like to keep the shopping cart close at hand. The same is true online — shoppers want to be able to return to their electronic shopping cart from any page.

The Init Functions

Let's turn our attention to the top-level functions dbconnect() (shown in the next code listing) and dbdisconnect(). JavaScript supports many options to connect to databases. For JSShop, I've chosen the simplest approach, which opens a separate connection for each request. This approach may not be the most efficient, but it's the easiest to write. To adopt a more efficient strategy, it suffices to rewrite dbconnect() and dbdisconnect(), because I was careful to isolate all the connection code in these two functions.

```
function dbconnect()
{
    if(isBlank(client.orderid))
        client.orderid = ssjs_generateClientID();

    database.connect("ODBC","JSShop","SYSDBA","masterkey","");
    if(database.connected())
        return database;
    else
    {
        reporterror("could not connect to database");
        return null;   // Makes the compiler happy.
    }
}
```

dbconect() also creates an order identifier using JavaScript's ssjs_generateClientID() function. Note that the code checks for the order identifier on every page. It's wise not to assume that users always enter the shop through the home page.

In addition, I've defined some utility functions, such as `isBlank()`, which tests if an object exists, and several variations of `reporterror()`, which redirects to an error page. The next bit of code shows these functions.

```
function isBlank(o)
{
   if(null == o)
      return true;
   else if(o.toString().length == 0)
      return true;
   else
      return false
}
function reporterror(msg,conn,cursor)
{
   dbdisconnect(conn,cursor);
   redirect(addClient("error.html?msg=" + escape(msg)));
}
```

Session Management

The search form, located near the bottom of the index page, has a special hidden field — NETSCAPE_LIVEWIRE_ID — that's used for session management.

HTTP is connectionless; that is, it treats each page request as separate. However, in an e-shop application, it's important to know whether two requests come from the same shopper or from different ones. JSShop associates an order identifier with each shopper session so that if a shopper views 20 pages during a session, all the pages have the same order identifier. The same technique also supports statistics, although this use isn't currently implemented in JSShop.

JavaScript offers no fewer than five solutions to manage sessions. Each has unique strengths and weaknesses, but my favorite for an e-shop is server-url, in which the Web server retains session data in memory and uses a session identifier in the URL to match requests with sessions. I particularly like it for these reasons:

- **It doesn't use cookies.** Cookies don't deserve the bad press they've received, but the customer is king: f customers don't like cookies, you shouldn't use them.

■ **It's not based on IP addresses.** Relying on IP addresses to track users isn't practical on the Internet, where some users sit behind proxies that change their IP addresses.

■ **It doesn't store all the information in the URL.** This is good because you don't want to store credit card or other sensitive information here. Browsers retain a list of previously accessed sites, and the same information is available in the server log. Such lists and logs may fall into the wrong hands, and if they do, you don't want them to lead someone to sensitive information.

`Server-url` is less convenient than other solutions for the programmer because it requires that you explicitly pass the session identifier in several cases. But JavaScript provides two functions for that purpose: `addClient()` and `ssjs_getClientID()`.

Parameters versus Session Properties

It's not always easy to decide which values should be passed as parameters to a page (such as the category identifier) and which values should be stored as properties of the client object (such as the order identifier). My rule of thumb is that page parameters are like function parameters, whereas session properties are akin to global variables. Any information that's specific to the page being called is a candidate for a parameter (with one exception in the checkout page for security reasons). It's a good software engineering practice to minimize the use of global variables.

Whether using parameter or session variables, never assume they have been properly initialized. With a limited effort, it's almost always possible to recover with default values. In the worst case, prompt the user but avoid error messages.

The Category Page

You'll remember that links to the category page include a category identifier. As illustrated in the next code listing, the category page will default to the first category if no such parameter is given. Why not print an error message? Because shoppers aren't responsible for errors and shouldn't be punished for them!

Chances are that other sites will link to the e-shop, and they may get the link wrong or use an outdated link. Still, those links bring in new customers, and you don't want to greet them with an error message. It always pays to be tolerant of errors, but this is especially true when building e-commerce applications. You should avoid anything that locks some customers out — a definite no-no in e-commerce!

```
<SERVER>
var conn = dbconnect();
var categoryid = isBlank(request.categoryid) ? "1" :
request.categoryid;
var category = conn.cursor("select name from category where
id = " +
categoryid);
if(!category.next())
    reportdberror(conn,category);
</SERVER>

<HTML>
<HEAD><TITLE>JSShop \
<SERVER>write(category.name);</SERVER>
</TITLE></HEAD>
<BODY>
<H1><A HREF="index.html">JSShop</A> \

<SERVER>write(category.name);</SERVER></H1>
<!-- ... -->
```

Also note that the navigation bar at the top of the page includes a link to the home page and shows which category we're in. It's important to help shoppers build the right mental model of the shop. The navigation bar is a sort of roadmap for them. On the product page (one level down in the shop), the category name becomes an active link. As a rule, the more navigational information you provide, the better.

Finally, the page lists all the products in the current category. The code isn't included here because it's very similar to the code in the index page.

The Product Page

Next we move to the product page. The product page expects two parameters: a product identifier and a category identifier. As usual, it goes to great lengths to compensate if either of these parameters is absent.

The product page is the most important page because it's where shoppers turn into buyers. It is important to provide enough information to help shoppers decide to place an order. If they hesitate, they're unlikely to follow through. How much information is enough? It depends on your product. JSShop assumes familiar products and supports only an image, a description, and an e-mail address where shoppers can request more information.

Further, make sure the buying process is as painless as possible. Include a simple form and use clear labels such as "Buy now!" Fill in the quantity field with a reasonable default.

```
<FORM ACTION="shoppingcart.html">
<INPUT NAME="qty" VALUE="1">
<INPUT TYPE="SUBMIT" VALUE="Buy Now!">
<INPUT TYPE="HIDDEN" VALUE='`product.id`' NAME="productid">
<INPUT TYPE="HIDDEN" VALUE='`ssjs_getClientID()`'
NAME="NETSCAPE_LIVEWIRE_ID">
</FORM>
```

Stay away from cryptic icons, and add explicative labels to graphics. Remember that if shoppers don't recognize the graphics, they won't know how to order.

For some e-shops, it makes sense to attach another order form to the category page — that is, one level up. E-shops that sell common articles such as pens will find that their customers don't need many details and are likely to order most goods from the category page. Shoppers familiar with the products will appreciate the faster turnover.

The Shopping Cart

As we've seen, the shopping cart can be called from any page to display information on the current order. However, when it's called with a product page identifier, it will add the product to the current order. Note that if no quantity is given, it defaults to one. Again, this is better than presenting an error message.

Before adding a new orderline, the code may have to insert a row for the current order in the orders table. This is done in a transaction as illustrated in the next code example:

```
<SERVER>
```

```
var conn = dbconnect();
var productid = request.productid;
if(!isBlank(productid))
{
   var qty = isBlank(request.qty) ? "1" : request.qty;
   conn.beginTransaction();
   var existingorder = conn.cursor("select * from orders
where id = '" +
getOrderID() + "'")
   if(!existingorder.next())
   {
      conn.execute("insert into orders(id) values('" +
getOrderID() + "')");
      if(conn.majorErrorCode() != 0)
         rollbackreportdberror(error,conn,existingorder);
   }
   existingorder.close();
   var product = conn.cursor("select * from product where id
= " + productid);
   if(!(product && (conn.majorErrorCode() == 0))
      rollbackreportdberror(error,conn,products);
   product.next();
   conn.execute("insert into orderline (orderid, name,
price, qty) values
('" + getOrderID() +
                "', '" + product.name + "' ," +
product.price + ", " + qty
+ ")");
   if(conn.majorErrorCode() != 0)
      rollbackreportdberror(conn,null);
   else
      conn.commitTransaction();
   product.close();
}
</SERVER>
<HTML>
<HEAD><TITLE>JSShop \ Shopping Basket</TITLE></HEAD>
```

```
<BODY>
<H1><A HREF="index.html">JSShop</A> \ Shopping
Basket</H1>
<!-- ... -->
```

The actual display of the shopping cart is done by the `writeShoppingCart()` function. It is most convenient to use a function because the same printout is necessary on the confirmation page. Currently, JSShop assumes that shipping costs and taxes are included in the product prices, but it wouldn't be difficult to modify `writeShoppingCart()` to process them.

When called from the shopping cart page, `writeShoppingCart()` adds a delete button to the right of each line. The delete button isn't present on the confirmation page, for obvious reasons.

```
if(addDelete)
{
    write(addClient("<TD><FORM ACTION=\"delete.html") +
                    "\"><INPUT TYPE=\"SUBMIT\"
VALUE=\"Delete\"><INPUT TYPE=\"HIDDEN\" VALUE=\"" +
                    products.name + "\" NAME=\"name\"><INPUT
TYPE=\"HIDDEN\" VALUE=\"" +
                    ssjs_getClientID() + "\"
NAME=\"NETSCAPE_LIVEWIRE_ID\"></FORM>");
}
<SERVER>
var conn = dbconnect();
if(0 != conn.execute("delete from orderline where orderid =
'" +
                    getOrderID() + "' and name = '" +
request.name + "'"))
    reportdberror(conn,null);
dbdisconnect(conn,null);
redirect(addClient("shoppingcart.html"));
</SERVER>
```

From the shopping cart, customers can either return to the shop or proceed to checkout. There's a specific button to return to the shop in addition to the usual link in the navigation bar. Without seeing this button, some shoppers may not re-alize they can return to shop for more goods. It's essential to provide clear guid-ance for navigation. On this page, an extra button makes a lot of sense.

The Checkout Page

Shoppers eventually proceed to the checkout page, which is probably the most complex one because it's called in no fewer than three ways:

- From the shopping cart, when a shopper decides to buy

- From the confirmation page, when a shopper requests a lookup (see below)

- From the confirmation page, when a shopper has entered invalid data

The checkout page provides shoppers with a form where they can register themselves. Depending on where it was called from, the form may be partially filled in. If it's called from the shopping cart, the form is empty. The form calls the confirmation page, but the confirmation page will redirect to the checkout page if the shopper requested a lookup or entered invalid data.

For return customers, JSShop provides a simple mechanism to look up their data based on their e-mail address. No password is required (a relief to shoppers who are tired of having to remember passwords) because the lookup works only with nonsensitive information such as name and address. Credit card information isn't automatically reloaded, so thieves can't use this solution to order goods. Of course, with this mechanism, it is possible to discover whether somebody has al-ready shopped at JSShop.

Finally, if the confirmation page detects an error, it stores customer data in ses-sion properties and redirects to the checkout page. We use session properties in-stead of parameters for security reasons: because customer data related to credit card payment is sensitive, it's not safe to pass it as parameters in a URL. The form on the checkout page uses the POST method, which is safer in this case. Unlike the GET method used with other forms, the POST method doesn't use the URL to pass data to the server.

The checkout page uses a helper function, asString(), to make sure that un-defined properties appear empty:

```
<TR><TD>Name:<TD><INPUT NAME="name"
VALUE='`asString(client.name)`'>
```

By default, JavaScript prints "undefined."

The Confirmation Page

The confirmation page serves to confirm the customer's order. It validates the checkout form, updates the database, and prints a summary of the order. Finally, it resets the session properties with

```
client.destroy();
```

Form validation is done by the validateCheckout() function. As you saw with the checkout page, if data isn't valid, the confirmation page redirects to the checkout page. JSShop does little validation, but it's easy to adapt validateCheckout() to your specific needs.

The confirmation page also checks whether the user requested a lookup. In this case, it redirects to the checkout page, this time passing the e-mail address as a parameter.

```
if(!isBlank(request.lookup))
    // I will just have to put it in the query string (build
it myself).
    redirect(addClient("checkout.html?email=" +
escape(asString(request.email))));
```

The confirmation page would be a good place to generate a confirmation e-mail.

Other Pages

JSShop has three other pages: the error page, the search page, and the delete page.

- The error page is called by other pages when there's an error. It apologizes and prints an error message.

- The search page lists all products that match the search criteria specified by the customer in the search form on the index page.

- The delete page is called from the shopping cart when the user presses the delete button. It deletes one item and redirects to the shopping cart.

All these pages are based on techniques we've seen elsewhere.

Caring for the Customer

As mentioned earlier, an e-shop doesn't need the sleekest design to be effective. What it does need is a philosophy of caring for the customer. The e-shop defines how the customer perceives your business, and customers like businesses that go the extra mile to please them.

The main problem when building SSJS applications is to keep track of the links between the various pages — which page is called when, which parameters are required, and so on. It's easy to make mistakes, and some of these may not be identified until the site is in production. Furthermore, other sites may link directly into your site and introduce errors. It's best to prepare for the worst and make copious use of default values.

JSShop is a simple yet effective e-shop framework. Throughout the chapter, I've hinted at possible improvements you might make. You may want to visit different e-shops online and then incorporate those features that you find the most effective. As long as you keep shopper satisfaction in mind, your e-shop will be successful.

29

Error-Handling Techniques for Web Applications

JJ Kuslich — *application developer, Application Methods, Inc.*

So you think you've written the perfect application? Well, if your application works perfectly with perfect input, you're really only half done. Reliable applications must also consider interacting with imperfect users and imperfect external systems, such as database servers. In fact, it's so important for your application to be able to handle bad user input or errors produced by other systems that you must design it to handle errors from the start. You must adjust your notion of what's perfect and build from there.

In the software world, a "perfect" system is one that handles most of the cases most of the time; it's one that asymptotically approaches an error-free system but never quite reaches it. In other words, perfect doesn't mean "error free" but "as error free as possible given time, budget, and other constraints." Don't dismiss this notion of perfection as cynical or pessimistic. It's simply realistic and must be understood before you start designing your application. Otherwise, you could wind up spending too many resources trying to provide complete protection against application Armageddon. Of course, you don't want to swing too far in the other direction either, leaving it up to service packs or point releases of your software down the road to provide sufficient error handling.

Because it's often hard to determine just how much error handling is enough, this chapter presents several techniques that you can use alone or in combination to provide varying levels of protection. Though this chapter focuses on server-side JavaScript (SSJS) applications, you can use several of the concepts and many of the code samples in client-side JavaScript (CSJS) logic as well. And note that the techniques apply not only to JavaScript development but also to Web development in general. You can apply just about all the error-handling tips to projects in Microsoft's Active Server Pages (ASP) and Sun's new Java Server Pages (JSP), and even to CGI scripts.

Detecting Errors

Regardless of the level of protection you wish to provide, detecting error conditions is the first step in handling errors. Error conditions are usually generated by users, by interactions with external systems, or by your own application logic. Let's look at user-generated errors first, then consider database errors, and finally examine the important issue of error levels.

User-Generated Errors

Users can generate errors by entering invalid data, selecting invalid program options, or performing operations out of sequence. You can detect any of these error conditions by validating user input. However, in most cases you'll want to use validation only to detect data entry errors. Overusing validation can be expensive in terms of processing power and can lead to inflexibility in application design because it often ties application logic to the user interface.

For instance, suppose you were to perform some validation each time users select a program option, such as "Edit Employee Records," to make sure that users are able to select this option from the page they're on or from the point they're at in some sequence of operations. Validating every one of these operations for every user of the system would require a lot of conditional code and would also effectively hard-wire application sequences and interfaces to the underlying code. It would be far more effective to prevent user interaction errors than to detect them after the fact. From a user interface perspective, it's much more effective to design an interface that guides users through valid choices than to build one that inundates them with error messages every time they select an invalid option. Again, such decisions are fundamental to how you design your user interface and must be made during the design phase of a project.

For data entry errors, validation works well, and in many cases it must be performed to prevent bad data from being sent to a critical system, such as a database. Data entry validation involves developing acceptance criteria that identify the type and format of data allowed for each data field. Once the acceptance criteria for all data fields have been determined, you can write routines that check to see if data entered fits the acceptance criteria.

You can perform data validation in the browser with CSJS, on the server in an SSJS page, or to varying degrees in both places. CSJS validation of form fields, for example, gives you the ability to provide immediate feedback to users should they enter data that fails the acceptance criteria. In addition, as you may already know, performing validation on the client side reduces network traffic and server-side processing, giving the appearance of a faster, more responsive application.

The code below shows the underlying JavaScript code for a form field that accepts only numeric characters and reports an error if the user attempts to submit the form with invalid data. The form itself, with the error message it generates if the user fills it out incorrectly, can be seen in Figure 29-1.

```
function validateFields(theForm) {
    // Where IsNum() is a custom function that checks a
string to see if
    // it contains only numbers.
    if (IsNum(theForm.numbers.value))
        theForm.submit();
    else
        alert("The numbers field contains invalid
characters.");
}
```

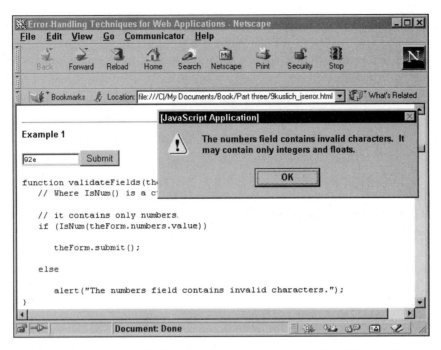

Figure 29-1: A JavaScript form that reports an error when invalid data—in this case, any nonnumeric character—is entered

Of course, validation doesn't apply just to processing HTML forms. You can also validate parameters that are passed to any SSJS function, object constructor, or custom method that you write. For instance, if you can't trust that the caller of a custom function will pass arguments of the proper data type, you can use the typeof operator to check the type of the arguments before attempting to use them in your function. Such simple validation checks, as shown in the next code example, can save you from crashed applications and blank screens caused by an inexperienced user's passing in a null where a string value was expected.

```
function ReverseString (forwardStr) {
    var revStr = "";
    // Validate the argument here.
        if (typeof(forwardStr) == "string") {
            // Without validation, if forwardStr were null, the
attempt to access

            // the length property would fail and cause the
application
```

```
        // to crash.  Because we validate above, we're
protected from that

        // error.
        for (var i=forwardStr.length; i >= 0; i--)
            revStr += forwardStr.charAt(i);
    } // End if.
    return revStr;
}
```

Database Errors

No matter how much we like to complain about users, they're not the only players who generate errors. If you access an external system, such as a database server, you should plan for the unexpected. Database connections can mysteriously disconnect, system administrators can trip over power cords, and database servers can have bugs. The SSJS `Connection` object has four methods that will help you detect and gather detailed information about database server errors: `majorErrorCode`, `majorErrorMessage`, `minorErrorCode`, and `minorErrorMessage`.

You can call `majorErrorCode` after performing a database operation, such as inserting a row in a table, to see if any errors have occurred. If the operation is successful, it returns a value of zero; if an error occurs, it returns a nonzero integer that represents the actual vendor-specific error code. Once you've detected the error, you can call `majorErrorMessage` to retrieve a related vendor-specific error message that the database server might have generated. Additionally, you can call `minorErrorCode` and `minorErrorMessage` to try to find more detailed error information.

The codes and messages returned by the four methods can change every time you interact with the database, so you should check for errors immediately after performing an operation that you wish to monitor. Keep in mind when using these methods that not all database servers provide messages for every error, and that `minorErrorCode` and `minorErrorMessage` may not return useful information in many cases.

In addition to the four methods mentioned above, many methods in the SSJS database API return error codes that can tell you whether you should look to `majorErrorCode` and `majorErrorMessage` to provide you with more detailed error messages. For more information about detecting database errors from SSJS, see Chapter 12 of the Netscape SSJS developer's guide, *Writing Server-Side JavaScript Applications*, which you can find on the CD-ROM that comes with this book in the materials that support Chapter 3.

Error Levels

So far I've discussed errors as if they were a binary condition — either you have an error or you don't. However, some applications may require more sophisticated error detection than this. You may need to know what kind of error occurred and how severe it was before you can determine how to handle it. For this reason, when you're designing your application you should think about errors in severity levels such as "warning," "input error," and "fatal error." For instance, in a data entry application, a warning might be used to report to the user that he or she hasn't filled out any optional fields in an input form, though he or she will still be permitted to submit the form. By contrast, an input error could require the user to fill in all mandatory fields before he or she can submit the form and proceed to the next part of the application.

Differentiating among error levels can also be useful as a debugging tool. For example, you could design your application to output detailed warnings and status conditions while debugging but silence this noncritical feedback during normal execution.

Defining a hierarchy of error levels, codes, and messages can take a lot of planning, especially for large applications. Once again, let me stress that this planning shouldn't take place as an afterthought but rather should be a normal part of any application design process.

Handling Errors

Once you've detected an error, you must decide what to do with it. Your options include reporting the error to the user and allowing him or her to take some action, taking some action (such as rolling back a database transaction) automatically, failing gracefully and then halting the application, or any number of other responses. In most cases, you'll want to let users know what happened and what they can do about it.

Constructing an Error Page

One way you can handle error reporting is to redirect users to a special page, `error.html`, whenever your application detects an error. This special page reports that an error has occurred and gives details about the error and possibly tips on how to resolve it. For example, suppose a form in your application has several required fields, and you want to ensure that they're all filled in before accepting the information. If your form handler detects that some of the required fields are blank, it can redirect the user to a page that says some of the fields haven't been filled in and possibly lists the blank fields. Of course, you can first perform any number of other actions, such as closing a connection to a database that you might have opened to insert a record.

Constructing such an error page is fairly straightforward. From the page where the error occurred, you need to send details about the error such as error codes, error messages, and suggestions for resolving the problem. Depending on your application, you might not need to report all this information, so it's up to you to decide how far you want to go.

One of the simplest ways to send information to the error page is to send your error message as part of the URL query string. When you redirect to your error page, you'll have to provide a URL anyway, so you might as well append a query string and send along an error message. Don't forget to URL-encode the message, using the JavaScript function `escape()`, in case it contains spaces, special characters, or punctuation, none of which are allowed unencoded in URLs. For example, the following redirect statement sends the URL-encoded text of an error message to error.html:

```
errMsg = "Some of the required fields are missing.";
errMsg += "Please click the Back button on your browser and
try again.";
redirect("error.html?myerror=" + escape(errMsg));
```

The error page could then dynamically write out the value you sent over, `request.myerror`, and possibly provide some static information such as Webmaster e-mail addresses, links to online help, or other contact information. Keep in mind that SSJS automatically decodes the URL-encoded value of the `myerror` property for you before storing it in the `Request` object. You can include as many parameters as you like in order to pass more information, such as error codes and tips on resolving the error.

This method for handling errors works fine in simple cases. Next I'll explain some more robust ways to return errors from your functions.

Returning Multiple Values in a Result Object

Returning error information from a page such as a form handler can be a simple matter, but returning an error code or message from a JavaScript function can be tricky since JavaScript functions can return only a single value or object. What do you do if you need to return both an error message and a return value from the function? Because a single object can hold many values, you can return a custom JavaScript object that contains as many values as you need to return, including error codes and messages. This trick can be used not only for error handling but also anytime you need to return multiple values from a function.

The next code example shows the definition of a typical result object that you can return from your functions. Every application is different, so feel free to modify the object to fit your needs.

```
function ResultObj (result, errorMsg) {
    // Define object properties.
this.result = result;
this.errorMsg = errorMsg;
}
```

To use this object, simply instantiate it in your function, set the `errorMsg` and `result` properties, and return the object, as shown in the following code:

```
// Assume the variable stockVal contains the number of items
currently
// in stock and was set prior to calling the following lines
of code.
var result = new ResultObj(stockVal, "Stock value is below
the minimum level.");
return result;
```

Creating an Error Object

Now suppose that you want to enable your result object to return more sophisticated error information than just an error message. You could modify the result object to do this, or you could create a separate object to handle error information.

I recommend creating a separate error object and storing an instance of it in your result object in order to separate the behaviors of storing and manipulating results from those of storing and reporting errors. Once you separate the duties out into an object, you can think about assigning methods that look up error messages based on error codes returned, and customizing error output.

The next example defines a basic error object, which you can modify and expand to suit your needs. Notice that the methods getErrorCode and getErrorMessage are just basic get methods and don't do anything special. Later you'll see how you can expand these methods to perform additional operations.

```
function ErrorObj (errorCode, errorMsg) {
    // Define properties of the object.
    this.errorCode = errorCode;
    this.errorMsg = errorMsg;
    // Define methods of the object.

    this.getErrorCode = eoGetErrorCode;
    this.getErrorMessage = eoGetErrorMessage;
    this.serialize = eoSerialize;
    this.deserialize = eoDeserialize;


}
function eoGetErrorCode() {
    return this.errorCode;
}
function eoGetErrorMessage() {
    return this.errorMsg;
}
function eoSerialize() {

    var resultStr = "";
    // Delimit the code and message values with a semicolon
(;).
    resultStr = this.getErrorCode() + ";";
    resultStr += this.getErrorMessage();
    // URL encode the string so it can be added to a URL.
    resultStr = escape(resultStr);
```

```
        return resultStr;
    }
    function eoDeserialize(serStr, decode) {
        var valArray = new Array();
        if (typeof(serStr) == "string") {
            if (decode)
                serStr = unescape(serStr);
            // Split the string into two strings using the
            // JavaScript split() method of the String object.
            valArray = serStr.split(";");
            this.errorCode = valArray[0];
            this.errorMsg = valArray[1];
        }
    }
```

To use the error object effectively, you must recognize that as an object, it has its own behaviors. For instance, notice that the object has a method called serial-ize() that "flattens" out the object into part of a URL-encoded string, which you can then append to a query string and send to an error page. The next example shows how you could use the ErrorObj object with a form handler to report a database connectivity error.

```
var error = new ErrorObj(7, "Invalid password");
redirect("errorpage.html?err=" + error.serialize());
```

The example just after this paragraph shows how the error page would reconstitute the ErrorObj object based on the URL-encoded values and generate the error messages. You can experiment with this code and try to find the right balance between using a simple error handler and full-blown error objects.

```
// Initially construct an empty object.
var error = new ErrorObj();
// Because the Request object automatically decodes its
properties,
// simply pass the serialized string contained in
request.err to
// the deserialize () function and tell it not to decode it.
error.deserialize(request.err, false);
```

```
write("Error code: " + error.getErrorCode() + "<br>");
write("Error message: " + error.getErrorMessage());
```

The examples above show only one type of error object. In keeping with languages such as Java, you can think of these error objects as more like exception objects and specialize them to contain custom information and even methods depending on the type of exception they represent. For instance, you could create a specialized error object called DBError that knows how to report specific information about database errors. Instead of forcing the user to call majorErrorCode and majorErrorMessage, it could override the standard ErrorObj object's getErrorMessage method and automatically call majorErrorMessage as part of its built-in functionality.

To specialize error objects, you'll need a way of determining which type of error object is returned so you know which interface to rely on when you start working with it. For this, you add an exceptionType property and corresponding getExceptionType method. The following code example shows the definition of such a DBError object, which inherits from the base ErrorObj object. (In case you don't already know it, you can use inheritance with user-defined JavaScript objects.)

```
function DBError(connObj) {
    this.dbConnection = connObj;
    this.exceptionType = "DBError";
    this.getExceptionType = dbeGetExceptionType;
    // Override the ErrorObj getErrorCode and getErrorMessage
methods.
    this.getErrorCode = dbeGetErrorCode;
    this.getErrorMessage = dbeGetErrorMessage;
}
// DBError gets its prototype from the ErrorObj object.
// NOTE: This statement must be executed in an SSJS page,
client-side page, or
// client-side .js include file.  It will NOT work in an
SSJS .js include file.
DBError.prototype = new ErrorObj;
function dbeGetExceptionType() {
    return this.getExceptionType;
}
```

```
function dbeGetErrorCode() {

    // Return a database error code.

    return this.dbConnection.getMajorErrorCode();
}
function dbeGetErrorMessage() {
    // Return a database error message.
    return this.dbConnection.getMajorErrorMessage();
}
```

Cleaning up with CleanRedirect()

Finally, before you leave the page you're on and redirect to an error page, don't forget to perform any cleanup operations that might be needed. In database applications, for example, simply zipping off to an error page without first closing cursors and releasing connections can cause some real problems. However, you certainly don't want to write the same cleanup code several times on every page where you might need to redirect to an error page. Instead, you should write a function that will perform common cleanup tasks and that you can call from anywhere.

The next example is a reusable function, CleanRedirect(), that can close cursors and result sets and release database connections automatically, and then redirect to your error page (or any URL, for that matter) when it's done. This function closes only one cursor and releases only one connection, but you can modify it to close several without too much trouble.

```
function cleanRedirect(url, connObj, cursor, rsObj) {
    if (rsObj != null)
        rsObj.close();
    if (cursor != null)
        cursor.close();
    if (connObj != null)
        connObj.release();
    redirect(url);
}
```

The following code example shows how to use CleanRedirect() in a typical database application:

```
// Assume hrdbPool is a stored DbPool instance that was
initialized
// in the application's initial page.
var hrconn = project.hrdbPool.connection("HRConn", 15);
var hrcursor = hrconn.cursor("SELECT * from EMPLOYEES where
CITY='Seattle');
// Perform database operations ...
// Ready to close and redirect to a results or error page.
var url = "errorpage.html?err=" + escape("A database error
has occurred.");
CleanRedirect(url, hrconn, hrcursor, null);
```

Design Error Handling in the Design Phase

I hope you'll find the error-handling tips and tricks presented in this chapter as useful as I have in my own projects. Whatever platform you use, just remember to plan your error-handling mechanisms in the design phase, not at the end of the implementation phase. Designing code that performs a task is only half the battle. Customers want applications that meet their list of functional requirements, but they also want applications that don't fall apart every time someone sneezes.

30

Extending the Capabilities of the Server-Side JavaScript File Object

Duane K. Fields — *internet systems engineer, Tivoli Systems*

Many Web developers are familiar with server-side JavaScript's built-in File object, which enables reading and writing to files on the Web server. Java and Perl aficionados may feel that the File object lacks some of the power and elegance of their file access implementations. In this chapter, I'll show you how to use SSJS's object inheritance model to extend the functionality of the File object in a powerful and elegant way.

Throughout this chapter, I'll be working with the SuperFile module, which you can find on the CD-ROM that accompanies this book. You can compile this module straight into your applications and take advantage of the new capabilities the `SuperFile` object offers, or extend it further to meet your specific needs. The approach I use here — building on the functionality of an existing object — can be applied to any of JavaScript's built-in objects, or even to objects that you've created yourself.

ON THE CD-ROM

The SuperFile module, around which the discussion in this chapter is based, can be found on the CD-ROM that accompanies this book in the file Chapter 30 SuperFile_js; follow the path: Sample Code and Supporting Documentation ➪ Part III ➪ Chapter 30.

If you've never used the `File` object, the excellent documentation in Chapter 7 of Netscape's *Writing Server-Side JavaScript Applications* (available on the CD-ROM in the materials that support Chapter 3; follow the path: Sample Code and Supporting Documentation ➪ Part I ➪ Chapter 3) will get you up and running quickly. You should be familiar with basic file operations before reading this chapter since I'll be showing you how to add to (and in some cases enhance) existing functionality.

Taking Advantage of JavaScript's Object Model

Although Java uses a class-based system for creating objects and their relationships, JavaScript employs a prototype approach. In Java, you define classes that describe objects, then create instances of each class to bring the objects themselves into being. Object classes can inherit functionality from each other through subclassing — defining a class as being built upon an existing class. Under JavaScript's prototype approach, by contrast, there are no classes, just objects. But objects can inherit the properties of their "prototype object" in a way analogous to the class-subclass relationship in Java. So the object inheritance relationship in Java and JavaScript is architecturally the same, if not syntactically so.

I'll be using a Java-style object-oriented programming (OOP) vocabulary throughout this chapter; when I refer to classes and subclasses in JavaScript, I mean the words in the OOP sense, not literally.

The File Object

SSJS's file system services are provided through the `File` object. To work with a file, you must first create a File object (an "instance," if you will) by invoking the `File()` function and passing in the filename:

```
myFile = new File("/tmp/data.txt");
```

The `File()` function is a constructor — a special type of function that returns an object with properties and methods (functions that operate on objects) defined inside the constructor. So the `File()` constructor returns an instance of the `File` object, which we call `myFile`. As an instance of the `File` object, `myFile` will have properties and methods associated with it.

For example, the following statement uses the object's `getLength()` method to print the length of the file represented by the `myFile` instance of the `File` object:

```
write ("Length is " + myFile.getLength() + " bytes.");
```

The `getLength()` method is defined as part of the `File` object and has no meaning outside it. A full complement of methods and properties associated with the `File` object enable you to open the file, read data from it, and so on. In the rest of this chapter, I explore adding file-related functionality to our programs by building on the existing `File` object.

Creating a New Superfile Class

When defining a new class, you don't have to start from scratch each time — you can build on an existing class through inheritance. Inheritance, simply stated, means that a subclass automatically has all the same properties and methods as its parent. Thus, an instance of the subclass has a ready-made set of data and operations. You can add entirely new methods to this object as well, or alter existing methods to specialize, refine, or customize their behavior.

SSJS already has the basic functionality you're looking for — the capability to read and write to files on the server. Suppose you want to add some new functionality and create customized operations. You'll create a new `SuperFile` class based on the existing `File` object to avoid having to rewrite all the existing, and perfectly good, `File` object methods. You'll define our constructor to create a `File` object and pass it back directly.

```
function SuperFile(filename)
{
    var f = new File(filename);
    return f;
}
```

Now that you've defined our `SuperFile` object as a subclass of JavaScript's built-in `File` object, you can create a new `SuperFile` instance just as we would create a regular `File` object:

```
myFile = new SuperFile("/tmp/data.txt");
```

The `myFile` object can now be used just as if it were a `File` object — as a subclass of `File`, `SuperFile` has inherited all the properties and methods of `File`. Of course, this becomes useful only when you begin extending the capabilities of `SuperFile`.

Adding New Methods to Superfile

Now you will want to extend the functionality of our `SuperFile` object by adding new methods. You'll create a `getContents()` method that will enable you to read the contents of the entire file in one step. You'll make use of existing methods such as `readln()` to get the job done.

The first step in adding a method to our `SuperFile` class is to create a function that's designed to operate on a referenced object rather than to receive an explicit object through its arguments. To refer to the object you're working with inside the function, use the `this` keyword. Once the function is assigned to a particular object (such as your `SuperFile` object), the `this` keyword can be used to act on the object's properties. For example, `this.x` would refer to property `x` of whatever object the function was assigned to.

So you create the `getContents()` function — referring to the `SuperFile` object's `readln()` and `eof()` methods (inherited from the `File` object) through the this keyword — as follows:

```
function SuperFile_getContents()
{
   var contents = "";
   var line = "";
   while (! this.eof())
   {
      if ((line = this.readln()) &&
!this.eof())
         contents += line;
   }
   return contents;
}
```

It's common practice to name functions that will be used as methods of objects in the form `Classname_function`. This lets anyone working with the code know that this is a method to be used in association with an object, and that the method is not to be called directly.

Once the function has been defined, you tie it to our `SuperFile` object by mapping the function name to an object property in the constructor:

```
function SuperFile(filename)
{
   var f = new File(filename);
   this.getContents = SuperFile_getContents;
   return f;
}
```

Notice that you don't say `SuperFile_getContents()` or `this.getContents()`, because in this case (with the parentheses added) JavaScript would try to evaluate the function immediately. Instead, you're simply mapping the function's name to the object.

Once you've set up this mapping, you can call the method on the object just as you would call native methods. For example, with your `myFile` object, you could say

```
contents_of_file = myFile.getContents();
```

This is a powerful technique indeed. You can create as many methods as you need, encapsulating all the added functionality directly into the object. By keeping our routines generic, you open the door to code reuse. Anytime you need to perform file operations in the future, for example, you can just throw our `SuperFile` object into the mix.

Using LiveConnect to Call Java Methods

The Java programming language's `File` class has a number of very useful methods. For example, the class contains the `canRead()` and `canWrite()` methods, which test a file to determine if the system can access it. But because these are methods of a Java (not a JavaScript) `File` object, you can't access them directly in JavaScript.

What you need, then, is a way to somehow associate the complementary Java-accessible version of the `File` object with our JavaScript one. LiveConnect can provide you access to Java objects (as described in the TechNote *Java to JavaScript Communication Using Server-Side LiveConnect*, which is on the CD-ROM), so this is the likely solution. All you have to do is provide instances of our `SuperFile` class with access to the Java `File` object corresponding to the file you're working with. This will open up most of the Java `File` object's methods.

ON THE CD-ROM
The Netscape Technote *Java to JavaScript Communication Using Server-Side LiveConnect* can be found on the CD-ROM that accompanies this book in the file, Chapter 30 Server Live Connect.

Let's modify the `SuperFile()` constructor to include a new property called `javaFile` that gives ready access to the Java version of our `File` object:

```
function SuperFile(filename)
{
    var f = new File(filename);
    this.getContents = SuperFile_getContents;
    f.javaFile = new java.io.File(filename);
    return f;
}
```

You may be tempted to do something like this in your program now:

```
if (myFile.javaFile.canRead())
    write ("File is Readable!");
```

This will work, but it forces you to remember the details of the Java method and doesn't allow you to add any functionality (such as trying alternate paths or printing debugging information) to the canRead() operation. A better way to approach this problem is to add a method to your SuperFile class to handle the canRead() test. By encapsulating the Java calls inside your own method, you're defining an interface, or set of operations, that won't have to change if you wish to add functionality later to the canRead() test itself.

```
function SuperFile(filename)
{
    var f = new File(filename);
    this.getContents = SuperFile_getContents;
    f.javaFile = new java.io.File(filename);
    f.canRead = SuperFile_canRead;
    return f;
}
function SuperFile_canRead()
{
    return this.javaFile.canRead();
}
```

One thing to keep in mind when working with Java calls through LiveConnect is that any arrays or strings returned from Java calls will be Java (not JavaScript) objects and as such will have to be converted. This can be accomplished with simple utility functions such as the following:

```
function javaArrayTojsArray(javaArray)
{
    var jsArray = new Array();
    for (var i=0; i < javaArray.length; i++)
        jsArray[i]=javaArray[i];
    return jsArray;
}
function javaStringTojsString(javaString)
```

```
{
    var jsString = javaString + "";
    return jsString;
}
```

Booleans, dates, and integers will automatically be converted into the appropriate JavaScript object, and thus don't require special handling.

Overloading Parent Class Methods

Many of the operations you'd like to perform on files are already defined by the `File` object. However, you might wish to alter an operation's behavior or add functionality to it. For example, you might want the operation to record debug information, perform additional validity checks, or modify data before or afterward.

Say you want to modify the `File` object's `open()` method to verify that the file is indeed readable and to log an error message if it is otherwise. You first need to modify the constructor to assign the built-in File object's `open()` method to SuperFile objects because you're about to create our own `open()` method. If you fail to do this, you won't be able to make calls back to the "old" `open()` method because you're essentially redefining it.

```
function SuperFile(filename)
{
    var f = new File(filename);
    this.getContents = SuperFile_getContents;
    f.javaFile = new java.io.File(filename);
    f.canRead = SuperFile_canRead;
    f.parent_open = f.open;
    f.open =  SuperFile_open;
    return f;
}
```

You can then define your own `open()` method, with whatever extras you like:

```
function SuperFile_open(args)
{
    if (this.canRead())
```

```
        return this.parent_open(args)
    else
        java.lang.System.out.println("Cannot
read"+this+", read access not allowed");
    }
```

Going Further

Although the `File` object isn't available in client-side JavaScript, the techniques introduced in this chapter can generally be applied to any objects in order to extend their functionality. You can extend the `Array` object, for example — adding your own methods to replace any functionality you feel is missing or confusing. Or you can add new features to the `String` object.

CROSS-REFERENCE

For further exploration of the concept of extending the capabilities of server-side JavaScript, see Chapter 33, "Extending Server-Side JavaScript Prototypes."

By packaging functionality into reusable objects, you can develop robust code modules once, and then reuse them from project to project. This style of programming not only gets you up and running quickly but also encourages elegant, clear, robust program design. The `SuperFile` object included on the CD-ROM is a good start. Simply compile the `SuperFile.js` module into your own projects and invoke it to instantiate your own `SuperFile` objects.

31

Accessing LDAP from Server-Side JavaScript

Mark Wilcox — *Web administrator, University of North Texas*

By promising to bridge incompatible directory services, Lightweight
Directory Access Protocol (LDAP) has taken the Internet world by storm.
Netscape's Directory Server was the first commercial LDAP server to hit
the market, but others have steadily followed. For example, the two most common
proprietary network directory services, Novell's NDS and Sun's NIS, can now be
accessed using LDAP, further fueling the LDAP fire. Already, personal search databases such as BigFoot and Four11 have become LDAP enabled. Since Version 3.0,
Netscape's Enterprise Server has used LDAP as the base protocol for its user data-

base, and from the beginning, an LDAP client-side application, the "Search a Directory" applet, was included with Communicator.

CROSS-REFERENCE

If you're not yet familiar with LDAP and the Netscape Directory Server, read Chapters 4 and 9 before you read this chapter.

This chapter shows you how to access LDAP from Netscape Enterprise Server using server-side JavaScript, with the help of the Netscape LDAP Java SDK (also known as the *Directory IFC*) and a library I provide (called *LDAP.js Library*). The LDAP.js Library is available on the CD-ROM; for the LDAP SDK and Netscape Enterprise Server, you'll have to go to the Netscape Web site and download them — they're free. For directions on how to do so, go to the files on the CD called *Welcome and Software Download*.

ON THE CD-ROM

The LDAP.js Library is available on the CD-ROM that accompanies this book. To find it, follow the path, Sample Code and Supporting Documentation ➪ Part III ➪ Chapter 31. To take full advantage of it, you'll need to use the Netscape LDAP Java SDK and Enterprise Server, both available for free download from the Web. For download directions and links, see the file on the CD called *Welcome and Software Download*.

I start with a look at the LDAP record structure; you will need to understand this in order to search an LDAP database.

Using the LDAP Record Structure

The database in an LDAP server is hierarchical in nature and may contain both textual and binary data. The root directory branches down into individual entries.

If you're familiar with Novell's NDS or the X.500 protocol, you're already familiar with the basics of the LDAP record structure. Table 31-1 shows an example of a record containing textual data about a user.

TABLE 31-1: AN LDAP RECORD

TABLE ENTRY	EXPLANATION
dn: cn=John Doe,o=UNT,c=US	Dn = the distinguished name, the unique key for the record.
objectclass: top objectclass: person objectclass: organizationalPerson objectclass: inetOrgPerson	Objectclass attributes denote the type of record.
givenname: John	Givenname = the user's first name. A user can have multiple givennames.
sn: Doe	Sn = surname, the user's last name. Typically, there is only one per record.
cn: John Doe	cn = common name, the name the user is typically known by in the organization. It is traditionally part of the dn, and there is only one per record.
uid: jdoe	uid = a user's id, used for authentication purposes.
mail: nobody@unt.edu	A user's e-mail address. There can be multiple addresses per record.
telephone: 940-555-5555	A user's telephone number. There can be multiple telephone numbers per record.
creatorsname: uid=entadmin,o=UNT,c=US	The dn of the user who created this record.
createtimestamp: 19980225160825Z	The time when record was created, in GMT.
description: This entry was modified with the LWLDAP program by jdoe at 05-Mar-98 7:35:22 AM	A note field. It can be anything, and there can be multiple entries per record.
userpassword: {SHA}NWdeaPS1r3uZXZIFrQ/EOELxZFA=	The user's password. This example is stored in secure hash algorithm format, but passwords can be stored in clear-text or MD5 hash format.

Continued

TABLE 31-1: *(continued)*

`modifytimestamp:` `199803132010039Z`	The time when record was last modified, in GMT.
`modifiersname: uid=` `entadmin,o=UNT,c=US`	The dn of the user who modified this record.
`title: Marketing Rep`	The title of the user.

Each record can be thought of as an object. User objects can belong to groups of unique members (such as organizational units); groups can in turn belong to other groups.

Table 31-2 shows an example of a group record, in the form used by the Netscape Enterprise Server. Note that a group record has several field elements in common with a user record.

TABLE 31-2: A GROUP RECORD IN NETSCAPE ENTERPRISE SERVER FORM

TABLE ENTRY	EXPLANATION
`dn: cn=padm5530,o=UNT,c=US`	The distinguished name of the group; in this case a class of students.
`objectclass: top`	Shows where in the database hierarchy the record fits.
`objectclass:` `groupOfUniqueNames`	Denotes a group of users.
`cn: padm5530`	The group's common name.

`description: Dr.`
`Smith's Public`
`Administration class`
	A note field.

`creatorsname:` `uid=entadmin,o=UNT,c=US`	The dn of the creator of this record.
`createtimestamp:` `199802161840024Z`	The time of creation in GMT.
`uniquemember:` `cn=John Doe,o=UNT,c=US`	A member of this group. Of course, there can be multiple entries of this type per record; each entry must be in the form of a dn.

TABLE ENTRY	EXPLANATION
owner: cn=classadmin, o=UNT,c=US	An owner of the group. There can be multiple entries. Could denote special privileges, such as the capability to add or remove unique members. The Enterprise Server does not consider an owner to be a "member" for access purposes; you must add an ACL per owner if you restrict access to a Web site on your server.
modifytimestamp: 19980311171903Z	The time when the record was last modified, in GMT.
modifiersname: cn=Directory Manager, o=UNT,c=US	The dn of the user who last modified this record.

The LDAP database structure is an object-oriented hierarchy. Each element of the dn and the `objectclass` attributes helps determine where in that hierarchy the record fits.

Let's look more closely at the distinguished name (dn) field. The dn usually contains at least the user's first and last names (common name, cn), the organizational unit (ou) the user belongs to, and the base field of the user's organization's hierarchy (known as the *directory base*, consisting of the organization name, o, and country, c). You can also include a user's id or Social Security number or some other field to help provide uniqueness to a given dn. Here's an example of such a dn:

```
cn=Mark Wilcox+uid=mwilcox,ou=ACS,o=UNT,c=US
```

If you don't specify any special attributes in the dn like uid or ou, it is assumed that the dn is at the top of the hierarchy.

Searching an LDAP Database

Most LDAP servers provide a publicly accessible search interface with which a client can interact. The LDAP specification allows for Boolean, wildcard, and case-insensitive searching. The LDAP syntax currently is obscure and arcane, so it does take some time to get used to. The "Search a Directory" applet provides an easier-to-use search interface.

A search normally has two parts. First, you specify where in the hierarchy you want to search, called the `Search Base`. For example:

```
Search Base: o=UNT,c=US
```

All searches start from the Search Base, which in this case is the root of the UNT (University of North Texas) LDAP hierarchy.

Second, you specify a search filter. Here are some examples of filters:

```
cn=Mark Wilcox
sn=Wil*
(&(cn=Ma* Wilcox)(ou=Accounting))
```

The first filter looks for a common name (`cn`) matching Mark Wilcox. The second filter searches the LDAP server for all users that have a surname (`sn`" with "Wil" as the first three letters. It will return Wills, Wilcox, and Wilson, but not Goodwill. The third filter, an example of a Boolean `AND` search, returns all users who have a first name that starts with "Ma" and a last name of Wilcox and are a part of the organizational unit (`ou`") Accounting. The Boolean LDAP operators are `&` for `AND`, `|` for `OR`, and `!` for `NOT`. Notice that the operator is placed first inside a group of parentheses.

The code listing that follows is an example Java method that takes a search base, a user name, and an attribute to search for and returns an array of any matches it finds.

```java
public synchronized String[] getAttrib(String searchBase,
                                       String username,
                                       String attribute){
    // Returns an array of attributes.
    String [] myAttrib= null;
    try{
      // Sets up the LDAP filter.
      String MY_FILTER=
"(|(uid="+username+")(cn="+username+"))";
        // Sets up to pass back only the attribute(s) you want
        String[] attrNames = { attribute };
        if ( searchBase == null ){
          searchBase = MY_SEARCHBASE;
        }  // Performs the actual search.
```

```
    LDAPSearchResults res = ld.search(searchBase,
                               LDAPv2.SCOPE_SUB,
                               MY_FILTER,
                               attrNames,
                               false);
        /* Loops on results until finished; will only be
one! */
    if (res.hasMoreElements() ) {
       LDAPEntry findEntry = (LDAPEntry)res.nextElement();
       /* Gets the attributes of the entry. */
       LDAPAttributeSet findAttrs =
findEntry.getAttributeSet();
       Enumeration enumAttrs = findAttrs.getAttributes();
       /* Loops on attributes. */
       while ( enumAttrs.hasMoreElements() ) {
          LDAPAttribute anAttr =
(LDAPAttribute)enumAttrs.nextElement();
          String attrName = anAttr.getName();
          if ( attrName.equals(attribute) ) {
             Enumeration enumVals = anAttr.getStringValues();
             Vector myVector = new Vector();
             while ( enumVals.hasMoreElements()){
                myVector.addElement((String)
enumVals.nextElement());
             }
             myAttrib = new String[myVector.size()];
             try{
                // Will speed up stepping through enumVals.
                for(int i=0;;i++){
                 myAttrib[i] = (String)myVector.elementAt(i);
                }
             } catch(ArrayIndexOutOfBoundsException z) {}
          }
       }
    }
}
```

```
        catch (LDAPException e) {
          switch( e.getLDAPResultCode() ) {
            case e.NO_SUCH_OBJECT:
              System.out.println( "The specified user does not
exist." );
            case e.INVALID_CREDENTIALS:
              System.out.println("Invalid password for user: "+
username);
            default:
              System.out.println(e.toString());
          }
        }
        return myAttrib;
      }
```

Creating an LDAP SSJS Application

Applications developed with SSJS have two major benefits to developers. One is that SSJS applications are fairly easy to create and set up. The other is that the LiveConnect mechanism provides an easy way to connect to individual Java classes. LDAP and SSJS make good company because you can hide the complex LDAP API in a Java class (or classes) that is easily accessed by SSJS.

Because you can place your SSJS code in standard HTML files, you can quickly develop several different LDAP applications that use your existing page design re-sources/creators. Some examples of possible applications are:

- A public search interface for users who don't have access to the Communicator LDAP applet

- A way for users to modify their attributes

- A way to provide different levels of access to the records (for example, anyone has access to e-mail addresses, but only managers have access to employees' home telephone numbers)

An LDAP application generally follows these steps when interacting with an LDAP server:

1. Initializing a session with the LDAP server

2. Authenticating itself to the LDAP server

3. Performing LDAP operations

4. Closing the connection to the LDAP server

Initialization

During initialization, as shown in the next long code listing, a number of variables need to be set for your environment. It's best if you add a new entry (or entries) to your directory server that you can use for all these types of applications. I chose not to use the "Directory Manager" here; instead I created a user that has read and write permissions on the database.

The default listening port is 389 if you're not using SSL, and 649 if you are.

The redirect at the end of the code is irrelevant when this initial page is called during application or server startup. I've included it simply so that I can reuse the code should project.ldap need to be reinitialized. Thus, in the start page (login.htm), I've included the following lines:

```
if (project.ldap == void(0)){
    redirect('init.htm');
}
```

This checks for the existence of project.ldap and redirects back to this page if needed. Here's the complete listing:

```
// Set to your LDAP host.
  project.host  = "directory.phoenixgroup.com";
  // Set to your LDAP port.
  project.port  = 389;
  // Set to your directory base.
  project.searchBase = "o=Phoenix Group,c=US"
  // Set to the distinguished name you are going to use.
  project.mgr_dn      = "cn=SSJS LDAP,ou=Information
Services,o=Phoenix Group,c=US"
  // Set to the password for the distinguished name.
  // May be blank for mgr_dn & mgr_pw if directory allows
anonymous searches.
  project.mgr_pw      = "<MGR DN PASSWORD>"
```

```
/* Grab an LDAP connection. */
var ldap          = connect(project.host,
                              parseInt(project.port),
                              project.searchBase,
                              project.mgr_dn,
                              project.mgr_pw);
if (ldap == null){
  /* Connection could not be made. */
  write("Failed to connect to LDAP server. See error log
or Java Console<br>");}
  else{
    /* Store the connection in the project object. */
    project.ldap = ldap;
    redirect("home.htm");
  }
```

Authentication

When you connect to an LDAP server, you have the option to connect as an authenticated user or to connect anonymously. If you want to perform any LDAP operations (such as password checking or changing a record's attribute), you must be an authenticated user. In some instances, you're granted extra rights depending on which group you're a part of.

When your application authenticates itself to an LDAP database, the LDAP API expects the call to be in the form of a user's dn and password. Users can't be expected to remember their full dn, but they can usually provide their user id. So an LDAP-based authentication should first perform a search to retrieve the user's dn and then make the authenticate method call, as shown in the next code example:

```
var passwd = request.pwd;
var login  = authenticate(project.ldap,user,passwd);
debug('<B>'+user+'</B>');
debug('<B>'+passwd+'</B>');
debug('<B>'+login+'</B>');
if (login == true){
  client.user = user;
```

```
    // I'm doing this instead of a redirect.
    write('<FORM  NAME="redir" ACTION="attrib.htm"
METHOD=POST>');
    write('<INPUT TYPE="hidden" NAME="junk">');
    // We need at least one field for this to work.
    write('</FORM>');
  }
  else{
    // I'm simulating a redirect because I don't want to
pass
    // these values on the URL line.
    write('<FORM  NAME="redir" ACTION="login.htm"
METHOD=POST>');
    write('<INPUT TYPE="hidden" NAME="relogin"
VALUE="YES">');
    write('<INPUT TYPE="hidden" NAME="badpw" VALUE="YES">');
    write('</FORM>');
  }
```

LDAP Operations and Disconnection

Though most data in an LDAP server is in a binary format, you do most of your interaction with the LDAP server in an intermediate data format called LDAP Data Interchange Format (LDIF). This is an ASCII text representation meant to foster the capability to transfer LDAP data between servers and to manipulate LDAP records with a variety of clients.

It's easy to access the Netscape LDAP Java SDK from SSJS. However, because of the number of exceptions and objects that are provided currently in the JavaScript language, it's better to have a Java middle-ware class that actually handles all the calls to the Netscape LDAP Java SDK.

By default, SSJS applications are like standard HTML files or CGI applications — that is, they're free and open to the world. There are two basic ways to protect your SSJS application. The Netscape TechNote, "Protecting Your SSJS Applications with a Directory Server," which you can find on the CD-ROM, shows one way to protect an application with LDAP so that anyone trying to access the application will need to enter a user name and password.

ON THE CD-ROM

The Netscape TechNote, "Protecting Your SSJS Applications with a Directory Server," can be found on the CD-ROM that accompanies this book. To find it, follow the path, Sample Code and Supporting Documentation ⇨ Part III ⇨ Chapter 31.

The code in the test suite below shows how to provide a login page that uses the Netscape LDAP Java SDK to protect your SSJS application. It also shows an interface to an SSJS application that enables users to change a preference in their records, such as their password or e-mail address. This example shows the code to change a password.

```
user    = client.user;
  oldpw    = request.oldpw;
  newpw    = request.newpw;
  newpw2   = request.newpw2;
  if (newpw != newpw2){
    redirect("changepw.htm");
  }
  else{
    var goodpw = authenticate(project.ldap,user,oldpw);
    if (goodpw == true){
      // Change password will also test changeAttrib because
      // changePW is actually a wrapper to that method.
      var didChange =
changePW(project.ldap,user,user,newpw);
      if (didChange == true){
        write("Password changed for user: "+user);
        write("<br><a href=\"home.htm\">Login as a different
user</a>");
      }
      else{
        write("***ERROR*** Password change failed. Check
error logs.");}
      }
    else{
      redirect("changepw.htm");
    }
  }
```

The `LDAP.js` library on the CD-ROM provides a function to disconnect from the server.

Using the LDAP.js Library

To make it easier to write LDAP-enabled JavaScript applications, I've created a library of JavaScript functions called `LDAP.js`, which you can find on the CD-ROM. To use the `LDAP.js` library, you must include an additional Java class (`SSJSLDAP.class`) with your code. This class acts as a wrapper class to help trap `LDAPExceptions` that can be thrown by the underlying LDAP Directory Package, making it easier to provide meaningful messages to both JavaScript and the developer.

You can use one of two methods to install the necessary class files. The first method involves getting a small subset of the Netscape LDAP Java SDK from the most recent Netscape Communicator release, whereas the second method has you download the entire SDK. The first method is easier, but the second method gives you the most complete package of classes.

Here is the first method:

1. Retrieve the `ldap10.jar` file from the classes directory in the most recent Netscape Communicator release. It can be found in the Communicator directory at `Program Files\Netscape\Communicator\Program\Java\Classes`.

2. Go to the directory *server root*`\plugins\java`.

3. Make a directory there called `local-classes`, if it doesn't already exist.

4. Copy the `ldap10.jar` file into the local-classes directory and then unzip it. This creates a Netscape directory with a bunch of class files in it.

5. Place the `SSJSLDAP.class` file in the *server root*`\plugins\java\local-classes` directory.

6. Restart the Enterprise Server.

7. When you compile your Web file for your SSJS applications, make sure that you include the `LDAP.js` file when you run the JavaScript Compiler.

Here is the second method:

1. Retrieve the Netscape LDAP Java SDK from the web (see the file at the root level of the CD called *Welcome and Software Download*) and install it on your system.

2. Go to the directory *server root*\plugins\java.

3. Make a directory there called local-classes, if it doesn't already exist.

4. Copy the ldapfilt.jar and ldapjdk.jar files into the local-classes directory and then unzip them. This creates a netscape and a com directory.

5. Place the SSJSLDAP.class file in the *server root*\plugins\java\local-classes directory.

6. Restart the Enterprise Server.

7. When you compile your Web file for your SSJS applications, make sure that you include the LDAP.js file when you run the JavaScript Compiler.

When using the LDAP.js library, you'll first have to call the connect() method. This method is passed all the necessary information to connect to the LDAP server. It will return an LDAP object that's a reference to the SSJSLDAP.class, and you'll pass this LDAP object to each method you call in the LDAP.js library.

To help the developer out, the LDAP variable is stored as a variable in the project object. This makes it available (and keeps the connection open to the LDAP server) between applications. The library takes care of this action. All you have to do is call the connect() method at the start of your SSJS application. Note that this one connection method is ugly because of a bug in the way Enterprise handles LDAP connections, but without this fix, your Directory Server may crash.

The code example below shows the LDAP.js Library. Another file called SSJSLDAP.java is needed to make the library work and is included on the CD-ROM with the rest of the LDAP.js Library.

```
// Due to a bug in the LDAP code in Enterprise 3.x
servers, we create
// one shared connection in the project object.
function connect(host,port,searchBase,mgr_DN,mgr_PW){
  var ldap = Packages.SSJSLDAP(host,
                               parseInt(port),
                               searchBase,
                               mgr_DN,mgr_PW);
  var conn = ldap.connect();
  if (conn){
    return(ldap);
```

```
    }
    else{
      return null;
    }
  }


  // Returns an array of values for a given attribute.
  function getAttrib(ldap,
                     searchBase,
                     user,
                     attrib){
    var nullArray = new Array();
    nullArray[0] = "";
    myArray = new ldap.getAttrib(searchBase,user,attrib);
    if (myArray == null){
      return nullArray;
    }
    else{
      return myArray;
    }
  }


  // Returns true if attribute is set, false if not.
  // Pass it the user who's making the modification,
attribute to change,
  // value to change to. The user must have rights in the
database to actually
  // make the change.
  function setAttrib(ldap,user,mgr_DN,attrib,value){
    var results = ldap.setAttrib(user,mgr_DN,attrib,value);
    return(results);
  }


  // Change a user's password.
  function changePW(ldap,user,mgr_DN,newPass){
    var results =
setAttrib(ldap,user,mgr_DN,"userpassword",newPass);
```

```
    return(results);
}

// Return a list (array) of groups the user is a part of.
function getGroupArray(ldap,searchBase,user){
  var nullArray = new Array();
  nullArray[0]  = "";
  var myArray = new ldap.getGroups(searchBase,user);
  if (myArray == null){
    return nullArray;
  }
  else{
    return myArray;
  }
}

// Boolean function that returns true if the user is a
member of a group.
  function isMember(ldap,searchBase,user,group){
    var groupArray = getGroupArray(ldap,searchBase,user);
    var holder = "";
    for (var i=0; i<groupArray.length; i++){
      holder = groupArray[i];
      if (holder.indexOf(group) != -1){
        return true;
      }
    }
    return false;
}

// Boolean function that returns true if the user is
authenticated.
  // false if not
  function authenticate(ldap,user,pwd){
    var passed = ldap.authenticate(user,pwd);
    return(passed);
}
```

```
// Returns user's distinguished name.
function getUserDN(ldap,user){
  var myDN = ldap.getDN(user);
  return (myDN);
}


// Disconnect from server.
// Due to current bug in Enterprise 3.x servers,
// only call when application dies.
function disconnect(ldap){
  ldap.disconnect();
}
```

Using the Test Suite for the LDAP.js Library

The test suite for the LDAP.js library consists of these files, all of which are on the CD-ROM:

- `attrib.htm`

- `authenticate.htm`

- `changepw.htm`

- `commitchange.htm`

- `home.htm`

- `init.htm`

- `login.htm`

To install this test suite, you must have a copy of the Netscape Enterprise Server and the Netscape Directory Server (Versions 1.0*x* or 3.*x*). These examples will not work with the default database that is shipped with the Enterprise Server. You must make sure that the class files are accessible by the Enterprise Server by following either the first or second method outlined above.

Next create a directory called `ldaptest` and place the `LDAP.js` and all of the `.htm` files in this directory. Compile them with the server-side JavaScript Compiler (`jsac`) that comes with your Enterprise Server into a Web file called `ldap.web`. See the SSJS documentation for more information.

Start up your SSJS application manager and create a new SSJS application called `ldap`. Give it the path to the `ldap.web` file you created. The initial page should be set to `init.htm`, and the default page should be `init.htm`.

Then you should be able to browse to `http://your.server/ldap/` and login.

32

Interleaving JavaScript with HTML

Robert Husted — *intranet technical lead, Qwest Communications*

You're creating a server-side JavaScript (SSJS) application and find that you need to embed HTML in your JavaScript code in order to present users with truly dynamic pages. You use the `write()` function to explicitly print the required HTML, but your code ends up looking insanely messy with all those quote (") and escape quote (\") characters. If you accidentally forget to escape a quote, you'll introduce a bug into the code. And if you ever need to edit the HTML in your application, you'll find it difficult to read and to spot mistakes, which means you'll be spending a lot of time debugging while your friends play Quake II on the net.

Isn't there an easier way? Well, yes, there is. Unknown to many developers and even to some folks at Netscape, you can "interleave" SSJS code with HTML, just as you can do with competing products. Although not publicized, and not even mentioned in much of the existing documentation, this capability has been available since the inception of SSJS and it's included with the Netscape Enterprise Server. Indeed, interleaving was included in SSJS by design. With interleaving, the SSJS code and the HTML are distinctly separate units; it's obvious where one stops and the other starts. The application looks cleaner and is easier to maintain.

You can also clean up your JavaScript code by using presentation templates to separate out the HTML, as detailed in Chapter 24, "Changing a Web Application's Look and Feel without Touching the Source Code." In the chapter you're reading now, I show you how to use interleaving by comparing interleaved HTML with embedded HTML in three different situations that you might run into when developing an SSJS application.

Example 1: Displaying HTML Text Based on User Input

Okay, so in your SSJS application you want to display different HTML text depending on what the user has entered. Let's suppose that you want to display a search form when the user first accesses a given page, and on subsequent accesses you want to display database information (and not the form). How will you do it? Well, if you don't interleave the JavaScript code and the HTML, you'll have to embed the HTML in JavaScript `write()` statements as shown in the following code:

```
<BODY>
...
<SERVER>
if (request.search) {
    // STATEMENTS THAT DISPLAY DATABASE INFORMATION GO HERE
}
else {
    write "<FORM NAME=\"myForm\" ACTION=\"thisPage.html\"
METHOD=POST>";
    write "<INPUT NAME=\"search\" SIZE=30 MAXLENGTH=60>";
```

```
       write "</FORM>";
   }
   </SERVER>
   ...
   </BODY>
```

The <SERVER> tags mark the beginning and end of the SSJS code executed by the server. Notice that the HTML is sandwiched between quotes in the `write()` statements. Any quote marks (") appearing in the HTML must be escaped (\"); otherwise, they'll cause JavaScript errors when you try to compile your application.

Using `quote` and `escape quote` characters makes your code all but unreadable. It's really difficult to pick out where the HTML begins and ends. If you later want to edit the HTML on the page, you'll have to worry about HTML and SSJS. I can't tell you how many times this has caused me grief when creating an application.

To make the code more readable, what you can do is to end the SSJS code preceding your `write()` statements with a `</SERVER>` tag, dispense with the `write()` statements and instead insert the plain HTML, and then start the next section of SSJS code with another `<SERVER>` tag. This results in the interleaved code shown in this example:

```
<BODY>
...
<SERVER>
if (request.search) {
    // STATEMENTS THAT DISPLAY DATABASE INFORMATION GO HERE
}
else {
</SERVER>
<FORM NAME="myForm" ACTION="thisPage.html" METHOD=POST>
<INPUT NAME="search" SIZE=30 MAXLENGTH=60>
</FORM>
<SERVER>
}
</SERVER>
...
</BODY>
```

Notice how much easier it is to read the HTML in this fragment. The HTML looks like HTML now, rather than like some bizarre mutation. If you have to alter the form, you can do it easily. Without having to worry about escaping quotes, you've just monumentally reduced your chances of creating bugs in the application. Now, if only you could do this with client-side JavaScript! (You can't.)

Example 2: Displaying Database Query Results in a Form

Okay, now I assume you want to do something trickier. You want to query a database and display the results in a form so that the user will be able to edit the database information easily. Normally, to do this you'd have to write something like the code shown in the next example.

```
<TABLE BGCOLOR=BLUE>
<TR BGCOLOR=LIGHTYELLOW>
   <TD><B>NAME</B></TD>
   <TD><B>JOB</B></TD>
   <TD><B>SALARY</B></TD>
   <TD> </TD>
</TR>

<SERVER>
if (dbConnection.connected()) {

    // EXECUTE SQL STATEMENT
    var cur = dbConnection.cursor(mySQLStatement);
    while (cur.next()) {
        write("<TR><FORM METHOD=POST
ACTION=\"update.html\">" +
        "<TD><INPUT TYPE=TEXT NAME=\"employee\" " +
        "VALUE=" + cur.ename==null?'':cur.ename) +
        " SIZE=20></TD>" +
        "<TD><INPUT TYPE=TEXT NAME=\"job\" " +
        "VALUE=" + cur.job==null?'':cur.job +
```

```
            "SIZE=20></TD>" +
            "<TD><INPUT TYPE=TEXT NAME=\"salary\" " +
            "VALUE=" + cur.sal*12 + " SIZE=20></TD>" +
            "<TD><INPUT TYPE=HIDDEN NAME=\"empno\" " +
            "VALUE=" + cur.empno + ">" +
            "<INPUT TYPE=SUBMIT NAME=\"UPDATE\" " +
            "VALUE=\"Update\" SIZE=20></TD>" +
            "</FORM>" +
            "</TR>";
        }
        cur.close();
    }
</SERVER>


</TABLE>
```

That sure doesn't work very well! Try to figure out where the HTML form starts — kind of hard, isn't it? If you need to change our HTML to do something such as add another column to the table, you've got to read the messy JavaScript code very carefully and make your changes without introducing new bugs.

There's an easier way to do it. You simply interleave your HTML inside an SSJS `while` loop. To put the database values directly into your form fields as you display them, you put JavaScript variables inside `backquote` characters (`` ` ``) in the HTML tags. Here's how the code looks:

```
<TABLE BGCOLOR=BLUE>
<TR BGCOLOR=LIGHTYELLOW>
    <TD><B>NAME</B></TD>
    <TD><B>JOB</B></TD>
    <TD><B>SALARY</B></TD>
    <TD> </TD>
</TR>


<SERVER>
if (dbConnection.connected()) {
    // EXECUTE SQL STATEMENT
    var cur = dbConnection.cursor(mySQLStatement);
    while (cur.next()) {
```

```
</SERVER>

<TR>
  <FORM METHOD=POST ACTION="update.html">
  <TD><INPUT TYPE=TEXT NAME="employee"
VALUE=`(cur.ename==null?'':cur.ename)` SIZE=20></TD>
  <TD><INPUT TYPE=TEXT NAME="job"
VALUE=`(cur.job==null?'':cur.job)` SIZE=20></TD>
  <TD><INPUT TYPE=TEXT NAME="salary" VALUE=`cur.sal*12`
SIZE=20></TD>
  <TD><INPUT TYPE=HIDDEN NAME="empno" VALUE=`cur.empno`>

  <INPUT TYPE=SUBMIT NAME="UPDATE" VALUE="Update"
SIZE=20></TD>
  </FORM>
</TR>

<SERVER>
    }
    cur.close();
}
</SERVER>

</TABLE>
```

Again, the HTML in this code actually looks like HTML. You can edit the HTML or the SSJS easily without worrying about causing problems in the JavaScript code. Even adding another column to this table will be remarkably easy because you can clearly see the HTML.

Example 3: Querying a Database Column and Generating a Select List

Now let's try one last example. Certainly you've created forms that have list boxes in them (select lists). How do you use this technique to query a column in a database and then generate a select list? Well, first let's look at how you would do it without interleaving:

```
<FORM ACTION="db2.html" METHOD="GET">
. . .;
<SELECT NAME="state">
<SERVER>
if (dbConnection.connected()) {
    sql = "SELECT NAME FROM LU_STATE";
    // EXECUTE SQL STATEMENT
    cur = dbConnection.cursor(sql);
    while(cur.next()) {
        if (cur.name == request.name) {
            write("<OPTION SELECTED VALUE=\"" +
            cur.name + "\">" + cur.name);
        }
        else {
            write("<OPTION VALUE=\"" +
            cur.name + "\">" + cur.name);
        }
    }
    cur.close();
}
dbConnection.release();
</SERVER>
</SELECT>
. . .
</FORM>
```

Now, take a look at how you can improve the readability of your code with interleaving, as this example shows:

```
<FORM ACTION="db2.html" METHOD="GET">
. . .
<SELECT NAME="state">
<SERVER>
if (dbConnection.connected()) {
    sql = "SELECT NAME FROM LU_STATE";
```

```
    // EXECUTE SQL STATEMENT
    cur = dbConnection.cursor(sql);
    while(cur.next()) {
        if (cur.name == request.name) {
</SERVER>
<OPTION SELECTED VALUE=`cur.name`>
<SERVER>
            write(cur.name);
        }
        else {
</SERVER>
<OPTION VALUE=`cur.name`>
<SERVER>
            write(cur.name);
        }
    }
    cur.close();
}
dbConnection.release();
</SERVER>
</SELECT>
. . .
</FORM>
```

Okay, so this last example isn't as dramatic as the previous one. However, notice that by interleaving in this last example it is much easier to quickly spot the <OP-TION> tags and read them.

Making Your Code Easier to Read and Maintain

If you've never looked at a .web file, try it sometime — it will help you better understand how interleaving works on the Enterprise Server. Basically, the JSAC compiler concatenates all of your HTML and JavaScript code into a single .web file. The SSJS code is compiled into JavaScript byte-code and appears intermixed with the HTML and client-side JavaScript. So your `.web` file is one big file with a bunch of HTML pages, JavaScript libraries (`.js` files), and compiled SSJS. When you request an HTML page within an application, the server parses this big `.web` file (which is resident in memory) and locates the specific page you want. As the page is sent to you, the server executes all the SSJS byte-code it finds.

Interleave SSJS and HTML in your applications to make the code easier to read and understand. You can use this technique to conditionally display parts of a page without having to rely on JavaScript `write()` statements. This makes your maintenance efforts much easier and will greatly improve the readability of your code. For those of you who have asked why Netscape hasn't provided this capability as its competitors have, here's your answer. Netscape has always provided it — this is where the competition got the idea.

33

Extending Server-Side JavaScript Prototypes

Robert Husted — *intranet technical lead, Qwest Communications*

In Chapter 30, "Extending the Capabilities of the Server-Side JavaScript File Object," Duane Fields explains how to extend an instance of the server-side JavaScript File object. He even shows how to use Java to do this so that you can get the file type, last-modified date, permissions information, and so on. These techniques work wonderfully for extending individual instances of an object, but what if you want to extend all instances of an object on the server (all those you'll create, as well as those you've already created)? What about special objects such as SendMail, where you can't add JavaScript functions as properties of the object? In such cases, you must extend the JavaScript "prototype" for that object using its constructor's `prototype` property, as I discuss in this chapter.

The prototype for `SendMail` (for example) is an object that is pointed to by `SendMail`'s `prototype` property, and whose properties and methods apply to all instances of `SendMail`. Here's an analogy that may help clarify this: A JavaScript prototype is like a blueprint of a house, whereas a single instance of an object is like a house built with the blueprint. Chapter 30 talks about the `File` object and shows you how to modify the house — how to add a room, for example. I'm going to explain how to change the blueprint so that every new house you build has the additional room. (Because of the way JavaScript works, even the older houses you've already built from the blueprint will suddenly have the additional room.)

ON THE CD-ROM

The `SuperMail.js` file built in this chapter is available on the CD-ROM that accompanies this book. Look for the file, Chapter 33 SuperMail_js.txt. You can find it by following the path Sample Code and Supporting Documentation ⇨ Part III ⇨ Chapter 33.

Please note that although JavaScript prototypes are based on object-oriented programming (OOP) principles, they are not the same as the Java or C++ implementation of a "class."

Modifying the SendMail Prototype

The following example creates an instance of the `SendMail` object and assigns it to the JavaScript variable `myMail`:

```
var myMail = new SendMail();
```

If we add methods or properties to `myMail`, we're simply modifying a single instance of `SendMail`:

```
myMail.myProperty = "my initial value";
myMail.myMethod = myJavaScriptFunction;
```

Now `myMail` (and only `myMail`) has a new property named `myProperty`, and a new method named `myMethod` that points to an existing JavaScript function.

Notice that when adding a method you don't use parentheses or include any function arguments. In the above code, myJavaScriptFunction refers to a JavaScript function that is called with myJavaScriptFunction(args), where args is a list of arguments passed to the function. When you assign the name of a JavaScript function to SendMail, the function is thereafter treated as a method of SendMail.

In contrast to this, if you change the SendMail prototype, you'll be modifying all instances of SendMail, including myMail — because myMail was constructed from the SendMail prototype. You see, SendMail has a constructor that in turn has a property named prototype (see Figure 33-1). SendMail's prototype property points to an object whose properties and methods are added to all instances of SendMail. (The same is true for Array, Date, DbPool, and so forth.)

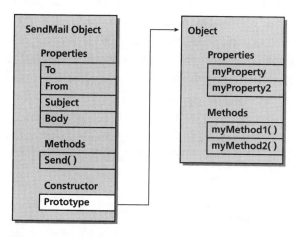

Figure 33-1: SendMail and its prototype

If you want to add properties and methods to all instances of SendMail, you would do this:

```
SendMail.prototype.myProperty = "my initial value";
SendMail.prototype.myMethod = myJavaScriptFunction;
```

Now every existing instance of SendMail (including myMail) has a property named myProperty and a method named myMethod, and every instance created thereafter will likewise have this property and method. You'd use myProperty and myMethod just like any existing property or method. For example:

```
var myMail = new SendMail();
myMail.myProperty = "some new value";
myMail.myMethod(arg1, arg2, ...);
```

An Example: Sending E-mail Attachments

Suppose you want to apply this concept to something useful — for example, to make it easier to send e-mail attachments with your messages. You can simply write some functions that will add MIME-encoded or text attachments to a message, and then add these functions as new methods of the `SendMail` prototype. This way, every time you create an instance of the `SendMail` object in any SSJS application on your server, you'll have access to the methods that you've added.

How do you do this? Well, for starters, you need to write the JavaScript functions that create the file attachments and their associated headers. The attached files have to be either text files or Base64-encoded files (text representations of binary files) because MIME messages must be text only. You'll store the attachments in an array so that you can later package them up when you send your e-mail message. (You'll combine the original message with all the attachments and then send the resulting message.)

Creating File Attachments

Let's write a function (shown just below) to add text files as attachments to our message. By adding a `SuperMail_` prefix to the function names, it is easy to identify them as new methods of `SendMail`. I won't go into the gory details of what this function does because the focus is on extending SSJS prototypes. It's sufficient for your purposes to note that the function reads the contents of a text file, creates an appropriate MIME header, and puts the resulting string in attachments (an array that holds our file attachments until you're ready to send your e-mail message). The code for this function (and those that follow) is commented, so you can browse through it to better understand what the function does.

```
// CREATE A TEXT FILE ATTACHMENT

function SuperMail_attachTextFile(fullFilename) {
```

```javascript
  // CREATE FILE ATTACHMENT ARRAY IF IT DOES NOT EXIST
  if (this.attachments == null) {
    this.attachments = new Array();
  }
  var filename = fullFilename;

  // SET THE INITIAL CONTENT TYPE OF THIS TEXT FILE
  var contentType = "text/plain";

  // IF THE TEXT FILE IS AN HTML FILE, CHANGE THE CONTENT
TYPE
  if (filename.indexOf(".htm") != -1) {
    contentType = "text/html";
  }

  // GET JUST THE FILENAME, REMOVE THE EXTRA PATH
INFORMATION
  if (filename.indexOf("/")) {
    filename = filename.substring(
filename.lastIndexOf("/")+1,
      filename.length);
  }
  // CHECK FOR WINDOWS-STYLE PATH INFORMATION AS WELL
  if (fullFilename.indexOf("\\")) {
    filename = filename.substring(
filename.lastIndexOf("\\")+1,
      filename.length);
  }

  // CREATE A NEW JavaScript File OBJECT
  var inFile = new File(fullFilename);
  var contents = "";

  // ENSURE THAT WE CAN READ THE FILE
  if (inFile.open("r")) {

    // GENERATE A HEADER FOR THE TEXT FILE
```

```
        contents = "Content-Type:" + contentType +
          "; charset=us-ascii name=\"" +
          filename + "\"\n" +
          "Content-Transfer-Encoding: 7bit\n" +
          "Content-Disposition: inline; filename=\"" +
          filename + "\"\n\n";

        // READ ENTIRE CONTENTS OF FILE INTO THE VARIABLE
"contents"
        contents += inFile.read(inFile.getLength());

        // ADD THE ATTACHMENT TO FILE ATTACHMENTS ARRAY
        this.attachments[fullFilename] = contents + "\n";

        // CLOSE THE FILE
        inFile.close();

        return true;
    }
    else {
        return false;
    }
}
```

Note that the `this` keyword is used in this function and the others you'll create. At present, `this` doesn't refer to anything. However, when you add the functions as methods of `SendMail`, `this` will refer to the `SendMail` prototype. And when you create an instance of `SendMail`, `this` will refer to the current instance.

If you want to attach a MIME-encoded (Base64) file to your message, you'll need a second function because MIME files are markedly different from text files. Both are text-based, but MIME-encoded files are in Base64 format (an encoding where binary files are converted to a special text format) while text files are generally in 7-bit ASCII. Most mail clients can convert files back to binary format using a Base64 decoder. Here's the code for the second function:

```
// ATTACH A MIME-ENCODED FILE

function SuperMail_attachMIMEFile(fullFilename, mimeType) {
```

```
// CREATE FILE ATTACHMENT ARRAY IF IT DOES NOT EXIST
if (this.attachments == null) {
  this.attachments = new Array();
}

var filename = fullFilename;

if (filename.indexOf("/")) {
  filename = filename.substring(
filename.lastIndexOf("/")+1,
    filename.length);
}
if (fullFilename.indexOf("\\")) {
  filename = filename.substring(
filename.lastIndexOf("\\")+1,
    filename.length);
}

var inFile = new File(fullFilename);

// ENSURE THAT WE CAN READ THE FILE
if (inFile.open("r")) {

  // READ ENTIRE CONTENTS OF FILE
  this.attachments[fullFilename] =
inFile.read(inFile.getLength());

  // CLOSE THE FILE
  inFile.close();

  // IF THE FILE DOES NOT HAVE A HEADER, CREATE ONE
  var header = this.attachments[fullFilename];
  if (header.indexOf("Content-Type:") == -1) {

    if (mimeType == "") {
      mimeType = "application/octet-stream";
    }
```

```
                    // GENERATE A HEADER FOR THE FILE
                    this.attachments[fullFilename] =
                      "Content-Type: " + mimeType + "; name=\"" +
                      filename + "\"\n" +
                      "Content-Transfer-Encoding: base64\n" +
                      "Content-Disposition: attachment; filename=\"" +
                      filename + "\"\n\n" +
                      this.attachments[fullFilename];
                }
                return true;
            }
            else {
                return false;
            }
        }
```

Adding and Clearing All File Attachments

You need a function to combine all the file attachments into a single message body, and you also have to be sure not to discard your existing message body because you may want to include a text or HTML message with your file attachments. The `SuperMail_addAttachments()` function does all this, and here's what it looks like:

```
// ADD ALL ATTACHMENTS TO THE OUTGOING MESSAGE

function SuperMail_addAttachments() {

  // GENERATE THE BOUNDARY THAT SEPARATES PARTS OF THE
MESSAGE
  this.Boundary = this.generateBoundary();

  // GET MESSAGE TYPE OF MAIN MESSAGE (TEXT OR HTML) BEFORE
  // CHANGING THE TYPE OF THE ENTIRE MESSAGE TO
multipart/mixed
  if (this["Content-Type"]) {
    mainMessageType = this["Content-Type"];
  }
  else {
```

```
    mainMessageType = "text/plain";
 }


 // CREATE REQUIRED MIME HEADER INFORMATION FOR ATTACHMENTS
 this["Content-Type"] = "multipart/mixed; boundary=\"" +
this.Boundary + "\"";
 this["MIME-Version"] = "1.0";


 // ADD INITIAL MIME-SECTION HEADER
 var msgBody =
   "\nThis is a multi-part message in MIME format.\n" +
   "--" + this.Boundary + "\n" +
   "Content-Type: " + mainMessageType + "; charset=us-
ascii\n" +
   "Content-Transfer-Encoding: 7bit\n\n" +
   this.Body + "\n\n";


 // ATTACH ALL FILES TO THE OUTGOING MESSAGE
 for (i in this.attachments) {

   // ADD BOUNDARY
   msgBody += "--" + this.Boundary + "\n";

   // ADD FILE CONTENTS
   msgBody += this.attachments[i];
 }

 // ADD FINAL BOUNDARY
 msgBody += "--" + this.Boundary + "--" + "\n\n";
 this.Body = msgBody;
}
```

The above function calls SuperMail_generateBoundary(), which creates a unique boundary for your mail message. The boundary is important because it's what separates the different parts of the e-mail message. The code is simple: You just add up a bunch of random numbers to create the boundary. Here's what SuperMail_generateBoundary() looks like:

```
// GENERATE A MIME BOUNDARY FOR FILE ATTACHMENTS

function SuperMail_generateBoundary() {

  boundaryDate = new Date();
  boundary = "--------------MIME";
  boundary += boundaryDate.getSeconds();
  boundary += Math.round((Math.random() * 100));
  boundary += "A";
  boundary += boundaryDate.getMinutes();
  boundary += Math.round((Math.random() * 100));
  boundary += "B";
  boundary += boundaryDate.getHours();
  boundary += Math.round((Math.random() * 100));
  boundary += "C";
  boundary += Math.round((Math.random() * 100));
  return boundary;
}
```

Sending the Message

The SuperMail_send() function, shown next, calls the addAttachments() method of SendMail to package up your e-mail message and attachments, and then clears the attachments array (which you no longer need because you've added the attachments to the message). Finally, it calls SendMail's existing send() method to send our email message.

```
// PROCESS AND SEND THE EMAIL MESSAGE

function SuperMail_send() {

  // IF ATTACHMENTS EXIST, ATTACH THEM TO THE OUTGOING
MESSAGE
  if (this.attachments != null) {
    this.addAttachments();
    this.attachments = null;
  }
```

```
  // SEND THE EMAIL MESSAGE
  if (this.send()) {
    return true;
  }
  else {
    return false;
  }
}
```

Adding the Functions as SendMail Methods

Now comes the fun part: adding these functions as methods of the SSJS `SendMail` prototype and using them to send e-mail messages with file attachments. As shown in the next code example, you add the following methods. (Remember that when you add function names to the `prototype` object, you don't include the parentheses.)

Three methods:

- `attachTextFile()`, which puts a text file and header into attachments

- `attachMIMEFile()`, which puts a Base64-encoded file and header into attachments

- `Send()`, which packages and sends our email message

Two private methods (used by other methods in `SendMail`, but not used directly by you):

- `addAttachments()`, which adds all of our file attachments to the outgoing message

- `generateBoundary()`, which creates a unique MIME boundary

And here's the code where you add the methods:

```
// EXTEND THE JAVASCRIPT SENDMAIL PROTOTYPE

function SuperMail()  {

  // METHODS
  SendMail.prototype.Send = SuperMail_send;
  SendMail.prototype.attachTextFile =
SuperMail_attachTextFile;
```

```
SendMail.prototype.attachMIMEFile =
SuperMail_attachMIMEFile;

    // PRIVATE METHODS
    SendMail.prototype.addAttachments =
SuperMail_addAttachments;
    SendMail.prototype.generateBoundary =
SuperMail_generateBoundary;
}
```

Every `SendMail` object instance on the server will contain these methods. This includes any new `SendMail` instances that you create as well as any existing ones. All you need to do is make a single call to the `SuperMail()` function from within the initial page of one of our SSJS applications, as follows:

```
SuperMail();
```

You can now use all the methods as if they had been built into `SendMail`, as shown in the next code example. You never have to use the `SuperMail()` function again; it has done its work of extending the `SendMail` prototype.

```
// CREATE A NEW SENDMAIL OBJECT INSTANCE
var myMail = new SendMail();

// SET SOME OF THE SENDMAIL PROPERTIES
myMail.To = "husted@netscape.com";
myMail.From = "someone@netscape.com";
myMail.Subject = "Test Message";
myMail.Body = "This is a test, it is only a test...";

// ATTACH A TEXT FILE
myMail.attachTextFile("C:/TEMP/myTestFile.html");

// ATTACH A MIME-ENCODED FILE
myMail.attachMIMEFile(c:/temp/calendar.mme,"image/gif");

// SEND THE EMAIL MESSAGE
myMail.Send();
```

You can easily add text or MIME-encoded files to any outgoing email message. This means that you can attach text files and even entire HTML pages from the server. (Note that if you add an HTML page to your outgoing message, all the form actions and hyperlinks must be fully qualified URLs and not relative to the server or they won't work properly.) Take a look at the `SuperMail.js` file — it's on the CD-ROM — and start using it in all of your email-enabled Web applications.

Now It's Your Turn

This chapter has shown you how to extend a JavaScript prototype, specifically the `SendMail` prototype. All object instances constructed from this prototype on the server contain the methods added in the example.

You can use this same technique to extend the prototypes of objects such as `Array`, `Date` (to add your own application-specific date formats), `Window` (on the browser), and so on. You might even want to extend the prototype of the SSJS cursor object to create a `SuperCursor` that enables you to call `next()` and `prev()` to loop through all of your returned database values. The possibilities are limitless.

IV

Server Development, II: Building Applications for Scalability

IV

Server Development, II: Building Applications for Scalability

If you've developed small workgroups applications that you want to grow to serve more users, this section will help you get started. It focuses on the specific issue of moving applications from Netscape Enterprise Server to run on Netscape Application Server. A future version of NAS is supposed to make this migration easier, but in the meantime, the chapters in this part will help. The chapters will also give you other ideas for developing applications that can scale to meet the needs of thousands — even millions — of users.

We've focused on stable APIs rather than on cutting-edge technology because we want to give you solutions and ideas that work today (as in the rest of the book). The programming ideas presented here are in use in real-live applications as you read this.

The chapters in this section can only scratch the surface of this large, complicated topic. Be sure to visit *View Source* magazine at `http://developer.netscape.com/viewsource` for a lot more ideas about how to build large-scale Web applications.

34

Building Scalable Server-Side JavaScript Applications, Part 1: A Layered Approach

JJ Kuslich — *application developer, Application Methods, Inc.*

In addition to being a buzzword used in every software marketing datasheet and brochure on the planet, *scalability* has a very tangible meaning to software developers. It refers to the ability of an application to scale up, or grow, to meet some anticipated increase in demand on system resources, often because of growth in the number of users. Scalability is of particular concern to Web developers because there is often no way to accurately forecast just how many users will visit a site, especially when a site first opens to the public.

Netscape Enterprise Server can scale up as a content server to handle large numbers of requests for static Web pages and other documents, but the server-side

JavaScript (SSJS) engine within Enterprise Server that handles application requests is designed to handle only smaller loads for workgroup-sized applications. This means that if you're using Enterprise Server, you'll reach the limits of SSJS scalability, and thus Enterprise Server's limits as an application server, long before you reach its limits as a content server.

This chapter and Chapter 35 are based on the theory that you can make your SSJS applications scalable by making them portable to a more scalable platform or a so-called runtime environment, like Netscape Application Server (NAS). They'll introduce you to how you design portable SSJS applications using a layered approach and how you can best prepare them for porting to the new runtime environment.

CROSS-REFERENCE

To obtain an understanding of the differences between Netscape Enterprise Server and Netscape Application Server, see Chapter 6.

Not all applications need to be designed to scale up to heavy-duty application servers. If you're just building a simple Web storefront for small merchants who don't expect overwhelming amounts of traffic, SSJS may be the only platform you need. However, if you're building an application that you want to deploy in multiple market segments — say, a small business version, a midmarket version, and an enterprise version — you'll need a scalable platform for your application. (Keep in mind that when I refer to *platforms*, I mean the SSJS and NAS platforms, not operating systems.)

In this chapter, I describe how to build a multitiered SSJS application. In Chapter 35, I present more specific techniques for designing your SSJS applications so that they can be ported to a more scalable application server, like NAS. If you're interested only in learning how to build multitiered SSJS applications, you can skip this chapter and read the next one. However, if you want to build SSJS applications that can scale up to a server like NAS, you'll want to read both.

Building Scalable Apps: A Strategy

The overall strategy for building scalable SSJS applications is a process that combines elements of multitiered application design, object-oriented design, and common sense. As you'll see, many of the ways you can achieve portability involve traditional good design techniques, so they aren't as intrusive or specialized as you might think. The process has the following three steps:

- **Separate presentation, application, and data logic.** SSJS and NAS present information to the client in different ways and use different database APIs. Keeping the logic in separate layers, known as *multitiered programming*, and isolating SSJS-specific code into specialized classes or objects makes it easier to upgrade the application to work with NAS or another application server when the time comes to scale up. How to do this is covered in this chapter.

- **Build a bridge between SSJS and the application server.** In this step, you design the interface points between your application layers and between objects within each layer to be as platform-independent as possible. Isolating platform specifics into implementation details and away from public interfaces helps improve portability. This is discussed in Chapter 35.

- **Generate dynamic output as HTML.** Resolving HTML generation incompatibilities between SSJS and NAS improves portability. Once again, creating platform-independent interfaces between your application's layers helps isolate incompatibilities into implementation code and away from public interfaces that are used throughout the application. This also is covered in Chapter 35.

The design choices you make within each step vary based on the solution you choose, but the steps remain the same. I'll illustrate each of the steps with a simple example of how you would perform the required operations for a typical SSJS application. The examples are all drawn from the same fictional business, introduced later in this chapter. This chapter discusses step 1 in detail, while Chapter 35 discusses steps 2 and 3.

Taking a Multitiered Approach

Multitiered programming, also called *multilayered programming,* refers to the logical or physical separation of application responsibility into different layers, or tiers. Typically, you might have a thin client running on the top tier, an application server running on the middle tier, and a database server running on the bottom tier. The thin client handles presentation logic, which deals with presenting information to the user in a user interface. The application server handles application logic, which might perform calculations, check business rules, and transfer data between the client and the database server. The database server holds the data, and may perform data validation.

The Alternatives

The alternative to multitiered programming is client-server programming, in which you typically have a fat client, which handles most presentation and application logic, communicating with a dedicated server, like a relational database server, which handles most data logic. One of the advantages of multitiered programming is that, in theory, it's very scalable. If you have a bottleneck at any tier, you can upgrade or change that one tier and limit the effect on the other tiers. In a traditional client-server application, if your fat client gets too fat, you have to upgrade, retest, and redistribute the entire client to all of your users.

In my experience, many Web developers using scripted application servers like Microsoft Active Server Pages (ASP) or Netscape SSJS tend to write Web applications as if they were writing a fat-client application. Most of their application logic resides in each page, completely intertwined with presentation and data logic. Sometimes the logic is separated out into function libraries, but often this is done inconsistently, so that the application, data, and presentation layers are still inseparable. Just because ASP and SSJS let you put all of your logic right in the HTML page, doesn't mean that you have to put it there, or that you should.

Logically separating your SSJS application into layers may not directly give you more scalability, but it does improve scalability indirectly by making your application more portable, as I suggested earlier. And separating presentation logic from application logic has other acknowledged benefits beyond scalability. It sets the stage for improved performance, enables code reuse, improves maintainability, provides greater flexibility for future upgrades, and makes code easier to understand. For moderate to large applications, these are all benefits that customers look for, because they lead to a decrease in maintenance and upgrade costs in the long run. So in general, you should already be employing a layered approach in your SSJS application designs.

A Closer Look at the Layers

Let's look a little more closely at what I mean when I refer to presentation logic, application logic, and data logic. *Presentation logic* is code that controls how the application looks and to some degree how it interacts with the user. This includes HTML, style sheets, client-side JavaScript, and so on. SSJS code can be considered presentation logic when it's responsible for generating output for the browser. For example, a function `PlotStarChart()` that generates a graph to plot astronomical objects would be presentation logic. It doesn't analyze data or retrieve data from a database; it knows only how to use data passed as function arguments to create a star chart on a Web page.

Application logic (or business logic), on the other hand, consists of code that performs application-specific functions not directly related to the user interface. This can include data validation, execution of business rules, calculations, manipulation of data, and so on. A function `CalcPlanetPos()` that calculates the orbital position of a specified planet on some future date would be considered application logic. It may call out to a database that contains historical astronomical data on the orbit of the planet passed in as a function argument and then apply a formula for extrapolating the position of the planet in the future. It doesn't know anything about how the information it returns will be used or presented. It simply acts as a specialized provider of information to any information consumer that requires such information.

To tie the presentation and application logic functions together, an SSJS page could call `CalcPlanetPos()` and pass the result to `PlotStarChart()` to render a page with the desired plot, as this code example shows:

```
<HTML>
<HEAD><TITLE>Star Chart</TITLE></HEAD>
<BODY>
<SERVER>
// Call specialized business logic to calculate
// the position of Jupiter on November 12, 1999.
coord = CalcPlanetPos("Jupiter", 11, 12, 1999);
// Call presentation logic and plot the provided coordinates
// on the standard star chart in the color blue.
PlotStarChart(coord, "blue");
</SERVER>
</BODY>
</HTML>
```

The two layers are tied together through the APIs that come out of the process of building up libraries of functions and objects within each layer. Figure 34-1 illustrates this relationship and also shows where a layer of data logic might fit in to round out the picture of a typical multitiered application.

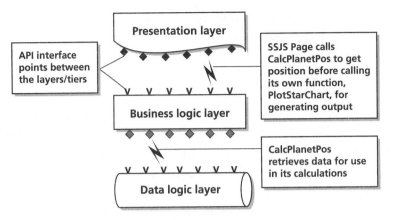

Figure 34-1: How the different layers of an SSJS application communicate through public APIs

What happens if you need to calculate the position of Jupiter in some other application? Suppose you want to use the position information in a Java applet instead of in an SSJS page. If you mingle presentation logic with application logic in the SSJS page, you'll have to pull the calculation information out of the page, put it into a new context, retest the code, and so on. However, if you separate the logic, you can reuse the calculation function directly and feed the information to the Java applet.

Similarly, it's a good idea to separate data logic from application logic. If your function directly accesses a database, you might have to modify it if you switch database servers or modify your schema. Also, because SSJS and NAS use different database APIs, you'll have to change the code that accesses a database when you move from SSJS to NAS. Finally, not all developers who may be capable of writing presentation and application logic may be familiar enough with SQL or stored procedures to write good data logic. So the limitations of your development staff may motivate you to have a small group of database specialists handle the data logic while your other developers focus on less data-intensive tasks. You'll make your life easier by separating out data logic into a distinct layer.

Separating an SSJS Application into Layers: An Example

In this section, I'll illustrate in detail how to take a typical SSJS application that is-n't layered and turn it into a layered application that uses distinct objects and functions. The example that I'll use is a simple two-page application that looks up the status of orders for Snigley Toys, a fictional retailer of toys for pets.

The Scenario

Snigley Toys has been in business for more than a hundred years and has only recently started moving operations to the Web. For the past several years, the firm has outsourced some of its customer service operations and used a slow and overly complex client-server application to give this outside firm access to their customer and order databases. At a recent board meeting, the Chief Information Officer (CIO) complained about the amount of money being spent to outsource customer service operations and suggested using the Web to give customers direct access to order information. Eventually, the CIO hopes to build an online store complete with do-it-yourself customer service functionality, such as automatic order processing.

The company decides to start out small by extending to its customer service firm some of the functionality it would eventually like to build into its Web store. The initial SSJS application will service only a few dozen users, yet should be able to grow to meet the needs of a busy online store servicing hundreds of thousands of customers. When Snigley is ready to build its online store, it will invest in Netscape Application Server and port its SSJS application to NAS. Unfortunately, when Snigley finished the first phase of the project, it found that its developers didn't really understand how to design for portability. Now the firm has hired you to help it straighten out the application before it goes any further.

The Initial Application

The initial application uses a simple HTML form, shown in Figure 34-2, to enable customer service representatives to enter orders placed by phone or fax. When a representative enters order information, the application attempts to insert the order into the database and, if successful, returns a page that summarizes the order information, as illustrated in Figure 34-3. If an error occurs, the representative is redirected to an error page that contains more information about the error.

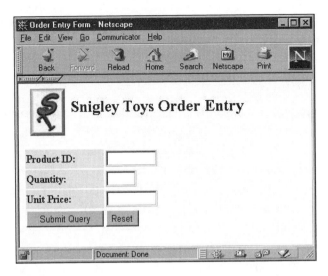

Figure 34-2: A form used to enter customer service representatives

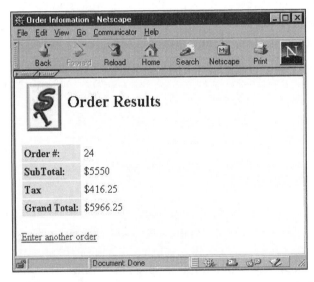

Figure 34-3: The order summary page that's returned when the order is inserted into the database

The next code listing shows the code that produces the order entry form page:

```
<HTML>
<HEAD><TITLE>Order Entry Form</TITLE></HEAD>
```

```
<BODY bgcolor="#FFFFF9">
<H3><IMG SRC="stlogo_sm.jpg" ALIGN="absmiddle"
HSPACE=10>Snigley Toys Order Entry</H3>
<FORM ACTION="orderform_handler.html" METHOD="POST">
<TABLE BORDER=0>
<TR>
<TD BGCOLOR="#EEEECC">Product ID: </TD>
<TD><INPUT TYPE="Input" NAME="productID" SIZE=8></TD>
</TR>
<TR>
<TD BGCOLOR="#EEEECC">Quantity: </TD>
<TD><INPUT TYPE="Input" NAME="quantity" SIZE=4></TD>
</TR>
<TR>
<TD BGCOLOR="#EEEECC">Unit Price: </TD>
<TD><INPUT TYPE="Input" NAME="unitPrice" SIZE=8></TD>
</TR>
<TR>
<TD><INPUT TYPE="Submit" NAME="Insert"></TD>
<TD><INPUT TYPE="Reset" Name="Reset"></TD>
</TR>
</TABLE>
</FORM>
</BODY>
</HTML>
```

The following bit of code shows the SSJS form handler, which is also responsible for creating the order summary page. Please note that the way this sample code retrieves the next available ID from the database is not ideal. I've used this retrieval method to help illustrate multilayered design techniques, not to show the best way to write code for guaranteeing unique database identifiers.

```
<HTML>
<HEAD><TITLE>Order Information</TITLE></HEAD>
<SERVER>
var TAXRATE = 0.075;

// Grab a database connection.
```

```
pool = new DbPool("ODBC", "MyAccessDSN", "", "", "", true);
conn = pool.connection();

// Validate the form data.
if (request.productID == null || request.productID < 1 ||
    request.quantity == null || request.quantity < 1 ||
    request.unitPrice == null || request.unitPrice <= 0)
        redirect("Error.html");

// Attempt to insert the order into the database.
project.lock();
        var nextOrderID = GetNextOrderID(conn); //
GetNextOrderID is a custom function.
        var result = conn.execute("INSERT INTO Orders
(OrderID, ProductID, Quantity, UnitPrice, Tax) " +
                " VALUES (" + nextOrderID + "," +
                request.productID + "," +
                request.quantity + "," +
                request.unitPrice + "," +
                request.unitPrice*TAXRATE + ")");
        project.unlock();
conn.release();
pool.disconnect();

// If the insert was successful, write out a confirmation.
if (result != 0)
        redirect("Error.html");
else {
// Write out the order confirmation.
</SERVER>
<BODY bgcolor="#FFFFF9">
<H2><IMG SRC="stlogo_sm.jpg" ALIGN="absmiddle"
HSPACE=10>Order Results</H2>
<TABLE BORDER=0 CELLPADDING=3 CELLSPACING=2>
<TR>
<TD BGCOLOR="#EEEECC"><B>Order #:</B></TD>
<TD><SERVER>write(nextOrderID)</SERVER></TD>
```

```
</TR>
<TR>
<TD BGCOLOR="#EEEECC"><B>SubTotal:</B></TD>
<TD>$<SERVER>var sub = request.unitPrice * request.quantity;
write(sub)</SERVER></TD>
</TR>
<TR>
<TD BGCOLOR="#EEEECC"><B>Tax</B></TD>
<TD>$<SERVER>var tax = request.unitPrice * request.quantity
* TAXRATE; write(tax);</SERVER></TD>
</TR>
<TR>
<TD BGCOLOR="#EEEECC"><B>Grand Total:</B></TD>
<TD>$<SERVER>write(sub + tax)</SERVER></TD>
</TR>
</TABLE>
<BR>
<A HREF="OrderForm.html">Enter another order</A>
<SERVER>
} // End else statement.
</SERVER>
</BODY>
</HTML>
```

This code listing exemplifies the design of a typical application that's fast, simple, and straightforward to write, a design used by many Web developers. Unfortunately, if you write your code this way, you'll wind up rewriting your entire application when you want to move to a more scalable platform like NAS. Even if you don't want to move to another platform, upgrading code like this won't be pleasant, especially if you didn't write it in the first place.

Clearly, this hasn't been designed with a layered approach. Let's examine some of the problems with it:

■ Calculations (in other words, business logic) have been mixed with the presentation logic. In general, it's not a good idea to bind business rules to user interfaces, especially if you may eventually need more than one interface to respect your business rules. If you keep business rules tucked away in business logic, all user interfaces that access the same business logic will be guaranteed to respect the same business rules in the same way.

- Data validation code has all been jumbled together into one large Boolean OR clause. Application logic should be written in distinct, compact form so that changing a particular business rule doesn't require altering code that processes other business rules.

- The calculations and data validation code directly reference form elements by name. What happens if you build a different form in the future that uses this same form handler, but change the names of the form fields? The input form shown in Figure 34-2 is fairly sparse; it assumes that the users from the customer service center are trained. However, when the online store is built, the interface will have to service novice users and will certainly need to be redesigned. But you don't want to have to rewrite the form handler just because you've changed the look and feel of the form. Or what if new forms use different names for the form elements? In either of these cases, you have to change every single reference to the form elements made in the form handler.

- Some calculations are performed in the midst of constructing the SQL statement, tying business logic to data logic. Should calculations need to be changed, the SQL statement will need to be adjusted as well.

- The code refers directly to database fields, thus mixing business and data logic. If the database schema changes, all code for tables or fields that have changed will need to be updated to reflect the changes.

- The code has redirects embedded in the business logic. Redirects are really presentation logic, as they determine where the user will be sent and what page will be presented next. In general, page redirection should be performed only at the very end of a form handler. Remember that a `redirect` call is really just a `goto`, and that using a `goto` is one of the seven deadly sins of programming.

SSJS and NAS handle form input in different ways and perform data operations differently. So when you port to NAS, you'll have to completely rewrite the code that handles the form input if you don't first separate out the common business logic from the proprietary form-handling code. Porting this form handler will be a lot easier if the application logic is separated from the other logic. When you move to NAS, the application logic should stay pretty much the same and you'll only have to rewrite the portion that handles form inputs to follow the NAS specifications.

The Layered Application

Now I'll transform this standard, but messy, application for Snigley Toys by decoupling the presentation, application, and data logic. I'll make these major changes to the form handler with the goal of separating the logic:

■ Decouple the HTML form from the application code. To avoid problems in the future caused by maintenance changes, upgrades, or new user interfaces being added, I reference the form elements by name only at the very top of the form handler and never again. This will decouple the HTML form from the application code in the form handler, thus making the application code more portable.

■ Move the business logic out of the presentation code in the result output. The form handler actually contains two distinct entities—an application logic module and a user interface generator. You should decouple the application logic from the summary form, for the same reasons that you want to decouple the input form from the application. The first step in this is to remove the business rule from the grasp of the presentation logic.

■ Decouple all application logic from presentation code that outputs the results. Once you isolate the business logic, you can fully separate business logic and presentation logic. In fact, you can even move the presentation logic to an entirely new SSJS page by rearranging the page redirection.

■ Decouple data logic from application logic. You want to isolate the logic that actually updates the database from the business logic in the application. Not only will doing so keep you from having to modify business logic when the database API changes in the move to NAS, but if Snigley decides to switch database servers or modify their database schema at some point, your business logic will be nicely isolated from such changes in data logic.

The following code example shows a new SSJS form handler that has clearly identifiable sections of presentation, application, and data logic. Once the inputs are processed, the form handler redirects to the summary page, where the results are displayed dynamically with SSJS.

```
<SERVER>
// Initialize local variables.
var tax = 0;
var error = false;


// Separate presentation logic from the business logic
below.
// In effect, the variables are business logic and
// the request properties are presentation logic.
var productID = request.productID;
var quantity = request.quantity;
```

```
var unitPrice = request.unitPrice;

// BUSINESS LOGIC:
// The tax rate may change or could vary from state to
state.
// For now, we'll just visually separate it.
var TAXRATE = 0.075;

// BUSINESS LOGIC: Validate values with business rules.
if (productID == null || productID < 1)
    error = true;
if (quantity == null || quantity < 1)
    error = true;
if (unitPrice == null || unitPrice <=0)
    error = true;

// If we passed the business rules, insert the record.
if (!error) {
    // BUSINESS LOGIC: Calculate the tax.
    tax = unitPrice * quantity * TAXRATE;

    // DATA LOGIC: Insert the record.
    pool = new DbPool("ODBC", "MyAccessDSN", "", "", "",
true);
    conn = pool.connection();

    project.lock();
    var nextOrderID = GetNextOrderID(conn); // GetNextOrderID
is a custom function.

    // Now we're just inserting data that's ready to go.
    var result = conn.execute("INSERT INTO Orders (OrderID,
ProductID, Quantity, UnitPrice, Tax) " +
        " VALUES (" + nextOrderID + "," +
        productID + "," +
        quantity + "," +
        unitPrice + "," +
```

```
        tax + ")");
        project.unlock();
    conn.release();
    pool.disconnect();


//If the insert failed, set the flag.
if (result != 0)
    error = true;
}


// PRESENTATION LOGIC:
// Redirect to the proper page depending on the outcome.
if (error)
    redirect("Error.html");
else
    redirect("Confirm.html?orderID=" + escape(nextOrderID))


</SERVER>


<HTML>
<BODY>
If you see this page, a server error has occurred.  Please
contact the
webmaster.
</BODY>
</HTML>
```

Now, here's the code for the new summary page:

```
<HTML>
<HEAD><TITLE>Order Confirmation</TITLE></HEAD>
<SERVER>
var error = false;
var quantity = 0;
var subTotal = 0;
var total = 0;
var orderID = request.orderID;
```

```
    // BUSINESS LOGIC: Validate orderID.
    if (orderID == null || orderID < 1)
        error = true;

    if (!error) {
        // DATA LOGIC: Connect to the database and execute a
    query.
        pool = new DbPool("ODBC", "MyAccessDSN", "", "", "",
    true);
        conn = pool.connection();
        curs = conn.cursor("SELECT * FROM Orders WHERE OrderID="
    + orderID);
        curs.next();

        // BUSINESS LOGIC: Calculate the subtotal and total.
        subTotal = curs.unitPrice * curs.quantity;
        total = subTotal + curs.tax;
    </SERVER>

    <BODY bgcolor="#FFFFF9">
    <H2><IMG SRC="stlogo_sm.jpg" ALIGN="absmiddle"
    HSPACE=10>Order Results</H2>

    <TABLE BORDER=0 CELLPADDING=3 CELLSPACING=2>
    <TR>
    <TD BGCOLOR="#EEEECC"><B>Order #:</B></TD>
    <TD><SERVER>write(orderID)</SERVER></TD>
    </TR>
    <TR>
    <TD BGCOLOR="#EEEECC"><B>SubTotal:</B></TD>
    <TD>$<SERVER>write(subTotal)</SERVER></TD>
    </TR>
    <TR>
    <TD BGCOLOR="#EEEECC"><B>Tax</B></TD>
    <TD>$<SERVER>write(curs.tax);</SERVER></TD>
    </TR>
    <TR>
```

```
<TD BGCOLOR="#EEEECC"><B>Grand Total:</B></TD>
<TD>$<SERVER>write(total)</SERVER></TD>
</TR>
</TABLE>
<BR>
<A HREF="OrderForm.html">Enter another order</A>
<SERVER>
   curs.close();
   conn.release();
   pool.disconnect();
} else
   redirect("Error.html");
</SERVER>
</BODY>
</HTML>
```

If you look at the code, you'll see the separation of logic is definitely improved, but it could be better. Recall from Figure 34-1 that you're actually striving to build APIs for each layer, where the API functions represent interface points between the layers. This form handler still knows an awful lot about what the tax rate is, how to calculate taxes, and how to apply business rules to validate values; and it knows what the orders table looks like. The form handler doesn't need to know these specifics, and these operations might need to be reused in other parts of the application. For that reason, you should at least pull the reusable snippets out into reusable functions as part of our layer APIs, as shown here:

```
<HTML>
<HEAD><TITLE>Order Information</TITLE></HEAD>
<SERVER>
// Initialize local variables.
var tax = 0;
var error = false;

// Separate presentation logic from the business logic
below.
// In effect, the variables are business logic and
// the request properties are presentation logic.
var productID = request.productID;
```

```
var quantity = request.quantity;
var unitPrice = request.unitPrice;

// BUSINESS LOGIC:
// The tax rate may change or could vary from state to
// state. For now, we'll just visually separate it.
var TAXRATE = getTaxRate();

// BUSINESS LOGIC: Validate values with business rules.
error = isValidProductID(productID);
error = isValidQuantity(quantity);
error = isValidPrice(unitPrice);

// If we passed the business rules, insert the record.
if (!error) {
    // BUSINESS LOGIC: Calculate the tax.
    tax = calcTax();

    // DATA LOGIC: Insert the record.
    var pool = new DbPool("ODBC", "MyAccessDSN", "", "", "",
true);
    var conn = pool.connection();

    project.lock();
    // Now we're just inserting data that's ready to go.

insertOrder(OrderID, ProductID, Quantity, UnitPrice, Tax);
    project.unlock();

    conn.release();
    pool.disconnect();

    // If the insert failed, set the flag.
    if (result != 0)
        error = true;
}
```

```
// PRESENTATION LOGIC:
// Redirect to the proper page depending on the outcome.
if (error)
    redirect("Error.html");
else
    redirect("Confirm.html?orderID=" + escape(nextOrderID))

</SERVER>
```

In the next chapter, I expand on this example further. For now, there are some points you should consider after looking through the code listings.

First, writing a layered application can take a long time compared with writing applications where you use a less-defined approach. You had to introduce more steps in the process to respect the layers, and that took time and effort to do.

Second, calling `redirect` can be an expensive operation, so you might not want to use it as a way to keep your application and presentation logic separate. Snigley Toys currently doesn't have many users accessing its order lookup application, so for now it will stay with the calls to redirect. If you don't want to use redirect in your application, you can simply visually separate your calls to application logic from your calls to presentation logic in the form handler. This way, the calls are all on one page, but you still have your application and presentation logic isolated into distinct functions and objects. However, if you're going to do this, make it the standard way you write all of your form handlers for any one application so that your form handlers are designed consistently.

Third, you still need to turn our functional approach into an object-oriented approach. This issue is addressed in the next chapter because using an object-oriented approach from the start with SSJS will improve the application's portability as you move it to the object-oriented NAS platform.

Now that the data logic is separated from the application logic, the act of processing an order is no longer dependent on where the order information comes from. It can come from any number of databases, and the application logic doesn't have to worry about handling special cases that certain databases might require. The data logic handles database specifics. When you're ready to scale up to NAS, you also won't have to worry about harming the basic algorithm of the application or business rule because of changes in the way SSJS and NAS deal with databases. When you modify the data logic, you won't directly affect the business logic with any bugs you might introduce. It will also help your testing efforts when you port to NAS because you'll be able to more easily isolate any bugs you might introduce down to either the application logic or the data logic without having to sort through the intermixed code. This testing advantage is significant because you'll have to completely retest our application when we port it to NAS and you want to make sure you don't spend any more time or money tracking down bugs than you have to.

Finding the Right Solution to Meet Your Needs

In this chapter, I've laid the foundation for building scalable SSJS applications by showing you how to design a layered SSJS application. Without a layered approach to your design, you'll have a difficult time building a scalable SSJS application. In Chapter 35, I build on the concepts presented here to show you some techniques you can use to handle specific differences between SSJS and NAS that must be addressed to further improve portability, and thus scalability. Keep in mind that there are many possible solutions for building a scalable SSJS application. I hope that from these chapters you'll take away enough techniques and information about the risks and pitfalls that you'll be able to find the right solution for your needs.

35

Building Scalable Server-Side JavaScript Applications, Part 2: Designing for Application Server Portability

JJ Kuslich — application developer, Application Methods, Inc.

In Chapter 34, I explain how to design and build layered server-side JavaScript (SSJS) applications in preparation for migrating to a more scalable application platform, such as Netscape Application Server (NAS). I propose the theory that although there's currently no direct migration path from SSJS to NAS, you can still take steps to build SSJS applications that will be more portable to NAS. As the theory goes, the more portable an SSJS application is to a scalable platform like NAS, the more inherently scalable it is.

In this chapter, I explain and illustrate how to build portability into a layered SSJS application. I start by recapping the scalability strategy outlined in Chapter 34, and then compare the way SSJS and NAS work, as a prelude to discussing several specific portability techniques and giving a detailed example. As I point out along the way, the task of building portable SSJS applications is greatly simplified by starting off with a layered application design.

Recap: The Strategy Explained

In Chapter 34, I define the three-step strategy that follows for building more portable, and thereby scalable, SSJS applications. I then describe how to implement the first step. In this chapter, I demonstrate how to implement the other two steps of the strategy.

- **Separate presentation, application, and data logic.** SSJS and NAS present information to the client in different ways and use different database APIs. Keeping the logic in separate layers, known as *multitiered programming*, and isolating SSJS-specific code into specialized classes or objects makes it easier to upgrade the application to work with NAS or another application server when the time comes to scale up.

- **Build a bridge between SSJS and the application server.** In this step, you design the interface points between your application layers, and between objects within each layer, to be as platform-independent as possible. Isolating platform specifics into implementation details and away from public interfaces helps improve portability.

- **Generate dynamic output as HTML.** Resolving HTML generation incompatibilities between SSJS and NAS improves portability. Once again, creating platform-independent interfaces between your application's layers helps isolate incompatibilities into implementation code and away from public interfaces that are used throughout the application.

Separating business logic from presentation logic is essential for portability because SSJS and NAS produce HTML output in very different ways. If your business logic is tightly coupled with your SJSS presentation logic, you won't be able to port the business logic without modifying it significantly, thus increasing the chance of introducing bugs into critical code. For similar reasons, pulling the data logic out of the business logic is equally essential because of the differences in the way SSJS and NAS talk with databases. Following the first step of the strategy, as discussed in Chapter 34, significantly decouples business logic from other logic that's tied to the underlying application services.

I'm going to approach the problem of implementing the final two steps of the strategy by discussing how to build each of the three application layers. Building the data and business layers will implement the second step of the strategy, and building the presentation layer will implement the third step. First I'll discuss some portability techniques that will apply at all layers, and then I'll return to the Snigley Toys example from Chapter 34 to show you how to use the techniques in each layer of the application.

Comparing SSJS with NAS

Before I describe the portability techniques, you need to know some things about how NAS works compared to SSJS. These are the differences you'll have to overcome when porting SSJS applications to NAS. The primary differences are in these areas:

- **Implementation languages**—SSJS applications use, well, SSJS, whereas NAS uses Java or C++ code.

- **Programming models**—SSJS uses a page-centric model, whereas NAS uses a component-centric model.

- **HTTP request processing models**—An SSJS page uses application objects to process requests; in NAS, requests are handled by AppLogic objects.

- **HTML output generation models**—SSJS directly mixes static HTML with server-side code, whereas NAS uses a merged HTML template scheme.

- **Platform APIs**—SSJS and NAS each provide their own proprietary API.

I won't cover NAS in depth here; to learn more about it, see the Netscape Application Server documentation on DevEdge Online at `http://developer.netscape.com/docs`.

Implementation Languages

SSJS and NAS use different languages for server-side programming. In SSJS, you write code in the server-side variant of JavaScript, but in NAS you can write code in Java or C++. Unfortunately, this means that no matter what kind of portability tactics you employ in your design, you'll ultimately have to rewrite or at least check every line of code when you move to NAS. Still, how you design your SSJS application can greatly influence how straightforward or complicated this rewriting will be. The techniques I present in this chapter should significantly tilt the scales toward the straightforward side.

NOTE

This discussion refers to Netscape Application Server 2.x. Netscape Application Server 4.0 introduced a modified application architecture based on the Enterprise JavaBeans standard described in Chapter 7. For details about NAS 4.0, please see DevEdge Online at `http://developer.netscape.com`.

If you move from SSJS to a Java-based NAS implementation, you'll have an easier time because JavaScript and Java share some similar syntax. Some code might even be directly compatible under both servers. Just don't let the similarities fool you into thinking that code should be the same under both languages, thus causing you to miss subtle differences and introduce bugs along the way.

Programming Models

SSJS uses a page-centric programming model, where all server-side processing takes place between `<server>` and `</server>` tags or backquotes (`` ` ``) inside .htm or .html pages. SSJS pages both handle requests and generate dynamic output. You can build libraries of server-side functions inside .js files, but the processing still initiates inside an SSJS page.

Under the NAS programming model, all initial processing of requests takes place inside an AppLogic component. For example, the URL for form submissions refers directly to an AppLogic by name or by its GUID. It doesn't refer to a page name as SSJS does. An HTML result is then returned to the browser by the AppLogic, either through direct HTML generation or by merging dynamic data with an HTML template, as I'll discuss shortly.

Although you can't change SSJS so that it uses a component-centric model, you can still design your SSJS applications with a component-centric approach. Later in this chapter, where I extend the Snigley Toys example from Chapter 34, I show you how to build form handler pages in SSJS with a component-centric approach so that the form handler looks less like a page and more like code that a component such as an AppLogic might use to process a form request.

HTTP Request Processing Models

At a high level, request processing by SSJS and NAS looks the same, as Figure 35-1 illustrates.

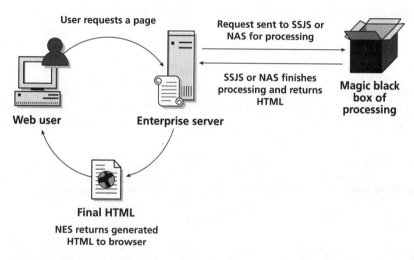

Figure 35-1: The basic Web request model

However, once you look inside that magic black box, you discover that SSJS and NAS actually process requests and retrieve submitted information differently. Under the SSJS model, as shown in Figure 35-2, requests are submitted to ordinary SSJS pages. Any SSJS page can handle requests simply by referring to a session management API object, the *request object*, to retrieve the information submitted through a form or URL query string.

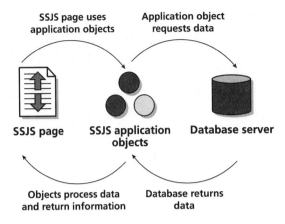

Figure 35-2: Request processing in a multitiered SSJS application

Under the NAS model, as shown in Figure 35-3, AppLogic objects handle HTTP requests. They handle request input through special objects that implement the IValList interface and contain the name/value pairs passed in the request. So an AppLogic doesn't go through a similar session management API to find request information, and an AppLogic is a component, not a page with server-side code.

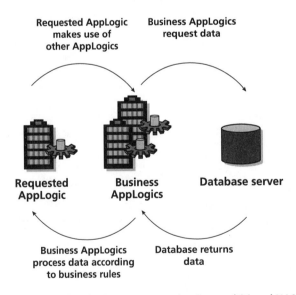

Figure 35-3: Request processing in a multitiered NAS application

HTML Output Generation Models

SSJS generates HTML output in a straightforward manner by directly mixing static HTML with server-side code that dynamically generates HTML using the `write()` function and backquotes.

NAS also lets you either generate dynamic HTML from an AppLogic object or merge dynamic data with static HTML. However, the way you use each generation scheme is very different from the way you generate HTML under SSJS. First, if you want to generate all the HTML for a page from an AppLogic, you can do so through methods similar to the SSJS `write()` statement. However, you can't mix these write statements directly with static HTML. If you want to mix dynamic data with static HTML, you have to use HTML templates. (You can also use another kind of template called a GXML template, but normally for HTML output you would use HTML templates.) HTML templates are created using a combination of HTML and a special markup language that's proprietary to NAS. You control the merging of the templates with dynamic information through special methods called from an AppLogic.

In your SSJS applications, you can use a merged HTML template scheme for generating output, and you might want to consider doing this to achieve greater portability. However, you'll have to build and implement such a scheme yourself. Glen Long's contribution to this book, Chapter 24, " JavaScript," describes an SSJS template technique that can help you build your own template generation engine.

Platform APIs

Every application server worth its salt provides APIs to make working with the server easier. SSJS and NAS are no different in this respect, and each provides its own proprietary set of APIs. This is great when you're writing exclusively to one application server or the other, but it causes problems if you write an application under one set of APIs and later move that application to a server with a different set of APIs. In the next section, I demonstrate some techniques for isolating API specifics.

And Now . . . the Portability Techniques

Now that you understand the differences between SSJS and NAS that you'll need to consider when you port an application, I'm going to describe some general techniques for enhancing portability that apply to all layers of code. The ultimate goal of this stage of the design process is to build a bridge between the application code written on the SSJS platform and the code you'll have to write on the NAS platform. You can reach this goal by following these general design guidelines:

- **Isolate SSJS API methods and objects from your application-specific code.** The more you tie your application-specific code to SSJS-specific APIs, the harder it will be to port to NAS and its own APIs.

- **Design object and function interfaces in SSJS that you can reuse in NAS.** Even though you'll have to port the implementations of your application objects from SSJS to NAS, you can make the process simpler by defining interfaces in SSJS that change as little as possible when you move to NAS. The less you have to change the structure of your objects and methods, the less you'll have to change code that uses those objects and methods.

I've managed to slip the word *object* into this chapter several times, and for good reason. NAS is very much an object-oriented application server, and an object-oriented approach will help you design portable applications within these two guidelines. JavaScript is also object-oriented to a degree, and you can take advantage of this to achieve greater portability.

Isolating SSJS API Calls

NAS has its own APIs for the functionality handled by the SSJS APIs, so when you port your application you'll have to rewrite any code that references any of these. Isolating any calls that are specific to the SSJS APIs into specific areas of your application will help make this rewriting process easier.

When I refer to SSJS APIs, I don't mean basic language elements like loops, conditionals, and so forth. I'm referring instead to the built-in APIs that give SSJS its real server-side power, including:

- Session Management Service

- LiveWire Database Service

- File System Service

- Mail Service

- LiveConnect API

- External Library API

You can isolate API calls in a number of ways, depending on the API itself, the frequency with which you use it in your application, and your overall application needs. Some ways to isolate SSJS API calls are by using helper functions/objects and wrappers. If you write your application objects in Java and access them through LiveConnect, you have even more options for improving portability. Using Java in the first place already improves your application's portability to NAS. Because NAS fully supports Java, you should be able to reuse most or all of your Java code when you scale up to NAS. And because Java is a fully object-oriented and class-based language, you can also use abstract classes to improve portability.

I'll describe each of these approaches in turn. Note that using helper functions/objects increases portability the most, but also takes the most time to implement. Conversely, using abstract classes increases portability the least but takes the least time to implement.

Helper functions/objects or proxies

When you encounter a piece of application code that must make some API calls, you can delegate the work of making the API call and returning the proper value to a helper object. By isolating API calls inside helper objects, you build a well-identified API that can be ported more easily than if your API calls are scattered throughout your code. Helper objects can be considered proxies for the real, underlying SSJS API calls. They may simply pass through calls to the API and pass back the results, or they may perform some other processing beyond just the API calls. Figure 35-4 illustrates the difference between embedded API calls and isolated API calls from the application's perspective.

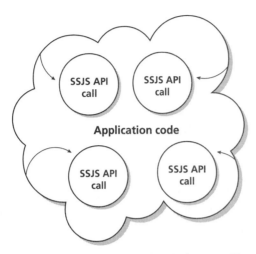

Application code is directly tied to platform-specific APIs

Figure 35-4: Using helper objects to isolate platform-specific API calls

Wrappers

You can also wrap SSJS API calls in generic utility functions or objects and have
your application code call only these utility functions or objects, rather than making API calls directly. Depending on the size of the API that you need to wrap, this
method may be impractical. However, if you intend to build a number of SSJS applications that will scale up to another platform like NAS, it may be worth it in the
long run to write complete wrappers for the APIs that you commonly use. This
case differs from the helper objects case in that helper objects can do more than
just pass through calls to SSJS API functions. They can also perform business logic,
whereas wrappers simply wrap up the functionality of SSJS API calls and pass information back and forth for the purpose of hiding SSJS API specifics.

Abstract classes

You can build application objects that will require different SSJS and NAS implementations through the use of abstract classes. By defining a generic abstract class,
such as `ProductsAbstract`, you can construct a common object interface. You
can then subclass `ProductsAbstract` into two concrete classes, `ProductsSSJS`
and `ProductsNAS`, each having the same interface but its own platform-depen-
dent implementation. In most cases, you'll need only two concrete classes because
you're porting between only two platforms.

As Gamma et al. point out in the classic book *Design Patterns*, using abstract classes for the purposes of abstracting platform-specific implementations has drawbacks. For one thing, every class that requires platform independence requires two concrete classes. For example, suppose the Snigley Toys application represents an order with an abstract class called `Order`. Using this class to abstract away platform-specific implementations of the class then requires that you create two concrete classes — for instance, `OrderSSJS` and `OrderNAS` — that inherit from the `Order` class and implement platform-specific details. However, suppose there are several kinds of abstract `Order` classes in the application. In this case, you may also have to implement two concrete classes for each type of `Order` object, as illustrated in Figure 34-5. That could lead to a lot of coding, depending on the application.

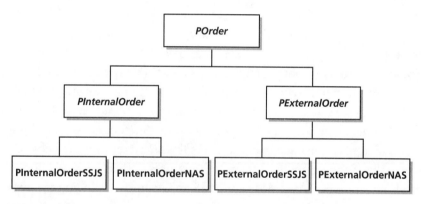

Figure 35-5: How using abstract classes can lead to a lot of coding

More important, although use of abstract classes isolates calling code from platform-specific details, it ties that calling code to the concrete classes that were made for each platform. So because the SSJS application will refer directly to objects of the `OrderSSJS` class, you need to change all these references when you port to NAS to refer instead to the `OrderNAS` class. You've isolated platform-specific details but tied yourself to platform-specific concrete classes. It's one step closer to a solution, but might not work well for all applications. The usefulness of this solution really depends on how much platform-specific code you need to abstract.

Designing Portable Interfaces

Using the benefits of robust, object-oriented languages like Java goes a long way toward providing portable interfaces to your application logic classes, and even your presentation and data logic classes. However, using Java through LiveConnect may not be feasible for everyone. If you're one of those people who prefer not to use Java classes through LiveConnect, don't worry; you can still build portable interfaces using JavaScript objects if you're building SSJS applications with pure JavaScript. You won't achieve the same level of portability with this technique if used apart from the other techniques mentioned previously, but every bit of portability you can introduce should help. Note that you can also combine portable interfaces with helper objects, proxies, or abstract classes for maximum portability.

Designing a portable object interface begins with the concept of *information hiding*, which object-oriented programmers are already familiar with. You build interfaces that don't overexpose object internals by hiding the data and implementation details from any objects and methods that don't need to know those details. Then the object can be reused in many places even though its internal implementation may change. This concept applies because you want to be able to change the internal implementation details — porting from SSJS to NAS — while limiting the changes to application code that references the interfaces of ported objects. And incidentally, if you carefully design your interfaces in this way, you'll notice a pleasant side effect for both your SSJS and NAS applications: Changing the implementations of your methods becomes easier, resulting in lower maintenance and upgrade costs.

Though JavaScript has object-oriented features, it does lack two features in particular that Java and C++ developers are familiar with, and that directly affect an object's interface:

- Explicit data types for data members, method parameters, and method return values

- The notion of public, private, and protected data members and methods

An object interface is a combination of its public data members, or properties, and public method signatures. A method signature is generally defined by the method name, the number of parameters, the data types of the parameters, and the data type of the return value. However, JavaScript is a loosely typed language, so variables and properties can generally hold values of any type at any time.

Further, JavaScript doesn't support any explicit declarations of public versus private data members or methods. If a property or method is part of an object, any other code can access it. As with most of the techniques in this chapter, the solution for building portable object interfaces in SSJS is one of applying good design techniques and setting development standards.

Enforcing good design techniques and standards is harder than letting a compiler handle things like data types for you, but it's not too difficult to enforce these practices by hand. And if you're going to build for portability, you really don't have much choice, so don't whine! Here are the basic rules you should follow to support portable interfaces:

- Determine in advance which properties and methods of an object will be available to the entire world, and which ones will be used internally by the object itself. Mark the public and private properties and methods with comments and separate their declarations in the code.

- Determine the data types that each of your public properties, parameters of public methods, and return values of public methods will have. Then document these return types and stick to them.

- Keep platform-specific objects, such as the SSJS session objects, out of your public method interfaces. If you tie platform-specific code to the public interfaces of your objects, you'll not only have to change the interfaces when you port to NAS, but you'll also have to change all the application code that refers to the objects.

- Make sure you expose only the properties and methods that the outside world must know about to work with an object. Hide all other details. This is a general guideline, not an absolute.

The following code listing illustrates some of the basic rules just outlined for building portable interfaces. The application example later in this chapter will further illustrate these rules.

```
function PMyObj (params)
{

// Public properties
this.name = params.name; // String
this.maxConn = params.packagerName; // Integer
```

```
this.DBConnection = params.DBConnection; // SSJS connection
object

// Private properties
this.cursor = null; // SSJS cursor object
this.sql = null; // String

// Public methods
this.getCurrentCursor = qu_GetCurrentCursor; // Returns:
SSJS cursor object
this.emitProperties = qu_EmitProperties; // Returns: String

// Private methods
this.openCursor = qu_OpenCursor; // Returns: Boolean
} // END PMyObj constructor
```

Keep in mind that these guidelines will still not give you completely portable object interfaces because of the differences between the JavaScript language and the Java or C++ used in NAS, but every bit of portability you can introduce helps. Also note that this technique isn't specific to NAS; should you want to migrate to Java servlets, for example, the general rules outlined here should also improve portability and reuse.

Additional Portability Tips

For maximum portability, consider porting your SSJS code to Java instead of C++ when you ultimately move to NAS. JavaScript code isn't directly portable to Java, but you'll find that you can reuse some JavaScript code either directly or with minor modifications when porting to Java. Of course, Java isn't appropriate in all cases, but it does provide you a high degree of portability.

If you decide you'll eventually be using Java on NAS, consider using the JDBC database API that NAS provides rather than the proprietary NAS database APIs. You'll find that the JDBC API and the SSJS database APIs are structured similarly in many ways, and this may make porting your SSJS database code easier.

Be aware that instances of AppLogic objects under NAS are created differently from object instances in SSJS. In SSJS, you use the new operator to create a new instance of an object. Under NAS, you typically don't use the new operator. You may want to consider wrapping your object instantiation calls in SSJS so that they're more compatible with the NAS instantiation calls.

Even though SSJS has a garbage collector that cleans up object references when objects and variables go out of scope, typically after a page has been processed, you should still explicitly close database connections and clean up object instances before leaving a page. If you're moving to a Java-based implementation under NAS, the Java garbage collector should still handle the cleanup of your instances, but under high-load scenarios you don't want to wait for the garbage collector to catch up with you. If you're planning on porting to a C++ implementation, implementing explicit cleanup code in your SSJS application will remind you where you need to implement similar memory management code in your C++ code.

There are many possibilities for bridging the gaps between SSJS and NAS, ranging from disciplined JavaScript programming to more elegant OOP solutions in Java. The solution you choose depends on the skills of the developers you have available to you at the time, their comfort level with developing object-oriented solutions, and other project-specific factors. Different projects may require different solutions.

Building a Portable Application: An Example

I know, I know — all these design tips are nice, but you want to see some code, right? I'm going to continue the Snigley Toys example from where I left off in Chapter 34, so you might want to review it before you read further.

Recall that I transformed the fictional Snigley Toys order entry application from a page-centric SSJS application with almost no portability into a layered application using functions to separate the presentation, business, and data layers. The second to last code example in Chapter 34 shows the code for the order summary page where most of the presentation logic for producing output is written. The last code example shows the final form of the order form handler, which is where most business logic and data processing takes place. Before I start applying the techniques I just mentioned, I want to take the order form handler one step further by building some SSJS business objects. This will make it easier to apply the portability techniques, and in any case I highly recommend using objects in your SSJS code whether you're concerned with portability or not.

First, let's talk about the pieces of the Snigley Toys order entry application. It has three pages: an order entry form, a form handler, and an order summary page. The order entry form is purely a presentation-layer entity. However, the form handler currently contains business and data logic, and the order summary page currently mixes data and presentation logic. Ultimately, you should structure the application so that the form handler contains purely business logic and the order summary page contains purely presentation logic. With this kind of a structure, you won't have to deal with any SSJS or NAS database API issues at the presentation or business logic level when we port to NAS. In other words, you're isolating SSJS database API specifics out of the presentation and business layers, which is one of the portability techniques.

To evolve this application from a layered SSJS application into an application that's more readily portable to NAS, I'll follow these steps:

1. Encapsulate the presentation, business, and data logic into objects.

2. Further decouple the three layers by building specialized objects for each layer.

3. Abstract the SSJS API specifics into proxy, or helper, functions within the objects.

4. Design the objects with portable interfaces.

When I'm through, I'll have transformed the form handler from a page-centric entity into an SSJS page that looks like what you might find inside an NAS AppLogic object's execute method under a component-centric model. Note that I'm not using the abstract classes technique. That's because I don't want to use Java through LiveConnect for this example, to keep things simple.

Step 1: Encapsulate the Logic into Objects

To transform the simple layered function-based application into a portable object-based application, you need three business objects, one data object, and one presentation object that will encapsulate the layers of functionality that were previously performed inside functions or inside the form handler itself. The structures for these objects, including their method signatures, are shown in Table 35-1. Objects are listed in bold, and their methods are listed underneath them in plain text. Because JavaScript is an object-oriented language based on prototypes rather than classes, I prefix all object constructor functions with a P for prototype so I can tell them apart from my other methods and functions. In real life, these objects might have many more objects, properties, and methods than I'm showing.

But here, I'll describe only objects and methods that I'm actually going to use in the sample application.

TABLE 35-1: ORDER ENTRY APPLICATION OBJECT STRUCTURES

BUSINESS OBJECTS

Porder	A business object representing an order
IsValidOrderID	Validates an order ID
IsValidQty	Validates an order quantity
CalcSubTotal	Calculates the subtotal for an order (product price × quantity)
CalcTax	Calculates the tax for an order (subtotal × tax rate)
CalcTotal	Calculates the grand total for an order (subtotal × tax)

GetOrder	A proxy method for retrieving order information from the database
InsertOrder	A proxy method for inserting order information into the database
Pproduct	A business object representing a product
IsValidProductID	Validates a product ID
IsValidPrice	Validates a product price
Pstore	A business object representing the Snigley Toys online store, used to encapsulate storewide operations
GetTaxRate	Gets the tax rate, which for this example is a constant value

DATA OBJECT

PorderData	Handles all database interactions for orders
GetOrder	Retrieves an order from the database
InsertOrder	Inserts a new order into the database
GetQuantity	Gets the quantity of an existing order from the database
GetTax	Gets the tax of an existing order from the database

Continued

TABLE 35-1: *(continued)*

GetUnitPrice	Gets the unit price for the item in an existing order from the database

PRESENTATION OBJECT

PorderForm	A presentation object representing the order entry form
GetProductID	Gets the product ID passed by the form from SSJS
GetQuantity	Gets the quantity passed by the form from SSJS
GetUnitPrice	Gets the unit price passed by the form from SSJS
RenderOrderResults	Renders the results of the order entry request in the user's browser

The following code listing shows the revised form handler, using the new objects. I'm not going to show how the objects are implemented because those details aren't important. In fact, if you're working on a large, multitiered application with a large group of developers, chances are you won't see the code for most of the objects you work with. The implementations are basically copied and pasted from the listings in Chapter 34 into the appropriate methods of the new objects. The only exception is in the implementation of POrderData, which was reimplemented, as I'll discuss in a moment.

```
<HTML>
<HEAD><TITLE>Order Information</TITLE></HEAD>
<SERVER>
// Initialize local variables.
var error = false;
var result = 0;
var orderForm = new POrderForm();
var order = new POrder();

// project.snigleyStore holds a global PStore object
instantiated in
// the application's initial page.
```

```
var store = project.snigleyStore;

// Hide HTML form details and presentation logic by
delegating to the
// orderForm object.
var productID = orderForm.getProductID();
var quantity  = orderForm.getQuantity();
var unitPrice = orderForm.getUnitPrice();

// BUSINESS LOGIC:
var TAXRATE = store.getTaxRate();

// BUSINESS LOGIC: Validate values with business rules.
error = isValidProductID(productID);
error = isValidQuantity(quantity);
error = isValidPrice(unitPrice);

// If we passed the business rules, insert the record.
if (!error) {
   // BUSINESS LOGIC: Initialize the object once we've
validated the
   // data and have found no errors.
   order.productID = productID;
   order.quantity  = quantity;
   order.unitPrice = unitPrice;

   // BUSINESS LOGIC: Calculate the tax.
   order.tax = order.calcTax();

   // Insert the record and delegate the data logic to the
proxied
   // insertOrder method.
   result = order.insertOrder();

   // If the order object says the insert failed, set the
error flag.
   if (result != 0)
```

```
        error = true;
    }


    // BUSINESS LOGIC:  We don't care how it does it, just tell
    the
    // POrderForm object to show the results.  It could redirect
    to
    // another page, or it could just start generating HTML.
    The form
    // handler doesn't care.  We pass it the order object so
    that it
    // can reprint order information in the order summary if the
    insert
    // was successful. orderForm will know whether or not the
    insert
    // was successful based on the value of the error variable.
    orderForm.renderOrderResults(order, error);

    </SERVER>
```

Step 2: Build Specialized Objects for Each Layer

I've used the layered design to isolate knowledge of how HTML results are presented from the business logic in the form handler. The description of the renderOrderResults method of the POrderForm object says that it renders the order entry results. In Chapter 34, the form handler was responsible for determining whether or not to display an error or a transaction receipt, and the order summary page printed the results. However, if the form handler is to be a business-layer entity, it should defer any decisions about how to render results of its transaction to a presentation-layer object. The form handler shouldn't care how results are generated or where the code for displaying the results lives. This separation of responsibility will be important for portability since SSJS and NAS produce HTML output in very different ways. If you were to leave the HTML output up to the form handler, you'd have to change that part of the form handler code when we port to NAS. But since the form handler now delegates responsibility to the POrderForm object for producing its own results, you shouldn't have to touch the business logic in the form handler when you port the presentation code to NAS.

Step 3: Abstract the SSJS API Specifics into Helper Functions

POrderForm is also responsible for understanding how its corresponding HTML form is structured. In SSJS, form values are passed to the server through one of the SSJS session management objects, the request object. Although you could isolate session management API details into yet another object, for this example I've decided to let POrderForm know about the SSJS session management API and therefore directly reference the request object when it needs to retrieve values submitted through the form. The important thing is to isolate session management API details from business and data logic, which I've done. In your applications, you might choose to isolate these details in another object or set of objects.

Notice that the descriptions of the getOrder and insertOrder methods of the POrder object state that they're simply proxies. A proxy doesn't actually do the work requested but rather passes off its responsibilities to some other object. In this case, I've created a corresponding object in the data layer that represents an order, POrderData. As I mentioned earlier, using the notion of a proxy is one way to isolate SSJS API calls from business logic, and it doesn't require the use of more advanced languages like Java. When the getOrder or insertOrder methods of the POrder object are called, they simply call the getOrder and insertOrder methods of the corresponding POrderData object and marshal the results back to the caller, which in this case is the form handler. Now you don't need the form handler to directly reference the SSJS database API at all. All those details about connections, DbPools, and cursors are tucked away in the implementations of the POrderData object. When you port the application to NAS, you won't have to risk damaging the business logic when you change the data logic to work with the NAS database API.

I could have implemented this another way and not used proxy methods at all, but instead I just let POrderData handle all the details. However, recall that I decided to hide all the data objects from the rest of the application so that only the corresponding business objects know about them. I did this because you already know you're going to have to reimplement the data logic, and that reimplementation might require changing the interfaces of the data objects. You don't have to follow this same methodology in your applications; it's just one way of achieving data logic isolation.

Step 4: Design the Objects with Portable Interfaces

Though you can't tell from the code in the new form handler, I've actually reimplemented the data logic in POrderData such that all the queries and insert statements are processed in stored procedures rather than in the SSJS object itself. You'll have to trust me that I really did change the underlying implementation, just as you may have to trust developers on your team who are implementing the data layer and giving you back only objects with no implementation details. I intentionally hid those details from you because I wanted to illustrate the point that at the form handler level, neither you nor the form handler should care how POrderForm implements its data. Clearly, the form handler doesn't need to know! You didn't know either, but it didn't change your understanding of the business or presentation logic. It didn't change your understanding of how to use the POrderData object to execute data processing logic because you understood the interfaces as they were outlined in Table 35-1. That's the whole intention of building a layered application — isolate implementation details into layers so when you want to change the implementation, other logic isn't affected because the interfaces stay the same. Neat, isn't it?

The Result

Here's what's happened as a result of the work I've done on the Snigley Toys order entry application:

- Only POrderData contains SSJS API calls for connecting to the database, calling stored procedures, passing parameters, and retrieving return values.

- Only stored procedures running on the database server contain data processing logic, such as queries and inserts.

- Only POrderForm performs SSJS-specific HTML generation.

- Only POrderForm contains SSJS-specific session management API calls and performs SSJS-specific request processing.

- The business objects, where the bulk of the code resides, perform only pure business logic. They have no direct ties to any specific platform (other than the fact that they're written in JavaScript).

The net effect of all this reimplementation work is that when you port to NAS, in the worst case you'll have to rewrite `POrderData` and `POrderForm` to comply with the NAS APIs. You should have to port only the business objects from JavaScript to Java for the most part, not completely rewrite them. Business logic is the most critical part of your application because it models all of your customer's business processes. If you break the business logic, you can seriously damage the integrity of the application. Fortunately, using the techniques described in this chapter and the previous one, you've significantly limited the amount of risk in porting the business code.

Data logic is equally important to the integrity of the application. By pushing basic data processing — such as queries and inserts — into stored procedures on the database server, you limit the amount of data processing in the application to simple stored procedure calls and parameter passing. Yet you're still keeping business logic up in the business objects and out of the stored procedures. So when you port `POrderData` to NAS, you won't be altering the queries or sensitive data-processing logic. You'll simply have to rewrite the SSJS database API calls to conform to the NAS database APIs for performing the simple operations of connecting to the database, calling a stored procedure, and passing parameters and results back and forth.

As for the presentation logic, you may recall from Chapter 34 that you knew you were going to have to change or rewrite the user interface anyway when you moved from the small, internal SSJS application to the public consumer-oriented online store application hosted in NAS.

So I've laid all the groundwork for an SSJS application that works well under SSJS and is portable to NAS. When it comes time to scale up, all the SSJS objects can be ported to equivalent NAS AppLogic objects of the same name. Additionally, I'd port the SSJS form handler page to an AppLogic object and place all the code in the execute method of the AppLogic.

Growing Wiser, Stronger — and More Scalable

In this chapter, I built on the layered approach covered in Chapter 34 to describe specific techniques for designing portable SSJS applications. I described how to isolate platform-specific APIs, how to use Java to build abstractions, and how to design portable object interfaces. I finished off by applying these techniques in the Snigley Toys order entry application. You now have a complete framework for building portable SSJS applications. You can also apply these techniques to existing SSJS applications and to the process of migrating these applications to another platform.

Any decent novelist will tell you that in a good story, the protagonist must experience some growth and follow a path of transformation through the trials and tribulations of the plot. In stories with happy endings, the protagonist ends up wiser, stronger, or somehow changed for the better. The protagonist in this two-part story of mine at first appears to be the archetypal SSJS application, and my plot twist required that it be prepared for transformation into an NAS application someday. However, you're actually the protagonist of this story. I hope these chapters have not only helped you come to a better understanding of how to design SSJS applications through a layered approach but also prepared you for the time when you have to move that application to an entirely new application server such as NAS.

36

Java Servlets for JavaScripters: Expanding Your Server-Side Programming Repertoire

Duane K. Fields — *internet systems engineer, Tivoli Systems*

Don't get me wrong — I love developing in server-side JavaScript. I'm lazy by nature and appreciate JavaScript's relaxed approach to variable typing and declaration. LiveConnect gives me access to Java's unique functionality when I need it, and I've created a good number of reusable libraries that speed the development process. I develop many of our internal tools here at Tivoli Systems with Netscape Enterprise Server's JavaScript capabilities and use it for rapid application development. But for our more complex, multitiered applications developed using a team approach, I've begun employing Enterprise Server's Java capabilities — through servlets.

In this chapter — written primarily for those currently developing on the server in JavaScript — I explain the basics of working with Java on the server through Sun's Java Servlet API. I start with a brief overview of servlets and their role in server-side software development. Then I compare JavaScript applications with servlets in a number of crucial areas of program design. I'm assuming that you're already familiar with Java programming, but if not, I hope this chapter will encourage you to begin exploring the possibilities offered by Java servlets. Once you're comfortable with basic Java programming, it's fairly easy to extend that knowledge to include servlet development. Additionally, if you have experience developing in server-side JavaScript, you're already familiar with all the application design concepts necessary to work with servlets.

Servlets and Their Place in the World

Servlets are the first standard extension to Java released by Sun Microsystems. The classes that constitute the Servlet API are typically not distributed with the core Java classes, but are controlled and managed by Sun itself. What this means to Web developers is that support for servlets isn't included in every Web server out there, but the API is stable, easily obtainable, and consistent with the rest of the Java API. And almost every Java-enabled Web server can support servlets with just a little retrofitting, described in the next section. Remember, too, that since all of your Java servlet code will be running on the server, not the client, no particular requirements for Java are placed on the end user's browser.

The benefits of developing applications in Java or JavaScript instead of with the more traditional CGI scripting method have long been touted. CGI, by comparison, is a slow and inefficient architecture for Web applications, requiring as it does that a unique instance of the executable or script interpreter be invoked to handle each incoming request. Persistence and state maintenance are other problems not easily handled by CGI applications. Both Java and JavaScript applications provide good data-persistence options and much-improved performance.

If Java and JavaScript are both attractive development environments, why should JavaScript developers consider servlets for more complex application projects? First and foremost, Java is a richer, more structured language better suited to complicated programming tasks — especially those being handled by a team of developers. Java's strong typing and memory-access protection create the safer, more predictable run-time environment demanded by mission-critical applications. Working in Java also gives you access to Java's rich core APIs, as well as the ability to easily build on the efforts of others by reusing their classes. Last, Java servlets are portable — not just across platforms, but across vendors.

Equipping Yourself for Servlet Development

As mentioned earlier, though very few Web servers (Sun's Java Web Server being a notable exception) support the latest edition of the Servlet API out of the box, it's relatively easy and cheap to retrofit a Web server with a servlet engine. A servlet engine is a server extension, written in a server-specific API such as NSAPI or IS-API, which acts as a harness for running servlets on the Web server. Although Netscape Enterprise Server 3.5.1 does provide support for the 1.0 release of the Java Servlet API, the 2.0 API now available adds some essential new features, so your best bet is to upgrade to the 2.0 level of support with a servlet engine.

Servlet engines are available for Enterprise Server on most platforms, and for many other Web servers as well. Each has its own relatively straightforward interface for configuring, starting, and stopping servlets. The most popular of the engines currently available are the following:

- LiveSoftware's Jrun, available at `http://www.livesoftware.com`

- IBM's WebSphere, available at `http://www.software.ibm.com/webservers`

- New Atlanta's ServletExec, which you can find at `http://www.newatlanta.com`

Chapter 37 shows how to add the JRun Servlet Engine to a Netscape server.

To develop servlets, you'll also need a copy of Sun's Java Servlet Development Kit (JSDK), version 2.0 or later. You can download it from the Web at `http://java.sun.com/products/servlet/index.html`. The JSDK contains the Java classes necessary to develop servlets, as well as ServletRunner, a standalone application that enables you to test your servlet code without a Web server.

NOTE

The ServletRunner documentation isn't too clear on a couple of things. First, when you specify the location of your servlet directory with the -d option, you need to specify the full path. Second, if you need to specify an alternative document root, use the -r option.

Designing Your Application

In this chapter, I discuss working with servlets in their most popular form, which is similar to working with a CGI script: You write the servlet, put it on the server, and let it handle requests. However, more advanced options modeled after features that were until recently unique to Sun's Java Web Server are becoming available. One such feature, Server Side Include, enables you to embed references to servlets in a Web page in much the same way you would embed an applet. At delivery time, this embedded statement is replaced with the output of the corresponding servlet. Another option, Java Server Pages, follows the JavaScript application model even more closely by enabling you to distribute Java code throughout HTML documents. Because these features aren't as commonly available as servlets and build on the basic concepts anyway, I won't go into any detail on them here.

Once you're comfortable with basic Java programming, switching gears from JavaScript development to servlets isn't as hard as you might think. The development techniques involved share many aspects, although beginning Java programmers might have some difficulty getting their minds around the idea of one instance of the servlet object being called by multiple, simultaneous threads. Like JavaScript, servlets are built around a request/response model. When a page request comes into the Web server, it's routed to the servlet for handling, and the servlet's output is returned.

To get an idea of what a Java servlet looks like, take a look at the ever-popular "Hello World!" program in the following code listing:

```
import java.io.*;
import javax.servlet.*;
import javax.servlet.http.*;

public class HelloServlet extends HttpServlet
{
```

```
    public void doGet (HttpServletRequest  request,
HttpServletResponse response) throws ServletException,
IOException
    {
        // Prepare the client to receive HTML and get our
output stream.
        PrintWriter out = response.getWriter();
        response.setContentType("text/html");
        out.println("<HTML><BODY>Hello World!</BODY></HTML>");
    }

    public void doPost (HttpServletRequest request,
HttpServletResponse response) throws ServletException,
IOExceoption
    {
        // Dispatch this to the doGet() method to make post
and get synonymous.
        doGet(request, response);
    }
}
```

This example shows a pretty typical servlet implementation that extends the HttpServlet class and overloads the doGet() and doPost() methods. For an example of an even simpler servlet implementation, see the first code example in Chapter 37. In that example, the service() method (whose job is normally to dispatch the request to either the doGet() or the doPost() method) is overloaded to handle outputting the "Hello World" statement.

As you can see, the basic model for a servlet is to provide methods to handle the doGet() or doPost() methods, using the request object to gather information and the response object to return it. Once compiled, the resulting HelloServlet. class file can be configured through your servlet engine's configuration panel. Any request (either GET or POST methods) will return the earth-shatteringly thought-provoking "Hello World!" message.

Don't worry about the details just yet; we'll delve into these later on. Let's first step back and look at how a Java application is put together.

In JavaScript, you start by creating a set of HTML documents. Some of these documents are plain HTML, whereas others contain embedded JavaScript designated for use on the server. You generally have some data-entry documents that collect data through a form, and some form-handling code to interpret and work with the data. These are all compiled into a single `.web` package and placed on the server, mapped to the URL specified in JavaScript's application manager. For example, say you have a two-document application called `dbtest`. Its two documents, `query.html` and `show_results.html`, would be compiled into a single package called `dbtest.web`. You would then use the application manager to set up our `dbtest` application. To query the database, the user would visit `/dbtest/query.html`, which when submitted would post the data from its input form to the `/dbtest/show_results.html` URL, to be handled by the code inside the `show_results.html` document.

Thus, JavaScript has a structured system for combining multiple documents (some containing code) into a discrete application file. By contrast, there's no standardized system for compiling a collection of servlets into a single application. Servlets are generally independent of each other, and a collection of servlets is an application only in the mind of the developer and the spirit of the design. For convenience, related servlets can be combined into a JAR file — (a Java Archive) for easy shuffling between servers, but as far as the server is concerned, this is just a packaging ploy.

If your `dbtest` application were developed with servlets, you would probably make the query page a plain HTML page, call it `query.html`, and design a Java servlet called something like `ResultsServlet`. The `ResultsServlet.class` file would be installed on the server through your servlet engine's configuration interface and mapped to any valid URL you wanted, typically something like `/servlet/ResultsServlet`. (Notice that unlike in JavaScript, you're usually not passing control to a file with an `.html` extension file but to the servlet class itself.) The `query.html` input form file would be placed on the Web server (or any Web server, for that matter) as a regular document. Although there's no particular benefit in doing so, you could have used a servlet to generate the HTML form that made up the query. Or you could define the `doGet()` method to return the HTML form, and the `doPost()` method to handle the results. This has been a common tactic in the CGI programming world for some time.

If you're familiar with developing CGI applications, it's helpful to look at servlets from that design perspective. You can think of servlets as Java CGI scripts, but with an important distinction. A servlet is instantiated and initialized only once, at startup, and then handles requests from the main Web server as needed. Unlike CGI scripts or programs, which are evoked separately to handle each incoming request, a single instance of the servlet handles multiple requests simultaneously. The servlet isn't brought up and torn down with each request. This application persistence happens when JavaScript code is executing — the server dispatches a separate thread to process the code. I discuss how to avoid conflicts that may arise between competing threads later.

Configuring Your Application's Startup Parameters

In JavaScript, one of the challenges programmers face is managing host- or application-specific initialization parameters. For example, if you have one application that's used on multiple hosts, its data files might live on different paths on each. Or perhaps you have configuration parameters that need to be changed depending on the exact behavior desired. Other than recompiling the application each time, JavaScript can accomplish this by creating routines to manage persistent INI files on the server, or retrieving configuration data from a database. Unfortunately, this means more work for you, the developer, because none of these techniques are built into the core language.

Servlets, on the other hand, do have a built-in mechanism for passing in initialization parameters. Although it's implemented a little differently by each servlet engine, the basic idea is the same across all of them. A collection of name/value pairs is associated with each servlet on the server. When the servlets are first initialized (say, at a reboot), each servlet's init() method is called. Within the init() method, you can use the getInitParameter() method to access t hese configuration parameters and can alter the behavior of your application accordingly. Likewise, Java provides a built-in class for handling INI-style configuration files — java.util.Properties.

Communicating Between Client and Server

One of the critical elements of application design is passing information from the user (on the client) to the server for processing. Let's first review how you pass this information in JavaScript. Form data from a GET or POST action surfaces automatically as properties of the request object on the receiving JavaScript page. Variables that may have multiple values, such as a select list, are accessed through the getOptionValue() function, which takes an identifier string and an index variable. To access information from a named form element, you simply read the corresponding property of the request object, which returns a string representing the property's value (or a null if it's undefined).

Java also employs the concept of a request object that's passed into the receiving code. In Java, an object that's an instance of HttpServletRequest is passed into the servlet's doGet() or doPost() service method, depending on the request method used. This object encapsulates any incoming form data as well as information about the request itself. In typical Java style, form data isn't accessed directly, but through the getParameter() method. A slew of other methods likc getRemoteHost() and getRemoteUser() are available to obtain other specifics about the request. For variables that may have multiple values, use the getParameterValues() method, which returns an array of string values. All in all, it's a very convenient and clean way to get to the incoming data.

Take a look, in the following example, at a snippet of JavaScript code that retrieves some form data stored in the request object, and at its Java equivalent. Assume that the form you're accessing was configured with the following HTML:

```
<INPUT TYPE="text" NAME="username">
<INPUT TYPE="text" NAME="userid">
```

Now, take a look at the JavaScript snippet:

```
username = request.username;
if (request.userid)
    userid = parseInt(request.userid);
else
    userid = 0;
```

And here's the Java version:

```
String username = request.getParameter("username");
int userid;
try
{
```

```
    userid =
Integer.parseInt(request.getParameter("userid"));
}
catch (NumberFormatException e)
{
    userid = 0;
}
```

Notice that in both languages the values come through as strings, and integers (or other nonstring data types) must be parsed out of the parameters. I present some examples of this a little later. (Yes, catching exceptions is a pain, but it's for your own good.)

Getting Environmental Information

Information about the environment a request was delivered in, such as the IP, hostname, and other request- or server-specific values, is necessary for lots of common tasks in Web development. JavaScript uses its server and request objects, along with the `ssjs_getCGIVariable()` function, to expose such information. In Java, this information is provided through access methods of the request object passed to your service methods. A few examples of common attributes are given in Table 36-1, along with the JavaScript properties/functions and Java methods used to retrieve them.

TABLE 36-1: ENVIRONMENTAL ACCESS METHODS

PROPERTY	JAVASCRIPT PROPERTY/ FUNCTION	JAVA METHOD
Hostname of server	server.hostname	getServerName()
Port number of server	server.port	getServerPort()
IP of client	request.ip	getRemoteAddr()
Remote username	request.auth_user	getRemoteUser()

Continued

TABLE 36-1: *(continued)*

PROPERTY	JAVASCRIPTPROPERTY/ FUNCTION	JAVA METHOD
Query string	`ssjs_getCGIVariable ("QUERY_STRING")`	`getQueryString()`
Request type (get/post)	`ssjs_getCGIVariable ("REQUEST_METHOD")`	`getMethod()`

As you can see, everything you're used to working with is still there, but in Java it's been corralled into a more consistent and manageable interface. In JavaScript, the server object is also used to store global data — information accessible by all applications running on the server. I look at how Java handles global data later in this chapter.

Maintaining State Across Requests

Now let's see how you can keep some of your information around between requests: persistent data. Both JavaScript and Java applications are built around a series of stateless requests — that's the nature of HTTP — but it's critical that you somehow maintain client-specific data from request to request. JavaScript accomplishes this through its client object, which it uses to store data for a particular user and application across requests. You can keep information, such as a shopping basket, in a client object that's unique to each user. This data is maintained with cookies, either on the client or the server, depending on the options you've selected. JavaScript takes care of sharing the data and moving the cookies around.

JavaScript's client object can store only string values. Any other values, such as numbers, dates, or Booleans, must be parsed out of the resulting string. More advanced techniques can be employed to get around the string-only limitation: You can access the `ssjs_getClientID()` method and use it as a user-specific key to data stored on the project object. However, you the developer are responsible for creating, managing, and destroying this data on the project object, making this a somewhat daunting task.

The 2.0 release of the Java Servlet API provides for session-specific data management through a technique similar in design to the `ssjs_getClientID()` indexing idea in JavaScript. A client-specific identifier serves as a key to accessing a pool of stored data. Fortunately, Java does most of the cleanup and data shuffling for you. To work with session-specific data, you need to associate the servlet with the session identifier early in its code, before writing any output or working with the response object. To establish a session, call the `getSession()` method of the request object. Once you have a reference to the user's session object, you can use this object's `getValue()` and `putValue()` methods to retrieve and store Java objects. Any type of object, not just strings, can be stored in a session object. Be warned, however, that you may need to cast the data as you get it back out to let the compiler know what you're intending. You may also need to use wrapper classes like `Integer` or `Boolean` to store data primitives because `putValue()` accepts only objects.

The following code provides an example of a simple servlet that remembers your last visit by storing a `Date` object in your session object.

```
import java.io.*;
import javax.servlet.*;
import javax.servlet.http.*;
import java.util.Date;

public class GuestLogServlet extends HttpServlet
{
    public void doGet (HttpServletRequest request,
    HttpServletResponse response) throwsServletException,

IOException
    {
        // Retrieve the session object or create a new one if
it doesn't exist.
        HttpSession client = request.getSession(true);

        // Prepare the client to receive HTML and get our
output stream.
        PrintWriter out = response.getWriter();
        response.setContentType("text/html");
```

```
        out.println("<HTML><BODY>");

        // In case this is a new visitor...
        if (client.isNew())
           out.println("Welcome first-time visitor!");

        else
        {
           Date lastVisit = (Date)
client.getValue("GuestLog.lastVisit");
           out.println("Your last visit was on " + lastVisit);
        }


        out.println("</BODY></HTML>");

        // Now store the current date and time for next time.
        client.putValue("GuestLog.lastVisit", new Date());
     }


  }
```

Although the hash key used by the session-tracking object's getValue()
and putValue() methods can be any string, you must remember that unlike
in JavaScript, the client-specific session object is shared by all servlets running
on the server and isn't partitioned by application. Therefore, you must be sure
to avoid collisions between servlets by establishing a consistent naming scheme.
A useful technique is to append the servlet or application name to the front of
the key to assure a unique entry.

One important difference between Java's session-tracking capabilities and
JavaScript's client object is how the information is stored between requests.
JavaScript can be configured to store its information in client-side cookies —
which are stored on the end user's machine and passed back and forth between
requests. As covered in detail in the Netscape document *Writing Server-Side
JavaScript Applications*, which can be found on the CD-ROM in the materials
that support Chapter 3, client-side cookies have storage and speed limitations
but maintain the information across servers and through server reboots.

By contrast, Java's session-tracking technique stores only the client's session ID information through client cookies. The actual data itself is maintained in memory on the server. Java provides a mechanism to use cookies for the data as well, though a little less transparently than through JavaScript. You must instantiate a cookie object and set its attributes directly. Another option is URL rewriting, which passes the information around in the URL itself, the only option available if your application must support users who can't or won't use cookies in their browser. Fortunately, Java provides methods that determine the cookie-storing capabilities (and preferences) of the client, allowing a single application to support cookies where available and URL rewriting where necessary.

The lifetime of the session object is configured by the Web server's servlet engine and typically defaults to something short — 30 minutes or so, since it's primarily intended for "life of transaction" style values. If the servlet or server is restarted, the session is cleared and your data will be lost. If you need persistence over a longer period of time, or beyond the life of the servlet, you need to employ more advanced options such as storing the client's information in a database or server-side file. One way to do this is to override the servlet's `destroy()` method, which gets called before the servlet is shut down (unless your server crashes unexpectedly). This is a good place to clean up any open resources or temporary files, and to save any state information. This information can then be restored during the `init()` phase of the servlet as it starts up.

Sharing Data Globally

JavaScript provides a project object as a mechanism to hold global data and share information among clients accessing an application. You simply assign properties to a project and access them later. The persistent nature of Java gives you a natural way to share information among clients accessing a particular servlet — the class's instance variables. Because servlet classes are instantiated only once, you can store data of interest to all clients accessing the servlet in the instance variables of the servlet itself. You need to protect writable instance variables from collision since they're accessed simultaneously from multiple threads, as described later. The following code listing is example of a servlet that can track the number of times it's been accessed. The counter is maintained in an instance variable, accessible by all threads that call on the servlet.

```java
import java.io.*;
import javax.servlet.*;
import javax.servlet.http.*;

public class CounterServlet extends HttpServlet
{
    int counter;
    public void init(ServletConfig config) throws
ServletException
    {
        super.init(config);
        counter = 0;
    }

    public void doGet (HttpServletRequest request,
HttpServletResponse response) throws ServletException,
IOException
    {
        response.setContentType("text/html");
        PrintWriter out = response.getWriter();
        out.println("<HTML><BODY>");
        synchronized(this)
        {
            counter++;
            out.println("Page has been accessed " + counter + "
times.");
        }
        out.println("</BODY></HTML>");
    }
}
```

Because servlets are generally independent of each other, this technique won't work when the data needs to be accessed from more than one particular servlet instance. Suppose you need to have an instance variable that's accessible by threads accessing any servlets on the server. In JavaScript, you might use the project object as a storage bin for such a variable because all files that make up the JavaScript application have access to it. In Java, a good strategy is to employ a programming technique called the *singleton*. In this model, you create a class that can be instantiated only once per virtual machine. The instance itself is accessible through static methods of the class, giving any servlet access to the singleton object. The following code listing shows the counter example again, this time implemented through a singleton class so that any servlet can access it. This makes it a counter that can report its access count to any servlets on the server.

```java
public class CounterSingleton
{
    private static CounterSingleton theInstance = null;

    private static int counter;

    public static CounterSingleton getInstance()
    {
        if (theInstance == null)
            theInstance = new CounterSingleton();
        return theInstance;
    }

    private CounterSingleton()
    {
        counter = 1;
    }

    public synchronized void incValue()
    {
        counter++;
    }

    public synchronized int getValue()
    {
        return counter;
    }
}
```

Then, from within a servlet access method you could work with the current counter value, as shown in the following snippet of code:

```
CounterSingleton accessCount =
CounterSingleton.getInstance();
out.println("I have been accessed " + accessCount.getValue()
+ " times.");
accessCount.incValue();
```

The singleton model ensures that only one actual counter object is ever instantiated; thus, everyone using the class is accessing the same instance. This strategy often comes into play during the design of applications that connect to databases. In JavaScript, you might instantiate a dbPool object and store a reference to it in the project object. In Java, however, we would access our pool of database connections through a singleton-style class.

Protecting Data Integrity at Runtime

JavaScript's locking feature is used to ensure that shared data on the project or server object isn't corrupted by simultaneous modifications from competing threads. In Java, each request that comes in for the servlet accesses the servlet object's methods and instance variables in its own thread. Servlets, therefore, must be written to handle multiple service requests simultaneously, making it the servlet writer's responsibility to control access to any shared resources through Java's synchronization techniques. Such resources include in-memory data such as instance or class variables of the servlet, as well as external components such as files, databases, and network connections.

In JavaScript, if there were a variable stored in the project object — say, an access-tracking variable referenced by project.counter — that you wanted to increment, you would protect the code with a lock on the project object, make our changes, and then remove the lock. Here's an example:

```
project.lock();
project.counter++;
project.unlock();
```

In Java, locking is handled through Java's thread synchronization methods. Routines or blocks of code should be prefaced with the synchronized keyword if they're attempting to access or modify data that could potentially be in use by another, simultaneous thread.

Accessing a Database

One of the big benefits of server-side JavaScript is its built-in support for communicating with a wide variety of databases. Rest assured that Java provides equally powerful (if not more so) database support through its JDBC (Java Database Connectivity) package in combination with platform-specific drivers provided by each database manufacturer. Java also provides support for ODBC (Open Database Connectivity), a cross-vendor abstraction layer, enabling you to create truly platform- and vendor-independent database applications.

JDBC works very similarly to JavaScript's LiveWire interface. Once you've created a valid connection object, you can execute queries and access cursors of information through it. As in form-data passing, data is retrieved through access methods rather than as direct properties of a cursor object as in Java Script. Here's a quick snippet of Java code, just so you can get the idea:

```
Connection con =
DriverManager.getConnection("jdbc:odbc:mydb.db");
Statement stmt = con.createStatement();
ResultSet rs = executeQuery("SELECT name, id FROM users");

while (rs.next())
{
    String name = rs.getString("name");
    Int id = rs.getInt("id");
}

stmt.close();
con.close();
```

Though I won't attempt to cover the details of JDBC here, you may be wondering about that getConnection() method. Notice that Java has mapped database connection calls into a URL-style syntax. This gives you a vendor-independent way to address a database as a network resource.

One particularly cool thing about JDBC is that the interface to the underlying data is the same no matter what type of database you're actually working with. And since the interface is extensible, any manufacturer can create drivers to tie into JDBC. For example, there's a JDBC driver that stores all of your information in simple flat files but gives you RDBMS-style access to the information.

Keys to the Future

Java's rich APIs and good formal structure make it an ideal language for the team development of complex Web applications. Looking ahead, it's likely that servlets (or their offspring) will become essential components in the development of Web-based applications, as well as one of the key methods of extending functionality in Web application servers and other multitiered architectures. That's reason enough for Web developers to pick up this important technology.

37
Adding Java Servlet API Capability to Netscape Servers

Paul Colton — *president and CEO, Live Software, Inc.*

The Java Servlet API from JavaSoft offers a way to extend the functionality of Web servers, like other Web server APIs, such as CGI and Netscape's NSAPI. Introduced as a means of standardizing the use of Java with Web servers, the Java Servlet API is becoming a de facto standard for Web server programming.

At first, the Java Web Server was the only server to fully support the Servlet API, but with its release of Enterprise Server 3.5.1, Netscape introduced basic support for the Servlet API through the use of Sun's reference implementation, the Java Servlet Development Kit (JSDK). The only problem is, the JSDK is already outdated: it supports version 1.0 of the Servlet API, but not version 2.0 with its many new features, including user session tracking.

Fortunately, there's a product freely available from Live Software that adds full Servlet API capability to all Netscape servers, including FastTrack and Enterprise Servers 2.*x* and 3.*x*, on all platforms. Called the *JRun Servlet Engine*, or simply *JRun*, this product is a Web server extension that makes Netscape servers totally compatible with the Servlet API and enables them to run Java servlets. JRun combines a Netscape plug-in that interfaces directly and immediately with your Web server with a collection of Java classes that provides the interface layer between your server and the servlets that you run.

In this chapter, I briefly discuss servlets and their benefits before telling you how to install and configure the JRun Servlet Engine. Then I'll take you through a tutorial designed to get you up and writing your own servlets in no time. For this discussion, I assume you already know the basics of Java.

What's a Servlet, Anyway?

Just in case you haven't read Duane Fields's terrific explanation in Chapter 36, I'll start with a really basic question: What exactly is a servlet? It's a server-side component written in Java that basically replaces CGI scripts. Servlets provide the usual HTTP services of retrieving files, creating directory listings, and performing basic CGI functions, yet they involve only about 900 lines of code, far fewer than a CGI script. Because servlets are written in Java, they're more flexible and stable than CGI scripts and give developers an interface that can be used on any platform without additional porting. As a result, servlets enable users to dynamically extend the functionality of their Web server on the fly.

CROSS-REFERENCE
Be sure to read Chapter 36 for a complete description of servlets, especially if your previous experience with server-side programming focused on writing server-side JavaScript.

Servlets can be used to provide a limitless range of customized services. For example, you can use them to look up records in a database in order to generate a Web page on the fly. System administrators can upload administration servlets on demand, such as log servlets that monitor visitor activity at a Web site or proxy servlets that perform traffic characterization and filtering. You can also use servlets for load balancing in multitiered applications. In a three-tier system, for example, the first tier could be a Java-enabled browser on a thin client, the second tier could consist of servlets that encapsulate specific business rules and logic, and the third tier could comprise legacy database information.

Why Use Servlets?

Servlets offer many benefits to the developer, including ease of development, automatic garbage collection, fast throughput and response, interservlet communications, and all the features inherent in Java. The HTTP services provided in the Servlet API are very convenient, and the API model and methods appear logical and clean, like most of the standard Java API.

Overall, Java is an easier and friendlier development environment than any of the other languages traditionally used to develop CGI scripts (C, C++, and the favorite, Perl). For instance, in a servlet, you need only a few simple print statements to output information to the Web. Working in Java, you also have available the power of Java's large API (including JDBC and LDAP).

Using servlets relieves you of the need to worry about the inner workings of the server. The Servlet API comes standard with a set of classes specifically oriented toward HTTP processing. Form data, server headers, cookies, and such are all handled for you by these classes. Additionally, because servlets are written in Java, you can move them from one platform to another for deployment and not worry about the operating system, as long as it supports Java. This advances Java's whole notion of "write once, run anywhere."

Servlets are modular, offering a true component model for building server-side applications. You can assemble any number of different servlets, perhaps from different vendors, and they'll work together seamlessly, each performing a specific task. Servlets can talk to each other, and they can also be chained together in a feature known as *servlet chaining*.

Servlet chaining is the capability whereby one servlet's output is "piped" into another servlet as its input. This can continue for multiple servlets. For example, a spelling-checker servlet could be chained after any other servlet to check spelling in the output sent to the client. Or a servlet that produces text could be chained to the spelling-checker servlet, then to a language-translation servlet. Each servlet need not know about the capabilities of the others, yet all can work seamlessly together. This is made possible by the use of a consistent server-side API.

In the end, the biggest difference between CGI and servlets is performance. A Web server's CGI interface incurs heavy expense by launching full-fledged programs to handle each user's request. By contrast, when you use servlets, there's a single Java Virtual Machine (JVM) running on the server and the servlet is loaded once when it's called. It's not loaded again until the servlet changes, and a modified servlet can be reloaded without your having to restart the server or application. The servlet stays resident in memory and is very fast. And static or persistent information can be shared across multiple invocations of a servlet, allowing you to share information among multiple users.

Installing and Configuring the JRun Servlet Engine

Before installing JRun, you must make sure you've turned on Java support in your Netscape server. Do this as follows:

1. Enter your Netscape administration server and select the Programs menu.

2. Select the Java option from the menu.

3. Click Yes to activate the Java interpreter.

Figure 37-1 shows what your screen should look like when you've performed the above steps.

The next step is to download JRun from the Live Software Web site at `http://www.jrun.com`. You can download either the UNIX version or the Windows version.

- The UNIX version comes as a `.tar.gz` file. Uncompress (using `gzip -d filename.tar.gz`) and untar (using `tar -xf filename.tar`) the file, then follow the instructions in the README file to start the connection wizard.

- The Windows version comes as a `.zip` file. Unzip the file (using WinZip or another unzipping program) and run the `setup.exe` program. The `setup.exe` will run an installation wizard that will copy the files onto your hard drive, and then launch the connection wizard.

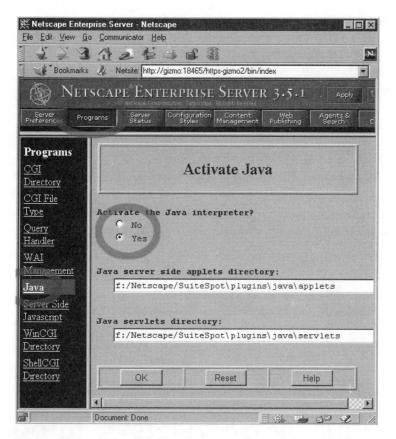

Figure 37-1: Turning on Java support

The JRun Connector Installation Wizard is used to link JRun to your Netscape server. Figure 37-2 shows the wizard's settings for installing the connector for Netscape servers. Note that you can choose either Java-based or NSAPI-based (native) connectors, and specify the version of Netscape server you're running. Once you proceed with the Connector Installation Wizard, it will automatically adjust your Netscape `obj.conf` file to properly run servlets. More information on the wizard can be found in the JRun documentation, which is available for downloading or can be viewed online.

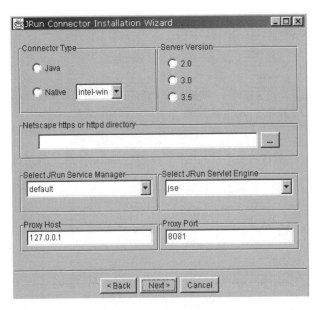

Figure 37-2: Connector Installation Wizard settings for Netscape servers

Now that you can run servlets, the next section shows you how to start writing your own servlet-based applications.

Writing Your Own Servlets: A Tutorial

The best way to explain the basics of any programming language and API is with the help of the simplest program possible. This tutorial starts with a "Hello World!" program. As I tell you more about the Servlet API, I'll modify the program, ending up with a large yet easy-to-modify program that covers the primary aspects of the API. By the end of this tutorial, you'll have a basic understanding of the Servlet API and all the tools necessary to develop any servlet.

The Basic Program

Start the tutorial by taking a look at the program in the following code example. The first lines import all the packages necessary to implement the servlet interface. The lines of code that may not be familiar are `import javax.servlet.*` and `import javax.servlet.http.*`. These are just packages from the Servlet API.

```java
import java.io.*;
import javax.servlet.*;
import javax.servlet.http.*;

public class HelloWorld extends HttpServlet
{
    public void service(HttpServletRequest servReq,
HttpServletResponse servRes) throws IOException
    {
        ServletOutputStream out = servRes.getOutputStream();
        out.println("Hello World");
    }
}
```

Next, the "Hello World!" program extends the `HttpServlet` class and doesn't explicitly implement the servlet interface just mentioned. The reason is that the `HttpServlet` class implements the servlet interface. It's a common practice for the servlet developer to extend the `GenericServlet` or `HttpServlet` class instead of implementing the servlet interface. When to extend from `GenericServlet` instead of `HttpServlet` will become clear as you learn more about the Servlet API.

The `service()` method implemented in the example is called repeatedly. The first parameter of the `service()` method is an `HttpServletRequest` object that provides an `InputStream` so that servlets can read client requests. The second parameter of the `service()` method is an `HttpServletResponse` object that provides an `OutputStream` so that servlets can write a response back to the client.

The rest of the program is self-explanatory. At this point, all you need to do is compile the Java code to get your servlet class file. After successfully compiling the code, put the servlet class file in the appropriate directory so the Web server can have access to it.

The simple "Hello World!" servlet is the most basic program that can be created using the Servlet API. From this program, you learned that all servlets must implement the servlet interface and that it's customary to do so by extending either the `GenericServlet` or `HttpServlet` class, both of which implement the interface.

The Servlet's Life Cycle

Now let's address what happens when a client invokes a servlet. When this happens, the servlet goes through a three-stage life cycle: initialization, service, and destruction.

- During the *initialization* stage, the servlet is initialized via the init(ServletConfig) method, which gets called only once. At this stage, it's a good idea to allocate all the resources the servlet will need throughout its life cycle.

- During the *service* stage, the servlet takes care of all incoming requests via the service(), doGet(), or doPost() methods. If you're not familiar with the HTTP protocol, which method to implement will become clear as you continue with the tutorial. In this example, I use the service() method, but I could have used the doGet() or doPost() methods, which are explained later in this tutorial.

- During the *destruction* stage, the destroy() method gets called either implicitly or explicitly. Inside the destroy() method is where you free all the allocated resources that the servlet was using during its life cycle. As soon as the destroy() method gets invoked, the class can be garbage-collected.

Now that you know more about the servlet life cycle, let's rewrite the "Hello World!" example program using the appropriate methods. The next listing shows the same example as the previous one, but with the init(), service(), and destroy() methods in place. At this point, these methods aren't doing anything, but as you'll see in future examples, they can be very useful.

```
import java.io.*;
import javax.servlet.*;
import javax.servlet.http.*;

public class HelloWorld extends HttpServlet
{
    public void init(ServletConfig config) throws
ServletException
    {
    // This method initializes the servlet and gets called
only once.
    // Allocate all of the servlet resources here.
```

```
      super.init (config);
  }

  public void service(HttpServletRequest servReq,
HttpServletResponseservRes) throws IOException
  {
      ServletOutputStream out = servRes.getOutputStream();
      out.println("Hello World");
  }

  public void destroy()
  {
  // Once this method is called, any instance of this class
can be garbage-collected.
  // Here is where all servlet resources can be
deallocated.
  }

}
```

Regular Parameters

The example program I've been using up to this point always outputs the same string value. Obviously, this isn't a very useful program. What you really need is a servlet that allows you to interact with it. You can easily interact with servlets by using parameters. Servlets have two types of parameters: initialization parameters and regular parameters. This section covers regular parameters; initialization parameters are explained later on in the tutorial.

If you wanted your example program to print "Hello <your name>" instead of just "Hello World," you would accomplish this task by using parameters. For simplicity, from now on the examples will implement only the methods necessary to make the servlet work. This will help keep the examples easier to read and the tutorial small and easy to follow.

The next listing shows how you would retrieve a parameter's value using the getParameter(String) method. If the parameter name you're trying to retrieve isn't defined, the getParameter(String) method returns a null value. As simple as it looks, this is all that's required for getting the parameter's value.

```
import java.io.*;
import javax.servlet.*;
import javax.servlet.http.*;

public class HelloWorld extends HttpServlet
{
    public void init(ServletConfig config) throws
ServletException
    {
        super.init (config);
    }

    public void service(HttpServletRequest servReq,
HttpServletResponse servRes) throws IOException
    {
        String userName;
        ServletOutputStream out = servRes.getOutputStream();

    if( (userName = servReq.getParameter("userName")) !=
null)
        out.println("Hello " + userName);

    else
        out.println("Hello, who are you?");
    }
}
```

Now that you know how to retrieve parameters, you need to learn how to specify them. There are various ways to specify parameters. The most basic way is via a GET query string, which enables you to specify parameters in the following way:

```
http://host/servlet/HelloWorld?userName=Mary
```

Another method of specifying parameters is through Server Side Include (SSI) and using the <servlet> tag, as in the following example:

```
<servlet code="HelloWorld" >
<param name="userName" value="Mary">
</servlet>
```

The most common method of specifying parameters is in an HTML form. For example, you could use the following form to send your name and address to a servlet:

```
<form action="/servlet/MyServlet" method="get">
Name: <input name="name"><br>
Address: <input name="address"><br>
<input type=submit>
</form>
```

Initialization Parameters

Now that you know how to retrieve and specify regular parameters, you can look at an example that requires initialization parameters. For simplicity, I'll continue using the same example program, with added features. Assume that you need a counter to keep track of how many times a specific home page is accessed. Furthermore, you'd like to be able to print the counter's value in a different font size. To accomplish this task, as shown in the next listing, you need two extra variables: counter and fontSize.

```
import java.io.*;
import javax.servlet.*;
import javax.servlet.http.*;

public class HelloWorld extends HttpServlet
{
    //Default values
    private static final int FONTSIZE = 3;
    private static final int COUNTER = 0;

    //Default variables
    public static int fontSize;
    public static int counter;

    public void init(ServletConfig config) throws
ServletException
    {
```

```
            super.init (config);

      if (getInitParameter("fontSize") != null){
         try{
            this.fontSize =
Integer.parseInt(getInitParameter("fontSize"));
         }
         catch (NumberFormatException e){
            this.fontSize = this.FONTSIZE;
         }
      }

      else
         this.fontSize = this.FONTSIZE;

      if (getInitParameter("counter") != null){
         try{
            this.counter =
Integer.parseInt(getInitParameter("counter"));
         } catch (NumberFormatException e){
            this.counter = this.counter;
         }
      }

      else
         this.counter = this.counter;
      }

      public void service(HttpServletRequest servReq,
HttpServletResponse servRes) throws IOException
      {
      // Set the content type.
      servRes.setContentType("text/html");
         String userName;
         ServletOutputStream out = servRes.getOutputStream();

      if (servReq.getParameter("userName") != null)
```

```
        userName = servReq.getParameter("userName");

    else
        userName = new String("Stranger");
        out.println("<HTML><HEAD><TITLE>Hello
World</TITLE></HEAD><BODY>");
        out.println(userName + "This page has been accessed
<FONT size=+" + fontSize +">" + counter++ + "</font>
times<BR>");
        out.println("</BODY></HTML>");
    }

}
```

Right away, you can see that the previous code includes some methods you haven't previously seen. I'll explain the program piece by piece. Because I assume you know the basics of Java, I won't explain the constants and variables declarations. After the declarations, the first method we encounter is the init(ServletConfig) method. This time, however, you're using the init(ServletConfig) method to retrieve the initialization parameters with the getInitParameter(String) method, and to initialize the global variables.

At this point in the program, let's review a couple of things. First, you know that servlets remain in memory until the server is restarted or until they're reloaded dynamically. Second, because the init() method is called only once during the initialization stage, the global variables are going to be initialized only one time (when the servlet is first invoked). With those two points in mind, you can see that once the global variables are initialized, they'll be available throughout the life cycle of the servlet, keeping their state through different client requests.

So following the code in the init() method, you can see that if the user declares valid initialization parameters, the global variables will be set to those values. On the other hand, if the user doesn't specify initialization parameters, or specifies the wrong ones, the global variables will be set to the default values (the constants). This flexibility allows you to start counting at whatever value you wish. It also allows you to specify the font size for the value of the counter display. With a little imagination, you can see how useful this can be in almost any application.

Besides the changes in the init(ServletConfig) method, the method service(HttpServletRequest, HttpServletResponse) also introduces another method: servRes.setContentType(String). The purpose of this program is to display the user name and the number of times the page has been accessed. Furthermore, you want to display the counter's value in a different font size, so you need to use HTML. As you can see, the HTML is embedded in the print statements. You need to let the browser know that we're going to be displaying HTML. The `servRes.setContentType("text/html")` method is provided so you can set the content's MIME type. Once you set the MIME type, the rest of the code is self-explanatory; you get the parameters and then print to the browser.

Now that we know how to retrieve initialization parameters, you also need to know how to set these parameters to the servlet. In JRun, you set initialization parameters with the JRun Admin tool. Consult the JRun documentation for details on how to do this.

Server-Side Development Made Fun

Servlets are the future. Blurring the differences between platforms, servlets help to realize Java's promise of "write once, run anywhere." They also make server-side application development fun. Now that you've installed the JRun Servlet Engine on your Web server and read through the tutorial, you should be able to start developing your own simple servlets.

38

Embedding Netscape Directory Server in Your Application Using the C and Java Directory SDKs

Mark Wilcox — *Web administrator, University of North Texas*

One of the first things I realized when I started working with the Netscape Directory Server was just how easy it is to embed it in an application. In fact, it was just as easy as Netscape said it would be in its promotional materials, and that's one of the reasons I use the product in the applications I've developed.

To embed Directory Server, start by downloading either the Java or C versions of the Netscape Directory SDK, both available for free from Netscape's DevEdge Online Web site at `http://developer.netscape.com/tech/directory/in-dex.html?content=downloads.html`. You can also obtain a trial copy of

Netscape Directory Server from Netscape; to find out how, see the file at the root level of the CD called "Welcome and Software Download."

Note that usefulness of the SDKs is enhanced by the fact that Netscape has made the source code available, also free. Using either version of SDK decreases your development time; in addition, as you use the source code, you can better see how the SDK works, and it allows you to customize the SDK to meet specialized needs. For more about what you gain from Netscape's release of the Directory SDK source, see the section "Importance of Open Source and the Directory Server SDKs."

In the rest of this chapter, I show you how simple it is to add in support for using the Directory Server and the Lightweight Directory Access Protocol (LDAP) as the authentication database for your application, using both C and Java. Unlike previous chapters, which have been heavier on tutorial information, this chapter consists mostly of just the code you can use to accomplish these tasks. My purpose is simply to get you up and running with Directory Server and LDAP as quickly as possible.

CROSS-REFERENCE
Before reading this chapter, we recommend that you read Chapter 4 and Chapter 9, which will introduce you to the Netscape Directory Server and LDAP.

The application described here is very simple. You pass it a userid and password on the command line, and it tells you if the userid and password authenticate to the Directory Server. This is authentication at its most basic level. Of course, the Directory Server and the Directory Server SDK also enables you to do more advanced forms of authentication, including making use of client certificates. You can also restrict access based on departments or teams/groups in your organization. LDAP does not eliminate any of the possible means of authentication you may need; it just makes it easier to do so. LDAP implements the "make the simple things simple and the hard things possible" credo that has made Internet technologies so viable.

To install these examples, you need the Netscape Directory C and Java SDKs. These examples use Netscape's Directory Server 3 with the default `Airius.ldif` file installed as the LDAP database. Copy and paste this code into your favorite text editor. Save it as `authenticate.c`. Follow the directions provided in the Read Me file for your OS and compiler for building C executables with the C SDK.

For the Java examples, copy and paste the code into your favorite text editor. Save it as `ldapAuth.java`. Make sure that the Netscape Directory Java SDK is in your `CLASSPATH`. Then type `javac ldapAuth.java`. To run the example, type **java ldapAuth** as your userid password. Make sure you use JDK version 1.1.5 or later; I use JDK 1.1.6.

Looking at the Code

The first long code shows the code you'd use to this in C; the second listing provides a Java code sample you can use to do the same thing. Both examples are very simple introductory examples. Yet they use the same basic algorithm that Netscape Enterprise Server uses to access the Netscape Directory Server for authentication.

Here's the algorithim in pseudo-code:

- Get the userid and password.

- Search the LDAP server using the userid as the search filter. The search filter is `uid=userid`.

- If the search results come back with an entry, grab that entry's Distinguished Name (DN) attribute. Note that a userid should be unique in any particular database. For example, there should be only one user named mewilcox in the Ace Industries database. If this is not the case (for example, if your company is merging with another company), you will need to do some extra work to determine which user is trying to log in. That is left as an exercise for the reader.

- Pass the user's DN and password to the LDAP SDK authenticate routine.

- If the DN and password match, you can proceed. Otherwise, you should tell the user that the userid and password combination failed. Note the LDAP authentication routine doesn't pass back a Boolean true/false value. Instead it throws an error if the authentication operation failed. Also, the Netscape Directory Server uses special functionality to handle passwords, including restricting the number of times users can try to log in before they're denied.

- Continue with your program if the authentication operation passed; otherwise, handle this error condition (for example, by asking for the user to login again, log the login failure, call the police, etc.).

Here's the first example, showing how to embed the Netscape Directory Server in your application using C:

```
/*authenticate.c
This is a very simple example to show how easy it is to
provide authentication in
your applications with LDAP. This application assumes that
you have a Directory server
installed on your local machine and that you have the
default Airius.ldif file installed. It's
a very trite example. You just pass it a userid and password
on the command line. Then it tests
if those pass. You can configure it for your needs.
Questions: Mark Wilcox mewilcox@hotmail.com

usage: authenticate uid password
*/

#include <stdio.h>
#include <stdlib.h>
#include <string.h>
#include <time.h>

/* standard C ldap libary */
#include "ldap.h"

#define MY_HOST         "localhost"
#define MY_PORT         389
#define MY_SEARCHBASE   "o=airius.com"

int authenticate();

int
main( int argc, char **argv )
{

  // for test we will "set" the uid and passwords here
```

```c
    // had this been a real program, you would get them
externally
    // from a prompt

    const char *uid = argv[1];
    const char *passwd = argv[2];
    char uid_filter[100]="uid=";
    int results = 1;
    if (argc < 3){
       printf("usage: authenticate uid password\n");
       exit(1);
       }

   printf("Testing Authentication\n");

    // Need to build the search filter
strcat(uid_filter,uid);


   printf("search filter is %s\n",uid_filter);

   results = authenticate(uid_filter,passwd);

   if (results == 0){
     printf("you authenticated!\n");
     }
   else {
     printf("userid %s failed!\n",uid);
     }

  }

 int authenticate(char *uid_filter,char *passwd)
 {

   LDAP            *ld;
   LDAPMessage     *result, *e;
```

```
char            *dn;
int             value= 1;
const char      *MY_FILTER = uid_filter;

/* First setup a LDAP connection */
 if ( (ld = ldap_init( MY_HOST, MY_PORT )) == NULL ) {
  perror( "ldap_init" );
  return( 1 );
 }
  printf("connected to LDAP host %s on port
%d\n",MY_HOST,MY_PORT);

    /* In LDAP v2 We must always authenticate as someone to do
an operation.
      Here we authenticate as anonymous
      In LDAP v3 which Directory 3 & 4 support, you don't
have to bind first,
      but it's good form.
    */
 if ( ldap_simple_bind_s( ld, NULL, NULL ) != LDAP_SUCCESS )
{
   /*Special error method for LDAP */
   ldap_perror( ld, "ldap_simple_bind_s" );
   return( 1 );
 }

     /* A bind in LDAP is accomplished by passing a
Distinguished Name (dn) and
  the password. Of course people can't be expected to
remember their dn. So
  instead we ask for their userid (uid) and then search for
the first entry
  that matches that userid
  */

 if ( ldap_search_s( ld, MY_SEARCHBASE, LDAP_SCOPE_SUBTREE,
   MY_FILTER, NULL, 0, &result ) != LDAP_SUCCESS ) {
```

```
     ldap_perror( ld, "ldap_search_s" );
     return( 1 );
    }


    /* Either LDAP Connection handle is bad or there are more
 than user entries that match
         the results
         */
     if (ldap_count_entries(ld,result)!= 1)
       {
           ldap_perror(ld,"ldap_count_entries");
           return(1);
         }
       if (e = ldap_first_entry(ld, result)){
     if ( (dn = ldap_get_dn( ld, e )) != NULL ) {
         printf( "dn: %s\n", dn );


         /* if dn or password is empty but not null we need to
 throw it out here otherwise
             someone will successfully authenticate anonymously
 */


           if ((dn == "") || (passwd == "")) {
             printf("dn or password are empty.\n");
     return(1);
      }


         /* To test for authentication in LDAP, we do a bind.
 If it fails, the server
           will throw an error
           */
     if ( ldap_simple_bind_s( ld, dn,passwd) != LDAP_SUCCESS )
 {
        /*Special error method for LDAP */
       ldap_perror( ld, "failed to authenticate" );
       return( 1 );
      }
```

```
          value = 0;
          /*call this to free memory */
          ldap_memfree( dn );
   }
  }
//}

 ldap_msgfree( result );
 ldap_unbind( ld );
 return( value );
}
```

Now, here's the example showing how to do the same thing using Java:

```
import netscape.ldap.*;

/**
   ldapAuth.java
   usage: ldapAuth uid password

   A simple command line example to show how to use LDAP for
user authentication for
   an appliction.
*/

public class ldapAuth {

 public static boolean authenticate(String uid,String pwd)
  {
    boolean status = false;
    LDAPConnection ld = new LDAPConnection();
    LDAPEntry findEntry = null;
    String dn = null;
    String MY_HOST = "localhost";
    int MY_PORT = 389;
    String MY_SEARCHBASE = "o=airius.com";
    String MY_FILTER = "uid=" + uid;
```

```
        try {
            ld.connect( MY_HOST, MY_PORT );
            LDAPSearchResults res = ld.search(
MY_SEARCHBASE,LDAPConnection.SCOPE_SUB,MY_FILTER,null,false)
;

            System.out.println("getCount is "+res.getCount());
            // more than 1 user matching filter, fail.
            if (res.getCount() != 1) { return false;}

            if (res.hasMoreElements()) {
                findEntry = res.next();
                dn = findEntry.getDN();

                System.out.println("dn is "+dn);
                //prevent anonymous connections
                if ((dn == "") || (pwd == "")) { return false;}
                //now attempt to bind to server
            ld.authenticate(dn,pwd);

            //if ld.authenticate doesn't throw an exception we passed
            status = true;
            }
        } catch(LDAPException e) {
                System.out.println(e.toString());
                }
                catch(Exception x) {
                x.printStackTrace();
            }
        return status;
        }

    public static void main (String args[]) {

        if (args.length <2) {
            System.out.println("usage ldapAuth userid password");
            System.exit(1);
```

```
        }

    String uid = args[0];
    String passwd = args[1];
    boolean status = authenticate(uid,passwd);
    if (status) {
        System.out.println(uid+" authenticated!");
    }
    else {
        System.out.println(uid+" failed!");
    }
    System.exit(0);
    }


    }
```

Feel free to use either of these examples in your application, depending on whether you need to use C or Java.

Innovating with Open Source and the Directory Server SDKs

Before I finish up, I want to give you some food for thought about Netscape's release of the source code for the SDKs because down the road some of you might find the need to do more complex, customized installations of the Directory Server.

The reason the open source release of the Directory Server SDKs is important is that SDKs are the essential building blocks of applications. They are the tools developers use to build applications. Most SDKs are "black boxes," which means developers are given the documentation and then use the SDK without knowing how the internals work. Most of the time this works great. However, building anything without understanding how the tool works can lead to disaster, especially if there is a bug in the tool.

By having an open source to the SDKs, you can learn how they work, gain a better understanding of how LDAP works, and learn good programming practices. It also means that if you discover a bug in the SDK or if there's a feature that hasn't been implemented, you can fix the bug or implement the new features without waiting for the original developers to release an update.

Further, it means that you can modify the SDK so that when you ship your application you can ship a customized version of the SDK to make your application customizable. This could mean enabling extra features (for example, special calls to dynamically configure your application using LDAP data), or you can make a smaller SDK by eliminating features you or your customers don't need.

Using an SDK without an open source is like an operating a saw with a blindfold on. You can saw wood that way, but you're likely to lose a few fingers in the process. Using an SDK with open source is sawing without a blindfold. Or to follow another saying: An open source SDK doesn't give developers an LDAP toolbox; it teaches developers how to build better LDAP toolboxes. If you're interested in checking out the source code for the Java and C Directory SDKs, see the Netscape Directory SDK page at `mozilla.org`, which also contains the source code release of Netscape Communicator. You can find it on the Web at `http://www.mozilla.org/directory/`.

All You Need to Get Started

That's really all you need to know to get going with Netscape Directory Server and LDAP. See Chaper 39 for another way of programming the Directory Server, a Netscape-invented technology called PerLDAP.

Now you can start doing all the cool things the Directory Server lets you do. Some of them are discussed in Chapter 9, but your imagination is really the limit for how you can add to application functionality with Directory Server.

39

Developing Your Own WWW/LDAP Gateway with the PerLDAP SDK

Mark Wilcox — *Web administrator, University of North Texas*

S ince its early days, Netscape Directory Server has shipped with a default Directory Server Gateway. This gateway is a series of HTML pages and CGI programs that provides an interface to the server. In the beginning this was important because none of the major browsers (Navigator included) provided support for the LDAP protocol. A Web-based CGI interface was the best one at the time.

The gateway is still with the server, and it has improved. However, the default gateway doesn't always fit the bill. Maybe you don't want to wade through all the special comments needed to customize the gateway. Perhaps you've found a dusty old Pentium-90 in the closet on which you've placed a copy of Linux, and you've decided that will be your interface server. Or you could be like me: You think the existing gateway interface is nice, but you get a small burn in your stomach when you run software on your Web server that the "public" uses and you don't have its source code. Finally, you may just want to learn more about LDAP. Writing your own interface is called for in all these cases. This chapter tells you how.

What You'll Need

For this exercise you need Perl5, the PerLDAP SDK (available at `http://www.mozilla.org/directory/perldap.html`), and the CGI.pm module (from `http://stein.cshl.org/WWW/software/CGI/cgi_docs.html`). CGI.pm is shipping with modern Perl distributions, and you probably already have it if you've ever done any CGI programming. If you've been doing CGI programming in Perl without this module, go get it right now.

You also need to configure two directories for your use: a place to put CGI programs and a place where you can stick HTML documents. Most likely you already have these directories set up. If not, consult your server's documentation on how to do this.

To install the scripts described in this chapter, find the files supporting this chapter on the CD-ROM and copy the `simplesearch.pl`, `search.pl`, and `mod.pl` files to the directory for CGI programs.

ON THE CD-ROM

The files referred to in the preceding and following paragraphs are available on the CD-ROM that accompanies this book. You can find them by following the path, Sample Code and Supporting Documentation ⇨ Part IV ⇨ Chapter 39.

You'll use the other directory to store three text files, which can also be found on the CD-ROM; these files will contain HTML you can use for display:

■ A header file, called `header.htm`, that will be the header for all the forms.

■ A search file, called `simplesearch.htm`, that will contain the search form. This must have a text box called "filter" and a drop-down box called "attribs."

■ A footer file, called `footer.htm`, that will be the footer for all the forms.

Put these files in the directory for HTML documents where your Web server process can read them, and put their locations in the gateway scripts.

A Simple Search Interface

The script `simplesearch.pl`, shown in the following listing, performs the search provided by the simple interface in the `simplesearch.htm` file. The interface consists of a Web page with a single form with a single-line text field named "filter."

```
use strict; # Encourage good programming.
use CGI; # CGI library
use CGI::Carp qw(fatalsToBrowser); # Echo error messages to
browser and server log.
use URI::URL;
use Mozilla::LDAP::Conn;  # LDAP module
use Mozilla::LDAP::Utils; # LDAP module

# Some variables to set
my $www_host = "localhost";
my $www_port = 80;
my $ldap_host = "localhost";
my $ldap_port = 389;
my $ldap_base = "o=airius.com";

# We're doing an anonymous search.
my $dn = "";
my $pwd = "";
my $query = new CGI;

# Print necessary headers so the server can send back a web
page.
```

```
print $query->header;
print $query->start_html(-title=>'Search Results');

# Get our search form parameter.
my $filter = $query->param('filter');

# Now do the search.
my $ldap = new
Mozilla::LDAP::Conn($ldap_host,$ldap_port,$dn,$pwd) ||
    die("Failed to open LDAP connection.\n");
my $entry = $ldap->search($ldap_base, "subtree",$filter);
print $query->h1("LDAP Search Results");

# Print out results.
print "<PRE>";
if (! $entry) {
    print "$filter did not return any results";
}
else {
    while ($entr {
        $entry->printLDIF();
        $entry = $ldap->nextEntry();
    }
}
print "</PRE>";
print $query->end_html();
```

All the script does is import the necessary modules, declare some variables needed for the LDAP search, and use CGI.pm's built-in methods to start printing out HTML for display. Then it creates an LDAP object, performs the search, and displays the results of that operation.

This very simple form might be handy for testing out LDAP queries, but you probably want something meatier. In the rest of the chapter, you develop a more complete gateway example.

A More Advanced Search Interface

The search.pl script, shown here, displays both the search form and the search results. This is possible because the CGI.pm module makes it easy to check to see if the script was called with a GET or a POST. If you're not familiar with this concept, I suggest that you read up on CGI programming. A good place to do that is from Perl-related articles at *Web Review* magazine, available at http://webreview.com/wr/pub/98/06/12/perl/index.html.

```perl
use CGI;     # CGI library
use CGI::Carp qw(fatalsToBrowser); # Echo error messages to
browser and server log.
use URI::URL;
use Mozilla::LDAP::Conn;  # LDAP module
use Mozilla::LDAP::Utils; # LDAP module


# Some variables to set
my $www_host = "localhost";
my $www_port = 80;
my $cgi_bin = "pdsgw-bin";
my $ldap_host = "localhost";
my $ldap_port = 389;
my $ldap_base = "o=airius.com";
my $ldap_scope = "subtree";


# Display variables
my $header = "f:/pdsgw/cgi/header.htm";
my $body = "f:/pdsgw/cgi/search.txt";
my $footer = "f:/pdsgw/cgi/footer.htm";


# We're doing an anonymous search so we don't need to set
the dn and the password.
my $dn = "";
my $pwd = "";


### Start work here. ####
```

```perl
my $query = new CGI;
print $query->header;
open (HEADER,"$header") || die("Failed to open
$header.$!\n");
open (FOOTER,"$footer") || die("Failed to open
$footer.$!\n");
my $header_txt;
my $footer_txt;
while (<HEADER>) {
   $header_txt .= $_;
}
close (HEADER);
while (<FOOTER>) {
   $footer_txt .= $_;
}
close (HEADER);

# Display search form.
if ($query->request_method() eq "GET") {
   print $header_txt;
   open (SEARCH,"$body") || die("Failed to open
$body.$!\n");
   while (<SEARCH>) {
      print $_;
   }
   close (SEARCH);
   print $footer_txt;
}
else {
   print $query->start_html(-title=>'Search Results');
   print $header_txt;
   my $filter = $query->param('filter');
   my @attribs = $query->param('attribs');

   # Now do the search.
   my $ldap = new
Mozilla::LDAP::Conn($ldap_host,$ldap_port,$dn,$pwd) ||
```

```perl
        die("Failed to open LDAP connection.\n");
    my $entry = $ldap-
>search($ldap_base,$ldap_scope,$filter,0,@attribs);
    print $query->h1("LDAP Search Results");
    if (! $entry) {
        print "$filter did not return any results<br>";
    }
    else {
        # I hacked this routine from the printLDIF routine.
        while ($entry) {
            print "<TABLE border=3>";
            my $dn = $entry->getDN();

            # Make an LDAP URL out of the dn. This will make it
easier
            # to get the entry for modifications.
            my $ldap_url = "ldap://".$ldap_host."/".$dn."???";

            # Modify the LDAP URL for transport.
            $ldap_url =~ s/=/||/g;
            $ldap_url =~ s/, /\~/g;
            my $url =
"http://$www_host:$www_port/$cgi_bin/mod.pl?entry=$ldap_url"
;
            print "<TR><TD>DN:</TD><TD> $dn </TD>";

            print "<TD><a href=\"$url\">Modify Entry</a></TR>";

            print $query->br();
            my $attr;
            my @vals;

            # This was hacked from PerLDAP internals.
            foreach $attr (keys(%{$entry})) {
                @vals ="";
                next if ($attr =~ /^_.+_$/);
                next if $entry->{"_${attr}_deleted_"};
```

```
                    grep((push(@vals,$_)), @{$entry->{$attr}});
                    my $value;
                    foreach $value(@vals) {
                        print
       "<TR><TD>$attr</TD><TD>$value</TD></TR>"
                            unless $value=~ /^$/;
                    }
                }
                print "</TABLE>";
                $entry = $ldap->nextEntry();
            }
        }
        print $footer_txt;
    }
    print $query->end_html();
```

To start this script, type the following in your browser:

http://myserver/my-cgi/search.pl

The first lines of this script set some variables needed for the rest of the script. Then the script loads the header and footer files.

If the script is called with a GET, the script prints out the header, opens the search text file, prints out the search text file, and then prints out the footer.

Of more interest to us is what happens when the form is called with the POST method. First, the script sets a scalar variable called $filter to the contents of the form's "filter" value. Then it loads an array called @attribs with the values of the contents of the form's "attribs" values, if any. Then it must create a new Mozilla::LDAP::Conn object before we can perform any LDAP operations. The following line sets this up:

```
my $ldap = new
Mozilla::LDAP::Conn($ldap_host,$ldap_port,$dn,$pwd) ||
    die("Failed to open LDAP connection.\n");
```

Notice that in PerLDAP you must pass the distinguished name (dn) and the password of the user you wish to authenticate as. In the search.pl script, you wish to do this anonymously, so set the dn and password to " ".

The next line performs the search:

```
my $entry = $ldap-
>search($ldap_base,$ldap_scope,$filter,0,@attribs);
```

This line starts the search at the point that's contained in the `$ldap_base` variable. The scope of the search is set in the `$ldap_scope` variable. The search filter is contained in the `$filter` variable. The "0" means display the names of attributes.

The `@attribs` array contains the attributes you want the search to return. If the `@attribs` array is empty, all the attributes will be returned. If the search returns with anything, the `$entry` variable will contain something; if it doesn't, a message is printed saying that the search failed. If the `$entry` variable does contain something, the results are printed out in a tabular form. Each entry gets its own table.

You should note two things here. One is that I got the results to come out the way I did by hacking my own `printLDIF()` method. In the PerLDAP module, the `printLDIF()` method prints out the contents of the entry in the LDIF format — that is, the format Netscape Directory Server uses for its database entries. This is a quick-and-dirty output. You also have the option of getting particular attributes by name, but because I want to print out all the attributes of the entries that are returned, I want to use the `printLDIF()` method. However, I want the output to be "pretty," so I need to hack something together so that I can control the output of the LDIF itself.

To do this, I actually peered into the PerLDAP source code to see what the `printLDIF()` method did, and then copied that code and modified it for this script. I didn't actually make any changes to PerLDAP itself — I just made my own display code. It's not good practice as taught in strict object-oriented programming, but the result is something that works.

The other thing I'd like to point out is that I want a "Modify Entry" link to appear next to each entry in the search form. When a user clicks on this link, it will call the `mod.pl` script so that the user can modify the entry. To make it easier to look up the entry, I decided to pass an LDAP URL to the `mod.pl` script.

LDAP URLs, created as part of the LDAP version 3 specifications, are an easy way to specify a particular entry contained in an LDAP server. Netscape Communicator supports LDAP URLs natively in the browser, but not many other browsers support LDAP URLs (a reason why WWW/LDAP gateways are popular). An LDAP URL takes the following form:

```
ldap(s)://host:port/base?attributes?scope?filter
```

For example, let's plug in the following values:

```
host: ldap.myserver.com
port: 389
base: ou=People,o=myserver.com
attributes: cn,mail
scope: sub
filter: sn=Carter
```

The LDAP URL with these values will look like this:

```
ldap://ldap.myserver.com/ou=People,o=myserver.com?cn,mail?su
b?sn=Carter
```

If the port is the standard LDAP port (389 for non-SSL transactions), you can leave the port out of the URL. If the LDAP server is using SSL, you need to specify the LDAP protocol with `ldaps://` instead of `ldap://`.

In the `search.pl` script, the LDAP URL is built in the section following the comment "Make an LDAP URL out of the dn." You must do some text mangling to pass the LDAP URL from the search.pl script to the `mod.pl` script over an HTTP URL. This is because of the CGI protocol, which separates elements by =, and because certain other elements can cause the `mod.pl` to get false or nonexistent values. So you mangle the text into something that looks ugly but is easily passed to the `mod.pl` script.

A Script to Modify a Search Form Entry

The `mod.pl` script, shown in the following listing , follows the same steps as the `search.pl` script. The only difference is in the display — all the values are displayed in a form text box, separated by a | as the delimiter. This makes it easier to modify attributes that have multiple values without having to worry about replacing all of them.

```
use CGI;    # CGI library
use CGI::Carp qw(fatalsToBrowser); # Echo error messages to
browser and server log.
use Mozilla::LDAP::Conn;  # LDAP module
```

```perl
use Mozilla::LDAP::Utils; # LDAP module

# Some variables to set
my $www_host = "localhost";
my $www_port = 80;
my $cgi_bin = "pdsgw-bin";
my $ldap_host = "localhost";
my $ldap_port = 389;
my $ldap_base = "o=airius.com";
my $ldap_scope = "subtree";

# Display variables
my $header = "f:/pdsgw/cgi/header.htm";
my $body = "f:/pdsgw/cgi/search.txt";
my $footer = "f:/pdsgw/cgi/footer.htm";

# We're doing an anonymous search so we don't need to set
the dn and the password.
my $dn = "";
my $pwd = "";

### Start work here. ####
my $query = new CGI;
print $query->header;
open (HEADER,"$header") || die("Failed to open
$header.$!\n");
open (FOOTER,"$footer") || die("Failed to open
$footer.$!\n");
my $header_txt;
my $footer_txt;
while (<HEADER>) {
    $header_txt .= $_;
}
close (HEADER);
while (<FOOTER>) {
    $footer_txt .= $_;
}
```

```
close (HEADER);
if ($query->request_method() eq "GET") {
    print $query->start_html(-title=>'Modify Form');
    print $header_txt;
    my $ldap_url = $query->param("entry");

    # Turn the URL back into a real LDAP URL.
    $ldap_url =~ s/\|/=/g;
    $ldap_url =~ s/~/\, /g;

    # Can modify if the entry is not a person,
organizationalPerson, or inetOrgPerson objectclass.
    my $action = $query->url;
    print $query->startform(-method=>'POST',-action=);
    my $ldap = new
Mozilla::LDAP::Conn($ldap_host,$ldap_port,$dn,$pwd) ||
        die("Failed to open an LDAP connection.");
    if (! $ldap->isURL($ldap_url)) {
        die("$ldap_url is not an LDAP URL!<br>");
    }
    my $entry = $ldap->searchURL($ldap_url);

    if (! $entry) {
        die("Oops. You didn't enter a valid person filter.");
    }
    else {
        # Do the modifications.
        my $ldap = new
Mozilla::LDAP::Conn($ldap_host,$ldap_port,$dn,$pwd) ||
            die("Failed to open an LDAP connection for
modification.");
        my $entry = new Mozilla::LDAP::Entry();
        print $query->header;
        print $header_txt;
        my @attrs = $query->param;
        my $mgr_dn;
        my $mgr_password;
```

```perl
foreach my $value (@attrs) {
    if ($value eq "mgr_dn") {
        $mgr_dn = $query->param($value);
        next;
    }
    if ($value eq "mgr_password") {
        $mgr_password= $query->param($value);
        next;
    }
    if ($value eq "dn") {
        print $query->h1("Attempting to modify:");
        # Another way to get a particular entry.
        $entry = $ldap->search($query->param($value),"base","(objectclass=*person)");
        if (! $entry {
            die("Entered bad entry");
        }
        next;
    }
    else {
        my @vals = split(/\|/,$query->param($value));
        foreach my $val(@vals) {
            $entry->addValue($value,$val);
        }
    }
}

# Don't allow empty strings.
if (($mgr_dn =~ /^$/) || ($mgr_password =~ /^$/)) {
    die("Failed to enter manager dn or password.");
}

# Rebind as an authenticated user.
$ldap = new
Mozilla::LDAP::Conn($ldap_host,$ldap_port,$mgr_dn,$mgr_password) ||
```

```
        die("Failed to open an LDAP connection for
modification.");

    # Do the actual modification.
    $ldap->update($entry);

    if ($ldap->getErrorCode()) {
        print $query->h1($ldap->printError());
    }
    else {
        print $query->h1($entry->getDN());
        print $query->h1("Entry updated");
    }
    print $footer_txt;
}
```

In the initial GET call, the search is performed with the searchURL() method using the unmangled LDAP URL you got in the call to mod.pl. Here's the searchURL() call in the mod.pl script:

```
my $entry = $ldap->searchURL($ldap_url);
```

Then the script steps through the results just as the search.pl script does.

A new wrinkle in this output is the addition of the DN and PASSWORD fields at the bottom. These fields are necessary because to update an entry in LDAP, you must be bound as a particular entry and that entry must have the ability to update that particular entry.

Netscape Needs Your Help

That's about it for this gateway. You could add a form that would enable someone to create an entirely new entry or remove an entry. Check out the PerLDAP docs at the Mozilla directory site at http://www.mozilla.org/directory/ to see how to add and remove entries with PerLDAP.

Because PerLDAP is one of the Netscape Directory SDKs and thus has been released as an OpenSource product, you have full access to the source code. Netscape is looking for volunteers to help out with PerLDAP 2, which will include modules for schema management, group management, and Netscape Suitespot management. Netscape could also use help with developing tools that use the PerLDAP SDK or any of the Netscape SDKs. (For more about tools like this, please see the mozilla.org Web site at http://www.mozilla.org/directory/tools/ldaptools.html.) If you have anything to offer, I encourage you to join the discussion at the Mozilla directory discussion group, available through news://news.mozilla.org/netscape.public.mozilla.directory.

If you liked what you saw about PerlDAP in this chapter, be sure to read Michelle Wyner's contribution, Chapter 41. And, of course, we'll be talking a lot more about PerLDAP in *View Source* at http://developer.netscape.com/viewsource. Stop by and check us out next time you're on the Web.

40

Storing Preferences for a Personal Homepage Using LDAP

Michelle Wyner — *technology evangelist, Netscape-Sun Alliance*

The word *portal* used to mean something as simple as a *door* or *entrance*. Now if you say "portal," especially if you're in high-tech (and even sometimes if you're not), people think of Web sites such as Yahoo, Excite, and Netcenter. These portals are popular because they let users create their own personal home pages, incorporating everything from headline news and stock information to sports scores. The sites enable users to pick the stocks they wish to track, decide whether or not they want to see sports information, and choose from an array of information and services. Most sites use a combination of DHTML, including Cascading Style Sheets, and JavaScript that enables users to select what they want.

I'll show you a simple way to enable users to design their own personalized pages and position where on the page each element should be. Once they've done this, users can save their preferences, using LDAP, into their directory entry on a Directory Server. Then in subsequent session, they'll be able to bring up their personalized page from the stored preferences.

ON THE CD-ROM

Complete source code for Personal Homepages in DHTML described in this chapter is available on the CD-ROM that accompanies this book. To find it, follow the path: Sample Code and Supporting Documentation ⇨ Part IV ⇨ Chapter 40.

I'm going to assume that you know Netscape Directory Server basics (see Chapters 4 and 9 to start), such as how it works and some of the terms (like objectclass and schema). Because the Common Gateway Interface (CGI) is written in Perl, I'm also going to assume you know Perl. (Check out the Perl Web site at `http://www.perl.com/pace/pub` for more information.) By the same token, if you're not familiar with PerLDAP, you should become familiar with it. It's extremely easy and provides hooks into the Directory SDK C API using Perl. A great place to start learning about PerLDAP is in Chapter 39 of this book. (More information on PerLDAP can be found on the mozilla.org site at `http://mozilla.org`.)

NOTE

You'll want to be sure to read Chapters 4, 9, 38, and 39 before reading this chapter. Also, be sure you've installed the Netscape Directory SDK C version, which you can find at `http://www.mozilla.org/directory/tools/ldaptools.html`.

The Software I Used

This is the software I used to build the code.

- Netscape Directory Server 4.0, under Linux, which you can find at `http://home.netscape.com/download/prodinfonfs_102.html`

- Netscape Directory SDK 3.0 for C, available at `http://www.mozilla.org/directory/tools/ldaptools.html`

- PerLDAP Version 1.2.2., located at `http://www.mozilla.org/directory/perldap.html`

- Perl 5.0 or later, from `http://www.perl.com/pace/pub`

- The CGI.pm Perl library, which is at
  `http://stein.cshl.org/WWW/scftware/CGI/cgi_docs.html`

The CGI.pm module is a Perl library that enables your CGI scripts to easily pull information out of HTML pages or write information to them. It also offers functions for creating forms, pulling information out of existing forms, and more. It's an extremely useful package if you're going to be doing anything with HTML and Perl.

About the Files

As I mentioned, the files you need to run this example are included on the CD-ROM. Here's a quick explanation of each file; I will go more into greater detail on each file later.

- `search.html` is a blanket starter page where users enters their username and password and chooses whether to view their page or change their page preferences.

- `prefs.js` contains the JavaScript code for setting up the preferences page.

- `getprefs.pl` is the CGI script that does the actual work of connecting to the Directory Server and it either reads preferences from the Directory Server or saves preferences there.

Known Bugs

There's a bug in Linux under the Apache server. Occasionally, when saving the directory preferences, you'll get a CGI Misconfiguration Internal Error caused by a core dump. You can work around this by reloading the page with the error message, and after you do this, everything should be hunky-dory. The code has been tested on Solaris and also on Windows NT, and the bug wasn't reproducible on these platforms.

I also found a lot of bugs when I ran the code on Internet Explorer, although I believe I've worked around most of them. One thing you may have to do before running the code on IE is to change the positioning of the DIV elements on the Preferences page.

The Directory Server

To make things on the Directory Server side clearer, I chose to add my own objectclass and attribute to the server schema, and I did this directly through the administration console. I first created a multivalued attribute named prefsselection. Then I defined the objectclass as follows:

```
objectclass personalprefs
oid personalprefs-oid
superior person
allows prefsselection
```

You must do this step before running the script, or you run the risk of getting a schema violation on the Directory Server. Obviously, you don't have to use my naming standards, but remember that whatever you call your objectclass and attribute, you need to change those values in the getprefs.pl script. One other thing to be aware of is that values stored in the prefsselection attribute look similar to this example:

```
stocks:visible:100:100
```

The parts of this value separated by colons are:

- The name of the content area, such as *stocks, news, weather,* or *fun*

- An indication of whether or not the content area is going to be visible to the user

- How far from the left side of the page the upper-left corner of the content area should be placed

- How far from the top of the page the upper-left corner of the content area should be placed

The Starter Page: search.html

The page shown in Figure 40-1 is written in standard HTML. It's a form with a couple of text fields for users to enter their Directory Server username and password. There are also two radio buttons that let users choose whether to view their saved page or change their preferences. In the form action, I call the getprefs.pl script with the POST method so that the username and password are not passed in the URL as parameters that can be viewed by everyone.

```
<html>
<head>
<title>Get User Prefs</title>
</head>
<body bgcolor="#FFFFFF">
<h2>Your Own Page</h2>
<form name="searchform" action="/cgi-bin/getprefs.pl"
METHOD=POST>
<b>UserName: </b><input type="text" name="username"><br>
<b>Password: </b><input type="password" name="password"><p>
Do you wish to:<br>
<input type="radio" name="choose" value="view" CHECKED>View
Your Current Page<br>
<input type="radio" name="choose" value="change">Change Your
Preferences<p>
<input type="submit" name="submit" value="submit">
</form>
</body>
</html>
```

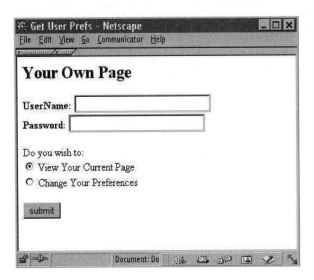

Figure 40-1: The Search page, written in standard HTML

The External JavaScript Code: prefs.js

The JavaScript code stored in the external file enables users to set up their personal pages by dragging and dropping different content areas. The code has been tested on both Internet Explorer 4.x and Netscape Communicator 4.x. (And it should also work with the next-generation versions of both products.) Also, please note that, in many cases, I reference a style sheet definition. I cover the style sheet definition is when I talk about the `getprefs.pl` script because this is where the style sheet is defined. Figure 40-2 shows a personal home page.

The first aspect of the script is the global variable definitions. They are as follows:

- `currentX`: the current X coordinate position of the event

- `currentY`: the current Y coordinate position of the event

- `oldLeft`: the original left-hand side position of the element before it is dragged

- `oldTop`: the original top position of the element before it is dragged

- `theElement`: the current element on the page being dragged

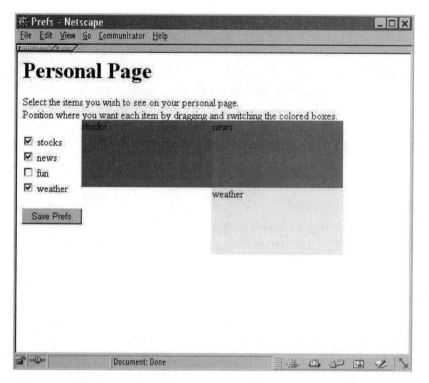

Figure 40-2: Our personal home page

- `oldElement`: the last element on the page to be dragged

- `Draggable`: an array to keep track of which objects on the page are capable of begin dragged

- `isNav4` and `isIE4`: used to determine which browser is being used

And here's what the part of the script I just described looks like:

```
currentX = currentY = oldLeft = oldTop = 0;
var theElement;
var oldElement;
var Draggable = new Array();
var temp;
var isIE4 = document.all;
var isNav4 = document.layers;
```

The setUp() Function

The setUp() function, which is called when the HTML document loads, has two purposes. The first purpose is to initialize and assign values to the Draggable array, and because there are four elements on the page that you want to be draggable, you're going to put the name of each element into the array. The second purpose is to control the checkboxes on the page. Users can control which items they can or cannot see on their personal page via a series of checkboxes. If the news checkbox is checked, the news area becomes part of the page but the news checkbox is unchecked; it disappears so that the users won't see it. When the Preferences section is loaded back, these checkboxes are automatically checked or unchecked, depending on which areas the users chose to view during their previous session. The for loop loops through the items in the Draggable array (which contains all the content areas users can choose from) and checks their visibility attribute. What this attribute is set to determines whether the associated checkboxes are checked or unchecked.

```
function setUp() {
   Draggable[0] = "stocks";
   Draggable[1] = "news";
   Draggable[2] = "fun";
   Draggable[3] = "weather";

   for (i=0; i<Draggable.length; i++) {
     if (isNav4) {
        if (document.layers[Draggable[i]].visibility ==
"hide")
              eval("document.finishedForm." + Draggable[i] +
".checked=false");
     } else if (isIE4) {
        if (eval(Draggable[i] + ".style.visibility") ==
"hidden")
              eval("document.finishedForm." + Draggable[i] +
".checked=false");
     }
   }
}
```

The isDraggable() Function

The isDraggable() function is passed an element on the HTML page and determines whether that element is in the Draggable array. If it is, it's considered an element that can be dragged, and the item is returned.

```
function isDraggable(item) {
  for (j=0; j<Draggable.length; j++) {
    if (item.name==Draggable[j])
      return item;
  }
  return null;
}
```

The begindrag() Function

Next is the begindrag() function, which is called whenever the mouse button is pressed. The code is noticeably different between Internet Explorer and Communicator. Under Communicator, you find out where on the page the mouse button was pressed, and set the currentX and currentY variables. The first for loop is going to cycle through all the elements in the document.layers array. This is so you can determine the layer where the mousedown event took place. The second if statement is used to determine if the current element you're looking at from the document.layers array is something you've set with the capability to be dragged or not. If it is, then you can look at where the mouse event actually took place. Obviously to be the element you want, the mouse event needs to have taken place within the boundaries of this element. If the current element checks out, you set the theElement variable to be this element and oldLeft and oldTop so you can keep track of the element's original position (before any dragging takes place).

Under Internet Explorer, you find the element that was clicked by using the built-in event.srcElement variable and checking to see if it's draggable. If it is, you set theElement and find the exact coordinates where the mousedown event fired. You then set oldLeft and oldTop. By doing this, the event.returnValue is set to *false* to prevent any normal action by the element from taking place. (For example, if there were a link inside the element that was clicked to invoke the mousedown event, the event.returnValue = false statement would prevent this link from being navigated to.) Finally, you set cancelBubble to *true* in order to prevent the event from propagating up the element container hierarchy.

```
function begindrag(e) {
  if (isNav4) {
    currentX = e.pageX;
    currentY = e.pageY;
    for (i=0; i<document.layers.length; i++) {
      temp = document.layers[i];
      if (isDraggable(temp) != null) {
        if ((currentX > temp.left) && (currentX < temp.left
+ temp.clip.width) &&
            (currentY > temp.top) && (currentY < temp.top +
temp.clip.height)) {
          theElement = temp;
          oldLeft = theElement.left;
          oldTop = theElement.top;
          break;
        }
      }
    }
  } else if (isIE4) {
    var tempObject = isDraggable(event.srcElement);
    if (tempObject != null) {
      theElement = tempObject;
      distanceY = (window.event.clientY -
theElement.style.pixelTop);
      distanceX = (window.event.clientX -
theElement.style.pixelLeft);
      oldLeft = theElement.style.pixelLeft;
      oldTop = theElement.style.pixelTop;
      window.event.returnValue = false;
      window.event.cancelBubble = true;
    }
  }
}
```

The moveIt() Function

The moveIt() function is called when the user moves the mouse by holding the mouse button down. This function is used to drag the selected item for placement. When dragging your element over another element, you want to make sure yours is shown as being dragged on top. To do this, you need to change the zIndex values of both the element that was previously dragged and the element you're currently dragging. Before you assign the left and top edges of the element new coordinates, find out how far the element was dragged across the page. Then you can change the two edges officially to the new coordinates based on the newly found distance.

```
function moveIt(e) {
  if (theElement) {
    if (isNav4) {
      if (oldElement)
        oldElement.zIndex=0;
      theElement.zIndex=5;
      distanceX = (e.pageX - currentX);
      distanceY = (e.pageY - currentY);
      currentX = e.pageX;
      currentY = e.pageY;
      theElement.moveBy(distanceX,distanceY);
    } else if (isIE4) {
      if (oldElement)
        oldElement.style.zIndex = 0;
      theElement.style.zIndex = 5;
      currentX = window.event.offsetX;
      currentY = window.event.offsetY;
      if (window.event.clientX >= 0) {
        theElement.style.pixelLeft = window.event.clientX-
distanceX;
        theElement.style.pixelTop = window.event.clientY-
distanceY;
      }
      window.event.returnValue = false;
      window.event.cancelBubble = true;
    }
```

```
        }
    }
```

The enddrag() Function

The last function that deals with drag and drop is enddrag() is called when the user releases the mouse button. At the beginning of the function, you check to see if there's actually anything in the theElement variable. Why? Because you're capturing the mousedown and mouseup events for the entire document, the two events will fire not only when you want a layer dragged but also when one of the checkboxes is selected or unselected. If you run a quick check to see if you actually selected a layer, rather than a checkbox, none of the code in the enddrag() function is ever called.

Once you've determined that a layer was actually dragged, you check to see if you dropped this layer on one of the other three layers. If so, you want these two layers to switch places. To do this, check two things: First, check to see if the user ended up dragging the layer, but dropped it in the same place (essentially dropping it on itself). If the user did not do this, then find out if the layer was actually dropped on another layer; if so, switch the two layers. If the layer was dragged and dropped someplace on the page other than on top of another layer, move the dragged layer back into its original position. Last, release the mousemove event because you don't want to capture it anymore.

Another thing I should mention is that in the Internet Explorer code, I use two hard-coded values when I check to see whether one element has been dropped on another: *200* refers to the width of each element, and *100* refers to the height of each element. These are hard-coded because of an IE 4 bug. If a DIV's style elements are defined in a style sheet in the HEAD of the HTML document, then these values, when accessed, return null, even though the DIVs are positioned correctly on the page. For instance, because I set the height and width of each element in the style sheet, if I then try to get the value of, for example, stocks .style.width, no value is returned. Here's what the code looks like for the feature I just described:

```
function enddrag(e) {
    if (theElement) {
        // Determine whether you dropped the layer on another
    layer.
```

```
    for (i = 0; i<Draggable.length; i++) {
      if (theElement.name != Draggable[i]) {
        if (isNav4) {
          temp = document.layers[Draggable[i]];
          if ((currentX>= temp.left) &&
(currentX<=temp.left+temp.clip.width) &&
              (currentY>=temp.top) &&
(currentY<=temp.top+temp.clip.height)) {
            // Switch places.
            theElement.left = temp.left;
            theElement.top = temp.top;
            temp.left = oldLeft;
            temp.top = oldTop;
            break;
          } else {
            theElement.left = oldLeft;
            theElement.top = oldTop;
          }
          } else if (isIE4) {
            temp = eval (Draggable[i]);
            if ((window.event.clientX >=
temp.style.pixelLeft) &&
                (window.event.clientX <=
temp.style.pixelLeft+200) &&
                (window.event.clientY >=
temp.style.pixelTop) &&

(window.event.clientY<=temp.style.pixelTop+100)) {

theElement.style.pixelLeft=temp.style.pixelLeft;
              theElement.style.top=temp.style.pixelTop;
              temp.style.pixelLeft=oldLeft;
              temp.style.pixelTop=oldTop;
              break;
          } else {
            theElement.style.pixelLeft=oldLeft;
            theElement.style.pixelTop=oldTop;
```

```
            }
          }
        }
        if (isNav4)
          releaseEvents(Event.MOUSEMOVE);
      }
      oldElement = theElement;
      theElement="";
    }
  }
```

The changePage() Function

The changePage() function handles what happens when users click one of the checkboxes to either hide or show an element. If users uncheck the *news* preference, the news layer is hidden; otherwise, it is visible. Notice in the IE code that I actually get the value of the passed-in checkbox element, set it to lowercase, and use this to find the visibility of the DIV element. This is another bug I ran into with IE: The problem wasn't getting the names of the checkbox elements but getting the values. Because the values are the same as the names, with the exception of those values that start with uppercase, I just went from here.

```
function changePage(somename) {
  if (isNav4)
    document.layers[somename.name].visibility =
      ((somename.checked == true) ? "show" : "hide");
  else {
    temp = (somename.value).toLowerCase();
    eval(temp + ".style.visibility=" +
        ((somename.checked == true) ? "'visible'" :
"'hidden'"));
  }
}
```

The getReadyForCGI() Function

The getReadyForCGI() function is called when users click the *Save Prefs* button, after changing all of their preferences. The way PerLDAP works is that if you want to set a multivalued attribute with all the attributes at once, you can do something like this:

```
$entry->{prefsselection} = ["value1", "value2", "value3"];
```

In our case, the values are "stocks," "news," "weather," and "fun," with all the associated extras we're saving along with that — visibility, left coordinate, and top coordinate. All these can be referenced from the Preferences page and passed in to our CGI script. To make life easier, you take all the values, put them in the correct format, and place them in a hidden field so that the CGI can automatically reference the values without worrying about formatting.

Also, remember the format for how each content area's characteristics are saved in the Directory Server:

```
stocks:visible:100:100
```

The `arguments` variable is what's going to hold your string. Since you need to save the visibility of each content area, you cycle through the checkbox elements on the page to see whether they're checked or not. You then pull out the left and top values and add those to your string as well. You may notice that at the end of each content area section I add a comma; it's what separates one value from the next in a multivalued attribute. However, this means that once your string is completely built, you're going to have a trailing comma. To get rid of it, you can take a substring of the entire built string and subtract the last character (which is the comma). Once our string is complete, set the value of the hidden form field, which is called `varToPass`. Then the form submit continues on its own.

```
function getReadyForCGI(finishedForm) {
  var arguments = "";

  for (i = 0; i< Draggable.length; i++) {
    someVar = eval("finishedForm." + Draggable[i]);
    arguments += (Draggable[i] + ":");
    if (someVar.checked)
      arguments += "visible:";
    else
      arguments += "hidden:";
    if (isNav4)
```

```
            arguments += document.layers[someVar.name].left + ':'
  +
                    document.layers[someVar.name].top + ',';
        else if (isIE4) {
          arguments += (eval(Draggable[i] + ".style.pixelLeft"))
  + ':' + eval(Draggable[i] +
                    ".style.pixelTop") + ',';
      }
    }
    temp = arguments.substring(0,(arguments.length-1));
    finishedForm.varToPass.value = temp;
  }
```

The CGI Script: getprefs.pl

As stated earlier, the getprefs.pl file contains the code that does most of the work. This is the code that loads the user's personal page or saves users' preferences.

The file begins with the package importing. The first use CGI statement says not only to import the CGI.pm package, but also that if there is a problem with the CGI, write the error message directly to the browser window. The second use CGI statement says you're going to use some HTML3-specific tags; these are needed for any style sheet definitions you'll use through the CGI.pm package. The two use Mozilla statements are PerLDAP package calls, and the use strict statement tells the Perl compiler to make sure all of your variables are first declared somewhere in your script before they're actually used (the rules of compilation are stricter).

```
#!/usr/bin/perl5 -T

# Stuff is stored like this in the directory:
#
# name of pref,
# visible or hidden,
# left position,
# top position
```

```
use CGI::Carp qw(fatalsToBrowser);
use CGI qw/:standard :html3/;
use Mozilla::LDAP::Conn;
use Mozilla::LDAP::Utils;
use strict;
```

Next are the global configuration variables. These are variables that you need to configure in order to get the script to run correctly on your server. They're pretty self-explanatory. The scriptURI variable refers to the HTML form's action when users click the *Save Prefs* button.

```
#
# Configuration part; edit this.
#
my $webhost = "localhost";
my $ldaphost = "localhost";
my $ldapport = "389";
my $ldap_base = "o=mcom.com";

my %colors = ( "stocks"  => "red",
               "fun"     => "blue",
               "weather" => "yellow",
               "news"    => "green"
             );

my $scriptUri = "/cgi-bin/getprefs.pl";
```

Finally, there are some random global variables, which you'll learn more about later when they come up in the code. The $query variable creates a CGI object, which contains the parameters passed to the CGI script from our HTML form.

```
#
# Global variables
#
my $query = new CGI;
my ($filter, $tmp, $i, $numVals, $entry, $ldapcon, $ret,
$password);
```

The createHTML() and createStyle() Subroutines

There are two subroutines (functions) in this script. The first one, called cre-ate_HTML(), creates the user's personal page — not the Preferences page, but the full-blown finished personal page. One variable, that contains information for the prefsselection attribute is passed in. To get the specifics of this value (the DIV name, visibility, left coordinate, and top coordinate), you need to parse the string on the delimiter, which happens to be a colon. One thing to realize is that the left and top coordinates, which are stored in the directory, are specific to the Preferences page. This means that both coordinates are used to place a small content area in the middle of the page (because this is how the Preferences page looks). You need to change these coordinates so that users' finished home pages use the entire page instead of only a portion of it. Once you have the new coordinates, the HTML for the DIV is written to the page. Notice that the width and height coordinates have been changed as well.

```
sub create_HTML {
  my $prefsstring = shift;
  my ($divName, $visible, $left, $top) = split(/:/,
$prefsstring);
  my $curColor = $colors{$divName};

  $left = ($left - 100) * 2;
  $top = ($top - 100) * 3;

  print "<DIV ID='$divName' STYLE='position:absolute;
  visibility: $visible; left: $left; top: $top; layer-
background-color: $curColor;
  width: 400; height: 300; background-color :$curColor;
  clip: rect(0 400 300 0)'>$divName</DIV>";
}
```

The second subroutine, create_Style(), writes the entire "change your preferences" page. The value passed in is the user's entire LDAP entry, which is immediately set to the variable thing. One of the local variables declared is a hash array called vElements; it is going to contain the key/value pair of each content area name, and its visibility attribute. I use this array because of the same IE bug that I mentioned earlier (when explaining the prefs.js file). Unless I set the visibility directly in the DIV definition, I can't get the visibility property in order to see whether the checkboxes on the page should be checked or unchecked (in the JavaScript code). I create the empty hash array, which will be filled with key/value pairs in the for loop.

```perl
sub create_Style {
  my $tmp = "";
  my $thing = shift;
  my $numVals = $thing->size("prefsselection");
  my ($newStyle, $prefsstring, $i, $divName, $visible,
$left, $top,
      $curColor);
  my %vElements = ( );

  for ($i = 0; $i < $numVals; $i++)
    {
      $prefsstring = ($thing->{prefsselection}[$i]);

      ($divName, $visible, $left, $top) =
split(/:/,$prefsstring);
      $curColor = $colors{$divName};
      $tmp .= ".$divName {position:absolute;
visibility:$visible;
      left:$left; top:$top; layer-background-
color:$curColor;
      background-color:$curColor; clip:rect(0 200 100 0);
width:200;
      height: 100; zIndex:1}\n";
      $vElements{$divName} = $visible;
    }
  print $query->start_html(-title      => 'Prefs',
                           -style      => {-code=>$tmp},
                           -script     => {-
language=>'JavaScript1.2',

                                            -
src=>'/prefs.js'},

                           -onLoad=>"setUp()");
```

```
print $query->h1('Personal Page');
print "Select the items you wish to see on your personal
page.";
print $query->br;
print "Position where you want each item by dragging and
switching ";
print "the colored boxes.";
print $query->startform(-name          => 'finishedForm',
                        -method        => "POST",
                        -action        => $scriptUri);
print $query->checkbox(-name           => 'stocks',
                       -checked        => 'checked',
                       -onClick        =>
'changePage(this)',
                       value           => 'Stocks');
print $query->br;
print $query->checkbox(-name           => 'news',
                       -checked        => 'checked',
                       -onClick        =>
'changePage(this)',
                       value           => 'News'
                       );
print $query->br;
print $query->checkbox(-name           => 'fun',
                       -checked        => 'checked',
                       -onClick        =>
'changePage(this)',
                       value           => 'Fun');
print $query->br;
print $query->checkbox(-name           => 'weather',
                       -checked        => 'checked',
                       -onClick        =>
'changePage(this)',
                       value           => 'Weather');
print $query->br;
print $query->hidden(-name=>'varToPass');
```

```
  print $query->hidden(-name=>'username', -
default=>$main::filter);
  print $query->hidden(-name=>'password', -
default=>$main::password);
  print $query->br;
  print "\n";
  print $query->submit(-name=>'Submit', -value=>'Save
Prefs',

onClick=>'getReadyForCGI(this.form)');
  print $query->endform;
  print $query->br;
  while (($divName, $visible) = each(%vElements)) {
    print $query->div({-class     =>        $divName,
                       -id        =>        $divName,
                       -name      =>        $divName,
                       -style     =>
"visibility:$visible"},
                       $divName);
    print "\n";
  }
  print "<SCRIPT>\nif (document.captureEvents != null)\n";
  print "document.captureEvents(Event.MOUSEDOWN |
Event.MOUSEUP | Event.MOUSEMOVE);\n";
  print "document.onmousedown=begindrag;\n";
  print "document.onmouseup=enddrag;\n";
  print "document.onmousemove=moveIt;\n</script>";
}
```

The first for loop goes through the user's LDAP entry and gets each value of
the prefsselection attribute. You split on the string again, just as you did in
create_HTML(), and get a color out of the colors array. The $tmp variable
string is going to be added to each time through the loop; this contains a style definition (which will go in the HEAD of your HTML page) for each DIV you're going
to define. Each time through the loop, you also add the visibility information of
each DIV to the vElements array.

Using the wonder of the CGI.pm package, you start writing information to your HTML page. The style sheet definition and the external JavaScript file definition are all defined in the `start_html` line.

Inside this HTML page definition are three hidden fields, which are defined at the bottom of the newly created form. The first, `varToPass`, contains the full text string that you're going to use to set the user's new preferences (as explained earlier for `prefs.js`). The next two are the username and password that were passed in from the `search.html` form. You pass these variables in hidden fields to prevent the user from having to type the username and password twice. (You can also use cookies to prevent this.)

After the form is written, you iterate through our new hash array and actually write each DIV definition to your new page. Then comes the JavaScript code that actually captures the events. Remember, you're capturing three events: `onMouseDown`, `onMouseMove`, and `onMouseUp`.

The Meat of the Code

Now you come to the main part of the code and take care of the directory calls. I'll explain this code a piece at a time, with commentary explaining what the next piece does.

First you open a new LDAP connection to the Directory Server, saving the connection information in the `$ldapcon` variable, and do an anonymous search to get back information about the user's entry (saving the user's info in the `$entry` variable). You do this so that you can get the user's DN, and then authenticate using this DN and the user's password so that users can modify their own entry. Before the user authentication occurs, though, you check to make sure that only one entry corresponding to the user's ID was returned. If more than one was returned, this means the user didn't enter a unique ID and you will not know which entry to use.

```
$filter = $query->param('username');
print $query->header;

# First we need to get the dn by binding anonymously to the
server.
$ldapcon = new Mozilla::LDAP::Conn($ldaphost, $ldapport) ||
   die ("Failed to open LDAP connection");
```

```
$entry = $ldapcon->search("$ldap_base", "subtree",
"uid=$filter");

# Check to see that we got only one entry back.
if ($entry && !$ldapcon->nextEntry()) {
  $password = $query->param('password');
  $ret = $ldapcon->simpleAuth($entry->getDN(), $password);

  exit(-1) unless $ret;
```

Once you've established that the user has entered a unique ID and you've been able to authenticate to that user's entry, you need to know if the user is viewing his or her personal page, has selected changing his or her preferences on the personal page (but hasn't actually done so), or has just changed his or her preferences and is now saving them back to the directory entry. The same CGI is called in all these three cases, so you need to make some distinction between what's going on. To differentiate, you can check to see whether the hidden form field varToPass exists. If it does, the user is saving preferences and has just clicked the *Save Prefs* button; otherwise, the user is coming off of the first search.html page and either wants to change preferences or wishes to view his or her personal page.

Before you show a user his or her page, however, you need to check to make sure the user actually has preferences saved in his or her directory entry. You can determine this by checking to see if the objectclass personalprefs is part of the user entry. If it's not, the user has not saved preferences before and cannot really view his or her personal page. You add the objectclass to the user entry, design a stock personal page, and bring the user to the preferences page so that he or she can change user preferences to his or her liking.

```
  # Are we getting prefs, or saving them?
  if ($query->param('varToPass') eq "") {
    # We're getting prefs.
    # Check to make sure the user has saved prefs before. If
not, give
    # him the default page.
    if (!$entry->hasValue("objectclass", "personalprefs")) {
      $entry->addValue("objectclass", "personalprefs");
      $entry->{prefsselection} = ["stocks:visible:100:100",
                                  "news:visible:300:100",
```

```
                                        "fun:visible:100:200",
                                        "weather:visible:300:200"
                                    ];

        $ldapcon->update($entry);
        create_Style($entry);
        print $query->end_html();
    }
```

If you're coming from the first search.html page, you need to know whether the user wants to only view his or her page or to change his or her page preferences. You can tell by looking to see which of the two radio buttons the user has selected. If the *change* button is selected, the user first wants to change his or her preferences. In this case, you call the create_Style() subroutine to show the user his or her current preferences. If the change button is not selected, the user wants only to view the page and you call the create_HTML() subroutine.

```
    else {
        # Read the prefs back since they've been saved
previously.
        # Is the user changing prefs, or viewing them?
        if ($query->param('choose') eq 'change') {
          create_Style($entry);
          print $query->end_html();
        }
        else {
          foreach $i (@{$entry->{prefsselection}}) {
            create_HTML($i);
          }
        }
      }
    }
```

The next else statement applies when the user has just clicked the *Save Prefs* button and wants to save new page preferences to his or her directory entry. You take the contents of the now-filled hidden form field varToPass and split on the comma because this differentiates one value from another. You save everything to the user's prefsselection attribute, and then you show the user his or her personal page using the user's new preferences, by calling call the `create_HTML()` subroutine. But wait! Do not forget that you haven't actually saved the user's entry; you have only modified the entry. So now you must update the user's entry so that the new preferences are permanently part of it.

```
else {
    # since we already did the check for the object class,
we can
    # assume that the user already has prefs stored, so we
can just
    # modify them.
    $entry->{prefsselection} = [ split(/,/, $query-
>param('varToPass')) ];

    print $query->start_html("Personal Page");
    foreach $i (@{$entry->{prefsselection}}) {
      create_HTML($i);
    }
    print $query->end_html();

    $ldapcon->update($entry);
    undef $entry;        # Kludge, don't know if it helps on
Linux...
    }
}
```

The final `else` statement is called if the user does not enter a unique Directory Server value. Once everything on the Directory Server is complete, you close the connection.

```
else {
   die ("Loser! Put in a unique ID!");
}
# Close the LDAP connection.
$ldapcon->close() if $ldapcon;
```

After all the preferences are saved, the user can view his or her own personal page. Figure 40-3 provides a quick picture of the way I've set up mine.

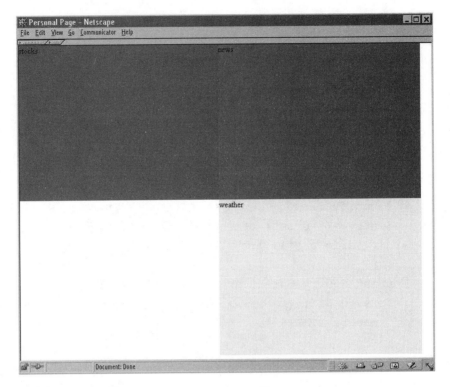

Figure 40-3: The way I've set up my personal home page

Using LDAP Creatively

This chapter illustrates one creative use of LDAP. (I began by showing you some DHTML so you could sneak into this with something easy.) As I hope I've shown, LDAP and the Netscape Directory Server can be used for a lot more than just storing your users' names. It's a terrific way to build persistence into a Web application by storing information about the application itself. What I've shown is pretty simple, but it will also work for much more complicated applications. The speed, power, and adaptability of LDAP make it a great tool for building all kinds of advanced functionality into your application. Now that I've given you a simple idea, go see what more you can do with it!

41

CORBA in the Enterprise, Part 1: Object-Oriented System Design

Bob Schlicher — *software architect, AlterNet Communications*

n an article I wrote for *View Source* magazine, "CORBA in the Enterprise: Introduction," I discussed the basics of *object-oriented* (OO) modeling and design, outlined a generic software development methodology, and described the artifacts that are produced as a result of the problem analysis phase of the development process. I went on to detail and illustrate how to perform a problem analysis in the enterprise, applying the Common Object Request Broker Architecture (CORBA) to this analysis. I urge you to have a look at this article, which is included on the CD-ROM that accompanies this book. Additionally, if you haven't done so already, please see Chapter 5, "CORBA: Theory and Practice," for a general introduction to CORBA.

ON THE CD-ROM

The *View Source* article "CORBA in the Enterprise: Introduction," can be found on the CD-ROM that accompanies this book. To find it, follow the path Sample Code and Supporting Documentation ⇨ Part IV ⇨ Chapter 41.

In this and the next chapter, I'd like to turn your attention to the system design phase of the development process, which involves mapping the analysis artifacts to the actual implementation code. I begin with some general comments on OO design, discuss what you need as you get started, describe the activities and steps involved in design, and list the design artifacts, the fruits of your labor. Then I look more specifically at designing with CORBA and consider the decisions about scale, interface granularity, and interface integration that it entails.

I'm emphasizing the up-front efforts — the analysis and design — that are necessary before you start doing any IDL language binding, code generation, and coding. There are enough resources that explain CORBA at a code level. My intention is to help you integrate CORBA activities into a development methodology.

Some General Comments on OO Design

The primary purpose of an OO design is to provide sufficient description and specification to enable developers to build, deploy, test, and reuse software. The design should be flexible enough to respond to changes in the business requirements and the implementation.

Developing any OO design requires the ability to compromise. The designer must bridge the gap between the analysis artifacts, which should directly meet the requirements gathered in the phase before the problem analysis, and the limitations of reality — that is, the constraints of the target software environment. Making those come together is all about tradeoffs. For instance, the target environment usually includes the CORBA services that your application will use and rely on for support — services such as locating components over the distributed network and transactional management, to name a couple. The problem analysis that the designer receives may not make any mention of these services, but the system design must take them into account.

Design involves a significant amount of work and covers a broad range of concerns, from refining the OO analysis artifacts to identifying and building with programming idioms and design patterns, to extending existing frameworks and objects, to considering the physical packaging and the dependencies (especially in C++) among programming modules. I'll cover only the key basics here, but if there's any one thing you should remember from this chapter, it's the following: *Design is an engineering problem.* Maintain discipline, make it simple, strive for balance, and keep it stable.

- **Maintain discipline:** Work with your project team and stay in sync with the rhythm of your release plan.

- **Make it simple:** Solve complex problems through the integration of simpler parts. Seek out patterns and apply them where they make sense.

- **Strive for balance:** Ensure that no one part of your architecture is tasked with too much to do.

- **Keep it stable:** Document your work in the artifacts and make them stick. Make changes through a controlled process.

As You Begin the System Design

As you begin the system design, it's important to have a fairly mature set of analysis artifacts, as described in "CORBA in the Enterprise, Introduction" (on the CD-ROM), and what's normally called an object-oriented design guide. This design guide directs you and your fellow designers in several aspects of design.

- It tells how to capture your design in *Unified Modeling Language* (UML), or your chosen notation, in the familiar object model, sequence, and state diagrams.

- It identifies useful design rules and heuristics, such as "Use cache objects to improve performance." Patterns are included.

- It documents tactical policies—that is, policies for using the underlying, sometimes called infrastructure, services.

For the design guide, it's important to establish tactical policies and develop an understanding of some useful software patterns. I'll describe tactical policies and software patterns here.

Tactical Policies

You'll need to formulate tactical policies that support the system architecture and vision. These policies should address concerns such as the following:

- Error processing

- Memory management

- Data storage management

- Approaches to control

- Initializations

- Internationalization

- Distributed communications

- Integration with third-party products

For instance, the memory management policy may identify the use of a specific factory pattern and implementation for creating business objects. As another example, a distributed communications tactic may indicate the usage of CORBA and distinctly identify the level of granularity for the IDL interfaces (I'll discuss this in more detail later).

Software Patterns

A pattern is a common solution to a problem within a given context or set of constraints. Using a pattern can reduce not only the time and effort required to produce a design but also the complexity of your software model. If you haven't already been using them knowingly, you've probably been using them anyway, without being aware that there were names for them.

There are quite a few books and articles on this subject. One of the most referenced and useful books is *Design Patterns* by Erich Gamma et al. I further recommend *Pattern-Oriented Software Architecture* by Frank Buschmann et al., *Analysis Patterns* by Martin Fowler, and articles or books written by Douglas Schmidt.

Some of the patterns I use quite often across several industries are the following:

- **Observer:** In this pattern, an object, called an observer, registers and interest in another object, called an observable. When the observable changes, the observer is notified.

- **Façade:** In this pattern, a form of a wrapper serves as an interface to a logically grouped set of objects. Invocations on the façade's interface are passed on to the appropriate object that it wraps.

- **Protocol:** This pattern provides a consistent-looking interface for classes with similar behaviors.

- **Interpreter:** This pattern interprets sentences of a language, where a class is used to represent each grammar rule.

- **Memento (specification-engine):** This pattern captures the internal state of an object so that the object can be restored at a later time.

- **Strategy:** This pattern defines a set of algorithms that can be used interchangeably. One algorithm is assigned per class.

- **Broker:** This pattern acts as an intermediary between two or more objects, such that the objects interact by remote service invocations and are independent of each other.

- **Agent:** This includes a whole range of patterns from proxies to intelligent visitors. For example, an agent can be a representation of another object or an entity that navigates and reasons across a set of objects.

Many patterns have in common what can be called the metapattern of delegation. Delegation is a relationship between two or more objects, where a delegator object relinquishes parts or all of its behavior and/or structure to a delegate object or set of delegates. The delegator object is the object that clients use. The real power of delegation is that the delegate can be swapped out at runtime, effectively changing the structure and behavior of the delegator. Remembering this one metapattern will help you understand and identify patterns quickly.

Activities and Steps in the Design Process

There's no brief and concise way to capture all the aspects and complexities involved in the design process. And design approaches can vary, depending on your requirements and your computing environment. Nevertheless, OO design should involve at least these three activities:

1. **Architecture development:** This involves refining the analysis classes and clustering them into components, with reuse in mind. The refinement process may include changing, rearranging, removing, and adding classes to get to a buildable design. Details that shouldn't be overlooked are navigability, cardinality, attributes and their types, function signatures and function return types, container classes, and replacing analysis concepts or patterns with design patterns.

2. **Tactical design:** This involves integrating and modifying your objects to comply with your tactical policies.

3. **Release planning:** This involves developing a release plan, which prescribes scheduled incremental releases and establishes priorities, setting the rhythm of your development cycle.

OO design can proceed through these steps:

1. Refine the classes arrived at during the analysis phase.

2. Modify the design model to accommodate your tactical policies.

3. Cluster classes whose relationship forms some larger architectural pattern or that perform a specific and reuseable function. Allocate the clusters into layers. Clusters that build upon one another belong in separate layers; clusters that interact as peers should be in the same layer.

4. Build a little and test a little. Explore key risk areas and critical architectural components through prototypes and proofs of concepts.

5. Construct, test, and evaluate your product based on your release plan.

6. Iterate as required.

Using Design Artifacts

The fruits of your design effort should be your design artifacts:

- Class diagram
- Sequence diagram
- State diagram
- Release plan
- Test plan
- Design guide

I recommend that coding or at least prototyping begin when you have some, but not necessarily all, of the design artifacts in hand. It's unwise to wait for completion — actually, I'm not really sure what that is. Over the life cycle of your product, you'll need to do design on a continuing basis. It's important to regularly update the design and verify key design areas with executable components.

Designing with CORBA

CORBA is a specification that addresses the distribution of an object-oriented system across a network of computers. Designing with CORBA involves all the considerations I've just outlined, and then some. As I explained in "CORBA in the Enterprise: Introduction" (on the CD-ROM), your CORBA design is expressed primarily by classes, and the CORBA objects that run in your computer are produced from those classes. Furthermore, a CORBA-based object is produced from a class that's specified in the Interface Definition Language (IDL). (For a review of IDL, see Chapter 5.)

As you develop a design based on CORBA, a good place to start is with a consideration of the scale of your problem. You can then go on to consider interface granularity, partitioning, interface integration, and integrating business objects and CORBA objects. I'll describe each of these considerations in turn.

Understanding the Scale of Your Problem

Because you're developing an object-oriented design, you may assume that most of the design issues you encounter will be focused at the object level. But although your design is implemented at the object level, it may also solve a problem at another level of scale. For instance, at the object level of a problem, you might be concerned with how the objects in your design are initialized and/or the exact signature for the interface (methods). But at the system level, you might create a design for applications to share systemwide information.

I've found it useful to organize a software problem by applying a separation of concerns based on scale. This organization, suggested in *CORBA Design Patterns* by Thomas Mowbray and Raphael Malveau, is referred to as the scalability model. It describes seven levels, from the object level to the global level. The goal of the scalability model is to assist software engineers by focusing their discussions and design efforts at the appropriate level of scale. At each level, a problem can be isolated, priorities can be identified, and the appropriate pattern and solution can be applied. Table 41-1 provides a summary description of each of the levels of the model.

TABLE 41-1: THE SCALABILITY MODEL

ARCHITECTURAL LEVEL	SUMMARY DESCRIPTION OF CONCERN
Global	Issues that are applicable across multiple organizations that cooperate and interoperate through well-established standards. An example of a global system is the Internet.
Enterprise	Coordination within a single organization. The organization may be distributed geographically and interoperate using heterogeneous systems; however, it has control of its resources and policies.
System	Integration of multiple applications through interoperable technologies. Distribution strategies such as client-server, application-to-application cooperation, multitiered architectures, and layering are considered system-level issues.

ARCHITECTURAL LEVEL	SUMMARY DESCRIPTION OF CONCERN
Application (subsystem)	Providing a set of functionalities as specified in the business requirements. Applications principally capture business clusters of objects and make use of the services provided in frameworks. Patterns at this level are concerned only with solving a particular business problem.
Macroarchitecture (framework)	Providing a solution to a collection of related and generalized requirements, sometimes referred to as a domain. In practice, a framework consists of integrated components (microarchitecture) that are designed to be configurable or completed by applications.
Microarchitecture	Providing a set of objects to solve a limited but recurring problem. At this level, components are designed and built for reuse by providing an encapsulation via a stable interface to the component's service.
Object	Determining an object's attributes, behavior, and relationship with other objects, as well as its life cycle and possibilities for reuse. The object is the unit of abstraction for object-oriented modeling.

Applying a separation of concerns by scale is not to be confused with using the Object Management Architecture (OMA) to separate business from infrastructure concerns. The OMA differs from the scalability model in that the OMA is organized into units of functional layers, where each layer is dependent on some lower layer for services. Each level above the object level in the scalability model encompasses the levels below it (for example, an application-level solution may contain several frameworks and other components from the microarchitecture).

Depending on how you utilize CORBA, you can have design concerns at nearly all the levels — from the object level up to and including the enterprise level. Table 41-2 lists by level some problems concerning CORBA that you might find yourself addressing during your design activities. In general, these problems are driven by the desire to partition and distribute your software and to improve performance. This table should serve as a guide to identifying patterns and/or strategies that can be appropriately applied to provide solutions, as has been done in *CORBA Design Patterns*.

TABLE 41-2: SOME CORBA DESIGN PROBLEMS AT VARIOUS LEVELS OF SCALE

SCALABILITY MODEL LEVEL	CORBA DESIGN PROBLEM
Enterprise	Ensuring uniform access to services
	Managing enterprise resources
System	Discovering and reconfiguring services dynamically (at runtime)
	Integrating legacy system modules
	Improving performance of access to shared resources
	Sharing systemwide information among applications
	Interfacing with other distributed computing technologies
	Controlling the visibility of the server interface
	Reducing complex interfaces for integrating applications
Application	Improving concurrency and loading across the network
	Obtaining reference data or instances in the environment
	Interacting with legacy systems
	Managing concurrent access to services
	Reducing unnecessary invocations on remote interfaces
	Identifying the proper level of interface granularity
Macroarchitecture	Identifying the interfaces to CORBA services that a client uses
	Providing implementations for client-side interfaces (to complete a framework)
Microarchitecture	Identifying fine-grained modules (captured as patterns) that are distributed (for example, object factories)

SCALABILITY MODEL LEVEL	CORBA DESIGN PROBLEM
Object	Integrating IDL interfaces into the implementation code
	Integrating CORBA objects and business objects

Deciding on Interface Granularity and Partitioning Your Solution

Suppose you've completed an OO application design that's composed of a collection of classes, microarchitecture components, and frameworks. Which one of these parts of your application should be captured in IDL? This dilemma is the essence of interface granularity. IDL interfaces can be either fine-grained or coarse-grained. In general, I consider IDL interfaces at the framework level and above to be coarse-grained and at the micoarchitecture and object levels to be fine-grained, although in practice, where you draw the line really depends on your project and should be noted in your design guide.

For obvious performance and partitioning reasons, I don't recommend that each class in your application be in IDL, unless you have unique requirements for doing so. At the microarchitecture level, there are many instances where it makes good design sense to express a component in IDL. What this means is that the component interface is the way to utilize the services provided by the object that the component contains. The interfaces of the contained objects themselves aren't in IDL, but this is invisible to the client. Such an arrangement is categorically described as the façade pattern (see *Design Patterns* by Erich Gamma et al.).

A similar argument can be made for the framework and application levels. However, note that a framework can contain one or more IDL-ized components, and an application can contain multiple IDL-ized frameworks and components.

Another part of CORBA design that must be discussed is how you partition your software solution to get the best use out of the CORBA technology, which should enable considerable code reusability. One simple approach is as follows:

1. Build the one or two logical partitions (subsystems) that you identified during your OO design activities. Consider that your partitioning may not be correct or optimized for performance.

2. Study the patterns of communication among the objects in the subsystem(s).

3. Group together (capture in a coarse-grained interface) the objects or components (fine-grained interfaces) with a high volume of interaction so that their interactions can occur locally (that is, local to the same machine or process). This will possibly redefine your initial partitioning and clustering. Implicitly, interactions among coarse-grained interfaces should be small.

4. Ensure that your new partitioning doesn't violate your architecture.

5. Hide the fine-grained interfaces behind the coarse-grained interfaces. That is, make the coarse-grained interfaces into IDL interfaces and implement the fine-grained interfaces as regular objects of the chosen language. Your coarse-grained interfaces are your level of granularity to be used as CORBA application objects.

Integrating IDL Interfaces into Your Code

Many previous CORBA articles and books focus on the object level of design, describing how objects are created, initialized, distributed (for example, for load balancing), and destroyed, and how they interact. I won't repeat any of that here but will instead concentrate on another important design aspect — integrating IDL interfaces into your implementation code.

For most OO programming languages, the language binding for an IDL interface is a class. There are two approaches to implementing this class:

- Inherit from a base class that offers the interface for the Basic Object Adaptor (BOA) services. This is known as the inheritance, BOA, or standard implementation approach.

- Implement the class as an IDL-based delegator that receives remote calls but forwards the calls to a delegate, which is a regular application object. This is called the TIE approach, so named because the IDL-based delegator and the delegate are essentially tied together.

From a developer's perspective, the inheritance approach requires one class, and the TIE approach requires at a minimum two classes (delegator and delegate). Each approach has its strengths and weaknesses, although most would argue that neither approach has any major advantage over the other. Which one do you choose? That depends on several factors, including infrastructure independence, memory management, and multiple interface views.

- **Infrastructure independence:** On some projects, you'll find that the business objects—the ones that make up the application—are guarded as pure business objects. That is, the companies declare that these objects are not to be tainted or modified by any underlying infrastructure service, including persistence, rules engines, and distributed computing services. This makes a tremendous amount of sense. Infrastructure independence contributes to the long-term survivability of your business applications. The TIE approach naturally gives you that independence, since the IDL-based object is simply a pass-through to the delegate business object. Furthermore, the TIE approach frees the business object from having to potentially inherit from multiple classes—a problem for Java. On the other hand, you can design an interface that implements the BOA approach, but additional programming is required.

- **Memory management:** Because the TIE approach requires two classes, it can lead to an inadvertent dangling pointer (for C++), depending on the ORB vendor and the programming language. By default, if the TIE object is deleted, it will delete its delegate; however, the delegate object isn't necessarily responsible for deleting the TIE object if the delegate is deleted. The solution is straightforward: The delegate needs to have a reference to the TIE object so that it can delete it if necessary.

- **Multiple interface views:** A common problem faced by designers is that a business application must accommodate several different types of clients, each with its own service and hence interface needs. A business application might need to support a GUI client and also be able to support back-end processing for automated billing, rule evaluation, or agent searches. In most OO programming languages, the interface that can be used by one client can also be used by any other because that's the way the language works. In the distributed environment, a TIE object can expose or hide any interface for its delegate, and multiple TIE objects can refer to the same delegate. The net effect is that different clients (communicating via CORBA) can invoke only the interfaces available to them for the same delegate object. The inheritance approach can be employed to provide a similar configuration, but additional programming and control are required.

Integrating Business Objects with CORBA Objects

In "CORBA in the Enterprise: Introduction" (on the CD-ROM), I discussed how to use the OMA to separate business objects from those concerned with the infrastructure. The business usage of infrastructure services is illustrated in a UML sequence diagram. Since the interface to the services is specified and standardized in IDL, I recommended they be shown as invocations in their exact name on the analysis sequence diagram. To the designer, this immediately indicates a CORBA boundary that represents an eventual language binding to a CORBA object.

If we apply some understanding of CORBA, it appears these invocations imply that the business object that invokes the CORBA object must itself be a CORBA client (object). Recall that the CORBA terminology refers to objects involved in an invocation as clients and object implementations. Herein rests an important question for CORBA design: How do you integrate business objects with CORBA objects?

Keep in mind that CORBA objects can be located on any system in your environment. Thus, integration involves an understanding of partitioning your software problem and an appreciation of distributed computing performance. It also involves these steps:

1. Learn your requirements (for example, are business objects pure?)

2. Understand the scale of your problem.

3. Select the appropriate granularity by forming logical partitions of the problem and capture your interfaces in IDL.

   Choose either the BOA or the TIE method to integrate your IDL-ized objects.

Next: A Business Scenario

In this chapter, I've provided a general discussion of how to do OO design, followed by a discussion of considerations involved in designing with CORBA. Three primary activities are involved in design: architecture development, tactical design, and release planning. Within these activities, CORBA design is concerned with identifying the scale of the distributed computing problem and imposing some tactical policies for IDL and business object integration. Based on the seven levels of the scalability model, a set of patterns, expressed through the use of CORBA, can readily be applied.

To help clarify the OO design techniques I've presented here, in the next chapter, I'll briefly describe a possible business scenario based on generating an invoice for a customer. I'll also describe other design considerations, elaborate on the topic of utilizing the CORBA Query and Event services, and discuss some approaches to wrapping legacy interfaces.

42

CORBA in the Enterprise, Part 2: Applying Object-Oriented and Component Design

Bob Schlicher — *software architect, AlterNet Communications*

I n this chapter, I'll illustrate how to apply the object-oriented design principles discussed in Chapter 41. I'll do this by further extending the billing system example introduced in "CORBA in the Enterprise: Introduction" (on the CD-ROM). This illustration will incorporate the use of certain CORBA services, so I'll preface the illustration with a description of those services.

CROSS-REFERENCE

Before reading this chapter, it's highly recommended that you read "CORBA in the Enterprise: Introduction," which can be found on the CD-ROM in the files that accompany Chapter 41, as well as in Chapter 41. To find "CORBA in the Enterprise: Introduction," follow the path Sample Code and Supporting Documentation ⇨ Part IV ⇨ Chapter 41.

A Look at Some CORBA Services

At present, there are 15 CORBA services, along with several drafts that will eventually be adopted by the Object Management Group (OMG). Over the past several years, object relation broker (ORB) vendors have increased their product offerings to include most of these services. As shown in Table 42-1, CORBA services are organized into four categories: infrastructure services, information management, task management, and system management. The services in boldface are the ones I'll discuss in more detail here.

TABLE 42-1: THE CORBA OBJECT REQUEST BROKER OBJECT SERVICES (ORBOS)

SERVICE CATEGORY	DESCRIPTION	CORBA SERVICES
Infrastructure services	Services related to the ORB mechanisms	Security, **Time**
Information management	Services to retrieve and manipulate data	Collection, Externalization, Persistent Object, Property, **Query**, Relationship
Task management	Services to manage distributed object events and transactions	Concurrency, **Event**, Transactions
System management	Services to manage metadata, licensing, andobject life cycle	Licensing, Lifecycle, Naming, Trader

Some services depend on others or utilize the features of others, as you'll notice in the discussions that follow (specifically, Query uses Collection, and Time uses Event). Development professionals have been known to spend hours at a time arguing about which services are most important. I argue that it depends on your requirements and your target environment. Nevertheless, I've chosen three useful services to describe here: the Query, Event, and Time services. The billing system example makes use of these services.

The Query Service

The Query service is used to find objects in a collection whose attribute values meet the criteria specified in a query. A query contains the expression (in a string) of the criteria along with an identification of the query language used for that expression. Although the OMG set as the initial goal for this service that a query would be independent of any specific query language, the reality is that a query must support at least either SQL-92 or the Object Query Language (OQL-93).

According to the CORBA specification, a query, which is performed via the QueryEvaluator interface through the `evaluate()` operator, returns a type any (any CORBA object). In implementations, the result is typically a collection, so you initially query a collection and get a collection back that you can continue to query, and so on.

To get to a specific object, you interact with the returned collection via a collection interface that provides the minimal specification allowing you to add, insert, retrieve, and delete objects and obtain an iterator for navigating the collection. The collection can be extended to provide a richer interface set. The interfaces for the Query service are specified in the COSQuery module; the class diagram (captured in UML using Rational Rose) is shown in Figure 42-1.

The Event Service

The Event service permits objects to register and unregister interest in events from other objects. This service specifies the familiar observer pattern, sometimes called the publisher-subscriber pattern, which I briefly introduced in Chapter 41. Recall that the observer registers interest in an observable. When the observable changes, the observer is notified through an event and processes the event as needed. In the CORBA Event service specification, a slight variation on this pattern, identified as supplier-consumer, is used. Supplier-consumer implements the observer pattern but includes additional elements so that the supplier(s) and consumer(s) aren't directly dependent on each other. This is useful for integrating objects and services that may reside on separate machines and networks, at the application, system, and enterprise levels.

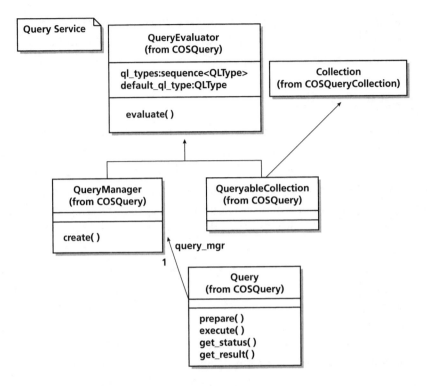

Figure 42-1: The Query service class diagram

In the Event service, the supplier and the consumer are strongly separated through the use of what's called an event channel, which implements the proxy pattern. An event channel is a CORBA object to which a supplier and zero or more consumers attach. The supplier communicates its changes or notifications to the channel. The channel relays the notice as an event to the attached consumers. Thus, the channel serves as a proxy, or placeholder, for the supplier and controls access to it. In this scheme, the objects involved don't need to know about each other.

Two models are used in the Event service: push and pull. In the push model, the supplier initiates the transfer of the event. In the pull model, the consumer initiates a request for an event from a supplier. The push model is the preferred choice to meet most requirements in a supplier-consumer situation. The pull model may require a polling mechanism to obtain the event, and in a distributed computing environment this can be expensive — it can increase the network traffic, leading to unnecessary response-time delays.

In general, the channel doesn't have any understanding of the contents of the data it's transporting. It treats all data as a type *any* (any CORBA object). However, the Event service specification does identify typed events, some of the contents of which are known and available for the channel to process. This permits a form of event filtering and facilitates the consumer's subscribing to a specific typed event.

A partial view of the class diagram for the Event service is shown in Figure 42-2.

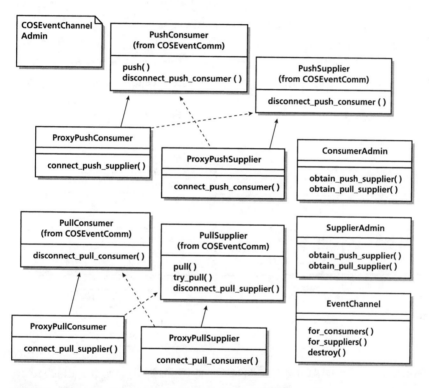

Figure 42-2: Partial view of the Event service class diagram

The Time Service

The Time service provides time information based on the standard Universal Time Coordinated (UTC) representation. The important thing to remember about this service is that it always uses Greenwich mean time. The Time service provides interfaces for these four important functions:

- Supplying the current time with an estimate of the error

- Determining the order of event occurrences

■ Generating time-based events for timers and alarms

■ Computing the interval between events

To generate time-based events for timers and alarms, the Time service provides the `TimerEventHandler` and `TimerEventService` interfaces. The `TimerEvent Service` interface makes it possible to create `TimerEventHandler` objects that are registered with an event channel from the Event service. The `TimerEvent Handler` object contains the time when an event is to be triggered, such as an alarm. The timer can be reset, canceled, or set to be periodic or relative.

A partial view of the class diagram for the Time service is shown in Figure 42-3. Note that the Universal Time Object (UTO) interface represents a fixed point in time.

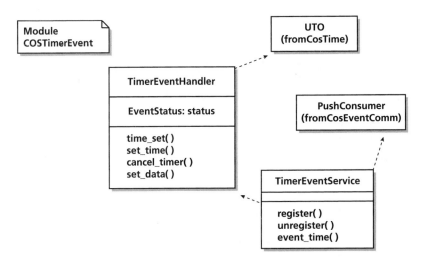

Figure 42-3: Partial view of the Time service class diagram

Applying Object-Oriented Design to a Billing System

Now let's apply the design considerations discussed in Chapter 41 to an aspect of the billing system introduced in "CORBA in the Enterprise: Introduction" (on the CD-ROM). Specifically, let's focus on the bill generation scenario, described as follows: A timer periodically alerts the bill generator to create invoices for those customers who are at the end of their billing cycle. The amount that a customer owes is calculated based on usage of the service (or product) and the fee for that service. The invoice provides an itemized list of usages by service, determines subtotals, and calculates summary information showing all the totals.

Establishing the Scale of the Problem and the Interface Granularity

In the analysis of the bill-generation scenario in "CORBA in the Enterprise: Introduction," I established that the `BillGenerator` object makes use of the CORBA Query service. Let's apply the scalability model from Chapter 41: The bill generator best matches the criteria for the application level of scale because it makes use of CORBA services, it represents an interface to a cluster of related objects, and most important, it's concerned with solving a particular business problem.

Based on this decision on scale, we know that the bill generator is a CORBA application object with a coarse interface granularity. This means that it acts similar to the façade pattern for a related set of non-IDL objects (usually called just Java or C++ objects). Recall that the façade pattern involves an object that serves as a wrapper to a logical set of objects. Invocations on the façade's interface are passed on to the appropriate object(s) that it wraps.

Reviewing the Partitioning of the System

Before proceeding with reviewing the problem analysis and discussing the system design, a review of the system will further help us understand this problem. In "CORBA in the Enterprise: Introduction," I discussed how to use the OMA (Object Management Architecture) to separate business objects from those concerned with the infrastructure. Figure 42-4 is an illustration of the application objects, CORBA clients, and CORBA services in the familiar OMA configuration.

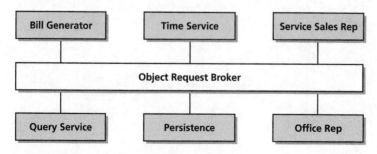

Figure 42-4: OMA view of the billing system

The clients communicate through the ORB service layer with any of the billing system application objects. In this architecture, which is typical for CORBA environments, clients can invoke all the services and application objects. However, in this design, clients are expected to interact with the application objects that use the services as required. The `BillGenerator_I` application object (the `_I` notation is explained in the next section) represents the coarse-grained interface that we identified earlier when considering scale.

Reviewing the Analysis Sequence Diagram

The analysis sequence diagram for the bill generation scenario, shown in Figure 42-5, includes two obvious candidate CORBA services: the Time and Query services. The Time service notifies the bill generator to create bills or invoices for those customers at the end of the billing cycle. To identify these customers, the bill generator prepares query or search criteria and invokes the search on the Query service. The Query service returns with a collection of customers from the customer data store. The bill generator obtains individual customers from the collection and creates an invoice for each by invoking the invoice factory. The behaviors involved in the invoice factory include obtaining the customer's service usages, assessing the fees, and creating the bill.

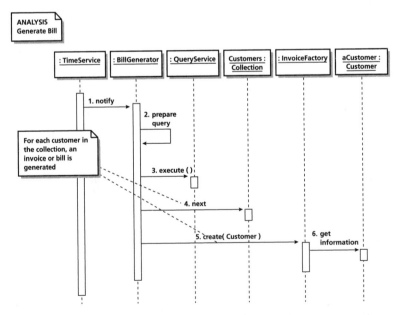

Figure 42-5: Analysis sequence diagram for the bill generation scenario

Reviewing the Design Sequence Diagram

As you'd expect, the design sequence diagram, shown in Figure 42-6, provides significantly more details than the analysis sequence diagram. It's not my goal here to show you all the details but rather to convey to you some of the differences between analysis and design. Nevertheless, recall from Chapter 41 that one of the principal aims of design is to have a close correspondence to the actual software code so that the design illustrates some language-specific representations. In Figure 42-6, the CORBA services are labeled `TimerEventHandler` and `Query Manager`. The `TimerEventHandler` object (from the Time service) notifies the bill generator by invoking the `push()` method. Note that this indicates that at some time prior to this event, the bill generator registered or subscribed to the `TimerEventHandler` using the event channel mechanism described earlier.

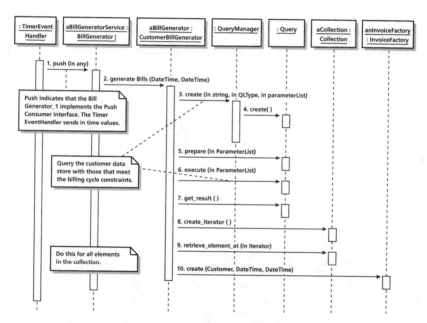

Figure 42-6: Design sequence diagram for the bill generation scenario

Similar to the analysis sequence diagram, Figure 42-6 represents the bill generator as a CORBA application object, but with some differences. The bill generator is actually shown as two objects: one that represents the coarse-grained interface that can be invoked by other CORBA objects (labeled `BillGenerator_I`) and the other, the delegate, that represents an implementation for the interface, which is a Java or C++ object (called `CustomerBillGenerator`). I've used `_I` to indicate the IDL-based object. This object could be either a TIE object or a BOA object (see Chapter 41); however, the design implies that I'm using the TIE method.

In response to the event received via the push, the `BillGenerator_I` object invokes the `generateBills()` function on the `BillGenerator` object. The `BillGenerator` object uses the CORBA Query service objects (`QueryManager` and `Query`) to obtain a collection of Customer objects that need to be invoiced for their service consumption for the given billing period. Using this collection, the `BillGenerator` object obtains an iterator and sequentially navigates through the collection.

For each customer, the `BillGenerator` object creates an invoice through the invoice factory. The sequence diagram for the behaviors in the invoice factory is shown in Figure 42-7. This factory obtains the customer's service usage (`CustomerUsage`, incorporating both usage and credits) for each service and the rates for that service (via `ServicePricePlan`) and determines the amount due (via `PricingEngine`), which is captured in a `ServiceUsageSummary`. `ServiceUsageSummary` is part of the invoice.

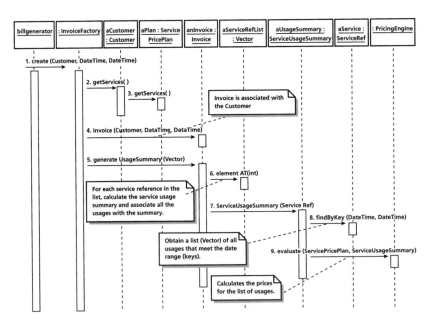

Figure 42-7: Design sequence diagram for the invoice factory

The class diagram for this specific bill generation example is shown in Figure 42-8. One interesting set of relationships in the class diagram is that among `ServiceRef`, `CustomerUsage`, and `ServiceUsageSummary`. `ServiceRef` contains a collection of all the `CustomerUsage` instances that were recorded for a specific customer. Using the qualified association, `ServiceRef` provides a method for obtaining a subset of the collection using `BillStartDate` and `Bill EndDate` for keys. `ServiceUsageSummary` uses this method to obtain the customer usage for a given bill period in preparation for producing the invoice.

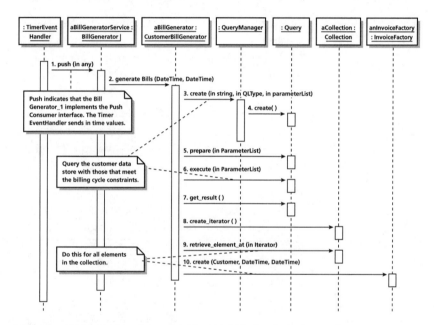

Figure 42-8: Design class model for the bill generation scenario

Table 42-2 lists the analysis objects in Column 1 and the corresponding design objects in Column 2 ("Design classes and changes"). Column 3 ("Design explanation/rationale") is an explanation of the decisions that were made to arrive at the design. Notice that several classes have been added to the design that weren't in the analysis. This is usually the norm, since the analysis may not consider support classes or the details of a particular concept.

TABLE 42-2: A SUMMARY OF THE CHANGES MADE TO THE ANALYSIS IN THE DESIGN

ANALYSIS CLASSES	DESIGN CLASSES AND CHANGES	DESIGN EXPLANATION/ RATIONALE
Customer	Customer, made a subclass of Party	Party is an abstract class used to illustrate that the system can handle more than just customers such as an organization can.
CustomerUsage	CustomerUsage, moved away from Customer to Service Ref, used by Service Usage Summary	The term CustomerUsage previously indicated only usage of the service and not other actions such as credit. The definition has been broadened. CustomerUsage is closely tied to the customer's service—the design is an interpretation of it as a link class that would have been in the analysis.
Communication Service	Communication Service, also a stereo type of reference objects; ServiceRef introduced to refer to the reference objects	Reference objects are created to indicate a specific typeof an object. A service provider will have a finite set of services, with each one in the set representing a specific type of service. This type is only instantiated once and then stored. References to these objects are achieved through ServiceRef.
Invoice	InvoiceFactory and ServiceUsage Summary added for creating invoices	In addition to creating invoices, the factory creates service usage summaries, which are aggregated. Factories are used to create new objects, initialize them, and track their runtime life cycle. ServiceUsage Summary is used to present a summary of all the events that occurred for the customer for a given service.

ANALYSIS CLASSES	DESIGN CLASSES AND CHANGES	DESIGN EXPLANATION/ RATIONALE
Fee	`PricingEngine,` `ServicePricePlan`	Used to calculate large numbers of events and fees for customer usage. Fees are a part of `Service PricePlan`.
Billing Cycle	Implemented via the CORBA `TimerEvent` Handler from the Time service	No change from analysis— details added for design.
Bill Generator	Changed to two classes: `BillGenerator_I` and `BillGenerator`	BillGenerator_I is a coarse-grained interface that serves as an entry into the billing system service. BillGenerator is the delegated member implemented in C++ that processes received invocations.
Customer data store, usage data store	Integration with the data store(s) is done via the Query service	Business and application objects interact with the Query service and are insulated from the details of the specific data store.

Identifying the Patterns in the Design

Are there any patterns in the design? Before answering this question, notice that in Figure 42-6, six out of nine objects are objects from CORBA services — specifically, from the Time and Query services. This simple measure not only indicates the utility of CORBA for the billing system problem domain but also serves to highlight the reusability of such infrastructure components. This reuse was facilitated by the technique that I used in the analysis, separating business from infrastructure concerns.

In the CORBA services, several patterns have already been described: The Event service uses the observer (supplier-consumer) and proxy patterns, and the Query service uses iterators for traversing collections. Among the application objects, delegation is used at the IDL interface (between the `GenerateBill_I` and `Genera teBill` objects) and two design patterns are identified: façade for the IDL interface and a variation of factory for the `InvoiceFactory` object.

Moving from Design to Code: Integrating IDL/CORBA Objects and Business Objects

Design is an iterative process. One of the primary activities you face when designing is that of making tradeoffs. After several passes on this simple example, we'd be ready to produce the code and begin the compiling, testing, and integration. After several iterations of code development, we expect to modify or update the design to continue with the iterative nature of the object-oriented development process. The IDL classes, such as `BillGenerator_I` and not including the available CORBA services from your ORB vendor, are generated or coded in IDL code, which is then compiled in the coding language for your environment. The other classes, the non-IDL classes, are generated or coded directly in your environment's programming language.

Finding CORBA Programming Content

This and the previous chapter have been intended to provide some general design considerations to help you when it comes to designing CORBA — or any other object-oriented — applications. The considerations when it comes to writing code are so vast that we can't even begin to describe them here. If you want to get going with CORBA application coding, we recommend you visit the extensive CORBA resources available through your bookstore or library. If you visit *View Source* magazine on the web at `http://developer.netscape.com/ viewsource` and read the CORBA articles, you can find a wealth of pointers to web-based CORBA programming content.

43

Object Pooling in NAS: An Architecture for Caching Objects

Mike Abney — *senior engineer, NetExplorer, Inc.*

Netscape Application Server (NAS) provides a form of caching that works well for results that are static for a given set of parameters. Problems arise, however, if the data those results are based on changes over time, thus invalidating any cached results. The only other standard alternative is to load data from the database (or some other form of persistent storage) for each request, which seriously degrades system performance. This chapter outlines a philosophy for building object-oriented systems and then applies that philosophy toward a solution that enables even rapidly changing data to be cached.

The Problem

NAS has some very good functionality for caching the results of requests to its AppLogics. Typically, for each request to NAS, the server first checks to see whether the results are already cached. If not, the AppLogics load data from persistent storage, put it into a so-called GXML template, and give the results back to the application server, which caches them (if caching is turned on) and then streams them to the user. But the caching is basically "all or nothing": if the results may change over time (because of changes in the data they're based on), there's no way to cache the subset of them that won't change. This means that if the data is mutable, caching is not possible and all the data will have to be loaded for each request. Thus, when making database calls is slow (and when is it not, relative to object-to-object calls), any mutable data significantly degrades the performance of an application.

NOTE

The techniques here were designed to work with Netscape Application Server 2.x; NAS 4 and its support for Enterprise Java Beans obviates the need for the solution proposed in this chapter.

There are several ways to partially alleviate this problem. For instance, the called AppLogic could build its results based on the results of several other AppLogic calls (using the `newRequest()` method). Some of the AppLogics would be able to cache their results, thus reducing the number of database requests. This solution works but can be slow because of the expense of inter-AppLogic communication and is simply not appropriate (or possible) in a large number of cases. There's a need for a more thorough solution. The first part of this chapter discusses a basic design philosophy. The second part builds on the first to describe a solution; an architecture called object pooling. This architecture enables more of the data (in object form) to be cached in memory between requests, rather than read from persistent storage each time. This chapter does not attempt to provide a complete, "prepackaged" solution but instead provides direction and suggestions that should enable you to create your own solutions more quickly.

This chapter assumes a working knowledge of NAS application development, some knowledge of design patterns, and an awareness of the workings of hashtables; however, some benefit may be derived from reading the chapter without those prerequisites. NAS knowledge is best gained through experience, but a quick read of the documentation that comes with Netscape Application Builder should provide enough background for this chapter; you can find it online at `http://developer.netscape.com/tech/appserver/index.html?content=/docs/manuals/appserv/`. For information on design patterns, use the Portland Pattern Repository at `http://www.c2.com/ppr/index.html` as a starting point.

CROSS-REFERENCE

We strongly recommend you read Chapter 6, "Netscape Enterprise Server and Netscape Application Server: What's the Difference," before reading this and the next two chapters. It provides a technical introduction to Netscape Application Server (NAS). In addition, please be sure to read the first two chapters in this section, Chapters 34 and 35.

First, Some Philosophy

Before we look at the design of the object pool, some groundwork must be laid in the form of design philosophy. Many developers (and possibly even more managers) expect that just because Java is an object-oriented language, reuse and proper design will be almost automatic. This is very much not the case. Object-oriented programming (OOP) and object-oriented design (OOD) are methodologies that can make proper design easier, but they do not, by themselves, cause all designs to "automagically" become good design. So, how do you design for reuse?

Separation of Concerns

Reuse is the cornerstone of the design philosophy used at Net Explorer, Inc. This philosophy categorizes objects into three layers based on their roles: *human interface* (HI), *problem domain* (PD), and *data management* (DM). See Figure 43-1.

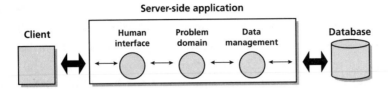

Figure 43-1: Three object role layers

HI objects are responsible for handling communication with the user. They convert user requests into messages to the problem domain. They also convert the data in, and messages from, the problem domain into a form that makes sense to users. In NAS HTML-client applications, this generally involves accepting input parameters, making appropriate PD method calls, putting the PD responses into `TemplateDataBasic` objects, and using the `AppLogic.evalOutput()` method to generate the HTTP response. The HI layer isolates the problem domain from changes in the user interface. If the application is converted to an OCL client, it is the classes in the HI layer that need to change, while the PD layer remains untouched (as does the DM layer).

The problem domain layer has many aliases: business rules and business logic, to name two. PD objects perform calculations, contain a "live" version of some data, and contain rules that pertain to that data. Generally, if an application has anything going on that is algorithmically interesting, it will be in the problem domain. PD objects are the ones that most laypersons will mention if you ask them about a system without talking about the user interface.

The data management layer handles the saving and loading of PD objects to and from persistent storage. This layer would need to change if the database changed. For instance, you would need different DM objects to create objects from an Oracle database from those you would need from a Sybase database. A change of database would not, however, affect the PD objects. (Only if the data structure were changed and new attributes were needed would changes to the PD objects be necessary.) The DM layer would also know about stored procedures, as well as things like LDAP and communication through CORBA.

Here's an example that may help clarify the distinctions: A person who is asked to list the important parts of a car might mention the engine, the drive train, the tires, and the steering wheel. These would be PD objects for a system that modeled a car. That same person would not be likely to immediately mention the fact that you turn the wheel to steer a car (steering is part of the HI layer) or that an internal combustion engine powers a car (where the power comes from is a DM issue).

How This Works in NAS

Now that we've laid down the basic foundation, how do we use it in NAS? The way NAS is designed, the client (via a Web server) talks to the NAS AppLogic, which then reads query files that tell it how to save and read information to and from a database. The AppLogic then takes the data, reads a GXML template, and prepares an HTTP response to send back to the user (via the Web server again) by putting the data into the template. This structure is shown in Figure 43-2.

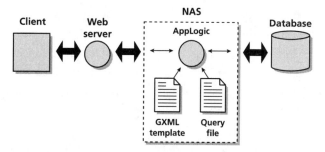

Figure 43-2: The typical NAS architecture

This does not quite fit with the separation of concerns mentioned earlier. To some extent, it could be said that the template, AppLogic, and query files are the HI, PD, and DM layers, respectively. This breaks down in several cases. For instance, if a non-HTML client is required, the template does not perform the HI duty of protecting the PD from changes in interface. A second, even worse, example is trying to use the same business rules (PD) in non-NAS applications: It's not possible at all. This second example implies that the AppLogics should not be in the PD layer but in either HI or some combination of HI and DM. A diagram of one potential breakdown is shown in Figure 43-3.

This breakdown fits with our design philosophy, but it has a few problems. First, how do the DM objects get their database connections? Simply making sure they have a reference to an AppLogic solves this problem, since they can then use the built-in database connection functionality in NAS (as well as use query files if that's desired).

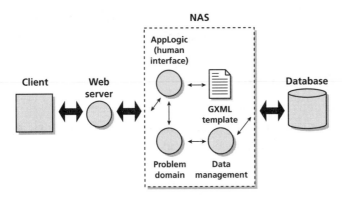

Figure 43-3: Separation of concerns in NAS

A second problem is how to keep the PD objects alive between requests. If a major change isn't made to the design, each request to each AppLogic will cause the PD objects that are needed to be loaded from the database. This is similar to the original problem mentioned in this chapter — that is, that the data would be reloaded each time and not cached. In performance terms, this is probably worse than the original design! This is where object pooling comes to the rescue.

Now, on with the Show

We now have a foundation to build on, but, as we just saw, building an application based on just this foundation is not likely to be very successful. Here's a brief review of the problems:

- Results often cannot be cached because parts of the data that make up the problem domain might change.

- All needed PD objects get reloaded for each request.

- Each request will get a different copy of the PD objects and therefore could become out of sync with the other requests.

The remainder of this chapter will propose a fairly complete solution for the first two problems. The third problem will be only partially solved (for a single server); a full solution (for multiple servers) is beyond the scope of this chapter. The Improvements section at the end of the chapter provides a few possible directions to take in solving the remaining problems with this architecture, including the synchronization of data on multiple servers.

Making a Cache

Barring creating a separate server (or using NAS extensions, which might be a valid solution), the easiest way to keep something in memory — thus solving the first two problems on the above list — is through the use of the static keyword. It's also desirable to make sure that only one instance of the cache exists (partially solving the third problem). Therefore, the class for the cache will implement the singleton pattern. (As described in the book *Design Patterns: Elements of Reusable Object-Oriented Software*, by Erich Gamma et al., singleton pattern ensures that only one instance of a particular class exists and that all parts of the system have access to that one instance.) An example implementation of the singleton pattern is shown here:

```
{
    private static Singleton instance = null;
    private Singleton() {}
    public static Singleton getInstance() {
        if (instance == null)
            instance = new Singleton();
        return instance;
    }
}
```

Appropriate additions for thread safety must be made, of course, but the above code demonstrates the basics of creating an object that will stay in memory as long as its corresponding class is not "cleaned" by the ClassLoader.

To avoid having too many static objects in memory, the singleton object is made to store all the other cached objects in a "pool." It's therefore called the PoolManager. The PoolManager could store all the objects in a single hashtable; however, some groups of similar objects might be treated differently from others. For example, it might be desirable to update objects whose data comes from an LDAP database less frequently than those whose data originates in an Oracle database. Therefore, the PoolManager holds a table of PoolHashtable instances that store these different groups of objects (called categories). Each PoolHashtable instance then has its own set of performance-related attributes.

Adjusting Performance

Performance adjustment requires exposing the previously mentioned performance-related attributes. We can identify these attributes by asking the following question: What are the operations needed for the `PoolManager` and its `PoolHashtable` instances? Here's a list of required capabilities:

- Adding and removing objects

- Adding and removing categories of objects

- Automatically removing unused objects to save memory

- Dynamically adjusting the characteristics of their internal storage mechanism

Addition or removal of objects or categories does not require adding attributes to either class. Automatic removal of objects that are unused, however, does. For the object pool, "unused" means that the pool has not been notified of any access to a given object within a specified amount of time (called the lifetime of objects in the pool).

The last item in the capability list, dynamic adjustment, is a little more difficult to grasp at first. Basically, the `PoolManager` must have some way of storing its `PoolHashtable` instances that allows the attributes of the storage mechanism to be adjusted over the lifetime of the pool. In a Java implementation, a `Hashtable`, keyed on the categories' names, is a likely candidate. Similarly, each `PoolHashtable` could store its objects in a `Hashtable` keyed on some unique identifier for the individual objects (generally the primary key or index from the database). However, an instance of the `java.util.Hashtable` class can accept the specification of only two attributes that affect performance — load factor and initial capacity — and those only at the time of instantiation. Consequently, the `AdjustableHashtable` class was created; its interface is shown here:

```
implements Cloneable, Serializable
{
    public AdjustableHashtable(int initialBucketCount,
        float expansionMultiplier, float loadFactor);

    public int size();
    public int getSize();
```

```
    public boolean isEmpty();
    public synchronized Enumeration keys();
    public synchronized Enumeration elements();
    public synchronized boolean contains(Object value);
    public synchronized boolean containsKey(Object key);
    public synchronized Object get(Object key);
    public int    getBucketCount();
    public void   setBucketCount(int bucketCount);
    public float getLoadFactor();
    public void   setLoadFactor(float loadFactor);
    public float getExpansionMultiplier();
    public void   setExpansionMultiplier(float
expansionMultiplier);
    public synchronized Object put(Object key, Object value);
    public synchronized Object remove(Object key);
    public synchronized void clear();

    public synchronized Object clone();
    public synchronized String toString();
}
```

In addition to the regular attributes (the load factor and "bucket count," a more accurate term for capacity), there is new one: the expansion multiplier. This attribute actually already existed to some extent in the regular Hashtable but was not accessible. It controls the amount by which the bucket count increases when the table is rehashed. During the rehashing process, the expansion factor is multiplied by the current bucket count to determine the new bucket count.

The other difference — and the much more important one — between this version and the regular Hashtable is that this version allows all three of these attributes to be adjusted (within valid ranges) at any point in the lifetime of the table. Therefore, the PoolManager and its PoolHashtable instances can expose those attributes as well.

The next example shows the interfaces of the PoolManager and Pool Hashtable classes. Notice from the first three lines of the PoolManager interface that it's a singleton.

```
{
    private static PoolManager instance;
```

```
    private PoolManager();
    public static PoolManager getInstance();

    public boolean containsId(ObjectId id);
    public boolean containsObject(Object poolObject);
    public Object getObject(ObjectId id);
    public int getPoolSize();
    public int getCategorySize(String categoryName);
    public int getCategoryCount();
    public void putObject(ObjectId id, IPoolObject
poolObject);
    public void updateObject(ObjectId id);
    public void removeObject(ObjectId id);
    public void removeCategory(String category);
    public void removeAll();
    public void removeExpiredObjects();
}

public class PoolHashtable
{
    public PoolHashtable(int initialBucketCount, float
loadFactor,
        float expansionMultiplier, long objectLifetime);

    public int getPoolSize();
    public boolean containsId(ObjectId id);
    public boolean containsObject(Object poolObject);
    public Object getObject(ObjectId id);
    public void putObject(ObjectId id, IPoolObject
poolObject);
    public void updateObject(ObjectId id);
    public void removeObject(ObjectId id);
    public void removeExpiredObjects();
    public void removeAll();
}
```

There are two new types in the `PoolManager` interface that have not been described. The first is the `ObjectId` class, which is simply a wrapper for the category name and object identifier. The second is the `IPoolObject` interface, which objects that are to be placed in the pool must implement to ensure that they can return an `ObjectId` when it's required.

Most of the methods are self-explanatory. There are only two that might raise eyebrows. The `updateObject()` method is the one to call when a "pooled" object is accessed. This method first uses the specified `ObjectId` to find the object and then causes the object's lifetime to be reset, thus saving it from expiration for a while longer. This description hints at the meaning of the `removeExpired Objects()` method, which checks all the objects in the pool (or a specific category) to see if they've lived past their lifetime since the pool was notified of any access.

Using the Object Pool

Use of the object pool is relatively straightforward. It simply becomes necessary to have the DM objects check the pool (using the `getInstance()` method to find the `PoolManager` and then the appropriate `contains()` or `getObject()` method) for existing objects before loading from persistent storage. If the object sought is not found in the pool, the DM objects simply load the PD objects from the database as usual and then stores them in the pool for later before returning. Figure 43-4 shows the new architecture.

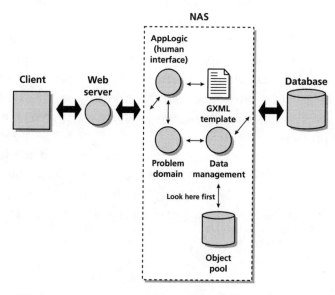

Figure 43-4: Object pooling in the NAS architecture

Problems Solved?

A review of the problems is necessary to determine whether all this work is worth the time. The first two problems were the inability to cache results for data that might change, and the fact that all the needed PD objects had to be reloaded from the database for each request. These problems are definitely lessened. Instead of depending on NAS to cache the complete results of an AppLogic call, individual objects are cached. Even better, those objects can use the DM layer to save any changes made to them. This means that the new data will still not have to be loaded from the database unless it expires from lack of use. Furthermore, since the PD objects are cached in a singleton, they do not disappear unless the `PoolManager` class is unloaded.

Is the unloading of the `PoolManager` class a problem? This question has a somewhat tricky answer. After much experimentation, we determined that non-AppLogic classes in NAS will not be unloaded unless there's a change to an AppLogic that references them, or unless all classes that reference it have been un-loaded. To put it another way, when a change is made to an AppLogic, a special class loader makes note of this and reloads that AppLogic the next time it's called. In doing so, it also unloads all the other classes (regardless of whether they're HI, PD, or DM classes) and then loads them again, as they're needed. Unloading classes causes any static data in those classes to be lost. This includes the singleton `PoolManager` class and thus the pool itself.

Therefore, the basic solution to the problem of unloading the `PoolManager` class is to limit the uploading of new AppLogics to times when a reload of the pool would not be harmful. Regardless, the most harm that will be done is that the `PoolManager` would be instantiated again, and all the pool's objects would be re-loaded as needed. This would cause a temporary slowdown in response time for applications using the pool.

The third of the original problems was that each request could end up with a different copy of the PD objects. Since the `PoolManager` is a singleton, this should no longer be a problem — almost. The problem resurfaces when more than one server is used. A singleton can ensure its singleness only within its Java Virtual Machine (JVM).

Improvements

Here we'll look at some suggestions for solving the remaining problems with this architecture. One solution to the class-unloading problem might be to make the pool a NAS extension. Another might be to make the pool its own server, but that would tend to make passing objects a bottleneck similar to the bottleneck of database communication, which was one of the original problems being solved.

Two Solutions

The problem of data synchronization on multiple servers is a bit more complex. Currently there is no "golden" solution for this, but the following solutions work with varying degrees of success.

Use a Time Stamp

Use a time stamp in the database. Every update made to the database has to pass back this time stamp. If the time stamp in the update request doesn't match the one in the database, exceptions are raised that cause the object to be reloaded (thus getting rid of the old data). Appropriate messages are then sent to the user (or attempts are made to recover more gracefully without the user's intervention). Once a change is successfully made, the time stamp in the database is updated and the DM layer tells the pool that the object has been updated. The pool then calls to any pools on other servers and tells them to remove that object so that the new data will be loaded in the next time it's needed. Problems with this method include finding an efficient way for the pools to communicate with one another and the increase in the total number of messages that get sent between the pools as more and more servers are added.

Create a Server

Create a server (possibly an AppLogic) that manages locking of objects that are being written. This server must have only one instance in use at a time. It could, however, back up its data to a second instance that would take the place of the first if the first became unreachable. Regardless, the lock server would be concerned only with attempts to update objects, not attempts to read them. It essentially becomes a simple transaction manager, in that it allows only one process to update an object at a time and allows locks to be either committed or canceled. Upon a successful (committed) update, the lock server would notify each of its client pools to remove the object to allow the new data to be reloaded when it's needed. This method is somewhat safer and uses a more efficient communication strategy than the previous one, but it does have the potential for slowing down applications and causing a form of deadlock if care is not taken.

But Does It Work?

The only answer to this question that could possibly be satisfactory is a demonstration. The best site that currently uses an implementation of this design is the Oakley O-Store, an application designed and written by Net Explorer. You can find it on the Web at `http://ostore.oakley.com/`.

44

Partial Content Caching in Netscape Application Server: A Framework for Reusable Content and Caching

Vishi Natarajan — *principal designer, e*solutions*
Roni Korenshtein — *consultant, e*solutions*

Caching is a valuable feature of Netscape Application Server (NAS) that enables AppLogics to retrieve data from memory rather than query the data source each time, often significantly improving performance. Mike Abney introduces this concept in Chapter 43. However, NAS provides caching of only a whole HTML page — the entire HTML result set — and not part of a page. If a page contains dynamic content and some of the content doesn't need to be updated as often as other content, you'll want these different parts of the page to be cached separately, but this isn't possible with NAS's standard "all or nothing" caching. For partial caching, you need a different solution.

 NOTE
The information in this chapter pertains to NAS 2.*x*.

One way to do partial caching involves using the `newRequest()` method, but this can be expensive, making the net performance gain insignificant. In this chapter, we'll look at an alternative, more effective solution for partial caching that's built on a framework for reusable content — that is, a component architecture that enables pieces of dynamic content to exist as reusable components, each of which can be cached separately. We'll start by describing the framework we've developed for this, and then (along with reviewing other caching techniques) we'll discuss how you can build on such a framework to cache these reusable components in the NAS state layer, thereby solving the partial caching problem. Finally, we'll look at the results of our performance test on some of the caching techniques described.

Before reading this chapter, be sure you've already read Chapter 43 and followed the cross-references to further web-based information. You'll need an understanding of NAS programming to truly benefit from the techniques described here.

A Framework for Reusable Content

NAS already incorporates a component architecture into its presentation layer, by allowing templates within templates — that is, a request made of NAS can load a template, which in turn can load other templates. This architecture enables high reusability of templates if the page content is static, but it doesn't work so well if some of the content is dynamic. In that case, the templates contain GX markup tags (parsed by the Template Engine) that specify how the dynamic content is to be merged with the page, and values for all the GX variables have to be available in the AppLogic. There lies the problem: a nondeveloper (such as someone in Marketing or the user interface group) who wants to place a new dynamic component in a page can't just add the corresponding GX tag in the template; the AppLogic code would also have to be changed. A framework is needed that will allow the same high reusability of dynamic content as is possible with static content.

A common approach to reusing dynamic content is to create a separate AppLogic to generate that content and then use the `newRequest()` method to call it from within other AppLogics. For example, suppose a bank wants to develop a component that publishes account balance information, and the Marketing group wants this component to be placed in multiple pages. An AppLogic could be written to get the balance information and `newRequest()` calls to that AppLogic added in other AppLogics. However, this method still has the disadvantage that if a nondeveloper wants to add the dynamic component to a new page, a developer will have to modify, recompile, and test the AppLogic code. Furthermore, using `newRequest()` adversely affects performance because of the high overhead of communication between AppLogics.

At e*solutions, we've implemented an architecture that uses object-oriented technology for true reusability of dynamic components and doesn't compromise performance or maintenance. As shown in Figure 44-1, this architecture uses the template callback mechanism provided by NAS (whereby the template calls back the AppLogic for the data it needs). The id attribute of the GX tag specifies which component (object) is to be instantiated. The following is a sample template for calling a component:

```
%gx type=cell id=TransComp %/gx%
```

This template calls back the AppLogic, passing it the id value `TransComp`. The AppLogic then instantiates the `TransComp` object using a factory, and the object streams the result.

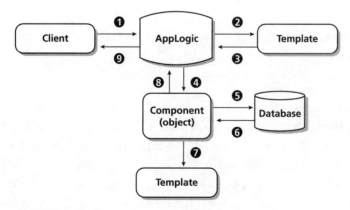

Figure 44-1: The component architecture

The architecture's process is as follows:

1. Calls AppLogic

2. Loads template

3. Via GX tag, calls back for component (object)

4. Instantiates object

5. Connects to database

6. Returns data

7. Merges data with template

8. Returns merged result

9. Streams back result

Let's look at our `TransComp` example more closely. The AppLogic code just below creates a `TransComp` object and also an `ObjectHash` object. It then stores the `TransComp` object along with the corresponding template tag in the `ObjectHash` object, which it passes to the `evalTemplate()` method.

```
{
    // Create the transaction component
    TransComp tc = new TransComp(this);
    ObjectHash oh = new ObjectHash();
    oh.put(TRANS_TAG, tc);

    return evalTemplate(MY_TEMPLATE, (ITemplateData) null,
 oh);
}
```

When the NAS Template Engine queries the `ObjectHash` object for a value for the template tag (which happens to be associated with the `TransComp` object), the `ObjectHash` object will call the `TransComp` object's `execute()` method, which will result in the desired streamed output. The next example shows the code for the `TransComp` object. This object behaves just like an AppLogic, but it's not an AppLogic, and it will be created a lot faster than if `newRequest()` were called.

```
{
    super(appLogic);
}

public int execute() {
    int ret = -1;  // Assume errors.
    com.kivasoft.IHierQuery hierQuery = buildQuery();
    if (hierQuery != null)
        // Merge the hierarchical query results with a
template.
        if (evalOutput(MY_TEMPLATE, hierQuery, null, null,
null) != 0)
            result("<HTML><BODY>Unable to evaluate "
        else
            ret = 0;
    return ret;
}
```

TemplateMapBasic — the next example — is a simple Hashtable-like class that's used by the Template Engine to get values for GX tags. Here's where template extension comes in: The ObjectHash class extends TemplateMapBasic to allow a GX tag to be resolved to an object. When the Template Engine calls get() on a key whose value is an object rather than a simple string, ObjectHash passes control to the object, letting the object stream its value; the way ObjectHash passes this control is by calling the object's execute() method.

```
class ObjectHash extends TemplateMapBasic {
    private ITemplateMap tmb_;
    private Hashtable hash_;  // Used for ESAgent storage
(below)
    public ObjectHash() {
        tmb_ = GX.CreateTemplateMapBasic();
        hash_ = new Hashtable();
    }
    public void put(String key, ESAgent agent) {
        hash_.put(key, agent);
    }
```

```
// Implementation of ITemplateMapBasic
public IBuffer get(String tag, IObject dummy, IObject
dummy2) {
    IBuffer res = null;
    ESAgent agent = (ESAgent) hash_.get(tag);
    if (agent == null)
        res = tmb_.get(tag, dummy, dummy2);
    else {
        int rc = agent.execute();
        res = GX.CreateBuffer();
    }
    return res;
}
}
```

Using this methodology, you can include real objects and not just simple strings in any page and reuse them in any context.

Caching

With a framework (like the one just described) for reusing dynamic components on a page, partial caching becomes feasible. We'll explore this further after reviewing AppLogic caching and partial caching using newRequest(). We'll also touch on the option of developing your own caching mechanism.

AppLogic Caching

NAS provides caching of AppLogic results (and the corresponding input parameter values). When NAS gets a request for an AppLogic from the web server, it checks the cache manager to see if the corresponding AppLogic result has been cached (see Figure 44-2). The cache manager looks at the ValIn parameters of the request to see if they match the current caching criteria for the input parameters. If there is a match and the AppLogic result is cached, NAS streams the result back to the client; if the result is not cached, NAS executes the AppLogic (saving the result in the cache) and streams the result back to the client.

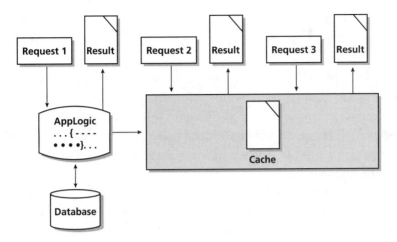

Figure 44-2: How AppLogic caching works

AppLogic caching has many advantages:

- It's fast and efficient and can significantly improve performance.

- It optimizes memory usage by removing the least-used cache.

- The cached result is streamed to the client.

- You can choose caching criteria using the `setCacheCriteria()` method, which allows flexibility in the kind of data that can be cached.

- You can monitor the cache usage with the NAS Admin tool.

A limitation of NAS AppLogic caching, as already mentioned, is that it's "all or nothing": You can't cache only part of a page's content. Also, when you deploy applications in a cluster of servers, the cached data isn't shared across all servers, so you can't take full advantage of the cached data. For example, if the data is cached in NAS server 1, it's not available in NAS server 2; NAS server 2 builds its own cache. You can't control which server a request comes back to (to ensure that it comes back to the server where the data was cached) because caching is only one of the parameters that determine which server is chosen during load balancing.

Partial Caching Using newRequest()

One of the problems with AppLogic caching can be alleviated by using the newRequest() method. If you want to cache a dynamic component in a page — for instance, the top ten bidders for an auction site — you could make it an AppLogic by itself (say, topbidders), which any other AppLogic could call using the newRequest() method. The separately cached data on the top ten bidders could then be streamed back.

This approach works, but since AppLogic-to-AppLogic communication is expensive, the performance gained by it may be insignificant. Our experience has shown that this method of caching doesn't improve performance much — and it can become expensive if the request gets routed to another server in the cluster. This approach, which will also use more threads, works well only in a low-volume environment.

Using the NAS State Layer for Caching

NAS provides global state information that resides in memory and can be shared across multiple users in a cluster. NAS's sophisticated state management, which includes destroying data in the state tree under specified timeout conditions, can be used for caching data. When combined with a framework for reusable components like the one described earlier, this mechanism enables dynamic parts of a page to be cached separately.

The data that's stored in the state tree can either be the result set from the data source or the merged result output from evalOutput(). Here's an example of where caching the data would be useful: A user gets transaction data from the database (causing it to be cached) but then decides he or she wants it sorted in a different order. So the user gets the data again, specifying a different sort order this time. If the data is cached in the state tree, the AppLogic can call evalOutput() on the cached data instead of retrieving the data from the database again. If the result set is large, you can stream the first page and store the rest of the data in this user's session information in the state layer; then, when the user asks for each subsequent page of data, you can stream the next page to the client.

The next example is a snippet of code that implements caching using the state layer.

```
{
```

```
        super(appLogic);
    }
    public int evalOutput(String templatePath, IHierQuery
query, ITemplateMap map,
        IStream stream, IValList props) {
      int res = 0;
      String key = getValIn().getValString("acctnum");
      String results = getResultsFromState(key);
      if (results == null) {                    // Not in the
cache (state layer)
        res = evalOutputAndCache(templatePath, query, map,
stream, props);
        results = getResults();                 // Return the
results just streamed.
        outputResultsInState(key, results);  // Save the
results in the cache.
      } else
        res = result(results);
      return res;
    }


    /** Retrieves from the cache **/
    public String getResultsFromState(String key) {
      String ret = null;
      IState2 node =
appLogic_.getStateTreeRoot(GXSTATE.GXSTATE_LOCAL, key);
      if (node == null)
        appLogic_.log("Can't get state tree root for " +
key);
      else {  // Got the root OK
        IValList vals = node.getStateContents();
        if ((vals != null) && (vals.count() >= 1))
          ret = vals.getValString(key);
      }
      return ret;
    }
```

```
/** Stores in the cache **/
public void putResultsInState(String key, String value) {
   IState2 node =
appLogic_.getStateTreeRoot(GXSTATE.GXSTATE_LOCAL, key);
   if (node == null)
      appLogic_.log("Can't get state tree root for " +
key);
   else {   // Got the root OK
      IValList vals = GX.CreateValList();
      vals.setValString(key, value);
      node.setStateContents(vals);
      node.saveState(0);
   }
 }
}
```

It's very easy to implement caching criteria using this method. As you can see from the code, key is used for setting up the caching criteria. The key can be generated as a combination of criteria. If a state node is present for that key, cached information in the state is streamed back to the client; otherwise, a new node is created for that key and the result is cached in that node. The state timeout feature can be used for deleting unused data in the cache.

The state layer method of caching is best suited for data that's going to be read many more times than it's written. If data put in the state layer is updated very often, the cost of doing so can be great, whereas if there are few (or no) updates of and many reads on that data, the cost of writing becomes insignificant. Also, performance can be adversely affected when the state data gets replicated, since at that time any updates to the data have to be made across multiple servers; if the data isn't changed frequently, this may not be a problem.

Note that an object that's not serializable cannot be cached using this method — and if you serialize an object before storing it in the state layer, there's overhead associated with serializing it (and unserializing it).

Developing Your Own Caching Mechanism

You can develop your own mechanism to do object caching and pooling, using NAS extensions, the static keyword and constant pool in the JVM, or other techniques. (An example of the static keyword technique is discussed in Chapter 43, "Object Pooling in NAS: An Architecture for Caching Objects.")

A custom caching mechanism can be helpful when you need to connect to a data source and, for better performance, you want to reuse the connection. Using the NAS state layer for caching isn't as effective in this case because you can't serialize all connection objects. And, although developing a mechanism to share a cache across multiple servers can be expensive, we found that the performance was comparable to that of using the state layer for caching. (Note that if you use the JVM for caching, you need to do "sticky" load balancing — redirecting NAS to use the server where the JVM is running — which offsets the benefits of NAS's sophisticated load balancing.)

A Performance Comparison

Table 44-1 shows the performance results (in transactions per minute) that we observed in our test of some of the caching methods described in this chapter. For this test, we used a Solaris 2.6 server running NAS 2.1 SP4 with two CPUs; Netscape Enterprise Server 3.6 was used as the web server and Oracle 7.3.4 as the database server. The khc load generator was used for generating user requests.

TABLE 44-1: CACHING METHODS: PERFORMANCE BENCHMARKS

CACHING METHOD USED	TRANSACTIONS PER MINUTE
No caching	100
AppLogic caching	547
Caching in the state layer	184

We found that the number of bytes cached didn't make much difference. It would be a useful exercise to see what the effect of the back-end communication is on caching — that is, to run profiling on an AppLogic and plot the relationship between time spent in back-end data source retrieval and the improvement in transactions per minute when caching is used.

AppLogic caching is clearly the most efficient approach, as discussed in this chapter, but that doesn't mean it's always the best choice. You should consider the special needs of your situation before choosing a caching method. If you need the ability to do partial content caching, you may want to build a framework for reusable content like the one we designed at e*solutions, and use the NAS state layer for caching reusable components. We hope this chapter will help you make the caching decision that's right for you.

45

Using LDAP with Netscape Application Server for User Authentication

Tony Dahbura — *lead systems engineer, Netscape Communications*

Although Netscape Application Server (NAS) has its own method of storing users and groups, the scalability and wide availability of Lightweight Directory Access Protocol (LDAP) directories across intranets, extranets, and the Internet make the use of LDAP a logical adjunct to the development of robust network applications. This chapter describes how to use LDAP to handle authenticating users of NAS applications.

I briefly review LDAP and NAS and then look at some code that uses LDAP directories (via the Netscape Directory SDK) to do user authentication. This code is available for your use. Since no single method of authentication will fit every application's needs, we'll look at three different authentication methodologies.

NOTE

If you haven't downloaded Netscape Directory Server SDK yet, now's a good time to do so. You can find it on the Web at `http://developer.netscape.com/tech/directory/index.html?content=downloads.html`

This chapter assumes that you have some familiarity with the Netscape Directory SDK, which you can gain from reading Chapter 38, and with NAS and NSAPI. You should know how to build NAS AppLogics, how to insert them into a NAS project and set up the calling sequences, and how to build parameter lists for callable AppLogics. Chapters 43 and 44 contain information on building NAS applications. For more information on NAS and NSAPI, visit the DevEdge Online Library at `http://developer.netscape.com/docs`.

About LDAP and NAS

LDAP is a protocol that's widely supported on the Internet. A large number of corporations are taking advantage of its availability and robustness to manage user information within their communities. A wide variety of tools are available that can query and write to LDAP directories. Many vendors are providing support for LDAP in their products and making their own systems accessible via LDAP.

LDAP's ability to handle rapid read requests makes it perfect for high-performance Internet applications. LDAP provides tools for adding, modifying, and locating information contained in a directory. Programming methods and descriptions of the routines in the LDAP API are supplied as part of the Netscape Directory.

Netscape Application Server is Netscape's high-performance application server, which was introduced in Chapter 6. Netscape Application Builder (NAB) is a standalone single-user version of NAS for designing and developing NAS applications. Many of the highest-performance Internet applications are based on NAS's three-tiered development architecture (the client, NAS, and database tiers). Using NAS for high-performance application processing, combined with LDAP for authentication and user management, provides a highly robust, scalable environment for meeting the demands of today's network applications.

You can write NAS AppLogics in both C++ and Java, and the Netscape Directory SDK supports software calls in both languages. This chapter focuses on the Java platform; however, the necessary libraries are available in either language, and the code provided here could easily be ported to C++.

Methods of Authentication

At the most basic level, the purpose of authentication is to identify someone accessing a resource and to bar unauthorized access. With NAS and LDAP, the application developer has multiple options for authenticating users. Table 45-1 lists the methods of authentication available, along with some of their features and faults.

TABLE 45-1: AUTHENTICATION METHODS

METHOD	PROS	CONS
Web server username/password authenication — based on Web server access control	Takes advantage of Web server security Minimal client requirements Access rights in LDAP directory Easily to switch to certificate authentication Secure Sockets Layer (SSL) use optional	Password not known to applications
Certificate authentication — Web server-based with digital certificates	Same as username/password authentication, except SSL use required Enables access to multiple servers without having to authenticate again	Requires client digital certificate

Continued

TABLE 45-1: *(continued)*

METHOD	PROS	CONS
HTML authentication —based on an HTML form	Simple Presentation can be customized Additional information (such as hints) can be provided Password can be made available for other uses across applications Passwords are exposed to applications, creating potential security problems	Does not take advantage of Web server security (security solution must be implemented entirely by the developer)

This chapter explains how to use each of these methods as an authentication model. The code you write and place under NAS access control will be the same regardless of which authentication model you choose to implement; thus you can change your authentication model later without having to modify or rearchitect your code.

The Architecture of Authenticating with LDAP

Figure 45-1 depicts the architecture of standard Web server-based username/ password authentication. (The architecture diagrams and their descriptions are oversimplified; later sections provide additional details.)

In the process illustrated by Figure 45-1, a user comes to a Web site and requests a Web page from the Web server (Step 1). The Web server in return requests a username and password (Step 2); a username/password dialog box appears on the screen. After the user enters his or her username and password, this information is sent to the Web server (Step 3), which in turn uses it to authenticate the user against the LDAP server (Step 4). If the user is authenticated, he or she receives the initially requested page (Step 5). Note that at this point the application server has no idea who the user is.

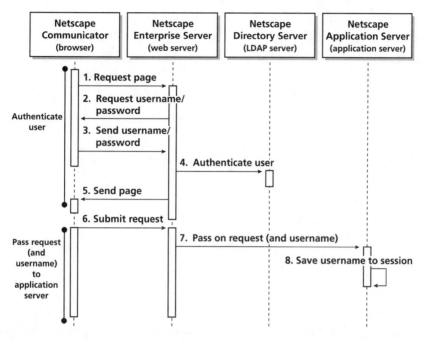

Figure 45-1: Web server-based authentication via username and password

Now suppose the user clicks a link on the Web page. This submits a request to the Web server (Step 6), which then has to pass the request on to the application server. Because the application server doesn't know who the user is, the Web server also passes the username along with the request (Step 7). The first time a request is submitted to the application server, the AppLogic in the application server takes the username and saves it in the session — that is, places it in a secure session, a concept supported by NAS (Step 8). After the session is saved, the distributed state management of the application server will keep track of the username, so it will be accessible to any AppLogic called on behalf of the user during the current session.

Certificate-based authentication (Figure 45-2) proceeds in a similar manner: The authentication is taken care of by the Web server against the LDAP server, and the storing of the username is done at the first request to the application server. The only difference is that instead of the username and password, a digital certificate is used to authenticate the user. The Web server requests a certificate (Step 2) and the user sends his or her certificate (Step 3). The Web server first checks that the certificate itself is valid by making sure it was issued by an approved Certificate Authority (Step 4). The e-mail address is extracted from the user's certificate and used to authenticate against the LDAP server (Step 5). (Other criteria can be used to authenticate against the LDAP server as well.) On Netscape Enterprise Server 3.*x*, this is done by modifying the `certmap.conf` configuration file. Everything else about this type of authentication is the same as for the previous method.

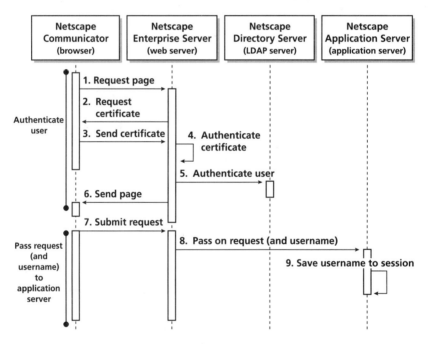

Figure 45-2: Web server-based authentication via digital certificates

Figure 45-3 depicts HTML authentication. The user enters his or her username and password in an HTML form on a login page. This information is then passed to the application server, which in turn validates it against the LDAP server. The big difference between this method and the other two is that the authentication is done by the application server against the LDAP server (Step 5), instead of by the Web server against the LDAP server. In this scenario, the username is saved in the session right after the authentication is performed (Step 6).

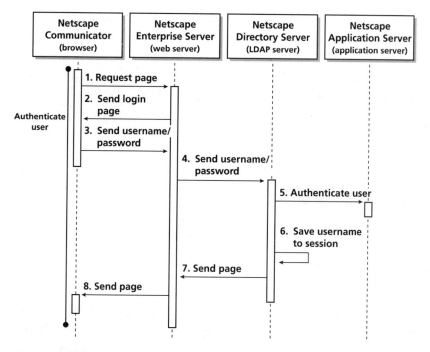

Figure 45-3: Authentication based on an HTML form

Notice that if you use a server-based authentication method, you can access usernames from your application, but you cannot access passwords. However, if you use HTML authentication, you can access both usernames and passwords, which enables you to seamlessly log in to other applications for the user — meaning the user has to log in only once. Although HTML authentication does pose a potential security risk (because the application has direct access to usernames and passwords), it's preferable if the application will access two or more systems that require username/password authentication. Otherwise, the user will be prompted for a username and password multiple times while using your application and may find this frustrating.

Setting up the Authentication Scheme

To use a Web server-based authentication method, you must make modifications to NAS so that it can pass the username to the AppLogic. (You must also place your application's code and HTML under Web server access control, as described in the Netscape Enterprise Server documentation, available at `http://developer.netscape.com/docs`.)

To set up the NAS NSAPI plug-in to communicate the username to the AppLogic, you must modify the configuration information stored in the central registry. Here, you're interested in passing the `auth-user` attribute (the username authenticated by the Web server); to do this, you need to edit the registry as follows:

1. Using `regedt32` on Windows NT or `kregedit` on Solaris, navigate in the registry tree to the following key: `HKEY_LOCAL_MACHINE/SOFTWARE/KIVA/Enterprise/2.0/CCS0/HTTPAPI/INPUTNSAPI`

2. Create a `String` value with the name as `auth-user` and the data as `REMOTE_USER`.

3. Reboot the machine.

To see the `auth-user` attribute value from within the AppLogic code, you must place the `cgi-bin` directory (containing the `gx.cgi` module) under Web server access control. If you don't, when the AppLogics get called, they won't have access to the ACL information, because the caller is not under Access Control List (ACL) control, even though your NAS application's HTML is under ACL control. Figure 45-4 shows the Enterprise Server `docs` directory after a default installation of NAS or NAB; the `cgi-bin` directory is highlighted. When deploying applications on the Internet or an extranet, you should probably place the whole `docs` directory under ACL control. Because most high-use situations have a series of Web servers to serve the application's HTML and forms, this shouldn't overload your servers.

The user attribute is passed into an AppLogic as a name-value pair within the `valIn` parameter. Given the example of passing in the `auth-user` attribute as `REMOTE_USER`, you can access the value of `auth-user` with the following code:

```
String user = valIn.getValString("REMOTE_USER");
```

This value is passed to an AppLogic named `login.java`. If you use HTML authentication, these steps are not needed. The HTML form that prompts for the username and password passes this information in form variables named `userid` and `passwd`.

Note that because of the different setup requirements, there is a separation of logic and flow until after authentication has occurred. Once authentication has been completed, the application continues with the main flow of execution regardless of the original authentication scheme.

Figure 45-4: Enterprise Server docs directory

Although a common AppLogic is used here to handle both Web server-based and HTML authentication, once you've decided on a security scheme, the logic should be coded to prevent the other method from being used. For example, if you choose Web server-based authentication, the entire application should be under access control to prevent someone from entering the logic in the middle. On the other hand, if you use HTML authentication, you must ensure successful validation to the LDAP server.

Writing the AppLogic Code

Enough on theory and practice; let's take a look at the code to accomplish authentication via LDAP. Figure 45-5 shows the NAB project files that make up the system.

The process is initiated by the index.html file, which enables you to select the method by which to authenticate. In practice, the application developer would choose a method, and this page would instead be the main entry into the network application. Upon selecting the method, you're routed to either the htmlauth page for HTML authentication or the webauth page for Web server-based authentication. The Webauth page is under ACL control of the Web server (validating credentials from the LDAP server); if you select that route, you're immediately presented with the standard user authentication dialog.

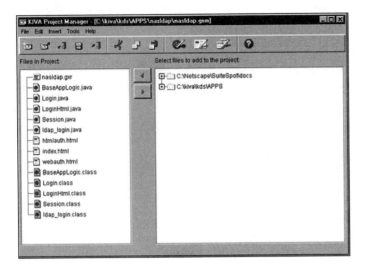

Figure 45-5: The NAB project files

ON THE CD-ROM

The files mentioned in this chapter are available on the CD-ROM that accompanies this book. To find them, follow the path: Sample Code and Supporting Documentation ⇨ Part IV ⇨ Chapter 45.

Now I'll look at the AppLogics in detail. In the AppLogic code that follows, I've omitted the NAS Java header information for brevity. Notice that the source makes heavy use of the NAS `log()` function, which writes values to the system console log and enables you to see the flow of the code, binds, and so on; these calls should be commented out in a production version.

The following shows the `login.java` AppLogic, which is called to perform Web server–based authentication. Again, in order for this to work correctly, the application has to be placed under Web server ACL control, and the NSAPI plug-in for NAS has to be configured to pass the user credentials into our service. Remember that the username is coming in under REMOTE_USER.

```
public int execute()
{
    String k1;  // Temporary string variables used for
logging messages
```

```
    String k2;

    log("*****inside login.java");
    nasldap.Session session = getSessionProxy();
    if (session == null) {
        return result("Call to getSessionProxy() failed in
login");
    }


    // Verify correctness of valIn criteria.
    // For extra security, the referrer and host should
probably also be validated.
    log("********************************");
    k2 = "";
    valIn.resetPosition();
    while ( (k1 = valIn.getNextKey()) != null)
        log(k1 + "=" + valIn.getValString(k1));
    log(k2);
    String authuser = valIn.getValString("REMOTE_USER");
    if (authuser == null || authuser.trim().length() == 0) {
        // We have a problem -- redirect user back to
authentication page.
        ...
    }


    // Call the common LDAP AppLogic (lookldap.java) to do
the search.
    IValList paramsTo = GX.CreateValList();
    IValList paramsFrom = GX.CreateValList();
    log("inside login.java %%%%% authuser=" + authuser);
    paramsTo.setValString("host", "natasha.mcom.com");
    paramsTo.setValInt("port", 389);
    paramsTo.setValString("searchroot", "o=Airius.com");
    paramsTo.setValString("searchstring", "uid=" + authuser);
    paramsTo.setValString("criteria",
"cn,uid,mail,telephonenumber");
```

```
    newRequest("{6ad81114-0142-11d2-810d-0060974ad69f}",
paramsTo, paramsFrom);

    if ( (paramsFrom.getValString("status")).equals ("found")
) {
        // Save login criteria in the session.
        session.setUsername(valIn.getValString("Username"));
        session.setDN(valIn.getValString("dn"));
    }
    else {
        session.setUsername("");
        session.setDN("");
    }
    session.saveSession();

    String temp;
    temp = "<HTML><HEAD></HEAD><BODY>";
    temp += "Welcome " + paramsFrom.getValString("cn") +
"<br>";
    paramsFrom.resetPosition();

    // Iterate return set, and display all values so that we
see something.
    String k;
    while ( (k=paramsFrom.getNextKey() ) != null)
        if ( !((k.substring(0,2)).equals("GX")) )  // Don't
dump GX tags.
            temp += k + "=" + paramsFrom.getValString(k) +
"<br>";
    temp += "</BODY></HTML>";
    return result(temp);
}
```

The code in this listing is executed when the URL that refers to the AppLogic calls it. The URL is of the form

```
http://hostname/cgi-bin/gx.cgi/GUIDX-GUID_for_the_AppLogic
```

The GUID, or globally unique identifier, is a number that uniquely identifies the AppLogic within the environment and is generated either automatically by the development tool or by a command-line utility.

The code begins execution at the execute( ) method. The first thing it does is gain access to the session handler so that it can later use the handler to store information to maintain across requests. It then writes all the passed values to the log (again, this is for debugging and educational use — remove this code when you're done learning). It takes the username that was passed to it from the Web server and checks whether it's blank or null; if it is, it means that ACL control was not set up correctly.

Next the code builds the parameter list for calling our common LDAP AppLogic, passing information such as the host name and the port number. Calling newRequest( ) with the GUID is how you call another AppLogic. Details on calling AppLogics from other AppLogics are provided in the section "Calling AppLogics from Code" in the Netscape document *Developing KIVA Applications*, available at http://developer.netscape.com/docs/manuals/index. html?content=appserv/2_1/pg.htm. When the called AppLogic returns, login.java verifies that the user was found and saves the settings in our session variable.

The code then generates an HTML page showing the results of the LDAP lookup. For an actual application, you would process the next phase of your system, such as by presenting the initial entry into the business-processing end of your application.

The AppLogic for doing HTML authentication, loginhtml.java, is very similar to the login.java AppLogic; the next example shows only the build of paramsFrom. Notice how the username and password entered by the user is passed in to the common LDAP AppLogic.

```
String Username = valIn.getValString("Username");
if ( Username == null || Username.trim().length() == 0 ) {
  log("Input error on Username");
  return result("Username should not be null!");
}
String Password = valIn.getValString("Password");
if ( Password == null || Password.trim().length()== 0 ) {
  log("Input error on Password");
  return result("Password should not be null!");
```

```
}

log("inside loginHTML.java");

// Call the common LDAP AppLogic (lookldap.java) to do the
search.
IValList paramsTo = GX.CreateValList();
IValList paramsFrom = GX.CreateValList();

paramsTo.setValString("host", "natasha.mcom.com");
paramsTo.setValInt("port", 389);
paramsTo.setValString("searchroot", "o=Airius.com");
paramsTo.setValString("searchstring", "uid=" +
Username.trim());
paramsTo.setValString("criteria",
"cn,uid,mail,telephonenumber");

paramsTo.setValString("authid", "uid=" + Username.trim() +
","
   + paramsTo.getValString("searchroot"));
paramsTo.setValString("authpw", Password);

newRequest("{6ad81114-0142-11d2-810d-0060974ad69f}",
paramsTo, paramsFrom);
```

What's especially convenient about authenticating via an HTML page is that you can provide a very rich user interface for entry of the information. One service I use quite regularly even enables you to provide a hint to yourself if you forget your password. Given the number of passwords we all have to remember, this is a handy feature, and it certainly reduces the number of requests to fix a lost password.

After successfully authenticating the user, the login.java and loginhtml. java AppLogics set two session variables that maintain the username and the fully distinguished name (DN) of the user who has been authenticated. The DN is important because it allows you to do very fast lookups if you need further information about this user later in the application's processing—for example, the user's full common name (such as John Doe).

The login.java and loginhtml.java AppLogics call another AppLogic, lookldap.java. The lookldap.java AppLogic (the next listing) has the sole purpose of providing a common, simple interface to a variety of applications that require LDAP queries for authentication purposes. It also provides a code model for the use of LDAP services in general. (The code in the next listing has been shortened for the sake of readability; the log() statements and other peripheral pieces are not shown.)

```
import java.util.*;

// ...Other standard NAS imports...

import netscape.ldap.*;

public class ldap_login extends nasldap.BaseAppLogic
{

    public int execute()
    {
        // Verify correctness of valIn criteria.

        // We pass the following in valIn: host, port,
searchroot, searchstring
        boolean fndone=false;
        String  authid = valIn.getValString("authid");
        String  authpw = valIn.getValString("authpw");
        String  lhost = valIn.getValString("host");
        int     lport = valIn.getValInt("port");
        String  lsrchroot = valIn.getValString("searchroot");
        String  lsrchstring =
valIn.getValString("searchstring");
        String  lcriteria = valIn.getValString("criteria");
// Skip for now.

        // Turn criteria into array of attributes we want from
the LDAP server.
```

```
            String[] myAttrs = parse(lcriteria, " ,");

            // Do the search in the LDAP directory.
            LDAPConnection ldap_conn = null;
            int status = -1;
            try {
                ldap_conn = new LDAPConnection();   // Build
connection.
                ldap_conn.connect(lhost, lport);    // Connect to
LDAP server.

                if (authid == null) authid = "";
                if (authpw == null) authpw = "";
                if (authid.length() > 0 || authpw.length() > 0) {

                    try {
                        ldap_conn.authenticate(authid, authpw);   //
Bind by username and password.
                    } catch (LDAPException e) {
                        switch ( e.getLDAPResultCode() ) {
                            case e.NO_SUCH_OBJECT:
                                valOut.setValString("status", "The user
does not exist");
                                break;
                            case e.INVALID_CREDENTIALS:
                                valOut.setValString("status", "Invalid
password");
                                break;
                            default:
                                valOut.setValString("status", "some
other auth error");
                                break;
                        }
                        if ( (ldap_conn != null) &&
ldap_conn.isConnected() ) {
                            try {
                                ldap_conn.disconnect();
```

```
            } catch (LDAPException e) {
                ;
            }
        }
        return 0;
    }
}


        LDAPSearchConstraints cons =
ldap_conn.getSearchConstraints();
        cons.setBatchSize(0);  // Block till all results
are back.
        LDAPSearchResults res = ldap_conn.search(lsrchroot,
LDAPConnection.SCOPE_SUB,
            lsrchstring, myAttrs, false, cons);

        // Loop through result set -- we actually only want
first result.
        if ( res.hasMoreElements() ) {
            LDAPEntry findEntry =
(LDAPEntry)res.nextElement();
            valOut.setValString("status", "found");
            valOut.setValString("dn", findEntry.getDN());
            fndone = true;

            // Get the attributes of the entry.
            LDAPAttributeSet findAttrs =
findEntry.getAttributeSet();
            Enumeration enumAttrs =
findAttrs.getAttributes();

            while ( enumAttrs.hasMoreElements() ) { // Loop
on attributes for this entry.
                LDAPAttribute anAttr =
(LDAPAttribute)enumAttrs.nextElement();
                String attrName = anAttr.getName();  //
=cn,mail etc.
```

```
                    // Loop on values for this attribute --
should only be one.
                    Enumeration enumVals =
anAttr.getStringValues();
                    while ( enumVals.hasMoreElements() ) {
                        String aVal =
(String)enumVals.nextElement();
                        valOut.setValString(attrName, aVal);

                    }
                }
            }
            status = 0;
            if (!fndone)
                valOut.setValString("status", "none found");
        } catch (LDAPException e) {

            ;

        }

        // Done with connection, so disconnect us.
        if ( (ldap_conn != null) && ldap_conn.isConnected() )
{

            try {
                ldap_conn.disconnect();
            } catch (LDAPException e) {

                ;

            }
        }
        return 0;

    }

}
```

This is the main code for handling the LDAP processing requests from the two previously described AppLogics. Note the use of import netscape.ldap.* near the beginning of the code; this allows you to call the LDAP Java-language methods using the short-form syntax (that is, to refer to the routines in the

netscape.ldap library without having to spell out netscape.ldap.
methodname each time). I included the try clause because I needed to control
exits very carefully so that the status field could be set with correct values.

First, the code pulls the values for the host, port, and so on. Next, the search
string is pulled, and a connection to the LDAP server is built. If the password
and username have been specified, an LDAP authentication is attempted (if the
authentication fails, we exit with an appropriate message). The search is then
performed, and the values requested are returned as a ValList. The code uses
the Java tokenizer to parse the string for desired return values.

AppLogics expect data to be passed in and out using valIn and valOut. You
pass the information listed in Table 45-2 to the lookldap.java AppLogic.

TABLE 45-2: INBOUND VALUES TO LOOKLDAP.JAVA

PARAMETER NAME	DESCRIPTION
host	The LDAP host name to use
port	The port number the LDAP server is listening on; must be passed as int type
searchroot	The LDAP search root to begin the search in the directory—in most cases, the top of the tree (for example, "o=mycompany,c=us")
searchstring	How to form a prefixed search string (for example, "uid=userid_we_want" if searching by username)
criteria	Comma-separated list of attributes and values we want returned (for example, "cn,uid,mail" to have those values returned)
authid	The user to bind as (for anonymous binding, pass null; when binding with username, pass the full DN to bind—for example, "uid=test,o=ace,c=us")
authpw	The password for the user to bind as

The return results are passed back as a keyed value pair, with the keys listed in
Table 45-3.

TABLE 45-3: RESULTS FROM LOOKLDAP.JAVA

PARAMETER NAME	DESCRIPTION
status	A text message describing the result: "The user does not exist"; "Invalid password" Some other authentication error message: "found" — everything is OK (we validated the user); "none found"
dn	The full dn of the authenticated entry
cn	The cn of the authenticated entry
uid	The uid of the authenticated entry
Other requested values	The values you requested

Setting up the Software on Your System

To compile and build these modules, you need the appropriate libraries. For the Java-based Netscape Directory SDK, the critical file is ldapjdk.jar. This file needs to be added to the CLASSPATH environment variable of NAS or NAB so that the file can locate this library. Note that JAR files, unlike class files, need to be listed in CLASSPATH with the JAR file fully specified (for example, /usr/libs/java/ldapjdk.jar). On the NAB server, you can easily check this by asking the Project Manager to compile one of the sample AppLogics; if the library is not found, your CLASSPATH is wrong.

The full source of the AppLogics presented in this chapter is available on the CD-ROM; look for the files associated with Chapter 45. But you need to modify the host, ou (organizational unit), searchroot, authid, and authpw attributes for your purposes. Also, remember to comment out the log( ) statements in an operational environment.

ON THE CD-ROM

The files mentioned in the previous paragraphs are all available on the CD-ROM that accompanies this book; follow the path: Sample Code and Supporting Documentation ⇨ Part IV ⇨ Chapter 45.

What's on the CD-ROM?

The CD-ROM bundled with this book contains working sample code that illustrates the concepts and techniques described in *Netscape DevEdge Web Developer's Library*. It also includes additional information — most of it official Netscape documentation — which provides in-depth information about the technology described in the book. You'll also find a searchable, electronic version of this book on the CD-ROM.

The CD-ROM does not include the Netscape software products you'll need to use the sample code. Those products can be downloaded at no charge from the Netscape Web site. See the file on the CD called "Welcome and Software

Download" for a list of the software you'll need as well as links to Web locations where you can download the software for free.

The following table describes the CD-ROM contents in detail:

ITEM OR PACKAGE	DESCRIPTION
Welcome and Software Download	Read this HTML file before you try to use any of the sample code on the CD-ROM. You'll find a list of the Netscape Communications software you need to use the code examples as well as links to the Web locations that contain free copies of the software.
	This file also includes a guide to the sample code and documentation that illustrate or support the book's chapters. (Those files are in the directory "Sample Code and Supporting Documentation" on the CD-ROM.)
	It's recommended that you print this HTML file and use it to help guide you to the files on the CD-ROM.
Sample Code and Supporting Documentation	This large directory contains the sample code and documentation that illustrate and support the book's chapters. The directory contains four folders/directories, one for each of the book's four main parts. Folders/directories for each chapter with supporting code and documentation can be found within those four directories. Note that only 25 of the book's 45 chapters have corresponding directories/folders on the CD-ROM.
This book	A complete PDF version of *Netscape DevEdge Web Developer's Library*. This version is especially useful if you're trying to find a particular section of the book: Use Adobe Acrobat Reader to search for what you want to find.
Adobe Acrobat Reader 4.0	This utility from Adobe Acrobat Reader lets you read, search through, and print electronic documents saved as .PDF files.

ITEM OR PACKAGE	DESCRIPTION
WinZip 7.0	An evaluation version of the compression utility for Windows-based personal computers. WinZip is a straightforward zipping and unzipping utility that includes built-in support for popular Internet file formats such as TAR, ZIP, UUencode, XXencode, BinHex, MIME, and Unix-compressed files. If you're a Windows user, use this software to decompress the files on the CD-ROM.
Aladdin Stuffit Expander	A freeware version of the utility for Mac OS users that decompresses just about any file (including StuffIt, Compact Pro, BinHex, and MacBinary files) that you come across while on the major commercial online services, surfing the Internet, or receiving email with compressed files attached. If you use a Mac OS system, use StuffIt to decompress the files on the CD-ROM.
Netscape License Agreement	A statement limiting Netscape's responsibilities and warranties regarding the software, sample code, and documentation in the book and on the CD-ROM. This agreement also gives you permission to use, copy, modify, and distribute the sample code on this CD-ROM for any purpose without a fee.

Index

A

Abort event, 144
absolute positioning of elements, 162
abstract classes, 485
accelerator key combinations, 156
access control scheme, 287
access privileges, 30
access speeds, improving, 94
accessing URL data, 238
Acrobat Forms object model, 13
ad hoc queries, 276
addAttachments() method, 450–451
addClient() function, 380
additive JavaScript, 213
Adobe Systems, 13
agent pattern, 591
aggregate calculations, 23
Airius.ldif file, 534
alarms, 606
alert() function, 130
Amazon.com, 76
American Internet Corporation, 101
American National Standards Institute (ANSI),
      78, 81, 85–86
ampersands, ASCII character code equivalent,
      254
analysis artifacts, 588
analysis sequence diagram, 608
andprev(), 453
animation, 12
ANSI. *See* American National Standards
      Institute
API. *See* Application Programming Interface
Apple Computer, 39
applet-generated hot spots, 15

application architectural level, 595
application logic, 302–303, 460, 461
application name uniqueness, ensuring, 338
application objects, 24
Application Programming Interface (API), 31,
      112, 152
application run-in process, 9
application-to-application communications, 77
AppLogic, 483, 490, 616
   AppLogic.evalOutput() method, 618
   components, 480
   modules, 59
   NAS, 10
   partial content caching, 634–635
   user authentication, 649–660
applying object-oriented and component
      design, 601–614
appointment calendars, 175
approaches to control, 590
appVersion, 209
architecture development, 592
array objects, 5, 411, 453
arrayObj.join(), 228
arrays, 289
ASCII character code equivalents, 254
asString() helper function, 385
asterisk (*), escape() function, 254
astronomical observations, 178
asynchronous messaging layer, 42
at sign (–), escape() function, 254
atomic clocks, 178
attachMIMEFile() method, 451
attachTextFile() method, 451
attrib.htm, 429
attributes, positional thingies, 107
authenticate.c, 534

Continued

E

S

IDG Books Worldwide, Inc.
End–User License Agreement

4. **Restrictions on Use of Individual Programs.** You must follow the individual requirements and restrictions detailed for each individual program in Appendix D of this Book. These limitations are also contained in the individual license agreements recorded on the Software Media. These limitations may include a requirement that after using the program for a specified period of time, the user must pay a registration fee or discontinue use. By opening the Software packet(s), you will be agreeing to abide by the licenses and restrictions for these individual programs that are detailed in Appendix D and on the Software Media. None of the material on this Software Media or listed in this Book may ever be redistributed, in original or modified form, for commercial purposes.

5. **Limited Warranty.**

   (a) IDGB warrants that the Software and Software Media are free from defects in materials and workmanship under normal use for a period of sixty (60) days from the date of purchase of this Book. If IDGB receives notification within the warranty period of defects in materials or workmanship, IDGB will replace the defective Software Media.

   (b) IDGB AND THE AUTHOR OF THE BOOK DISCLAIM ALL OTHER WARRANTIES, EXPRESS OR IMPLIED, INCLUDING WITHOUT LIMITATION IMPLIED WARRANTIES OF MER-CHANTABILITY AND FITNESS FOR A PARTICULAR PURPOSE, WITH RESPECT TO THE SOFTWARE, THE PROGRAMS, THE SOURCE CODE CONTAINED THEREIN, AND/OR THE TECHNIQUES DESCRIBED IN THIS BOOK. IDGB DOES NOT WARRANT THAT THE FUNCTIONS CONTAINED IN THE SOFTWARE WILL MEET YOUR REQUIREMENTS OR THAT THE OPERATION OF THE SOFTWARE WILL BE ERROR FREE.

   (c) This limited warranty gives you specific legal rights, and you may have other rights that vary from jurisdiction to jurisdiction.

6. **Remedies.**

   (a) IDGB's entire liability and your exclusive remedy for defects in materials and work-manship shall be limited to replacement of the Software Media, which may be returned to IDGB with a copy of your receipt at the following address: Software Media Fulfillment Department, Attn.: *Netscape DevEdge Web Developer's Library*, IDG Books Worldwide, Inc., 7260 Shadeland Station, Ste. 100, Indianapolis, IN 46256, or call 1-800-762-2974. Please allow three to four weeks for delivery. This Limited Warranty is void if failure of the Software Media has resulted from accident, abuse, or misapplication. Any replacement Software Media will be warranted for the remainder of the original warranty period or thirty (30) days, whichever is longer.

(b) In no event shall IDGB or the author be liable for any damages whatsoever (including without limitation damages for loss of business profits, business interruption, loss of business information, or any other pecuniary loss) arising from the use of or inability to use the Book or the Software, even if IDGB has been advised of the possibility of such damages.

(c) Because some jurisdictions do not allow the exclusion or limitation of liability for consequential or incidental damages, the above limitation or exclusion may not apply to you.

7. **U.S. Government Restricted Rights.** Use, duplication, or disclosure of the Software by the U.S. Government is subject to restrictions stated in paragraph (c)(1)(ii) of the Rights in Technical Data and Computer Software clause of DFARS 252.227-7013, and in subparagraphs (a) through (d) of the Commercial Computer—Restricted Rights clause at FAR 52.227-19, and in similar clauses in the NASA FAR supplement, when applicable.

8. **General.** This Agreement constitutes the entire understanding of the parties and revokes and supersedes all prior agreements, oral or written, between them and may not be modified or amended except in a writing signed by both parties hereto that specifically refers to this Agreement. This Agreement shall take precedence over any other documents that may be in conflict herewith. If any one or more provisions contained in this Agreement are held by any court or tribunal to be invalid, illegal, or otherwise unenforceable, each and every other provision shall remain in full force and effect.

my2cents.idgbooks.com

Register This Book — And Win!

Visit **http://my2cents.idgbooks.com** to register this book and we'll automatically enter you in our fantastic monthly prize giveaway. It's also your opportunity to give us feedback: let us know what you thought of this book and how you would like to see other topics covered.

Discover IDG Books Online!

The IDG Books Online Web site is your online resource for tackling technology — at home and at the office. Frequently updated, the IDG Books Online Web site features exclusive software, insider information, online books, and live events!

10 Productive & Career-Enhancing Things You Can Do at www.idgbooks.com

- Nab source code for your own programming projects.

- Download software.

- Read Web exclusives: special articles and book excerpts by IDG Books Worldwide authors.

- Take advantage of resources to help you advance your career as a Novell or Microsoft professional.

- Buy IDG Books Worldwide titles or find a convenient bookstore that carries them.

- Register your book and win a prize.

- Chat live online with authors.

- Sign up for regular e-mail updates about our latest books.

- Suggest a book you'd like to read or write.

- Give us your 2¢ about our books and about our Web site.

You say you're not on the Web yet? It's easy to get started with IDG Books' *Discover the Internet*, available at local retailers everywhere.

CD-ROM Installation Instructions

The CD-ROM that accompanies this book is divided into several directories that contain code examples, text files, a PDF version of this book, and other tools and utilities. Before you use any of them, it's strongly recommended you read the HTML file on the CD-ROM called *"Welcome and Software Download"* to determine what software you will need to run the examples and to download them from the Web.

The code examples and text files are contained in the CD-ROM directory called "Sample Code and Supporting Documentation." The contents of that directory are described in detail in the file called "Welcome and Software Download."

To use the code examples on the CD-ROM, either copy the files from the CD-ROM to your hard drive or copy the contents of the file and paste it into your editor of choice. Note that all CD-ROM files are read-only. When you copy a file from the CD-ROM to your hard drive, it retains its read-only attribute. To change this attribute after copying a file, right-click the filename or icon and select Properties from the shortcut menu. In the Properties dialog box, click the General tab and remove the checkmark from the Read-only checkbox.

Some of the files on the CD are contained in .zip files, and you will have to expand them. Be sure to unzip them to a file on your hard disk, as follows:

1. Double-click the .zip file to open it (this assumes that you have WinZip or another extracting utility).

2. Click Actions ⇨ Extract from the WinZip menu.

3. In the lower pull-down list, select your hard disk.

4. Scroll through the upper pull-down list and select the directory where you would like to store the data from the .zip file.

5. Click the Create Directory button, and name the new directory whatever name you'd like.

6. Click Extract. All the files from the .zip file will now appear in the directory you just created. Follow the instructions in the book and/or in the file on the CD called *"Welcome and Software Download"* to determine which file to open.

Adobe Acrobat Reader (used for viewing the PDF files) has its own folder with an installer and instructions.

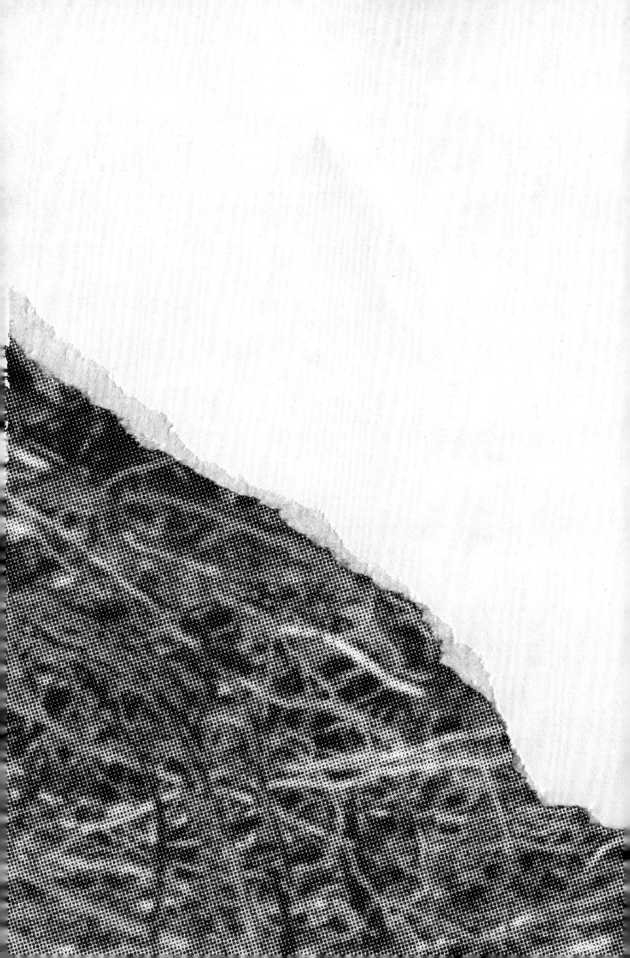

LUNCH 15

LUNCH is the design research journal of the UVA School of Architecture.

Published by Applied Research and Design Publishing, an imprint of ORO Editions.
Gordon Goff: Publisher

www.appliedresearchanddesign.com
info@appliedresearchanddesign.com

Editors: Colleen Brennan, Leah Kahler, Chris Murphy, and Ben Small
Faculty Advisors: Brad Cantrell and Sneha Patel
Book Design: Colleen Brennan, Leah Kahler, Chris Murphy, and Ben Small
Project Manager: Jake Anderson

10 9 8 7 6 5 4 3 2 1 First Edition

ISBN: 978-1-957183-12-1

Color Separations and Printing: ORO Group Ltd.

Printed in China.

Typeface: Bau Pro

AR+D Publishing makes a continuous effort to minimize the overall carbon footprint of its publications. As part of this goal, AR+D, in association with Global ReLeaf, arranges to plant trees to replace those used in the manufacturing of the paper produced for its books. Global ReLeaf is an international campaign run by American Forests, one of the world's oldest nonprofit conservation organizations. Global ReLeaf is American Forests' education and action program that helps individuals, organizations, agencies, and corporations improve the local and global environment by planting and caring for trees.

LETTER FROM THE EDITORS

Dear reader,

When the editorial team came together in late 2019 to develop the call for submissions for LUNCH Journal's fifteenth issue, the world was a different place. That time, the "pre-pandemic," found us ruminating on the thickness of lines, the thinness of our computers' screens, and the tantalizing possibility of that which refuses oversimplification in pursuit of complexity. Sitting knee to knee, breathing with blissful and maskless comfort, we chattered on about vibrant bikini-crowds sweating on each other at the beach, the crushing thickness of walls in dummy crash tests videos, ogled the cushiony depth of Iceland's moss-covered rock formations, and pondered the fortitude of braided strands. These images, we decided, were thick, and we liked it.

In the coming months, the editorial team, our contributors, and the entire rest of the world bore witness to what felt like radical, pivotal shifts in the trajectory of reality. Almost overnight, those thick crowds sweating at the beach disappeared; ushering in eighteen months of a pandemic that revealed to us the shocking thinness of our own skin. The porosity of our bodies changed everything about how we interacted with our friends, loved ones, and neighbors. It upended the way we move through the world and how we understand the air that we breathe. Then in the summer of 2020, the murders of George Floyd, Breonna Taylor, Ahmaud Arbery, Tony McDade, and too many since, ignited a conversation on the long history of race-based violence in the US and around the world.

As we collectively grieved, the range of things we believed were possible became far more expansive, in ways that inspired both incredible fear, but also incredible hope. Calls for examining institutional entanglements with white supremacy grew, and we began to see cities across the south toppling, dismantling symbols of white supremacy in court houses, schools, and public spaces. Finally in July of 2021, nearly four years after white supremacists marched on the University of Virginia's campus, occupied downtown Charlottesville, and killed Heather Heyer, the monument at the heart of the conflict was removed.

When we began ruminating on the playful aesthetic of THICK for the fifteenth issue of LUNCH, we couldn't have imagined what we would experience together over the next year. But our contributors offered us a beautiful breadth of ways to think through this time and its thickness and thinness as it waxed and waned. Thickness isn't always the goal. In fact, "You need thin. Thickness all the time would be exhausting," as Garnette Cadogan reminded us. Sometimes thinness just is. It can't or won't thicken, but in its own stubbornness, the strands that bind us together bend and give with flexibility and the strength of many.

Dear reader, we've been through it; through thicket and thin wood. But we're still not out of the woods. Through thick and thin, slice the bread so there's more to go around, even if it means we each get less. Neither are easy, but since when has anything worth doing been easy?

Yours through thick and thin,
Ben Small, Colleen Brennan, & Leah Kahler

PLACES

MATERIALS

REPRESENTATION

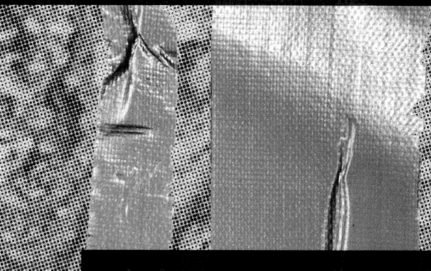

RELATIONS

PLACES

A THICK DESCRIPTION OF THE SCHOOL OF ARCHITECTURE
A Case for Turning

ALISSA UJIE DIAMOND

This piece begins with questions arising from the School's celebrations around the 100th Anniversary of its founding in 1919. Unmentioned in this year's laudatory missives was the fact that in 1919, Paul Goodloe McIntire, a wealthy local man and "philanthropist," most infamously known for the donation and installation of many statues featuring explicitly racist imagery, provided the funds to found the School of Art, the precursor institution to today's School of Architecture.[1] Philanthropy derives from a Greek origin: philanthropos,[2] translating to man-loving, which in this case describes a particular kind of love that Black spatial scholars like Sylvia Wynter, Katherine McKittrick,[3] and others[4] critique. Wynter states that these projects of producing the "ideal man" served to:

> invent, label, and institutionalize the indigenous peoples of the Americas as well as the transported enslaved Black Africans as the physical referent of the projected irrational/ subrational Human Other to its civic-humanist rational self-conception.[5]

She calls this figure Man2, replacing a racialized religious ideal of human perfection (Man1) with a scientific one. These ideological projects used emerging "scientific" and "rational" logics to produce the tropes of the racialized "Others" necessary for the project of imperial-industrial modernity. These ideologies used modern science as the new unquestionable, greater-than-human Truth. Many mainstream thinkers of the time used this bulwark to hide constructed racial-political systems behind a curtain of scientific expertise and physical "proof."

Within architectural and spatial discourse today, many scholars call for a turning, both towards a reckoning with the fraught legacies of architecture's role in producing racial hierarchies,[6] and a recovery of spatial practices that have undergone erasure in mainstream design practice and pedagogy.[7]

This piece prods one avenue for historically grounded "turning," through a thick description of the institutional history of the School of Architecture. My writing reflects my experiences as an undergraduate architecture student, a graduate landscape architecture student, a local alumna, an instructor in the school, and now a PhD candidate in the Constructed Environment. I've put experiential accounts in *italics*, to show how I have lived the culture and history of the School.

FOURTH YEAR UNDERGRADUATE STUDIO, FEBRUARY 2002

*I've spent four years strategizing about bathrooms. If I wait until class change, the line is so long. I'm reviewing Campbell Hall as-built drawings for studio. Campbell went up in 1970, the first year that UVA became fully co-educational, but the studios still have the original bathroom layou*t (Fig. 1).

An informal straw poll: men never worry about timing their restroom visits. The building was made for them, even though the explicit messaging of the school insists that I am welcome. This same semester, I go to a "medallion party" organized by my friends. I go dressed as "Asian Flava Flav." I wear a Chairman Mao alarm clock around my neck and dance, poking "fun" at my own ancestry. While we do not yet realize I am echoing a long tradition of racial minstrelsy[8] in Virginia (Fig. 2).

UVA SARC + THE CULT OF THE PERFECT MAN

University of Virginia, well before the establishment of the School of Art in 1919, was highly imbricated in racializing cultural currents at multiple scales. Nationally, during the late nineteenth century, post-bellum world's fairs had tremendous influence on the design fields. These events provided a vision of the past, present, and future that served the goals of American imperial capitalism. Robert Rydell argues that these events, which drew over 100 million people between 1876 and 1916, provided a model of orchestrated heterogeneity,

> "inseparable from the larger constellation of ideas about race, nationality, and progress…[They were] ideologically coherent 'symbolic universes' confirming and extending the authority of the country's corporate, political, and scientific leadership."[9]

Designers translated and elaborated the principles explored in world's fair planning in many American cities during the course of the City

Fig. 1 *(opposite, top) Campbell Hall third Floor Studio Restroom Layout per as-built drawings, annotation of restrooms added by author.*

Fig. 2 *(opposite, bottom) Blackface (1920s) with inset of detail of attendees in blackface, and yellowface (1956) at UVA's Beaux Arts Balls.*

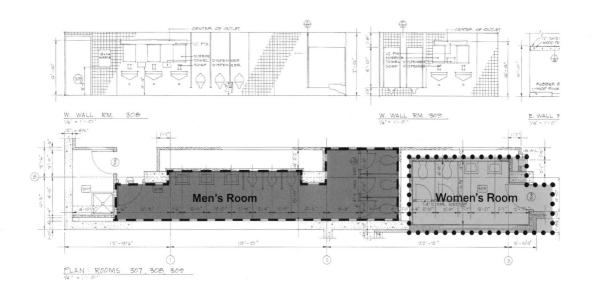

CENTER OF OUTLET

LT. FIX
MIRROR
TOWEL DISPENSER
SOAP DISPENSER

W. WALL RM. 308
1/4" = 1'-0"

CENTER OF OUTLET

LT. FIX
MIRROR
TOWEL DISPENSER
SOAP DISPENSER

W. WALL RM. 309
1/4" = 1'-0"

E. WALL F
1/4" = 1'-0"

Men's Room

Women's Room

PLAN : ROOMS 307, 308, 309
1/4" = 1'-0"

THE SCHOOL OF
ARCHITECTURE

Beautiful Movement, based on the physical forms of monumentality, axiality, racial-spatial segregation, and Neoclassical architecture. At these fairs, the "perfect" architectural form was deeply connected to an idea of the "perfect" body, and those not "fit" were marked for either progress or extinction. These fairs often included athletic events, like Olympic games, demonstrating that "sports and anthropology were nodes in an interconnected network united by a shared ideology of civilizational progress,"[10] and these ideologies spread through the men that orchestrated fairs. William A. Lambeth, later Superintendent of Grounds at UVA beginning in 1905, served first as the Vice President of the Department of Physical Education at the 1893 world's fair.[11] A director of one fair noted:

> human culture is becoming unified, not only through diffusion but through the extinction of the lower grades...white and strong are synonymous terms.[12]

The fair designers juxtaposed this image of the white, European-descended "perfected" man with carefully designed ethnographic exhibits housing "savage" non-white people in areas outside the neoclassical "white cities," giving palpable form to developing ideologies of anti-Blackness based in social Darwinism. At the same time, sporting events supposedly "measured" human difference and performance.

Social and architectural developments in Charlottesville were bound up in these larger trends, but also embedded in the political projects of the post-bellum South, especially through the figure of Thomas Jefferson. At the time, Jefferson was "at best a 'forgotten man,' at worst, a scoundrel in the public mind" nationally,[13] but Democratic politicians throughout the late nineteenth century and early twentieth century began to recognize the utility of Jefferson's image to bridge regional sectarian and class divides within potential constituents: "to hold together factions: northern and southern, urban and rural, nativist and immigrant."[14] Historian Nell Painter terms this formation the second enlargement of American whiteness, when German and Irish European immigrants and their descendants were ushered into the ranks of American white identity.[15]

Jefferson's historic role as designer of UVA's Academical Village resonated strongly both with the Neoclassical iconography of fairs and with emerging narratives of Pan-European identity as tied to American "greatness." Daniel Bluestone notes that in the wake of the destruction and economic stagnation following the Civil War, Virginia leaders aimed to reassert the state's primacy in an emerging national narrative of historicity and progress represented architecturally in National Fairs.[16]

Connecting to the emerging cult of founding father worship through local association with Jeffersonian architecture served this purpose for Charlottesville. The University of Virginia, before the establishment of the School of Art, was highly entangled with these dynamics, and campus development in the late nineteenth century evidences these connections. In 1893, the year of the famed Chicago Columbian Exposition, UVA built philanthropically funded Fayerweather Hall as its new gymnasium. The architect of the building Kevan Peebles expounded on his connections to both the classical architectural traditions that were selectively chosen by enlightenment-era humanists like Thomas Jefferson, and the contemporary grandeur of world's fair architecture.[17]

The building, in its form and daily use as a gymnasium (Fig. 3), gave institutional and physical form to ideologies connecting the "ideal" man, neoclassical architecture, and physical and cultural evaluations of human "fitness."[18] Further, Peebles' other work, including an unbuilt triumphal arc to Confederacy (Fig. 4), designed for the south end of the Academical Village, evidences his stake in Lost Cause narrative North/South cultural bridging through architectural form.
Later influential figures in UVA's campus development further

Fig. 3
Physical perfection (Gymnastics Team) and architectural perfection (Fayerweather Hall) pictured together.

Fig. 4
Proposed Memorial Arch to the Confederacy from Corks and Curls 1895.

elaborated the ideology of Jefferson, and ideas of human 'fitness' that spanned built and human physical form. William A. Lambeth, as building and grounds superintendent from 1905, used Jefferson as a founding figure for the fledgling profession of American architecture: "acknowledge him as the pioneer in an infant profession, and with one acclaim hail the Godfather of the American Architect."[20] Lambeth's interests also spanned to sports, as he developed the budding athletic program at UVA.[21] In 1915, UVA President Edwin Alderman called for the establishment of a department of art and architecture.[22] Sociologists note that at this time, the design fields were narrowing recognized expertise to those in racial, economic, and gendered power:

> the need for standardized credentials kept those who were socially marginalized from professional rank, their adoption as the basis for entry to a profession can be understood as an acquisition of social power... by keeping the 'irregulars' out of competition...(women and amateur gardeners in landscape architecture [not to mention racial minorities]), a controlled base of operation could be delineated, and power firmly established over not only the market, but also over the production of future professionals.[23]

In this way as well, the fields' originators built the design fields to consolidate their own power through exclusion of rival forms of spatial knowledge. In 1919, Paul Goodloe McIntire donated $155,000, and UVA hailed him as the founder of the School of Fine Arts.[24] McIntire is best known for his other donations: Stonewall

Jackson, Robert E. Lee, and other statues. But this endowment of the school, well before his donation of any physical statues, and before his donation to establish the McIntire School of Business show the centrality of art, spatial practice, and aesthetics in the project of city building. Journalists of the time focused on his selfless love of art and aesthetics gained from his travels in Italy.[25] Later scholars, however, point out that he was likely also influenced by the reach and rhetoric of world's fairs, having lived and worked in Chicago during the 1893 World Columbian Exposition.[26] McIntire's donations across the city reveal a racialized agenda made physical through design:

> City Beautiful aesthetic vision merged seamlessly with a dominant racial ideology...The pattern of racial separation in McIntire's provision of public [facilities]...lends credence to the idea that improvements...supported the white ideals of racial separation in the structure and embellishment of the civic landscape.[27]

Local coverage of donations in the period show that McIntire was not the only philanthropic interest on the scene. Campus development at UVA attracted the agglomerated donations of businesses, white supremacist organizations, and regional cultural institutions. In 1921, President Alderman accepted monetary pledges from three entities: the youngest descendant of Thomas Jefferson represented by his father; a rector at a Roanoke, Virginia, church; J.P. Morgan; and the Ku Klux Klan.[28] That Centennial fund paid for Memorial Gymnasium, whose construction allowed architectural education to move into Fayerweather Hall.

In terms of curriculum, most of the UVA School of Architecture's early faculty trained in the Beaux-Arts curricular model, adapted from the Ecole de Beaux-Arts in Paris. UVA used this curriculum into the early 1950s.[29] The system's French-derived terms, including *charette*, *parti*, and others still appear in design studios today. Other aspects of this system of training have fallen away, but reveal the imbrication of design curriculum in the creation of particular human hierarchies. Advanced students were Class "A," and more novice students were "Class "B." Beginner students were required to do rendering and other work for advanced students, and this practice went by the verb form of a racial epithet: n***ering. Mirroring paternalist justifications for racialized labor exploitation in societal discourse, design textbooks of the time insisted this type of unpaid work was "good" for younger students: "Do not think that 'n***ering' is doing a favor for someone else. The good in it is largely to you..."[30]

SECOND YEAR UNDERGRADUATE, FEBRUARY 2000

It's my first year of studio. The students tell me: "The Architecture School...those kids never sleep." My professor told me to rest, but in the same breath gave me a long list of deliverables, and I can do it. I can't remember when I last slept, and I just realized I'm hallucinating. As I call for a ride home, I see that my eyelashes have fallen out, leaving a hairy smile on my index finger.

As late as 1978, architect James Stirling reflected on his Beaux-Arts training alongside Colin Rowe, and his desires during studio reviews in the late 1970s:

> Colin Rowe and I have fantasized quite often on the making of a conversation along these lines at the rarefied revues [sic] at Yale or Harvard. Would we dare ask a bad project student, 'Couldn't you get any n***ers to help you?'[31]

As a person who has been assigned readings by Colin Rowe in multiple design theory courses, I was surprised by this statement, which evidences unspoken aspects of the inertial exclusivity of design culture, and the persistence of older models for design processes. First, the prod at "bad" students betrays the ongoing alignment of racial and gendered ideologies and who "counts" as an architect. Why did you fail? Because you couldn't master others.

Our design precedents are imperial models: Hadrian's Villa, Palladio's works, and their Jeffersonian legacies, baked into contemporary perspectives on "good" urbanism and design. We are still working toward an incredibly specific "universal" ideal: a newly re-digested set of slightly broadened histories of the powerful applied to today's spaces. Second, the jest insists we must be as productive as a plantation master's operation. These attitudes persist today in the idea that one must work at an ever-faster pace, be ever more productive, and sacrifice self and communal care to enable the "excellence" of a design product. These histories show up in our lives and educations every day, in myriad ways varying with positionalities of the people engaging with this institution.

ON LEAVE FROM LANDSCAPE ARCHITECTURE, MARCH 2016

I'm on maternity leave with my second child. I grew up in Lexington, Virginia, the "Shrine of the South." Images of Confederates are like wallpaper to me, I've seen them my whole life, and I no longer think much of it Fig. 5). Fifteen-year-old high school activist Zyahna Bryant's letter to Charlottesville's city council snaps me out of it:

> *When I think of Robert E. Lee I instantly think of someone fighting in favor of slavery. Thoughts of physical harm, cruelty, and disenfranchisement flood my mind. As a teenager in Charlottesville that identifies as black I am offended every time I pass it. I am reminded over and over again of the pain of my ancestors and all of the fighting that they had to go through for us to be where we are now. Quite frankly I am disgusted with the selective display of history in this city. There is more to Charlottesville than just the memories of Confederate fighters.*[32]

BEGINNING WITH QUESTIONS, TURNING TOWARD THE DIFFICULT

As an undergraduate who entered the UVA architecture program in 1998, I walked daily to class. Having grown up in central Virginia, UVA echoed the spaces where I grew up: elite, white, eternal institutions. But this fall I encounter Jeffery Hantman's Monacan Millennium, where he observes that indigenous people have continuously inhabited the region encompassing Charlottesville for at least 10,000 years.[33] The 400 years of "permanent" European colonization of this land amounts to at most a mere four hundredths of the time human societies have interacted with this place. The buildings I see are a recent crust over a living social system that reaches across countless generations.

Fig. 5 *(left)*
The Author (right) and her Father and Sister at Lee Chapel at Washington and Lee University, 1989.

As our school passes its first centennial, we have choices about what we turn toward. We must engage our fraught histories to frame future questions, to understand where we come from and where we want to go. Will we stay on the incredibly specific, invented, and exclusive historical trajectories that are given to us based on the historical sediments of institutional design culture? What questions would we need to ask to turn in productive directions that undermine rather than reinforce imbalances of power? How can we examine the histories of our everyday spaces in ways that reveal ongoing construction of the highly specific "universal" systems we take for granted? And in exploring these histories, can we explore ways of living more fully in relationship to our pasts, our presents, our futures, and each other? Could we destabilize our notions of what space is, whom it is for, whom it belongs to, and what it should become?

ALISSA UJIE DIAMOND
Alissa Ujie Diamond, PLA, is a landscape architect and a PhD candidate in the Constructed Environment program at the University of Virginia. Her research concerns race, space, and capitalisms in Central Virginia.

Notes

1 John S. Patton, "Paul Goodloe McIntire, 79, Founder of the School of Fine Arts," University of Virginia Alumni News, April 1919, 182–84.

2 "Philanthropy | Definition of Philanthropy by Lexico," accessed November 7, 2019.

3 Katherine McKittrick, ed., *Sylvia Wynter: On Being Human as Praxis* (Durham: Duke University Press, 2015), 281.

4 Cedric J. Robinson, *Black Marxism: The Making of the Black Radical Tradition* (Chapel Hill, N.C: University of North Carolina Press, 2000); Edward W. Said, *Orientalism, 1st Vintage Books ed.* (New York: Vintage Books, 1979); Alexander G. Weheliye, *Habeas Viscus: Racializing Assemblages, Biopolitics, and Black Feminist Theories of the Human* (Durham: Duke University Press, 2014).

5 Sylvia Wynter, "Unsettling the Coloniality of Being/Power/Truth/Freedom: Towards the Human, After Man, Its Overrepresentation-An Argument," CR: The New Centennial Review 3, no. 3 (n.d.): 281.

6 Lesley Naa Norle Lokko, "Introduction," in *White Paper: Black Marks* (Minneapolis: University of Minnesota Press, 2000); Mabel O Wilson, "Dancing in the Dark: The Inscription of Blackness in Le Corbusier's Radiant City," in *Places through the Body*, ed. Heidi J. Nast and Steve Pile (New York: Routledge, 1998), 133–52.

7 George Lipsitz, "The Racialization of Space and the Spatialization of Race," Landscape Journal 26, no. 1–07 (2007); J. T. Roane, "Plotting the Black Commons," Souls, January 2, 2019, 1–28, https://doi.org/10.1080/109999 49.2018.1532757; Craig L. Wilkins, *The Aesthetics of Equity: Notes on Race, Space, Architecture, and Music* (Minneapolis: University of Minnesota Press, 2007).

8 While I do not thoroughly engage the topic of racial minstrelsy and its centrality in Virginia's culture in this piece beyond this anecdote, further reading: Rhae Lynn Barnes, "The Troubling History behind Ralph Northam's Blackface Klan Photo - The Washington Post," The Washington Post, February 2, 2019, https://www.washingtonpost.com/outlook/2019/02/02/troubling-history-behind-ralph-northams-blackface-klan-photo.

9 Robert W. Rydell, *All the World's a Fair: Visions of Empire at American International Expositions, 1876–1916*, Paperback ed (Chicago: Univ. of Chicago Press, 1987).

10 Susan Brownell, ed., *The 1904 Anthropology Days and Olympic Games: Sport, Race, and American Imperialism, Critical Studies in the History of Anthropology* (Lincoln: University of Nebraska Press, 2008),19.

11 Lyon G. Tyler, *Men of Mark in Virginia*, vol. 5 (Washington, DC: Men of Mark Publishing Company, 1909), 250.

12. Robert W. Rydell, All the World's a Fair: Visions of Empire at American International Expositions, 1876–1916, Paperback ed (Chicago: Univ. of Chicago Press, 1987), 161.

13 Patricia West, *Domesticating History: The Political Origins of America's House Museums* (Washington, [D.C.]: Smithsonian Institution Press, 1999), 112.

14 Ibid., 103.

Notes

15 Nell Irvin Painter, *The History of White People* (New York: W.W. Norton, 2011).

16 Daniel M. Bluestone, *Buildings, Landscapes, and Memory: Case Studies in Historic Preservation*, 1st ed. (New York: W.W. Norton & Co, 2011), 44-45.

17 John Kevan Peebles, "Thomas Jefferson, Architect," The Alumni News Bulletin, May 15, 1894.

18 For more on the connections between physical fitness, anthropology, evolutionary theory, and scientific racism, see Susan Brownell, ed., *The 1904 Anthropology Days and Olympic Games: Sport, Race, and American Imperialism, Critical Studies in the History of Anthropology* (Lincoln: University of Nebraska Press, 2008). For the connections between fatphobia and white supremacy, *Fearing the Black Body: The Racial Origins of Fat Phobia* (New York: New York University Press, 2019).

19 "The Romantic Picturesque," *From Village to Grounds; Architecture after Jefferson at the University of Virginia*, University of Virginia Library, 2009, https://explore.lib.virginia.edu/exhibits/show/architecture-after-jefferson/the-romantic-picturesque/9.

20 W. A Lambeth and Warren H Manning, *Thomas Jefferson as an Architect and a Designer of Landscapes* (Boston, New York: Houghton Mifflin Company, 1913), 95.

21 Lyon G. Tyler, *Men of Mark in Virginia*, vol. 5 (Washington, DC: Men of Mark Publishing Company, 1909), 250.

22 Edward K Lay and Boyd Coons, "The Early Years of Architectural Education at the University Part I," Collonade: The Newsjournal of the UVA School of Architecture, 1988.

23 Timothy C. Baird and Bonj Szczygiel, "The Sociology of Professions: The Evolution of Landscape Architecture in the United States.," Landscape Review 12, no. 1 (2007): 6.

24 John S Patton, "Paul Goodloe McIntire, 79, Founder of the School of Fine Arts," University of Virginia Alumni News, April 1919, 182–84.

25 Ibid., 183.

26 Daniel M. Bluestone, *Buildings, Landscapes, and Memory: Case Studies in Historic Preservation*, 1st ed. (New York: W.W. Norton & Co, 2011), 222.

27 Ibid, 223.

28 "Several Gifts to University," Daily Progress, March 23, 1921.

29 Edward K Lay and Boyd Coons, "The Early Years of Architectural Education at the University Part II," Colonnade: The Newsjournal of the UVA School of Architecture, Winter 1989.

30 John F Harbeson, *The Study of Architectural Design, with Special Referrence to the Program of the Beaux-Arts Institute of Design,* vol. 1926 (New York: The Pencil Points Press, 1926), 177.

31 James Stirling, "Beaux-Arts Reflections," Architectural Design 48, no. 10–11 (1978): 88.

32 Zyahna Bryant, "Petition, Charlottesville City Council: Change the Name of Lee Park and Remove the Statue in Charlottesville, Va, Change.Org," 2016, www.change.org/p/charlottesville-city-council-change-the-name-of-lee-park-and-remove-the-statue-in-charlottesville-va.

33 Jeffrey L. Hantman, *Monacan Millennium: A Collaborative Archaeology and History of a Virginia Indian People* (Charlottesville: University of Virginia Press, 2018).

Figure Credits

Figure 1 Campbell Hall 3rd Floor Studio Restroom Layout per As-Built Drawings, annotation of restrooms added by author.

Rawlings and Wilson Architects, Pietro Belluschi, and Kenneth Demay of Sasaki, Dawson, Demay Associates, Inc., "Fine Arts Center Phase 1," Charlottesville, VA, As-built drawings January 15, 1970. Base files courtesy of UVA Facilities Management.

Figure 2 Blackface (1920s) with inset of detail of attendees in blackface, and Yellowface (1956) at UVA's Beaux Arts Balls. Ruth Severn Smith of the Daily Progress published the lower image after Governor Ralph Northam's blackface scandal in 2019.

Top image: Beaux Arts Ball at University of Virginia, Nonprojected Graphic (Charlottesville, VA: University of Virginia Library, n.d.), https://search.lib. virginia.edu/catalog/uva-lib:2160625.

Bottom Image: 1956 UVA Corks and Curls yearbook.

Ruth Severn Smith's article: Ruth Severn Smith, "UVa Yearbooks in 1920s, 1950s Feature Depictions of Blackface, KKK," February 27, 2019, www. roanoke.com/news/education/uva-yearbooks-in-1920s-1950s-feature-depictions-of-blackface-kkk/article_03b7b65e-b27d-5d84-b00b-9095896fc349.

Figure 3 Physical perfection (Gymnastics Team) and architectural perfection (Fayerweather Hall) pictured together.

Rufus W. Holsinger, "Gymnastics Team University of Virginia," 1913. Special Collections at University of Virginia.

Figure 4 Proposed Memorial Arch to the Confederacy from Corks and Curls 1895. Carpenter and Peebles, Architects, "Proposed Memorial Arch to the Confederacy" from Corks and Curls, 1895, illustration by T. McK. Sharpe.

Figure 5 The Author (right) and her Father and Sister at Lee Chapel at Washington and Lee University, 1989. Alissa Ujie Diamond, 1989.

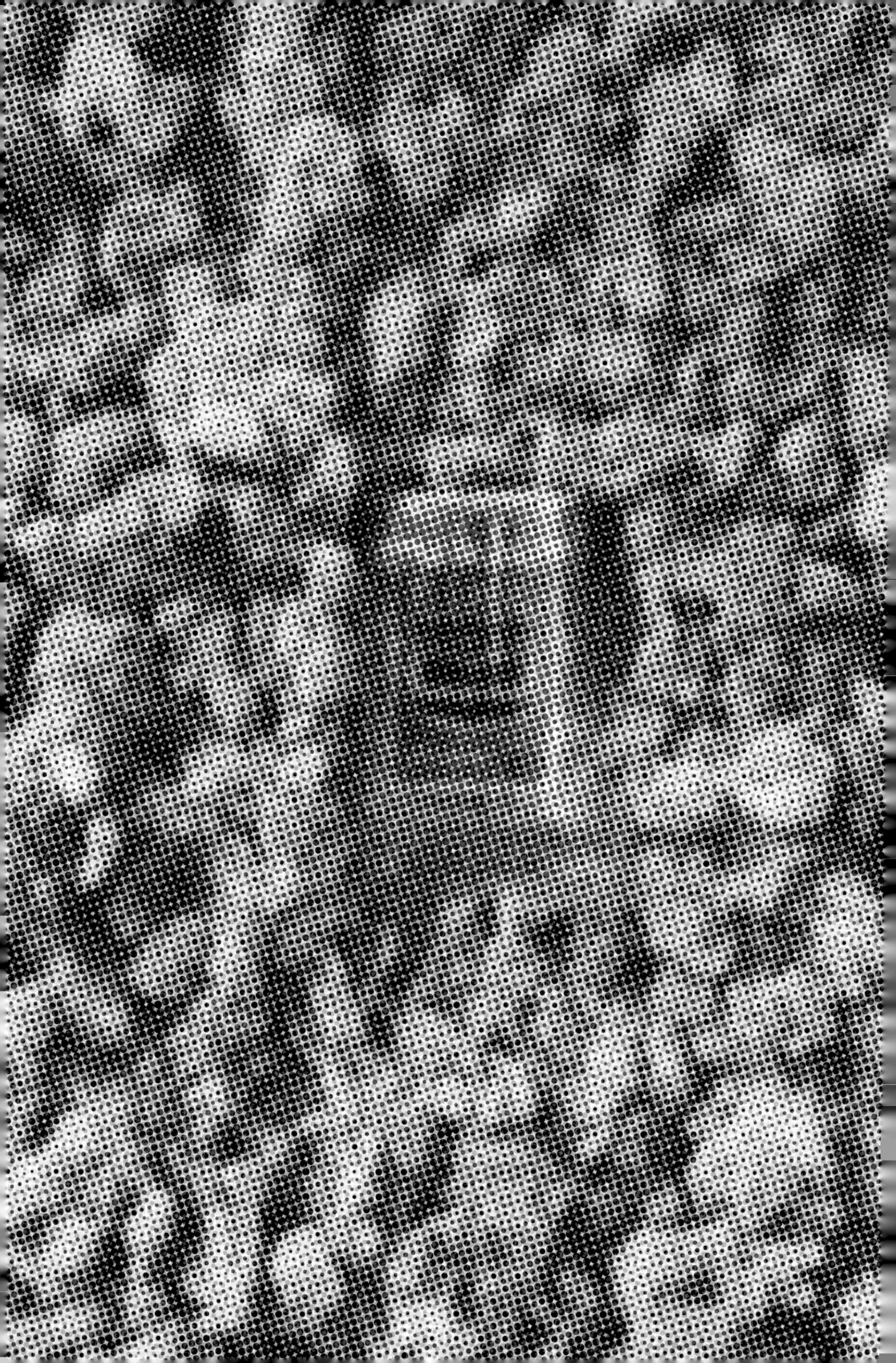

NO MUSS, NO FUSS

Erin Besler & Ian Besler

What follows is a selection of excerpts from our ongoing project, Best Practices, which examines how contemporary issues of agency and authority impact the design of the built environment. Using Los Angeles as a case study, and drawing on the history of architecture, design, media theory, and cultural anthropology, Best Practices pairs photographic documentation with text and citations to define a territory between the sanctioned and the unsanctioned, the tasteful and the tacky, the novel and the nonsense, and asserts that interest, knowledge, and meaning are more often generated on the lines that divide such categories. In visually cataloging the endearing and enigmatic ways in which the built environment takes shape, the project proposes a new way of thinking about neighborhoods, housing, streetscapes, and storefronts, not so much as places defined by regulations and dimensions, but as assemblages of impromptu interventions by advocating for a more thorough consideration of how meaning is constructed in contemporary urban spaces by looking at the messy relationships between building materials, signage systems, communication equipment, plant life, and people.

Extrusions By SketchUp[1]

Uncanny valley²

Trompe l'fire marshal[3]

Helpful labeling[4]

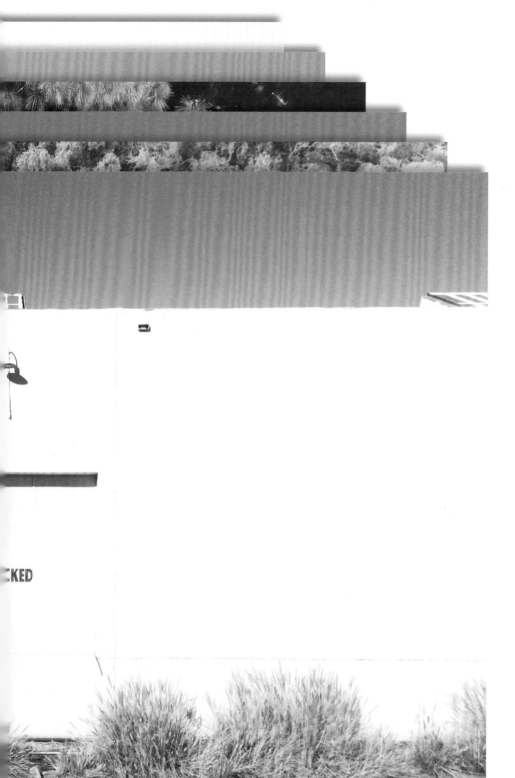

Charismatic megaflora[5]

Camouflage-ish[7]

Rubberneckers[8]

"House"[9]

Notes

1 Los Angeles is replete with buildings that embody the formal qualities of digital models created with SketchUp software, which is available for free online and primarily marketed to amateur, rather than professional, practitioners. This visual association, of course, has nothing to do with the design or fabrication of these buildings (presumably the vast majority of buildings in the world have never existed as digital models, at least not as part of the design process, but rather, were likely planned to the minimum degree specified by local building codes). The "SketchUp look" is characterized by unorthodox relationships between proportions and surface treatments, as if imagined and iterated exclusively on the screen of a small laptop computer. Perhaps a canonical exemplar of the "SketchUp look" can be found in architect Rafael Viñoly's 432 Park Avenue tower, completed in 2015. The overall proportions are uncomfortably narrow and tall,* and the enormous and unarticulated window openings only emphasize the sense of visual discord: As if a low-resolution rendering for a tower was suddenly dropped into place at the edge of Central Park.

*Note: 432 Park Avenue is currently among the first results that return in an internet search for the phrase 'Pencil Building.'

2 The unending charm of Masahiro Mori's term* is in the poetically evocative tint that it casts on what could have otherwise been an obtuse and dispassionate observation. Pointing out that there's a varying degree of creepiness to things that seem to reproduce facial expressions, postures, and gestures (such as robots, androids, or other automata) isn't especially novel, but to articulate it with a level of precision and a terminology that so strikingly expresses both an emotion and a place is what elevates the label and embeds it indelibly in the imagination; it's a term that can't be unheard, or unremembered. Rather than simply describing the relationships of two values on a coordinate plane (the "valley" derives from the graph that accompanies Mori's article describing the phenomenon), it brings to mind a haunting and hazy emotion tied to some specific destination and experience; The Uncanny Valley sounds like a setting torn directly from the fabric of a dream or a distant memory. It lets the mind wander, stumbling upon the eponymous Valley on a map, like the Badlands or the Barrens, it's a place that evokes an emotion just in the evocation of its name. The staying power and provocative potential of the term leads one to imagine an entire expanded category of sensations or impressions in which representation and interactive overlay seem to have callously wandered too close to the boundary that neatly divides the real from the unreal, or the living from the inanimate. We might more appropriately start to describe ourselves as having momentarily tumbled into the Uncanny Valley when we drunkenly try to double-tap a sunset viewed through a window, or sleepily swipe-left a glossy portrait in a magazine.

*See: Masahiro Mori, "The Uncanny Valley," Energy, Vol. 7, No. 4 (1970): 33–35.

3 The quirkiest applications of prosaic interior details—such as trim plates, molding, ventilation covers, fire egress signs, and strobes—are found in transitory spaces, particularly convenience stores, airports, and fast-food chains. Conversely, places that self-consciously assert some cultural or historical novelty, like the Getty Villa, also brim with bizarre accents and fittings. In resolving surface finishes, the richest outcomes happen when the stakes are either incredibly low or delightfully high; as if attempting to render the incidental into invisibility.

4 The blunt immediacy of language in labels that are applied to buildings ("BLOCKED") seems especially reserved for points of ingress or egress.* The management company for a building in the Jewelry District in Los Angeles hangs signs across the glass entryway doors at night that read: "THIS DOOR IS CLOSED," which seems to aspire for the blunt utility of "BLOCKED," but falls amusingly short of its aim due to the absurd obviousness of the message. Anyone can see that the doors are closed just by looking at them ("THIS DOOR IS LOCKED" is probably the less ambiguous message that the management company intended to convey). As with the filler copy usually reserved for blank storefront signs, it's interesting to imagine the other uses to which this kind of labeling could be applied, or to imagine a cityscape cluttered with equal amounts of labeling and building. Such graphic applications start to turn buildings themselves into signs, billboards, and diagrams, in a way confusing the distinction between the plan and the built object.

*See, for instance: "ENTER" or "EXIT," "OPEN" or "CLOSED," "CAUTION" or "CUIDADO."

5 While the creeping spread of the not-quite-living "living green wall" (the name itself positively vibrates with a sense of barely repressed threat) seems to have had an out-sized impact in hotel lobbies and the occasional corporate office interior, the otherwise institutional entryway of a historic greenhouse conservatory on Chicago's West Side, of all places, strikes a discordant tone. I spent an afternoon lurking in the lobby, trying to seem nonchalant while watching with rapt fascination as a disinterested facilities member opened bag after bag of dried lichen and hot-glued it to the wall. Your vision wanders around the periphery of the surface and your eyes can so easily create the impression that you're hovering at low altitude over a charmingly even-tinted forest in a helicopter or perhaps a small prop plane. The stubborn impropriety of the fire alarm, which seems rudely unaware of its presence in disrupting the scene, can easily be redacted by closing one eye and holding up a thumb to blot-out the scale, and suddenly the forest seamlessly reemerges.

6 The digital turn in typesetting, more typically referred to as the advent of 'desktop publishing,' didn't simply reach its conclusion with the banality of holiday newsletters and "Lost Dog" signs. Like movable type and the standardization of lettering and punctuation before it, every technological shift deprives us of some nuance or irreproducible quirk in the interest of convenience. If the mood struck them, people used to simply make up their own punctuation marks when they had pen and paper to work with! The implications for the built environment, how our neighborhoods and streetscapes look and feel, continue to reflect and synthesize the outsize influence of those moments in the '80s and '90s when the palette of letterforms started to become locked-in: perhaps starting with the typeface Chicago in Apple systems, and expanding to include dreary storefront evocations set unimaginatively in Helvetica, Mistral, Copperplate, and other charmless palettes of letterforms. Cooper is the only one with any redeeming character to speak of, and typically the ludicrously inept are the only signs worth noticing. There's a dentist office down the street that decided to imitate the Coca-Cola lettering and ribbon in their signage for God only knows what reason: the words "Dental Implants" written out in loopy curves and swoops. Occasionally, while looking at historic photography, you might notice the tender care and character evident in hand-painted advertising murals and other signs prior to rapid reproduction.* With digital lettering in retail signage today, it seems like the only marks of distinction come from the incomprehensible choices.

*Note: Some technical schools still offer sign-painting classes, and inevitably the school building itself becomes the display surface for the classes' efforts: Ever the selfless martyr, the building is offered-up in the interest of educational development.

7 Like Ecce Homo (c. 1930)* or "Ecce Mono,"† the fresco in Borja that was woefully altered, with hilarious consequences, in a good faith attempt at amateur art restoration by Cecilia Giménez in 2012 (what the church diplomatically referred to as "una intervención" on her behalf‡), camouflage also seems like a completely reasonable goal for an amateur painting "intervention." One can't help but feel sympathy for the custom automotive painter responsible; what makes the project seem so easy is what simultaneously makes the final outcome so vulnerable to scrutiny, because camouflage is both vague and specific. We all recognize camouflage immediately when we see it, but particularly so when it's poorly executed. Judging from the repetition of the forms, the alterations here seem to have been accomplished with a stencil, but a stencil of what exactly?

*See: Elías García Martínez, Ecce Homo (c. 1930), Santuario la Misericordia, Borja, Spain.

†See: Cecilia Giménez, Untitled ("Ecce Mono"), Aug. 25, 2012, Santuario de Misericordia, Borja, Spain.

‡See: "Un hecho incalificable," Centro de Estudios Borjanos, Institución Fernando el Católico (Aug. 7, 2012) [http://cesbor.blogspot.com.es/2012/08/un-hecho-incalificable.html].

8 The satellite dish on the side of the building is so incredibly prosaic, yet the satellite in orbit is so extraordinarily surreal. Is there any greater odd couple in the built landscape than the dish and the satellite? But then again, aren't these types of odd couplings just what globalization is best at achieving? Something so massive and abstract distilled down to something so unremarkable? A piece of out-of-season produce or a cheap t-shirt in itself isn't extraordinary, but the production and circulation of capital and resources that they represent is downright miraculous, if not perverse. At every moment of contemporary life we're thrust into contact with forces and phenomena that so vastly outscale us. But the points of contact that mediate the relationship are so inane: monotonous aisles of products, fluorescent lights, store shelving, or a gaggle of aluminum parabolas staring dumbly into outer space.

9 As with any act of modeling and depiction, choices have to be made regarding accuracy and fidelity in relation to the source material, evidenced here in a mock-up of a residential house exterior, used for practice by ConEd employees. So, while the vinyl siding, soffit, and conduit remain roughly true to scale, the roof, gable, and depth of the structure itself have each been shrunken, resulting in a bizarrely mis-proportioned building, which feels otherwise insistently recognizable and stubbornly bland. It's a sort of "austerity" version of the iconic shape of a home, where certain dimensions are accurate, but others appear strangely stretched and skewed like a JPEG image that's circulated one too many times across screenshots, social media platforms, and devices—it's starting to show the sum of every little transfiguration. The fussy attention to detail, evident in the choice of siding, trim, and the single-hung window is incredibly endearing, as if to say that the depth of a structure is simply an optional variable, but cladding details are specially privileged in the interest of depiction and simulation. It's an icon of a house. A simple graphic logo. But somebody misread the icon, mistaking it for a plan, and then they built the logo to scale.

ERIN BESLER

Erin Besler (they/them/theirs) was born in Chicago, Illinois. They are an Assistant Professor of Architecture at Princeton University School of Architecture.

IAN BESLER

Ian Besler (he/him/his) is a designer, educator, and writer whose work is situated at the edges between interfaces, media, software, and cities.

DESIGNING DECOMMISSION
Plum Island, New York

Chloé Skye Nagraj

Plum Island in the Long Island Sound is, as islands go, more inaccessible than most. The famously opaque identity of the 840-acre island is thanks to the Plum Island Animal Disease Center (PIADC), operated by the Department of Agriculture since 1954 and since 2001, the Department of Homeland Security. The Montauk Monster is said to have originated here. Lyme disease truthers are adamant that the tick-borne illness was created and intentionally spread by a tick lab (the existence of which is unconfirmed) at PIADC. Clarice Starling offers Hannibal Lecter's transfer to Plum Island in exchange for information on Buffalo Bill in Silence of the Lambs, to which he responds, "Plum Island Animal Disease Center. Sounds charming." Its shape even mildly resembles a question mark (Fig. 1).

What we do know is this: the facilities are to be moved to a site in Manhattan, Kansas, in 2022, at which point the island may be sold to the highest bidder and redeveloped, maintained as a "mothball" site by the government, or, as environmental groups are advocating, be preserved as a refuge.[1] There is widespread contamination from PIADC and military activity on the island, the true extents of which are unknown. The island is, because of its relative isolation from humans over the past 122 years, incredibly biodiverse. While the story of Plum Island seems unique, it is quintessentially American; it is a story that is typically told beginning with the genocide of Indigenous people and settlement by colonizers, one that is deeply tied to military power and government secrecy. With the decommissioning of the island potentially set for 2022, the island's future is up in the air.

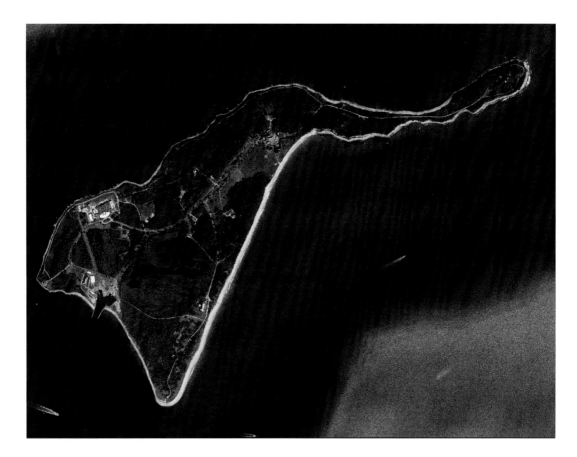

Fig. 1
Plum Island, New York.

This moment of transition can be an opportunity to reckon with the overlapping, opaque, and seemingly contradictory stories embedded in the landscape of Plum Island.

On the conversion of the former plutonium factory, Rocky Flats, into a wildlife preserve, Shiloh Krupar writes, "ambiguity is what must be explored to contest routinized recitations of evidence and established truths." How can ambiguity be more deeply explored through the decommissioning of Formerly Used Defense Sites [FUDS][2] like Plum Island? If decommission were to be treated as design, how might a process that makes space for ambiguity inform the often-indeterminate futures of these landscapes? Might this positioning enable us[3] to better mitigate the social impact of the entangled histories so common to these sites? There are hundreds of thousands of military and industrial sites where these questions are worth asking; Plum Island is one character within this larger national narrative.

MYTH AND HISTORY

In order to reframe decommission as design, site analysis must accommodate the unruly ways of knowing that complicate opaque landscapes. Unruliness, here, is knowing in spite of a prescribed site narrative or history; knowing in spite of inaccessibility; knowing in spite of forced removal; knowing as a radical act of interpretation. Such a relational framework is absent from the myriad environmental, historic, and economic assessments undertaken during decommissioning by the FUDS program. In the case of Plum Island, the resulting conflicts over future land use and development articulate the need for a relational understanding of site history that makes room for unruliness.

The Harbor Hill Moraine created Plum Island approximately 22,000 years ago. Thick layers of sand and gravel make up the bulk of the island, with outwash channels forming flat and fertile areas. A subsequent advance of the glacier deposited silt, sand, gravel, and glacial till to create the hilly topography of the northern end of the island, where forests and scrublands thrive. Over time, erosion carried fine sand particles to the southern end of the island, where freshwater swales, marshes, and wetlands formed as a result.[4] These varied types of outwash and glacial till created a diverse array of soils and habitats. The island has been valued by humans for millennia, due in no small part to the biodiversity stemming from its geologic formation.

The island was first known by the name Manittuwond, "the island to which we go to plant corn."[5] It was an important fishing site for Algonquian peoples of the Corchaug, Manganese, Montaukett, Shinnecock, and Pequot tribes due to the high velocity of water flowing through the narrow and deep Plum Gut.

Plum Island has long resided in the minds of imperialists and colonizers. Adriaen Block, the Dutch trader, included Plum Island in his 1614 map documenting his last voyage of the Americas, the first to represent Long Island cartographically. The data collected on this trip was used to create Willem Janszoon and Joan Blaeu's famous 1635 map Nova Belgica et Anglia Nova, which indicates Plum Island as land occupied by Matouwac/Metoac/Montaukett peoples of the Algonquian nation. Dutch colonial maps such as this laid the groundwork for the colonization that would occur later in the century (Fig. 2).

Between 1637 and 1639, Indigenous peoples used the island as a refuge for women and children as well as a safe place to grow and harvest food during the bloody Pequot War, when 800 Pequot people were killed or imprisoned. Declaring victory in 1638, colonizers declared the Pequot tribe extinct.[6] Samuel Willis III, son of the governor of Connecticut at the time, lay claim to the island in 1652, purchasing it from Wyandanch of the Montaukett tribe for a coat, a barrel of biscuits, and 100 fishhooks.[7] The island was used primarily for agriculture through the late eighteenth century.

Plum Island's military history began in 1775, during the Revolutionary War. The island was used for recreation during the mid to late

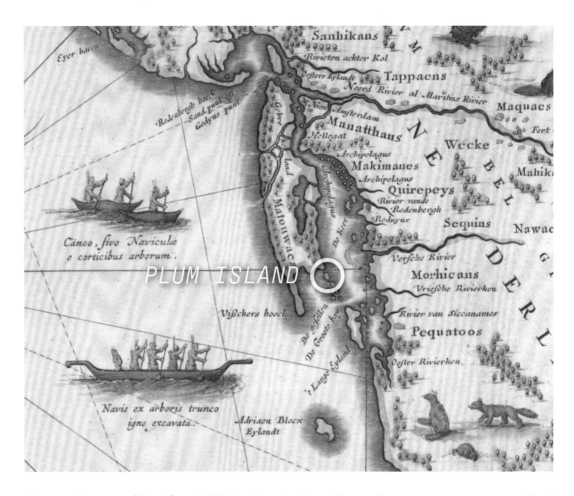

PLUM ISLAND

nineteenth century (Fig. 3) until 1898, when the Army Corps of Engineers bought 150 acres to establish Fort Terry (Fig. 4). In 1901, they bought the rest of Plum Island to defend Gardiners Bay and the Long Island Sound: from this point on, Plum Island has been largely inaccessible to private citizens. In 1952, the Army transitioned Plum Island to be used by the Chemical Corps to research germ warfare, as well as by the USDA to establish the Plum Island Animal Disease Center, a foot and mouth disease research lab (Fig. 5). The germ warfare operation was presumably shut down two years after it was announced. Unexploded ordnance, acid, and buried fuel have been uncovered and removed from Fort Terry as recently as 2005.[8]

With the establishment of many Environmental Protection Agency acts through the 1970s and 1980s, the ramifications of this research on the landscape began to be acknowledged in the early 1990s. The facility's largely unregulated waste management practices and groundwater contamination first came to light in 1993, when the EPA cited the Research Center $250,000 to determine how extensive of a cleanup would be needed. And yet, the largely undeveloped island is designated as a critical natural resource area by the Fish and Wildlife Service. It is home to regionally rare plant species and over 200 bird species, including the federally endangered Piping Plover (Fig. 6).

Fig. 3
Lighthouse keepers at
Plum Island, 1870s.
Collection of Southold
Historical Society
Southold, NY.

After September 11, Plum Island was transferred to the Department of Homeland Security, as part of its chemical, biological, radiological, and nuclear countermeasures division. In 2009, it was announced that the Plum Island research facilities would be moved to Manhattan, Kansas, in 2022, opening the door for speculation as to the island's future. Due to the upcoming closure, real estate developers, including Donald Trump, have expressed interest in the site, offering visions of golf courses, luxury waterfront properties, and mixed-use development. Environmental groups, community organizers, politicians, and preservationists have banded together to halt the sale of the island, forming the Preserve Plum Island Coalition. In December 2019, the US Senate passed a bill stating that the sale of Plum Island would be put on hold for one year until 2021.

Like many former military sites, the opacity of Plum Island has given rise to a web of mythologies. What is known, unknown, and speculative blend together depending on who you ask. Landscapes like Plum Island are known in spite of—sometimes, because of—their opacity.

Fig. 4 (above)
*New York Tribune, Training
Camp at Fort Terry, 1916.*

Fig. 5 (bottom)
*Dr. Charles Allen, Breeding
Habitats of Fish Hawks
on Plum Island, 1892.
Courtesy of The Auk.*

Fig. 6 (opposite)
*Entangled narratives
at Plum Island Animal
Disease Center: scientific
research, contamination,
and conspiracy.*

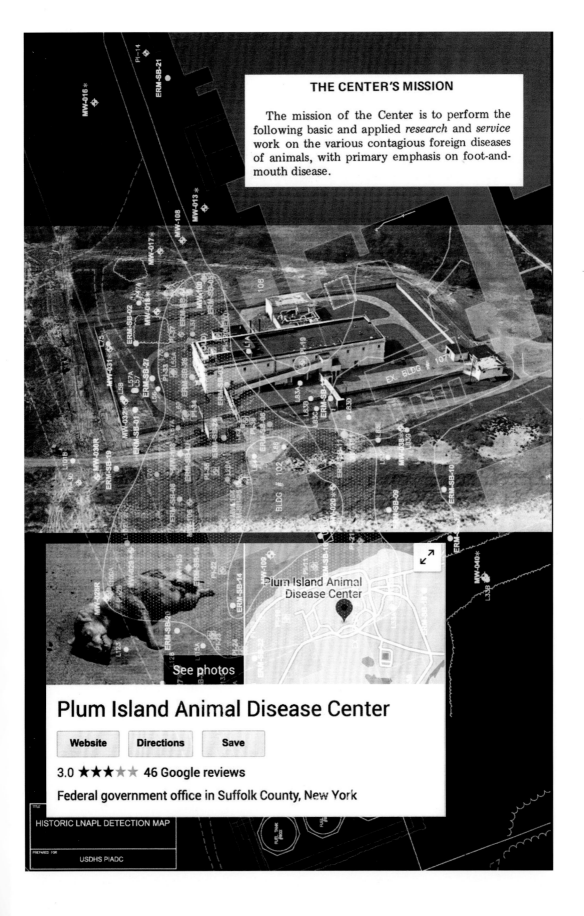

THE CENTER'S MISSION

The mission of the Center is to perform the following basic and applied *research* and *service* work on the various contagious foreign diseases of animals, with primary emphasis on foot-and-mouth disease.

See photos

Plum Island Animal Disease Center

Website   **Directions**   **Save**

3.0 ★★★★★ 46 Google reviews

Federal government office in Suffolk County, New York

HISTORIC LNAPL DETECTION MAP

PREPARED FOR
USDHS PIADC

CURRENT   1954   1930s

Tradescantia sp.

Vica faba

Remediation mix

THE MULTIPLICITY OF OPACITY

Decommissioning is a broad term that can be applied to military, nuclear, and industrial sites as well as infrastructure. To put it simply, to decommission is to take something out of service, a process that typically includes deconstruction; disarmament; and the removal, disposal, and remediation of wastes. Existing remediation technologies are intended to resolve a specific contaminant in a specific area. While these technologies are necessary, they do not address the unruly political, cultural, and perceptual entanglements also present. Opacity can conceal site contamination—it can also exacerbate suspicions of it. Actual and perceived contamination— what Jennifer Gabrys calls "the 'social imagination' of pollution"[9]— affects how landscapes are used and designed.

We have seen landscapes with similarly entangled histories emerge from decommission and redevelopment sanitized and greenwashed. No matter how much regrading, reseeding, and rebranding occur through these processes, landscape still embodies the physical traces and social stigmas of contamination and mystery (in other words, their history). For Plum Island, this moment is, as acknowledged by the community and activist groups mobilizing for its preservation, one of contestation and potential transformation.

UNRULY FUTURES

So far, the decommissioning activities that have occurred or are slated to occur on Plum Island focus on three things: analysis, removal, and treatment of waste and contamination:

> removal and disposal (including contents) of fourteen (14) open rusted 55 gallon drums (unknown contents), three (3) 55 gallon drums with unknown contents crystallized in form,

Fig. 7
Making groundwater contamination visible at Plum Island's Lab 257.

eight (8) 5 gallon drums (unknown contents) and estimated thirty one gallon cans of 3% malathion. The project also includes the removal and disposal (including contents) of abandoned one 75 KVA and two 50 KVA transformers. Removal and disposal of contents of 34 acid batteries...[and] further investigation of possible hazardous toxic waste at the former location of four (4) dump sites, motor pool, and firing range. The investigation will consist of soil augering, soil sampling, and water sampling to determine the extent of possible soil and groundwater contamination on the areas stated above.[10]

The truth is decommission is already designed. But it does not account for the sociocultural effects of operating opaque sites.

And it does not account for the material, political, and historical complexity of these landscapes. Opacity is multiplicitous. Shouldn't decommissioning—the first actionable step towards reconciling this multiplicity—take this into account?

What would an expanded decommissioning process—one that considers the sociocultural effects of military site occupation in addition to the physical—look like on Plum Island? How can this approach create a new space for design within the decommission process motivated by a relational understanding of site history?

One strategy might be to acknowledge the unknowability[11] and agency of groundwater contamination by introducing publicly accessible long-term monitoring data that is physically marked above ground (Fig. 7). When decommissioning opaque sites, it becomes much easier to flatten this complexity out of them, covering up the material entanglements[12] that continue to exist. By introducing long-term monitoring that is marked above ground, traced over time, the boundaries and bleeding over between humans and nonhumans become visible.

Rethinking preservation of the Fort Terry–era gun battery structures is another opportunity to consider a relational history of landscape through decommission. The unmaintained batteries are not on the National Register for Historic Places and have fallen into disrepair. Rather than focusing on the structures as the historical sites that deserve preservation, how could a guideline for preservation and management focus instead on geologic, climatic, non-human, and human drivers of change that have shaped the landscape? This approach would resist the knee-jerk urge to preserve or restore a snapshot, or what is traditionally perceived as "historic."

Most urgently, this approach can inform acknowledgment of Indigenous stewardship and connection to this landscape, which several Native tribes are currently advocating for (Fig. 8). Indigenous

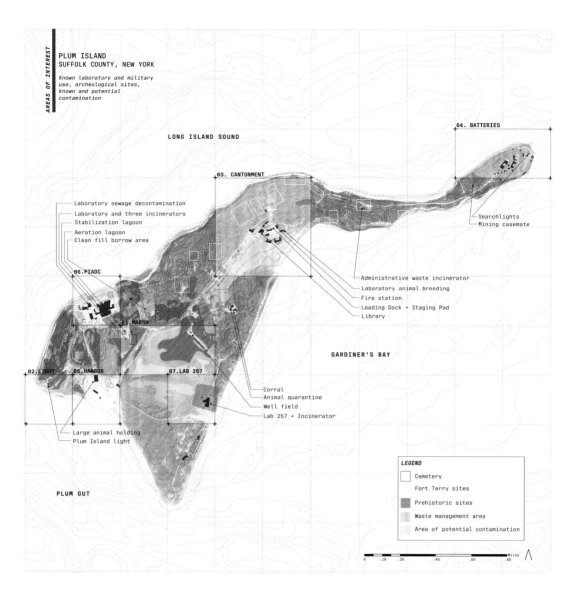

PLUM ISLAND
SUFFOLK COUNTY, NEW YORK

*Known laboratory and military
use, archeological sites,
known and potential
contamination*

LONG ISLAND SOUND

04. BATTERIES

03. CANTONMENT

Laboratory sewage decontamination
Laboratory and three incinerators
Stabilization lagoon
Aeration lagoon
Clean fill borrow area

Searchlights
Mining casemate

06.PIADC

Administrative waste incinerator
Laboratory animal breeding
Fire station
Loading Dock + Staging Pad
Library

01.MARSH

GARDINER'S BAY

02.LIGHT   05.HARBOR   07.LAB 257

Corral
Animal quarantine
Well field
Lab 257 + Incinerator

Large animal holding
Plum Island light

PLUM GUT

LEGEND

☐ Cemetery
☐ Fort Terry sites
▨ Prehistoric sites
☐ Waste management area
☐ Area of potential contamination

Miles
0   .10   .20   .40   .60   .80

stewardship should be acknowledged onsite no matter what, not if
the site becomes public. Opaque sites like Plum Island are more
often than not sites of disappropriation and injustice. Policy and land
management practices reproduce these injustices. Waste is viewed
as something that is critical to manage in the landscape through
decommission policy—disappropriation should be treated with the
same weight.

Fig. 8
*Plum Island
animation still.*

CHLOÉ SKYE NAGRAJ

*Chloé Skye Nagraj is a 2020 graduate of the University of Virginia
Master of Landscape Architecture program. She believes landscape
architects are translators of sociocultural, material, and ecological
histories and seeks to recognize these often-obscured narratives
through her research and design work.*

Notes

1 A 2012 Environmental Impact Statement prepared by the US General Services Administration and the Department of Homeland Security laid out five options for Plum Island after its public sale: a "no action alternative," which would place the island under mothball status with limited maintenance activities; and four "action alternatives" centering around redevelopment and reuse. These consist of: adaptive reuse of the existing facilities onsite, low-density zoning with ninety residential units, high-density zoning with 750 residential units, and a conservation/preservation option with the goal of managing and enhancing natural and cultural resources.

2 The FUDS program is the environmental restoration program for properties "formerly owned by, leased, or otherwise possessed" by the US Department of Defense. Established in 1986, this program is administered by the Army Corps of Engineers. There are more than 10,000 FUDS properties throughout the world.

3 "Us" being: designers, communities, consultants, academics, policymakers who are or should be involved with decommission.

4 Schlesinger, M. D., E. L. White, S. M. Young, G. J. Edinger, K. A. Perkins, N. Schoppmann, and D. Parry. Rep. *Biodiversity Inventory of Plum Island, New York*. Albany, NY: New York Natural Heritage Program and SUNY College of Environmental Science and Forestry, Syracuse, NY, 2016.

5 Bramson, Ruth Ann, Geoffrey K. Fleming, and Amy Kasuga Folk. *A World unto Itself: The Remarkable History of Plum Island*, New York. Southold Historical Society, 2014.

6 The myth of extinction of Indigenous peoples in Long Island (and throughout the US) persists today. A 1910 Suffolk County Supreme Court case ruled that the Montaukett Indians were extinct, to the shock of the many Montaukett people sitting in the court room. In 2019, Governor Andrew Cuomo vetoed the "Montaukett Indian Recognition Bill" for a third time. The bill sought to overturn the 1910 ruling. The Montaukett Indian Nation is still not recognized by New York State.

7 The validity of land transactions between settlers and Indigenous people have been studied and called into question by many Indigenous activists and scholars.

8 BMT Entech, Inc. 2005. *After Action Report: Military Battery Drain, Gun Pit, and Roadbed Sediment/Soil Removal Project, Plum Island Animal Disease Center, Suffolk County, New York.*

9 Gabrys, Jennifer. "Sink: The Dirt of Systems." *Environment and Planning D: Society and Space* 27, no. 4 (August 2009): 666–81.

10 Formerly Used Defense Sites [FUDS] Program Management Action Plan [MAP] for Plum Island, New York.

11 Matthias Gross hints at this concept of unknowability in his chapter Layered Industrial Sites: Experimental Landscapes and the Virtues of Ignorance: "These [processes] lead to many sets of nonknowledge—that is, not merely unknown unknowns (complete unknowns) but more or less clear knowledge of what is not known (e.g. it is unknown exactly what types of chemicals are in the ground, but it is known that they are there)."

12 Barad, Karen Michelle. *Meeting the Universe Halfway: Quantum Physics and the Entanglement of Matter and Meaning*. Durham: Duke University Press, 2007.

13 Paglen, Trevor. *Blank Spots On the Map: The Dark Geography of the Pentagon's Secret World*. New York: New American Library, 2010.

INDUSTRIAL THICK
Northwest Indiana & the Machined Landscape

Jonah Pruitt

Industrial history of America is inherently thick. Economy, ecology, culture, technology, geography, and our relationship with the natural world are mediated by the depth of ties and connections we have to industry. This anthropogenic reality we find ourselves in is seen in incredible fidelity in Northwest Indiana. Lake, Porter, and Laporte Counties are spiritual centers of the rust belt and at one point produced one quarter of the world's steel immediately after World War II. It is an expansive landscape made of patches of National Park, steel mills, factories, harbors, beaches, cities, dunes, towns, highways, and railroads to connect it all. The juxtaposition of these elements is complicated and born from generations of development. Northwest Indiana, my home, is also a place in flux. Industries are changing hands, industrial sites are being abandoned, and crisis after crisis has left the people who choose to remain weary. What is the future of a place where the smokestacks have long vanished?

Northwest Indiana is a region thick with meanings, borders, relationships, and layers far beyond my personal experiences. The borders between industry and the more 'natural' elements are paper thin, but the thickness of biodiversity and ecological richness of the Indiana Dunes National Park cannot be overstated. There is no buffer between conditions of industry, human occupation, and ecological space. When thinking about ways to alter this landscape in a post-carbon, climate-changed world, this line between these altered landscapes needs to expand and envelop more area.

The thickness of all these components led me to making collages.
One constructed collage for each of the main sites that dominated the
culture and economy of Northwest Indiana: Inland Steel, U.S. Steel
Garyworks, Midwest Steel, the NIPSCO Michigan City Generation
Station, and the railways that connect it all. Collages are the making
of thickness on a page, just as thickness needs to be applied to blur
the lines between the industrial and the landscape. This projective
thickness is a new understanding of a future where the industries of
yesterday provide a backdrop for new kinds of experiences, parks,
infrastructures, lives, economies, and culture. This understanding,
deep and subjective, is a way to rethink how and why we design in
post-industrial areas that need attention and care.

The collages themselves all started the same way: an acetone transfer of historic imagery onto a page. It is a low-fidelity type of printmaking that leaves the final product feeling ghostly and tonal over figural. After the transfer, layers of plants, people, and new conditions were added in successive increments. The final products are dreamlike moments of pure, subjective speculation. In them, I can hear the waves on the beach, the hum of cicadas, the dull roar of highways, trains clattering, birds, wind blowing through trees and smokestacks, and I feel at home in a new future. I made these to understand and project my imperfect understanding, desire, and love of a future that could be. I love this place and its people, though damaged and hurting, I can feel the resilience to the bone.

The history of Northwest Indianians emerges from our special relationship with the southern tip of Lake Michigan. Following many of the ancient trading routes of the Native American Potowatamie Tribes, tracks were laid to connect Detroit and the exploding city of Chicago in the 1840s. The area along the coast stayed relatively sparsely populated for decades despite the growing railways. The combination of cheap, swampy land and easy connection to the concentrated railroads created massive incentive to relocate and expand industry to Northwest Indiana from Chicago.

Rapid takeovers of windswept dunes for industry began in the 1890s. Standard Oil, Inland Steel, U.S. Steel Garyworks, Bethlehem Steel, and four coal power plants took dominance over the crescent of lakeshore. They brought people by the thousands to work and build on a scale difficult to fully comprehend. Worker's Progress Association writers wrote about Northwest Indiana, "This region, within a few miles of the eastern city limits of Chicago, lay dormant during the nineteenth century waiting for electricity and the machine age to give it life.[1]"

By the time World War II began, steel felt like an inextricable part of
the Calumet River Corridor. At the time, steel and its support industries
ran the show and the steel needed for the war effort supercharged
the need for production and growth. Postwar, the linking of small
shops and huge mills made much of this area read as the continuous,
industrial mesh to this day. For years, the paradigm of generations
of steel workers and public patronage continued. The identity of
Northwest Indiana became the buckle of the Rust Belt, a center for
steel in America, where men were tough and unions were tougher.

Irreversible environmental damage went on uncontrolled for many years, even after the establishment of the EPA. My mother has stories of orange fogs that would roll through Chesterton, Indiana, a few miles from most of the mills. On cloudy nights, you can see the orange reflection of the open hearths on the undersides of the clouds. Smoke bellowed and people worked round the clock, and everything seemed like it would remain that way. All signs pointed to Northwest Indiana being the steel hub of America for generations to come, with jobs for all who wanted them.

Nothing is meant to last forever, even steel.

During the 1980s, the industry entered a free fall due to inefficient mills, international competition, and falling demand. Steel is still a large part of life in Northwest Indiana, but it no longer employs the same numbers it used to. People have transitioned to service jobs or other light industry. The communities of Gary and East Chicago never truly recovered from this drop in employment. When the center of a community vanishes, it has to evolve or die. Currently, Gary is still limping along, with vacant buildings dotting every street and smoke continuing to rise over the mills. It may be 50 or 100 years from now, but someday these industrial landscapes will need to transform. The steel industry will never return to what it was, and no amount of bargaining or empty promises will change that.

Now is the time to begin looking to what this land could be for future generations. The creativity, engineering prowess, determination, and hard work that went into not only building the mills, but making them the largest in the world in a matter of around 20 years is difficult to fully comprehend. The people and these companies transformed the landscape around them into a massive machine. This transformation came at an enormous cost, one that residents continue to bear. I am one of those residents contending with the histories of this case study in American industrialism and burnout.

My grandfather was a mill worker, and my high school was built directly from tax revenue from the mills. No matter how objective and academic I try to be in this research, it will always be tinged with my memories of hot summers on the lake with smokestacks in view. The train rides to Chicago through national parkland, abandoned neighborhoods, and brownfields color my entire understanding of home. My chances of developing cancer are three to four times higher than average, and I'm a privileged person from a richer, smaller town further from the mills. In doing this research, my subjective, tainted, and personal history provided me a chance to envision a new future through thick understanding of a place that only comes from calling it home.

These industries have an expiration date, and we need to consider what comes next before the sites are vacant. Thickening and thinning the lines between industrial buildings, waste, and life provide an alternative future for the area. The depth we study, speculate, and hope about this place, and so many others like it, determines what kind of landscape we make. Architectural research is a way to build a thickness of understanding and empathy with a place. It is from this thickness that decisions and design can be drawn from. Northwest Indiana is a massive machined landscape and nothing we do will ever change it back to the way it was. Instead, we must retool it to create a new future.

At the risk of being too sentimental, the postscript is a poem my brother, Jake Pruitt, wrote about Northwest Indiana.

JONAH PRUITT

Jonah Pruitt is a native of Northwest Indiana, the buckle of the Rust Belt. He holds a Bachelor of Science in Architecture from the University of Cincinnati and a Masters of Architecture from the University of Virginia. Working with the editors of Lunch at the University of Virginia's Architecture School allowed him to delve deeper into where he's from and what the role of research has in the practice of architecture. He is currently working on his second book of research documenting his masters thesis. For the future, Jonah will continue researching and documenting life in the American Midwest to contribute to the work of making it a more just and beautiful place.

EVERYTHING THAT FALLS
BENEATH THE FEET OF DEER

Where I'm from, the earth is held
And burned above the lake

Where I'm from, the bottom coal knows the black earth best
And blackens it more

The meek will not inherit the earth

In winter, when the lake freezes
And the dunes are snow and sand,
God is a deer, and she walks through the dunes

Her eyes watch the power burn above her
Her feet are cold and her breath is steam
Her footsteps blanket the earth

The meek will not inherit the earth
For the earth is wild

Notes

1 The Calumet Region Historical Guide: Containing the Early History of the
Region as Well as the Contemporary Scene Within the Cities of Gary,
Hammond, East Chicago (including Indiana Harbor), and Whiting. United
States: German printing Company, 1939.

REMEMBERING HER HOMECOMING
From the North Atlantic to Leigh Street

Nastassja Swift

The mobility and displacement of the Black body, from port to holding cell, to ward and out, is a history that is embedded in our communities socially, culturally, and geographically. Evoking feelings of pain, otherness, power, and triumph, "Remembering Her Homecoming" is a collaborative performance in Richmond, Virginia, that remembers and reflects on the Black women who have roamed these spaces before us, and how their stories affect those of the present and tomorrow. Dancing and singing through some of Richmond's racially historical spaces, the performers give a face to our ancestral mothers while becoming a portal for their journey, and shaping an experience of storytelling and history.

In the summer of 2018, I led a collaborative workshop and public performance that consisted of masked Black women and girls who traced the ancestral footprints of the arrival of the Black body in the city of Richmond, Virginia. As a Black female artist working and learning within what was once the center of slave trading in the region, my work explores the journey of the Black female in Richmond, and how that journey has contributed to the stories and history of Black girlhood in the city. Operating similarly to a women's march, the mobile, 3.5 mile outdoor performance began in Shockoe Bottom (the site of the importation of slaves into Richmond, and one of the largest sources of slave trade in America); stopped along the Untold RVA 11:11 Portal, the African Burial Ground and Devil's Half Acre (Lumpkin's Slave Jail); and concluded in the Jackson Ward neighborhood (once one of the largest Black communities in Richmond).

The project produced performance masks, photography, a mini documentary, and short film, which premiered at the 2019 Afrikana Independent Film Festival and was screened at the Virginia Film Festival and Current Art Fair.

IN COLLABORATION WITH

Torian Urgworji, Film
Kyara Massenburg, Film
Cameron Hopkins, Film
Marlon Turner, Photography
Sanchel Brown, Choreography
Alicia Phillips, Dance
Raven Wilkes, Dance
Jourdan James, Dance
Kennijah Waller, Dance
Kyata Johnson, Dance
IdaLease Cummings, Dance
Christina Irby, Dance
Kristin Davis, Wardrobe
Rob Gibsun, Instrumentation
Free Egunfemi, Untold RVA Site
Barbara Jones, Voiceover

PHOTO CREDIT
Marlon Turner

NASTASSJA SWIFT

Nastassja Swift is a visual artist holding a BFA from Virginia Commonwealth University. She is the recipient of a Virginia Commission of the Arts Fellowship in Craft, and recently the Black Box Press Foundation, Art as Activism Grant. Nastassja has participated in several national and international residencies and exhibitions, including her first solo exhibit in Doha, Qatar, in 2016, and fellowships at the Vermont Studio Center and MASS MoCA.

MATERIALS

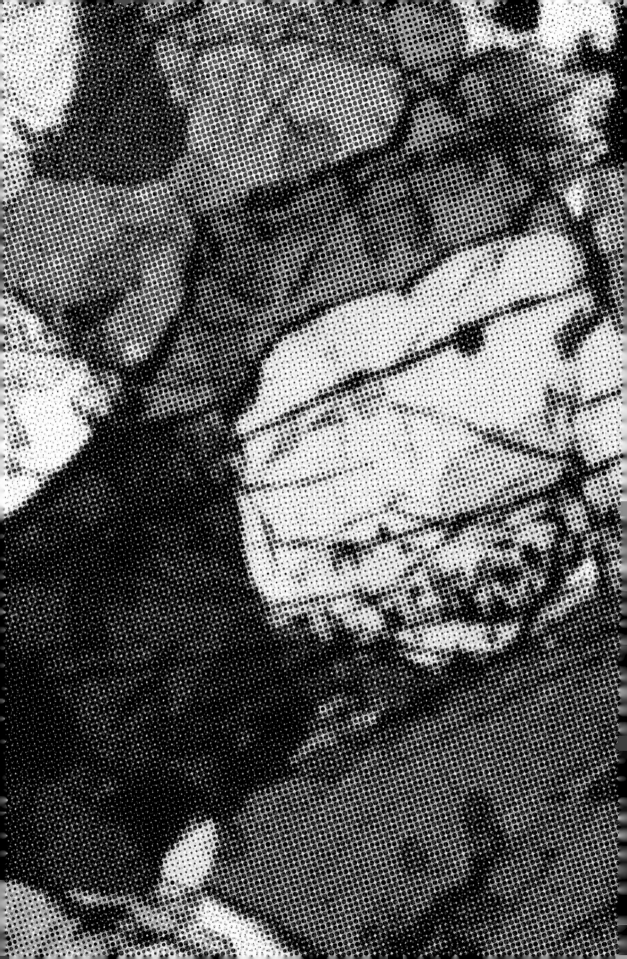

BORROWING: LIBRARIES, METHODS, & BOUNDARY OBJECTS

An Interview with Shannon Mattern and the LUNCH 15 Editorial Board

LK: Our first question: THICK or THIN?

SM: I would say THICK. Do I have to explain or is that good enough?

CB: That's good for now—we'll have to circle around to it at the end and see if you slice things differently. For now though, we're curious about the idea of the public that runs as a kind of through line in your work, everything from public engagement in the design process to rethinking publics through the framework of technological change. Could you talk a little bit about the thick- and thin-ness of ideas of the public in your work?

SM: Well, let me start with publishing because it's something that doesn't feel all that radical to me, though some of my colleagues who publish mostly peer-reviewed journal articles think that it is this "life-choice" that I have made. For me, I was legitimated in choosing to publish in public venues after I got tenure because I had just spent so much time jumping through the hoops to prove I could meet the standards of peer review. But there was so much that was more rewarding about publishing in public venues, para- and pseudo-academic and sometimes non-academic publications. There are so many advantages to it. First of all, you reach a much larger audience, you get feedback from a wider array of people, and invitations to participate in different kinds of discussions or forums that are way beyond your own disciplinary training and outside the academy. In publishing online, you also get an immediate response and potentially international distribution. So your interlocutors are much broader and more widely strewn.

Online platforms are also great because you're not dealing with the time and expense of physical printing. For example, I have an article that's coming out in December that I submitted to a peer review journal article on invitation five years ago. I'm glad I wasn't writing about current events! With digital venues, if you are still going through with rigorous editing with professional editors, the whole process can be a couple months, and by that time the event may not be still timely, still fresh.

The other thing I'll say about public engagement is that most of my students in my classes come from different disciplines, something I really enjoy. A lot of them are really engaged in how they think about their training. The world they are preparing themselves for goes beyond the academy. A lot of our course activities are focused on helping them think through how what they're learning in the classroom has public impact. Or we engage directly in public events. Or we go out and visit people who are performing the everyday labor of the things we are talking about. So that's a very simple thing too—another means of engaging with the "public," whatever that means in reference to what you're doing in the classroom.

Other modes of scholarly production or public engagement take place too, through working on exhibitions, working with different kinds of public institutions, or on collaborative projects. I actually wrote my dissertation 20 years ago on public engagement in the design process, and it's been a thread throughout my work. That said, I have mixed feelings about it sometimes. I feel like it's performative or obligatory and can actually be exploitative in some cases. On the whole, I think it's really important to think critically about how it is done.

CB: Your work has more recently started to bridge into the design education world, and I think we're all very interested in hearing from you about how your work in communication and media studies has started to become spatialized in terms of

> "I was just as much interested in the material culture of text as I was in the meaning and semantics of the words on the page. Later... I would think about space itself as a communications medium."

infrastructure and materialized in terms of geology. Can you talk a little about that path?

SM: So I grew up in a family that ran a hardware store. My dad has built all the houses we lived in, one uncle is an architectural engineer, and the other is a contractor. So my upbringing was in a "build your own space" environment, and I got to learn a little bit of woodworking. My friends and I, back in the days when not everyone had video games, we built spaces all the time. We built drive-thru restaurants in the backyard and farm stands in the front yard. I know it all sounds sort of romantic, but those were really formative experiences for me. Then when I was an undergrad, I had a bunch of different majors but ultimately wanted to think about texts and literature. I was very interested in literature as an imaginary or virtual space. I was just as much interested in the material culture of text as I was in the meaning and semantics of the words on the page, which is what my undergrad thesis was about. Later, while pursuing my PhD, I would think about space itself as a communications medium.

I wrote my dissertation about the design process behind OMA's, Rem Koolhaas's, Seattle Public Library. I got to be there for some of the public forums, looked at the evolution of the design over several years. It allowed me to bridge those interests as well because this was a space being designed to span the transition from library as a print institution to library as digital institution. They were making all these formative decisions and discussions about how prominent should books be in an era of Amazon and e-books and other

Fig. 1
Crest Hardware Art Show, 2012.
Garrett Ziegler.

types of digital formats. There were questions about what kind of furniture you'd need when you don't know how big computers are going to be five years from now when the building opens. There were also questions about the building itself as a symbol for a city that was redefining its image as a hub of the digital economy. I had media and urban studies scholars and architectural historians on my dissertation committee.

After that, I went on to do a post-doc in architectural history, which was actually not by choice. I submitted a general call for a post-doc and the architectural historians chose me. It was kind of validating. I never would have self-identified that way, but they found some value in what I was doing. I then went to the New School, a large and well-known design school that offered all kinds of pedagogical and research opportunities. I realized there was great potential for legitimate forms of cross-pollination here. So I moved from architecture, which I suppose was my first design field,

to which I tethered media studies, and I kind of scaled up and down from there.

I look at objects as communicative media and how they're designed in a way to facilitate communication and to convey cultural values. Start with interfaces, databases, and data structures, and then scale it all up to the urban scale and the infrastructural scale. I guess when I think retrospectively about all the stuff I've done over the past two decades it has me really thinking about how we design the built world to facilitate communication and to embody our epistemologies.

I think a lot about libraries.[1] You want your data model to be reflected in the interface of your catalog, but also to be intelligible to the way the building is designed, the way you circulate throughout it, and to the logistical system. So a well-functioning system has a consistent logic and aesthetic through all of these different layers of interfaces.

CM: It sounds like making data tangible

is an important thing for you. How would you want designers to think about data or to approach it differently?

SM: Well I know that there are a lot of different methods. I was just at a conference recently where someone was doing a publicly engaged urban design project, and they described their method as "We went out and gathered data," and that was it. There was no discussion as to what that meant. I wasn't physically present—I was livestreaming it—but if I was there I would have asked "What does that mean? Did you go out and just do a convenience sampling and ask three people what they thought? Did you do ethnographic research? Was there some type of a survey?" And I have sat in on some crits in design studios where they are essentially told "go get some data." I am wondering how you think critically about what those methods are and the affordances and differences of those methods.

I had this discussion really briefly on Twitter recently because I tweeted that aforementioned quote, saying that I would love to know more about what this means, and some architects chimed in to say that we realize there should be more methodological training in architecture schools, but at the same time there is only so much you can be an expert in. Because if you have to design buildings that stand up and are structurally sound and are sustainable and all these things, you cannot be a methodologist in all fields. This is maybe where collaboration and participation becomes more useful. That said, I know that there is also a rising industry of engagement consultants, and I want to learn more about that. Is that something that resonates with all of you?

LUNCH: Yeah, yes!

LK: I'm fascinated by the way that you're talking about methodology. We're here in design school where community engagement is spoken about as something that we should do, but the sheer pace of research studios, even theses, makes that really hard to do reciprocally. I'd love to hear you talk a little about how you think about rigorous design research. What role might community engagement play in that, and how might we translate those ideas into space?

CB: Yeah, I'm also really curious about methods. I don't know a whole lot about media studies, so could you tell us about the way methods are thought of in that field?

SM: There is communication studies which is drawing on a lot of social scientific methods. Media studies tends to lean more towards cultural analysis, which I don't think is any less rigorous. It just doesn't necessarily have a codified set of protocols as the other strains do. There is also the risk of fetishizing methods, which I think some fields do; if you read the outcome you think, "Well that's not really surprising," but you spent 20 pages outlining your complicated, bespoke methodology, which itself is maybe an interesting contribution.

BS: This was the topic that I was really excited about. I think the term you use is "methodolatrous."[2] I come up against this a lot where you say that architects and professional designers have to be generalists in all things and specialists in no things. Methods and disciplinary boundaries are so fluid, and we situate them in a really positively expansive way. But those boundaries get really hazy. Where does accountability come in when everyone is doing everything? Where does the role of architect end and where does the role of the geographer or social scientist come in? And then when you start to borrow these methods, you start to get self-critical of your own methods where you are doing mostly things that are very aestheticized. Can you talk a little more about this "methodolatrous" area of behavior?

SM: Well, I'm really interested in locating "the good enough." You know what is good enough to get done the job you need to get done. Rather than saving every piece of data at the highest resolution, why don't we make more judicious decisions about what is worth saving. There are much larger systematic consequences to all of these decisions regarding rigor. This connects to the fetishization of fieldwork that you get in some social sciences. I don't know that architects have the time or the desire, or if it is even useful to go sit in the field for three years before you can gather a "good enough" amount of data to actually make a responsible design proposal.

But there's also this idea of borrowing methods. I was asked to start a new track in the anthropology department focusing on the anthropology of design and technology. There, we're exposed to lots of questions about when we can say we have done our duty as ethnographers. In my own training, I wasn't accustomed to focusing on these temporal standards. I think borrowing is fine. I think triangulating multiple methods is a great value to incorporate. Even just purely the aesthetic experimentation gives you a new lens through which to look at the research environment or subjects or collaborators that you are working with—so messily mixing about different methods.

Some may say well, that is not very rigorous. But as I have progressed I have become much less concerned with that, and I see the value of having more experimental, less codified methods. I've seen how they can productively inform one another. I am also not terribly concerned with developing jurisdictions. I don't know that ownership of methods is really a productive way of serving the public.

LK: I think there gets to be a problem in design where, not necessarily where people are messily combining all of these methodologies, but instead with how they communicate those findings. The way that we draw can claim to have more rigor than there really is in a way that justifies our work.

SM: Exactly. It's basic reflexivity. It's a way to articulate what you have actually done. Several years ago, and even back when I was looking at early OMA stuff, translation from data visualization to design. In some practices, you could see a formal parallel: they might take their data, without being explicit about how it was gathered, and use it to make a data visualization—and then you see those formal morphological parallels in the building itself. It can certainly appear very convincing presented to a public in a way that reifies or naturalizes the progression of design development, but it's not very open about the processes by which these decisions were made.

LK: That's got me thinking about the granularity of data now. OMA was looking at a specific scale of data that seems more rectilinear and larger grained but now we have these point clouds and the forms that come out of parametric computational methods, ones that possesses a much finer grain.

SM: Right! And then you have firms like KPF (Kohn Pederson Fox) which is working on a lot of smart city design. They have their own bespoke platform that makes

> "I think borrowing is fine. I think triangulating multiple methods is a great value to incorporate. Even just purely the aesthetic experimentation gives you a new lens through which to look at the research environment or subjects or collaborators that you are working with."

parametrics intelligible to a client. So I could see how they could take their software, show it to a big developer like Related, who developed Hudson Yards, to show building height or material, or the sun's position and shading, or the energy use- this would be really attractive to a developer. I wonder about the methods that are behind such work, and I wonder how trustworthy a lot of those models actually are.

BS: We're thinking about data as a THIN description of really THICK reality, I think. In that same piece about methodology you talk about this idea about solutionism in that it's not just that we need to generate more data points or finer granularity, but taking a step back and being more intentional with the type of data we analyze. What would be a THICK methodology for this approach to gathering data?

SM: *Solutionism* is typically attributed to Evgeny Morosov.[6] In terms of thick data and thick description, it goes back to Clifford Geertz and a long line of anthropologists. Some folks have advocated for the combination of thick data with thin data. A lot of people working on decolonial data and data feminism these days are also thinking about thicker modes of data collection, and sometimes it involves combining the use of open data sets with ethnographic research. Some people have also proposed that you can use a cell phone to allow people to do self- or community-engaged data gathering. People can collect their own photographs documenting their own pathways they take throughout the day or voice recorded notes that provide real-time impressions of a place. There are ways of using the phone to allow people to collect data. There a lot of ways of using the phone to collect thicker forms of data and combine

I'm building on some Black feminist theory that argues that we can light things differently— metaphorically cast light upon them—illuminate colonial and racial histories of geology and natural history and all the various social scientific fields that are entangled with the museum.

that with other data sets.

CB: None of us have a background in Communications or Media Studies, and I was wondering if you could talk to us about what we or others don't understand about your field. What do you want us to know?

SM: When I was doing my dissertation there was research about architecture as a medium and cities as a media. But most of my own research drew on architects writing about media. I feel like there always has been a very robust discussion within urban and architectural studies, design studies, architectural history, and criticism about how media technologies have informed the design processes, how we see them reflected in the urban screen, the façade as a communicative medium, how print informs classical architecture. So there has long been a consideration of the mutual constructedness of architecture and media technologies.

In terms of what you may not understand is the importance of historicizing the new, though I think architectural historians are well aware of the value of questioning "newness."

BS: I want to talk a little bit about the subject of the work you'll be sharing with us tonight in your lecture.[3] In addition to the exhibiting of rocks, you have a piece on the big data of ice.[4] What struck me about that is that ice core samples, these physical data points to understand climate change, are really aggregated layers that are this additive process of history that becomes this object in an ice core and that the Anthropocene is going to be a layer at

Fig. 2 *Lamont-Doherty Core Repository*

some point too.

SM: The piece I'm sharing tonight was commissioned by the editors of LA+, the landscape architecture journal, for their "Geo" issue, which explores intersections of geometry, geology, and geography. They asked me specifically to do a follow up on my piece on soils, sediments, and rocks.[3] They wanted to see how matter can embody knowledge. We see this in media history, too: how can we take a chemical sample from a medium that would tell us when or how a book or clay tablet or photograph was made? What happens, then, if we're working with an archive of a different sort? How do standard archival principles apply to something like a sediment or an ice core sample, and how do they function as archival objects in similar or different ways? In trying to rethink this piece, I found that light was a key tool in so many of the methods, and it became a theme that tied this piece together. Light shining on something, light shining through, in the case of optical petrology, and then light deployed in experimental methods–

both metaphorically and literally. I'm building on some Black feminist theory that argues that we can light things differently—metaphorically cast light upon them—illuminate colonial and racial histories of geology and natural history and all the various social scientific fields that are entangled with the museum.

Whether you're talking about a sediment sample or a rock, they cast their thickness differently. For a sediment sample, you can read striations. Although it's not always so neat and simple because geological strata have all kinds of entanglements and messiness, with lower levels of geological time jutting up through the contemporary, so we problematize the neat striation of the sample. For rock, it is more about compression and a more concentric record. For crystals, there's a very different geometry than we find with concentric rings or linear type of striation. So, we have these different geometries of thickness manifested in these different objects.

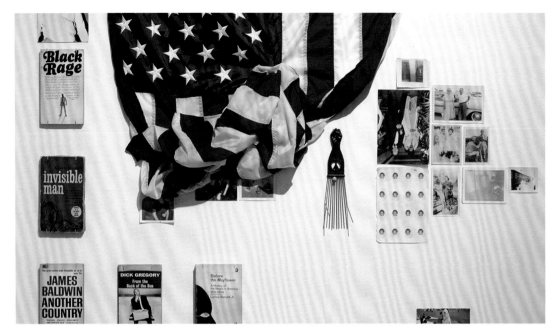

Fig. 3
Kameelah Janan
Rasheed,
No Instructions for
Assembly (Activation I),
installation shot, 2013.

BS: I love that idea and the different ways you used it can reveal different things about an object. It enhances the tangibility of the object.

SM: This reminds me of Marshall McLuhan[5] who makes a distinction of "light on" media and "light through" a media. For example, the book is a "light on" medium, you cast light on the book to read it. And the television is a "light through" medium; light flows through the screen. Or he also draws historical parallels to things like stained glass, which allowed the church—the architecture itself —to serve as a communications medium for the illiterate. Stained glass is light through medium. Different illumination methods cultivate different modes of reading or methods of engagement, which have different pedagogical and epistemological implications.

BS: Great, the medium is the message for McLuhan. If you have a rock and have a particular way of displaying it, that affects, even becomes the message.

SM: Everything we've talked about: the library contains media but it is also its own medium communicating what a culture values. And if you have a transparent façade, you want to be able to look in and see what the program is from the street to know that you're welcome. Rocks and ice core samples are a medium that are also their own message. Everything we've talked about embodies this central McLuhan principle.

Media studies has been a marginalized field; it hasn't been taken seriously in all institutional and cultural contexts, but I think it's incredibly valuable. McLuhan has waxed and waned in popularity and legitimacy. He was the patron saint of Wired magazine when it started in the early 1990s and has also been regarded as a bit of a quack who's harbored some questionable views about other cultures. And yet, a lot of what he has said in the past around cultural gender biases is actually pretty prescient and has come to fruition through the digital era.

CB: When we go home for the holidays, I feel we spend a lot of time trying to explain to other people what it is we do. Do you find that with Media Studies?

SM: Yeah, especially since I grew up in a very conservative family, and they read the Wall Street Journal that loves to trash things like Women's Studies and Literature and Cultural Studies which is right where my field fits in. They have concrete things they can latch onto like my parents will say "Oh she studies libraries and archives." Those are concrete things that make sense. Even if they don't want to validate public funding of them they at least know what kind of service they could provide. This is again, something I talk with students about all the time, is that one of the techniques that has been really helpful for me in doing interdisciplinary work is to always have a concrete thing at the center of it that people can latch onto. Susan Leigh Star has a concept of the "boundary object" which is an object that a geologist, a landscape architect, a landscaper, a laborer in a quarry, all have some way of connecting with. It's that thing which gives you something to wrap the discourse around.

CM: Going back to how you talk about libraries and epistemology and how knowledge is organized, you use the term *fugitive libraries*. Can you talk a little bit about that?

SM: Sure, this was just after the 2016 election. I had felt for a long time that I wanted to say something about race and libraries, but I didn't think that as a white woman anyone needed to hear what I had to say about it. Following Twitter discussions, particularly by a lot of Black feminists, has really made me waffle on this because in some cases I was thinking "I should really use my platform" to elevate the voices of others. But then there are concerns that white female scholars in particular are co-opting the work of others and using it to package it in their new theory and while mining the experience and suffering of another population. So, I really have had mixed feelings about this.

This is something I was thinking about when writing my most recent piece on fugitive libraries which came out about three weeks ago.[6] I felt that I could create a framework for them to speak in their own words. So that's how I really looked at that article. It was an opportunity for me to maybe provide some historical and critical framing–about the history of racial segregation in American libraries–and let my article be a window through which these other practitioners, these fugitive librarians, could shine their light *through.*

I've written about libraries for a couple decades. They're beloved because they purportedly represent the last free, democratic, egalitarian spaces in American culture. This is of course, in large part, true, but it also obfuscates the fraught history of that institution and the fact that there still exists segregation in this beloved institution today. Including the fact that close to ninety percent of workers in the field are white, and in many libraries we see evidence of ongoing racial prejudices; it's manifested in everything from what books are on the shelves, to how people of color are treated within the institution. So I wanted to look at this history of fugitivity.

> "Whether you're talking about a sediment sample or a rock, they cast their thickness differently.
> For a sediment sample, you can read striations...
> For rock, it is more about compression...
> For crystals, there's a very different geometry than we find with concentric rings or linear type of striation."

There has been a lot of interesting theory about fugitivity in critical race studies in the past few years in particular. And it's a useful framework to consider both the resourcefulness and resilience of African American communities to build their own institutions when the "official" one had no place for them. And even if our contemporary institution has made a great deal of progress, we must recognize that there is still enough wrong—still enough racism—to necessitate that African American communities and Black women in particular make their own fugitive kind of parallel institutions that serve their needs better than the "formal" institution can.

BS: Very cool. Thank you so much for your time, Shannon. Any closing comments?

SM: Just a note on studying across majors and disciplines. I was having the same conversation with two different groups in the past couple weeks. "If you were to start college over again what would you major in?" I said I would have had like three majors and it would have taken me like seven years.

LUNCH: **laughter**

SM: So here's my answer: Geography, Landscape Architecture, and Graphic Design.

CB: Last question: THICK or THIN?

SM: Still THICK!

Notes

1 Shannon Mattern, "Library as Infrastructure," Places Journal, June 2014.

2 Shannon Mattern, "Methodolatry and the Art of Measure," Places Journal, November 2013.

3 Shannon Mattern, "The Big Data of Ice, Rocks, Soils, and Sediments," Places Journal, November 2017.

4 Shannon Mattern, "Glimmer: Refracting Rocks," UVA School of Architecture, November 2019.

5 McLuhan, Marshall. *Understanding Media: The Extensions of Man.* Cambridge, Mass: MIT Press, 1994.

6 Shannon Mattern, "Fugitive Libraries," Places Journal, October 2019.

7 Morozov, Evgeny. *To Save Everything, Click Here: The Folly of Technological Solutionism.* New York: PublicAffairs, 2013.

SHANNON MATTERN

Shannon Mattern is a columnist for Places. She is a professor of anthropology at The New School in New York City.
Mattern's research and teaching address how the forms and materialities of media are related to the spaces (architectural, urban, and conceptual) they create and inhabit. She writes about libraries and archives, media infrastructures, the material qualities of media objects, media companies' headquarters and sites of media-related labor, place branding, public design projects, urban media art, and mediated sensation.

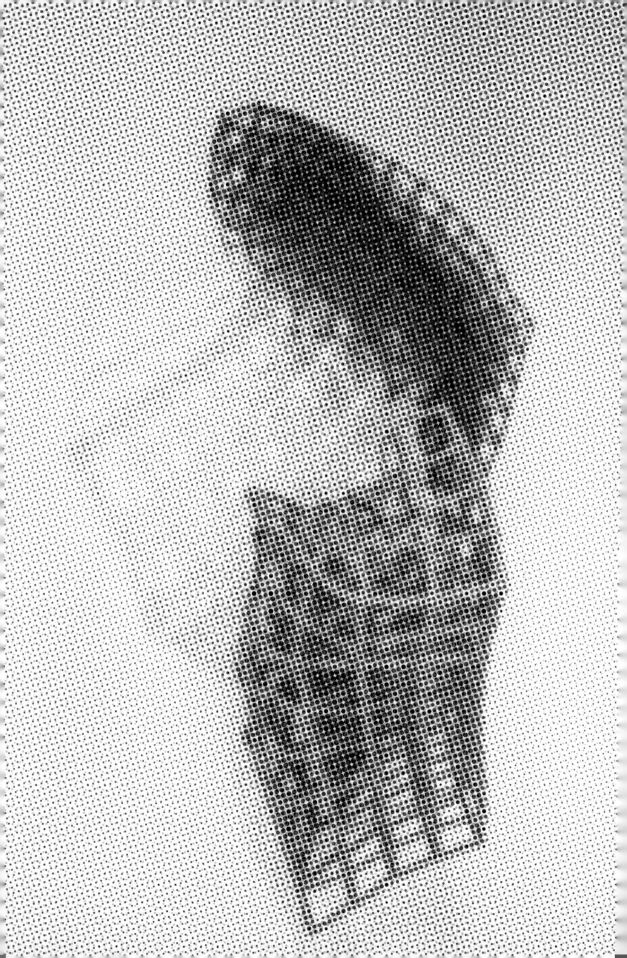

GRAINY AND SMOOTH
Ideas About Matter About Ideas, for the Designer

Bjørn Sparrman

Design hinges largely on our material imagination, our ability to envision the pliability and composition of matter. We do so with sketches, models, textual descriptions, renderings, vocalizations, formulas, etc. Our relationship with material hinges on the theories of matter through which our imagination operates, allowing us to foresee new material compositions or designs. In this brief text, we question our relationship with materials in the practice of design by comparing two competing material types and two theories of matter. Embodied creatures, such as ourselves, are forced to manage our relationship with materials through disincorporated ideas and advanced theories. In this process, our style and ideologies are drawn into the light.

Materials and ideas are always co-present in the moment of design. To put it another way, design consists of ideas and their implications. The transition from ideation to material embodiment is strongly dependent upon our understanding of matter and our direct experience with materials. The idea of craft and the crafts-person or master has been widely used to describe an ideal or perfected relationship with material. In the mythology of the master, the distance between material and master approaches nothing, understanding of the character and structure of material is fully internalized, the mind of the carpenter becomes wood, the potter's clay, the weaver's threads. While the craft master presumably manipulates and absorbs understanding of material through their own hands, eyes, noses, and ears, of the non-masters among us, understanding of matter is driven by theories, concepts about how matter works, and through methods of representation,

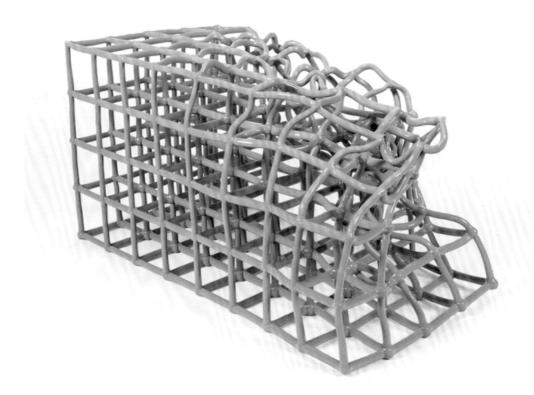

ideas about materials made material with other materials. While the mythical craft-master may be a sincere practitioner, where form, processes, products, and materials are paired for a good match, we mere designers intentionally violate convention and material theories ironically and with good humor.

I would like to identify two types of matter that we encounter, as both theory and material, with which we design: homogeneous and heterogeneous materials. These terms are heavy, so we may also call them smooth and grainy, or liquid and structured matter.

Grainy materials dominate our logical discerning minds. We understand matter to be irregular in consistent and patterned ways: wood is grainy, photographs have grains or pixels, woven fabric stretches on the bias. Atomic theory reinforces our understanding of grainy materials. Matter breaks down into small and smaller particles or distinct structures. If anything, we are, all is, a sponge of energy and particles. We know, understand, and appreciate grainy matter. As much as we believe and are told that materials are in some fundamental way structured, we are confounded by the difficulty of understanding these structures.

Fig. 1
3D-printed matrices.

Throughout history, the classical atomic theory has developed into the insanely complex yet confoundingly incomplete standard model of particle physics. We respect both people with PhDs and craft-masters for their understanding and manipulation of grainy difficult materials: carpenters, civil engineers, sushi chefs, physicians.

Despite ourselves and despite knowledge, we maintain a belief in smooth materials, homogenous pure substance. This confusion is forgivable. While the field of physics has worked to describe the nuances and structure of matter, industry has been homogenizing and standardizing at full tilt for 200 years. Grainy wrought iron has been replaced by hot-rolled steel, wooden planks became plywood, and then oriented strand board, and eventually fiberboard. Nothing has been stronger in advancing our belief in homogenous materials than polymer science. Plastics and resins have recalibrated our understanding and relationship with materials. These materials assume any form, have no direction nor scale. We are economically incentivized to embrace the homogeneity of material, its ideation, and its representation. Standardization and homogenization leaches into nearly every aspect of our society: agriculture, manufacturing methods, languages, and aesthetics. In effect, the mindset and theory that has fundamentally shaped our very modern lives is fiction, a particularly operative story.

This smooth theory of matter has been advanced tremendously by digital tools of representation, namely rendering programs and physics simulators. Through the production of pure synthetic images, matter becomes pure math. With the limited computational power of the 1990s, math matter was simple and rough. Increases in computational power brought ever complex and textured digital matter, yet it also spawned perfected reality, perfect representations of physical matter lacking blemish, wrinkle, or grain. As the sophistication of these digital tools has begun to truly fool our senses, we have arrived in a strange zone where matter experienced through images needs no underlying structure or texture. To a point, we cannot differentiate our experience of representations and experiencing of the thing itself emotionally. While we have not completely crossed the uncanny valley and are able to distinguish or at least doubt purely synthetic representations, we find ourselves leaning into and often choosing perfected synthetic matter, our automatic airbrushed selfie, Japanese cheesecake.

At this point we admit that we are wading in a new material reality, disentangling forms of matter is moot. While this dualist "problem" may eventually blow over as our minds are uploaded onto the great server in the sky, we are currently straddling and constantly confusing these epistemes. We find ourselves with two robust and incompatible theories of materials. Yet these two theories are given spaces to exist and thrive without often interfering with each other. The grainy theory remains hard knowledge and the purview of some specialists. The smooth matter theory is a beautiful fiction, lubricating industry. Despite their practical differences, both theories play similar roles in the formation of our aesthetic sensibilities and are stoked by the types of representational images that we digest. We differentiate smooth and grainy matter, choosing at times one over another, for this or that reason: cabin porn one moment, goober candle the next.

Particle physics has delivered us a profound understanding of the deep underlying structure, and material scientists have delivered us polymers and matter without structure or direction. I have no desire to preach for or against any particular theory, there is value to the formless and the grainless. Formless materials are liquid, they take whatever form. Yet, at this extremity, what gives form? The container, surface tension, and gravity. More notably, our ideas and descriptions of structures themselves. What is PoMo but structuralism done in plasticine? The ideas of structure pass onto liquid/smooth materials. Reciprocally, the ideas of homogeneity pass onto structured materials. These incongruities and syncretic actions are the source of tension within the building trades and in the sensibilities of critics. Yet they are also the language of metaphor and humor. Designers are stuck with both modes, smooth and grainy, in our materials and in our representation, in our ideas and in the creations of our hands.

Fig. 2
Dressage #6
material: 3D-printed
silicone

BJØRN SPARRMAN

Bjørn Sparrman is an artist and design researcher working in the Boston/Cambridge area. As Research Lead at the MIT Self-Assembly Lab he developed fabrication techniques, machines, and systems. As an artist he is represented by the Yve Yang gallery in NYC with whom his work is shown internationally.

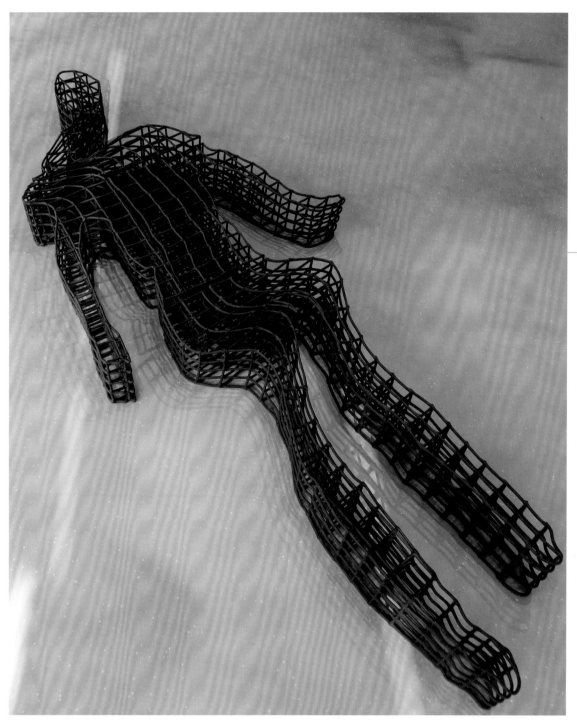

THE THICKENING OF THE MATTER

Ila Berman

What better contribution to THICK, than Aptum's Thinness pavilion—a structure, that through its very flirtation with the thinning of the thick (and the thickening of the thin), counters the basic tenets from which our architectural affair with thinness originated and evolved. To understand the thickening evident in the Thinness Pavilion, one might first delve a bit into the lineage of thinness within early-twentieth-century architectural history starting with Le Corbusier's Dom-ino House of 1914, the Maison Citrohan of 1922, and the publication Vers une Architecture (Towards an Architecture) of 1923. These emblematic works and latter collection of essays from L'Esprit Nouveau—which were consolidated into a manifesto on modern architecture—had an unparalleled influence within the discipline, aligning modernism with the thinness of an abstract and anti-gravitational three-dimensional geometric model of space; homogeneous manufactured materials such as concrete, steel, and glass; and repetitive standardized industrial processes out of which this metric spatial model was to be physically constructed. Notwithstanding the many transformations of this model over the past century (and Le Corbusier's own denunciation of thinness three decades later in the plasticity and thickness of Ronchamp, La Tourette, and Chandigarh), what is perhaps most fascinating is the persistence of the model's attributes
—its reliance on orthogonal geometry, industrialized processes, and manufactured components, as well as the pervasiveness of concrete, steel, and glass—in the making of our cities. The thinness of early modern architecture was not only exemplified by the curtain wall, but also a defining quality of the abstract dimensionality of cartesian space, the immaterial whiteness of the planes that delimited it, and the rarefaction of both the manufactured materials used and our

subsequent perception of the space produced.

This model of architecture, which simultaneously sublimated industrial production while abstracting the real, was intended to de-densify the thickness of the world by liberating architecture not only from gravity, but also from the density of information embedded in, and experienced by, all living earthly matters.

Aptum's Thinness pavilion is thus a fascinating counterpoint to this history, and a wonderful discursive object to reimagine architecture's relationship to both the thick and thin. A relatively small-scale pavilion, this work is highly experimental in its form, spatiality, structure, and use of material and fabrication methods, foregrounding larger implications for the future of building while reframing architecture's intrinsic relationship with matter. Despite its name, the Thinness pavilion is surprisingly thick in its conception, making, and experience. As a pavilion it operates within the realm of installation architecture, and is therefore freed from the normative scale of building and the permanence of its site to enable it to become a self-reflexive aesthetic object whose experimental tectonics move beyond standard modes of construction and whose experience and programming are unhindered by the typical constraints of utility. The pavilion's expansive thickening of the conception of architecture thus begins by questioning its relationship with utility and thus modernism's dictum that form should follow function, while simultaneously exploiting the potential of design and prefabrication to rethink both the typical uses of concrete and the making and experience of space.

The clarity with which one was to be able to perceive and understand modernism's striated world order, is thus complexified within the paradoxical nature of the Thinness pavilion that continuously oscillates between thick and thin. Although typically thick and heavy, concrete is deployed in this project as a highly perforated thin surface material rather than a weighty material mass, producing a lightweight structure that strategically replaces mass with volume. The thinness of this surface, which is carefully molded through the layering of digitally fabricated and precisely crafted materials, is also achieved through the complexity of the concrete material mix itself—a blending of concrete, steel fibers, and fiberglass and glass beads, the heterogeneous progeny of modern architecture's tripartite material palette. Unlike the disassociation of cladding from structure in modernism's skin and bones aesthetic, here the wall operates simultaneously as surface and structure, optimized for carrying loads by the way in which it is perforated—its pattern reflecting the trajectories of structural forces carried within—and the way in which individual 'columns' come together to form arches along the perimeter and within the interior. A thickened volumetric poché is rendered with the thinnest of material elements which are then folded and spatially manipulated to further amplify their structural capacity. The result is strangely paradoxical. Structure is generated by the thinness of surfaces and the emptiness of space yet is experienced as being surprisingly thick.

Solid and void are rendered equivocally, both in the alternation of space and structure within the perforated skin and in the relationship between the overall mass of the column-roof structure and the occupiable space that it encloses, entangling the figure of the pavilion with the environment it engenders. This massive yet lightweight voluminous form—an entirely new conception of a cathedral-like space—further thickens our sensorial experience of space by amplifying our haptic sensibilities within its dark, yet highly immersive, light-dappled interior.

Gridded in organization and in the clear demarcation of parts and their modular assembly, yet entirely non-cartesian in its continuous vaulted form, the pavilion thus inverts our expectations at every turn expanding our understanding of the very architectures it references as it conflates distinct historical trajectories and opposing values and qualities within a single work. The 10-foot by 10-foot by 10-foot cube that the pavilion defines is thus unlimited by the ways in which it is filled, just as the modern allusions to thinness that the work's name might seem to evoke operate as a veil to the structure's true thickness. A quasi-stable configuration that, like the paradox, always seems to move in two directions simultaneously, the Thinness pavilion is therefore anything but thin as it thickens the formal and spatial boundaries of the architectonic while calling into question the very matters out of which architecture is made.

Notes

1 Berman, Ila. "Didactic Objects and Immersive Events" in, *Expanded Field: Architectural Installation Beyond Art*. Berman, Ila, and Douglas Burnham. Novato, California: Applied Research and Design Publishing, an imprint of ORO editions, 2016.

ILA BERMAN

Ila Berman, DDes, is the Elwood R. Quesada Professor and former Dean (tenure, 2016–2021) at the School of Architecture at the University of Virginia.

THROUGH THICK OR THIN

Julie Larsen & Roger Hubeli

Architecture is driven by a fascination for the 'thin' with contemporary buildings often reduced to high-tech veneers enclosing mundane steel or concrete structures. In 2014 Venice Biennale, curator Rem Koolhaas stated that the architect's influence has "been reduced to a territory that is just two centimeters thick." Koolhaas's two-centimeter statement served as a provocation that when architecture must happen within two centimeters, what should a designer do? Thinness asks the question—is being "thin" something we created or just inherited? Are we fascinated with thinness or are we just forced to like it and actually fantasize about something thicker or more volumetric? We approach this question with the design of a three-meter cube pavilion, consisting of two-centimeter-thick concrete walls that, through thick or thin, is in pursuit of a more sustainable approach to one of the most ubiquitous materials on the planet.

BACKGROUND

As a material practice, our work privileges experimentation and collaboration rather than working with standard materials and systems, to discover innovative solutions that question the status quo of how we design. Our design approach is to synthesize computation and fabrication as methods to question material properties and behaviors of architectural elements in order to make the process of making instrumental to form-making. We unpack the relationship between materials and methods by not designing for existing materials, but designing beyond preconceived notions of those materials. In Material Presence, Sheila Kennedy speaks of designers' roles in material innovation:

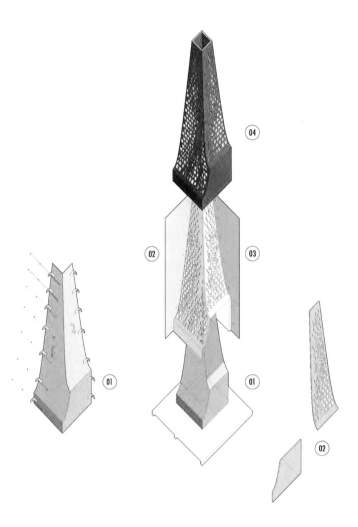

Fig. 1
*Axonometric of
Construction Layers
with lost wax formwork
technique*

The role of the architect is not so much to form these entities as it is to deform them from their standard applications and invent for them new definitions and uses. This reflects a practice that both accepts the economy of the standardized conditions of building materials as products, and deliberately seeks to exceed them.[2]

By partnering with the material industry, in this case Cemex Global R&D, at the research and development level, the process affords our office agency to bring a criticality and imaginative skill to the rapid development of new materials and discover new formal expressions.

CONCEPTUAL APPROACH

The aim of the pavilion was to interrogate thinness through the integration of a material, a digital strategy, a structural system, and a fabrication technique to challenge the thickness of concrete. This approach resulted in a pavilion that hybridizes structure and surface to become radically thin and light with the application of high-strength, lightweight concrete. With advancements in concrete technology, we embarked on a radically new approach to concrete being thin to achieve a thick poché without the need for mass.

Focusing on material experimentation and fabrication processes using high-performance concrete, which has far less cement and far greater recycled aggregates, our design strategy is a process of translation of concrete into a material that now resembles the structural capacities of steel, while maintaining the formal qualities of concrete that we hold dear—the allure, the texture, the volume, and the spatial thickness. As concrete has evolved into a material that is radically different than it was twenty years ago, shouldn't our response to the material evolve as well? If high performance concrete has the capability of being load bearing with far less material, what new and more sustainable possibilities emerge when a structural system can be conceptually as thin as paper?

To achieve this conceptually, we took baking as a reference to mixing concrete. Baking, with its slight variations to basic ingredients of egg, milk, and flour, can determine if you end up with a volumetric souffle or a thin crepe. With high-performance concrete, the recipe of the mix can also drastically determine how the concrete performs and ultimately, how thin the structure could become. Knowing we could achieve a much thinner structure by altering the mix and using small steel fibers, instead of typical steel reinforcement, we searched for other forms of inspiration to maximize the thinness of the structure. Inspired by a remarkably thin structure, the 'mille-feuille,' with its thin layers and hundreds of voids that comprise its volume, it challenged us to alter the concrete mix so that the structure could become volumetric without the need for heavy mass. To achieve a similar volume of space, the pavilion's load-bearing surfaces were thinned out to only two-centimeter-thick concrete walls (as opposed to typical twenty-centimeter concrete walls) while maintaining structural integrity, which questioned the potential of concrete to become a thin layer, rather than a thick poché, to encapsulate space.

A NEW APPROACH TO AN OLD MATERIAL

Fig. 2
Top view of pavilion

The tension of a thin veneer with a volumetric poché supports the notion of designing beyond a material's logic. Using advanced digital design and fabrication techniques, the pavilion defies the typical perception of concrete as a heavy and solid material to become so thin that it resembles the delicate and fine surfaces of one of the jalis at the Sidi-Saiyyed-Moschee, in Ahmedabad, India, where light passes through the exquisitely carved marble slab that forms one of the arched windows through an intricate pattern of voids rendering a tree and foliage motif. Thinness also attempts to dematerialize the already thin layer of the structural surface to create a visual finesse while maintaining its strength. And while in the jali, the pattern represents the structure of a tree, the Thinness Pavilion's pattern follows the branch-like form of the stress patterns that occur on the surface of the elements.

A CRAFTED DIGITAL SURFACE

Various patterns in Grasshopper were applied to the individual columns to find a composition of voids to thin out the surfaces of the elements. To determine where to place voids, according to the structural analysis, a "diffusion limited aggregation" technique in Grasshopper was used to create a parametric pattern outlining the stresses on the surface. The digital pattern was overlapped with the stress and load distribution for the horizontal and vertical position of the element. This generated a series of three-dimensional iterations to test the ability of the elements to maintain structural strength as the voids and shapes were altered. The pattern articulates a fine filigree of voids to capture a structural surface that allows for light to pass through. The pattern also creates a fluid connection between the arches on the elevation and the corners of the columns.

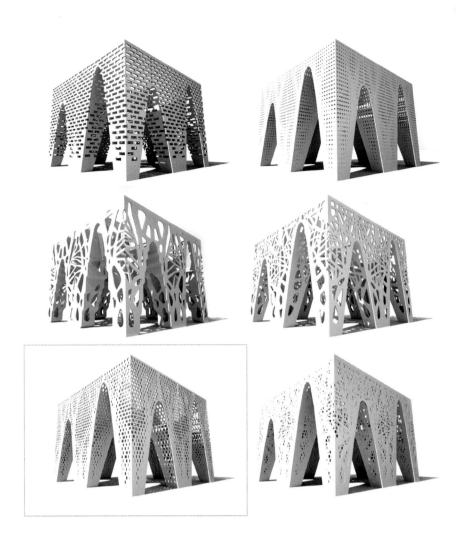

A THIN STRUCTURE

The combination of new digital fabrication methods and the high-performance concrete afforded us the opportunity to move beyond the surface to achieve structural integrity of the overall forms. To maintain vertical strength, the pavilion consists of a series of cross vaults split in half and made into separate columns to express the tectonic quality of the surface. Within the vaults, the strength relies on the surface rather than the integrity of the vault itself, thus embodying a new perception of concrete through its extremely thin structure.

Structural analysis of the elements and their surface patterns were studied to increase lightness and mobility of the pavilion. The elements were optimized to carry load in their upright and horizontal position. In order to accentuate that the surface held the strength, the digital pattern responded to stress and load patterns on the surface when the pieces were moved and rotated in a vertical or horizontal position. The structural moment diagrams located the highest stresses on each piece with the arc of the structural diagram informing where the pattern in Grasshopper became denser to ensure proper load distribution and reduction of shear and bending stresses and to distribute the voids in denser areas needing less material.

Fig. 3
A sampling of the iterations of applied grasshopper scripts to the surface of the columns.

Fig. 4
*Urban Speculation: A
Structural Ambition.*

A FABRICATION AND ASSEMBLY

To create a thin and light precast structural system that could be
stacked vertically to create a unique volumetric veneer, the hollow
column elements are light enough to be carried and assembled
with only two people and no heavy equipment. To achieve the
construction and assembly of a three meter cube, the challenge
was to find a method of casting that could achieve the fineness of a
thin surface with very little material without disturbing the surface
when demolding the formwork. Consisting of twelve columns and
four skylights, the formwork was reduced to only three molds for all
sixteen pieces in order to reduce waste and the amount of material
needed for the formwork. The resulting formwork is a combination of
digital fabrication techniques with water-jet-cut silicon in-lays along
with a prehistoric technique of 'lost wax molds' to cast wax formwork
that is melted and reused after each pour. Once the final concrete is
poured and cured, the lost wax formwork is melted and reveals the
intricate pattern of the surface. The result is a dematerialized surface
that expands our understanding of what concrete can achieve in the
future that historically it could not do.

Unlike shell structures that are known for being very thin while structural, because the concrete works solely in compression, the pavilion's vertical walls still resist buckling due to the high strength of the concrete with the fibers. Furthermore, shell structures are singular forms and cannot stack so the application of stacking thin elements to potentially become a vertical, urban form brings us one step closer to increasing the territory of control that architects have all but lost.

CONCLUSION

Rethinking the matter of architecture through translation of a material is a catalyst for new design innovation. In a time when architecture as a material practice is re-emerging with material science and technology at the forefront of innovation, it is a question of how to harness other expertise and translate new material technologies into applications and novel architectural expressions. Reconsidering form through the lens of material innovation has always been a key part of the evolution of architectural design. To transcribe Akos Moravanszky in Metamorphism, "matter becomes material with the intention to build and the gathering of knowledge required in order to be able to do so." The notion of Thinness allowed us to do just that.

Collaborations with industry, at the scale of matter, stretches disciplinary habits by harnessing knowledge from engineering and material science to invent a more emergent approach to architecture. This collaborative process questions the normative protocols of materials to expose what is possible when the fundamental matter of a material is questioned. As Sheila Kennedy states, "It may seem counterintuitive for a critical practice of material research to examine the material predicaments inherent in the culture of production as a source of inspiration. But it is precisely here that the greatest challenges to the imagination lie.[5]" In that sense thinness did not start with a formal agenda. That is not to say form didn't matter but the method was conceived as antithetical to the process in order to reconsider concrete as a material and as a system of construction.

Form follows Material.

JULIE LARSEN & ROGER HUBELI
APTUM is an award-winning design practice that focuses on material research and its influence on architecture. Their most recent research, teaching, and professional design work revolve around the notion of digital fabrication and tectonics and their potential to mediate between architecture, systems, and ecologies.

Notes

1 Wainright, Oliver. "Rem Koolhaas Blows the Ceiling off the Venice Architecture Biennale." The Guardian. Guardian News and Media, June 5, 2014. http://www.theguardian.com/artanddesign/architecture-design-blog/2014/jun/05/rem-koolhaas-architecture-biennale-venice-fundamentals.

2 Christoph Grunenberg and Sheila Kennedy, "Material Presence," in Material Misuse: Kennedy & Violich Architecture, (Architectural Association, 2001), 21.

3 Moravánszky, Ákos. *Metamorphism: Material Change In Architecture.* Berlin: Birkhauser, 2017.

4 Grunenberg and Kennedy, "Material Presence," 21.

5 Ibid.

WHAT THE TECHNOSPHERE AFFORDS
Toward Other Ecotechnical Logics

Kevan Klosterwill

In lush landscapes like those of the South, plants and animals move quickly to take advantage of every opportunity. Patient seeds sprout from disturbed soils and fill open canopies while worms and bugs devour fallen trees and branches. Often, these organisms appropriate one another: muscadines clamber up low branches to hitch a ride upward, and insects gnaw through living bark and leaf relentlessly. Such vigorous activity quickly softens the signs of human life too. Kudzu races across sidewalks and up telephone poles, draping them in coarse green. Cracks in the pavement offer refuge to their own unique ecosystems. And beneath the thick grasses, tumbling vines, and saplings of the seemingly untouched forest floor, each trying to catch as much of the warm light as it can, there are remnants of the human world, slowly being covered up. A walk through any local woodland landscape is inevitably a browse through the modern world's components—shards of plastic, old beer cans and coke bottles, wrappers, balls and toys, construction debris, and other shrapnel of modern life.

Chemical analysis of these entities would reveal an assortment of strange new petrochemical polymers and metallic alloys, many of which are unlikely to be decomposed quickly, and thus provide the base material for future geologic deposits. Other anthropogenic strata include landfills, cities, mining and agricultural sites, rubble, and ubiquitous pavement. Collectively, these human-made components form the primary geological signature of the Anthropocene, the proposed designation of our contemporary period as a distinctively human epoch on the long scale of planetary time.

But in addition to inaugurating a new time, these anthropogenic elements also open up a new world. Sometimes called the "technosphere," this planet-wide phenomenon is comprised of the marks of human activity.[1] To support their arguments for the inauguration of the Anthropocene, advocates present an array of quantitative evidence regarding the technosphere's presence. They suggest that this diffuse scattering of artifacts weighs about thirty trillion tons all told, unifying these fragments through acts of estimation.[2] Size is not the only measure: power and speed are invoked too. Summed together, the energy of human-generated technological forces might add up to about twenty terawatts—more powerful than all the world's rivers combined.[3] The technosphere has its own fossil record, which is evolving "orders of magnitude faster than biological evolution."[4] Other statistical instruments abound: parts per million of carbon dioxide equivalents, biomass of humans and domesticated animals, and classifications of land surface. Each in its own way testifies to the uniqueness of the present global condition.

These measuring gestures evoke Immanuel Kant's notion of the "mathematical sublime."[5] As one interpreter explains, for Kant

> "the experience of the sublime consists in a feeling of the superiority of our own power of reason, as a supersensible faculty, over nature...In the case of the mathematically sublime, the feeling of reason's superiority over nature takes the form, more specifically, of a feeling of reason's superiority to imagination, conceived of as the natural capacity required for sensory apprehension, including the apprehension of the magnitudes of empirically given things."[6]

Kant's use of terms like nature, imagination, reason, and sense is much more precise than our usual vernacular; however, his sense of the mathematical sublime as a way for uniquely human reason to conceptually contain the sensible, affectual world nonetheless resonates with critiques of the Anthropocene ideology, which suggest that it has far too often become something celebrated, rather than a caution against human hubris.[7]

But for all of the superlatives about its potent weightiness, analysis of the Anthropocene technosphere is so far relatively thin. It has yet to contend with the dynamic thickness of the relations of these and other layers that comprise the earth system.[8] Reason has yet to overcome the need for imagination and the sensible. In fact, it is the complexities of earthly interrelations—interferences, diffractions, and amplifications—and what they make possible that is far more interesting.[9] Just as dead bodies and live ones may weigh the same, so it goes with planets; health is a more holistic quality, requiring a synthesis of the relations between many organs and subsystems and their metabolisms.

Returning to the debris that litters the woods and roadsides, the signs of an eco-modernist "good Anthropocene" are hard to find. It is hard to conceive of how the beer cans, tangles of old wire, and scraps of plastic might be signs of any system that could eventually provide a compelling and even stabilizing force for the planet. Waste abounds. Confronted with the ubiquity of it, it is unsurprising that some choose to evaluate mass and impact and find no possibilities for understanding beyond those raw measurements. And yet, these fragments find new purposes. Tufts of fabric and string are woven into the nests of birds and mice, who find safe alcoves in the frame of a little-driven car. Saplings sprout from the gutter, in a well-watered soil formed from decaying leaves and the gravelly particles slipping off the asphalt shingles. Beavers build around culverts, finding them to be easy damming sites—if they're lucky and the humans are inattentive, a new wetland will blossom. Up and down the road, the signs of reuse are everywhere, by people too. Pie pans and scarecrows dressed in old clothes flap in the garden. Parts cars and bits of machinery lie dormant in many yards and fields, personal junkyards ready for re-purposing.

Technological materials are too often understood in terms of what they were meant to do and what happens to them when they don't work anymore and must be disposed of. Less often are the myriad potentials they offer given prominence and attention. But technological elements can offer many affordances, their creative possibilities as open-ended as the forms of life there are in the world.[10]

These decomposing fragments—albeit at slower timescales than organically-derived materials—offer new possibilities and configurations in the world. Similarly, disaggregating the concept of technology into its constituents offer potentials for more careful and open-ended theorization of the role that these human-made materials and objects play in the world. Are technical things purely defined by their function? Do they have an essence regarding how they relate humans to the world, potentially controlling us?[11] These are the questions that philosophers of technology have asked, but ultimately such arguments fall short when compared with the evidence of the scrappy world, where no one characteristic seems fully satisfactory as a way of drawing these things together and describing what they share.

Descriptions of the technosphere—and technology more broadly—include ideas and media, tools, and infrastructures; and occasionally try to grapple with notions of artificial intelligence. But each of these frames is defined or bracketed in some way to account for a human origin. In the case of the technosphere, its proponents argue that it is "budding off" from the biosphere.[12] The technosphere is a "parasite," but one that might perhaps eventually enter into a more symbiotic relationship with its bio-planetary host.[13] But rather than assuming that technology is a distinct phylum, nested below humans who are themselves a kingdom apart from other kinds of entities in our conceptual models of the world — whether in the spheres of the Earth System or the more simplistic nature-culture binary—I am interested in looking from another angle, asking how the technical might cut across such categories, or stand apart entirely.

Going back to the idea of a technology—a technical logic—as a system of managing practical knowledge suggests a method.[14] Technology could be interpreted geologically: not the speculative earth-systems geology used to argue for the Anthropocene, but a historically-minded geology interested in fossils and crystals as well as strata, capable of revealing previous worlds as they stand apart and flow together. Bracketed by the stratigraphical layers of silt and stone that demonstrate the surprising contingency and diversity of life, this geology applies its historical impulse and uses it to reveal diversity rather than unity, seeking out new species and using them to reveal particular patterns that emerge slowly. It explores the possibilities that alternative categorical gestures suggest, rather than reducing the material it analyzes to as crude a measure as gross weight. Such a technical history might lead to technological taxa as far apart as weather, minerals, vegetables, and animals were in early organizational schemes, permitting the multiplicity of relational modes technical materials create to appear.

Michel Foucault describes of the various kinds of questions drawn together around a given entity in earlier natural histories: not only its organization and components, but also its resemblances and uses, its symbolism and its associated stories and rumors.[15] The question for the entities compiled in a technology then becomes what kinds of phenomena these are, how they come to be, what effects they have, and which worlds they participate in. Such a line of questioning should not assume a certain directionality, but instead be open to relations as they come. Such an approach could offer a better understanding of the petrochemical fleece that lines the field mouse's nest or the role that a stick plays in a beaver's dam, as well as modern environmental and material manipulations, facilitating investigation of whether and how these things belong together at all as something distinct in the world. Rather than a single sphere, human-generated materials convene innumerable relational worlds that must be diligently observed and recorded in terms other than the quantitative. Other tools for detecting these relations and describing them in depth are ready at hand. These include the observational of methods of "nature" writers, who narrate worlds often far more complex and interwoven with human life than we realize;[16] practices of "reading landscapes" with an eye toward interpreting their complex patterns, as naturalist May Watts demonstrates so evocatively;[17] and especially of clearing our own human biases about intention and instinct as we evaluate the doings of other creatures.[18]

Technological choices have a politics that they bring with them, affording certain worlds and forms of life, at the expense of others.[19] There is something to the scrutiny of junk on its own terms, and the appropriations of other species that it in turn facilitates. But what is the health and quality like in these worlds in the long run? The kinds of measurements used to evaluate the Anthropocene can tell us something about the negative impacts of human activity, but they can also through their construction artificially compress that category, lumping differing cultures and ways of life into one species.[20] An attention to more localized affordances, meanwhile, opens the door to articulating the feasibility of other futures, good Anthropocenes that might be more bottom-up and diverse in their logics,[21] or alternative visions marked not solely by human agency, but the diversity of multispecies ecological relations that might emerge.[22] Potential collaborators abound, and the evidence of these novel, more-than-human worlds they have made are all around us. The question is what lessons we will draw from our own observations of this muddled world, and what actions and politics we might propose in response.

Notes

1 "Technosphere" was coined by geologist and engineer Peter Haff. P. K. Haff, "Technology as a Geological Phenomenon: Implications for Human Well-Being," Geological Society, London, Special Publications 395, no. 1 (January 1, 2014): 301–9, https://doi.org/10.1144/SP395.4.

2 Jan Zalasiewicz et al., "Scale and Diversity of the Physical Technosphere: A Geological Perspective," The Anthropocene Review 4, no. 1 (April 2017): 9–22, https://doi.org/10.1177/2053019616677743.

3 Mark Williams et al., "The Anthropocene Biosphere," The Anthropocene Review 2, no. 3 (2015): 196–219.

4 Jan Zalasiewicz et al., "The Technofossil Record of Humans," The Anthropocene Review 1, no. 1 (April 1, 2014): 38, https://doi.org/10.1177/2053019613514953.

5 Immanuel Kant, Critique of Judgement, trans. Werner S. Pluhar (1790; repr., Indianapolis, IN: Hackett Publishing Company, 1987).

6 Hannah Ginsborg, "Kant's Aesthetics and Teleology," in The Stanford Encyclopedia of Philosophy, ed. Edward N. Zalta, Winter 2019 (Metaphysics Research Lab, Stanford University, 2013), https://plato.stanford.edu/archives/win2019/entries/kant-aesthetics/.

7 Eileen Crist, "On the Poverty of Our Nomenclature," Environmental Humanities 3, no. 1 (2013): 129–47, https://doi.org/10.1215/22011919-3611266; Clive Hamilton, "The Theodicy of the 'Good Anthropocene,'" Environmental Humanities 7, no. 1 (May 1, 2016): 233–38, https://doi.org/10.1215/22011919-3616434.

8 "key characteristics of the Anthropocene-human agency, global social and economic networks and important feedback interactions between human systems and planetary processes-have not been dynamically represented or otherwise resolved in existing Earth System and integrated assessment models." Jonathan F Donges et al., "Closing the Loop: Reconnecting Human Dynamics to Earth System Science," The Anthropocene Review 4, no. 2 (August 1, 2017): 152, https://doi.org/10.1177/2053019617725537.

9 James Corner, "The Thick and the Thin of It," in Thinking the Contemporary Landscape, ed. Christophe Girot and Dora Imhof (New York: Princeton Architectural Press, 2016), 117–35.

10 James J. Gibson, The Ecological Approach to Visual Perception (Lawrence Erlbaum Associates, Publishers: Hillsdale, NJ, 1986).

11 Martin Heidegger, The Question Concerning Technology and Other Essays, trans. William Lovitt (New York: Harper & Row, 1977).

12 University of Leicester, "Earth's 'technosphere' Now Weighs 30 Trillion Tons," Science Daily, November 30, 2016, https://www.sciencedaily.com/releases/2016/11/161130085021.htm.

13 Williams et al., "The Anthropocene Biosphere," 208.

14 Leo Marx, "'Technology': The Emergence of a Hazardous Concept," Technology and Culture 51, no. 3 (2010): 561–77, https://doi.org/10.1353/tech.2010.0009.

15 Michel Foucault, The Order of Things: An Archaeology of the Human Sciences (London; New York: Routledge, 2005), http://public.eblib.com/choice/publicfullrecord.aspx?p=240649.

16 Lawrence Buell, *Writing for an Endangered World: Literature, Culture, and Environment in the U.S. and Beyond* (Cambridge, MA: Belknap Press of Harvard University Press, 2001).

17 May Theilgaard Watts, *Reading the Landscape of America, Revised and Expanded Edition* (New York: Collier Books, 1975).

18 Vinciane Despret, *What Would Animals Say If We Asked the Right Questions?*, trans. Brett Buchanan (Minneapolis: University of Minnesota Press, 2016).

19 Langdon Winner, *The Whale and the Reactor: A Search for Limits in an Age of High Technology* (Chicago: University of Chicago Press, 1986).

20 Janae Davis et al., "Anthropocene, Capitalocene, ... Plantationocene?: A Manifesto for Ecological Justice in an Age of Global Crises," Geography Compass, 2019, https://doi.org/10.1111/gec3.12438; Donna J. Haraway, "Anthropocene, Capitalocene, Plantationocene, Chthulucene: Making Kin," Environmental Humanities 6, no. 1 (January 1, 2015): 159–65, https://doi.org/10.1215/22011919-3615934.

21 Elena M Bennett et al., "Bright Spots: Seeds of a Good Anthropocene," Frontiers in Ecology and the Environment 14, no. 8 (October 2016): 441–48, https://doi.org/10.1002/fee.1309.

22 Haraway, "Anthropocene, Capitalocene, Plantationocene, Chthulucene"; Brian G. Henning, "From the Anthropocene to the Ecozoic: Philosophy and Global Climate Change," Midwest Studies In Philosophy 40, no. 1 (September 1, 2016): 284–95, https://doi.org/10.1111/misp.12061.

KEVAN KLOSTERWILL

Kevan Klosterwill is a Candidate in the PhD in the Constructed Environment Program at the University of Virgina, and holds degrees in Landscape Architecture from the University of Georgia. His research currently explores the efficacy of practices of multi-species care to regenerate local and planetary systems.

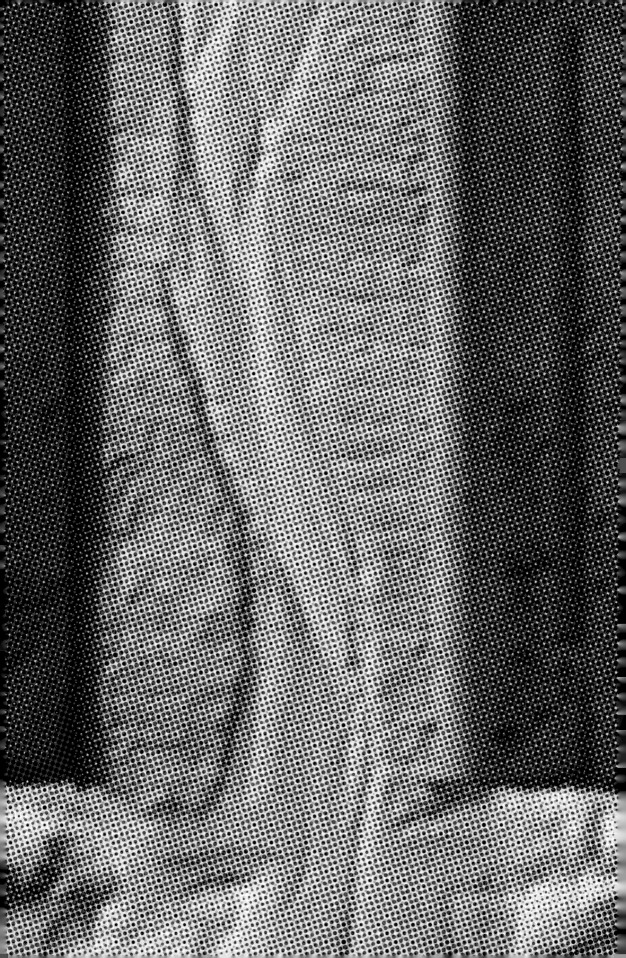

MORE MASSIVE AND MORE SUBTLE
The Asymmetry of Landscape II

Brian Davis

Mud. Sand, silt, clay, bits of broken-down plants and animals, trace chemicals, and industrial residues, all slurried together with salt or freshwater. Mud is one of the most fundamental, temperamental, understudied, and alluring landscape materials of modern life, and its aesthetics deserve our attention.

There is an irony in working with mud. The word connotes a vague, ambiguous quality. But working with it requires an excess of precision. Try to get a waterfront project permitted where mud moving around is a key part of the project. It is very difficult. You certainly can't draw it up in an Autocad section detail as neatly as you can a concrete curb or steel railing. The most sophisticated technical tools available for designing in river and coastal environments can grapple with solid, crystalline, and fibrous materials like large rocks, steel, wood, and concrete. But more plastic materials, of which mud is queen, largely evade description.

I work a great deal with mud; drawing it, listing out what might grow in it, modeling it, sitting in regulatory agency meetings figuring out how to permit its placement, out in the field with equipment operators. Despite this technical, often bureaucratic engagement, I have come to the belief that aesthetics is the most important, interesting, and powerful way to grapple with muddy landscapes on their own terms in ways that don't reduce them to solutions or images, but enroll our senses, tools, memories, and values to participate in the full realm of experience. Maybe aesthetics is first philosophy after all.[1]

By aesthetics I simply mean the philosophy of experience and value. I realized a couple of years ago that a practical aesthetics of landscape that related to these coastal and river places was needed in my

work, and that it should be based in technical and conceptual precision, derived through making instead of the modern tradition of critique. I am trying to follow Gottfried Semper in this. He argued that the conventions by which something is made mediate between the material and its form. Semper's concept of practical aesthetics positions technical concerns as a fundamental part of the cultural value and conceptual approach in the process of making. In my work this suggests that a focus on the tools and procedures applied to muddy landscapes—the mud and metal itself—offers a way forward. But just how might this lead to a practical aesthetic, and what would it be like?

THE WHITE RIBBON

The fast-eroding coastline of Illinois Beach State Park is one of the focus areas of Healthy Port Futures, a research project I run with Sean Burkholder and Tess Ruswick (University of Pennsylvania). Taking a walk here can do things to the senses and the mind. It is a stretch of nondescript beach with scrubby oaks and some weeds along low dunes repeating for miles, punctuated by old roads, mysterious concrete slabs. A complex and violent social history of indigenous dispossession, wartime imprisonment, and nuclear production exists alongside picnics and first kisses and rare sedges and amphibians, first boat rides, and working-class housing that fell

Fig. 1 (*above*)
Hart-Miller Island in the Chesapeake Bay

Fig. 2 (*right*)
A sediment drawing produced using a geomorphology table. This drawing led directly to the concept of the Illinois Beach State Park concept, the White Ribbon.

into the sea as the water levels rose on Lake Michigan in the '80s. It is mostly quiet. The decommissioned Zion Nuclear Plant is within its borders, its northern end holds Illinois' largest marina, while to the south is the Port of Waukegan. It is a landscape from the future.

When you stand on the beach, you have the vast horizon of Lake Michigan laid out before you, all sky and waves, sometimes with the crispest line separating the two, sometimes completely blending with one another. There are over 600 species of plants at Illinois Beach State Park, thanks to the unique ridge-and-swale topography at the lake edge. Undulating oak and pine strips grow on the dunes and a very special type of wetland called a panne in the swales. These qualities reveal themselves only slowly. They don't impress themselves upon a visitor as particularly interesting scenery. Even the nuclear plant reveals itself not as post-industrial sublime cooling towers, but simply large concrete pads and stacks of anonymous materials behind chain link.

Tess, Sean, and I discovered and developed our concept for this place, the White Ribbon, in the technical and bureaucratic context of the regulatory agencies of the state and federal government with its mandates on efficiency, measurement, and control. But the idea was aesthetic first. Dignity, more than beauty, more than performance, more than understanding or knowing, is the most important quality here.

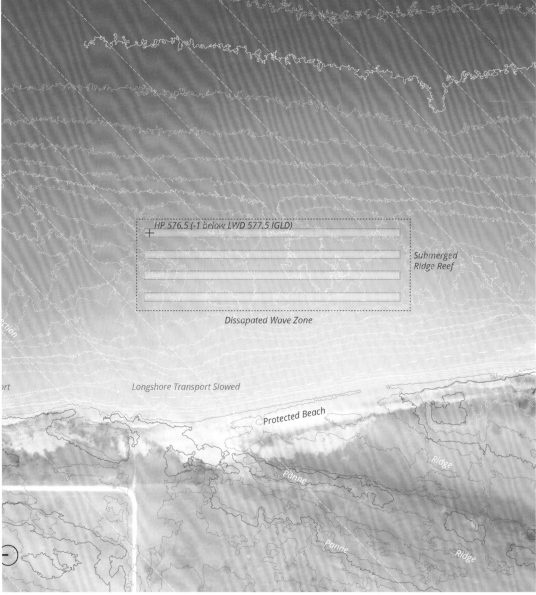

HP 576.5 (-1 below LWD 577.5 IGLD)

Submerged Ridge Reef

Dissapated Wave Zone

...ction

...ort

Longshore Transport Slowed

Protected Beach

Ridge

Panne

Panne

Ridge

The proposal was simple: extend the topographic characteristic of ridges and swales into the nearshore environment, (from zero to ten feet of The proposal was simple: extend the topographic characteristic of ridges and swales into the nearshore environment from zero to ten feet of water depth at high water. In recent years the high water levels and increased storms have led to excessive erosion of the beaches and dunes. Our analysis drew on science already underway in the area by coastal geologist Ethan Theuerkauf of Michigan State. There is something about the geological perspective, the way it focuses on the tiniest elements—bits of sand and plants and water—in the biggest temporal and spatial scale that is right for these landscapes. Together we determined that a reduction in the rate of longshore sediment transport and attenuation of wave energy in special spots along the coastline could be a good strategy for protecting the pannes and preserving the visual and hydrodynamic connection to the lake.

We aimed to unite the upland ridges and the rich swales together with the beach and the nearshore zone. This would create a thickened landscape that remained open and dynamic and that would widen the beach, protect the pannes, and create in-water habitat. This hinged on a series of simple, submerged rubble ridges parallel to the shore that would work in tandem to create a low-lying, high-friction field condition. A kind of entropic landscape, the underwater ridges would deform over time, attenuating less wave energy as the beach builds up, with any rocks that are flattened out by waves serving as habitat for fish.

Our proposal thickens the landscape as it diminishes the figure. The only thing we actually construct—the ridges—will likely never be seen. Only its effects will be experienced and even those will shift and change over time. If it works, the landscape will be a zone along the shoreline with a wider, dissipative beach and a gentler profile, with thriving panne wetlands, a still-unbroken horizon, and a nearshore zone with smaller, foaming, spilling breakers—the white ribbon. In this, I think, may be a key to the aesthetic I am pursuing. It is not about figures, though they may still be present. It is asymmetrical, about time.

THE IMPORTANCE OF ASYMMETRY

Symmetry might be the most fundamental, compelling principle in the history of design (and art and science). In architecture, math, and physics its use goes far beyond common meanings that refer to fairly simple forms of symmetry such as bilateral, rotational, or scalar; or conceptual descriptions such as balance, proportion, and harmony. These all are forms of symmetry of course. But symmetry can be understood to lie at the root of all figuration, and even composition itself.

Fig. 3 (above)
The shoreline of Illinois Beach State Park with the panne and dunes of the shoreline ridge-and-swale topography to the right, and protective rip-rap armor placed to reduce shoreline erosion in the center.

Fig. 4 (bottom)
The White Ribbon proposal, with constructed mounds extending the ridge-and-swale topography into the nearshore environment, nine feet deep at the deepest location given current water levels.

What I meant by asymmetry, then, is the absence of composition, of figures. Just how something can have form—true, specific difference—in the absence of figures or even composition is a central paradox of landscape, one I am only now beginning to peer into. But landscape has always been more circumspect in its discussion and use of symmetry. Mud, dirt, and water as well as people and their messy politics, histories, and rituals move through and rely on one of the most basic asymmetrical things in the universe—time.

Landscape architecture has long been committed to process and time. I believe it is the principle of asymmetry that explains how muddy landscapes in particular accrue their thickness, and what they are like. This essay expands on earlier writing in which I showed that you can sense the power and violence and growth that muddy landscapes embody, made vulnerable through the asymmetries of interactions and qualities of equal and unlike things.

The principle of asymmetry is evident in the proposal at Illinois Beach. Through an accident of the process—rocks being flattened by waves in our sediment drawing machine—we happened upon an idea. What if instead of a breakwater with just the right shape and size and orientation we create a field condition of rough, rocky ridges, one that is meant to form other fields—a wave field, the beach itself, the ridge-and-swale topography of the upland? This is what we proposed.

The White Ribbon is to be a field of ridges and swales some 200 feet wide and 700 feet long in the near-shore environment. Follow a wave in:

> Coming from a stormy lake you encounter the deepest ridge in about ten feet of water. You slow and spill a bit as your bottom drags on the ridge before your top. You start to set back up in the swale only to spill again, on and on for an area a bit wider than a football field, until you have dissipated half of your height and energy. You move up into the swash zone and run up on a low, broad beach face with a shorebird or two. As you begin to return to the water, you see up ahead a swale bracketed by two dunes. The swale is full of plants and birds, the dunes boast scrubby, windblown oaks.

Our team is using computational modeling alongside bathymetric analysis and construction limitations to help us locate this area and size the rocks that will constitute the ridges. Storm waves will be reduced, lessening their erosive power, while daily waves will pass over the ridges largely untouched, with their tendency to build the shoreline and dune system preserved. The power of the lake will be brought into a new relation with the pannes, converted to a beach-making mechanism.

PELOTROPHIC LANDSCAPES

What I am working on is nothing new in landscape. The unseen figure we create at Illinois Beach—the rubble ridges—has effects and works with contextual forces to help form a larger landscape over time. There is no way to know precisely what the effects will be beforehand, because the exact storms (their magnitude, duration, and direction), the exact choices of shorebirds and boaters, the precise plants that will succeed in the pannes have a specific agency that can't be predicted but can be worked with. These are maneuvers that have existed in landscape design for a long time. With something as simple as the planting of a tree or creation of a paving pattern, the point of the work is a secondary effect—the way people will move through a plaza according to their own choices and the rhythms of the city it is a part of; or the way the tree will grow, take root, attract birds, and sculpt space. The impulse to control these things exists within very limited boundaries in landscape design, though the form is affected over time by original design choices.[13]

In the drawings I've been doing and the projects with Sean and Tess; the field work in tide flats and wetlands; and the meetings with communities and technical bureaucrats and regulators; as well as my study of theorists, scientists, engineers, and artists such as Vija Celmins, Hiroshi Sugimoto, and the Oakes Brothers, a few common

Fig. 5 (below) Wave drawing for Port Bay, NY, using CMS-Wave, a two-dimensional wave spectral model.

qualities emerge. The first is vastness. These places are all massive in one way or another. They are also subtle, often with only very small variations in space and time, whether topographic or otherwise. These two conditions together produce a kind of banality that is teeming with life. They tend to be incredibly rich, with small shifts producing outsize effects in appearance, plant and animal species and density, wave attenuation, and human use. Despite this subtlety they change radically through time, punctuated by events such as storms or building, and the patient shaping of ongoing actions such as waves, or daily lives of humans. All of these things give form to the landscape.

But they do not feature the figure (though figures are sometimes present). They offer no overarching narratives, and composition is fleeting, if it exists at all. If asymmetry is the principle, the actual aesthetic that I want to offer is something like pelotrophic, meaning "mud-nourished." It is that sense you get spending time on the sea, or wading a mudflat, fishing a wetland, or hiking along a bog. There is no call to action, no narrative that stirs the soul. This aesthetic does not seek to resolve a landscape into a tidy narrative, or somehow absolve people (whether designers, caretakers, or users) from ongoing involvement with it. Wildness, or amongstness in the absence of control, is a key quality. There are no walls, no "out there." This is not an aesthetic theory descended from garden traditions, or modernist critique.[16]

A design idiom and set of techniques and approaches might work with these qualities, augmenting and extending them to create the cultural landscapes we desire. It is through this work that the aesthetic theory we need will cohere. In my work I use tools to find ways of inhabiting the watery, muddy landscapes of tomorrow; the working class neighborhood every year flooded by king tides, the riverfront park that strategically accumulates sediment deposited in floods, landscapes created as byproducts of port operations, and coastal landscapes where ecological preservation is possible in a time of massive biodiversity loss. In all of these, dignity is that which creates the allure and seems most essential. It will only become more so.

Fig. 6 (opposite)
A drawing from the series Asymmetry of Landscape, drawing from artists such as Vija Celmins and Sol Lewitt. A mechanical pencil is used on watercolor paper, with the lead width, line spacing, and slight variations in my mood or mechanical precision and speed as some of the main aspects of the drawing.

Fig. 7 (following page)
Drone captured point cloud of The White Ribbon after install.

BRIAN DAVIS

Brian Davis is an associate professor of landscape architecture at the University of Virginia. He is a licensed landscape architect, a member of the Dredge Research Collaborative, and a fellow of the American Academy in Rome. Brian's work focuses on large sedimentary systems as cultural, public landscapes, with a particular interest in the Great Lakes, the Chesapeake Bay region, and the Rio de la Plata.

Notes

1 Graham Harman, "Aesthetics as First Philosophy: Levinas and the non-human," Nake Punch: 09, Summer/Fall 2007; http://dar.aucegypt.edu/handle/10526/3073, accessed May, 2 2020.

2 Bruno Latour offers a compelling argument for why this tradition should be done away with entirely in Bruno Latour, "Why Has Critique Run out of Steam? From Matters of Fact to Matters of Concern," Critical Inquiry 30, no. 2 (Winter 2004): 225–48.

3 "The Performative Nature of Mud and Metal" was the title of my talk at the 10th Landscape Biennal in Barcelona in 2018.

4 "Healthy Port Futures," www.healthyportfutures.com.

5 The project is for and permitted by the Illinois Department of Natural Resources, with oversight from and collaboration with the Illinois State Geological Survey, the US Environmental Protection Agency, the US Army Corps of Engineers, the National Oceanic and Atmospheric Administration, and the US Environmental Protection Agency, and paid for by the Great Lakes Restoration Program.

6 While the Great Lakes don't have tides to speak of, they do experience seasonal, annual, and decadal fluctuations in water that can be as great as five feet in Lake Michigan.

7 Beginning with Vitrivius, up through Semper, and including more modern takes such as Colin Rowe, architectural theory offers a great discourse on the subject. While it is a bit out of fashion now, it is still present and important. As an example, one of the Architecture Fellows at the American Academy in Rome my year, Michael Young, has a whole series on the subject.

8 I draw this argument from the mathematician Herman Weyl's fantastic book *Symmetrie* (1938).

9 Francis Bacon's definition of what form actually is still works as one of the most precise and basic definitions of this critical term. Novum Organum, Book 2, Aphorism 1.

10 Studying the works of artists such as Vija Celmins and Tomas Saraceno, and imagery from NASA.

11 "The asymmetry of landscape: Aesthetics, agency, and material reuse in the Reserva Ecológica de Buenos Aires. Brian Davis," Journal of Landscape Architecture, Vol. 3, No. 13: 78-89.

12 "Accidents of process" are a key part of how I design. I am always looking for them and my methods for any innovative project attempt to create the conditions for them.

13 And thank God for that. Otherwise landscape architecture might have no value at all.

14 My early article "Landscapes and Instruments" discusses a concept of radical difference in landscape, which is what I mean here. Landscape Journal, 32:2, 2013, 293–308.

15 Elizabeth Meyer's "Beyond 'Sustaining Beauty': Musings on a Manifesto" (2015) as well as some of her other writings make this point, as do I in "Public Sediment" (*Towards an Urban Ecology*, ed. Kate Orff, Monacelli Press, New York, 2016).

16 In particular, the subject-object as a primary structuring device is the modernist legacy I am hoping to elude.

REPRENTATION

DRAWING TRANSLATION

Katie LaRose

To design is to rethink, redraw, and reconceive. To represent is crucial in this endeavor. There is a strong and undeniable link between the representational tools an architect uses and the spatial outcome of these architectures. Over time, architectural movements have shifted intentions in representation, resulting in unique spatializations of changing world views. As the agency of the architect in social conversations is changing, so too must her tools of representation.

How does the drawing translate to architecture, and furthermore what could be found in this space? The investigation of this representational change from drawing to building is analyzed in situ through case studies of center-built Roman monuments. Emanating from a single point, the center-built projects' strongest characteristic is their central axis. By redrawing existing projects and investigating their particular histories, intentions, realities, and experiences, a layered, thickened representation is created that itself can be inhabited. By occupying this in-between space, the unique worldview of Roman monuments can be made visible.

MULTIPLE CENTERS

In built examples that show clear favor to the compass including Piazza San Pietro, Piazza del Campidoglio, and Bramante's Tempietto, the translation from drawing to building is studied. The architect's compass, the technical drawing instrument used to inscribe circles, arcs, centerpoints, organizes not only a unique spatial worldview—one of man at the center—but the drawing and therefore the built monument. The compass uniquely connects the hand and body of the architecture to the architecture itself. With the handle between thumb and first two fingers, the leg sweeps

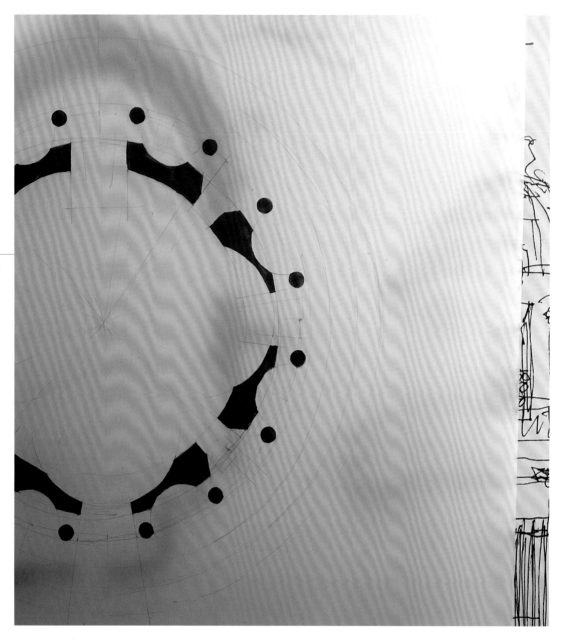

in a circular motion, following the movement of the wrist, elbow, and shoulder. The center point is marked by a rod, followed by the marking of the circle by tracking around it with a taut line. In this process, the whole body is utilized (Fig. 1).

Each center-built project will produce a unique reading of rebuilding −by way of isolating the plan, section, and perspective. By layering plan, section, and perspective, the case study is examined in reverse, revealing intended realities. The delamination of such drawings makes a thick space within, and reveals more slowly, this translation. The intentions of the drawing and the experience of the built environment are overlapped and thus reveal "edifices of power" and the centering of man.[1]

Fig. 1 (above)
Tempietto at San Pietro in Montorio.

Fig. 2 (opposite, top)
Center-built projects, Rome, Italy.

Fig. 3 (opposite, bottom)
Piazza del Popolo, Towards Basilica di San Pietro.

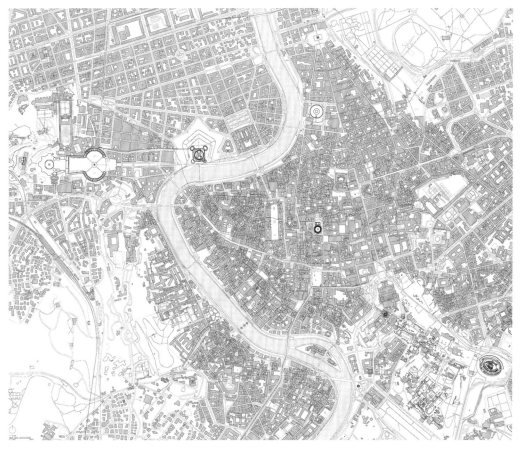

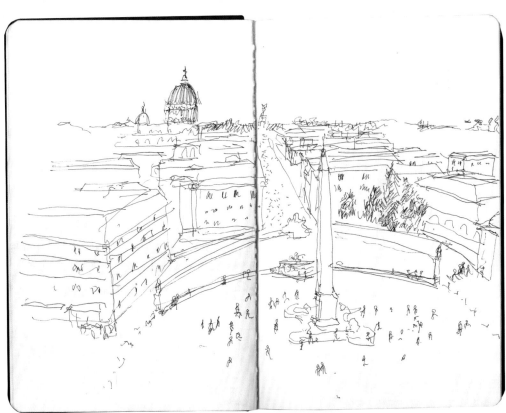

Projects of Rome's multiple centers are redrawn to investigate the ways in which single projects combine to create the urban fabric that shapes our collective experience of the built environment. Representation of multiple centers, a *dérive* through Rome, is a way of re-seeing projects utilizing the compass and the hand, and testing the translation from drawing to architecture.

A selection of Rome's center-built projects are highlighted on the map (Fig. 2). This urban scale was used to examine the use of the compass in the singular project as it relates to the larger fabric. These center-based monuments of Rome highlight the multiple centers of Rome's past (including Teatro di Marcello, Circo Massimo, Pantheon, Colosseo, Castel Sant'Angelo) and present. It is perhaps most apparent through the perspective drawing (Fig. 3, 4) in how these multiple centers influence one's movement through the city.

EDIFICES OF POWER

The "edifice of power" apparent in the Piazza San Pietro emanates from the centerpoint of its ancient Egyptian obelisk, towards the Vatican and the colonnade surrounding the piazza (Fig. 5). Four columns deep, the colonnade reinforces this center of Rome—one of power. The columns tower over the occupants of the piazza, and through its scale the base becomes a place for gathering (Fig. 6).

Fig. 4 (above)
Towards Capitoline Hill.

Fig. 5 + 6 (opposite)
Piazza San Pietro,
Vatican City.

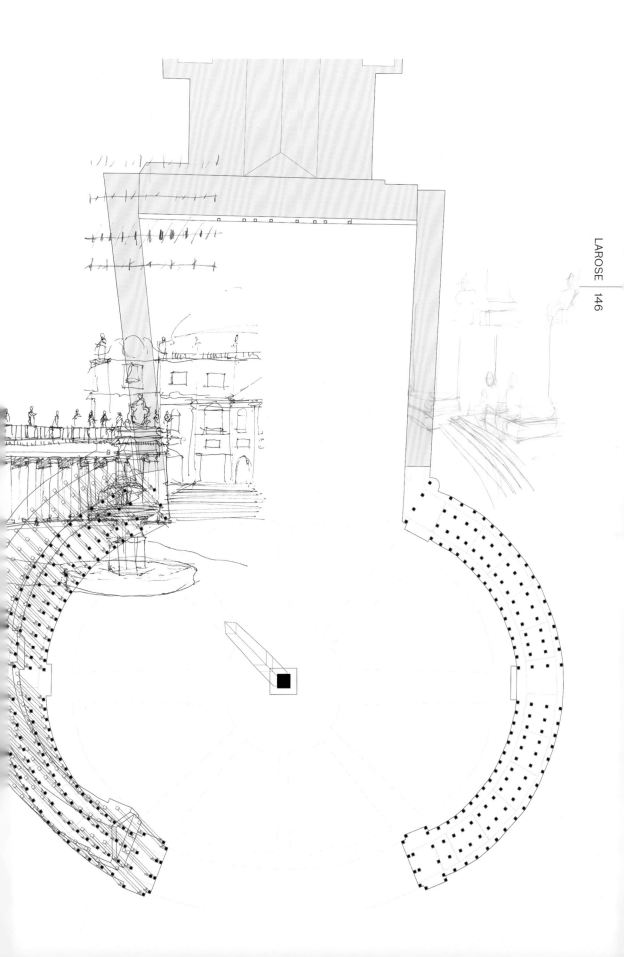

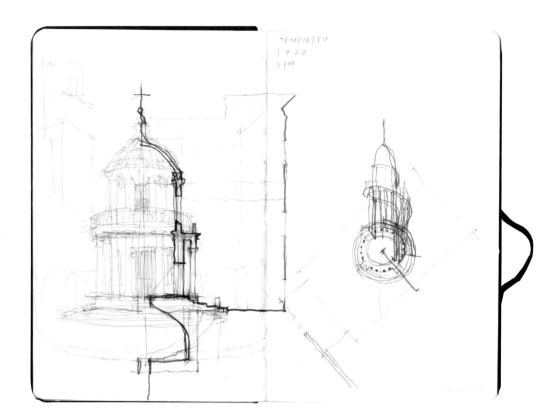

CENTERING IN TIME, IN PLACE

Bramante's Tempietto, considered the first architectural work of
the Renaissance, exemplifies the centering of man. The monument
was meant to be viewed at the courtyard's entrance–revealing a
masterpiece of proportions. It is in fact the only non-ancient work of
architecture in Palladio's Fourth Book of Architecture for this reason.[2]
The deep well of the Tempietto's grotto marks the martyrdom of St.
Peter, and connection to the ground (Fig. 9). Through its circular
nature, the building performs as a centering of man. The Tempietto
is an exemplification of the religious and political power of the
Renaissance and Rome itself, marking its location as a center in time
and space.

Disegno is an Italian word meaning both *to draw* and *to design*. The
spatialization of unique world views are made clear by the act of
drawing. These case study investigations could be described as a
"re-disegno" perhaps, by re-presenting multiple centers within Rome's
urban fabric, the relationship between drawing and architecture is
delaminated so that one may occupy this space of translation.

Fig. 7 + 8
*Tempietto at San Pietro
in Montorio.*

Notes

1 Carrie Mae Weems, "Roaming," Art21, "Extended Play," 2010.

2 Murray, P. Bramante's Tempietto. Charlton Lectures on Art Delivered in the University of Newcastle upon Tyne, 1972.

KATIE LAROSE

Katie LaRose is a practicing designer in Houston, Texas. She holds a Masters of Architecture from the University of Virginia and a Bachelors of Fine Arts in Interior Design from Virginia Commonwealth University. She was funded by the Carlo Pelliccia Fellowship in 2020, for research based in Rome, Italy. Her work investigates the mediation of the built environment, memory, and representation.

Fig. 9
Tempietto at San Pietro in Montorio.

THICK_FLAT

Charles Weak

Digital thickness seems like a bit of a misnomer. Image-making software, like Photoshop, is structured by organizational logics deployed by a software interface that allows users to edit Photoshop compositions, like the Layer interface. The Layer interface within Photoshop suggests a three-dimensional space through how Photoshop Layers seem to float on top of and below one another.[1] This assemblage of layers or layer "stack" creates the illusion that Photoshop uses foreground- and background-like analog modes of production (screen print, painterly effects), where layers of media are applied on top of one another. However, this is not the reality. Rather than subsequent layers of media sitting on top of one another, all content hosted within the space of a Photoshop (or PSD) file is nested somewhere, into the fibers or pixels of the assembled composition. There are no subsequent layers of media applique that generate a buildup in Photoshop. Instead there are pixels and color codes that toggle on and off based on the layer window interface.

The "toggling" is central to Photoshop materially, in understanding depth or "thickness" in a Photoshop file. The layer stack offers the ability to play through many different compositions quickly, and more flexibly than analog content. The trade-off being, Photoshop files can become heavier by importing more content into the file, making it difficult to toggle or manipulate the Photoshop interface. Photoshop files operate under principles of density rather than thickness (the analog system for buildup in compositional systems). Considering "density" as a spatial condition or compositional system might generate new readings of space and can create new techniques for designers to experiment with. Image-making software takes away some of the constraints of physical media and allows for designers to play with a composition more freely, before compressing and exporting a final image. Flexibility in this system plays a role in reshaping and opening up modes of working for designers. However, more than that, layer structures and image-making software encourages designers to work differently, and to think about how an image is a system of charged content laminated inside a frame at a particular moment in the design composition. If an image is a single moment in the time of a file, then a GIF portrays a short history of a compressed Photoshop file, blurring a series of compositions together, and doing work to deconstruct layers embedded in that file. The blurring creates a flickering, where users are allowed to see the construction of the Photoshop file from the back end, and to see the uncompressed construction within the analogical space of the image.

LAYERS AS THICKNESS

Working in Photoshop is uncanny. Layers seem to have thickness and depth, floating in planar relationship to each other in a 2.5-dimensional space. These qualities help to ontologically separate Photoshop from its predecessors. It's easiest to imagine the space of a Photoshop file as a separated axonometric, delaminating all layers into an exploded hierarchy, from foreground to background, top to bottom. While painting is the process of applying material successively onto a composition, as layers, Photoshop compositions grow through nesting more content but are never thicker than a single atomically thin layer. Images do not increase their thickness when they become more intricate, instead they increase in density as more data is collapsed into the file used to generate the image. A delaminated axon diagram expresses all the elements and effects within a file and how they would apply to each other moving backwards in space. "Off" content remains hidden within the interface, to not obstruct the in-progress composition. This content is kept close, if it might become useful again. There is never more information stored within the composition of a Photoshopped image, than what is seen on screen. However, the rest of the content of the PSD file still exists in the depths of the file, still conceptually nested inside the composition, flickering on and off via the interface. Photoshop files are interpretations and combinations of user intent and data, which are compressed and exported as the final step. Compression allows Photoshop files to be flexible compositionally. As signals change and layers are added or taken away from the PSD file, the thickness of the total composition stays the same.

Architects have only just become interested in the telematic qualities and potential of images; however, the mechanisms that are deployed within Photoshop come from art techniques (layers from Printmaking) and art movements (flickering and temporality in Cubism). Layering and flickering enter architecture through discussions of transparency in the writings of Colin Rowe and Robert Slutzky, and Peter Eisenman on the perception of depth through transparency, in the Transparency

Articles written in the middle of the twentieth century. The authors of the Transparency Articles employed formal analysis to investigate the relationship between the viewing subject and object on view, through an understanding of the body in space. Generally, the Transparency Articles focused on the spatial qualities of layers; their perceptual qualities, moving between foreground and background, as well as implied space between layers. In printmaking, Photoshop's ancestor layers are applied sequentially, one on top of another to generate the desired composition. When a layer is applied during the printmaking process, that layer cannot be removed or moved to another part of the composition. In a Photoshop file that functionality is available. Users can freely change the composition of a Photoshop file through the Photoshop interface's layer structure. This creates a situation where the limitations of physical media (material application) no longer apply to the generation of a file. Flexibility is a major asset to digital work and creates situations where designers or users can work and attempt compositions without concern for material ramifications of the application of material. Compression, the digital equivalent of application, happens at the end of the creation process, leaving all the layers in the Photoshop interface to sit analogically inside each other until the very final moment. Waiting until the final moment to create the composition might offer ideas of an epistemology on flexibility...or permanent unfinished-ness.

"Architects have only just become interested in the telematic qualities and potential of images; however, the mechanisms that are deployed within Photoshop come from art techniques...and art movements."

Examining the nature of the ancestors of image-making forms a basis for understanding some of the mechanisms around layers, temporality, and flickering. Interacting with the Photoshop interface, (turning layers on and off, changing the hierarchy of layers) creates a flickering condition within the composition of the Photoshop file, exposing the hidden content. GIFs (Fig. 1) are images that portray several instantiations of compositions native to a Photoshop file, operating as short, temporal compositions. A GIF's short history (two to six seconds) is not enough to elaborate on a full idea, but enough to express a feeling or have an effect. They portray a limited, compressed history that can be shared easily, sharing temporal information without requiring a video player. As GIFs cycle through compositions, they flicker, exposing each composition/frame as an individual, while simultaneously belonging to the assembled GIF. In two dimensions this appears as flickering layers that operate as a sequence, or in Photoshop through flipping on and off. In three dimensions flickering occurs when orbiting around projects like

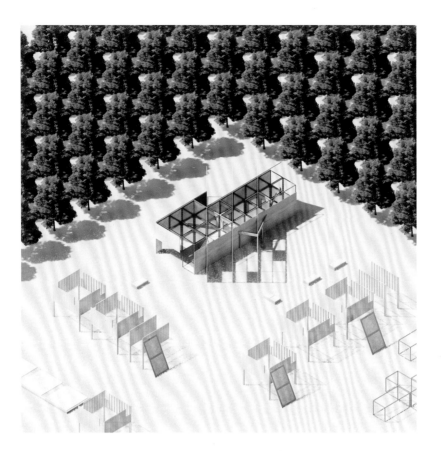

Hiromi Fujii's Mizoe Series. Flickering in both second and third dimensions is a product of shifting positions and dimensions. The flickering occurs when established elements within a moving composition shift out of an established alignment or into a new alignment. In the space between alignments, compositions find flexibility and a diversity of interpretations.

SURFACE CONSTRUCTION

In physical space, surface logics are analogous to the layer. Surfaces form the basis for all content that we have direct physical relationships with. In his book, *The Ecological Approach to Visual Perception*, psychologist James Gibson breaks down "terrestrial" (the word he uses in place of physical) material into three categories: Substance, Surface, and Medium. Substance and Medium represent "solid" and "ambient" matter respectively. Substance takes the form of the physical characteristics of an object, its material assemblage.[2] The category Medium plays an opposite role in subject / object relationship to substance. Media, such as air, light, or sound, play an integral role in our perception of phenomena. Gibson points out that the underlying nature of Substance (the characteristics and nature of objects to the atomic level) and Medium (viscera and other unseen entity like air, which play with ephemeral perception) are too abstract for most people to have interactions with, which leaves people to

Fig. 1 (above)
Shifting elements that relate to GIF compositions, built from individual frames that constitute short histories.

Fig. 2 (opposite)
Single composition frame, one of many.

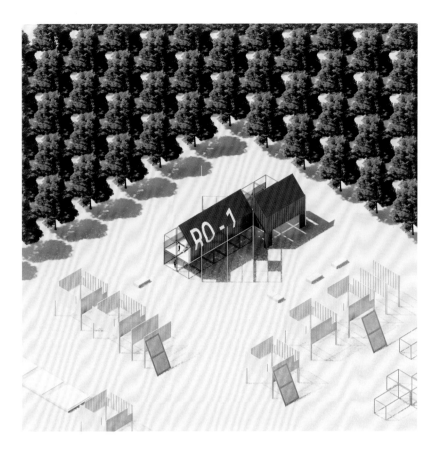

instead interact with the surface of objects. Surfaces represent the outermost layer of a substance, which is what's perceivable by a user or subject. They are the substrate that a subject interacts with and provide all visible and tactile information.

Image-making software inspires the work of artist Laura Owens. Owens' work examines the process for generating images, and through manipulating both physical and digital media, creates dense complicated compositions that question ideas on physical and digital ontologies. In her work, Owens creates a physical composition, scans that composition into the computer, edits that composition using software, prints out the new composition, and then continues to edit the composition. The oscillation between physical and digital means of working obscures the construction of the composition, causing it to flicker between media, and spatial organization. Owens creates a commentary on the intersection of physical and digital means of working, as she weaves the elements of her composition, physical and digital, into the foreground and background. These ontological and process games happen within the space of composition rather than on top of it. This interpretation of the thickness in Owens' work, as well as for image-making software, is focused on building up content within the bounds of the file. The density of the indexical systems in Owens' work comes in part through the translation that occurs when moving an image between physical and digital media, and then hiding or blurring the ontological characteristics of these systems, to create one flattened composition.[3] The game of interpreting the characteristics of her compositions seems to be more focused on understanding the hierarchical play between layers within the composition or even the space of the gallery, rather than understanding whether or not the particular effect was produced on a computer or by hand (although that game is still pertinent). Owens is interested in the viewing subject, and their interpretation of a thin, but incredibly dense, surface.

The speculative house projects T-Zone, Project Mizoe N. 4, and Project Mizoe Hall by Hiromi Fujii in the mid-1990s take on compositional ideas about surface construction and structure. Fujii's work was interested in the complex potential of built space. The surfaces of Fujii's Mizoe series shift and bend spatial elements through manipulating the surfaces that constitute the project. These surfaces slide into and next to each other; they share similar pattern language, suggesting indexical relationships (Fig. 2). However, as the frames and surfaces slide through one another, those indexical relationships are called into question. Mizoe's surfaces suggest different possibilities or compositions, as if moving or rearranging themselves. The screens of Fuji's houses retain strange scalar relationships, slip between one another, and disappear into the ground, or inhabit the same physical space as one another. Fuji's grids reference an organization that is thoroughly deconstructed by the arrangement of said grids and screens. They form surfaces that then form the enclosure for the house. The underlying logics and dislogic of the surface organization suggest that there may be several different compositions sitting on top of one another that are read as one would move around the exterior or interior spaces of the house. A flickering occurs and alignments and misalignments of different surface logics create and frustrate different organizations to create the house.

Fujii's house embodies the messy, unfinished nature of a Photoshop file. The flickering surfaces, shifting in locations and scale are reminiscent of digital modes of working, image-making software, and GIF files. GIFs, in particular, display a kinship with Fujii's work due to the GIF's relationship to cycling. GIFs begin with a single image/composition and then transition through a series of other images, before returning to the initial composition. Orbiting around the models of Fujii's Mizoe House has a similar effect; moving around the elevation of the model shows surfaces and indexical relationships appear through color and panelization, which then reset when you return to your original point of view.

GIFs deploy elements of structures no longer relevant to the construction of a single finished product. GIFs are instantiations of image-making's flexibility. Physical material operates differently from digital material, but the work of architect Hiromi Fujii as well as artists like Laura Owens deploy the layer logic systems in

Fig. 3
A composition of all the objects and elements modeled into the space of a Rhino file that I used to create a GIF, showing multiple temporalities and pointing to the work's unfinished nature.

physical space to question the nature of analog material, and build dense semiotic, indexical, representational, or perceptual systems into physical objects. They are ahistorical, reading the contents of compositions and constantly shifting through a compositional loop. In shifting through their contents, GIFs express some of the density embedded from the image-making software they were born out of, and the ontological nature of Photoshop files that focuses Photoshop on creating dense assemblages rather than final products. Software has begun to shape an aesthetic that puts digital effects, content, and tropes into physical space through laminating these effects on physical objects. Photoshop's flexibility and additional content structures new modes of working and thinking around the construction of file systems that generate multiple unique compositions, rather than a singular finished or frozen product. New spaces express their digital organizational origins, while retaining the physical material qualities, expressing qualities of both spaces at the same time (Fig. 3). Flexibility in the Photoshop interface lends itself to thinking about the process for constructing images and opens the interpretation of surfaces in physical space to thinking about flexibility and construction as something that is perpetually "cycling" or ongoing. A physical space that considers the nature of Photoshop layers and GIF cycling offers itself to interpretation and flexibility or understands that the process of building is ongoing, never quite finished.

CHARLES WEAK

Charles Weak is an architect practicing in Washington, D.C. His work centers around image-making and the software that generates images, and augmentation in existing and new modes of cultural paradigms and organizational logics. He's previously written for PLAT Journal at Rice University, Paprika at Yale, and See / Saw at University of Maryland, as well as Kooz/Arch and Malaparte Cafe. His work has appeared online at SuckerPunch, Refworks, IMadeThat, and Kooz/Arch.

Notes

1 In *Software Takes Command*, Lev Manovich takes an in-depth look at the models for which Photoshop systems operate, including how different types of layers work in Photoshop as well as how the Photoshop Hierarchy operates. "Understanding Metamedia," *Software Takes Command*, Bloomsbury Academic: 142.

2 Gibson's first chapter outlines in greater detail the different material instantiations. Gibson, James J. *The Ecological Approach to Visual Perception: Classic Edition.* United Kingdom: Taylor & Francis, 2014.

3 Godfrey offers a reading of Owens' work. Mark Godfrey, "Statements of Intent," Artforum, April 2014: 297.

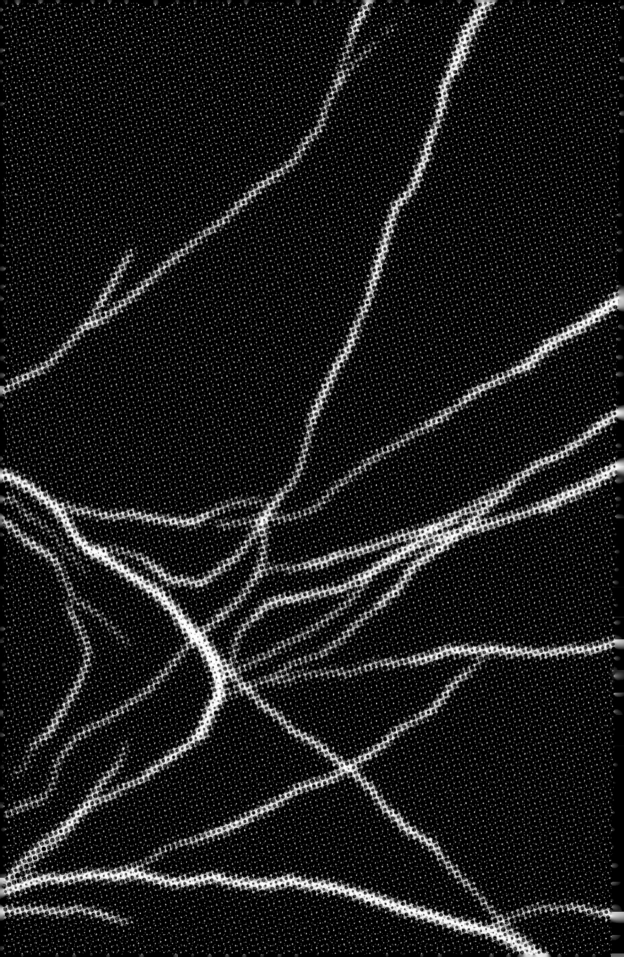

WHEN THE LINE THICKENS

Matthew Wilson

> The lines of various thicknesses are then drawn by hand. It takes a great deal of practice and skill to make a satisfactory hachure map. The generation of highly trained artists who did this kind of work is slowly dying out.[1]

The drawing of a line is the making of a world. It is this sense of mapmaking, as a post-representational practice, that both catalyzes and beguiles contemporary thought and action in cartography. However, all lines are not created equal. They may disguise or disclose the techniques of their making or the burden of significance they carry. Line widths and weights. Pattern and repetition. Then and now, the work of signifying the real begins with a simple question: how to re-present, well?

In the field of cartography, the headwaters of such training in America centers around the work of Erwin Raisz (1893–1968), cartographic instructor and map curator at Harvard University. The above epigraph originates from his General Cartography,[2] hailed by Arthur Robinson (1915–2004) in his 1970 obituary for Raisz as the first cartography textbook in English, and the first text that championed a systematic training of handborn cartography. Here, Raisz discusses the technical work of drawing a line by hand, noting the necessary practice and skill to arrive at a well-drawn line.

While the techniques of cartography a century ago were to produce a representation that would carry the signature of the cartographic artist, Robinson and his students would inject a modernist functionalism into cartographic practice in ways that would push the specific decisions of the designer below the map surface.

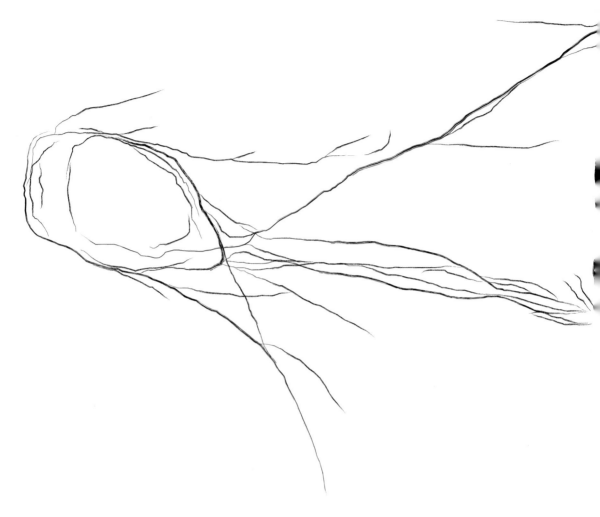

Today, however, cartographers' return to handdrawn methods, or methods that appear handdrawn, should be seen as a response to a Robinsonian over-purposing of the mapmaker-mapreader relation.

Attempting to draw lines that have the appearance of being hand-drawn with ink requires specific effects in drawing and rendering software. Here, I sheepishly submit "Cowlines," a gift given to my parents to memorialize a water retention pond on our family farm. The pond, beyond being seen through aerial imagery, is made visible through the paths wrought by the movements of cattle. These paths outline the pond, while bringing the pond into relation with the surrounding landscape. How to re-present these lines, well? How might one render the path not as a discrete vector, but as a line of discontinuous thickness?

Of course, I do not argue that my rendering is a great example
of thickness, but rather that the process of rendering using
digital software is conditional and ephemeral, that it attempts to
communicate the effect of a handborn craft, and of a craft that is still
developing. Raisz understood a forensics of this developing craft
and was able to diagnose a series of faults in drawing a line. I was
at some pains to digitally reproduce the appearance of faults in Fig.
3, faults that Raisz was at pains to train out of his pupils. The high
techniques of representation are perhaps fickle.

Thickness is regarded. Whether maintaining consistent thickness
or producing a bespoke variability, the drawing of a cartographic
line is weighty; it is responsible, and sometimes responsive. The
thickness or stroke weight of a line produces a further dimension of
its representational wake. Not only to define a limit, or bound an area,
but to specify the quality and quantity of that limit and boundary.

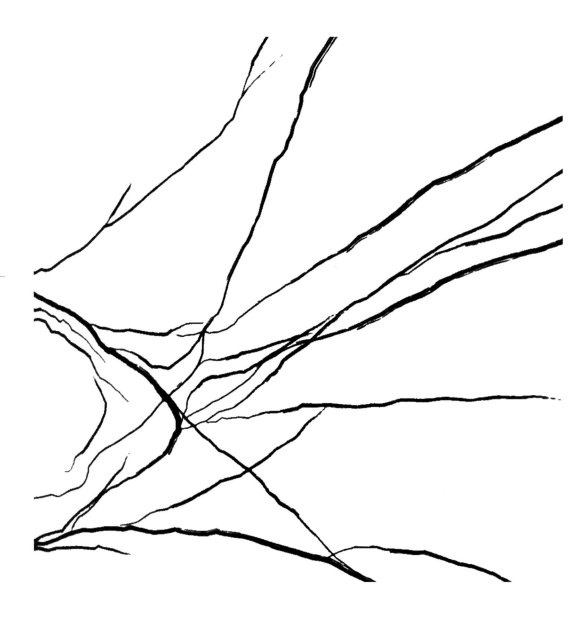

Guide slipped into wet line

Ink on outside of pen, ran under

Pen too close to guide. Ink ran under.

Ragged line. Pen sloped away from guide

Ragged line from dirty pen

Pen pressed too hard against guide

Pen too full   *Not enough ink*

Crooked line from using high guide

FIG. 103.—Beginners' common faults in the use of ruling pen. (*From Riggleman, Graphic Methods.*)

"A good ruling pen is very important," instructs Raisz. However, the pen is not sufficient. He continues:

> The ink is supplied between the two blades with a quill, and care should be taken that no ink shall stick on the outside. The lines are drawn with the pen held lightly in a perfectly vertical position. The two blades should never press against each other, for the ink must flow easily. If the pen is pressed down, it may clog with fibers of the paper. If contact with the paper fails, or the line becomes thick, the pen must be cleaned. If sufficiently fine lines cannot be obtained, the ruling pen should be sharpened on a fine honing stone.[3]

Care, comportment, contact. Cleaning and sharpening. When the line thickens, we are reminded that what is being represented is always sutured to how the representation proceeds. Such responsiveness, then and now, is the welcome aporia of the drawn line.

Notes

1 Raisz, Erwin. *General Cartography,* 124. New York and London: McGraw-Hill book company, inc, 1938.

2 Robinson, Arthur Howard. *"Erwin Josephus Raisz, 1893–1968,"* Annals of the Association of American Geographers 60 (March 1970): 189–93.

3 Raisz, *General Cartography*, 178-9.

Fig. 2 (top)
Enlarged, photographed section of "Cowlines."

Fig. 3 (bottom)
Explanation of common faults in the use of a ruling pen to draw lines with a guide, from Raisz's General Cartography (1938, 178).

MATTHEW WILSON

Associate Professor in the Department of Geography at the University of Kentucky and an Associate at the Center for Geographic Analysis at Harvard University. His most recent book is New Lines: Critical GIS and the Trouble of the Map *(University of Minnesota Press), and his current research examines early-twentieth-century thought on map-making and geographic education.*

THICK BODIES, THICK SPACES

Vic Mantha-Blythe & Brynne Day

Thick bodies in space are intrinsically radical. They challenge the social and physical norms of architectural design to make room for diverse people to exist. Architectural guidelines (e.g., building codes, reference guides, manuals) neglect to mention the role design standards can play in creating harmful spaces for thick bodies. "Comfortable" space guidelines, as defined by Neufert,[1] are created based on normative body sizes that exclude a vast percentage of the bodies that make up our communities. These guidelines base their minimum/maximum dimensions for space on what is considered 'sufficient' to provide comfort and ease of movement. This implies that people with bodies that do not fit comfortably within these standards are requiring more than 'sufficient' space, which normalizes and excuses the design of inaccessible spaces. Even accessible design guides lack recommendations for body size diversity, contributing to the exclusionary—and potentially harmful—spaces that are norms in most homes, offices, and public spaces.

People with fat[2] bodies are often pushed to the edges of space— hidden and isolated from spaces of power, wealth, attention, and desire. The lack of body size diversity represented within architectural visualization contributes to this erasure. Thick bodies deserve the right to take up space: to stretch, to make noise, to participate, to move, to feel just as comfortable as anyone else. Vector_Vault is a project we created as a call to action for the fields of architecture and design to uphold this right. Vector_Vault provides vectors of underrepresented peoples for free to the architecture and design community in an attempt to diversify architecture visualization. It aims to increase the presence of POC, fat bodies, people with visible disabilities, elderly, queer, and other marginalized peoples

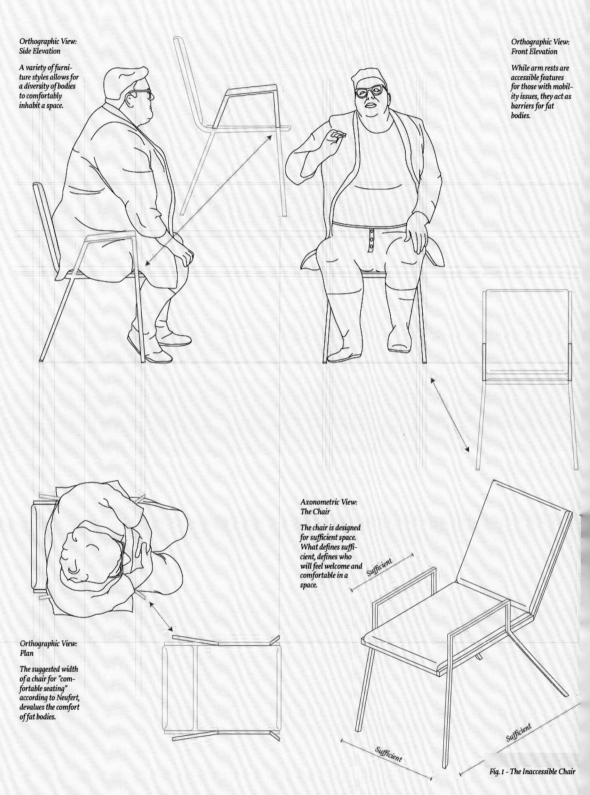

Orthographic View:
Side Elevation

A variety of furniture styles allows for a diversity of bodies to comfortably inhabit a space.

Orthographic View:
Front Elevation

While arm rests are accessible features for those with mobility issues, they act as barriers for fat bodies.

Axonometric View:
The Chair

The chair is designed for sufficient space. What defines sufficient, defines who will feel welcome and comfortable in a space.

Orthographic View:
Plan

The suggested width of a chair for "comfortable seating" according to Neufert, devalues the comfort of fat bodies.

Sufficient

Sufficient

Sufficient

Fig. 1 - The Inaccessible Chair

Fig. 1
The Inaccessible Chair.

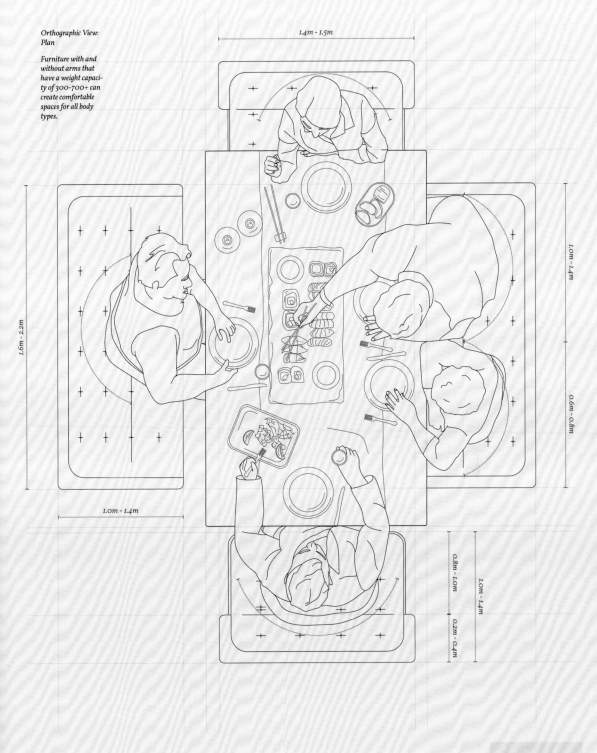

Orthographic View:
Plan

Furniture with and
without arms that
have a weight capaci-
ty of 300-700+ can
create comfortable
spaces for all body
types.

1.4m - 1.5m

1.0m - 1.4m

0.6m - 0.8m

1.6m - 2.2m

1.0m - 1.4m

0.8m - 1.0m

1.0m - 1.4m

0.2m - 0.4m

Fig. 2 - Redefining "Sufficient"

Fig. 2
Redefining Sufficient.

in architectural drawings with the intention of challenging existing spaces of exclusion. Vector_Vault is motivated by the belief that striving for diverse and inclusive spaces provides the opportunity for creative and engaging design solutions.

Vectors of thick bodies within architectural and design drawings can upset spatial norms in three distinct ways: they can call out physically inaccessible spaces; they can provide architects the opportunity to design spaces that are both physically—and by extension socially—inclusive; and they can normalize thick bodies in spaces that are typically socially exclusive.

CASE STUDY 1: THE INACCESSIBLE CHAIR
(Fig. 1)

The presence of people with fat bodies within architectural drawings forces designers to consider the ways in which their spaces are inaccessible. The chair has been a favored muse for design. It is a tool used to invite people to feel comfortable and welcome within a design. Chairs represent having a seat at the table—having a voice within a social setting. The chair is a symbol of acceptance; its size, weight limit, and shape signify to those in a space who is welcome to the privilege of comfort. Design guidelines privilege the comfort of people who fit within these standardized dimensions; they physically and socially exclude those who do not fit. Vectors of fat bodies challenge these standards by making visible their uncomfortableness in 'sufficient' chairs (see Fig. 1). A variety of chair styles depicted within a design is crucial to accommodating and inviting a diversity of bodies into a space. While a chair with arm rests is ideal for elderly people or those with mobility constraints, used exclusively, it is very effective at making those with fat bodies feel unwelcome in a space.

CASE STUDY 2: REDEFINING 'SUFFICIENT'
(Fig. 2)

It is within the capabilities of design to imagine spaces that people with fat bodies can occupy with the same ease and comfortability as any thin person might. Vectors that show people with fat bodies taking up physical and social space give designers the opportunity to propose responsive and creative spaces. In this process, they require designers to consider the furniture and room requirements needed to be sufficient. Sufficiency is predicated on what is needed by users of a space. If a space that claims to be 'sufficient' excludes a wide diversity of people, it sends the message that their voices and their presence are not valued or important. When a variety of bodies are represented in design drawings, it forces the designer to consider a broader range of users of a space. Fig. 2 demonstrates the way that a space (that has redefined what sufficient means) can be designed to provide comfortability for a wide range of body types. Dimensions indicate that seating can be comfortable for people with fat bodies

Fig. 3
*Physical activity
in social spaces.*

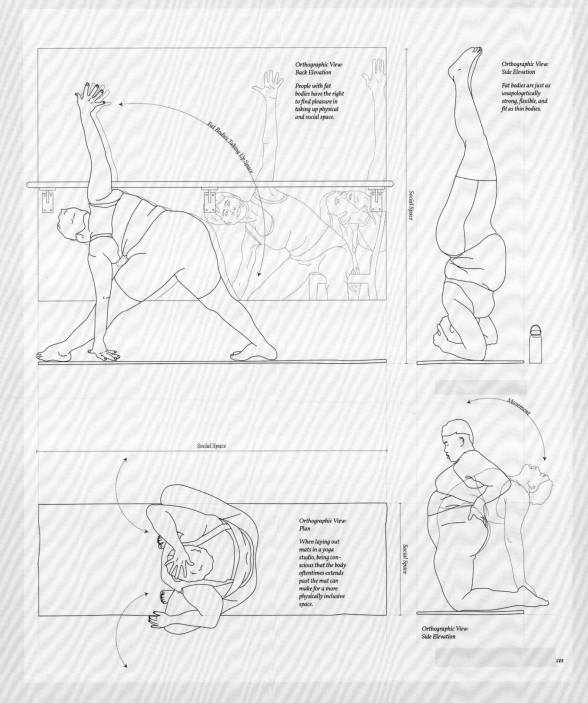

Orthographic View:
Back Elevation

People with fat bodies have the right to find pleasure in taking up physical and social space.

Fat Bodies Taking Up Space

Social Space

Orthographic View:
Side Elevation

Fat bodies are just as unapologetically strong, flexible, and fit as thin bodies.

Social Space

Social Space

Orthographic View:
Plan

When laying out mats in a yoga studio, being conscious that the body oftentimes extends past the mat can make for a more physically inclusive space.

Movement

Orthographic View:
Side Elevation

...ces

with some simple adjustments to standardized seating requirements. Simple adjustments have the potential to prompt exponentially improved design concepts.

CASE STUDY 3: PHYSICAL ACTIVITY WITHIN SOCIAL SPACES
(Fig. 3)

Including diverse representation in architectural drawings can also improve the social accessibility of spaces for physical activity. Architectural drawings of spaces that house fitness centers, gyms, fields, pools, dance studios, and other spaces for movement and activity consistently lack the portrayal of larger bodies. This exclusion furthers the notion that spaces for health are reserved for people with certain kinds of 'acceptable' bodies. Prioritizing the presence of thin bodies in spaces designed for high-energy, movement-oriented activities continues to feed the idea that bodies outside of the narrow qualifications for 'health' are unable to be active, strong, flexible, or healthy. Vectors of fat bodies that are engaging in activities such as yoga (see Fig. 3) disrupt these harmful prescriptions of who is allowed to partake in active social spaces. Vectors of fat bodies that unapologetically sweat, perspire, take pleasure in, and exert themselves through sports, yoga, dance, etc. challenge the social norms of exclusion that presume all fat bodies who exercise do so in the pursuit of thinness. In fact, people with fat bodies have the right to enjoy physical exertion as a form of pleasure and joy, just as any other person might.

Designers and architects have the responsibility to create spaces that promote equity and inclusion of the diverse peoples that make up our vibrant communities. These are but three examples of the ways in which increasing representation can improve design and positively influence the social impacts of our built spaces. Vector_Vault aims to assist in this mission by providing free vectors that reflect this diversity so that spaces can become more physically and socially accessible to all—including those with thick bodies. Visit vector-vault.org to download vectors and begin exploring the ways that these ideas can play out in your own designs. On the website you can read more about the project and contact us to get involved if you would like to contribute to the library of vectors.

Notes

1 Neufert, Ernst. *Architects' Data.* 4th ed. Chichester, West Sussex, UK; Ames, Iowa: Wiley-Blackwell, 2012.

2 In this text, the word fat is used as a value-neutral descriptor of bodies that experience systemic exclusion based on body size.

VIC MANTHA-BLYTHE & BRYNNE DAY

Vic Mantha-Blythe is a Master of Architecture candidate at the University of Waterloo and Brynn Day is a Master of Public Health candidate at the University of Alberta. They are the queer partnership behind Vector_Vault, a project that aims to increase the representation of diversity in architectural visualization, which can be found at vector-vault.org. They are interested in the social, equity, and health impacts of space and design.

RELATIONS

NARRATIVE, WALKING TOGETHER, & DESIGN AS PROVOCATION

An Interview with Garnette Cadogan, Elgin Cleckley, and the LUNCH 15 Editorial Board

LK: First Question: THICK or THIN?

GC: I say thick and thin. And I say thick and thin thinking alongside the sociologists. Here's why. In thin, I think of the sociological theory of third spaces and the one of weak ties. Both suggest that we need people whose names you don't know, with whom you have incidental relationships. For example, you walk past the same man every Thursday afternoon with his dog. The dog has a funny looking stride and a gait that is also cute. You stop. You have an exchange about the funny gait—600 times—and hardly anything much more than that. But that interaction is so absolutely crucial in terms of developing attachment to the neighborhood, in terms of civic vibrancy, even a sense of belonging. It's one of the things that is so important to civic participation, neighborhood activity and belonging, a sense of home. In other words, it helps transform a space into a place.

A lot of these incidental relationships are ones in which you have an exchange when you go into the elevator when you go into a building, a two- or three-minute talk with the doorman, or the doorman's friend, or the bartender who you always pass in the morning, or if you're headed home at night and he's shutting down, and there's another exchange with a smile. These weak ties are absolutely crucial, and these thin ways of knowing are so important because if we had to go through life with only thick ways of knowing, we would be beleaguered, exhausted, drained. We all have people who we absolutely love, but when their phone call is coming in, we say, "I don't want to talk to you right now." Not because we've lost affection, but because we know "I only have the bandwidth right now for a ten-minute talk. I would have to stay on the phone with you for two and a half hours when you call."

So those are weak ties, but they're also important to what are called *third space*. Third spaces are in the most intimate of settings; they are also the home, the barber shop, the coffee shop, the park bench, or a foodcart, or a pop-up lending library in a neighborhood. Third spaces, theorized by Ray Oldenburg,[1] are so crucial. Many third spaces are thin relationships. In other words, third spaces are crucial because they come up with their own network between communities and neighborhoods, within cities, within towns, that give you a sense of place but also a sense of civic attachment and belonging and a sense of civic health. They are absolutely crucial to the commons. Public spaces become public spaces in their interactions; it's in their interrelationship of both thin and thick ties. So you actually need public spaces that have a mix of thin and thick ties because some people, if you get to know them enough, you don't want to know them anymore. You get to know them just enough not to fight, not to bicker over the new skyscraper to be erected that would make the playground go away. Thin relationships are really good for coalitions but really bad for Thanksgiving dinner.

> "Thin relationships are really good for coalitions but really bad for Thanksgiving dinner."

And of course, the reason for thick is that we need these deep, interrelated connections, in which you're richly and deeply and sometimes exhaustively known. If anything, it gives you that real sense of being known, that sense of home, that sense of attachment, being seen in your full complexity and multiplicity. They're key in developing a rich sense of self, one that is also connected to other selves. So, yes to thin, and yes to thick. No to thin if it's the context of home. Yes to thin if it's the context of public space where incidental yet meaningful relationships are important.

EC: I think when you asked the question, I was laughing because we have this need

somehow to have absolutes—this or that—when everything is unknown. It's kind of a humorous thing. I don't know the answer. We're fighting inside of us, where we want to have absolutes, but there are so many things that we can't understand.

I did this with the word. I put thin inside of thick (Fig 1). That one piece there is one of a thousand layers. For instance, when I was a student here at UVA, I understood about that much, [gestures to a fraction of the stack] but now maybe I understand that much of it [gestures to a larger fraction of the stack].

I was talking to Garnette about that when I moved into this house. I moved in here, walked around, and went "Ok there's a thin layer to what I see, and there's a real thickness to what this place is." The more research I did, the more I learned about what this house is, where it is. All of a sudden, this is Nicholas Lewis' plantation, it's Meriwether's from King George III—oh wait, this is where the corn and tobacco fields were. The more research you do, the more you find out. Perhaps we are here in this moment because we are fighting to have absolutes in a space of uncertainty that is our lived experience.

BS: I read your diagram first as "THINK."

EC: Exactly, right. That's exactly it. Because yes, think about it. Think about what was here; think about who was here. Think about what was here. Monticello is amazing right now because you can take a self-guided tour. Without a tour guide, you find yourself filling in the blanks. It's actually kind of magical. As you're there, you just start thinking differently. Ok what

THICK

THIN

THI(N)CK

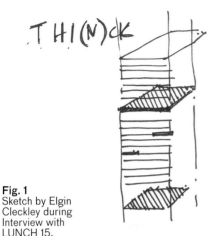

Fig. 1
Sketch by Elgin
Cleckley during
Interview with
LUNCH 15.

would it have been like? What would
this space have been like? It operates so
differently than when someone is telling
you what you should think or prompting
you towards what to think.

LK: That's something that we were
hoping to talk with you two about—
precisely this role of narrative. In the
worst cases, narrative can be didactic
and top-down, inherently erasive or
omitting some part of the truth. But
we're interested in how you see the
relationship between narrative and the
built environment. We're speaking to you
as an essayist and an architect. How do
you two work together as an essayist
interested in the built environment and
an architect interested in narrative?

EC: Garnette, can I just talk about when
we lived together?

GC: Yes! We need to make that podcast!

EC: We used to live in a house together.
The first moment I realized that Garnette
and I would get along together was when
I realized that we both walk and explore.
I do it as a questioning device, and
Garnette has some amazing essays on it.

GC: I'll start by saying some things

about Elgin. He has an essayist's soul. I'm
teaching a class now, and I think people
thought I would come and write a bunch
of essays. I think people are surprised
by how much design I'm asking of them.
A lot of that came about because of the
things Elgin has taught me. If you walked
into a room and decided you didn't like
where something was put, then you've
gone and thought about design. If you've
gone in and said "I'm going to sit in that
chair because that one hurts my back
and because that one is too high," then
you've begun to think about design in a
way that's very much oriented towards
narrative. "This chair is preferable to
that chair because of reasons having
to do with comfort or having to do
with accessibility, or having to do with
relationships." I'll sit there because I want
to see Garnette's face when I'm talking to
him. Or, like most people, "I don't want to
see Garnette's face in this case, so give
me a chair that's a little bit higher and I
don't have to look at him."

Elgin has been very insistent that we can't
see the built environment as this schematic
thing and then narrative as occupying
some other space. Both design and
written prose are very much interested
in and focused on making sense of the
world. We ask "How do we belong? How
do we move through the world? How do
we see our place in it, but also how do
we see ourselves in relation to others?"
He's always insisted that design is always
in the service of people, should be in the
service of people. The built environment
is an environment, meaning it tries to
inscribe itself in our imagination, as we
give it meaning through movements, and
giving over emotions to it. And all of this
is very much about narrative. Questions
of belonging, hope, the future, memory,
the past, likes or dislikes, affections and
frustrations, present sensibilities.

To think of past-future-present and the
interrelationship between each other is

to begin to think about narrative. How do we create a path and make sense out of things. Even though he hasn't said it now, it's one of the things he's been doing continually. I feel the great privilege of getting to learn from, both from talking with him and the great privilege of being able to sit in on his class, listen and learn and see also his own writing and work. Even the way he goes about his heuristic and comes up with designs is exciting.

It is so much a part of the class I'm teaching now, where I'm trying to get students to say "What is your design philosophy?" One of the learning objectives is by the end of this class, even if it's messy and imprecise, students will leave with an idea of their design philosophy, even if their design philosophy is first thinking about the environment and thinking about how tectonics should work. Or if their design philosophy is a question: "How do I serve people? What is in the best interest of people, community, belonging, encounter, interaction?" A lot of that is coming from Elgin. Even the way he goes about his own design philosophy, it's always about asking, "How do we meet or encounter the world?"

We begin always with intuition. If you like, we will begin with a flash of color, a particular song, a particular joke. All of these are proper starting places because it gives real credence to how we are as humans in our full humanity. Intuition is not some counter or messy or disorganized thing. Often intuition is a way of giving order and direction to our emotions and again, our desire to seek meaning. Again, we're talking about narrative. You can't think of meaning outside of narrative or attempts to find meaning in the world. The way we locate ourselves is some kind of narrative. "I once was this. And now I'm this. I am now here. I want to get there." The very sense of a path or a direction suggests movement. And so sometimes we're in a relationship where I can't tell

where he ends and I begin. Because of how we talk about the built environment and its relationship to narrative.

I almost feel like sometimes I'm a designer thinking about narrative because of his influence and in other times, the essayist in me, we often are not interested in story, unlike architects, planners, they are like, "What's the story?" where the essayists ask, "What's that particularity that you can hold on to and how do you give really rich meaning to particularity." The essayist is the meanderer, he picks up all the little particularities along the way in pulling all the different parts of the world that seem not to be connected, that seem to meander, and they all fit together at their root. In this way, you can know the place in a proper way, in a full way. The essayist in me looks at the built environment and asks, "What are the particularities? What is contained in these particularities? How can I meander? Let's look at everything in the world in its capaciousness." Nothing is out of the question. Nothing is out or irrelevant and disciplinary boundaries and ideas of genre in a working space are more about organizing than about proper ways of knowing. So the essayist in me is saying, "Oh if I'm thinking about this environment, I have to listen to Tupac who uses a Afropessimistic tone." Tupac has something to say along with Stevie Wonder's "Living in the City," along with Langston Hughes' "I, Too," along with my propensity to sit down in that field at sunset and take it all in. My particular affection for a particular plant or color or fragrance, all of this, comes together as part of a story, as an equal part of what it means to be alive in the world. Each of them has something to say. What it means to thrive, part of that capacious, multitudinous nature of the world helps give meaning and helps give a sense of belonging.

EC: So I'm going to talk about you, Garnette. The only reason why I'm really focused on my work and where I'm at is Garnette. I remember when we first met, there was that moment where you realize that you're seeing an understanding that the way you see the world isn't a foreign concept. Garnette's been such a great influence and inspiration for me because every once in a while, he keeps me in spatial and observational check. He says "Oh by the way, this is what you're doing." Sometimes he'll write me a little passage that shows me what I'm doing. I am thinking about ideas of "the canon," which can become a prescriptive thing, and if you're outside of that, you're always in the back of your mind wondering how your checks and balances are playing. When I met Garnette, I don't think it was ever an accident. All of the sudden, there's just a moment when a relationship becomes a collaborative space.

I think if we're going to talk about any topic of narrative here, you're often questioning your own practice because you know that it's not your idea. It's our idea. So you always want to feel like you're moving in a flow of things. And you want to be in a place where you know that those feelings that Garnette just mentioned are valid. Then, one day, the whole world shifts all of a sudden, and everyone is interested in what you do. You ask yourself, "What's going on?" because all of a sudden, the earth's axes have shifted. That's why people like Garnette mean so much to me, because it's a multilayered relationship. It's this idea of knowledge and support, in addition to intellectual support, friendship, design support, where you think to yourself, "Alright, this is it." You think to yourself, "Don't we all live in a large social experiment in which people connect together on a belief system to try to rethink how the world could

"If we're going to talk about any topic of narrative here, you're often questioning your own practice because you know that it's not your own idea. It's our idea."

be?" That possibility is that space between the thick and the thin that we're all talking about. And perhaps this new way of moving is it.

I will say though sometimes our conversations are the result of the fact that a lot people think thickly, or as we might see things, thinly. What's new to some people is not new to everybody. That's like the thinness of a glass window, versus the thinness of an opaque glaze. On the other hand, we know people run the race at their own pace, they come to things at their own time. So perhaps that's just another way of thinking about a new pedagogy, but there are moments where you kind of check yourself and say, "Wait a minute." It's a reality if you look at architecture and design education. Maybe that's part of it, you have to find your space and those layers and how to go forward. You have to find the narrative you tell yourself and the narrative you create.

BS: Hearing you talk about your friendship, there seems to be a real collaborative process in teaching and learning that begins with a simple invitation of "Let's go for a walk." How is this process of teaching and learning through exploring a narrative very much a thing that we do together?

EC: In the book I'm writing now, that's the core of the method. I'm writing to readers and practitioners who would actually practice this method with others. You're not going to work in a singular fashion. This work comes out of working as a collective group.

The idea is that you start with the idea of how you see a site, how you see a location, how you use this idea of empathy to drive design thinking. How do you analyze the different modes of design of site? Then you deconstruct it and then reconstruct. And then the last step is to imagine what it's like for others to be in a space. How does what's built in that public space respond to you, and how can you create new designs that respond back to it? The entire process is maximized when done in communion with others. Sure, you can do it on your own, but it's so much better with others.

The idea is if you're going to truly think about creating inclusive, public spaces, it's not a singular project. You've got to think about how to find yourself open to other ways of thinking. It's a different way of looking at pedagogy. It's always collaborative. I always think at the core, that's what a great design studio is—it's where you have your work and you're conversing and you're working back and forth. You're kind of creating new spaces with that.

"One of the beauties of thinking about pedagogy is that pedagogy rightly done...is a conversation."

It reminds me of the first job I had at a design firm in Washington state at a firm that designed elementary schools. I learned all of this from partners there. They told me the number one thing you need to do when you go down to these towns is to sit and listen, and if there's a meal going on, sit down and just listen. I would show up at the PTA meetings an hour early and just listen. And within an hour, you had design ideas because you were being completely open and listening. At the time, I thought those were soft skills, but they were actually the skills for collaboration. Any design we presented was a response back to the community. It was a back and forth, always.

GC: One of the beauties of thinking about pedagogy is that pedagogy rightly done and understood is a conversation. It is all embracing and in its own context, always expanding. This means it has to happen beyond the classroom, in our everyday lives. This is something Elgin does. His teaching happens in the classroom, but he will say next "Let's go take a walk on my street." And as we are walking, you actually have a sense of the spatial arrangement, but also the spatial history, or the history that has given a spatial character. You'll also have an ethnographic introduction to this street. You're also going to have musical introduction to this street in addition to an architectural introduction to it. You recognize how the pedagogy recognizes the multiple perspectives and disciplines and voices and conversation partners. It is a pedagogy that recognizes that it must extend beyond the usual fora in which we have these conversations. Are you going to have a panel about expanding pedagogy or are you going to get a group of people together and say "Let's walk, let's walk around the neighborhood and look and see." How can we design for, how can we build in, as an act of deep listening?

Something Elgin insists on, and something that's very much a part of my own approach to teaching, is it has to be very large ears, listening broadly. It demands of you to be a deep and close noticer. Henry James wrote about being a great noticer "for whom nothing is lost."[3] This is what pedagogy demands. It also demands to think of pedagogy as a conversation. That helps us get away from seeing a syllabus as a contract in which "Here's what I am going to do, and here's what is expected from you," versus "Here's this terrain of our hopes and aspirations. You, students, will also put down your hopes and aspirations, and they would dovetail each other and will genuflect in accordance to each others' needs. Together, we will try to find a way to make this space, this arena, in which we can both thrive, a place where we can see and understand each other, we will come to a richer understanding of each other but also to ourselves." We must also think how both of those will then lead to outside of the context we're meeting, other people, other communities, other environments to thrive even more, because of the way that we've learned to thrive in each other's company and each other's help.

So pedagogy then has to think about what it means to have open ears, big ears. Those big ears then mean listening through the walls that we normally have around us. It means being open to approaches that our peers, our colleagues might look at with some disdain. It also means that we have the sensibility of an amateur. That pedagogy can't be something that we've lifted up as a profession anymore. The person who is always sitting on their front porch and loves it would understand a lot of things about the relationship between public space and private space. They will understand something incredibly rich about the sensibility of the street and what it means to be in close touch to it and to draw from it, in ways that we may not, even with 16,000 precedents at our fingertips. We can no more say what public space is than anybody else. But a person who has been inhabiting it, who has been drawing from it and on it, that amateur, in many ways will have so much more to say and understand it than we will.

Having big ears then means looking for the amateur, being drawn to the amateur, and also striving to have the sensibility of an amateur. The first instinct is to listen. Sometimes it's not even to listen.

It's a sense of attachment to a place that sometimes means not even learning about the place. It means to ask what is it that we need to know about a place. How is it that we need to act so that the place can start inscribing itself on our imagination so that we can start inscribing our own equations on a place? An amateur often moves with love and with passion and enthusiasm and is quick to wander, meander, and linger. Often, they are not even afraid of being sentimental or nostalgic. Sometimes we need to give ourselves over to emotions like these because we're not unmoored from community, we're not unmoored from the collective. We're not unmoored from those who are inhabiting a place, but we're trying to find ways of inhabiting alongside them and listening with them. If only we could see the world closer to how they see the world or see them how they define themselves. Start paying attention to how they define themselves, how a neighborhood defines itself. This is absolutely crucial for our pedagogy and to think of what it means to design in these places. This kind of design requires an amateur's ear and eye and is why I don't feel a sense of insecurity or left out of the periphery in thinking about urban planning, design, and architecture, though I'm not trained officially in any of these disciplines. I think there's room for the amateurs to come and spend time and listen and inhabit and have something to say that may be fruitful to those who have been formally trained and will be thinking about it for the rest of their professional lives.

CB: The way you're talking about the amateur and the broader public being involved in the design process, reminds me of the ways the Paper Monument Project[1] allows people to participate in visioning a new public space. In the last year, we finally saw broad public support for the Black Lives Matter movement and growing calls for monument removal. Paper Monuments, and other projects like General Demotion / General Devotion[2] or the Cheats Movement,[3] all created images of monument removal. I wonder what you think of the role of design and image-making plays in provocation for calling the futures that we want to be a part of into being?

EC: It's been really surreal to be part of those projects through these past couple of years because I've found myself in these personal and public moments of watching this shift happen right in front of you. I'm realizing those competitions and projects like Paper Monuments are successful as design activism. They're helping push things forward, and at the center of it is public knowledge. The more everyone knows, the more we can actually start to rethink and make decisions. Without them, conversations like these and the design decisions wouldn't have happened to the extent that they have. More recently, though, I've been looking at highways, looking at environmental racism a lot recently. Monuments are fine. They're here, but next to them, there are all of these structural moments that need questioning just as much. I think about the bridge landing in Africville in Nova Scotia. I think about New Orleans; I think about Atlanta, DC, New York. The list goes on and on and you think to yourself, "Yes, a monument is one thing, it's symbolic. Yes, it's moving forward, but there are a stream of other systems, spaces, objects, products, graphics, and experiences to look at here as well." Who's to say that a highway that is purposefully segregating shouldn't be at home in the same conversation?

A lot of that comes from looking at urban design projects where highways were taken down to make a park, which sets into action a whole new chain of real estate that is unattainable. This is where I stop and I see Monument Avenue here, and you see that other project here. You can't help but think that perhaps our next move is to extend this thought process and ask "What

are the Paper Monuments that we can have for these other moments as well?" That's where I'm looking to go. I'm really excited to see these shifts and changes, but I think there's a larger picture we need to attend to at the same time.

I'll never forget. I was on the public event for the General Demotion General Devotion event, and I realized that I was one of the few Black people in the room talking about the removal of statues in the basement of the Valentine, with Edward Valentine's studios upstairs. I thought about the legacy of that time and place and thought maybe it's time to think about those competitions, to think about design as activism to shift these other moments too.

GC: One of the first things that designers have to do is ask, "How do we leave well enough alone?" There is often too quick a rush to have design begin to answer questions, ones that are deeply heavy questions, carrying the weight of hundreds of years of history, hundreds if not thousands of families and not even individuals. These are questions that deal with heavy wounds while at the same time try to clean and soak wounds that are being freshly made each day, wounds that have some relation to the earlier ones, that are made possible by the early ones, but with new slashes being made. How then can we begin to see multiple futures and multiple possibilities and multiple obstacles that could come and not suddenly try to cinch things in and create too clear or too organized or too narrow in terms of a future?

One of the first things is to think of the role of design in provocation, in calling futures into living or being. Maybe first, let's create spaces for us to begin to ask what futures are possible. Futures, rather than future. Often, the options presented by design tend to be too narrow. I think part of this is to begin to think how to create ground for people to start to

Fig. 2
Work by Andre
Hirschler.

discuss their futures or even sometimes not discuss the future yet, but to have reckonings or even the thing before reckoning, the possibility of catching their breath or taking in the scope of things. One of the things then, if I were to say our role in thinking about provocation is our role in care before provocation. I'm afraid that care, if it hasn't already, might become one of those quick catchwords. It's important to think "What are these structures of care, not what we're providing but already exist." First recognizing it and then also to give room or give ground for it to more productively happen. Care as repair. Thinking of care as even something more basic and sustained, care which is already existing. Care as mutual aid. Care as embrace. Care as warmth. Care as listening. Care as connection. Care as Elgin walking his good friend up the block and saying "Let me show you where everybody is and how everybody is doing, how this came

to be what it is," instead of considering what is this neighborhood now. One of the roles of design is to ensure that it creates possibilities that meet existing needs before we start thinking about orienting ourselves towards the future. Or for people who are already oriented towards the future, it'll be absolutely crucial for them to reckon with the past.

The role of design in provocation is to find a way to wed a provocation to care. It's almost a contradiction. The role of design is to acknowledge, support, extend, and then build structures of care. It helps acknowledge people's autonomy and gives a lot of room for them then to start making those provocations. Sometimes people are so beleaguered that an imagined future of possibilities might be more out of reach, out of grasp than it should be. Design can create provocation by reminding us that there is a narrative. That there are futures, there are possibilities. We ought not settle with the resignation that the sum total of what happens to us defines us or overly defines us. So the role of design in provocation is creating spaces for people to more richly experience their agency and allow different places of care to flourish. Part of that provocation is opening ways of thinking about the future and being reminded of the future, possibilities in which care is central, particularly where care is mutual aid, so people are suddenly reminded of the ways in which they're inextricably bound, the ways in which they've been supporting and working alongside each other, and then what it is about design that helps support and extend and give rich life to that.

EC: I wanted to add to this idea of visioning. It goes back to this idea of realizing that without those projects, design shows us who we can be. Andre Hirschler is one of the students in my seminar and who worked on the Richmond competition. He showed a future of the Lee statue coated in art all at the base (Fig. 2). If you take a photo of it now and put it next to it, it's a surreal experience because it's nearly identical to what Andre proposed. When it happened, Andre emailed me and I wrote back and went "Right?" and at the time, the critics said they couldn't see how this was possible. Andre's idea was that rotating through time, Richmond artists would come and use the statue as a canvas. When I read that, it was the most powerful piece of protest art, and Andre just smiled. Amazing. His visual from what he saw, born out of realizing that he had the ability to visually and empathetically tell the narrative. Once you take control of your sense of representation, things shift and change. I'm a product of that exact same thing. Design has that power to shift how we present ourselves out into the world and show us what those futures could be.

LK: We have to return to our thick or thin question before parting ways!

EC: I drew something new at the top.

GC: Both Elgin's responses but also the questions and the nature of the questions you've asked. I'm thinking thin, thick, thickthin, thinthick.

And another thing: Public space can have multiple of these happening, and sometimes you don't even know where. In other words, Elgin and I are sometimes having a thick relationship in public space, and there are other people around. There's thickness happening right before them but because of the thinness between them and us, they don't recognize it. This actually deepens the thickness. In other words, there's times when Elgin and I will have whole long conversations with our eyebrows and our chins.

We'll not have to say a word. I'll look at Elgin and say "Did he just say that?" and Elgin goes "He sure did," but we haven't said a single word, but in our chins and our eyebrows, we have a whole exchange. I know exactly what word I just said, and I know exactly what word he just said. Our relationship becomes even thicker through our ability to see, in the presence of others, it suddenly makes us both aware of just how thick this relationship is. It got thicker, because of our awareness of each other in the context of thin.

The presence of thin brings that recognition and deepens thick, and the converse is true sometimes. You might always pass the same person on the corner, but suddenly if you see a different congregation on the corner, it's a completely different reaction. It can motivate, make someone say "Ok, I want this to be thicker." Or you could say "Ok, it's thin, and I'm ok with that, and I don't want it to be thicker." In many ways,

I'm actually benefiting from your thick relationships, and it makes me grateful for my thin relationships but it also makes me think "I'm going to fight for your thick relationships" because the kind of thick relationships you have allows all these other thin relationships that you have to be that much more enriching. Some people recognize the need to fight for thick relationships, like in a city council meeting for example, even though it seems like it has nothing to do with them. But it's because they realize, it actually has everything to do with them. Those thick relationships have enriched all these other thin relationships through the neighborhood.

Notes

1 Colloquate Design, "Paper Monuments Final Report: Imagine New Monuments for New Orleans," October 18, 2019, https://issuu.com/colloqate/docs/pm_final_report.

2 Storefront for Community Design, "Monument Avenue: General Demotion/General Devotion," accessed December 17, 2021, http://www.storefrontrichmond.org/blog/2018/6/14/monument-avenue-general-devotiongeneral-demotion.

3 Spicer, Paul, and Marc Cheatham, *Voices: Critical Thought in a Challenging Time*, Vol. 1, 2 vols., 2020, https://thecheatsmovement.com/voices-critical-thought-in-a-challenging-time/.

GARNETTE CADOGAN

Born and raised in Jamaica, Garnette Cadogan is an essayist, a Visiting Fellow at the Institute for Advanced Studies in Culture at the University of Virginia, and a Visiting Scholar at the Institute for Public Knowledge at New York University. He was also a Martin Luther King Jr. Visiting Scholar (2017–18) at the Department of Urban Studies and Planning at MIT. Cadogan's work explores the dynamics of cultural change, particularly in urban settings. Cadogan's current research and writing explores the promise and perils of urban life, the vitality and inequality of cities, and the challenges of pluralism.

ELGIN CLECKLEY

Elgin Cleckley, NOMA, is an Assistant Professor of Architecture at UVA with an appointment in the Curry School of Education and the School of Nursing. He is a designer and principal of _mpathic design – a Design Thinking pedagogy, initiative, and professional practice. Elgin is the recent winner of the 2020 ACSA Diversity Achievement Award, and the 2021 Dumbarton Oaks Mellon Fellowship in Urban Landscape Studies. _mpathic design's practice includes collaborations with the City of Lynchburg, and the Albemarle County Office of Equity and Diversity. Elgin is also the Design Director at the UVA Equity Center, and the NOMA Project Pipeline: Architecture Mentorship Program.

THICK SECTIONS AS THICK RECKONING

Thaïsa Way

While many landscape architects and designers more generally are seeking to identify more productive approaches to climate change, biodiversity, sustainability, and environmental and public health, few acknowledge the critical role that history plays in shaping not only the challenges, but the potential of any response to be successful. If on the other hand we were to confront and engage deeply with the histories of places, people, and practices we might begin to deconstruct the very structures that lie at the core of our challenges and problems. Such histories include the violent displacement of indigenous peoples, the 1619 story and legacies of slavery, the internment of Japanese-Americans, and the vicious ways that we have treated those who worked in the mines, on railroads, and on farms and as domestic laborers across the nation among other stories. In such narratives, designers might identify the origins of contemporary inequities in environmental and public health, the deep reasons for climate change as well as why it will impact different communities in disparate ways, and the long history of erasing the traces of uncomfortable narratives in our landscapes. They might as well come to learn the powerful ways in which communities have built resistance and resilience in the face of extraordinary challenges. Addressing the complexity of designing sites begins with knowing history of the land, the people, and the place.

This focus on history as a lens into the future centers my essay on Gas Works Park[1] designed by Richard Haag and his firm Richard Haag Associates, in which I proposed the thick section as an alternative means to interrogate site, landscape, and place as intersectional narratives. Instead of seeing the site as only wasteland in need of remediation, Haag understood the power of its multitude of even divergent histories and narratives. A history of the site revealed an even thicker and more complex mesh of narratives, meaning, uses, and interpretations. As anthropologist Daniel Hoffman has described, for landscapes of urban war, not unlike post-industrial sites, the historical details and theoretical explorations are not layered onto narrative plotlines, but instead in relationships of space, use, form, and representation.[2] To design such a site begins by recognizing the inherent thickness of the landscape with taskscapes that as Tim Ingold argues, we might read as "constituted as an enduring record of–and testimony to–the lives and works of past generations who have dwelt within it, and in so doing, have left there something of themselves."[3] Every landscape is, to borrow from the work of Gilles Deleuze, "becoming,"[4] in which we find natural and cultural systems forming an emergent system and place. Such places hold memories both remembered and forgotten that comprise a history that we should know as we seek to change.

While my focus was on Gas Works, my intent was broadly focused on the intersections of history, place, and design, narratives that are often considered in isolation. I was concerned by how history is often relegated in design to timelining, setting a chronological list of events that are known, or as precedent. The timeline is a thin line, barely a thread, that constitutes little more than a list of names, dates, references. History as precedent is thinner, suggesting the past is nothing more than a series of flash cards. A place history requires thick reckoning with the intention to unravel the inherent complexities and read beyond the *tabula rasa* or erased site. It requires a rigorous untangling of the socio-ecological entanglements to steward the emergence of re-imagined experiences of places.

And yet to practice as such we find a limited set of tools, even today. We do not have the verbal or written language and corresponding vocabulary to engage in and reflect upon the rigorous inquiry into the entanglements of place. We do not possess the words to describe the thickness of places. David Whyte, a philosopher and poet, aptly describes how as a naturalist in the Galapagos Islands he found the scientific language to be imprecise for what he was observing. He turned to the language of poetry. In telling this story he suggests how "the language we have in that world is not large enough for the territory that we've already entered."[5] This is equally true for design and place histories. The words we have borrowed from architecture and science are not specific enough. They do not reflect the depth of human relationships to land, landscape, and place. Such thin language leads to equally vacuous narratives of history limited to stories we already know, not the other stories and poems. Our first challenge is to curate an enriched vocabulary that reflects the thickness of the world around us while encouraging us to navigate the knowledge with intelligence and care. This issue of LUNCH contributes to this effort.

An equally formidable challenge is the limited instruments of representation that compel us to engage with the thickness of landscapes. This is not for lack of trying. Over two centuries ago Alexander von Humboldt created his provocative cross sections, the Tableau Physique, illustrating the complex interconnectedness of climate, geography, nature, and humans. In the late nineteenth century, landscape architect Charles Elliott, in the office of Frederick Law Olmsted, developed layered maps to understand the relationships between natural and cultural systems to better plan for human uses and environmental health. The planner Patrick Geddes developed the Valley Section in 1909 representing descriptions of landscape to human activities, primarily productive, that take place on the surface of the earth. Ian McHarg in the 1960s expanded the drawing of layers to reveal the relationships between over and underground and the dynamics of change (Fig. 1).

Drawing landscape ideas remains an act with great potential to allow us to think anew. Landscape architect James Corner has rightly observed that "how one 'images' the world literally conditions how reality is both conceptualized and shaped."[6] With each invention of modified forms of drawing, design thinking and its boundaries correspondingly expand.

As Denis Cosgrove has asserted, "For many artists, it is the inventive capacity of representation that enables them to provoke new and alternative ways of seeing the world."[7] If we are to renew and recover landscape, designers need "new images and techniques of imagination."[8]

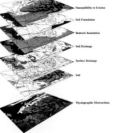

Fig. 1 *(top) Alexander von Humbolt, Chimborazo (1807); (left) Patrick Geddes, Valley Section 1909; (right) Ian McHarg, Design with Nature (1969).*

In 2012, Stephanie Carlisle and Nicholas Pevzner proposed what they called the deep section arguing that

> while landscape plans and perspectives have achieved high levels of graphic refinement over the last decade...sectional representation has lagged...[and that] [d]eveloping a fluency with "deep sections," or sectional representation techniques that make visible the wide range of site complexity while providing a critical tool for interdisciplinary collaboration and design exploration, can be a start of a shift towards a deeper grounding in how landscapes perform."[9]

Landscape architects including Meg Studer, Bradley Cantrell, and Matthew Seibert have experimented with alternative means and media for drawing that would expand inquiry and its intersections with place as explored through data-collection, analysis, and visualizations.

These drawings are evocative and powerful provocations that have moved ecological design in new directions grounded in an increasingly robust body of knowledge. Nevertheless the projects have focused on the richness of ecological and biological narratives of landscapes with barely a nod to the historical and cultural forces that are played out on and within landscapes. They have taken on a thickness of ecology and science of natural systems, but not to the same extent of that of cultural systems and history's inscriptions. To be explicit, the history, the narratives of occurrences, and meaning accumulated over time have not engendered a serious discussion in regards to tools of representation. To grapple with the conundrum of understanding the thickness of history, we need to imagine and construct a broader vocabulary and in turn a more dynamic toolbox for representing the stories and ideas that we cannot yet know or describe. Our engagement with history must be as robust and thick as that with ecology and natural systems.

The new tools must compel designers to engage with the thickness of history and socio-ecological entanglements visible and invisible, comprised of multiple, diverse, even conflicting narratives. Anthropologist Clifford Geertz wrote that reading the complex relationships of a place requires rejecting "thin descriptions," and instead, creating "thick descriptions" that engage a "multiplicity of complex conceptual stories, many of them superimposed upon or knotted into one another, which are at once strange, irregular, inexplicit."[10] That is any place, for every place holds the multiple and diverse narratives of nature, culture, humans, non-humans, the inert, and the living, all at once strange, irregular, inexplicit. New tools of thickness must lead to thicker practices grounded in rigorous inquiry into place history and a willingness to engage with the conflicting, confusing, and often oppressive complexity that is the stuff of humans and culture and nature as they shape and are shaped.

In the years since I proposed the thick section students and practitioners are exploring forms of representing thickness. They are experimenting with how to lift the skin of a landscape to see, read, and challenge what is unseen, erased, or ignored. They are attentive to the ground as a surface that stands between earth and sky as the most active of surfaces, in continuous generation.[11] The emerging thick sections bring to the fore what is below and above, between and among. Alison Hirsch's inquiry into "prosthetic landscapes," included in this issue, explores how digital tools might engage in sharing thicker readings of place, making visible what can no longer be seen without aids. In their book *Seattleness: A Cultural Atlas*, Tera Hatfield and Jenny Kempson create a thick book as an urban section.[12] Denise Hoffman, working with students at the City University of New York, has brought bodies of data into the section alongside geological and political threads to suggest alternative narratives of place, power, and potential futures.

In the work of these critical thinkers, we see evidence of their capacity to locate traces and threads of former and contemporary narratives, to bring the full site in all its messiness to the foreground. They engage in a thick reckoning with the history entangled within suggesting a complex mesh of forces and consequences, intended and unintended. The work collects and reckons a descriptive representation of what Elizabeth Meyer has called the "deep time—the *longue durée*, the thickness of time—embedded into spaces and surfaces."[13] This essential exploration into the potential of representation to tackle complexity, thickens the line to become a mesh comprised of multiple and diverse traces and threads of practices layered one with the other. From this, narratives emerge suggesting the inherent complexities and strangeness of historic engagements and entanglements with landscape and place.

In summary, we remain challenged to move forward without identifying the means to more fully and holistically understand history. Thick sections are one possibility, and yet the approach is not foolproof. To draw a thick section, it is imperative not to confuse the crowded with the thick. Thickness is not merely massive chaos, but rather emerges from chaos as a means of becoming. Lots of data points is not necessarily thick, rather thickness is the result of selected threads or muscles woven tightly together. Thickness when engaged, reveals thinness as well as mere crowdedness. Thickness, as I [14] and others including Andrea Kahn have argued, situates negotiations of distinct site knowledges and their relationships to one another.[15] Such thinking and inquiry requires a process of translation, mediation, percolation, and iteration as the data is sifted, questioned, and synthesized simultaneously into alternative questions and new knowledge. Such a thick section is legible to others, generating new perspectives, including from non-designers. This approach to inquiry and knowledge would oblige designers to contend with the wickedly complex, ambiguous, and unknown of places,[16] and the emerging relationships between what Peter Marcuse has described as the area of study and that of concern.[16]

A second significant challenge is the tempting path of thin tools, particularly in the digital world. The thin screen engenders a thin narrative that may, with its compelling images, turn out to be thinner and more deceptive than the printed book that at least allows for the imagination to engage. The purpose of the thick section is not a work of art but rather to explore the thickness of narratives, to understand the layers of traces and threads of stories accumulated over time by communities and individuals, sometimes merging, often conflicting, but always intersecting in place, whether visible or not.

Such a section develops thickness and complexity. It challenges the *longue durée* of cultural erasure and social flattening of sites and landscapes. The substantive edge that emerges to become the thick section divulges connections between traces, threads, and layers revealing both obvious and strange relationships, adjacencies, and narratives. The thick section is intended to suggest and coax alternative and provocative questions and observations. If our tools of representation are not intended to incite and reveal complex histories and their socio-ecological entanglements accrued over time, then we are not rigorously exploring these issues with the depth and breadth they necessitate.

Before I end, it must be noted that a thick section is not merely a document for representing the history. In provoking questions, it should confront any interpretation or intended design insertion or inscription, bridging site reading, writing, and thinking. Practicing a thick section should compel designers to engage in the inherently transdisciplinary work that leads to a more revealing reading of the socio-cultural-ecological entanglements of landscape. This is particularly true when encountering the violence that is so often embedded in the histories of places. When one identifies that a piece of land has been stolen from indigenous communities, then one must face the decision as to whether that is a narrative that calls for recognition and more. Hirsch's prosthetic landscape is one path worthy of further study as is that of Sara Zewde, whose work asks where are we, who is at the table, and what stories are being shared and what stories are being erased. When one acknowledges that the site was once the largest slave trading port in the world, as Zewde has done in Rio de Janiero, how does one design the public realm of this place?[17] One can no longer simply imagine nothing happened. By engaging with complex thick histories, designers will catalyze a thicker reckoning of all sites and places in our landscape leading to more responsible and responsive designs.

Now, let me end with a call for contribution of the thick section to the interdisciplinary engagement required for a thick reckoning of our public realm. No one discipline or practice can fix or even significantly respond to the challenges alone. We must work together, not merely in parallel, but as deeply committed members of transdisciplinary teams from which new knowledge emerges. This is not easy work as we each have our own vocabularies, lenses, and apparent roles. Thick sections offer one means to bring the needed bodies of knowledge together into the form of a shared work that might be used to provoke alternative questions generating the necessary depth and breadth of discourse. Drawing as a language is a powerful mode of thinking that designers claim, not merely to show a place but to convey ideas, knowledge, and the imagination. The thick section offers the possibility to enrich the sharing of questions, ideas, and knowledge among scholars, practitioners, and advocates. In turn the thick section asks how would one design differently if our knowledge was different. The thick section could well be one of our most powerful tools for practice, should we have the fortitude to develop it and better understand who we are and where we imagine we might go.

THAÏSA WAY

Thaïsa Way, PhD, FAAR, FASLA, is the Program Director of Garden & Landscape Studies at Dumbarton Oaks Research Library and Collection at Harvard University and Professor in Landscape Architecture in the College of Built Environments at the University of Washington. Her teaching and scholarship focuses on histories of urban landscape design practice and theory and their contributions to the public realm through the lenses of democracy, difference, and diversity.

Notes

1 Thaïsa Way, "Landscapes of Industrial Excess: A Thick Sections Approach to Gas Works Park." Journal of Landscape Architecture 8, no. 1 (2013): 28–39.

2. Danny Hoffman, *Monrovia modern: urban form and political imagination in Liberia*. Duke University Press, 2017, xix.

3 Tim Ingold, *The Life of Lines*. London, [England]; New York, New York: Routledge, 2015.

4 Gilles Deleuze, Felix Guattari, Michel Foucault, and Mark Seem, *Anti-Oedipus: Capitalism and Schizophrenia*. Translated by Robert Hurley. Illustrated Edition. New York, NY: Penguin Classics, 2009.

5 The On Being Project. "David Whyte — The Conversational Nature of Reality." Podcast, April 7, 2016. https://onbeing.org/programs/david-whyte-the-conversational-nature-of-reality/.

6 James Corner, *Recovering Landscape: Essays in Contemporary Landscape Architecture*. New York: Princeton Architectural Press, 1999, 153.

7 Denis E. Cosgrove, "Liminal Geometry and Elemental Landscape: Construction and Representation." In *Recovering Landscape: Essays in Contemporary Landscape Architecture*, edited by James Corner, 102–19. New York: Princeton Architectural Press, 1999.

8 James Corner, *Recovering Landscape: Essays in Contemporary Landscape Architecture*. New York: Princeton Architectural Press, 1999, 154.

9 Stephanie Carlisle and Nicholas Pevzner, "The Performative Ground: Rediscovering The Deep Section", *Scenario Journal 02: Performance* (Spring 2012). https://scenariojournal.com/article/the-performative-ground/. accessed 02/10/20.

10 Cliffor Geertz, *The Interpretation of Cultures: Selected Essays*. Harper Torchbooks ; TB 5043. New York: Basic Books, 1973.

11 Tim Ingold, *The Life of Lines*. London, [England]; New York, New York: Routledge, 2015.

12 Tera Hatfield, Jenny Kempson, Natalie Ross, and Timothy R. Wallace, *Seattleness : A Cultural Atlas*. Seattle: Sasquatch Books, 2018.

13 Elizabeth Meyer, "Seized by the Sublime" in *Richard Haag: Bloedel Reserve and Gas Works Park*. Edited by William S. Saunders, Patrick M. Condon, Gary R. Hilderbrand, and Elizabeth K. Meyer. Landscape Views 1. New York: Princeton Architectural Press, with the Harvard University Graduate School of Design, 1998.

14 Thaïsa Way, "Landscapes of Industrial Excess: A Thick Sections Approach to Gas Works Park." *Journal of Landscape Architecture 8*, no. 1 (2013): 28–39.

15 Carol Burns and Andrea Kahn, *Site Matters: Design Concepts, Histories, and Strategies*. New York; London: Routledge, 2005.

16 Peter Marcuse, "Study Areas, Sites, and the Geographic Approach to Public Action." In *Site Matters: Design Concepts, Histories, and Strategies*, edited by Carol Burns and Andrea Kahn, 249–80. New York; London: Routledge, 2005.

17 See Sara Zewde's work on Valongo Wharf at studio-zewde.com/valongo-wharf and in Reut, Jennifer. "Out of Time." Landscape Architecture Magazine, April 2018.

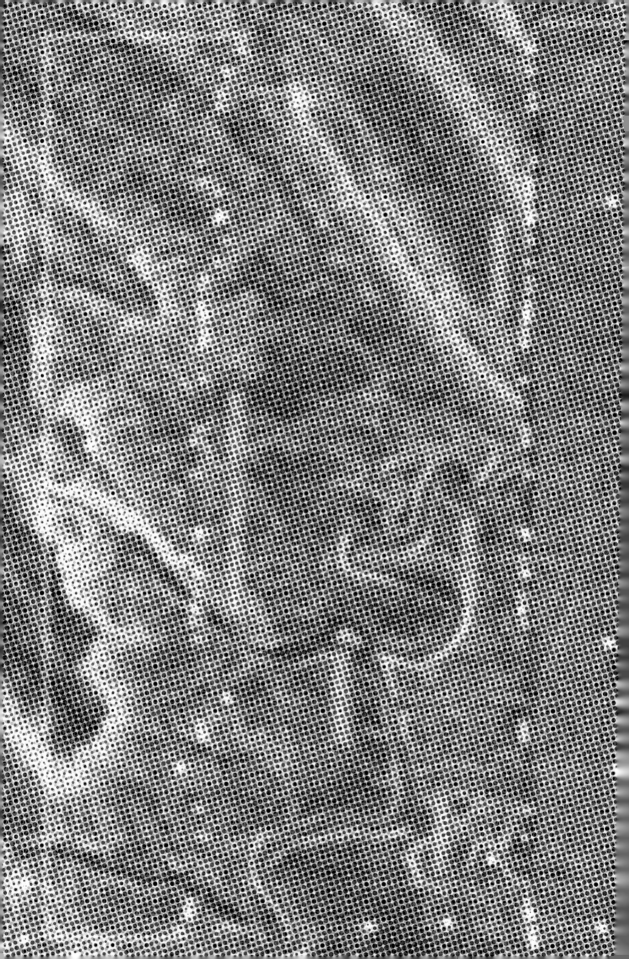

REPRESENTING RISK AND RESISTANCE
A Thick Sections Approach to the Mountain Valley Pipeline

Hannah Jane Brown

The Mountain Valley Pipeline is thick. With a diameter of forty-two inches, this high-pressure natural gas pipeline is over a foot larger than the infamous Keystone-XL. Currently under construction, the pipeline navigates a 303-mile route of mountain terrain in its journey from Wetzel County, West Virginia, to Pittsylvania County, Virginia, with 203 miles of the pipeline (sixty-seven percent) on terrain susceptible to landslides. The Mountain Valley Pipeline (MVP) is part of a new class of high-risk, mega-pipeline projects approved by the Federal Energy Regulatory Commission (FERC) since 2017.[1] Considered individually, each pipeline project poses an unprecedented, daunting risk. Considered together, they illuminate the frenzied rush to exploit the Marcellus shale fields at whatever cost necessary.

THICK

Representations of the MVP almost always appear in plan view. Plan representations belie the risk of the project by reducing the region's extreme topography and geology to mere surface. As such, representations in plan can be considered thin—intentionally excluding depth, both geologic and contextual, and proffering a subdued representation of risk.

I propose using Thaïsa Way's "thick sections" approach as an alternative to these insufficient representations. As Way writes, a thick section "suggest[s] that the surface is merely that which is at the top of a rich history of morphologies, natural and human."[2] For the MVP, a thick section collages the geomorphological and cultural, resulting in a more robust representation, built on relationality rather than omission, where risk and severity are more readily apparent.

To illustrate these risks, I examine the section of the MVP running through Giles County, Virginia, a particularly high-risk portion. In Giles County, the pipeline traverses a series of steep, landslide-prone ridges, underlying karst geology, and an active seismic zone. (Fig. 1). Acting alone, any one of these factors could pose disaster. But of course, they are linked, inextricable parts of systems that act in concert—synergistically. In a Deposition of Record for the FERC, Professor Ernst H. Kastning, a Virginia Certified Professional Geologist and karst expert, testified that the pipeline cannot be safely built through Giles County as doing so would "significantly threaten the structural integrity of the pipeline." He writes that "many of the potential hazards are immitigable; they cannot be adequately circumvented with engineering or construction practices."

One such immitigable risk is landslides, a common occurrence in Giles County where steep terrain and significant annual rainfall coincide. Unstable soils experience "soil creep," showing a propensity for downhill movement even under the most mundane of circumstances. As the pipeline in constructed, a 125-foot construction corridor is cleared and trenches are dug to bury this forty-two-inch behemoth. Removing forests and ground-cover, compacting soil, and altering grading further destabilize slopes and increase the likelihood of landslides.

Kastning notes that landslide risk is further increased by "weak" soils resulting from karst parent geology. Due to the difficulty inherent in documenting underlying karst, many significant geologic features in Giles County remain only tentatively mapped. As such, trenching for the pipeline could intersect with karst features, leading to collapse. Even if construction doesn't interact directly with karst features, it dramatically alters surface and subsurface water flows, which can spur subsidence, sinkhole collapse, and landslides.

Karst geology is characterized by the dissolution of soluble parent material, such as limestone, that produces underground drainage systems of caves and sinkholes. Regions underlaid by karst provide around twenty-five percent of the world's fresh water supply, and contain an estimated fifty percent of the world's hydrocarbon reserves. Perhaps too devasting to be considered ironic, karst geology is uniquely vulnerable to contamination. These vast, subterranean, and intensely vertical networks lack natural filters which allows for point-source contamination to spread quickly and broadly. The hydrological impacts of construction are already widely felt; pipeline spills will be far worse.

To make matters worse, Giles County sits at the center of an active seismic zone that in 1897 produced the second largest earthquake recorded in the eastern United States in the last 200 years. While an extreme event, Kastning posits moderate earthquakes are of equal

Fig. 1
The MVP through Giles County, Virginia.

NEW EDGE CONDITION

50 FT. EASEMENT

120 FT. CONSTRUCTION ZONE

300 FT.

KARST NETWORK

VERTICAL WATERSHED

*cave based on drawings of Clover Hill Cave
in Giles County, VA. The dimensions are
accurate, location is not.

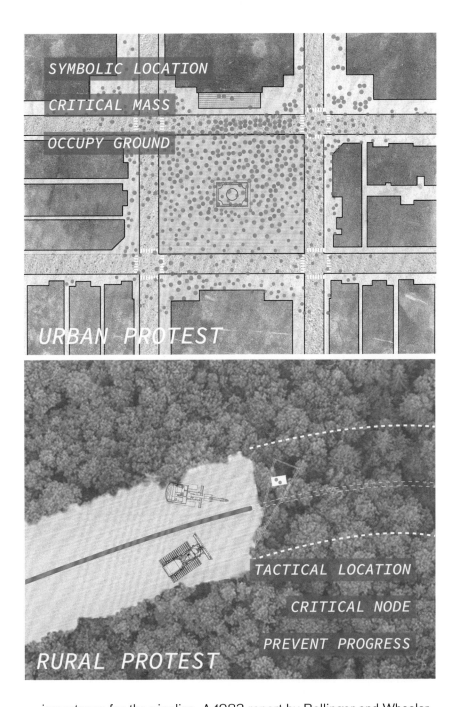

SYMBOLIC LOCATION

CRITICAL MASS

OCCUPY GROUND

URBAN PROTEST

TACTICAL LOCATION

CRITICAL NODE

PREVENT PROGRESS

RURAL PROTEST

Fig. 2 (left)
A thick cross section of the MVP.

Fig. 3 (top)
Spatial strategy in urban protests.

Fig. 4 (bottom)
Rural protest: making the thin operative.

importance for the pipeline. A 1983 report by Bollinger and Wheeler reports nine earthquakes that occurred near Giles County between 1959–81, the largest magnitude recorded at 4.6. Kastning writes, "on the basis of these reports, ground shaking of the magnitude 4.0 or higher is highly likely during the planned lifetime of the pipeline."

Represented and assessed in "thick section," interacting factors of surface relief, underlying geology and hydrology, and seismic activity are brought into focus, making the risk of the pipeline more readily apparent (Fig. 2). The question becomes not if a disaster will occur, but just how catastrophic it will be.

THIN

Here, I link geologic and human morphologies, bridging ancient material environments and contemporary industrial landscapes. This expanded geographic and historic scope situates projects like the MVP in a lineage of the commodification of natural resources in the Appalachian region. Appalachia, through which the MVP runs, has been conceptualized by sociologist David Walls as a "peripheral region within an advanced capitalist society." The core-periphery dynamic is inherently spatial, a topography of unequal political, economic, and socio-cultural power.

The processes by which Appalachia has been commodified are inextricably linked to representations—cultural constructions—of specific environments and those that inhabit them. Traci Brynne Voyles demonstrates the utility thin descriptions have in designating particular geographies and people as "sacrificial," thereby justifying and legitimizing projects of resource extraction. Voyles writes "wasteland discourses collect and sediment to give shape and power relations between peoples and geographies, creating a highly spatialized set of power relations that invoke place as well as race." As industrial landscapes are increasingly being located in rural periphery regions, we must assess how material environments and cultural constructions shape and "thin" efforts to resist landscapes of outsized risk, injustice, and harm.

We will now take a detailed look at three resistance tactics being used by communities along the pipeline's path. Rural resistance is a different beast than urban movements. The most iconic protest imagery is about mass, about turning out a crowd to take up literal and metaphoric space (Fig. 3). In Appalachia, critical mass is impossible to achieve and media attention made that much harder to attract. Rural protest must invoke a tactical spatial strategy, customizing interventions to specific sites and deploying hosts of unlikely "tools" in imaginative ways (Fig. 4). In each tactic featured here, activists have found opportunity in the particulars of their material environments and in the spatial qualities inherent to pipelines—they have made the "thin" operable.

SLOWING: TREE SITS

As the clearing of trees along the pipeline's route began in 2017, tree sits sprung up through West Virginia and Virginia in protest. Tree sits fashion small platforms in the canopies of trees in the path of the pipeline on which activists camp out, placing their bodies on the front line in an attempt to stop, or at least slow, construction (Fig. 5). One such effort, The Yellow Finch tree sit, is going strong some 591 days, at the writing of this, into their sit outside of Elliston, Virginia.

Acknowledging remote locations and an inability to gather a critical mass, tree sitters locate their protests above ground, suspended by

TREE SITS

systems of ropes and pulleys, knowing on-the-ground occupation would result in quick removal. Tree sits take advantage of the pipeline's narrow and linear path, strategically incising the route to halt progress while occupying a relatively small area. While construction can continue uninhibited on both sides of the tree sit, a pipeline doesn't work if a section of pipe is missing, no matter how small. The spatial quality of the pipeline is used to the advantage of activists—thinness is made operative.

In addition to, and often in proximity to tree sits, other peaceful protests have occurred where activists lock themselves to critical equipment, such as excavators and airplanes, halting construction for five to six hours at a time. It is easy for this to seem futile, but resistance takes all manners of temporal form. Perhaps it is crucial to be a "thorn in the side" and to do whatever you can to buy some time—and then to do it again.

STOPPING: BLUED TREES

In 2016, when the MVP project was announced, a slew of actions sprung up in an attempt to prevent the project from moving forward. One such attempt was a project led by Robin Boucher in Blacksburg, Virginia, and inspired by ecological artist Aviva Rahmani's work in Peekskill, New York, in protest of Spectra Energy's Algonquin pipeline. Rahmani painted trees in the proposed route of the pipeline

Fig. 5
A typical tree sit above the MVP.

BLUED TREES

with sinuous swathes of buttermilk-based blue paint (Fig. 6). Rahmani not only marked the trees, but recorded their locations, endeavoring to transcribe these spatial signifiers into a musical score. The score, which gives voice to these silent, sentient beings, came to be known as the Blued Tree Symphony. It was Rahmani's "hope that the copyrighted artwork might protect the trees, if only temporarily, from the pipeline's eminent domain claims to the land."

Rahmani's original Blued Trees in New York have since been taken down, but "The ideas in this project—the legal ideas, the aesthetic ideas — they can destroy every last trace of the project, but the ideas can't be killed because once you get an idea out there it's never lost," said Rahmani. Boucher likewise acknowledged the potential futility, or thinness, of the painted trees themselves, placing hope in the action and accompanying gallery show to spur community familiarity with the implications of the pipeline project and potential legal frameworks for stopping it. Here, thin gestures are the building blocks for constructing a thick community response.

MONITORING: CITIZEN WATCH

The Mountain Valley Watch launched in response to the start of pipeline construction as evidence of shoddy sediment and erosion control became visible. Mountain Valley Watch is a project of Protect Our Water Heritage Rights (POWHR), a coalition dedicated to developing a coalition of citizens to conduct research on the impacts of the fossil fuel industries work in the Appalachian region.

Fig. 6
A string of "blued trees" along the pipeline's path.

CITIZEN WATCH

The Mountain Valley Watch project brings together experts and citizens in an effort to "watchdog" pipeline construction. Their observations take many forms, including aerial monitoring via drone, water testing conducted by students, and photos taken by concerned citizens along the pipeline route. (Fig. 7).

The project engages citizens to contribute field observations. Volunteers have access to online training where they can "learn about erosion control best management practices used in pipeline development, specific examples of pollution to look for, and how to best document those problems." Citizens are asked to (safely) document any concerning sites, making sure to note date, time, and location of their images. A group of expert advisors made up of scientists and geospatial analysts translate field observations into GIS data, making a spatial record of violations and delineating areas of concern.

Collected data is ultimately compiled and reviewed for violations, with findings being collated into reports that are then submitted to the Virginia Water Control Board. These reports, publicly available online, include a list of notable incidents, annotated images, and a catalog of regulatory violations.

Fig. 7
Documenting poor construction practices.

Mountain Valley Watch overcomes the challenges of remoteness and low population density. Often banal citizen science work and image crowd-sourcing take on new meaning, fueling documentation that ultimately seeks more regulatory oversight and enforcement to reduce environmental damage.

IN CONCLUSION

Cutting through the Mount Tabor Sinkhole Plain, just north of where I grew up, the MVP is in my proverbial backyard. It slices through my home ground—my formative landscape. From the initial pipeline proposal, through rushed impact statements and legal proceedings, to each successive stage of construction, I have felt a profound disconnect between the staggering severity of the on-the-ground reality and benign, sterile representations of the project. The amazement I've felt seeing my otherwise politically "purple" county join forces in opposition to the pipeline is matched only by my shock at the "thin" representations employed by the pipeline parent corporation, FERC, and others to prop up and enable the pipeline.

Conducting the research for this essay, constructing the drawings included within, and reflecting on the purpose and potential of doing so has been, in the words of Rebecca Solnit, an exercise of "hope in the dark." This piece is both a rigorously researched study and a highly personal inquiry into how I might—as a student, as a young designer, and as a "remote" activist—cultivate agency in the face of the seemingly inevitable completion of the pipeline. How might designers better interpret, represent, and resist projects like the MVP? Here, I look to the thick section approach to study buried and unknowable systems, ponder feedback loops, composite geologic process and stochastic events, and to consider how representations of material environments and those that inhabit them collect and sediment, ultimately translating representation into reality.

Through the process of creating this piece, I believe I took the baby steps towards joining the ranks of those envisioning, manifesting, and demanding, an expanded role for designers. Here, this line of inquiry— of hope—probes the latent potentials for designers to intervene in the creation of, rather than inherit, harmful industrial landscapes.

HANNAH JANE BROWN

Hannah Jane Brown is a Master's of Landscape Architecture candidate at the University of Virginia. Hannah brings a fascination with intersections of the industrial, the ecological, and the agricultural to her work, with a particular interest in the Appalachian biophysical region.

Notes

1 Jacob Hileman, "Why the Mountain Valley Pipeline is uniquely risky," Virginia Mercury, August 22, 2019.

2 Thaïsa Way, "Landscapes of Industrial Excess: A thick sections approach to Gas Works Park," Journal of Landscape Architecture 8, no.1 (2013): 30

3 Ernst H. Kastning, "Geological Hazards in the Karst Regions of Virginia and West Virginia," Deposition of Record for the Federal Energy Regulatory Commission (2016): 5.

4 G.A. Bollinger, and Russell L. Wheeler, "The Giles County, Virginia, Seismic Zone," Science 219, issue 4588 (1983): 1,063–65.

5 Ernst H. Kastning, "Geological Hazards in the Karst Regions of Virginia and West Virginia," Deposition of Record for the Federal Energy Regulatory Commission (2016): 46.

6 David S. Walls, "Central Appalachia: A Peripheral Region within an Advanced Capitalist Society," The Journal of Sociology and Social Welfare 4, issue 2 (1976): 232.

7 Traci Brynne Voyles, *Wastelanding: Legacies of Uranium Mining in Navajo Country*, (University of Minnesota Press, 2015), 23

8 Madeline Sault, "Art raises awareness about trees in pipeline's path," The Roanoke Times (Roanoke, VA), November 18, 2016.

9 Ibid.

10 Rebecca Solnit, *Hope in the Dark* (Chicago: Haymarket Books, 2016)

THICKNESS AT THE NONPLACE
Travel, Ritual, and Elongated Entrances

Samantha K. Sigmon

A barrier is not just a structure, but instead a signal of in-depth and performative processes, thicker than they may seem. Spatial theorist Edward Soja described,

> a thick sedimentation of bounded spaces...powerfully shape[s] our everyday life. Above (and below) each of us is a stratification of almost innumerable and virtually invisible spatial authorities [that create] thick layers of spatial regulation that enmesh us...Every movement we make crosses some boundary whether we are aware of it or not.[1]

Physical structures, then, are markers of more expansive boundaries entangled with shifting power relationships between race, nationality, religion, gender and gender identity, class, and social and financial capital, veiled as normalized policies and procedures of control.

These boundaries are purposefully elongated in those sites built as in-between spaces, and perhaps most universally felt in the process of traveling long distance across geographic borders. These spaces of mass global movement—what for this essay I am simply calling "nonplaces" or "in-between spaces"—are over-planned, designed, and executed webs of many barriers that aggregate together to regulate access.[2] Entrances provide a weakened point across these barriers, needing to be controlled by what sociology professor Mimi Sheller calls unequal "mobility regimes" that govern "who or what can move (or stay put) when, where, how, and under what conditions" in which the violence and the freedom of mobility are equally at play.[3]

Those in power have long employed designers, architects, and planners to ensure security and control within the built environment. For instance, Christian Purgatory, a cosmic waiting room between heaven and hell, is one nonplace that the Christian world had designed and standardized to engross the mind, and then environment, of medieval Europeans. The concept was scaled up into a global money-making machine for the gain of state and religious powers. Medieval churches became physical gateways to the divine and reminders of purgatory, and were placed at power centers throughout the Christian empire for lay persons to travel to in order to experience less time in purgatory in the afterlife. Similar to churches' signaling a future purgatory, airports today are structures meant for mass waiting and movement to the next leg of a destination. These spaces display power, anxiety, and transformation as gateways in themselves, requiring performative actions to ensure successful passage. Both the nonplaces of church and airport are wrought with structured and ritualized systems of entering, moving, waiting, and consuming—mediated by personal means, corporate entities, and powerful regulations that serve as filtering apparatuses to differentiate between the privileged elite and "others," where human value is designed into systemic inequities.

PURGATORY, CHURCH, AND AIRPORT

While the symmetrical hierarchy of heaven and the chaotic fire-scape of hell are common images in medieval art, conjuring images of Purgatory as the mass, middle, waiting zone was harder to visually imagine. People were sometimes told to envision souls in a walled courtyard, inching toward heaven after death as they received prayers and gifts given from loved ones to the church in the name of the departed. Both death and life consisted of barriers that required a credit system of good deeds and donations to the church.[4]

Since one's life determined their initial placement in the Purgatorial field, this concept was not just imaginary, but very much lived and seen in the built environment. Churches served as a visual record of an official place where the living could amass good will while alive by praying for others' souls, convening with a saint, giving money, and reaffirming their virtue and piety as regulated by a clerical hierarchy.[5]

In part using the Purgatorial fear of prolonged detainment, Christian leaders officialized overarching processes and marked systems of repentance that had an internationalized spatial dimension on the many set pilgrimage routes leading to the center of a church. Each destination contains specific relics—commonly miraculous remains of saints—most likely located in its high altar. Some of the most extensive and popular pilgrimage sites had international routes, creating hubs of devotion all bound by the papal seat of Rome, before the Protestant Reformation began in the sixteenth century.

An experience in an international airport—located between nations as a send-off into the sky—is just one common example of a modern-day journey of crossing thick nonplaces co-opted by globalized, layered structures. These structures are standardized in design, require ritualistic actions, and are surveilled by many layers of policing. Like the powers of the church, the control in international airports is abstracted, almost beyond individual conception, and simplified to mass performative actions of rule following. Their designs take advantage of masses forcibly stuck waiting. Travelers give away rights and agency, as time, location within the space, and survival itself are in the hands of nameless other entities tied up in legal policy and capitalist enterprises.

TRAVEL ESSENTIALS FOR JETSETTERS

In order to cut time in Purgatory, Christian pilgrimages ideally had to be long and arduous, with bodily comfort purposefully sacrificed. The pilgrim seeks reflection of death, the well-being of loved ones, and forgiveness for sins, which includes praying for others in Purgatory— all culminating to a quicker process into heaven. The pilgrim must be Christian and must have done due diligence preparing their inner self to mirror their journey by fasting and praying. Location and ability to travel implies the traveler is most likely a man of Western European descent. Pilgrims commonly walked barefoot at least part of the way and wore a long tunic, a cross, a staff, a broad-brimmed hat, and leather pouch tied to the waist carrying food, utensils, and money, blessed by the pilgrim's priest (Fig. 3).[6] It was not above any class to undertake a pilgrimage; even kings made pilgrimages at times for publicity statements to declare their piety and thus fitness to rule.[7] The wealthy could also pay others to pilgrimage for them, yet reap the heavenly benefits, in a system where money could shirk the trials of the journey.[8]

Pilgrimages were gendered and racialized. Women were often discouraged from this display of public mobility, as their place was in the private spaces of the home, and they were commonly seen as too frail of mind and spirit to undertake this travel. Women had to gain permission from a male guardian and were not allowed at the same table or rooms as other pilgrims in stops along the way.[9] Additionally, pilgrims were assumed to be white and European because they were more ready for these trials and firm in their religion, thus excluding those considered foreign due to darker skin and Indigenous peoples, both who had to first be taught by Europeans the ways of the pious Christian before such travel.

For a twenty-first-century long-distance traveler—already a privileged luxury—getting there is a series of mini-destinations for which airports are crucial. The traveler must have readily-accessed currency, credit, phone, and the internet, or close friends or family that have these means to assist them. This assumes an already-built network. Also, the abler the body, the easier and quicker the process. Traveling with wheelchairs, medications, and internal devices requires extra effort and preparation, money to be paid for accommodation, and time and space to move through long terminals. A traveler must also look a certain way; in America, who is suspected of nefarious actions may often change based on what countries and cultures are seen as anti-American. Official documentation, Western clothes, a recognized binary gender, knowledge of the English language, and several sets of alternative plans might be necessary ways to conform to a "normalized" identity. International visas and passports provide varying degrees of access and create hard lines with regard to nationality, boiling individuals down to a card. Politicized rhetoric demonizing foreign migrants target people with brown skin who worry not just about TSA agents' scrutiny, but bias from the passengers around them.

These complicated aspects of the body in travel are not mentioned in blogs, magazines, and online advertisements of an effortless "jetsetter" style that shows us how women should look like a stylish model ready to party in a global city and men should wear a suit and carry a briefcase, each as a gendered marker of class. Both of these looks assume privilege that rarely encounter thick barriers imposed on others. We see the jetsetter as much different than the vagrant or the migrant, those who have no home or are forced into places with very little options.[10] Both of these examples assume a privilege of freedom to tell a personalized "making sense story" as theorist Zygmunt Bauman describes.[11] Both the pilgrim and the jetsetter have the capability to control their narrative and outcome. How you arrive— and how you prepare—mark your body with a willingness or need to conform in order to ease into the specific transactional purpose that unlocks aspects of the rest of the trip. In planning what you look like and what you bring, you signal what you hope to gain from crossing these borders, be they cosmic or global.

THE ENTERING: A REGULATED PORTAL TO MASS TRANSFORMATION

Like God's Earth is the center of the universe for Middle-Age believers, the principal church is often in the center of a medieval town with streets radiating toward it. Specifically, a Gothic church created during the medieval period is cruciform in shape with a grand entrance, called a portal, signaling the transition into the heaven-space as a transformation of the body, mind, and soul in preparation for interacting with the high altar or relic shrine (Fig. 1). Medieval churches architecturally celebrated entrances through a succession of ornate designs and towering scales, often displaying the Last Judgement as a complete lesson of cosmic hierarchy and human duty.

Like the church, the airport consists of portals functioning intentionally through their structure to seek mass group performance of action and pause. Yet, unlike cathedrals, airports are often far outside of town, consisting of a web of conjoining bypasses in themselves barriers of movement separating types of travelers. This in itself, according to Bauman, signals an elite system that segments whole populations where "mobility climbs to the rank of the uppermost among the coveted values."[12] Heavy fortification is all about the comfort of the elite, and it becomes a church-like enclave for them.[13] The nonplace spreads itself out here; as anthropologist Marc Augé states, "the installations needed for the accelerated circulation of passengers and goods...are just as much non-places as the means of transport themselves."[14]

Oftentimes the airport is flat, horizontal, and transparent on an open landscape, too large to comprehend its full expanse. The public door into a terminal is most likely automatic, sliding, and small-scale (Fig. 2). It is nondescript and meant for efficiency with signs that simplify space into letters, numbers, and arrows. This is the nondescript language of abstract authority, establishing the place where individuals are only interacting with official texts of "moral entities in institutions."[15] The texts and signs supersede the ornate church design meant to overwhelm.

After entering, the thickest layer of the journey into the terminal spaces is compressed by money, status, and appearance, from expedited service queues for airline preferred customers to TSA pre-check. Sheller, citing theorist Hagar Kotef, asserts that freedom in a liberal state "consists of submitting to a limited mobility regime in order to benefit from the security offered by the state, which effectively slows down movement into and out of the state as well as preventing and excluding the imagined other inside."[16] TSA agents are trained to corral actions, assuming anyone could be a terrorist. In 2011, the Guardian reported that in England, passengers from ethnic minorities were up to forty-two times more likely than white people to be stopped by police under counter-terrorism powers.[17] In 2019, Vox found that scanners have trouble reading thick hair and head coverings, causing continued racist profiling.[18]

This security, unlike massive built barriers, is not walled off, but a maze of see-through plexiglass where the other side is so close visually, yet of varying and uncertain distances and widths of thickness. It helps to have had previous lessons on the ritualized motions of when to take off shoes, what to take out of your bag, where to stand, and when to move. A passenger's belongings are their links to the outside world and their identity, and they move in concert with them through this process. Ideally, the passenger is united with their bags as the finale of this performance, but TSA agents are required to touch bodies or take bags whenever an alarm goes off. *Design Justice* author Sasha Costanza-Chock wrote about this experience as a non-binary, trans, femme-presenting person who always gets stopped in this line because the security scanner only sees binary, either male or female, bodies.[19] Trans or non-binary people, then, always get patted down at security for breaking this system, causing more policing on their bodies.

Fig. 1
*The Royal Portals
of Chartres, France,
Westfront, 1145–55.*

This is interactive security theater; we do it not because it actually makes us safe, but because we are supposed to feel safer for doing it. Inherent in this design are assumptions baked into the use of technology—creating machines that flag what doesn't fit in a world governed by patriarchy and white supremacy. On top of machines made to conform, increased facial scanning systems are becoming an official part of security checks, thus adding more data about your image and movements into the vast surveillance system, all in the name of convenience.[20]

AN INTERNAL/ETERNAL EXPERIENCE

Upon entering nonspace, you become a changed person—a non-person disjointed from place, possessions, rights, routine, and time. These spaces run entirely on their own other-worldly systems, funneled through interior architecture.

Upon entrance, the pilgrim, now under church rule and at the whim of heavenly time, passes ornate monuments and private chapels holding the remains of people who have ensured they are able to quickly move through Purgatory by commissioning elaborate tombs, purchasing space closest to the holiest relic, and endowing priests to pray around the clock for their souls. The drama of the large nave, tall clerestory, and side chapels all lead to the high alter where the most

Fig. 2
A terminal entrance into Dulles Airport.

treasured relic resides as a concentrated gateway between the living and the heavenly (Fig. 3).

Shrines were often built up specifically to hold large crowds of pilgrims and funnel them into a semi-circular museum of relics on view leading to the final or most important one in the system of liturgical theater. Once one made it to this central point through an ambulatory, they got a chance to pray for any causes they may have, and are expected to give money or precious goods to the shrine to seal the deal of their transaction. Treating this object with serious reverence was the utmost duty for the pilgrim, or they may return plagued and haunted by the saint.[21]

Like the inside of a cathedral, there is a multifaced array of stimuli in an airport, and each person is funneled into approved directions, with long terminal arms leading down paths of restriction or enticement. Like a church, it is a ritualistic place divided between the VIPs and the working-class. More money allows you more comfort, more time, less security, and more amenities. According to Sheller, citing geographer Lin Weiqiang, there is "a politics of uneven access to all global air travel, that is institutionalized within regimes of air rights, technical expertise, and aviation security."[22] Like the church, the airport is transactional with tickets, identification, and purchasing power all creating greater ease. Without common freedoms, but with strange,

Fig. 3
*Westminster Abbey,
Nave, Isaac Newton's
monument and grave in
the background, London,
England.*

novel liberties based on consumption, individuals can purchase tax-free luxury goods from countries with trade restrictions or a shame-free beer at six in the morning. While a pilgrimage is treated as a life-changing experience, it is not the ultimate destination, but a right step toward heavenly eternity. Similarly, each gate is a waiting room in the elongated passage of travel—a shrine without the gleaming jewels and beautiful processional. This gate is not elaborate; it is the same as any other, but it is, in a way, each traveler's temporary savior delivering them to their final destination. In both a plane and a holy place, the traveler surrenders their control to another power who denies their individual identity to best process this transcendental experience.

A THIN OPENING

Many stratifications of social, economic, or political boundaries rely upon design working in concert with legalized policies. These commonplace examples of how space and design are utilized to uphold the order, regulation, hierarchies, and compliance of a globalized power network in a nonplace might seem necessary on first glance, but by peeling back the thick layers, we are able to think through implications and imagine alternatives to mass corralling and movement that does not compartmentalize human value within the entering process.

These elite ways of traveling underscore that mobility is often not completely restricted, but used for managing exclusions—who should travel, who must stay in place, and what can be extracted from each.[23] The amount of funds needed; how someone looks; their background, language, race, or occupation are all factors within the mobile regime.

In these ways, one barrier is in fact often made up of many unseen constraints that bind together to create a thicker, more powerful structure than a single wall ever could. Thinking through this can start with what is taken for granted; as Sheller says,

> movements for mobility justice should be as concerned with dismantling systems of privilege...to air mobility, as with protecting the subaltern subject from the injustices of exclusion, detainment, eviction, or refusal of entry.[24]

In the capitalist, globalized world we are in, elite travel is at the expense of many others.

How we choose where we go, and where we feel varying amounts of comfort should serve as reminders that we are always in a process of testing our entry into different types of territories. Thick barriers and their layered entries have been tied to power structures for many hundreds of years. In tackling these issues as part of a larger purpose for equity across the board—in an increasing technologized world—we must all fight for security that does not imply a loss of personal agency and an othering of fellow humans. Designers must be trained as activists and represent all facets of human lived experiences so the discipline may be used to uncover many intersectional barriers within an invisible threshold. Sociologists and geographers have suggested a future of a "mobility commons," a protected free space through deregulation of the individual and regulation of the corporate or state powers; "it implies actions that are shared through acts of co-mobilization; it is unbounded and deterritorializing, it is ambiguous and amphibious."[25] Learning from history, and envisioning a future, what can our commons look like and how can it be designed to create an equal entering experience for all?[26]

SAMANTHA K. SIGMON

Samantha Sigmon is scholar, writer, and worker in the arts passionate about how art, space, and communities work together. She has Master's degrees in Museum Studies at Syracuse University and Architectural History at UVA. She has previously worked at Crystal Bridges Museum of American Art as Interpretation Manager, as well as within local galleries, do-it-yourself spaces, and arts organizations around her home region of Northwest Arkansas.

Notes

1 Edward Soja, *Seeking Spatial Justice* (Minneapolis: University of Minnesota Press, 2010) 44–45.

2 The term "non-place" has much more history behind its conception than there is space to delve into. For this essay, this term specifically refers to globalized areas of entrances that cross borders and increase control.

3 Mimi Sheller, *Mobility Justice: The Politics of Movement in an Age of Extremes* (London and Brooklyn: Verso, 2018) 115.

4 Jacques Le Goff, *The Birth of Purgatory*, Arthur Goldhammer, trans. (Chicago: University of Chicago Press, 1984) 143, 163, 167.

5 Clive Burgess, "'Longing to be prayed for': death and commemoration in an English parish in the later Middle Ages," in *The Place of the Dead: Death and Remembrance in Late Medieval and Early Modern Europe*, Bruce Gordon and Peter Marshall, eds. (Cambridge, UK; New York: Cambridge University Press, 2000) 60, 63; Carlos M. N. Eire, *A Very Brief History of Eternity* (Princeton: Princeton University Press, 2010) 91, 103–4.

6 April Munday, "The Medieval Pilgrim," February 19, 2017, https://aprilmunday. wordpress.com/2017/02/19/the-medieval-pilgrim/#:~:text=Pilgrims%20 came%20from%20all%20levels,a%20punishment%20from%20their%20 confessors.

7 Both King Henry II and King Henry VIII famously made these pilgrimages to English shrines.

8 Le Goff, *The Birth of Purgatory*, 330–1.

9 Nicole Chareyron, *Pilgrims to Jerusalem in the Middle Ages*, (New York: Colombia University Press, 2005) 50, 74.

10 Zygmunt Bauman, "Tourists and Vagabonds," in *Globalization: The Human Consequences*, (New York: Columbia University Press, 1998) 77-102.

11 Zygmunt Bauman, "From Pilgrim to Tourist—or a Short History of Identity," in *Questions of Cultural Identity*, Stuart Hall and Paul du Gay, eds. (Thousand Oaks, CA: Sage Publications, Inc, 1996) 23.

12 Bauman, *Globalization: The Human Consequences*, 2

13 Ibid., 102.

14 Marc Augé, *Non-Places: Introduction to an Anthropology of Supermodernity* (London ; New York: Verso, 1995), 34.

15 Ibid., 96.

16 Sheller, *Mobility Justice*, 123.

17 Michael White, "Airport security checks: More offensive to some than to others," May 24, 2011, The Guardian, https://www.theguardian.com/politics/ blog/2011/may/24/airport-security-checks-terrorism-act.

18 Gaby Del Valle, "How airport scanners discriminate against passengers of color," April 17, 2019, Vox, https://www.vox.com/the- goods/2019/4/17/18412450/tsa-airport-full-body-scanners-racist.

19 Sasha Costanza-Chock, *Design Justice: Community-Led Practices to Build the Worlds We Need* (Cambridge, MA: MIT Press, 2020) 1-5.

20 Jack Stewart, "Creepy or Not, Face Scans Are Speeding up Airport Security," November 21, 2018, Wired, https://www.wired.com/story/airport-security- biometrics-face-scanning/.

21 The icon of Sainte Foy in France is covered in jewels and stones given to her. When she does not receive her due, stories are passed down of threats and even murder that she has performed according to Bernard of Angers, who wrote in eleventh century on Sainte Foy's miracles.

22 Sheller, *Mobility Justice*, 130.

23 Ibid., 128.

24 Ibid., 130.

25 Ibid., 169.

26 Thank you to Zane Placke and Ghazal Jafari for being honest, kind, and impactful editors, and Rebecca Coleman for image guidance.

Image Credits

Fig. 1. Wiki Commons.

Fig. 2. Friscocali, licensed under CC BY-NC 2.0. Creative Commons Search.

Fig. 3. Herry Lawford, 2006. Wiki Commons, https://commons.wikimedia.org/wiki/File:Westminster_Abbey_Interior.jpg

PROSTHETIC LANDSCAPES

Aroussiak Gabrielian & Alison Hirsch

Responding to acts aimed at destabilizing dominant narratives of power, "Prosthetic Landscapes" is a proposition for the future of memorial-making that brings presence to sites or places whose stories have been erased or overlooked, and situates these site stories into larger webs of meaning–social, political, environmental. We use the term Prosthetic to imply the empathic task of taking on the experience of Other–to suture oneself into broader networks of history, experience, memory–landscape.

We, FOREGROUND DESIGN AGENCY, have long argued for adopting the interpretive role of critical ethnographer in the reimagining of landscape, particularly in a reclaiming of its expanded thickness (building from and critiquing Clifford Geertz's oft-cited "thick description"[1]). In her book *Critical Ethnography*, performance scholar D. Soyini Madison explains,

> The critical ethnographer...takes us beneath surface appearances, disrupts the status quo, and unsettles both neutrality and taken-for-granted assumptions by bringing to light underlying and obscure operations of power and control. Therefore, the critical ethnographer resists domestication and moves from 'what is' to 'what could be,'

as a projective practice.[2] Within the field of landscape architecture, the language of Landscape Urbanism (and its legacy) was largely dependent on the postmodern vocabulary of surface over depth, using the language of "staging surfaces" within the "horizontal field of urbanization."[3] While the global reach and horizontal spread of urbanization are significant to our practice, the emphasis is not an either/or formulation but an "and/also," in hopes of diversifying and opening up the limitations of binary thinking. It is for this reason that we look to "expanded 'thick description'" (expanded, from the Latin expandere, to spread out, and used here to respond to critique of the apolitical nature of Geertz's "thick description")-implying both broad understanding of the global spread of cultural flows and the planetary web of biophysical processes, and a deep search for both cultural meaning and the agency of physical matter in highly localized contexts.

"Prosthetic Landscapes" allowed us to linger on the tension between expansion and depth (thinness and thickness) through a reevaluation of contemporary memorial-making. The three propositions below question the traditional memorial as an inert monument dedicated to completed events of the past. Here we use the adaptable and ever-expanding digital database to commemorate ongoing processes of loss–situating sites in both the thickness of place and the thinness of expanded implications and impact. In other words, the singularity of event is situated within larger networks of memory–as a vehicle of mobilization and a form of collective reckoning.

A project that integrates digital capacities with physical specificities inevitably grapples with notions of place–as a register of the thickness of material and meaning, and often used as a safeguard against the disembodiment of the virtual. In her book, *One Place After Another: Site Specific Art and Locational Identity*, art historian Miwon Kwon identifies our familiar contemporary paradox:

> While the accelerated speed, access, and exchange of information, images, commodities, and even bodies is being celebrated in one circle, the concomitant breakdown of traditional temporal-spatial experiences and the accompanying homogenization of places and erasure of cultural differences is being decried in another. The intensifying conditions of spatial indifferentiation and departicularization—that is, the increasing instances of locational unspecificity—are seen to exacerbate the sense of alienation and fragmentation in contemporary life.[4]

With this collapse of traditional or habitual spatial and temporal modalities, the future of memory and memorial-making as a place-bound practice is called into question. In response to increasing "locational unspecificity," storytelling through geospatial and locative media has much to offer as an oppositional cultural practice. The thinness of the digital interface is thickened here by the thickness of the database's geographic and place-based content. While it does not re-place the power of place itself, storytelling through geospatial media has the potential to transport us virtually to sites of memory and, to some degree, transport memorial landscapes into the space of our everyday lives. Locational specificity–virtual and physical—becomes layered into the palimpsests of place and geocoded data situates memory not only in the singularity of site but in a dispersed (expanded or thin) and consistently updated network of remembrance. While we continue to recognize the potency of standing on "ground zero" to feel connected to past struggle, the following memorial musings attempt to optimize the synthetic potentials of geolocation in the context of new media in multiple ways. First their participatory and customizable nature—the expanding database accrues over time and alters the spatial narratives through the negotiation of multiplicity.[5] Second, understanding space as "stories-so-far" and place as heightened concentrations of those stories,[6] we are reminded that memory is in the process of becoming, thus the issues that are "commemorated" are as much about the future as they are about the past. Third, the memorials are at the same time portable experiences tethered to their locations in space, and deeply rooted in the particularities of place through the specificities of the stories they gather. Finally, the memorials are less about the singularity of sites as uniquely sacred, but are part of a larger network of memory that draws people together across geographies and "chasms of difference," as platforms for discourse.[7]

The "memorial" concept recognizes three ongoing issues at three scales, all aimed at stimulating a more active public realm through heated discourse and increased exposure to sources of national anxiety: Black Lives Matter (a national issue); Muslim Experience in America (an international issue, dealing with geopolitics across national boundaries); Landscapes Lost to Climate Change (a planetary issue, impacting all of the biophysical world). These three topics were chosen as critical to the political moment (2016/2017) with both deeply fraught histories and inevitably contentious futures, as well as representing a spectrum of resonance—from the national, to the international and the planetary—while clearly fueled by personal narratives of loss. As new stories are uncovered, new voices heard, and cultural and collective values shift, the shifting narratives become more robust and inclusive and the networks of memory expand. The dispersal and ongoing accrual of these commemorative experiences respond to the fragmentary, incomplete, and transitory nature of memory.

Passersby are alerted through the navigational system on their smart phones when crossing into sites of brutality. Pictured here is the intersection of W. Arbutus St. and N. Kemp Ave. in the ity of Compton, the site where Donta Taylor was shot and killed by the police

Memorial to Black Lives

Anonymous intersection of violence

Early interface studies

Recognizing victims of state violence

Mapping sites of police violence. Data culled from: https://fatalencounters.org/; https://mappingpoliceviolence.org/; https://www.washingtonpost.com/graphics/2019/national/police-shootings-2019/

MEMORIAL TO BLACK LIVES

The "memorial" to Black Lives is both a reflection on lives lost and dehumanized, and a vehicle for mobilization. Taking cues from the important work of the Equal Justice Initiative in bringing to visibility "terror lynchings" that occurred in this country between 1880 and 1940,[8] here we use both geodata and the physicality of the landscape to mark and remember what is an all-too actively expanding database of violence. The memorial is "discovered" and "experienced" via a georeferenced mobile app that guides the "visitor" to sites of state violence as well as historic Black insurgency. The intention is to catalyze a broad national conversation on the "validity of Black life." The memorial attempts to literalize the Black Lives Matter goal of "taking the hashtag off of social media and into the streets" by its organizing component where such places have the potential to be reclaimed as public space.[9]

While the project was initiated in 2016–17 in the face of then recent killings of Black men and women by law enforcement (Trayvon Martin, 2012; Michael Brown, 2014; Eric Garner, 2014; Freddie Gray, 2015; Sandra Bland, 2015; Alton Sterling, 2016; Philando Castile, 2016; Keith Lamont Scott, 2016; to name a few), our context is even more heightened in 2020 in national response to the murders of George Floyd, Breonna Taylor, Ahmaud Arbery, and many others.

On the left, mapping incidents of anti-muslim activity. Data culled from: https://www.newamerica.org/in-depth/anti-muslim-activity/;
https://www.splcenter.org/fighting-hate/extremist-files/ideology/anti-muslim; https://belonging.berkeley.edu/global-justice/islamophobia
On the right, Insertion of screens in everyday landscape in Garden City Kansas, near a site of recent anti-Muslim activity

Memorial to Muslim Experience in America

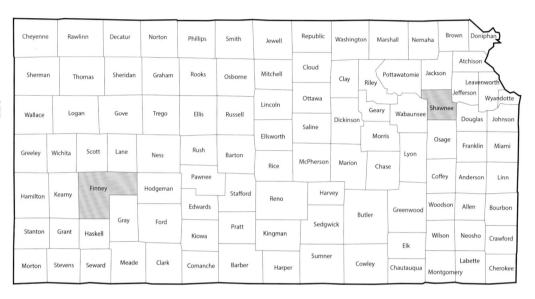

October 15, 2016
Garden City, Finney County, KS
Incident
Three men calling themselves the "Crusaders" were arrested and charged with conspiring to use a weapon of mass destruction in attacks targeting a mosque, an apartment complex, and specifically Muslim immigrants from Somalia. The men had frequently expressed their hatred for Somalis as well as immigrants and Muslims, whom the men called "cockroaches."

June 1, 2016
Topeka, Shanee County, KS
HB 2612
HB 2612 was introduced in the State House. Known as the "refugee absorptive capacity act," the bill would have allowed the state to declare refugee resettlement moratoriums in host communities that lack sufficient absorptive capacity. The bill died in committee.

November 16, 2015
Topeka, Shanee County, KS
Executive Order
Gov. Sam Brownback signed Executive Order No. 15-07, directing that "no state agency, or organization receiving grant money from the state, will participate in or assist in any way in the relocation of Syrian refugees in Kansas"

MEMORIAL TO MUSLIM EXPERIENCE IN AMERICA

The "memorial" to Muslim Experience in America addresses the Islamophobia that has emerged out of ongoing international conflict and how it has been portrayed in the media. It is about Islam throughout the world as a way of familiarizing and humanizing its multiple faces. Projection screens would be situated in unexpected parts of the American landscape that parallel the landscapes Muslim individuals are discussing in interviews.[10] Those individuals are asked to remember landscapes that brought them joy and are then re-"situated" in images of those landscapes in the video projection. The layers of mediation and dislocation are meant to reflect the blurry and disconnected nature of memory and the experience of displacement so many are undergoing today. The memorial is also meant to situate these individuals on both a physical and metaphorical common ground with those living in American locations where Islam is least familiar.

ALEPPO

ARDEN CITY, KANSAS

As the project continues to develop, this memorial may expand
into Immigrant Experience in America, more generally owing to
heightened forms of xenophobia and border control that has resulted
in walls, cages, family separations, and detentions for so many
living in the US particularly within the last four years of the current
administration (2016–20).

Ecologically threatened sites are seen in their future states, if left to unfold according to current trajectory, via an augmented reality app installed on their smart phones. Pictured above is a site in Mendota, CA which is faced with increasing water scarcity, and Lake Erie, below, whose increasing algal blooms suffocate aquatic life and threaten the water supply for more than 11 million people

Memorial to Landscapes Lost

Augmented experience showing landscapes in future states

Algal Bloom in Lake Erie, 2050 (projected)

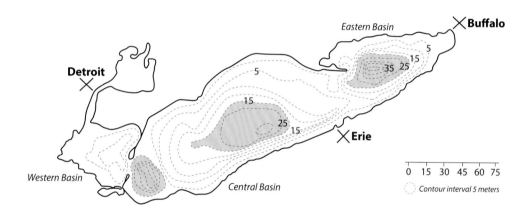

MEMORIAL TO LANDSCAPES LOST

The "memorial" to Landscapes Lost to Climate Change highlights human-natural ecologies that have been tangibly impacted by climate change. Using "augmented reality," vulnerable landscapes can be viewed in their future state if left to unfold according to current trajectory. It is thus a memorial to the future. This memorial will be constantly adapting and will not only serve as passive reflections on the loss of valued landscapes, but will address, through didactic elements, the impact of climate change on some of the world's (and nation's) most vulnerable species and populations. These "climate refugees" or "ecological migrants" embody the displaced presence and haunting absence in new landscapes of loss. The "memorial" tells the story of their possibly inevitable future. As a call to action and ethical thinking, the organizing component allows "visitors" to develop new collective rituals of commemoration in situ, such as acts of environmental care and stewardship.

MENDOTA, CA, 2050

The geography of memory, its narrative multiplicity, and dispersal across scales and territories, can only be comprehensively understood by connecting the tangibility of the local within a wider spatial and social context of impact. These memorial propositions are not suggestive that sites themselves no longer matter, but rather the opposite. They allow one to situate these places into a larger network of memory on a scale that has the capacity to incite empathy and mobilize action. While both the meaning latent in place and the often haunting absence of any trace of events that make that place significant has the potential to "jolt us out of complacency,"[11] in a world now mobilized by digitally-driven social movements, these expanded forms of media (geospatial, locative, immersive) provide increased opportunity for action—creating new collectives across geographies of difference.[12] They are thus less about reflecting on the past than mobilizing for a more equitable, more ethical, and more just future. 🐁

FOREGROUND DESIGN AGENCY

FOREGROUND DESIGN AGENCY is a transdisciplinary design practice operating between the fields of architecture, landscape architecture, urbanism and the arts. The diversity of their work finds its synthesis in the means, methods, and medium of landscape. Primarily engaged in design competitions, speculations and self-initiated design-research projects, FOREGROUND is a testing ground and ongoing collaborative platform between historian-designer Alison Bick Hirsch and futurist-designer Aroussiak Gabrielian. As such, their work is primarily invested in both the situated practice-of and projective prospects-for landscape architecture.

Notes

1 See Alison Hirsch, "'Expanded 'Thick Description': The Landscape Architect as Critical Ethnographer," in *Innovations in Landscape Architecture*, eds. Jonathon Anderson and Daniel Ortega (UK: Routledge, 2016). The term "thick description" comes from anthropologist Clifford Geertz (borrowed originally from Gilbert Ryle) in his essay "Thick Description: Toward an Interpretive Theory of Culture," in *The Interpretation of Cultures: Selected Essays* (New York: Basic Books, 1973). Geertz insisted on ethnography as an interpretive practice–a "thick description" of social and symbolic action–emphasizing the particular over the universal or cross-cultural. In the forty years since the publication of his essay, much criticism has been aimed at its political neutrality or the focus on locality at the expense of situating meaning into a broader context of political, economic and social structures.

2 D. Soyini Madison, *Critical Ethnography: Methods, Ethics, and Performance* (London: Sage, 2011), 5.

3 James Corner, "Terra Fluxus," in *The Landscape Urbanism Reader*, ed. Charles Waldheim (New York: Princeton Architecture Press, 2006), 28 and Charles Waldheim, "Introduction: A Reference Manifesto," in ed. Charles Waldheim (New York: Princeton Architectural Press, 2006), 15.

4 Miwon Kwon, *One Place After Another: Site Specific Art and Locational Identity* (Cambridge, MA: MIT Press, 2002), 157.

5 Here we have been inspired by "spontaneous memorials" that evolve through time and some of which have been digitally archived; see, for example, the Vietnam Veterans Memorial Collection: https://www.nps.gov/orgs/1802/vive.htm and the September 11 Digital Archive: https://911digitalarchive.org)

6 In her book, *For Space* (London: Sage, 2005), Massey argues for the conception of space as "stories-so-far," and places as spatio-temporal events–articulations or concentrations of narratives, histories, memories *in process*.

7 We also spent some time analyzing the potency of the mobile and ever-accruing AIDS Memorial Quilt as a tribute to loss across such difference.

8 Equal Justice Initiative, "Lynching in America: Confronting the Legacy of Racial Terror," http://eji.org/reports/lynching-in-america. Accessed August 17, 2016.

9 Latter two quotations from Black Lives Matter, http://blacklivesmatter.com. Accessed January 3, 2018.

10 Rather than screens, this has evolved since the project has been developed to be projection mapping onto existing built fabric of everyday life. We have not changed this in the text because the figures have not yet been updated.

11 This is a quotation adapted from one quoted by Max Page in *Why Preservation Matters* (New Haven: Yale University Press, 2016), 165. The original quote is from: Robert Scruton, *Beauty: A Very Short Introduction* (New York: Oxford University Press, 2011).

12 For an elongated perspective on *place* in the context of the digitization of memorials, see Aroussiak Gabrielian and Alison Hirsch, "Prosthetic Landscapes: Place and Placelessness in the Digitization of Memorials," *Future Anterior 15*, n. 2 (Winter 2018): 113-31.

University of Virginia
School of Architecture
www.arch.virginia.edu
www.lunch-journal.com

LUNCH is the design research journal
of the UVA School of Architecture.